"Accessus ad Auctores"
Studies in Honor of Christopher Kleinhenz

MEDIEVAL AND RENAISSANCE
TEXTS AND STUDIES
VOLUME 397

"Accessus ad Auctores"
Studies in Honor of Christopher Kleinhenz

Edited by
Fabian Alfie and Andrea Dini

ACMRS
(Arizona Center for Medieval and Renaissance Studies)
Tempe, Arizona
2011

Published by ACMRS (Arizona Center for Medieval and Renaissance Studies), Tempe, Arizona.
© 2011 Arizona Board of Regents for Arizona State University.
All Rights Reserved.

Library of Congress Cataloging-in-Publication Data

"Accessus ad auctores" : studies in honor of Christopher Kleinhenz / edited by Fabian Alfie and Andrea Dini.
   p. cm. -- (Medieval and Renaissance texts and studies ; v. 397)
   Includes bibliographical references.
   ISBN 978-0-86698-445-4 (alk. paper)
   1. Italian literature--To 1400--History and criticism. 2. Italian literature--15th century--History and criticism. 3. Italian literature--16th century--History and criticism. 4. Dante Alighieri, 1265-1321--Criticism and interpretation. 5. Renaissance--Italy. I. Alfie, Fabian. II. Dini, Andrea. III. Kleinhenz, Christopher.
   PQ4004.K54.A23 2012
   850.9--dc23
2011045518

∞
This book is made to last. It is set in Adobe Caslon Pro,
smyth-sewn and printed on acid-free paper to library specifications.
Printed in the United States of America

Tabula Gratulatoria

Gloria Allaire
Janice Aski
John C. Barnes
Fiora Bassanese
Elena Bender
Keith Busby
Maristella Cantini Malterer
Veena Carlson
Tania Convertini
The Dante Alighieri Cultural Society of Gainesville
The Department of French and Italian, University of Wisconsin-Madison
Chiara De Santi
Hillary Doerr Engelhart
Theresa Gualtieri-Clark
Douglas Kelly
Ilona Klein
Michael Lettieri
Nicole Lindenstein
Ernesto Livorni

Giancarlo Maiorino
Millicent Marcus
Jan Miernowoski
Enrico Minardi
Anthony Mollica
Leslie Zarker Morgan
M. Giovannella Moscovici
Sarah Nelson
Margherita Pampinella-Cropper
Alan Perry
Lino Pertile
Christina Petraglia
Elizabeth Poe
Guy Raffa
Paul Rockwell
Claudia Romanelli
Samuel Rosenberg
Chad Shorter
Madison Sowell
Tonia Triggiano
Dolly Weber

TABLE OF CONTENTS

Preface   xi
    ROBERT J. RODINI, *University of Wisconsin-Madison*

Christopher Kleinhenz's Curriculum Vitae   xiii

Section I:
Medieval Romances between France and Italy

The *Ordonnance* of the Quest in Jean Froissart's *Meliador*   3
    DOUGLAS KELLY, *University of Wisconsin-Madison*

From *Le Chevalier as deus espees* to the Prose *Yvain*   19
    NORRIS LACY, *Pennsylvania State University*

Chrétien in Italy   25
    KEITH BUSBY, *University of Wisconsin-Madison*

Tracce tristaniane nella lirica dei siciliani   39
    MICHELANGELO PICONE, *Università di Zurigo*

Galeotto Before the Fall   51
    SAMUEL N. ROSENBERG, *Indiana University*

Literary Afterlives in *Huon d'Auverne*: "The Art of [Dantean] Citation"   61
    LESLIE ZARKER MORGAN, *Loyola University, Maryland*

Section II:
Interpretations and Reception of Dante's Minor Works

The Narrative Structure of the *Vita Nova* 77
RICHARD LANSING, *Brandeis University*

Dream and Vision in Dante's *Vita Nova* 93
ERNESTO LIVORNI, *University of Wisconsin-Madison*

Re-Configuring the Self through Suffering, Violence, and Death in 115
Dante's *Vita nuova* and *Comedy*
DINO CERVIGNI, *University of North Carolina*

Sixteenth-Century Criticism of Dante's *Tenzone* with Forese Donati: 137
Vincenzo Borghini's "De' poeti antichi toscani"
FABIAN ALFIE, *University of Arizona*

Section III:
Interpretations and Reception of Dante's *Commedia*

Dante Equestrian 157
GLORIA ALLAIRE, *University of Kentucky*

"Quanto si convenia a tanto uccello" (*Inf.* 34.47): Dante's Satan as 169
Winged Phallus
MADISON SOWELL, *Brigham Young University*

Dal tema del pellegrinaggio alle icone della musica: per una rivisitazione 183
di *Purgatorio* II
EMILIO PASQUINI, *Università di Bologna*

Philomela: The "Civic" Rape of the Empire 195
MARGHERITA PAMPINELLA CROPPER

Appunti su Guglielmo Maramauro, sull'*auctoritas* e sulla "lettura" 223
di Dante nel Trecento
ZYGMUNT BARANSKI, *University of Cambridge*

"Quella Dolce Terra Latina": The Dantesque Landscape of Moravia's 239
La Ciociara ("Two Women")
MARY WATT, *University of Florida*

Section IV:
Studies on the Italian Middle Ages
(Thirteenth and Fourteenth Centuries)

The Portrayal of Falconry in Encyclopedic Literature: 253
The Sport Meets the Scholar
    Teresa Gualtieri-Clark, *University of Wisconsin-Madison (alumna)*

"Venite a laudare": Reflections of the Marian Cult in *Il Laudario di Cortona*   267
    Alan R. Perry, *Gettysburg College*

Il vi prometto—ve lo intendo dimostrare: Variable double object clitic   285
clusters in the *Decameron* and Medieval Florentine
    Janice Aski, *Ohio State University*

Literary Imagination and Mercantile Pragmatism in Goro Dati's *Sfera*   325
    Dario del Puppo, *Trinity College*

Section V:
Studies on the Italian Renaissance
(Fifteenth and Sixteenth Centuries)

The Newberry Library's Italian Prayer Roll: Evidence for Piety and Novelty   353
    Tonia Triggiano, *Dominican University*

Kairos: The Renaissance Reconstruction of the Best of All Possible Times   375
    Giancarlo Maiorino, *Indiana University*

Reading Through the Text: Lives of Saint Catherine of Alexandria   385
by Christine de Pizan and Pietro Aretino
    Dolly Weber, *University of Illinois at Chicago*

Walters MS W720: Chapters to Be Observed by the Singers of the   401
Cappella Giulia (1574)
    Ilona Klein, *Brigham Young University*

Section VI:
Renaissance Petrarchism and *petrarchiste*

Lettere di una Donna Incerta: Unpublished Letters and Sonnets of   439
Chiara Matraini
   VEENA KUMAR CARLSON, *Dominican University*

Sixteenth Century Petrarchiste and the Reinvention of the Medieval Blazon   459
   FIORA A. BASSANESE, *University of Massachusetts Boston*

Literary Pastimes of a Paduan Jurist: Boccaccio, Petrarca, and Marco   473
Mantova Benavides
   VICTORIA KIRKHAM, *University of Pennsylvania*

The Economics of Authority: Bembo, Vellutello, and the Reconstruction   493
of the "Authentic Petrarch"
   H. WAYNE STOREY, *Indiana University*

Preface

It is a pleasure to introduce this collection of essays in celebration of Professor Christopher Kleinhenz's retirement and to honor his distinguished service to the academic profession in his role as scholar, teacher, mentor, and university administrator. At the Modern Language Association meeting of 2006 his professional distinction was recognized when he received the annual ADFL Distinguished Service award, acknowledging, both nationally and internationally, his exemplary contribution to the academic community and his strong leadership in conjoining the scholarly worlds of North America and the European continent.

Professor Kleinhenz joined the faculty of the University of Wisconsin, Madison, in the 1969–1970 academic year upon completing his Ph.D. at Indiana University with a dissertation under the direction of Professor Mark Musa on the Pistoian poets of the thirteenth century. We soon became both good friends and collegial collaborators on many projects, both administrative and pedagogical. What, for example, began as a modestly enrolled course on Dante's *Commedia* became under our mutual collaboration one of the Department of French and Italian's most popular and successful courses. Always on the cutting edge of pedagogical innovations, Professor Kleinhenz , together with his colleagues, Professors Ullrich Langer, Jan Miernowski, and Jane Tylus, eventually developed an online course on the Middle Ages and Renaissance. The course has become a model for similar courses in other departments on the University campus.

Scholarly work aside, one of his greatest accomplishments in his teaching career was mentoring and nurturing both undergraduate and graduate students, many of whom, under his tutelage, have had distinguished academic careers. And for many, he has remained a "Virgilian" presence, advising them and assisting them in the thorny wood of academic life.

Chris's academic experience is too extensive to discuss in detail, but a summing up will certainly show the extent and breadth of his activities, both in the United States and abroad. He taught in Italy on many occasions and was active in developing the University of Wisconsin's affiliated programs in both Sesto Fiorentino and Bologna. While abroad he lectured extensively, as he has here in the United States and Canada. In addition to his numerous books, edited volumes, and his articles concentrating on medieval culture—which number more than seventy as of this writing—, he edited *Dante Studies* for several years (1988–2002), is the author of many encyclopedia entries, and has prepared bibliographies too numerous to mention. His career of tireless academic as well as administrative activity gained him several honors, most importantly perhaps his appointment as a Fellow at the Institute for Research in the Humanities (1974–1975) on the Madison campus.

To those who know Chris, it is patently obvious that what I have been saying is merely prefatory to what could be a recitation of his accomplishments as a scholar of medieval Italian and French literature, a paleographer, a linguist, and a bibliographer of the first order. If he is, as most would say, a *dantista*, he is an equally accomplished *boccaccista* and *petrarchista*, with essays on the entire canon of medieval and early Renaissance Italian literature, as well as ventures into Franco-Italian studies. And all would agree that in both subtle and in more openly humorous ways, Chris's work often touches on the comic, revealing his keen sense of linguistic play and puns.

The volume before you and the contributions to it represent the breadth and depth of Chris's interests as well as his professional links with some of academia's leading scholars in the field of medieval, early Renaissance, and linguistic / philological studies. Especially noteworthy is the splendid representation of his former students, all of whom hold him in high esteem and, as the titles of their essays suggest, reflect the overwhelming influence which his own interests and teachings have had on them.

The encomia which have followed his retirement have addressed the richness of his *curriculum vitae*, appended to this volume. One excellent example appears in the 19 September 2007 issue of *Wisconsin Week*, published by the University of Wisconsin. An article by Jenny Price splendidly highlights Chris's career and includes many of his own comments, especially in regard to his teaching of Dante. But perhaps the most significant tribute to his contributions to the academic world preceding the publication of this volume was a gathering of several hundred colleagues, former students, and university friends on 8 September 2007, on the University of Wisconsin campus when nearly thirty individuals spoke of his work, both academic and administrative.

I and my fellow colleagues in the Department of French and Italian long admired Chris's energy and his willingness to give unselfishly of his time to mentor students and to work with the Madison community as well as the University community to further underscore the significance of the humanities to the academic world.

ROBERT J. RODINI
Professor Emeritus

Abbreviated Curriculum Vitae

Christopher Kleinhenz

Education

A.B. 1964, Indiana University (Comparative Literature)
M.A. 1966, Indiana University (Comparative Literature)
Ph.D. 1969, Indiana University (Italian). Dissertation: *A Critical Edition of the Pistoian Poets of the Duecento*

Academic Positions

1964–65	Teaching Informant, Istituto Tecnico Commerciale "Amabile," Avellino, Italy
1965–68	Teaching Associate, Indiana University
1968–69	Instructor, University of Wisconsin
1969–70	Assistant Professor, University of Wisconsin
1970–71	Visiting Assistant Professor, Indiana University. Resident Director, Indiana University Study Program, Bologna, Italy
1971–75	Assistant Professor, University of Wisconsin
1975–80	Associate Professor, University of Wisconsin
1980–2007	Professor, University of Wisconsin (Department Chair, 1985–88)
2000–07	Carol Mason Kirk Professor of Italian, University of Wisconsin
2005–07	Director, L&S Honors Program
2007–	Professor Emeritus of Italian

Related Academic Experience

Resident Director, Indiana University Study Program, Bologna, Italy, 1970–71
Professor in residence, University of Michigan-University of Wisconsin Study Program in Florence (Italy) at Villa Boscobello, fall semester, 1984–85

Director and Professor in residence, University of Michigan-University of Wisconsin Study Program in Florence (Italy) at Villa Corsi-Salviati, May-June Summer Session, 1991
Visiting Professor, John Cabot University (Rome, Italy), Summer Session, 1997
Visiting Professor, Brigham Young University (Provo, Utah), Summer Session, 1998
Visiting Professor, Middlebury College (Middlebury, Vermont), Summer Session, 2000
Director, UW Summer Program in Perugia (Italy), June-July, 2002

Grants and Awards

Fulbright Fellowship, 1964–65, Avellino and Naples, Italy. Teaching and Research
Salary Support, Research Committee, University of Wisconsin Graduate School (Summer: 1971, 1983, 1989, 1991; Semester: 1974–75, 1978–79; Supplemental, Academic Year: 1995–96)
Fellow, Institute for Research in the Humanities, University of Wisconsin, 1974–75
Director, Development Grant, National Endowment for the Humanities, 1976–79, Medieval Studies Program
Co-Director, Research Tools Grant, National Endowment for the Humanities, 1980–84
Vilas Associate, University of Wisconsin, 1985–87
Sabbatical Leave, University of Wisconsin, 1988–89, 1995–96, 2002–03
Newberry Library/National Endowment for the Humanities Fellowship, 1988–89
Medal in Recognition for the Promotion of Italian in North America: Università per Stranieri di Siena, 1995
Medal in Recognition for the Promotion of Italian in North America: City of Genoa, 1998
Chancellor's Award for Distinguished Teaching (UW-Madison), 2004
Leonard Covello Educator of the Year Award, 2005
Hilldale Award in the Arts and Humanities (UW-Madison), 2006
AATI Distinguished Service Award, 2006
ADFL Award for Distinguished Service in the Profession, 2006

Publications

Books and Edited Volumes

1. *The Early Italian Sonnet: The First Century (1220–1321)*, Collezione di Studi e Testi 2 (Lecce: Milella, 1986).
2. *Medieval Manuscripts and Textual Criticism*, ed. with an Introduction. North Carolina Studies in the Romance Languages and Literatures, Symposia 4 (Chapel Hill: University of North Carolina Press, 1976).
3. *Medieval Studies in North America: Past, Present and Future*, co-ed. with Francis G. Gentry (Kalamazoo: Medieval Institute Publications, 1982).
4. *Saint Augustine, the Bishop: A Book of Essays*, with Introduction, co-ed. with Fannie LeMoine, Medieval Casebooks series (New York: Garland Publishing, 1994).
5. *Fearful Hope: Approaching the New Millennium*, co-ed. with Fannie LeMoine with an Introduction (Madison: University of Wisconsin Press, 1999).
6. *The Fiore and the Detto d'Amore: A Late 13th-Century Italian Translation of the Roman de la Rose, Attributable to Dante Alighieri*, co-tr. with Santa Casciani, with an introduction and notes (Notre Dame, IN: University of Notre Dame Press, 2000).
7. *Dante Encyclopedia*, Associate Editor; Richard Lansing, Editor (New York: Garland Publishing, 2000).
8. *Medieval Italy: An Encyclopedia*, Editor, 2 vols. (New York and London: Routledge, 2004).
9. *Movement and Meaning in the "Divine Comedy": Toward an Understanding of Dante's Processional Poetics*, Bernardo Lecture Series, 15 (Binghamton, NY: Center for Medieval and Renaissance Studies, State University of New York at Binghamton, 2005).
10. *Courtly Arts and the Art of Courtliness: Selected Proceedings of the Eleventh Triennial Congress of the International Courtly Literature Society*, co-editor with Keith Busby (Woodbridge: Boydell & Brewer, 2006).

Edited Journals

11. *Medieval and Renaissance Theater and Spectacle*, special issue of *Forum Italicum*, assistant editor; Robert J. Rodini, guest editor, 14 (1980): 275–492
12. *Dante Studies*, 106 (1988); 107 (1989); 108 (1990); 109 (1991); 110 (1992); 111 (1993); 112 (1994); 113 (1995); 114 (1996); 115 (1997); 116 (1998); 117 (1999); 118 (2000); 119 (2001); 120 (2002).
13. *Italian Culture*, 13 (1995) (co-editor with Mario Aste).

Exhibit Catalogues

14. *From Medieval to Modern: Italian Books and Manuscripts in University of Wisconsin-Madison Collections*, with John Tedeschi and John Dillon (Madison, 1994).
15. *Arrows of Time*, with Fannie LeMoine and Robin Rider (Madison, 1997).
16. *Chivalry*, with Keith Busby, Robin Rider, and Kelley Osborne (Madison, 2004).

Bibliographies

17. *Italian Language and Literature: A Guide to the Reference Resources in the Memorial Library*, with Charles Szabo. Occasional Papers of the University of Wisconsin-Madison Libraries, 1 (1978).

Textbooks

18. *Italian 104: Second Semester Italian* (Madison: University of Wisconsin Extension, 1989).
18a. *Italian 104: Second Semester Italian*, Completely Revised Edition (Madison: University of Wisconsin Extension, 1993).

Collaboration on Books

19. *Boccacciana: Bibliografia delle edizioni e degli scritti critici (1939–1974)*, Enzo Esposito (Ravenna: Longo, 1976). Responsible for the North American entries.
20. Dante, *Dante's Inferno*, tr. with an introduction, notes, and commentary by Mark Musa (Bloomington: Indiana University Press, 1971). Reprinted as *The Divine Comedy: Vol. I: Inferno* (Harmondsworth: Penguin Books, 1985).

Articles and Chapters in Books

"Esegesi del sonetto provenzale di Paolo Lanfranchi da Pistoia," *Studi e problemi di critica testuale* 2 (1971): 29–39

"The Interrupted Dream of Paolo Lanfranchi da Pistoia," *Italica* 49 (1972): 187–201

"Italian Literature in Translation: A Bibliography of Currently Available Texts," *Italica* 50 (1973): 349–74

"Dante's Towering Giants: *Inferno* XXXI," *Romance Philology* 27 (1974): 269–85

"Tristan in Italy: The Death or Rebirth of a Legend," *Studies in Medieval Culture* 5 (1975): 145–58

"Petrarch and the Art of the Sonnet," in *Francis Petrarch, Six Centuries Later: A Symposium*, ed. Aldo Scaglione. University of North Carolina Studies in the Romance Languages and Literatures and The Newberry Library (Chapel Hill and Chicago, 1975), 177–91

"A Nose for Art (*Purgatory* VII): Notes on Dante's Iconographical Sense," *Italica* 52 (1975): 372–79

"Stylistic Gravity: Language and Prose Rhythms in *Decameron* I, 4," *Humanities Association Review* 26 (1975): 289–99

"Infernal Guardians Revisited: 'Cerbero, il gran vermo' (*Inf.* VI, 22)," *Dante Studies* 93 (1975): 185–99

"Giacomo da Lentino and the Advent of the Sonnet: Divergent Patterns in Early Italian Poetry," *Forum Italicum* 10 (1976): 218–32

"The Nature of an Edition," in *Medieval Manuscripts and Textual Criticism* (#2, Books and Edited Volumes, above), 273–83

"Food for Thought: *Purgatorio* XXII, 146–147," *Dante Studies* 95 (1977): 69–79

"Italian Literature," *The Reader's Adviser*, Vol. II, 12th ed. (New York: Bowker, 1977), 273–311

"Giacomo da Lentini and Dante: The Early Italian Sonnet Tradition in Perspective," *Journal of Medieval and Renaissance Studies* 8 (1978): 217–34

"*Inferno* VII: Cariddi e l'avarizia," *Aevum* 54 (1980): 340–44. (with Gino Casagrande)

"Plutus, Fortune, and Michael: The Eternal Triangle," *Dante Studies* 98 (1980): 35–52

"Iconographic Parody in *Inferno* 21," *Res Publica Litterarum* 5.2 (1982): 125–37

"Iconographic Parody in *Inferno* XXI," in *Dante's "Inferno": The Indiana Critical Edition*, trans. and ed. Mark Musa (Bloomington: Indiana University Press, 1995): 325–39. (Revised version of #17)

"Medieval Journals and Publication Series in North America," in *Medieval Studies in North America: Past, Present, and Future* (#3, Books and Edited Volumes, above), 121–78.

"Reading the *Comedy*," in *Approaches to Teaching Dante's "Divine Comedy*," ed. Carole Slade (New York: Modern Language Association of America, 1982), 72–78

"Leggere la *Divina Commedia*: un approccio testuale," *L'Alighieri* 24.2 (1983): 54–58. [Italian translation of #20 above]

"Literary and Philosophical Perspectives on The Wheel of the Five Senses in Longthorpe Tower," *Traditio* 41 (1985): 311–27 (with Gino Casagrande)

"Dante and the Bible: Intertextual Approaches to the *Divine Comedy*," *Italica* 63 (1986): 225–36

"Notes on Dante's Use of Classical Myths and the Mythological Tradition," *Romance Quarterly* 33 (1986): 477–84

"The Art of Translation: Boccaccio's *Decameron*," *Yearbook of Comparative and General Literature* 36 (1987): 104–11

"A Half Century of Dante Scholarship in America," in *The Divine Comedy and the Encyclopedia of Arts and Sciences: Acta of the International Dante Symposium, 13–16 November 1983*, ed. Giuseppe Di Scipio and Aldo Scaglione (Amsterdam: Benjamins, 1988), 1–13

"Dante, Statius, and Virgil: An Unusual Trinity," in *Lectura Dantis Newberryana*, ed. Paolo Cherchi and Antonio C. Mastrobuono (Evanston: Northwestern University Press, 1988), 37–55

"*Inferno* 8: The Passage across the Styx," *Lectura Dantis* 3 (1988): 23–40

"*Inferno* VIII," in *Dante's "Divine Comedy": Introductory Readings, I: "Inferno,"* ed. Tibor Wlassics; Lectura Dantis Virginiana, vol. I (Charlottesville: University of Virginia Press, 1990), 93–109. [a reprint of #28 above]

"Le Riviste d'Italianistica nel Nord-America," *Revue des études italiennes* 34.4 (octobre-décembre, 1988): 116–29

"The Celebration of Poetry: A Reading of *Purgatory* XXII," *Dante Studies* 106 (1988): 21–41

"Deceivers Deceived: Devilish Doubletalk in *Inferno* 21–23," *Quaderni d'italianistica* 10.1–2 (1989): 133–56

"Dante and the Tradition of Visual Arts in the Middle Ages," *Thought* 65, No. 256 (March, 1990): 17–26

"The Poetics of Citation: Dante's *Divina Commedia* and the Bible," in *Italiana 1988: Selected Papers from the Proceedings of the Fifth Annual Conference of the American Association of Teachers of Italian, November 18–20, 1988, Monterey, CA*, ed. Albert N. Mancini, Paolo A. Giordano, and Anthony J. Tamburri. Rosary College Italian Studies 4 (1990): 1–21

"The Order of Santo Stefano in the Levant: An Unpublished Account of a Voyage in 1627," *Viator* 21 (1990): 323–47 (with Ilona Klein)

"Dante as Reader and Critic of Courtly Literature," in *Courtly Literature: Culture and Context: Selected Papers from the 5th Triennial Congress of the International Courtly Literature Society, Dalfsen, The Netherlands, 9–16 August, 1986)*, ed. Keith Busby and Erik Kooper (Amsterdam/Philadelphia: John Benjamins, 1990), 379–93

"Biblical Citation in Dante's *Divine Comedy*," *Annali d'Italianistica* 8 (1990): 346–59

"Gli studi d'italianistica negli Stati Uniti d'America," in *Lingua e letteratura italiana nel mondo oggi*, ed. Ignazio Baldelli and Bianca Maria da Rif (Florence: Olschki, 1991), 1:, 69–82

"Texts, Naked and Thinly Veiled: Erotic Elements in Medieval Italian Literature," in *Sex in the Middle Ages*, ed. Joyce E. Salisbury (New York: Garland, 1991), 83–109

"Cino da Pistoia and the Italian Lyric Tradition," in *L'imaginaire courtois et son double*, ed. Giovanna Angeli and Luciano Formisano. Pubblicazioni dell'Università degli Studi di Salerno. Sezione Atti, Convegni, Miscellanee 35 (Napoli: Edizioni Scientifiche Italiane, 1992), 147–63

"*Purgatorio* IV," in *Dante's "Divine Comedy": Introductory Readings, II: "Purgatorio,"* ed. Tibor Wlassics; *Lectura Dantis Virginiana*, vol. II (Charlottesville: University of Virginia, 1993), 53–69

"Perspectives on the Quest Motif in Medieval Italian Literature: Comic Elements in Antonio Pucci's *Gismirante*," in *Literary Aspects of Courtly Culture: Selected Papers from the 7th Triennial Congress of the International Courtly Literature Society*, ed. Donald Maddox and Sara Sturm-Maddox (Cambridge: D. S. Brewer, 1994), 249–56

"The Quest Motif in Medieval Italian Literature," in *Conjunctures: Medieval Studies in Honor of Douglas Kelly*, ed. Keith Busby and Norris J. Lacy (Amsterdam: Rodopi, 1994), 235–51

"L'Italianistica negli Stati Uniti," in *Italian Studies in North America*, ed. Massimo Ciavolella and Amilcare A. Iannucci. University of Toronto Italian Studies 10 (Ottawa: Dovehouse, 1994), 55–75

"Dante and the Art of Citation," in *Dante Now: Current Trends in Dante Studies*, ed. Theodore J. Cachey, Jr. (Notre Dame: University of Notre Dame Press, 1995), 43–61

"*Pulzelle e maritate*: Coming of Age, Rites of Passage, and the Question of Marriage in Some Early Italian Poems," in *Matrons and Marginal Women in Medieval Society*, ed. Robert R. Edwards and Vickie Ziegler (Woodbridge: Boydell Press, 1995), 89–110

"*Paradiso* XXX," in *Dante's "Divine Comedy": Introductory Readings, III: "Paradiso,"* ed. Tibor Wlassics, vol. 3 (Charlottesville: University of Virginia Press, 1995), 456–69

"Autorità biblica e citazione poetica: Osservazioni su Dante e la Bibbia," *Filologia e critica* 20.2–3 (maggio-dicembre, 1995): 353–64

"Italy," in *Medieval Arthurian Literature: A Guide to Recent Research*, ed. Norris J. Lacy (New York: Garland Publishing, 1996), 323–47

"Dante and the Bible: Biblical Citation in the *Divine Comedy*," in *Dante: Contemporary Perspectives*, ed. Amilcare A. Iannucci (Toronto: University of Toronto Press, 1997), 74–93

"Courtly Cooking *all'italiana*: Gastronomical Approaches to Medieval Italian Literature," in *The Court and Cultural Diversity: Selected Papers from the Eighth Triennial Congress of the International Courtly Literature Society, The Queen's University of Belfast, 26 July–1 August 1995*, ed. Evelyn Mullally and John Thompson (Woodbridge: D. S. Brewer, 1997), 343–56

"Michele Barbi (1867–1941)," in *Medieval Scholarship: Biographical Studies on the Formation of a Discipline*, vol. 2: *Literature and Philology*, ed. Helen Damico (New York: Garland, 1998), 325–38

"A Trio of Sonnets in Occitan: A Lyrical Duet and an Historic Solo," *Tenso* 13.2 (Spring, 1998), 33–49

"The Visual Tradition of *Inferno* 7: The Relationship of Plutus and Fortune," in *"Visibile Parlare": Dante and the Art of the Italian Renaissance*, ed. Deborah Parker. Special issue of *Lectura Dantis* 22–23 (Spring-Fall, 1998): 247–78

"Mito e verità biblica in Dante," in *Dante: mito e poesia*, Atti del secondo Seminario dantesco internazionale (Monte Verità, Ascona, Switzerland, 23–27 giugno 1997), ed. Michelangelo Picone and Tatiana Crivelli (Florence: Franco Cesati Editore, 1999), 367–89

"Virgil in Dante's *Divine Comedy*," in *The Author as Character: Representing Historical Writers in Western Literature*, ed. Ton Hoenselaars and Paul Franssen (Madison-Teaneck: Fairleigh Dickinson University Press, 1999), 52–67

"The Land of the Living and the Land of the Dead: Burial, Entombment, and Cemeteries in Dante's *Divine Comedy*," *Religion & Literature* 31.1 (Spring, 1999): 49–59

"Erotismo e carnalità nella poesia italiana del Due e Trecento," in *"Por le soie amisté": Essays in Honor of Norris J. Lacy*, ed. Keith Busby and Catherine M. Jones (Amsterdam: Rodopi, 2000), 293–310

"Comic Strategies in Early Italian Poetry: The *Contrasto* of Cielo d'Alcamo and the Anonymous *Detto del gatto lupesco*," *Italian Quarterly* 37, nos. 143–146 (Winter to Fall, 2000): 25–31

"The Status of Italian in the United States," *Forum for Modern Language Studies* 37. 4 (2001): 441–55

"Courtly Codes and Popular Diction in Medieval Italian Poetry," in *Word, Image, Number: Communication in the Middle Ages*, ed. John J. Contreni and Santa Casciani (Fiesole: Sismel-Edizioni del Galluzzo, 2002), 263–85

"Gli studi di italianistica nei 'colleges' e nelle università degli Stati Uniti," in *L'Italia nella lingua e nel pensiero*, 2 vols., ed. Anthony Mollica and Riccardo Campa. Ministero per i Beni e le Attività Culturali; Quaderni di Libri e Riviste d'Italia 46 (Roma: Istituto Poligrafico e Zecca dello Stato, 2002), 2: 713–29

"Tales of Ships and Seas: The Mediterranean in the Medieval Imagination," in *Alexander's Revenge: Hellenistic Culture through the Centuries*, ed. Jon Ma. Asgeirsson and Nancy van Deusen (Reykjavik: The University of Iceland Press, 2002), 181–208

"Newly Discovered Danteana from the Biblioteca Bengodiana," in *Proceedings of the Pseudo Society: First Series (1986–93)*, ed. Richard R. Ring and Richard Kay (Kalamazoo: Medieval Institute Publications, 2003), 157–73

"Tradition and Innovation in the Poetry of Guido Cavalcanti," in *Guido Cavalcanti tra i suoi lettori*, ed. Maria Luisa Ardizzone (Fiesole: Edizioni Cadmo, 2003), 131–47

"On Dante and the Visual Arts," in *Dante and the New Millennium*, ed. Teodolinda Barolini and H. Wayne Storey (New York: Fordham University Press, 2003), 274–92

"Andreuccio da Perugia (*Decameron* 2:5): Scatological Humor, the Odor of Sanctity, and Eschatology," in *Medusa's Gaze: Essays on Gender, Literature, and Aesthetics in the Italian Renaissance. In Honor of Robert J. Rodini*, ed. Paul A. Ferrara, Eugenio Giusti and Jane Tylus, Italiana 11 (Boca Raton, Florida: Bordighera Press, 2004), 233–51

"Rome and Florence in Dante's *Divine Comedy*," in *"De sens rassis": Essays in Honor of Rupert T. Pickens*, ed. Keith Busby, Bernard Guidot, and Logan Whalen, Faux Titre 259 (Amsterdam and New York: Rodopi, 2005), 339–52

"Alan of Lille and Dante: Questions of Influence," *Italica* 82.3–4 (Winter, 2005), 356–65 (with Gino Casagrande) (revised version of #15 above)

"Studies on Medieval Italian Literature in North America: Past, Present and Future," *Journal of English and Germanic Philology* 105. 1 (January, 2006): 245–56

"Italian Arthurian Literature," in *A History of Arthurian Scholarship*, ed. Norris J. Lacy (Cambridge: D. S. Brewer, 2006), 190–97

"Some Thoughts on the Early Italian Madrigal in Its Literary and Musical Contexts," in *Firenze alla vigilia del Rinascimento. Antonio Pucci e I suoi contemporanei. Atti del Convegno di Montreal, 22–23 ottobre 2004, McGill University*, ed. Maria Bendinelli Predelli (Fiesole: Edizioni Cadmo, 2006), 145–56

"Amore in città: le dimore urbane della poesia italiana del Due e Trecento," *Letteratura Italiana Antica* 7 (2006): 87–96

"Perspectives on Intertextuality in Dante's *Divina Commedia*," *Romance Quarterly*, 54 (2007): 183–94.

"*Purgatory* 22," forthcoming in the *California Dante*, ed. Allen Mandelbaum (University of California Press) (29 pp.) [a modified version of #31 above]

"Dante's Views on Judaism, Christianity, and Islam: Perspectives from the New (Fourteenth) Century," in *Poetry, Place, and Gender: Studies in Medieval Culture in Honor of Helen Damico*, ed. C.E. Karkov (Kalamazoo: Medieval Institute Publications, 2009), PAGES?

"Some Thoughts on an Old French Pastourelle" (with Keith Busby), in *"Chançon legiere a chanter": Essays on Old French Literature in Honor of Samuel N. Rosenberg*, ed. Karen Fresco and Wendy Pfeffer (Birmingham AL: Summa, 2007), 153–62.

"Adventures in Textuality: Lyric Poetry, the *Tenzone* and Cino da Pistoia," forthcoming in *Textual Cultures of Medieval Italy*, ed. William Robins and Lawrin Armstrong

Translations

1. "The Problem of Contamination in Prose Texts," by Cesare Segre, in *Medieval Manuscripts and Textual Criticism* (#2, *Books and Edited Volumes*, above), 117–22.

2. "Introduction to the Edition of Medieval Vernacular Documents (XIII and XIV Centuries)," by Egidio Rossini, in *Medieval Manuscripts and Textual Criticism* (#2, *Books and Edited Volumes*, above), 175–210.
3. Translations of fourteenth-century Italian poetry for inclusion in the materials accompanying the compact disk recorded by The Newberry Consort, *Il Solazzo: Music for a Medieval Banquet* (Harmonia Mundi 907038) (with Paul Gehl), 18–34.

Work in Progress

Volume on the minor literature of thirteenth- and fourteenth-century Italy
Volume for the MLA on "Approaches to Teaching Petrarch's *Canzoniere* and the Petrarchan Tradition"
Critical edition and translation of the poetry of Cino da Pistoia

Section I

Medieval Romances between France and Italy

The *Ordonnance* of the Quest in Jean Froissart's *Meliador*[1]

Douglas Kelly

The commonplaces of the Arthurian quest in Chrétien's romances as well as the adaptations of the motif in the different branches of the *Lancelot-Grail* cycle are well known today.[2] Less closely examined has been the influence of these two major collections of works as models for quests in later verse romances[3] such as—last but not least—Jean Froissart's *Meliador*.[4] I shall treat the quest motif in this romance, using Chrétien as model, although it is unlikely that Froissart knew his romances directly,[5] as well as some post-Chrétien romances in verse and especially in prose that he may have known.[6]

---

[1] An earlier version of this article was read at the 59th annual Kentucky Foreign Language Conference, Lexington, 20–22 April 2006.

[2] Annie Combes, *Les Voies de l'aventure: réécriture et composition romanesque dans le "Lancelot" en prose* (Paris: Champion, 2001); and, more recently, eadem, "Le Roman arthurien: le paradigme de l'aventure," in *Poétiques du roman d'aventures*, ed. Alain-Michel Boyer and Daniel Couégnas (La Mothe-Achard: Defaut, 2004), 31–43.

[3] Beate Schmolke-Hasselmann, *Der arthurische Versroman von Chrestien bis Froissart: zur Geschichte einer Gattung* (Tübingen: Niemeyer, 1980), chap. 2; Marie-Luce Chênerie, *Le Chevalier errant dans les romans en vers des XII*ᵉ *et XIII*ᵉ *siècles* (Geneva: Droz, 1986). See Richard Trachsler, *Les Romans arthuriens en vers après Chrétien de Troyes* (Rome: Memini, 1997), 315, Index s.v. "Quête".

[4] References are to Jean Froissart, *Méliador*, ed Auguste Longnon, 3 vols. (Paris: Firmin Didot, 1895–1899).

[5] Peter F. Ainsworth, "The Art of Hesitation: Chrétien, Froissart and the Inheritance of Chivalry," in *The Legacy of Chrétien de Troyes*, 2 vols. (Amsterdam: Rodopi, 1987–1988), 2:187–206.

[6] Alexandre Micha, "Miscellaneous French Romances in Verse," in *Arthurian Literature in the Middle Ages: A Collaborative History*, ed. Roger Sherman Loomis (Oxford: Clarendon Press, 1959), 358–92, here 392; Peter F. Dembowski, *Jean Froissart and His "Meliador": Context, Craft, and Sense* (Lexington, KY: French Forum, 1983), 96–97; Douglas Kelly et al., "Arthurian Verse Romance in the Twelfth and Thirteenth Centuries," in *The Arthur of the French*, ed. Glyn S. Burgess and Karen Pratt (Cardiff: University

Varieties of Movement in Space and Time

It is necessary at the outset to make some terminological distinctions regarding the quest and analogous or similar movements or kinds of progression by Arthurian knights in quest narratives. There are three common kinds of such movement not infrequently associated with or identified as quests, one of which is the quest itself; the two others are travel as voyage and *errances* or wandering. All three are found in Chrétien and *Meliador*. Travel is just that: travel or the passage from one place to another. Examples of such travel narratives are found in *Cligés*. Alexandre travels from Constantinople to Britain, Cligés from the city on the Dardanelles to Cologne; in a more strictly Arthurian example from the *Conte du graal*, Gauvain travels from Arthur's court to Escavalon in order to defend his honor against an accusation of murder. This is not a quest like that Gauvain begins upon leaving Escavalon in search of the Bleeding Lance. Similarly, in *Meliador* the titular hero travels from his father's castle in Cornwall to Arthur's court to be dubbed. From there he embarks on his quest for the hand of the princess of Scotland, Hermondine.

I shall return to the distinctive features of the *Meliador* quest after explaining *errances*. Calogrenant offers an example of *errances* in *Yvain*. He wanders about in search of adventures to test his mettle: he is a "chevalier errant / Qui aventure alast querant" (*Yvain*, v. 259–260).[7] Or, as Calogrenant later explains to the herder of bulls:

> – Je sui, çou vois, uns chevaliers
> Qui quier che que trouver ne puis;
> Assés ai quis et riens ne truis.
> – Et que vaurroies tu trouver ?
> – Aventures, pour esprouver
> Ma proeche et mon hardement.
> Or te pri et quier et demant,
> Se tu ses, que tu me conseilles
> Ou d'aventure ou de merveilles. (*Yvain*, v. 356–364)

Errances such as those a *chevalier errant* like Calogrenant embarks upon differ from the quest proper. Calogrenant seeks adventures or marvels that test his prowess. Any adventure, especially a marvelous one, will serve his purpose. In *Meliador* the closest example of *errances* is Sagremor's narrative. Towards the end of the romance this young knight sets out, like Calogrenant, in search of

---

of Wales Press, 2006), 393–460. The List of Proper Names in Langlois's edition also suggests some romances Froissart may have known.

[7] Chrétien de Troyes, *Le Chevalier au lion ou le Roman d'Yvain*, ed. David F. Hult (Paris: Librairie Générale Française, 1994).

adventures to test his mettle and prove his prowess to Sebille with whom he has fallen in love.

> Tant il fera
> Qu'il ara le grasce et le nom
> De chevalier et le renom.
> Saigremor, sus cesti pourpos,
> Ordonna ses besonges tos. (v. 26167–26171)

However, his undertaking is not entirely the same as Calogrenant's because he hopes in this way to win Sebille's love; this hope is a goal, but his actions recall *errances* in *Yvain*.

Querre aventures is not necessarily synonymous with *querre l'aventure*. The goal distinguishes the quest proper from *errances*. The quester is not *errant*. Rather the quester has a specific goal, a specific adventure that he hopes to achieve. In Chrétien, for example, Lancelot seeks the liberation of Guenevere in the *Charrette*, whereas in the *Conte du graal* Perceval seeks the Grail and Gauvain sets out in search of the Bleeding Lance; a more abstract goal is apparent in the quests of Erec and Yvain: reconciliation. Perceval occupies a middle ground between these two kinds of goal. In quest of the Grail Castle in order to ask the questions he failed to ask earlier, he wanders about seeking adventures and combat. In this he resembles Meliador. Perceval's errant quest lasts more than five years—it is longer than the *Meliador* quest—yet he fails to advance towards his goal until, by chance, he happens upon the Good Friday penitents and discovers his hermit uncle who actually answers one of the questions he intended to ask: whom one serves with the grail.[8] The *Lancelot-Grail* cycle contains many of these features in its numerous quests, including an allegorical level in the *Queste* and, occasionally, prior to that quest. The allegorical quest is missing in Chrétien and in later verse romances, including *Meliador*.

Ordonnance of the Chrétien Quest

Since Froissart probably did not know Chrétien, Chrétien will serve, provisionally, as an example that can reveal, comparatively, how Froissart fashions his own quests and what features the later author shares with his illustrious predecessor as well as in what ways his quests differ. I shall also introduce for comparison a few other Arthurian quests found in romances between Chrétien and Froissart. The broader implications will have to await a more thorough study of the quest motif

---

[8] See Chrétien de Troyes, *Le Roman de Perceval ou Le Conte du graal*, ed. Keith Busby (Tübingen: Niemeyer, 1993), v. 6217–6515.

that would include non-Arthurian quests such as those found in *Cristal et Clarie* and the *Sept Sages de Rome en prose*.[9]

Certain features of Chrétien's quests distinguish them from voyages and *errances*.[10] The quest has a specific goal that identifies its purpose. On the way to the goal the questing knight or knights encounter various adventures[11] that arise more or less coincidentally with the quest, but that are fundamentally distinguishable from one another as assistance or obstacle to the knight's progress. He confronts an episodic adventure only if necessary, a major difference between the quest and *errances*, wherein, as with Calogrenant, any adventure is suitable. An important exception to the quester's choice of adventures is his duty to aid maidens in distress or any other person in need of his protection. It is also improper for more than one knight to attack another at the same time, a custom[12] even robber knights observe in *Erec et Enide*. All knights quest incognito except for Gauvain, who is marked as an exception to this motif. Furthermore, the knight's reaction to adventure helps to define him and his relationship to the quest. He is always rushed, refusing to stop before nightfall unless ill, badly wounded, or imprisoned, or to stay for more than a single night before setting out again early the following morning; he also tries to take the most direct route to his goal. There may be companions, but not too many; the companions may have some relation to the knight's goal, as we see with Enide, the companions for Lancelot outside of and, then, inside Gorre, and Yvain's lion.

These commonplace features of the Chrétien quest remain more or less intact in the verse romances after Chrétien. Not in all of them, of course. Girart d'Amiens's *Escanor* has no quest although it is 'Arthurian'. But these romances

---

[9] See Keith Busby, "*Cristal et Clarie*: a Novel Romance?" in *Convention and Innovation in Literature*, ed. Theo D'haen, Rainer Grübel, and Helmut Lethen (Amsterdam and Philadelphia: Benjamins, 1989), 77–103; Douglas Kelly, "*Disjointure* and the Elaboration of Prose Romance: The Example of the Seven Sages of Rome Prose Cycle," in *The Spirit of the Court: Selected Proceedings of the Fourth Congress of the International Courtly Literature Society (Toronto 1983)*, ed. Glyn S. Burgess, Robert A. Taylor, et al. (Cambridge: Brewer, 1985), 208–16.

[10] What follows summarizes Douglas Kelly, "La Forme et le sens de la quête dans l'*Erec et Enide* de Chrétien de Troyes," *Romania* 92 (1971): 334–43.

[11] Philippe Ménard, "Problématique de l'aventure dans les romans de la Table Ronde," in *Arturus rex II: Acta Conventus Lovaniensis 1987*, ed. Willy Van Hoecke, Gilbert Tournoy, and Werner Verbeke (Leuven: Leuven University Press, 1991), 89–119: Chênerie, *Chevalier errant*, esp. 75–78 et passim; Erich Köhler, *Ideal und Wirklichkeit in der höfischen Epik: Studien zur Form der frühen Artus- und Graldichtung*, 2d ed. (Tübingen: Niemeyer, 1970), chap. 3.

[12] On custom and quests, see Donald Maddox, *The Arthurian Romances of Chrétien de Troyes: Once and Future Fictions* (Cambridge: Cambridge University Press, 1991); Matilda Tomaryn Bruckner, *Narrative Invention in Twelfth-Century French Romance: The Convention of Hospitality* (Lexington, KY: French Forum, 1980).

can also be original. Gauvain plays a prominent role in a variety of quests and *errances* in romances as diverse as *Meraugis de Portlesguez*, the *Atre périlleux*, and the *Chevalier aux deux épées*. What begins as travel to court in *Beaudous* opens up to a wide digression in which the titular hero comes to the aid of a lady in distress. The prose romances too offer, in the *Perlesvaus* and the *Lancelot-Graal* cycle, a multiplicity of quests whereas the *Prose Tristan*'s peregrinations resemble more those of travel and *errances*. The prose romances no doubt inspired the multiple quests in *Claris et Laris* and *Rigomer* as well as, perhaps, the multiple validated questers in the *Vengeance Raguidel*. Philippe Ménard notes cogently that "tout se renouvelle au gré des talents et des sensibilités."[13] So, as time passes, we may look for more and more variations on the quest motif in diverse romances.

Errances in Meliador: Sagremor

Froissart's *Meliador* is no different in this respect, except that it is set in time before the arrival of Gauvain's generation at the Round Table (*Meliador*, v. 1–7, 28–43, 11674–11699, 30597–30602), and, thus, of the epoch Chrétien writes about.[14] This adaptation is apparent when a few very young members of the next generation appear, notably Agravain, Gauvain's older brother in *Meliador*, as well as Sagremor during the quest, but not as a participant. Therefore, we may distinguish between the *chevalier errant* who, like Calogrenant and Sagremor, illustrate *errances*, and the *chevalier de quête* who is on a quest with a specific goal that influences his reaction to adventures he encounters en route to that goal.[15]

Once at Arthur's court, Sagremor acquires skill as knight, falls in love, and sets out to win his beloved, Sebille, by his prowess. His adventures (they are incomplete because the end of the romance is missing in the only nearly complete manuscript)[16] constitute *errances*. Like Calogrenant in *Yvain*, he is not actually

---

[13] Ménard, "Problématique," 100. He is referring to the notion of adventure, but the remark is valid for the quest motif as well; see "Problématique," 109–10.

[14] On this chronological adaptation and the problems it may raise regarding Froissart's approach to Arthurian romance, see Schmolke-Hasselmann, *Der arthurische Versroman*, 169–71; Michael Schwarze, *Generische Wahrheit-höfischer Polylog im Werk Jean Froissarts* (Stuttgart: Steiner, 2003), 141–43.

[15] Froissart uses various terms to refer to each kind of knight, for example, "chevaliers de queste" (v. 3344), "chevalier errant" (v. 6094), "chevaliers bien enventureus" (v. 21042), "compagnon de la queste" (v. 24538), "chevalier aventureus" (v. 27985). The specific connotation of such descriptions depends, of course, on whether, *errant*, the knight is on a true quest or is merely wandering about in search of adventures and marvels.

[16] Bibl. Nat. Fr. fr. 12557 offers the most complete version of *Meliador* known today; it is the basis for the Longnon edition. Bib. Nat. Fr. nouv. acq. lat. 2374 contains four fragments, the last of which relates part of an adventure of Sagremor that takes place after the end of ms. 12557.

in quest of a specific goal—he is not one of the *chevaliers de quête* (v. 27600) and is, for example, free to name himself (v. 28006)—but rather of adventures to test and prove his prowess.

> Besoing a, ce dist, d'aprendre.
> Si vodra travillier le mont
> Et aler aval et amont,
> Pour cognoistre les aventures,
> Car il dit que ce sont droitures
> Que tout jone chevalier doient
> Poursieuir, qui le monde voient. (v. 28012–28018)

Sagremor's adventures are also *enfances*, or the initial deeds of a young knight that show his mettle.[17] Like Calogrenant, Sagremor sets out in search of adventures (*querre aventures*). In this way his adventures conform to the definition of Calogrenant's *errances* in Chrétien's romance noted above: "Aventures, pour esprouver / Ma proeche et mon hardement." Sagremor too is *errant* in this sense. He encounters adventures and marvels in his wanderings, including rather fantastic dreams, perhaps a variant of Camel de Camois's somnambulism, and a supernatural stag that bears him away to captivity by three fairies.[18] The manuscript ends with Sagremor in Brittany, a prisoner of the fairies.

Ordonnance of the Meliador Quest

As we have observed, *Meliador* illustrates all three kinds of movement: travel, or knights like Meliador who goes to Arthur's court, *errances* like Sagremor's who seeks adventures and marvels, and the quest proper. A quest in this sense dominates the romance's narrative, as the narrator remarks in concluding the last Sagremor episode.

> Ailleurs que ci en parlerons,
> Mais nous avant parconclurons
> De la queste qui est emprise,
> Sur qui ceste matere est prise. (*Meliador*, v. 28828–28831)

In order to find a suitable husband for Hermondine, princess of Scotland, she and her cousin Florée announce a five-year quest. The immediate purpose of their plot is to eliminate an overweening pretender to her hand, Camel de Camois,

---

[17] Friedrich Wolfzettel, "Zur Stellung und Bedeutung der *Enfances* in der altfranzösischen Epik," *Zeitschrift für französische Sprache und Literatur* 84 (1974): 9–32.

[18] See Laurence Harf-Lancner, *Les Fées au moyen âge: Morgane et Mélusine. La Naissance des fées* (Paris: Champion, 1984), 231–33.

a particularly distasteful suitor because he is of lower nobility, which makes his proposal *oultrecuidant*, and because he is a sleepwalker, and a rather violent one at that.[19] In the hope of finding someone more suitable and thereby eliminate Camel, the two women instigate a five-year quest the goal of which is Hermondine's hand. Meliador successfully achieves the quest, is declared the winner, and marries the Scottish princess. Many other knights, or *chevaliers de quête*, begin the quest and the runners-up win the hands of maidens who are themselves ranked in a corresponding hierarchy.

The Hermondine quest has its own conditions. Here we may summarize the principal features of this quest. Froissart likens it to a 'chasse' or hunt (v. 2868, 7150, 7410, 23245). The *Meliador* 'hunt' differs from the exclusively erotic hunt in, for example, the *Roman de la rose* because the 'hunted woman', Hermondine, instigates the quest and is happy to be captured, providing it is by the best knight and that he marry her.[20] That knight will be so valiant that his prowess stands out before that of all other contestants; by the terms of the quest, that outstanding prowess explains why he alone achieves the quest so many undertake (v. 1725–1730, 1868–1873, 2802–2805). There are judges[21] who discuss and decide the outcome. The decision is unanimous in favor of Meliador, and so the judges award Hermondine to Meliador as well as other willing demoiselles to the runners-up: Phenonée to Agamanor, Florence to Gratien, and so on.[22] Apart from this goal of the quest, the actual quests and their adventures resemble more closely *errances* in Chrétien or Sagremor's similar *errances* in *Meliador*. The questers seek adventures, as Calogrenant does, in armed combat, but they do not see them as obstacles to progress or marvels to be overcome; they are the very stuff of the quest and the sole means to demonstrate prowess and excellence. The *chevaliers de quête* may also attack one another, an especially obvious way to demonstrate superior prowess. This accounts too for the prominence of tournaments in the *Meliador* quests as these permit more reliable eyewitness verification by a large body of witnesses. As the terms of the quest put it, the questing knights

---

[19] I discuss Camel de Camois in D. Kelly, "Analogie et anomalie dans la description de chevaliers: la *diverse ordenance* de Camel de Camois," in *Façonner son personnage au moyen âge: Actes du 31ᵉ colloque du CUER MA 9, 10 et 11 mars 2006*, ed. Chantal Connochie-Bourgne, Senefiance 53 (Aix-en-Provence: Publications de l'Université de Provence, 2007), 145–55.

[20] Contrast the quest in *Rigomer*, in which the successful knight will win the hand of Dionise, the lady of Rigomer castle. Gauvain achieves the quest but declines to accept the reward because he already has a beloved fay; he chooses another knight to wed Dionise and the lady accepts the bargain.

[21] Twelve *esliseurs* or *diseurs* (v. 2892–2893) are named by Arthur and Hermondine's father, Hermont, king of Scotland (v. 2878–2883).

[22] See Jane H. M. Taylor, "The Fourteenth Century: Context, Text and Intertext," in *The Legacy of Chrétien de Troyes*, 1: 267–332, here 303–4.

must "Par proece . . . conquerre" (v. 2792) Hermondine's hand. Prowess means prowess in arms: "uns preus chevaliers li venra, / Qui par armes le conquerra" (v. 2824–2825). Although such prowess may imply other honorable qualities, victory in armed combat is the single path to excellence because success reveals concomitant qualities that signal the knight's superior prowess (v. 2833–2835).[23]

There are adaptations of the quest motif because of the goal. Husbands are excluded in a rather jocular manner because they already have wives (v. 3049–3073). One knight, named Sorelais,[24] excludes himself because he already has a beloved; he enters the quest merely to prove his prowess (v. 7456–7470) and in this way win her love when she hears of his achievements. When Sorelais jousts with Meliador, the result is inconclusive as the contest has no purpose because Sorelais does not intend to marry Hermondine (v. 7485–7498). Another adaptation occurs when Agamanor turns from the goal of marriage to Hermondine after he falls in love with Phenonée, Meliador's sister. He loved Hermondine sight unseen; but when he sees Phenonée while winning the Tarbonne tournament a *coup de foudre* changes his inclination (v. 13274–13293). Phenonée later questions this change of heart before agreeing to their love and marriage provided Agamanor wins second place in the quest (v. 22800–22824).

Stationary Quests: Wales and Ireland

Two knights have virtually stationary quests. This is permissible in *Meliador* if the knight outposts himself on the border of his domain and jousts with any questing knight who happens by (v. 4412–4421). Clarin does so for a time before confronting Camel de Camois who defeats him (v. 5269–5282). The prime example of the immobile quester is Camel himself. In this way Froissart adapts what, in the Chrétien model, is an obstacle to the quester's progress towards his goal. If one has a domain, as Camel does—it is Camois, an otherwise vague geographical location in Wales—the knight may post himself there and await passing knights against whom he will try his mettle. Florée contrives in this way to keep Camel away from the tournaments, ostensibly at Hermondine's wish, but actually to keep his prowess out of view and thus reduce his chances of being elected the best knight and actually marrying Hermondine against her will (v. 3758–3766). Camel does as directed, either killing those he encounters or imprisoning them in Florée's castle Montgries. Questing knights like Clarin come to him in search of combat. In addition, Florée is required to scout about near Montgries in search of passing knights that she can send to do battle with Camel (v. 7859–7887). While fulfilling this obligation she encounters Meliador. Meliador defeats the upstart pretender to Hermondine's hand, liberates the prisoners

---

[23] Cf. Schwarze, *Generische Wahrheit*, 178–79.

[24] This name is missing in the *Meliador*'s Index of Proper Names; see v. 7368 et passim.

Camel took, and eliminates this undesirable somnambulant knight from competition and as a threat. Death in quests is more common in *Meliador* than in Chrétien's romances. Indeed, death in tournament or other combat is preferable to *recreantise* or other kinds of idleness (v. 4393–4403).[25]

In Ireland too border defense harks back to the traditional outpost as obstacle—for example, those who impede entrance into Gorre in the *Charrette* or to Rigomer castle in the romance of that name. Sicamont, the king of Ireland, is considered a barbarian. "Felles / Et a toutes raisons rebelles" (v. 24856–24857), he is opposed to quests, a commonplace of Arthurian civilization. Because of the king's opposition, his knights too are by and large uncivilized, or "rude" (v. 18796), a distinctive mark of inferior Irish civilization in *Meliador*. Sicamont tries in this way to prevent his son Sagremor, a sort of anti-Meleagant, from becoming a *chevalier de quête*.[26] Therefore, implicitly following the example of Camel, he posts his knights on the Irish border[27] and at various locations between the border and his seat in Dublin (v. 18998–19008) in order to prevent questing knights like Meliador from entering his realm. The Irish knights try unsuccessfully to stop questers who attempt to enter the kingdom. Meliador and Agamanor break through these defenses. Eventually they come to the attention of Sagremor, who escapes from his father's realm to Arthur's court. When his father dies of grief after learning what his son has done (v. 24878–24888, 26433–26445), the kingdom is given to Bondigal because Sagremor is absent (v. 26547–26549, 26583–26585). The denouement is not related in the incomplete romance, although Froissart suggests that Sagremor will overthrow Bondigal and recover his birthright (v. 26586–26591).

Marvels

As in Chrétien's romances, *merveilles* are experienced only as extraordinary, not supernatural obstacles.[28] In *Meliador* too the eponymous hero "fait merveilles" (v. 6875) in a tournament, that is, he accomplishes extraordinary feats of arms.

---

[25] For examples besides Camel (cf. v. 8792–8795, 9101–9105), who also kills many of his opponents (v. 5827–5828, 8597), see v. 13117, 13122, 16480, 23535.

[26] But he does permit his knights to participate in tournaments; see v. 12797–12798.

[27] In *Meliador* Ireland is separated from Britain by the river Clarence, which contradicts the earlier separation by the sea in the middle of which is found the Isle of Man (v. 11735). On this anomaly, see A. H. Diverres, "The Irish Adventures in Froissart's *Meliador*," in *Mélanges de langue et de littérature du moyen âge et de la Renaissance offerts à Jean Frappier*, 2 vols. (Geneva: Droz, 1970), 1: 235–51; and Schmolke Hasselmann, *Der arthurische Versroman*, 1: 229.

[28] An important exception is the Perilous Fountain in *Yvain*. See Kelly, "Forme," 332–34; Ménard, "Problématique," 115; Michael Schwarze, "Vom Artushof nach

In a different context, Camel's desire to marry Hermondine against her will is, to Meliador's way of thinking, "trop grant merveille; / Je n'ai point trouvé la pareille" (v. 8316–8317). The supernatural as *merveille* emerges in *Meliador* (if we discount Camel's somnambulism which may, like the Bisclavret's were-wolfishness, have seemed supernatural to Froissart's audiences, although Florée refers to Camel's dysfunction as a "visce" (v. 6317, 6358).[29] Phenonée interprets her mistaking Agamanor for her brother Meliador as "cose faée et nouvelle" (v. 19254). She becomes so overwhelmed by her experience that she cannot sleep and falls ill (v. 19266–19314). Her love for her brother is "oultre mesure" (v. 19548). The supernatural as such occurs in this romance during the *errances* of Sagremor when fairies abduct him with the help of an enchanted stag.[30]

Other Commonplaces in the *Meliador* Quest

Companions. There are other, more specific commonplaces in the *Meliador* quests. Some reflect those found in Chrétien, whereas others are unique to *Meliador* or derive from other post-Chrétien verse romances. In Froissart's romance, the questing knight may have only one companion, a squire (v. 2896–2897). Accordingly, Lansonnet accompanies Meliador, Bertoulet Agamanor, Manesier the Italian knight Gratien, and so on. The squires provide conversation and counsel, may negotiate the terms of combat, and comment on the artistic quality of the many songs by Wenceslas de Brabant that Froissart inserted into his romance, many of which the questers and their squires sing between adventures.

Incognito. The *Meliador* questers must remain incognito, as in Chrétien (v. 2898–2901).[31] For this reason they are often identified by armorial features like blazon and color. Besides Meliador as the "chevalier / Bleu, armé au solel d'or" (v. 7006–7007), Agamanor is the "[chevalier] rouge . . . / Qui portoit une blance dame" (v. 7122–7123); similar armorial colors and images identify the other

---

Arcadien: das *merveilleux* in Jean Froissarts *Meliador*," in *Das Wunderbare in der arthurischen Literatur: Probleme und Perspektiven*, ed. Friedrich Wolfzettel (Tübingen: Niemeyer, 2003), 113–25.

[29] There seems to be no word for somnambulism as such in Old or Middle French; see Michel Zink, "Froissart et la nuit du chasseur," in idem, *Les Voix de la conscience: parole du poète et parole de Dieu dans la littérature médiévale* (Caen: Paradigme, 1992), 129–31. *Visce* in *Meliador* also refers to Camel's overweening pride (v. 9207–9208), to Meliador's jealousy (v. 9842), and to the latter's skill at wrestling (v. 10659).

[30] One other minor because inconsequential exception occurs when a fairy casts a spell that causes passers-by to fall into deep sleep. This happens to Meliador and Lansonnet (v. 7961–7972).

[31] This can produce undesirable results, as when Gauvain and Yvain fight in Chrétien's romance. In *Meliador*, two brothers, Savare and Feughin, fight one another, with serious consequences (v. 9492–9505).

knights.[32] The pseudonyms are supposed to be unique so that the judges can identify successful questers while these remain incognito during the quest. For example, Camel's prisoners are liberated after Meliador slays the somnambulant knight; they report to the court the "proeces, de cief en cor, / Dou chevalier au soleil d'or" (v. 9343–9344), whereupon scribes consign their words to a register of illustrious deeds (v. 9339–9342), a motif probably adopted from the prose romances, but that is only implicit in Chrétien.[33] For this reason it is especially important that defeated knights report posthaste, and without any intervening combat, their misfortune at court, identifying the victor by his armorial signature; those who fail to do so are dishonored (v. 27677–27844). The armorial features permit official designation pending later revelation of the name at the end of the quest. Such pseudonyms for questers are commonplace in Chrétien's and other quest romances.[34] There can be no duplication of pseudonyms or armorial insignia lest the record of achievements and losses become skewed. This feature creates a problem and potential conflict when Agamanor meets Lyone wearing the same outfit and blazon he does. Agamanor pardons this young knight, who is a questing knight in quest of Agamanor, because Phenonée, whom Agamanor loves and marries as "second prize" in the quest, ordered Lyone to do so in order to facilitate his search for "cilz qui a les rouges draps / Et qui porte une blance dame" (v. 12886–12887) in order to transmit a message to her beloved. Later Agamanor and another knight, Morenois, fight because they have analogous blazons (v. 27960–27969).

Multiple Quests and Tournaments.

The quests in *Meliador* illustrate two additional novelties, one of which Chrétien anticipates: multiple quests and tournaments. Multiple quests occur in two late thirteenth-century verse romances, *Rigomer* and *Claris et Laris*.[35] Like *Rigomer*, but unlike *Claris*, Froissart does not (and says he cannot) relate the adventures of the ten times twenty-four knights (v. 4454–4466) who set out on the quest for Hermondine; he therefore opts to relate only the adventures of those who, "bon oultre l'ensengne" (v. 4465), are the most remarkable. These are also the quests of those who succeed in good order, as second-, third-, fourth-place knights and

---

[32] See Langlois, ed., *Meliador*, 3: 354–57.

[33] Combes, "Roman," 31–33. On the role of interdiagetic reports in the *Lancelot en prose*, see Bernadette Smelik, *Bijfiguren in de "Lancelot en prose": een studie over de verteltechnische functies van ridders, joncvrouwen, schildknapen, dwergen en kluizenaars* (Münster: Nodus, 2002), esp. chaps. 3–5.

[34] Chênerie, *Chevalier errant*, 132–35.

[35] Douglas Kelly, "Multiple Quests in French Verse Romance: *Mervelles de Rigomer* and *Claris et Laris*," *L'Esprit créateur* 9 (1969): 257–66.

beyond, winning correspondingly worthy damsels as wives and rewards for their achievements. Even they and almost everyone else falls into a predetermined, idealized place. In effect, these pre-Round Table knights constitute a group of stereotypes. I return to this feature of Froissart's quests below.

The tournament motif is not a feature of the quests themselves in Chrétien,[36] but does become an adventure in the prose romances and in verse romances like *Durmart le Galois* and *Rigomer*. In Froissart's romance the tournament becomes a major indicator of valor because it permits the "oultre preu ou dieu de bataille" (v. 4428) to display their prowess incognito (except for their armorial signs) before large audiences of connoisseurs, including the judges as well as knowledgeable spectators such as lords, ladies, and heralds. Peter Dembowski underscores the tournament motif's prominence and importance in *Meliador* by designating the tournaments as four acts in a play broken by "entr'actes" that relate the actual quests.[37] Tournaments provide a more objective venue to evaluate chivalric performance, hence the prominence Dembowski gives to them in the romance's *ordonnance* and in the individual quests.

Collective Heroism: Judging Stereotypes

How do the judges evaluate and rank the *chevaliers de quête*? The question is important and problematic. The multiple quests referred to above have as corollary what Dembowski and, in his wake, Jane Taylor term the "collective heroism" of the questers.[38] This collectivity resists identifying qualities that distinguish among the knights, an important feature of Chrétien's quests.

Collective quests like those in *Meliador* are a variety of multiple quests. This kind is adumbrated at the beginning of the second part of Chrétien's *Perceval* and receives its fullest elaboration in the verse romances *Rigomer* and *Claris et Laris*,

---

[36] There are tournaments in Chrétien's romances, but none occur during a quest (unlike in the prose romances). Gauvain's participation in a tournament at Tintagel in *Perceval* is not part of a quest but of a voyage as defined above. The closest action to a tournament occurs in the *Charrette*, but it is not a true tournament but rather a battle provoked by the insurgent prisoners in Gorre. "Tournoi" here describes the way battles are fought in the *Roman de Troie*: it is a "meslee," v. 2383: Chrétien de Troyes, *Le Chevalier de la charrette ou le Roman de Lancelot*, ed. Charles Méla (Paris: Librairie Générale Française, 1992). The same imprecision in language obtains in *Meliador*, which still uses both words to refer to tournaments; cf. that at la Garde (v. 6677, 6751, 6804), and Signadon (v. 15993, 16038, 16051). A duel is a "meslée" (v. 7404) as is a "luitier" (v. 10603–10604).

[37] Dembowski, *Jean Froissart*, chap. 2.

[38] See Dembowski, *Jean Froissart*, 62; Taylor, "Fourteenth Century," 301.

and in the *Lancelot-Graal* prose romances. Four features define collective heroism in the *Meliador* quest and serve to distinguish each knight from his peers.[39]

I. Order of appearance corresponds by and large to success and final ranking of the knights. Meliador is introduced before Agamanor, who precedes Gratien, and so forth; of course, Camel precedes them all because he is the first cause of the quest, but acts in the special way discussed above.

II. Social and chivalric status defines qualifications for noble standing; a major obstacle to Camel's candidacy is his inferior nobility.

III. Combat is a sign of chivalric excellence, including reporting to Arthur's court the names of victor and defeated. Meliador stands out because he defeats Camel, Agamanor, and Gratien; these of course have their own victories.

IV. Marriage is reward for the knight best meeting the aforementioned standards. Stereotype is the gauge. The knights are stereotypes given separate names and ordered, first, according to rank and, second, according to combat. Changing the names would change nothing essential except the romance's title. This is not the case in Chrétien or in many early thirteenth-century romances in verse and prose. Of course there are stereotypical features in his major characters. Chrétien distinguishes between what Erich Köhler terms the "Gleich Gestellten" but "nicht Gleich Gearteten" knights of the Round Table — that is, those knights of equal rank represented by their seating without precedence at the Round Table, but not of the same kind.[40] Chrétien ranks the Round Table knights in *Erec et Enide*: Gauvain is best, Erec second best, Lancelot third, etc.[41] But Erec is also different from Lancelot as Perceval is from Yvain. This is important, and I should like to conclude my remarks by analyzing these features of Chrétien's Round Table vis-à-vis *Meliador* hierarchy.

The distinction Köhler notes is Chrétien's most significant adaptation of Wace's Round Table to the quest motif. But other innovations are made in *Meliador* on earlier motifs, in part no doubt because of changes in knighthood between 1180 and 1400. For example, Meliador's combats and those of some others often include unhorsing an opponent by wrestling him to the ground,[42] a special prowess, or *apertise*. In one case, Agamanor unhorses Agaian with a shoulder blow (v. 4602–4605). In the tournament at la Garde castle, peasants are recruited

---

[39] Dembowski, *Jean Froissart*, 72, and Taylor, "Fourteenth Century," 303–4.

[40] Köhler, *Ideal und Wirklichkeit*, 90.

[41] Chrétien de Troyes, *Erec et Enide*, ed. Jean-Marie Fritz (Paris: Librairie Générale Française, 1992), v. 1683–1746. In all his romances tournaments, jousts, and duels tend to rank knights of the Round Table.

[42] V. 3992–4018, 4964–4967, 10593–10604, 10770–10782, 11095–11103, 18954–18958, 19173–19177, 26822–26835; see as well Camel against Lot (v. 1250–1260) and against Gratien (v. 5989–5996). There are some "luites" in the tournaments as well: v. 12920–12923 (Agamanor against Tangis) and 13042 (Gracien against a Norman knight).

to lift up fallen knights (v. 6608–6615), presumably because armor was heavier and, therefore, more cumbersome at the end of the fourteenth century than at the end of the twelfth.

But these are oddities in the romance tradition. We want to understand what if anything fundamentally distinguishes Round Table knights from one another in *Meliador*. "Distinguish" has, of course, two common connotations: on the one hand, to recognize as different or distinct, and, on the other, to make prominent or eminent. Chrétien's eponymous knights and ladies illustrate both senses of the word, Froissart's only the latter. That is to say that in Chrétien's case, Erec is different from Yvain and their adventures and other encounters are differently marked: the former demonstrates the prowess his alleged *recreantise* effaced, the latter shows himself worthy of becoming again the defender of his wife's fountain by defending various maidens in distress (and the lion, who then joins up with the Knight of the Lion as Laudine reunites with her husband Yvain at the end of the romance). Lancelot and Perceval are obviously of distinguished and distinct excellence. In the Lancelot-Grail cycle chastity and virginity define rank and success in the *Queste del saint graal*. The quest serves in the cases of all these knights to substantiate Köhler's description of Round Table knights as equal in rank, but different in kind. This is not the case in *Meliador*.

Of course, as we have noted, Chrétien ranks them too. However, his ranking does not appear to be based on the distinguishing features of their quests I have just summarized. In this he anticipates what Froissart does in *Meliador*. But the "collective heroism" of Froissart's knights is confrontational because, as in all multiple quests, they are in competition for the same goal and in *Meliador*, unlike *Rigomer* and *Claris et Laris*, they must fight one another to achieve it. This alters the commonplace according to which Round Table knights do not fight one another except in tournaments or under very special circumstances. In *Meliador* combat among questing knights is a feature of the quest's *ordonnance*. Meliador wins because he defeats all other prominent knights, both during his quest and in tournaments. The victory is arbitrary, as I indicated, for nothing distinguishes, that is, sets Meliador apart from the other knights except, perhaps, his skill at wrestling. To be sure, he occupies more narrative space, his adventures are related first in the plot, and so on. But the distinctive character we perceive in Erec and Yvain, Lancelot and Perceval, is missing. Or when it does appear, it is an anomaly or peculiarity that may characterize the knight, but it has nothing to do with success or failure in the quest for Hermondine's hand. That Gratien is Italian is of no use to him. Agamanor is a skilled artist, but it is useful only in facilitating his meeting Phenonée. All these knights are stereotypes. Their excellence is collective excellence. Only the author can mark the best. Meliador could have been named Agamanor, Agamanor Meliador; nothing else would have to be changed in the plot except, perhaps but not necessarily, the names of the damsels each marries. This matter deserves further study in the larger context of the evolution of post-Chrétien verse romance.

The Gauvain Factor

Finally, let me return to a point touched on above: the prominence of Gauvain in quest romances written between Chrétien and Froissart. Beginning with the *First Perceval Continuation*, that is, the various versions of the *Gauvain Continuation*, the extended exploits of Arthur's nephew are made to follow on the incomplete account in the *Perceval*'s second part. From the first place in the Round Table catalogue that Chrétien assigns to Arthur's nephew in *Erec* to murder he allegedly committed in the last romance, transformations begin in his person that continue in later verse and prose romances and culminate with Gauvain's being mentioned as one of the second generation of Arthurian knights identified in the *Meliador* Prologue. Froissart's romance makes no distinction among them. Although apparently not yet dubbed a knight (v. 25634–25635), Gauvain is at court like all the others; only his brother Agravain enters the Hermondine quest where he is good enough to win a wife: Florée, Hermondine's cousin. The thirteenth-century romances play on Gauvain's commonplace features: in the *Atre périlleux* he loses his name and cannot identify himself, as before when asked; he is accused, rightly or wrongly, of various crimes, usually murder, as in *Perceval*; he is or is not a desirable lover; he marries in two romances.[43] These anomalies distance Gauvain from the ideal that *Meliador* promotes: collective excellence arbitrarily evaluated by an author using new names that designate otherwise stereotypical knights. The *ordonnance* of the quest in *Meliador* is based on new principles that depart from unique excellence to fashion a community of stereotypical knights—a collective excellence. Only the anomalies—the pretentious sleepwalker Camel de Camois, the Irish king who doesn't approve of quests—are excluded arbitrarily, by death. They participate actively in the quests not as questers, but as obstacles standing in the way of collective heroism.

---

[43] Schmolke-Hasselmann, *Der arthurische Versroman*, chap. 4; Keith Busby, *Gauvain in Old French Literature* (Amsterdam: Rodopi, 1980), and idem, "Diverging Traditions of Gauvain in Some of the Late Old French Verse Romances," in *Legacy of Chrétien de Troyes*, 2: 93–109; Chênerie, *Chevalier errant*, passim.

From *Le Chevalier as deus espees* to the Prose *Yvain*

Norris J. Lacy

A few years back, taking my cue from what Wolfgang Müller called interfigurality (that is, the transformation that occurs inevitably when a character from one work is transplanted into another),[1] I examined what I called motif transfer, the related phenomenon that occurs when a motif firmly associated with one character is transferred to someone else.[2] I now wish to take the next logical step and offer some observations about the transfer of a complete narrative sequence from one text to another. Let us acknowledge from the outset that the phenomenon itself is entirely commonplace: Arthurian and other cycles regularly re-use earlier texts; the most familiar example in medieval French may be the scenes from Chrétien's *Lancelot* that are reconfigured and (literally) recycled in the Lancelot-Grail. This and other Arthurian compilations involve the recombination of sequences drawn from a number of sources; indeed, we sometimes have whole romances joined together—sometimes successfully, often uncomfortably.

However, the fact that this phenomenon is common and regularly acknowledged by critics cannot diminish either the importance or the interest of its analysis in a particular narrative environment. The borrowing gives us an opportunity to see what happens when a narrative unit—a subplot that is almost but not quite self-contained—is taken from one context and transplanted into (or grafted onto) another text.

The Prose *Yvain* is an early fourteenth-century composition that is still unpublished.[3] It consists of seven distinct episodes only loosely connected to one another. The first is a variant of Yvain's rescue of a lion, followed by episodes not drawn from Chrétien's romance. Several others are analogues of episodes from

---

[1] Wolfgang Müller, "Interfigurality: A Study on the Interdependence of Literary Figures," in *Intertextuality*, ed. Heinrich F. Plett (Berlin: de Gruyter, 1991), 101–21.

[2] Norris J. Lacy, "Motif Transfer in Arthurian Romance," in *The Medieval Opus*, ed. Douglas Kelly (Amsterdam: Rodopi, 1996), 157–68.

[3] The romance is transmitted in a unique manuscript (444D) in the National Library of Wales, Aberystwyth. I am in the process of editing it.

what Lynette Muir has termed the *Rusticien/Guiron* group,[4] and the sources of yet others are not known and may be original compositions by the author (or redactor) of this text.

The fourth and central episode is the longest (fols. 18v–34v) and most elaborate of the seven. It offers an analogue of a portion of the *Chevalier as deus espees*,[5] although there is no way to know if that romance was the immediate source or if there was an intermediate text. *Le Chevalier as deus espees*, from the thirteenth century, is a long (12,360 lines) and complex work featuring the eponymous hero (whose actual name is Meriadeuc, though we learn that only toward the end of the romance). Gauvain is the primary focus of an extended sequence, running some 3300 lines (vss. 2745–6050), that is borrowed and interpolated into the Prose *Yvain*. (However, this section of *Le Chevalier as deus espees* has interpolated into it another episode that is not included in the Prose *Yvain*.)

Gauvain is more prominent in the *Chevalier as deus espees* than in most other romances, though within the framework of the entire text he still plays his traditional role of counterpoise to the hero. In this work, he is sent off to seek the hero, and his role in that romance depends to a considerable extent on the effect generated by his juxtaposition to the Knight with Two Swords.

The redactor of the Prose *Yvain* (or, again, of his source), by extracting the episode from its immediate source and joining it to what we can call its "host text," discards that juxtaposition and radically modifies thereby the particular dynamic of the original.

As I noted, this author or adaptor uses that long sequence from the *Chevalier as deus espees* as the central episode of his composition.[6] Here is one of the few instances in which Gauvain, at least in the French tradition, is not secondary to any other Arthurian figure. An analysis of this sequence is intriguing not because there is a radical rewriting of the earlier romance, but precisely for the opposite reason: despite a fair number of alterations, most are far from momentous. As a result, we have an opportunity to assess the effect of some very modest changes as well as the two major ones: the transfer of a sequence from its original context into a new narrative environment and the complete excision of the hero of the earlier romance. The remainder of this essay will identify several of the modifications and will consider their effect.

---

[4] Lynette Muir, "A Reappraisal of the Prose *Yvain*," *Romania* 85 (1964): 355–65, here 361–64.

[5] All line references to this romance are from the edition by Paul Vincent Rockwell, ed., *Le Chevalier as deus espees* (Cambridge: D.S. Brewer, 2006).

[6] In addition, he presents the final battle as a struggle between Gauvain and Yvain, thus not only confirming the disappearance of the Knight with Two Swords but also forging what is virtually the only link between this sequence and the eponymous hero of the Prose *Yvain*.

In the earlier text, as indicated, Gauvain is sent to look for the Knight with Two Swords. Another knight, encountering Gauvain without immediately recognizing him, identifies himself as a vavasor's son (though he does not yet reveal his name, which is Brien). He explains that the lady he loves, the Queen of the Islands, will agree to marry him only if he can prove himself to be, as he had boasted, superior to Gauvain. More precisely, he had insisted that he is "plus biax et plus fors / Et mieldres de chevalerie / De lui [Gauvain] . . ." (vs. 2868–2870). The lady has serious doubts but suggests that he can demonstrate his superiority by finding Gauvain and either vanquishing him in combat *or* beheading him (vss. 2880–2881)—and the "either / or" is important here, as we shall see. After offering this background, the stranger learns Gauvain's identity and challenges him to battle but does not permit Gauvain to arm himself fully. With the advantage his, Brien seriously wounds Gauvain and thinks him dead. However, he elects not to behead Gauvain, because it would be, he says, a reprehensible act ("je feroie que villains," vs. 3076). (Oddly, he is not above battling an insufficiently-armed knight, but he will not stoop to beheading the unconscious Gauvain.)

In the Prose *Yvain*, the story is quite similar to that of the *Chevalier as deus espees*, though it is offered in the third-person narrative voice rather than by the knight himself. Moreover, in the Prose *Yvain*, the lady, a wealthy noblewoman but not a queen,[7] has flatly refused to marry Burian (the counterpart of Brien), and as a result he brutally wages war on her until, impoverished and desperate, she has no choice but to deal with him. She employs a subterfuge, sending for Burian and promising to marry him if he is able to find her "enemy" Gauvain, defeat him in combat, *and* bring her his head ("Qu'il m'aporte le chief de Missire Gauvain," fol. 19r). In fact, as my quotation marks (enclosing "enemy") indicate, she has fabricated the notion of Gauvain as her enemy, hoping and no doubt assuming that he will kill Burian. The result is double. First, Gauvain's reputation as an indomitable knight is underlined; second, and most notably, the Brien/Burian character becomes considerably more villainous in his transfer to the Prose *Yvain*: he is not simply a suitor but an attacker and enemy, explicitly described as cruel and spiteful.[8]

In the *Chevalier as deus espees*, there is no reference to a ruse involved in the lady's agreeing to marry Brien as an act of desperation or resignation. His boast—that he is superior to Gauvain—may not have been admirable, but it is

---

[7] She is initially identified as the daughter of a count, but later her father is said to be duke of Normandy. This discrepancy, though of no great significance (other than to call our attention more distinctly to the fact that she is not a queen), was first pointed out by Meta McRitchie, "A study of an Hitherto Unconsidered Yvain Manuscript. National Library of Wales. Add. Ms. 444-D." M.A. Thesis, Swansea, 1929, p. 142..

[8] This is not to suggest that Brien was an entirely virtuous knight in *Le Chevalier as deus espees*. Though largely honorable, he is occasionally characterized as arrogant and treacherous; see for example vss. 7102–7111.

little more than the presumptuousness expressed by many knights. Thus, already the alteration of the textual situation is obvious in the Prose *Yvain*, reflecting the stellar reputation of Gauvain but involving most notably the darkening of the character of Brien/Burian.

A telling example of this refashioning of the character occurs at the end of the sequence in the two works. In the earlier romance, Brien, defeated in the decisive battle, is required to agree that he will go to Arthur's court and serve the king. Once at court, he is welcomed and honored and lives on happily, known only as the Handsome Prisoner ("le Biel Prison," vs. 6125). In the Prose *Yvain*, however, he is defeated by Gauvain and simply disappears, riding off ignominiously into the sunset of shame.

The question of marriage figures doubly in both romances: in addition to the lady's possible marriage to Brien/Burian, both compositions raise the question of her eventually marrying Gauvain instead. In the *Chevalier as deus espees* (vss. 5980–6038), the Queen of the Islands raises with her advisors the prospect of her marriage to Gauvain, who she thinks is not married (". . . croi / K'encor n'a pas feme espouse," vss. 5990–5991). They discourage her from trying, both because they assume that a knight as noble and handsome as Gauvain must surely have a ladylove (an *amie*, vs. 6010) already and also that he doubtless hates the Queen of the Islands: after all, she sent a knight to kill him — and it was a knight whom, at least ostensibly, she considers superior to Gauvain (vss. 6010–6017). Reluctantly, she accepts their counsel and abandons her matrimonial ambitions.

In the Prose *Yvain*, however, she actually does propose marriage to Gauvain. Surprisingly, he replies that he is already married.[9] We have no information that will let us know whether he is simply concocting an excuse, but certainly a married Gauvain, especially in the French tradition, would be a significant innovation.[10] And if he is not in fact married, his excuse is at least novel — and no doubt amusing to a Gallic audience accustomed to Gauvain's reputation as a ladies' man incapable of commitment.

The major complication of the Prose *Yvain* involves a portion of the text that, ironically, remains very close to the corresponding passage of the *Chevalier as deus espees*. In this instance, the redactor was unable to innovate when his narrative design would seem to dictate it. In the Prose *Yvain* (fols. 21r–22r), as in the *Chevalier as deus espees*, Burian thinks it would be too great a *villanie* to cut off the

---

[9] Specifically, he offers a rather puzzling response: "je ne puis, car je sui mariés et ai outroié [*sic*, for *octroyé*] une dame de prendre la feme" (32r). That appears to suggest, curiously, that he is at the same time already married and yet engaged to marry someone. The line, though odd, makes sense if we take *marier* in its attested sense as "being married off" or to have a marriage arranged, to be espoused to someone. In that case the line is redundant and thus emphatic, but it is not a portent of bigamy.

[10] A married Gawain is not unknown, of course: that occurs in the Middle English Ragnell stories and on rare occasion elsewhere.

head of Gauvain, because Gauvain is too renowned and respected a knight, and it would be a shame for his body to be buried without the head (fol. 21r). Besides, he is persuaded that the lady will marry him because he has killed Gauvain; beheading him is unnecessary. This is an extremely intriguing point: by besieging the lady (and also by taking unfair advantage of Gauvain), Burian has shown himself to be dishonorable. His actions thus produce something of a shock when he honorably spares Gauvain's head. More important, we cannot help but wonder why he expects the lady to believe that he has defeated Gauvain when he has no tangible proof. Is a villain's word sufficient? He seems to think so, and the narrator chooses not to comment.

Here is a major crux. Obviously, Burian could *not* cut off Gauvain's head, specifically because Gauvain must survive to save the lady and more generally because beheading Gauvain is against Arthurian "rules": it just isn't done.[11] So we find ourselves confronting a problem: the author of the Prose *Yvain* has tried to show Burian as evil, but narrative circumstances require that he spare Gauvain and thus appear noble and chivalrous when we know that he is neither. And yet, the lady here, unlike her counterpart in the *Chevalier as deus espees*, has not offered her suitor a choice, but has demanded that Gauvain be killed *and* beheaded. Since Gauvain's destiny as well as narrative convention precludes his being killed, we can only wonder why, if the intent is to present Burian as a detestable character, the redactor had not had the lady offer the same choice as the *Chevalier as deus espees*: defeat him *or* behead him. Had he done so, Burian's sparing Gauvain would not produce the same shock. But since he *was* asked for Gauvain's head, his choosing not to take it is at odds with the redactor's conception of his character.

Here we have a fascinating, though not uncommon, situation: there is a factual or conceptual contradiction generated by the incompatibility of source material and narratorial design. Such problems are by no means surprising in general—they are to be expected—but in this instance the redactor has performed a double transformation and created an unnecessary contradiction. He departed from his source in requiring, logically enough, the defeat *and* the head of Gauvain, but because he had presented Burian as despicable, the reader experiences something of a shock when his character is sufficiently decent to spare Gauvain's head, thereby failing to meet the conditions imposed by the lady. Again, there is obviously no way to determine why the redactor made the initial innovation (defeat *and* beheading), but, once that decision was made, there seems to be no way for him to circumvent this difficulty. Either Burian is acting out of character in sparing Gauvain's head (and there is no indication that he possesses that decency), or else the result is an insoluble narrative dissonance.

---

[11] It is not done, of course, even by the Green Knight in Middle English.

Such problems are the most evident result of the extraction of a full sequence from one text for use in another. Even without such a dissonance—that is, if the narrator had made an effort to maintain not just the narrative contours of the text but also the precise features of his characters—the effect would inevitably be altered. But in this instance, where the redactor's design required him to reform Brien/Burian for the worse, he finds himself confronting a problem for which he—and we—have no solution.

We might contend that for this particular author, such a dissonance is hardly his most serious flaw, for he is far from a gifted author, and that is an understatement. Nonetheless, his text, both in the sequence I have discussed and in the other episodes borrowed and redacted from earlier texts, offers a revealing illustration of the literary migration, across textual boundaries, of an extended sequence. The segment I have discussed is easily identifiable as derived from *Le Chevalier as deus espees* (or from an intermediate text), and much of the borrowed material is narratively identical to its source, but even then the effect is altered by the new context. But where there are significant deviations, they are all the more conspicuous when measured against their source. And when they perturb both the texture and the internal consistency of the host text, they strikingly illustrate the inevitability of the process by which a narrative is reconceptualized and remade in the process of transplantation. At the hand of a more able author, the alterations might function more harmoniously or even, conceivably, improve the imported material. Elsewhere, as in the Prose *Yvain*, they create obvious disruptions. What even the most capable author *cannot* do, I suggest, is borrow a sequence and fit it seamlessly into a different work without modifying it in significant ways. Just as a character or a motif, once fitted to a new context, is itself transformed while also modifying that context, so does a full sequence inevitably mutate even as it reshapes, in tone, texture, or sense, its new narrative environment.

Chrétien in Italy

Keith Busby

One of the most curious aspects of the diffusion of medieval Arthurian literature is the apparent failure of Chrétien de Troyes's verse romances—and those of his epigones—to cross the Pyrenees and the Alps, where evidence for their presence and influence is slim, albeit not entirely absent. There are adaptations of Chrétien in Middle English, Middle High German, Middle Dutch, Old Norse, and Middle Welsh; manuscripts of his works circulated in the British Isles and much of the Continent, and there is one surviving Anglo-Norman manuscript of *Perceval* and an excerpt from *Erec et Enide*. Parts of the Continuations of *Perceval* were adapted into Middle English and Middle Dutch, and into Middle High German in the prose translation of the whole verse cycle by Wisse and Colin. Of the epigonal romances, there is a Middle Dutch version of *La vengeance Raguidel* and a Middle English text of Renaut de Bâgé's *Le bel inconnu*.[1] Yet even when French literature was at the height of its popularity in Italy, Arthurian romance was primarily a prose phenomenon, consisting of a large-almost industrial-scale copying of French prose romances, such as the *Lancelot-Graal*, the various versions of the prose *Tristan*, and some adaptations into Italian of the latter. The first phase of Arthurian romance in French, the verse tradition of Chrétien and his successors, was largely passed over *outre-alpes* when compared with most of the rest of western Europe.[2] This is even more striking when one considers that, despite the

---

[1] The bibliography in these areas is both enormous and easily accessible through well-known reference works. With regard to Spain, the possession of a manuscript of *Cligés* by Martin I of Aragon in 1410 is both little known and unique: see Roger Middleton, "The Manuscripts," in *The Arthur of the French*, ed. Glyn S. Burgess and Karen Pratt (Cardiff: University of Wales Press, 2007), 8–92, here 35. See also the recently published excerpt from *Erec et Enide* in London, British Library, Harley 4971 (s. 14^med.), which is in some ways comparable with the text edited below: Keith Busby, "Erec le fiz Lac (British Library, Harley 4971)," in *People and Texts: Relationships in Medieval Literature. Studies Presented to Erik Kooper*, ed. Thea Summerfield and idem (Amsterdam: Rodopi, 2007), 43–50.

[2] E. G. Gardner, *The Arthurian Legend in Italian Literature* (London: Dent / New York: Dutton, 1930) is now seriously dated and is supplanted by Daniela Delcorno Branca, *Tristano e Lancilotto in Italia: studi di letteratura arturiana* (Ravenna: Longo

chronology of composition, many of the surviving manuscripts of French verse romance date from that same heyday of French in Italy (ca. 1275–1350).[3] In this essay dedicated to a dear colleague and friend, I would like to suggest some possible reasons for Chrétien's general absence in medieval Italy and to examine more closely his rather modest presence.

That there are no Italian manuscripts of Chrétien does not mean, of course, that his romances were not read in Italy. On the contrary, there are at least two copies of *Perceval* known to have been owned by Italians, one by Francesco Gonzaga of Mantua, and the other by Valentina Visconti. The first of these appears in Francesco's *post mortem* inventory of 1407, with the hero's name corrupted, probably through an erroneously resolved abbreviation, as "Princivallis", but the work is securely identified by the full entry of "Princivallis le Galoys per versus," and the first line of the text: "Qui petit seme petit cheul". The last line of the manuscript is given as "Se il chierent par chemin," the end of Manessier's Continuation.[4] The second copy passed from Valentina to her son, Charles d'Orléans, and is mentioned as one of the books selected by the fourteen-year old Charles from his mother's estate in 1408; Charles's later tastes seem to have been resolutely modern.[5] It is surely significant that these two copies (as yet not identified with any of the extant manuscripts) are found in the highest echelons of Italian society of the north, the milieux with the closest personal and political ties with France and French culture, whose members and their representatives traveled frequently to France on business and diplomatic missions. Indeed, both of these copies of *Perceval* may have been acquired in 1389 when Francesco Gonzaga accompanied

---

Editore, 1998); Fabrizio Cigni, "Manoscritti di prose cortesi compilati in Italia (secc. XII–XIV): stato della questione e prospettive di ricerca," in *La filologia romanza e i codici*, ed. Saverio Guida and Fortunata Latella (Messina: Sicania, 1993), 419–41; and Marie-José Heijkant, *La tradizione del 'Tristan' in prosa in Italia e proposte di studio sul 'Tristano Riccardiano'* (Enschede: Sneldruk Enschede, 1989). I am especially grateful to Daniela Delcorno Branca for bringing some obscure allusions to my attention, to Gabriele Giannini, and to Maria Colombo Timelli. See most recently *Modi e forme della fruizione della "materia arturiana" nell'Italia dei sec. XIII–XIV, Milano, 4–5 febbraio 2005* (Milan: Istituto Lombardo di Scienze e Lettere, 2006).

[3] The Chrétien manuscripts are surveyed in Keith Busby, Terry Nixon, Alison Stones, and Lori Walters, *Les manuscrits de Chrétien de Troyes/The Manuscripts of Chrétien de Troyes*, 2 vols. (Amsterdam: Rodopi, 1993), and the epigonal romances in Keith Busby, *Codex and Context: Reading Old French Verse Narrative in Manuscript*, 2 vols. (Amsterdam: Rodopi, 2002), 1: 405–73.

[4] W. Braghirolli, "Inventaire des manuscrits en langue française possédés par Francesco Gonzaga I, Capitaine de Mantoue, mort en 1407," *Romania* 9 (1880): 497–514, here 410.

[5] Pierre Champion, *La librairie de Charles d'Orléans* (Paris: Champion, 1910), lxxiii-xiv.; G. Ouy, *La librairie des frères captifs* (Turnhout: Brepols, 2007).

Valentina to France, where she was to meet her future husband, Louis d'Orléans; Valentina's copy may never in fact have crossed the Alps into Italy.

These are exceptions which prove the rule, however, but a rule which seems to apply to Arthurian romances rather than other types of Old French narrative. The issue is clearly not one of prose being preferred to verse in general, as there are many Italian copies of *Le roman d'Alexandre*, Benoît de Sainte-Maure's *Le roman de Troie*, Aimon de Varennes's *Florimont*, and the anonymous *Athis et Prophilias*, for example. And the same is true of many *chansons de geste*, such as *Bueve de Hantone*, *La chanson de Roland*, and *La chanson d'Aspremont*, to cite just three. Much has been written about the *matière de France* and its attraction for medieval Italy, and I shall not repeat the arguments here. The other verse romances mentioned above all belong in varying degrees of proximity to the so-called "matter of antiquity", and there is no doubt that Italy's self-awareness as a home of classical culture gave such texts a real attraction in the peninsula. The taste for the *romans antiques* and the *chansons de geste* seems to be quite broadly based, judging from records of ownership, but tends, if anything, towards the great families. Families such as the Gonzaga, the Visconti-Sforza, and the Este also owned copies of Arthurian prose romances, some of them more luxurious than the run-of-the-mill manuscripts typical of the genre in Italy. Some of the more modest copies were owned by the urban patriciate and the *capitani di ventura*, whose connections with the more elevated ranks were as often as not in the nature of social aspirations and even fantasy. The desire to see themselves as members of a class which derived its status and identity from those courtly and chivalric ideals defining the prose romances goes a long way to explaining the attraction of such literature in the city-republics.[6]

One of the most francophile of Italian aristocrats from medieval Piedmont was Tomasso III di Saluzzo, author of the long *Le chevalier errant*, composed in verse and prose during his imprisonment in Turin by Amedeo III di Savoia in the years 1394–1396. I have tried to demonstrate elsewhere that Tomasso's reading in French was typical of the French-oriented northern Italian aristocracy, not so much of his time perhaps, but of an earlier generation.[7] It is perfectly possible that he used books from the Savoy library, as well as his own, during his incarceration as the sources for his own work. *Le chevalier errant* is on the way to being a nostalgic anachronism already at the end of the fourteenth century, although it also reflects a pronounced encyclopedic aesthetic to be seen elsewhere in narrative literature of the period. In addition to the Arthurian prose romances used

---

[6] For a survey of French manuscript production and ownership in medieval Italy, see Delcorno Branca, *Tristano e Lancilotto in Italia*, Cigni, "Manoscritti di prose cortesi," and Busby, *Codex and Context*, 2: 596–634, 766–97.

[7] K. Busby, "La bibliothèque de Tomasso di Saluzzo," in *"Qui tant savoit d'engin et d'art": Mélanges de philologie médiévale offerts à Gabriel Bianciotto*, ed. Claudio Galderisi and Jean Maurice (Poitiers: CESCM, 2006), 31–39.

by Tomasso, there is one verse romance that has left its mark. Not surprisingly, perhaps, this is Chrétien's *Perceval* and its First Continuation.

Tomasso rewrites in prose the Caradoc episode from the Continuation, and quotes wholesale, and in verse, passages from the Chrétien's episode of the Damsel in the Tent.

Two other Italian references to Perceval are clearly to Chrétien's romance and argue further in favor of the circulation of manuscripts in Italy. The Venetian troubadour Bertolomé Zorzi (fl. s. 13$^{3/4}$) alludes to Perceval's confession to his hermit uncle:

> Don convenra que l'arma l'enfern intra,
> Qu'el si gaudet, pois amors i mes l'ongla
> Com Percevaus tro qu'anet a son oncle.[8]

And Guittone d'Arezzo, in a poem possibly written before his conversion in 1265, alludes to Perceval's silence at the Grail Castle, comparing it to his own before his lady:

> Fallenza era demando
> far lei senza ragione;
> poi veggio che, sí stando,
> m'ha sovrameritato el meo servire.
> Però 'n tacer m'asservo, perché già guiderdone
> non dea cheder bon servo;
> bisogna i' n'ho, che 'l chere 'l suo servire,
> se no atendendo m'allasso;
> poi m'avvenisse, lasso!,
> che mi trovasse in fallo
> sì come Prezevallo — a non cherere.
> Verrei a presente morto!
> Ma non tal penser porto,
> né sí mala credenza,
> ché sola conoscenza — halla in podere.[9]

Although these references have specific meaning in the immediate context of the poems, it is equally important to note that they are both to what are now

---

[8] "En tal dezirs mos cors intra" (PC 74, 4), ll. 16–18 in Emil Levy, *Der Troubadour Bertolome Zorzi* (Halle: Niemeyer, 1883). The poem, preserved in the Italian *chansonniers I* and *K*, is a *sestina* in imitation of Arnaut Daniel. My thanks to Beth Poe for her help with Zorzi. Cf. also Gianfranco Folena, *Culture e lingue nel Veneto medievale* (Padua: Editoriale Programma, 1990), 131–32.

[9] Poem XXI, "Amor tanto altamente", ll. 65–80, in *Le Rime di Guittone d'Arezzo*, ed. Francesco Egidi (Bari: Giuseppe Laterza e Figli, 1940), 47–49. The poem is preceded by the heading "Non chiedendo, ma meritando si ottiene guiderdone in amore".

considered key moments in the narrative of Chrétien's last romance, suggesting that both Zorzi and Guittone had detailed knowledge and good understanding of the text.

The above is not Guittone's only allusion to Chrétien. In the undated letter XXI addressed to Orlando da Chiusi, he even includes a partial translation of a couplet from *Cligés*:

> Unde Cristiano là ove Allessandro Novello dice:
> 'Reposo e loda
> non concordano bene insieme'.[10]

I take "Allessandro Novello" to imply that Chrétien's character is a new Alexander the Great. The verbal detail here suggests intimate knowledge of *Cligés*, presumably either from a copy to hand or from memory owing to repeated readings of the text. This particular letter, which deals with response to adversity and its relationship to virtue and reputation, is full of allusions to, and quotations from, Latin, Old French, and Occitan texts: Aristotle, Cicero, Galen, Macrobius, Seneca, Socrates, Augustine, Bernard, Jerome, Gregory, Benoît de Sainte-Maure, Chrétien, Peire Rogier, and Peire Vidal. This letter may well have been written after Guittone's conversion, and in any case no earlier than 1261, the date which seems to mark the beginning of Orlando's conflict with Guglielmino degli Ubertini, bishop of Arezzo.[11] Whatever the precise dating of Guittone's poem XXI and letter XXI, there is a clear difference in the use to which Chrétien has been put, first, as part of a traditional amorous meditation, and second, as source of a moral *exemplum*. Indeed, the couplet translated from *Cligés* is essentially a moral dictum verging on the paremiological.

In contrast with its modern scholarly reception as the odd man out among Chrétien's romances, *Cligés* seems to have been relatively well known in Italy. In what appears to be an attempt by an Italian scribe to write an Occitan *salut d'amor* on the blank f. 60v of Florence, Biblioteca Mediceo-Laurenziana, Plut. XLIV 44 of *Le roman d'Eneas* (s. 12$^{ex.}$), the two pairs of lovers are mentioned in the company of Floire and Blancheflor:

> Per vos, donna vallenz,
> ch'eu non aus dir
> ni non pos dir
> a vos ma desiranza [. . .]

---

[10] Letter XXI, in *Guittone d'Arezzo, Lettere*, ed. Claude Margueron (Bologna: Commissione per i Testi di Lingua, 1990), 225–40, §16. Cf. *Cligés*, ed. Stewart Gregory and Claude Luttrell (Cambridge: D. S. Brewer, 1993), ll. 157–158: "Ne s'accordent pas bien ansanble / Repos et los, si con moi sanble."

[11] Cf. Margueron, *Lettere*, 225–26, who compares the letter with Guittone's poem XVIII, which also deals with Orlando's dispute with Guglielmino.

En am plus vos
de bon cor lialmenz
che Cliges non ama
Fenices verament
ne Floire Blancaflor
ne Alixandre Soredamors.[12]

L'Intelligenza, a curious and anonymous poem in three hundred and nine stanzas of *nona rima*, is probably Florentine, and dates from towards the end of the thirteenth century.[13] It consists of two principal sections, in the first of which the poet describes the seventy gems in the crown of his lady in the manner of a lapidary, and the second of which is a lengthy description of her palace. The ceiling is adorned with a series of paintings: a wheel of Fortune, the God of Love with a procession of famous lovers from classical, biblical, and romance traditions, the story of Cæsar's Civil War, the life of Alexander the Great, the destruction of Troy, and more lovers of romance (stanzas 70–288). If it is possible that the allusion to Guinevere and Lancelot in stanza 73 ("Èvi la bella Ginevra regina, / ed evv' apresso messer Lancialotto," ll. 1–2) is to Chrétien's *Charrette* rather than the prose *Lancelot*, it is certain that stanzas 74 and 75 refer to three of Chrétien's romances:

74
Èv' Allessandro e Ros[s]enna d'Amore,
Messere Erecco, ed Enidia davante,
ed èvi Trasia e 'l prenze Antigonore,
e d'Apollonio la lira sonante,
e Archistrate regina di valore,
Cui sorprese esto Amore al gaio sembiante;
èvi Bersenda e 'l buono Diomedes[se],
èvi Penelopè ed Ulizesse,
ed Eneasse e Lavina davante.

75
E non fallio chi·ffu lo 'ntagliadore
la bella Analidà e 'l buonn-Ivano;
èvi intagliato Fiore e Blanzifiore
e la bell' Isaotta Blanzesmano.
Si com' ella morio per fin amore,
cotanto amò Lancialotto sovrano,

---

[12] I am grateful to Gabriele Giannini for bringing these lines to my attention and for pointing out that they were published long ago by J. J. Salverda de Grave in his edition of *Le roman d'Eneas* (Halle: Niemeyer, 1891), iii.

[13] *L'Intelligenza, poemetto anonimo del secolo XIII*, ed. Marco Berisso (Parma: Fondazione Pietro Bembo / Ugo Guanda Editore, 2000).

èvi la nobile Donna del Lago;
quella di Maloalto col cuor vago,
e Palamidès cavalier pagano.

The first line of stanza 74 clearly refers to Alexandre and Soredamors from Chrétien's *Cligès*, although the form "Rossenna d'Amore" may be a contamination under the influence of the name Roxana, wife of Alexander the Great. It is also possible that "Rossena" derives from the notion that gold ("sor" = blond) has a reddish tinge; there is clearly an etymological word-play on "sora" and "rossa" here.[14] In any case, the occurrence of Erec and Enide, the central protagonists from Chrétien's first romance, in the following line confirms the identity. And could the author of *L'Intelligenza* be demonstrating detailed knowledge of *Erec et Enide* by his phrasing "Messere Erecco, ed Enidia davante"? The use of "davante" in the last line of stanza 74 could point to the disposition of the couples in the fresco, i.e., Eneas and Lavinia in the front of the line, as it were. Berisso's punctuation of line 2, however, suggests that he believes that Enide is shown in front of Erec, which might call to mind her preceding him on their "avanture".[15]

The second line of stanza 75 completes a trio of lovers from Chrétien with Yvain and his lady, although the form of the latter's name is, as in the case of Rossenna, problematic. The name, usually cited in *Yvain* scholarship as "Laudine", in fact only occurs in that form in two of the ten manuscripts, as "Laudune" in another, but as "la dame" in the rest.[16] It is perhaps therefore not surprising to find an apparently variant form here, although the name "Analida" itself is obscure, occurring to my knowledge elsewhere only in Chaucer's *Anelida and Arcite*, where its source is sometimes given as *L'Intelligenza*. Since the name Arcite is taken from Boccaccio's *Teseida*, Chaucer may have found Analida in an Italian text; whether this was *L'Intelligenza* or not remains moot. And in a note to these lines, Marco Berisso points out a second reference to *Yvain* in a somewhat earlier poem by Bonagiunta Orbicciani da Lucca:

E messere Ivano
e'l dolze Tristano
ciaschuno fue sotano
inver' me di languire.[17]

---

[14] See Berisso, *L'Intelligenza*, 263–64.
[15] *Erec et Enide*, ed. Wendelin Foerster (Halle: Niemeyer, 1890), ll. 2765 ff. Cf. "Devant s'est mise" (2777), "Et Erec, qui aprés venoit" (2934)
[16] See most recently, Chrétien de Troyes, *Le chevalier au lion*, ed. David Hult (Paris: Livre de Poche, 1994), 11–12.
[17] Berisso, *L'Intelligenza*, 265. The text of Bonagiunta's poem is to be found in D'Arco Silvio Avalle, *Concordanze della lingua poetica italiana delle origini*, vol. 1 (Milan: Riccardo Ricciardi, 1992). Dante, of course, meets Bonagiunta in Canto XXIV of the *Inferno*.

We can at the very least conclude from all these references in Zorzi, the Occitan *salut* from the Laurenziana *Eneas* manuscript, Guittone, Bonagiunta, and *L'Intelligenza* that Italian poets knew Chrétien and expected their audiences and readers to as well. If in France a clear but not absolute distinction was made between the verse tradition of Chrétien and the later rise of the great prose romances, in Italy—and certainly as far as this kind of allusive reference is concerned—the protagonists of verse romance stand alongside those from the prose cycles. Indeed, stanza 75 of *L'Intelligenza* has Chrétien's characters, Floris, Blanchefleur, and Iseut aux Blanches Mains (those probably alluding to verse texts) followed by a clear reference to the Prose *Lancelot* (the Dame de Malehaut) and the Prose *Tristan* (Palamède).

In addition to Chrétien's presence in medieval Italy which can be deduced from the library lists, rewritings, quotations, and allusions, some surviving manuscripts are known to have been in Italy for several centuries. One might have expected the extensive library of the House of Savoy, with its close geographical and cultural links to France, its domains straddling the Alps, to have contained manuscripts of Chrétien de Troyes, but such does not appear to have been the case according the surviving medieval inventories.[18] Turin, Biblioteca Nazionale Universitaria, L. I. 13 (Flanders-Hainaut, s. 14$^{2/4}$), which includes *Cligés* and the anonymous *Sone de Nansay*, was nevertheless given to the Turin university library by the dukes of Savoy in 1720, as was L. IV. 33 (Picardy, s. 14$^{ex.}$-s. 15$^{inc.}$), an unusual paper manuscript whose Arthurian verse texts are Raoul de Houdenc's *Meraugis de Portlesguez*, the anonymous *Gliglois*, the *lai* of *Melion*, and an episode from *Les merveilles de Rigomer*. It is not known at what moment these manuscripts were acquired by the dukes, but it is clear in any case from their northern French language that neither of them were produced in Italy. Both were severely damaged in the disastrous fire of 1904.[19]

Florence, Bibliotheca Riccardiana 2943 (eastern France [?], s. 13$^{2/4}$) of *Perceval* may have been acquired sometime before 1611 by the founder of the Riccardi family library, Riccardo Romulo Riccardi (1558–1611). The manuscript was already in Florence in 1739, where it was examined by La Curne de Sainte-Palaye, and whose description of it survives, together with that of Turin, BNU, L.

---

[18] However, Alessandro Vitale-Brovarone has cautioned us against taking as gospel the series of three articles on the Savoy ducal libraries by Sheila Edmunds ("The Medieval Library of Savoy (I-II-III)," *Scriptorium* 24 [1970]: 318–27, 25 [1971]: 253–84, 26 [1972]: 269–93), and argues for a return to the archives of the region: see his "Diffusione e testi letterari del Piemonte fra '400 e '500," in *Histoire linguistique de la Vallée d'Aoste du Moyen Âge au XVIIIe siècle: Actes du séminaire de Saint-Pierre 16–17–18 mai 1983* (Aosta: Région Autonome de la Vallée d'Aoste, Assessorat à l'Instruction Publique, 1985), 132–77.

[19] On L. I. 13, see Nixon in *Les manuscrits de Chrétien de Troyes*, 2: 78–79, and Roger Middleton, "Index of Former Owners," in *Les manuscrits de Chrétien de Troyes*, 2: 87–176, at 170. For L. IV. 33, see Busby, *Codex and Context*, 1: 87–93.

I. 13, in BnF, Moreau 1658 (itself copied in Moreau 1670).[20] The transcriptions Sainte-Palaye made or had made of some of the French manuscripts in Turin are particularly precious because of the destruction caused by the 1904 fire. And when Christina of Sweden abdicated and established herself in Rome in 1655, she brought the majority of her books with her, including the present Vatican City, Biblioteca Apostolica Vaticana, Reg. Lat. 1725 (Nièvre-Allier [?], s. 13$^{ex.}$-s. 14$^{inc.}$), containing Chrétien's *Lancelot* and *Yvain*, Jean Renart's *Guillaume de Dôle*, and Raoul de Houdenc's *Meraugis de Portlesguez*.[21]

The verse romances of Chrétien de Troyes and his epigones have thus played a minor role in Italian cultural history just as the manuscripts associated in one way or another with Italy are significant in the study of medieval French literature and French medieval studies. They were a small part of the vernacular literary culture of the Italian nobility, and the surviving manuscripts are associated with important figures and events in the history of the book, of bibliophilia, and of the rediscovery of medieval literature in the eighteenth century.

The popularity and influence of the Arthurian prose romance tradition, however, dwarfs that of the verse texts, again begging the question of why this should be so. In the light of the popularity of such older texts as the *romans antiques* and the *chansons de geste*, it is clearly not a matter of fashion in the sense of predilection for modern prose versions at the expense of those perceived as outmoded. What distinguishes Chrétien's romances (and those written in his wake) from later ones written in prose is their detailed and self-consciously rhetorical exploration of the subtle and shifting relationships between love, marriage, chivalry, courtesy, and, in the case of *Perceval*, religion and spirituality. In other words, they ask serious and subtle questions about the human condition and about the individual's place with personal and political relationships and within society as a whole. Such issues are not entirely absent from the prose romances (or from the *romans antiques* and *chansons de geste*, for that matter), and indeed, the relationships between rulers and their subjects may even define many of the French works, Arthurian and non-Arthurian, which achieved considerable popularity

---

[20] On this manuscript, see *Mostra di codici romanzi delle bibliotheche fiorentine (VIII Congresso Internazionale di Studi Romanzi, 3–8 aprile 1956)* (Florence: Sansoni, 1957), 167 (R 1); Nixon in *Les manuscrits de Chrétien de Troyes*, 2: 26–27, and Middleton, "Index of Former Owners," 163–64. For the scribal behaviour, see Busby, *Codex and Context*, 1: 108–19. Sainte-Palaye's visits to Florence and his relationship with the Riccardi's librarian, Giovanni Lami, are discussed by Lionel Gossman, *Medievalism and the Ideologies of the Enlightenment: The World and Work of La Curne de Sainte-Palaye* (Baltimore: Johns Hopkins University Press, 1968), 77–81.

[21] Reg. Lat. 1725 is described by Nixon in *Les manuscrits de Chrétien de Troyes*, 2: 62–63, and Middleton, "Index of Former Owners," 111–12; it had earlier been owned by Fauchet. On Christina, see Christian Kallmer, *Königin Christina, ihre Bibliothekare und ihre Handschriften* (Stockholm: Kungliga Biblioteket, 1977).

in Italy. But the world of prose romance is generally a simpler place than that in which Chrétien's characters live and move, and the love problematics of the verse romances were perceived in Italy as better suited to expression in lyric poetry, both Occitan and Italian. Despite the knowledge of Chrétien in Italy surveyed above, then, demand for copies of his romances seems to have been limited.

I should like to conclude this article with an edition of the one passage from a Chrétien romance known to have been copied in Italy in the Middle Ages. It is from *Cligés*, and is written in an Italian hand on a bifolium (fols. 71–72) added at the end of Florence, Biblioteca Riccardiana 2756, a manuscript whose primary contents are the Old French *Elucidarium*, *Les enseignements d'un père à son fils* (*Fables Pierre Aufors*), *La terre de promission*, and *La mort Adam*, written in a northeastern French dialect.[22] The main part of the manuscript dates from the second half of the thirteenth century, and fols. 71–72 from towards the middle of the fourteenth. On fol. 71v are five Italian sonnets in Florentine dialect, and immediately preceding the *Cligés* excerpt on fol. 72r, in the same hand, are the opening lines of the Occitan tale of *Las novas del papagai* by Arnaut de Carcassés.[23] The passage from *Cligés* was published in 1879 by Gaston Paris, who was unable to identify it since the whole romance had not yet then been edited. Paris had not seen the manuscript and informs us that the excerpt had been copied for him by "M. A. Stickney," whose transcription is not entirely free from errors.[24]

---

[22] See *Mostra di codici romanzi*, 172 (R 7), Nixon in *Les manuscrits de Chrétien de Troyes*, 2: 58–59, reproductions on 469–70 (figs. 253 [fol. 1r], 254 [fol. 71v], 255 [fol. 72r]), and Monica Türk, *'Lucidaire de grant sapientie': Untersuchung und Edition der altfranzösischen Übersetzung 1 des 'Elucidarium' von Honorius Augustodunensis* (Tübingen: Niemeyer, 2000), 18.

[23] For the sonnets, see Antoine Thomas, "Cinq sonnets italiens tirés du ms. Riccardien 2756," *Giornale di filologia romanza* 3 (1880): 107–10, and for the passage from the *Novas*, A. Wesselofsky, "Un nouveau texte des 'Novas del Papagay'," *Romania* 7 (1878): 327–29; Arnaut de Carcassés, *Novàs de papagai: novella provenzale del pappagallo*, ed. Daniele Barca (Rome: Salerno Editrice, 1992); and Arnaut de Carcassés, *Las nòvas del papagai*, ed. Pierre Bec (Mussidan: Fédéroc, 1988). Thomas ("Cinq sonnets," 107) states that the sonnets are in the same hand as the *Papagai* and *Cligés* excerpts, but this is clearly not the case, even though the two hands may well be contemporary. This article was practically complete by the time I was able to obtain a copy of Gabriele Giannini, "Il romanzo francese in versi dei secoli XII e XIII in Italia: il *Cligès* Riccardiano," in *Modi e forme*, 119–58, who re-edits the sonnets and the *Novas* except as well as the passage from *Cligés* (of which he provides a more critical edition than mine). Giannini dates the additions on fols. 71–72 closer to 1300.

[24] Gaston Paris, "Un fragment inconnu." *Romania* 8 (1879): 266–67. Foerster, preparing the first edition of *Cligés*, immediately identified the text, as Tobler reports the same year: "Foerster theilt mir mit, dass dieses Fragment von 28 Versen der Riccard. No. 2756, dem Cligés angehöre." Cf. Adolf Tobler, "Anzeige," *Zeitschrift für romanische Philologie* 3 (1879): 314.

Even though it has since been listed by editors and students of the textual tradition of *Cligés*, the passage was summarily dismissed by the poem's most recent editors as "corrompu et sans valeur,"[25] echoing Foerster's "verdorben."[26] Corrupt it may be insofar as the scribe was not apparently all that familiar with Old French, but one can at least agree with the great Gaston Paris when he wrote that: "Il est toujours intéressant de savoir quels sont ceux de nos anciens romans qui ont été connus et copiés en Italie."[27]

In some ways, Riccardiana 2756 is emblematic of the vernacular linguistic situation in fourteenth-century Italy. To a French book imported from across the Alps are added leaves containing the three main vernaculars of medieval Italy: Italian (in the dialect that was to become the Tuscan *koiné*), Occitan, and French. It is curious, perhaps, that the Occitan text is narrative rather than lyric given the Italian provenance of some of the major *chansonniers*, and curious that the French text is from an Arthurian verse romance rather than from a prose one, but the mixture of languages is no surprise.[28]

The first text below is a diplomatic transcription in which I have printed the text line-by-line as it appears on fol 72r of Riccardiana 2756. I have given all occurences of the raised *punctus* at the end of lines and have attempted to reproduce word-clustering. Resolved abbreviations are printed, as is customary, in italics. In the second text, I have divided the text into lines of verse, capitalizing the first letter, resolved abbreviations silently, distinguished between *u* and *v*, and applied modern word-division. I have not attempted to correct any of the errors but have rather printed in the right-hand column the critical text, with line numbers, of Stewart Gregory and Claude Luttrell, indicating where the Florence excerpt has missing lines. On occasions (e.g., ll. 363–364 and 370–372), the equivalence between the texts is approximate due to a combination of omissions and errors on the part of the Italian scribe.

Florence, Biblioteca Riccardiana 2756, f. 72r

Alisandre le roi salue · que lalanghe auoites molue · a biem parler et
sagge ment · rois fetil de vus ne ment · le renome che de vus nome ·
po che de fis le primerome · nonapusom de uettre puisançe ·
rois che n deus ad sa creançe · lere nome che de vus curt ·

---

[25] Gregory and Luttrell, *Cligés*, viii.
[26] *Cligés*, ed Wendelin Foerster (Halle: Niemeyer, 1884), xxxvii.
[27] Paris, "Un fragment inconnu," 267.
[28] To complicate matters further, there is one other example of an Arthurian verse romance copied in Italy: the Occitan text of *Jaufre* in Paris, BnF, fr. 12571 (copied probably in the Veneto, ca. 1280, by Johannes Jacobi, a scribe known to have copied in French, Occitan, Italian, and Latin).

si ma mene a uettre curt · p*ur* uuser uire do norer ·· et sel
moi ser uis ne serabie[1.] ge serai ciualier nouel · de uettre
ma*n* e no*n* tautrui · et se de ᵘᵉttre ma*n* no*n* sui · ge non serai
ciualier clamez ·
vusoiez letresbien uenuz bieudusamifet li rois chiet uus
sire de grece sumes · et chie ta*n* per · p*ar* mafoi sire le*n*p*er*er ·
et come tu nom e dimcresi medim battes me alixandre
mefu nomez alixandre bieu duxa mis mul me plet
et mul maet et mul mauez gra*n*t onor fet

Alisandre le roi salue
Que la langhe avoit esmolue
A biem parler et saggement
Rois fet il de vus ne ment
Le renome che de vus nome
Po che de fis le primer ome
Non a pus om de vettre puisançe.
Rois chen deus ad sa creançe
Le renome che de vus curt
Si ma mene a vettre curt
Pur vu servir ed onorer
. . . .
Et sel moi servis ne sera biel
Ge serai civalier novel
De vettre man e non tautrui
Et se de vettre man non sui
Ge non serai civalier clamez
. . . .
. . . .
. . . .
. . . .
. . . .
. . . .
Vu soiez le tres bien venuz
Bieu dus ami fet li rois
. . . .
Chi et vus sire de grece sumes
. . . . et chi et tan per
Par ma foi sire lenperer
Et come tu nom . . . .
E dim cresime dim battesme
. . . .
Alixandre me fu nomez
Alixandre bieu dux amis

Qui la leingue avoit esmolue 340
A bien parler et sagemant.
"Rois," fet il, "se de vos ne mant
Renomee qui vos renome,
Desque Dex fist le premier home 344
Ne nasqui de vostre puissance
Rois qui an Deu eüst creance.
Rois, li renons qui de vos cort
M'a amené a vostre cort 348
Por vos servir et enorer,
Et s'i voldrai tant demorer
Que chevaliers soie noviax,
Se mes servises vos est biax, 352
De vostre main, non de l'autrui,
Car se je par vos ne le sui,
Ne serai chevaliers clamez.
Se vos tant mon servise amez 356
Que chevalier me vuilliez faire,
Retenez moi, rois debonaire,
Et mes conpaignons qui ci sont."
Li rois tot maintenant respont: 360
"Amis," fet il, "ne refus mie
Ne vos ne vostre conpaignie,
Mes bien veignant soiez vos tuit,
Car bien sanblez, et je le cuit, 364
Que vos soiez fil de hauz homes.
Dom estes vos?"–"De Grece somes."
–"De Grece?"–"Voire."–"Qu'ist tes peres?"
–"Par ma foi, sire, l'emperes." 368
–"Et comant as non, biax amis?"
–"Alixandres me fu nons mis
La ou ge reçui sel et cresme
Et crestïanté et baptesme." 372
–"Alixandre, biax amis chiers

. . . .	Je vos retieng molt volantiers,	
Mul me plet et mul maet	Et molt me plest et molt me heite,	
Et mul mavez grant onor fet	Car molt m'avez grant enor feite,	376
Alixandres le roi salue,	[Quant venuz estes a ma cort.]"	

The only reading of the Florence excerpt which might indicate the place of its model in the transmission of *Cligés* is the inversion of ll. 351–352, which also occurs in mss. *NSBRT* (the Annonay fragments; Paris, BnF, fr. 1374; fr. 1450; fr. 1420; and Turin, BNU, L. I. 13). Even this, however, is the kind of variant which can occur independently in the copying process and may not be of great significance. As for the language, a number of features confirm the identity of the scribe as Italian: the use of double 'g' as in "saggement", the use of "gh" in "langhe", the use of "che" for "que" and "chi" for "qui", "come" for "com", "ed" for "et" before vowel, ç as in "puisançe : creançe", etc., although many of the more common Italianisms in transalpine French are wanting.[29] The omissions and the half-lines 367 and 369 and the apparently garbled line 370 may even suggest copying from dictation or memory.[30]

Why does the scribe of the added bifolium of Riccardiana 2756 choose to copy this particular part of *Cligés*?[31] In some of the manuscripts of *Cligés*, including Paris, BnF, fr. 794 (the notorious Guiot copy, the base manuscript of Gregory and Luttrell), the "A" of the first "Alixandre" is a pen-flourished initial, marking a new section of the narrative, an obvious place for the scribe to begin copying. Like the passage from the *Novas del papagai*, this scene is a dialogue, an encounter between strangers, in the *Novas*, between species, and in *Cligés*, between representatives of two geographic regions and empires; in neither case are there linguistic barriers of any kind, just as there appear to be no obstacles to the inclusion of three languages on the added bifolium. At the end of the opening section of the *Novas* copied here, the parrot tries to persuade the lady to accept Antiphanor's love by invoking the examples of Floire and Blanchflor, Tristan and Iseut, and Piramus and Thisbe, drawing her into the world of romance and transforming

---

[29] Giannini, "Il romanzo francese," 146–48, analyzes the language in somewhat more detail.

[30] Wesselofsky, "Un nouveau texte," 327, believed the same to be true of the *Papagai* fragment: "Il a été inséré au dernier feuillet du ms. par quelqu'un qui paraît avoir écrit de mémoire, sans avoir sous les yeux un texte quelconque, ce qui expliquerait selon moi l'omission de certains vers et la défiguration complète de certains autres."

[31] Giannini, "Il romanzo francese," 148–50, calls the sonnets, the *Novas* excerpt, and the *Cligés* passage "questo intelligente e singolare *collage*" (150) and believes that the two narrative passages provide illustrations of the moralizing and didactic themes of the sonnets.

her into a participant in a game of courtly love.[32] Alexandre requests that Arthur dub him knight, making him a member of Arthur's own prestigious social order (to which even the sons of Greek emperors can aspire), and bringing about the integration of the ancient and Arthurian worlds in a real-time *translatio imperii*. It may well have been the nature of *Cligés* as an Arthurian-classical, a blend of the modern and the ancient, which appealed to Guittone d'Arezzo, the author of *L'Intelligenza*, and the scribe of fols. 71–72 of Riccardiana 2756, all of whom were doubtless aware of Italy's historical place in the ancient world and and its role as intermediary between Greece and Arthur's Britain.

---

[32] *Pace*, Giannini, there seem to be no thematic links between the Italian sonnets on the one hand and the *Papagai* and *Cligés* excerpts on the other, not surprising perhaps given that we are dealing with two scribes. The sonnets, which Thomas ("Cinq sonnets," 109) thought might have been part of a larger work, resemble poeticized fragments of a courtesy book, the first three addressed to women, and the final two to young people.

Tracce tristaniane nella lirica dei siciliani*

Michelangelo Picone

È opinione diffusa nella critica specialistica che i "versi d'amore" e le "prose di romanzi" interferiscano in misura molto limitata nel Medio Evo italiano; più in particolare, che le allusioni romanzesche siano poco frequenti nell'antica lirica italiana. Bisogna però subito precisare che, se sono poche le allusioni scoperte, ciò non vuole affatto dire che esse siano poco significative; tutt'altro: esse risultano anzi essere decisive per la decifrazione del messaggio poetico. Come cercheremo di dimostrare, analizzando una piccola serie di luoghi della poesia italiana delle origini, non solo la dimensione romanzesca è presente nel discorso lirico, ma soprattutto essa ne rappresenta la novità più palese rispetto alla tradizione trobadorica. Possiamo dire che la presenza del romanzo (naturalmente del romanzo oitanico) costituisca uno dei fattori principali che permettono alle raccolte liriche—ai *Liederbücher* dei rimatori siciliani e toscani—di organizzarsi in senso macrotestuale, servendosi non solo di connettivi formali, di tipo metrico o retorico, ma anche di connettivi semantici, nella fattispecie narrativo-romanzeschi. È così che nella tradizione italiana il discorso lirico dell'io può diventare progressivamente il racconto o il romanzo dell'io. Il nostro compito è quello di scoprire le "tracce" di questo sviluppo in senso romanzesco presenti nella lirica italiana del Duecento: tracce che ci permettono di capire come si possa arrivare a capolavori tipo la *Vita nova* di Dante o i *Rerum vulgarium fragmenta* di Petrarca

---

* Mi è gradito offrire queste brevi osservazioni a Chris Kleinhenz che alla tematica qui trattata ha da sempre dedicato un'attenzione particolare (vd. la nota 4). Fra l'altro è proprio prendendo spunto dai suoi saggi che, nel lontano Winter Semester del 1994–1995, ho svolto un intero corso all'Università di Zurigo sulla presenza della leggenda tristaniana nella poesia italiana del Duecento; corso da cui sono tratte le pagine seguenti, che furono anche lette ad Ascona (Ticino) in occasione del Convegno organizzato dalle Università della Svizzera occidentale sulle "Forme del narrare poetico" (29 nov.–2 dic. 2005).

(io stesso ho recentemente enfatizzato l'importanza della tematica romanzesca in ambedue le opere).[1]

È con i poeti della Scuola Siciliana che l'amore ad una dimensione dei trovatori si movimenta, aprendosi verso la storia e il mondo esterno; possiamo dire che con i Siciliani lo spazio interiore comincia ad essere raffigurato come spazio esteriore, l'interno viene descritto come esterno, e il mondo soggettivo viene presentato come realtà oggettiva. L'amore senza tempo e senza storia dei trovatori entra così nel tempo e nella storia; si costruisce cioè come storia, che può imitare gli schemi esemplari della narrativa romanzesca.[2] Basta analizzare alcuni passi del Notaio Giacomo da Lentini, tratti dal suo piccolo canzoniere, per rendersi conto di questo mutamento epocale, del passaggio dalla lirica pura dei trovatori ad una lirica aperta verso la narratività, che si tinge di romanzesco. Le due strofe di canzone, qui sotto riprodotte, vogliono caratterizzare, oltre all'io lirico, anche la Donna, che non è più una figura astratta o ideale, ma diventa una figura concreta, vicina alla prospettiva storica in cui agisce l'io. La donna *de lonh* dei trovatori coi Siciliani diventa presente, si manifesta davanti al suo amante. Giacomo da Lentini si avvicina cioè alla sua donna non solo attraverso la *descriptio* della sua bellezza, o attraverso la tematica della lode, ma anche grazie alla *narratio*.

Giacomo cerca di stabilire un contatto con la sua donna, non diretto ma mediato, mediato attraverso l'immagine di lei riprodotta in una pittura o in una scultura. La pura essenza femminile in tal modo si incarna, diventa fenomenica:

> In gran dilettanz'era,
> madonna, in quello giorno
> quando ti formai in cera
> le bellezze d'intorno:
> più bella mi parete
> ca Isolda la bronda,
> amorosa gioconda
> che sovr'ogn'altra sete.[3]

È la grande "dilettanza", la grande gioia amorosa dell'io, quella che lo porta a rendere presente l'Assente, a dare realtà all'idea astratta dell'eterno femminino, e quindi a "formare in cera" la straordinaria bellezza della donna amata; che appare davanti al poeta come statua plasmata dall'artista. Giacomo annulla così la

---

[1] Mi sia permesso di rinviare a Michelangelo Picone, *Percorsi della lirica duecentesca: Dai Siciliani alla "Vita nova"* (Firenze: Cadmo, 2003), 219–65; e *Il "Canzoniere": Lettura micro e macrotestuale*, ed. Michelangelo Picone (Ravenna: Longo, 2007), passim.

[2] Si rinvia a quanto ha scritto a questo proposito Paolo Cherchi, "Il tempo degli amanti e il carrro di Febo," in *Studi di filologia e letteratura italiana: In onore di Maria Picchio Simonelli*, ed. Pietro Frassica (Alessandria: Edizioni dell'Orso, 1992), 51–61.

[3] Giacomo da Lentini, *Madonna mia*, vv. 44–48 (si cita secondo l'edizione approntata da Roberto Antonelli [Roma: Bulzoni, 1979], 159–69).

distanza dall'Oggetto del suo desiderio, creando un sostituto non simbolico ma reale dell'amata, e a questa realtà concreta tributa il suo amore. Messo davanti all'immagine della Donna riprodotta nella statua di cera, Giacomo non può fare a meno di esprimere tutta la sua ammirazione: essa (la statua, non la donna!) gli appare più bella addirittura di Isotta la bionda, la più paradigmatica delle bellezze femminili del Medio Evo. Ciò che fa del poeta un omologo di Tristano, un eroe proiettato in una avventura non solo lirica ma anche romanzesca. L'allusione letteraria è in questo caso manifesta: Giacomo vuole rievocare qui uno dei più suggestivi episodi del *Roman de Tristan* di Thomas: quello che Bédier ha ribattezzato come "la salle aux images."[4]

L'episodio romanzesco si riferisce all'esilio di Tristano nella piccola Bretagna, dove l'eroe ha sposato l'altra Isotta, quella dalle bianche mani, solo per il fatto che il suo nome gli ricorda l'Isotta assente. Ed è proprio questo ricordo angoscioso dell'amata assente che viene qui espresso. Nella foresta, dove cerca di svagarsi con la caccia, Tristano scopre un giorno una meravigliosa grotta scavata nella roccia. L'eroe decide subito di trasformare questo luogo in una specie di tempio segreto dove ritirarsi in meditazione amorosa. A questo scopo egli fa scolpire delle statue a grandezza naturale, rivestite di abiti preziosi; statue che rappresentano la sua storia d'amore. La statua più importante è naturalmente quella della regina Isotta, della donna amata e lontana. Questa statua diventa per Tristano una reliquia, viene fatta oggetto di un vero e proprio culto.[5] Ma la statua è anche uno strumento per rammemorare, e quindi per rivivere, la propria infelice storia d'amore. La grotta delle statue, la "salle aux images," diventa così anche un laboratorio artistico, dato che la rammemorazione di Tristano annuncia la rammemorazione dell'autore del romanzo di Tristano. È dunque possibile dare un'interpretazione

---

[4] Si tratta del frammento del ms. di Torino, ora perduto, corrispondente ai vv. 941–1196 del *Roman de Tristan* di Thomas; citato nell'ed. a cura di Felix Lecoy (Paris: Champion, 1991), 51–56. Sulla presenza della leggenda tristaniana nei poeti della Scuola Siciliana la bibliografia è molto ampia; si citano qui i lavori più importanti ai fini della presente indagine: Edmund G. Gardner, *The Arthurian Legend in Italian Literature* (London: J.M., Dent, 1930), 21–43; Christopher Kleinhenz, "Tristan in Italy: The Birth and Rebirth of a Legend," *Studies in Medieval Culture* 5 (1975): 145–58; Roberto Antonelli, "La scuola poetica alla corte di Federigo II," in *Federigo II e le scienze*, ed. P. Toubert e Agostino Paravicini Bagliani (Palermo: Sellerio, 1994), 309–23; Emanuele Trevi, "Introduzione" alla *Tavola ritonda*, ed. idem (Milano: Rizzoli, 1999), 9–85; Mario Mancini, "Giacomo da Lentini, Tristano, i trovatori," in *La poesia di Giacomo da Lentini: Scienza e filosofia nel XIII secolo in Sicilia e nel Mediterraneo occidentale*, ed. Rossend Arqués (Palermo: Centro di Studi filologici e linguistici siciliani, 2000), 214–41; Fabrizio Cigni, "Tristano e Isotta nelle letterature francese e italiana," in *Tristano e Isotta: La fortuna di un mito europeo*, ed. Michael Dallapiazza (Trieste: Edizioni Parnaso, 2003), 29–129.

[5] Cfr. Aurelio Roncaglia, "La statua di Isotta," *Cultura neolatina* 31 (1971): 41–67; e Claudio Galderisi, "Le récit du mariage avec la statue: Résurgences et modalités narratives," *Romania* 59 (2001): 170–95.

autoreferenziale di questo episodio, che assume il valore di una metafora dello stesso processo di creazione letteraria. Non si tratta solo di descrivere una patologia erotica, simile a quella celeberrima della *Gradiva* analizzata da Freud, ma di implicare dentro la narrazione gli estremi di una riflessione metanarrativa.

In questa prospettiva Tristano non è solo il protagonista della storia d'amore, ma anche l'iniziatore del processo di raccoglimento dei ricordi che afferiscono a quella storia: è quindi l'immagine dell'autore proiettato nel testo, l'autore che unisce insieme gli sparsi frammenti della storia d'amore di Tristano per farne un romanzo. Tristano è dunque il capostipite ideale non solo di Thomas o Béroul, ma anche dei poeti che, come Giacomo da Lentini, si identificheranno con lui nella loro vita e nella loro creazione artistica. È significativo che il frammento tristaniano che stiamo analizzando enfatizzi proprio questa funzione memoriale: davanti alla statua di Isotta Tristano "recorde," si fa scorrere davanti alla memoria gli eventi passati, e presagisce anche gli eventi futuri (ad esempio che Isotta possa dimenticarlo ["que ele mette lui en obli"] o possa addirittura dare il suo amore ad un altro cavaliere). Per questa ragione Tristano ha fatto scolpire la statua di Isotta, per poterle sempre manifestare il suo amore, per raccontarle la sua passione gioiosa e dolorosa al tempo stesso:

> Por içò fist il ceste image
> que dire li volt son corage,
> son bon penser e sa fole errur,
> sa paigne, sa joie d'amor,
> car ne sot vers cui descovrir
> ne son voler ne son desir.[6]

La statua diventa così la destinataria privilegiata del messaggio amoroso dell'eroe; Tristano infatti non sa a quale persona (meglio che a Isotta) svelare la forza del suo desiderio ("descoverir / ne son voler, ne son desir"). Solo Isotta può capire a fondo la storia d'amore di Tristano.

È nella canzone *Meravigliosa - mente* che il Notaio sembra aver assorbito a pieno la lezione impartita dall'episodio tristaniano che abbiamo appena analizzato. Questa canzone riprende chiaramente un motivo lirico già presente nella tradizione trobadorica: quello del cuore del poeta che è diventato la dimora dell'immagine dell'amata.[7] Motivo attestato, ad esempio, nella canzone di Folchetto che inizia *En chantan m'aven a membrar*. A chiusura della prima *cobla*

---

[6] *Roman de Tristan*, ed. F. Lecoy, vv. 985–90, (50).

[7] Così come hanno dimostrato, tra gli altri, Franco Mancini, *La figura del cuore fra cortesia e mistica: Dai Siciliani allo Stilnuovo* (Napoli: ESI, 1988); e Maria Luisa Meneghetti, "Il ritratto in cuore: peripezie di un tema medievale fra il profano e il sacro," in *Riscritture del testo medievale: dialogo fra culture e tradizioni*, ed. M.G. Cammarota (Bergamo: Edizioni Sestante, 2005), 73–85.

di questa canzone Folchetto afferma di portare "inz el cor," dentro il suo cuore, la "faisso," l'immagine dell'amata. In quanto custode dell'immagine della donna, il cuore non deve subire alcun danno, poiché ciò si ripercuoterebbe sulla donna stessa. La donna può dunque fare quello che vuole col corpo del poeta, ma deve salvaguardare il cuore, in quanto esso è la sua dimora (col solito gioco *cors/cor*).[8] Nella canzone del Notaio, però, questo motivo della lirica trobadorica si combina col tema romanzesco della "salle aux images" che abbiamo appena analizzato. Il cuore del poeta siciliano possiamo dire che si sia complicato rispetto al cuore del trovatore provenzale: esso è diventato l'equivalente della grotta delle statue tristaniana; il cuore del poeta siciliano è la sala dove è custodita non la semplice immagine mentale dell'amata, bensì la sua immagine "dipinta," il quadro a grandezza naturale della donna amata. Leggiamo la terza strofa della canzone *Meravigliosa - mente*:

> Avendo gran disio
> dipinsi una pintura,
> bella, voi simigliante,
> e quando voi non vio
> guardo 'n quella figura,
> par ch'eo v'aggia davante:
> come quello che crede
> salvarsi per sua fede,
> ancor non veggia inante.[9]

La figura della donna, impressa nel cuore del poeta, non è più una semplice metafora, come nella canzone trobadorica, ma è una realtà presentata come vera. Il Notaio usa non a caso un tempo storico per descrivere questa scena: "*dipinsi* una pintura." Pertanto la donna non è *come* dipinta nel cuore del poeta, essa *è* a tutti gli effetti dipinta in quel cuore, è un quadro gelosamente conservato nel museo interiore del poeta, come la statua di Isotta era gelosamente conservata nella grotta-sacrario di Tristano. Così facendo il Notaio inserisce la sua lirica in una prospettiva narrativa; egli narrativizza il processo attraverso il quale fa suo (o cerca di far suo) l'oggetto desiderato. L'io lirico agisce dunque sulla scena del mondo per colmare la distanza che lo separa dalla Donna; ed è questa azione che rende l'io lirico simile all'eroe romanzesco, che proietta la canzone sullo sfondo del romanzo.

Che si tratti di una vera e propria storia d'amore, quella che il poeta siciliano ci racconta in questa canzone, ce lo dicono gli ultimi versi di questa strofa. Qui infatti viene avanzata l'ipotesi di una fine positiva della storia: il Notaio prevede infatti che il contatto con la Donna, mediato dalla pittura, diventerà un giorno

---

[8] Folquet de Marselha, *Poesie*, ed. Paolo Squillacoti (Roma: Carocci, 2003), 112.
[9] Giacomo da Lentini, *Rime*, ed. Antonelli, 31 (sono i vv. 19–27 della canzone).

contatto immediato e diretto: "come quello che crede / salvarsi per sua fede, / ancor non veggia inante." Come il cristiano ha fede nella sua salvazione eterna, anche se non la vede davanti a sé, così il poeta amante ha fede nel raggiungimento dell'oggetto desiderato, anche se non ha davanti a sé la Donna reale ma la sua immagine dipinta (si noti il gioco oppositivo fra i sintagmi verbali in rima: *veggia inante* detto del cristiano, e *v'aggia davante* riferito al poeta amante). Questo presentimento di una conclusione positiva della storia amorosa è un altro segno evidente di una lirica che si avvia ad essere racconto e romanzo. Sarà precisamente questa la fine della *Vita nova* di Dante: lo spirito peregrino che ritrova nel Paradiso l'immagine della donna amata.[10]

Il terzo passo del Notaio che ora analizzeremo è tratto dal suo discordo *Dal core mi vene*: un componimento notevole per le sue novità formali, metriche soprattutto, ma anche per la sua forte accensione romanzesca. Troviamo infatti qui un'altra allusione al romanzo di Tristano: un'allusione incastonata dentro un chiaro movimento affabulatorio, dentro il racconto dell'io che ricerca il luogo in cui la Donna manifesta la sua presenza. L'allusione a Tristano è inserita cioè dentro quella che è la struttura fondamentale del romanzo, non solo oitanico: la struttura narrativa della *quête*, il campo semantico-ideologico della *peregrinatio*.[11]
Lo schema metrico della stanza che ci accingiamo ad analizzare (la seconda) individua i tre nuclei narrativi che compongono la storia che si vuole qui raccontare. Leggiamo il primo segmento (vv. 19–26), dove viene descritta la situazione amorosa vissuta dall'io lirico, la sua esperienza di una *fol'amor* simile a quella vissuta dal protagonista del romanzo tristaniano:

> Ca pur penare
> è disïare,
> già mai non fare
> mia diletanza:
> la rimembranza
> di voi, aulente cosa,
> gli ochi m'arosa
> d'un' aigua d'amore.[12]

Il desiderio amoroso (il "disïare") viene qui definito come "pur penare," un tormento continuo, che impedisce la "diletanza," il raggiungimento della felicità amorosa. Al poeta amante non rimane allora che la "rimembranza," il ricordo, la stessa rammemorazione che stava al centro dell'episodio tristaniano prima analizzato. Ricordo della donna amata, che viene caratterizzata come "aulente

---

[10] Si rinvia a Michelangelo Picone, *"Vita Nuova" e tradizione romanza* (Padova: Liviana, 1979), 129–92.
[11] Cfr. Picone, *Percorsi della lirica duecentesca*, 249–65.
[12] Ed. Antonelli, 224–25.

cosa" (anche questa costituisce un'allusione tristaniana: nello stesso episodio della "salle aux images" si dice che la statua di Isotta esala dalle labbra e dai capelli un profumo inebriante). La rimembranza dell'amata "arosa," fa bagnare di lacrime gli occhi del poeta.[13] Questa partizione metrica della strofa, così impregnata di risonanze tristaniane, esprime dunque la condizione di *impasse* dolorosa nella quale si trova l'io lirico a causa del suo amore impossibile.

Ecco però che già nella seconda partizione metrica, nel secondo segmento lirico-narrativo, la situazione si sblocca, l'*impasse* erotica sembra trovare una via d'uscita. Leggiamo i vv. 27–34:

> Or potess'eo,
> o amore meo,
> come romeo
> venire ascoso,
> e disïoso
> con voi mi vedesse,
> non mi partisse
> dal vostro dolzore.

L'io lirico veste qui i panni dell'eroe romanzesco, affronta cioè (seppur ottativamente) il viaggio che lo conduce nel luogo in cui si trova la donna amata. Anche se presentato in forma desiderativa ("Or potess'eo. . ."), si tratta pur sempre di un chiaro movimento narrativo: l'io esce dalla propria dolorosa interiorità e si proietta nello spazio esteriore, diventa un pellegrino *in itinere* verso il luogo della propria integrazione amorosa. Fondamentale questo brano nella prospettiva dei capitoli finali del libello dantesco, dove vediamo il protagonista trasformato in "romeo" che va alla ricerca del metaforico velo della Veronica, che nello specchio purissimo di Beatrice beata vede riflessa l'immagine stessa di Dio. Ma per il momento a noi interessa più quello che c'è a monte del passo del Notaio di cui ci stiamo occupando; e a monte troviamo di nuovo il *roman* oitanico di Tristano, un altro episodio altrettanto famoso di questo romanzo: episodio brevemente narrato nel *Tristan* di Thomas (ai vv. 2199–2216) e sviluppato nel poema altotedesco di Eilhart von Oberg.[14] Tristano, dopo aver passato un anno nella piccola Bretagna, lontano da Isotta, spinto da un violento desiderio di rivedere la donna amata, ritorna in Cornovaglia alla corte di re Marco, e per non farsi riconoscere dal re e dai cortigiani si traveste appunto da pellegrino, ciò che gli consente di avere un fugace incontro amoroso con Isotta. Diversamente da Tristano, il poeta siciliano si augura di rimanere più a lungo presso alla donna amata: egli anzi non

---

[13] Nel suo commento al discordo di Giacomo da Lentini, Gianfranco Contini (in *Poeti del Duecento* [Milano-Napoli: Ricciardi, 1960], 1: 69) richiama il v. 1145 del *Tristan* di Béroul ("L'eve li file aval le vis").

[14] Il richiamo si trova già nel commento di Contini (ibid.) e nel recente studio di Mancini ("Giacomo da Lentini, Tristano, i trovatori," 220–24).

si staccherebbe mai da quel luogo capace di produrre in lui tanta dolcezza ("non mi partissse / dal vostro dolzore").

Dopo questo segmento narrativo, dove il Notaio affabula la grande tematica romanzesca della *peregrinatio amoris*, nel terzo segmento si ritorna a parlare della condizione attuale in cui si trova l'io lirico, che viene ora esplicitamente paragonato a Tristano (vv. 35–42):

> Dal vostro lato
> [. . .] allungato,
> be·ll'ò provato
> mal che non salda:
> Tristano Isalda
> non amau sì forte;
> ben mi par morte
> non vedervi fiore.

Il Notaio afferma in questi versi che la lontannza dalla donna rappresenta per lui un male incurabile (un "mal che non salda"), come appunto dimostra il caso esemplare di Tristano che tenuto lontano da Isotta è morto. Anzi, l'amore del poeta per la sua donna è più forte di quello provato da Tristano per Isotta, e di conseguenza più tragica sarà la sua conclusione. Arriva del tutto naturale, dopo tanti indizi disseminati nel testo, questo coinvolgimento diretto, questa "citazione" esplicita degli eroi di Cornovaglia. Paragonandosi a Tristano (ma si tratta piuttosto di una *comparatio* che di una similitudine), mettendosi in gara con Tristano il poeta siciliano si propone anche lui come una figura paradigmatica della *fol'amor* romanza. La rima *salda* : *Isalda* mette in rilievo il fatto che solo Isotta è capace di curare, "saldare" la ferita amorosa di Tristano, e quindi dell'io lirico. La clausola finale, con l'accostamento della pulsione erotica a quella antitetica di *thanatos*, di "amore" accanto a "morte," sigilla questa *imitatio* da parte del poeta lirico del *pattern* romanzesco tristaniano, riproponendo appunto il binomio di "amore e morte."[15]

Parlerò solo brevemente di un altro testo siciliano, di una stanza tratta da un altro discordo attribuito dal Vat. 3793 a "messer lo re Giovanni," cioè a un membro molto altolocato della corte di Federico II; si tratta più precisamente di Giovanni di Brienne che aveva ereditato, tramite il suo matrimonio con Maria figlia di Corrado di Monferrato, il regno di Gerusalemme. Anche questo passo descrive l'amore come tensione verso l'Altro da sé, verso una Donna che viene identificata concretamente. Si giustificano così i richiami romanzeschi al Tristano oitanico: ad essere richiamati in questo caso non sono solo i personaggi del romanzo (i suoi protagonisti) ma anche precisi episodi della leggenda tristaniana:

---

[15] Per una accurata analisi di queste tematiche si veda Arianna Punzi, *Tristano: Storia di un mito* (Roma: Carocci, 2005), passim.

> Fino amor m'à comandato
> ch'io m'allegri tuttavia,
> faccia sì ch'io serva a grato
> a la dolze donna mia,
> quella c'amo più 'n celato
> che Tristano non facia
> Isotta, como cantato,
> ancor che le· fosse zia.
> Lo re Marco era 'nganato,
> perché 'n lui si confidia:
> ello n'era smisurato,
> e Tristan se ne godia
> de lo bel viso rosato
> ch'Isaotta blond' avia:
> ancor che fosse peccato,
> altro far non ne potia,
> ch'a la nave li fu dato
> onde ciò li dovenia.
> Nullo si faccia mirato
> s'io languisco tuttavia,
> ch'io sono più 'namorato
> che null'altro omo che sia.[16]

Benché all'inizio della strofa si parli di "fino amor," l'amore che viene qui praticato dal poeta siciliano è tutt'altro che "fino," risponde bensì alla tipologia opposta della *fol'amor*, dell'amore negativo e distruttivo, come l'allusione precisa ai tragici amanti di Cornovaglia sta ad indicare. Ai vv. 63–64 viene addirittura rievocato l'evento cruciale della leggenda tristaniana: quello del filtro d'amore bevuto da Tristano e Isotta sulla nave che dall'Irlanda li portava in Cornovaglia: "ch'a la nave li fu dato / onde ciò li dovenia." L'amore è dunque fino, positivo, in astratto; dato che nella concretezza della vita amorosa del poeta esso rivela tutta la sua tragica negatività. A ben guardare l'"amor" del primo verso è la stessa personificazione del dio d'Amore, e andrebbe quindi scritto con la A maiuscola. Questo Amore, che all'inizio della stanza comanda all'io di "allegrarsi tuttavia," cioè di essere continuamente felice, alla fine della strofa manifesta la sua vera natura: l'io lirico infatti al v. 66 "languisce tuttavia," soffre perennemente per il suo amore. Chiaro il rovesciamento della situazione iniziale, la trasformazione dell'atteggiamento euforico in disforico.

Ma vediamo come il re Giovanni narrativizza il suo amore (mi sembra a questo proposito significativa la parentetica del v. 53: "como cantato," che è

---

[16] Si cita, con alcuni lievi ritocchi alla lezione e alla punteggiatura, dall'edizione cumulativa curata da Bruno Panvini: *Rime della Scuola siciliana* (Firenze: Olschki, 1962), 85–88.

tutt'altro che una zeppa: il poeta lirico "canta" la sua storia d'amore, che ripete quella romanzesca di Tristano). L'amore, descritto nei vv. 47–50 in chiave lirica, come amore inappagato, come servizio dovuto all'amata senza attendersi nessuna ricompensa ("ch'io serva a grato": è questo l'ordine dato al poeta da Amore), viene proiettato nei versi successivi su uno sfondo chiaramente narrativo: l'amore viene cioè articolato secondo il *pattern* narrativo del romanzo di Tristano, ciò che permette di superare l'*impasse* lirica nella dimensione romanzesca. Il re Giovanni si paragona cioè a Tristano, che amava "in celato," di nascosto, Isotta, benché Isotta fosse la moglie di re Marco, zio di Tristano. Si tratta dunque di un "peccato" (come si dice al v. 61), di una relazione non solo adulterina ma addirittura incestuosa: Tristano, nel realizzare fisicamente il suo amore, nell'infrangere il codice cortese che escludeva la ricompensa, si pone fuori della legge morale e sociale; seguendo le sue orme anche il poeta siciliano si trova in un territorio minato, che vuole però attraversare.

Può essere utile a questo proposito analizzare una *cobla* di Raimbaut d'Aurenga, scambiata in tenzone con Bernart de Ventadorn e Chrétien de Troyes, trasformatosi per l'occasione in poeta lirico:

> De midonz fatz dompn'e seignor
> cals que sia·il destinada.
> Car ieu begui de la amor
> ja·us dei amar a celada.
> Tristan, qan la·il det Yseus gen
> e bela, no·n saup als faire;
> et ieu am per aital coven
> midonz, don no·m posc estraire.[17]

È qui, in questa *cobla*, che viene lanciata per la prima volta l'ipotesi di una soluzione romanzesca da dare al *paradoxe amoureux* tipico della tradizione trobadorica. Anche Raimbaut ama una donna sposata, destinata ad un altro uomo (v. 26), esattamente come Tristano aveva amato "a celada," di nascosto, Isotta. Come Tristano non aveva potuto resistere a quell'amore, perché azionato dal filtro amoroso, così anche Raimbaut "begui de la amor," ha bevuto alla stessa fonte della *fol'amor* tristaniana. Già in Raimbaut troviamo dunque proposti gli elementi fondamentali della leggenda tristaniana (amare "'n celato," il filtro magico, la consapevolezza della natura peccaminosa dell'amore), elementi che poi il re Giovanni riprenderà e svilupperà più sistematicamente.

Interessante al v. 55 del discordo del re Giovanni il riferimento al tema capitale del romanzo tristaniano che è quello dell'inganno d'amore ("lo re Marco era 'nganato"), tema che rimane inespresso nella *canso* di Raimbaut (lo si inferisce

---

[17] Si cita da *Los trovadores: Historia literaria y textos*, ed. Martín de Riquer (Barcelona: Editorial Planeta, 1975), 1: 431.

solo dal v. 26). Di inganni e controinganni è naturalmente pieno il *Roman de Tristan*, a cominciare dalla sostituzione di Isotta, non più vergine, con l'ancella Brangana nella prima notte di matrimonio. Con l'inganno, la storia d'amore che nella lirica aveva due soli personaggi (l'io e la donna), si trasforma in romanzesca, coinvolge un terzo personaggio (quello del marito tradito), si struttura secondo il canonico triangolo amoroso, sperimentato in versione tragica nel romanzo, e in versione comica nel *fabliau* e nella novella.[18] La stanza del poeta siciliano non si limita più, come la *cobla* trobadorica, a suggerire una prospettiva romanzesca tristaniana, ma attribuisce a questa prospettiva una profondità sociologica e una complessità diegetica.

A chiusura del mio discorso vorrei fare una rapida incursione nel campo della poesia siculo-toscana, dei rimatori che hanno trasferito, linguisticamente e culturalmente, i temi e i motivi della lirica italiana delle Origini dall'ambiente chiuso e elitario della corte siciliana all'ambiente aperto delle città e dei comuni toscani della seconda metà del Duecento.

La mia scelta è caduta sul fiorentino Palamidesse di Bellindote, il cui nome storico (o *de plume?*) richiama quello di un personaggio romanzesco, cioè di Palamedes, "le bon Sarradin," il prode e sfortunato cavaliere pagano rivale di Tristano nell'amore di Isotta, secondo il dettagliato racconto fornitoci dal *Roman de Tristan* in prosa.[19] In una tenzone con un altro rimatore fiorentino, Orlanduccio Orafo, Palamidesse viene definito "errante cavaliero, / de l'arme fero e de la mente saggio."[20] Ma è nell'unica canzone che di lui ci ha conservato il codice Vat. lat. 3793, *Amor, grande peccato*, che l'identificazione con il cavaliere antico viene portata alle sue estreme conseguenze: il poeta veste qui gli abiti di Palamedes, si presenta come l'amante disperato di Isotta. Nel congedo di questa canzone, infatti, Palamidesse si rivolge al suo rivale fortunato, a Tristano, che si trova (ovviamente in compagnia di Isotta) nel castello della "Gioiosa Guardia," per dedicargli appunto la sua "canzone dolorosa," ma anche per annunciargli il suo prossimo arrivo in quel luogo:

A la Guardia Gioiosa
ten va' al mio Tristano,
mia canzone dolorosa,
e di' che Speranvano
a lei tosto verà.
E, com'io credo, forse
n'averà doglia e paura:

---

[18] Cfr. Michelangelo Picone, "L'inganno d'amore tra romanzo e novella," *Rassegna europea di letteratura italiana* 5–6 (1995): 23–30.

[19] Su questo personaggio si vedano le fini osservazioni di Emmanuèle Baumgartner, *Le "Tristan en prose": Essai d'interprétation d'un roman médiéval* (Genève: Droz, 1975), 246–52.

[20] Edita da Contini, in *Poeti del Duecento*, 1: 473–74.

ché, s'una lonze fosse,
sì perderia natura
ed avriane pietanza.

Invece di essere indirizzata alla donna amata, la canzone ha come suo destinatario privilegiato l'avversario in amore (un altro poeta più famoso? è stato proposto il nome di Guido Guinizzelli[21]), che viene affettuosamente chiamato il "mio Tristano." Non si tratta in questo caso della "gran bontà de' cavalieri antiqui," bensì di una sorta di solidarietà fra i praticanti dell'amore passione, della consapevolezza che questo tipo di amore riserva a coloro che lo provano più afflizioni che gioie. Palamidesse, che si firma col *senhal* di "Speranvano," in quanto amante senza speranza di Isotta, sente una profonda affinità nei confronti di Tristano, il cui amore, sebbene ricambiato da Isotta, non può definirsi come pienamente felice, dato che gli è consentito di vedere l'amata solo in brevi, fuggevoli momenti. L'esperienza dolorosa dell'amore accomuna dunque i due cavalieri antichi, e di conseguenza i loro imitatori moderni.

La canzone viene inviata da Palamidesse al suo corrispondente (Tristano) che si trova nel *locus amoris* (la Gioiosa Guardia) in compagnia dell'amata contessa (Isotta). La sua funzione è precisamente quella di annunciare il prossimo arrivo in quello stesso luogo, e presso la stessa donna (il pronome *lei* del v. 65 sembra indicare infatti i due oggetti della *quête*, comunque collegati metonimicamente), del poeta che l'ha composta. Quando ciò avverrà, la donna, che fino ad ora si era dimostrata crudele nei confronti del poeta amante, potrebbe cambiare il suo atteggiamento, mostrandosi pietosa e compassionevole. Da "lonza," quale era stata fino a quel momento (la canzone è piena di immagini cavate dai bestiari), l'amata può diventare una creatura docile e devota. È quello almeno che si augura il poeta fiorentino nel congedarsi dalla sua canzone: che la "pietà" dell'amata costituisca il primo passo verso la reciprocazione dell'amore, e annulli quindi la distanza che lo separa dal rivale più fortunato.

Un ultimo elemento, non esplicitato nel nostro testo, ma decisivo per la sua stessa articolazione, va messo in evidenza a conclusione della nostra analisi. Nel romanzo francese tanto Tristano che Palamedes sono, oltre che valorosi cavalieri, anche abilissimi compositori di *chansons* e di *lais*, ai quali affidano il senso profondo della loro esperienza erotica. L'identificazione del rimatore fiorentino col personaggio arturiano è pertanto totale: non si riduce alla ripetizione delle stesse azioni e delle stesse passioni, alla semplice ripresa di temi narrativi, ma raggiunge il livello ben più complesso della riflessione sul proprio essere e sul proprio destino personale. Dall'intertestualità siamo così passati alla metatestualità. Per cui non si tratta più di motivi romanzeschi prestati alla lirica, ma di una lirica che comincia ad atteggiarsi come romanzo.

---

[21] La proposta è stata di recente avanzata da Roberto Antonelli, "Dal Notaro al Guinizzelli," in *Da Guido Guinizzelli a Dante: Nuove prospettive sulla lirica del Duecento*, ed. Furio Brugnolo e Gianfelice Peron (Padova: Il Poligrafo, 2004), 107–46.

Galeotto Before the Fall[1]

Samuel N. Rosenberg

Think of Galeotto, and the association that springs to mind is a mere reference, but a striking image, in Canto V of the *Inferno*. The lovers Francesca and Paolo, first brought together through their shared reading of the French tale of Lancelot and Guenevere, had reached the scene in which Lancelot's friend Galehaut brings the Arthurian pair together for their first kiss. At that point, Francesca tells the Pilgrim, she and Paolo imitated their literary model: "Galeotto fu il libro e chi lo scrisse; / quel giorno più non vi leggemmo avante" (ll. 137–138). Does the first line mean "The book was [entitled] *Galehaut* and its author was a Galehaut," or "The book was a Galehaut, as was its author"? It hardly matters, for the significant thing is that that particular book is identified as the mediating agent of the Italian couple's love just as the character Galehaut had made possible the love of Lancelot and the queen.

The Galeotto that thus metaphorically brings Francesca and Paolo together in the fifth canto of the *Inferno* has had a rather dismal reputation over the past several centuries, for Galeotto has come to be seen above all as an equivalent of Chaucer's Pandar, the very model of the procurer, the vile promoter of sexual indulgence. He has been censured with such labels as 'ruffiano,' 'seduttore,' 'infame sensale di amore,' 'vil entremetteur,' and the name has indeed been lexicalized in Italian with such meanings.[2] Despite the fact that some modern scholars, including Italian lexicographers, have adopted a more benign view of the character,[3] the

---

[1] This essay is an elaboration of Samuel N. Rosenberg, "Translation and Eclipse: The Case of Galehaut," in *The Medieval Translator* 8, ed. R. Voaden, R. Tixier, T. Sanchez Roura, and J. R. Rytting (Turnhout: Brepols, 2003), 245–55, which surveys literary treatments of Galehaut ranging through various languages, including English.

[2] See Heinrich Morf, "'Galeotto fu il libro e chi lo scrisse' (Dante, *Inferno* V, 137)," *Sitzungsberichte der Königlichen Preussischen Akademie der Wissenschaften, philosophisch-historische Klasse* 43 (1916): 1118–1138, at 1118.

[3] Aside from Morf, "'Galeotto'," see, for example, Branca's note in *Tutte le opere di Boccaccio*, ed. Vittorio Branca, 12 vols. (Milan: Mondadori, 1964–1998), 4:976; and Manlio Cortelazzo and Paolo Zolli, *Dizionario etimologico della lingua italiana*, 5 vols. (Bologna: Zanichelli, 1979–1988), 2: s.v. *galeòtto*.

common image of a morally corrupt Galeotto has hardly faded. One of the determinants of that pejoration has no doubt been the influence of a homonym, *galeotto*, a common noun belonging to the family of *galea* 'galley.' The word means, at its best, 'boatman, helmsman, pilot'—which gives Dante's metaphor 'Galeotto fu il libro' an even richer complexity than had been obvious earlier—and then, in a gradual depreciation, 'oarsman, galley slave, convict, scoundrel.'[4] Though this factor of pejoration is peculiar to Italian, its effect was bound to spread beyond that language, wherever the *Inferno* was read.

It is not clear how Dante wished to have the character understood, not clear whether, in that sole allusion, Dante was expressing a view of Galehaut as a force morally positive, nefarious, or even essentially beyond the reach of such judgment. Yet whatever controversy may have arisen over Dante's interpretation of the character and his behavior, the issue does not call for resolution here. The simple, objective fact is that Dante's brief but lapidary evocation presents the personage not in the fullness of his being as portrayed in the early thirteenth-century French Prose *Lancelot*—friend and lover, powerful knight and great warrior, and, in the end, a figure of high tragedy—but only in his narrow function as intermediary in an amorous relation. This limited use to which Dante reduced the figure of Galehaut was new to the Arthurian tradition as received in Italy.

Earlier, the treatment of the character had been more consonant with the considerably broader depiction offered in the French work, in which Galehaut, sire des Lointaines Isles (Lord of the Distant Isles), emerges for the first time in Arthurian literature in any language. He begins as an offstage character one evening in Arthur's dining hall, when a messenger arrives to announce that "le plus preudom qui orendroit soit de son eage, c'est Galahos, li fiex a la Bele Jaiande," wants Arthur to surrender his land to him and become his liegeman. If Arthur refuses, Galehaut will within a month invade and conquer the entire realm.[5]

The king, who has never even heard of Galehaut, is surprised by this challenge but is too confident of his own power to take it seriously. Of the many knights in attendance, only one, Galegantin the Welshman, has any knowledge of Arthur's new adversary: "'Sire, j'ai veu Galahot, il est bien plus grans demi piet que chevalier que l'en sache, s'est li homme el monde plus amés de sa gent et qui plus a conquis de son eage, car il est joines bachelers [. . .] et li plus jentix chevaliers et li plus debonaires del monde et tous li plus larges.'" In other words,

---

[4] See, for example, Cortelazzo and Zolli, *Dizionario* 2: s.v. *galèa*; and Barbara Reynolds, *Cambridge Italian Dictionary*, 2 vols. (Cambridge: Cambridge University Press, 1962–1981), 1: s.v. *galeotta*. Note that *galeotto* occurs twice in the sense of 'oarsman' or 'pilot' in Dante's *Commedia*: *Inf.* 8:17 and *Purg.* 2:27.

[5] For quotations and narrative material in this paragraph and the next, see Alexandre Micha, ed., *Lancelot: Roman en prose du XIIIe siècle*, 9 vols. (Geneva: Droz, 1978–1983), 7:439–41 (chap. 46a).

Galehaut is a perfectly worthy challenger to the mighty Arthur. In nobility and ambition, he is a veritable Alexander.

As the story unfolds, Galehaut proves that he is indeed capable of overthrowing Arthur and claiming the kingdom for himself. He chooses not to do so, however, turning a sure victory into a voluntary surrender. On the very battlefield, he has fallen in love with Arthur's chief defender, the new knight Lancelot, and in order to gain his companionship he has agreed to the unthinkable: he will renounce his military and political ambitions. What follows is a tale of love and self-denial, in which Galehaut figures as a major—indeed, as the pivotal—character: he becomes the doomed third person in a triangle otherwise composed of Lancelot and Queen Guenevere. Just as he has surrendered to King Arthur, he will give way before Guenevere, yielding the young Lancelot to her in one of the most memorable scenes in the whole romance—the very scene that will arouse the Italian lovers some decades later.[6]

Of all the personages in the story, Galehaut is the only one whose inner life the text explores at length and in depth, the only character whose trajectory is that of a classic tragic hero. If the first of the three sections of the cyclic Prose *Lancelot* has long been known as the Book of Galehaut, it is because its bounds are defined more clearly by his action and evolution than by anything else.

Galehaut gives profundity and complexity to the work's attempt to grapple with the meaning and expression of love, with its obligations and its consequences. He is unquestionably the richest creation in the narrative's immense cast of characters. Long after his death, brought about by love-sickness, Galehaut is remembered by everyone as a paragon of greatness. Lancelot, at the end of his own life, will be buried next to Galehaut in the magnificent tomb that the younger man had built to consecrate and eternalize their companionship. There is no question of the importance, even the centrality, of the character, whose invention was probably the unknown author's greatest act of genius.[7]

---

[6] See the episode of the Kiss in Micha, *Lancelot* 8: chap. 52a.

[7] For an appreciation of Galehaut as a tragic figure, see Roger Sherman Loomis, *The Development of Arthurian Romance* (London: Hutchinson, 1963; repr. New York: Norton, 1970), 94–95. For Galehaut as "among the noblest figures of mediaeval romance," see Edmund G. Gardner, *The Arthurian Legend in Italian Literature* (London: Dent and New York: Dutton, 1930), 85. For further, and similar, characterizations of Galehaut, see Jean Frappier, "Le personnage de Galehaut dans le *Lancelot* en prose," *Romance Philology* 17 (1965): 535–54, repr. in idem, *Amour courtois et Table ronde* (Geneva: Droz, 1973), 181–208; idem, "La 'mort Galehaut'," in idem, *Histoire, mythes et symboles: Études de littérature française* (Geneva: Droz, 1976), 137–47; Reginald Hyatte, *The Arts of Friendship: The Idealization of Friendship in Medieval and Early Renaissance Literature* (Leiden and New York: Brill, 1994); Gretchen Mieszkowski, "The Prose *Lancelot*'s Galehot, Malory's Lavain, and the Queering of Late Medieval Literature," *Arthuriana* 5 (1995): 21–51; Carol R. Dover, Galehot and Lancelot: Matters of the Heart," in Kathryn Karczewska and Tom Conley, eds., *The World and Its Rival: Essays on Literary Imagination in Honor*

Along with Lancelot and much of the Arthurian court, Galehaut reappears in the Prose *Tristan*, composed in the second half of the thirteenth century. Its depiction of Galehaut makes little room for the affective relationship between him and Lancelot. The character appears at various points through the long text and is identified as Lancelot's friend, but the work offers no more than a bare reminder that their encounter marked the end of his formidable threat to Arthur. The genesis and development of the special friendship are not recounted; nor does the text evoke Galehaut's role in self-effacingly favoring the rapprochement of Lancelot and Guenevere. To be sure, his death, when it is eventually reported, in passing, is attributed to his love for Lancelot, but the announcement is taken as a cue to speak above all of Galehaut's chivalric brilliance.[8] The Prose *Tristan* is innovative in elaborating a certain background for Galehaut which was markedly undeveloped in the *Lancelot*. He and Tristan are brought into serious conflict in an action that involves a family history previously unknown: Galehaut is called upon to defend a certain barbarous ancestral custom which he himself deplores. Thus, in addition to the rather mysterious mother, la Bele Jaiande (the Fair Giantess), mentioned but never presented in the *Lancelot*, he is now endowed with a father and sister, a family setting that tends to demystify and conventionalize the figure. Moreover, the *Tristan* invents a public social role for him that highlights his sophisticated graciousness along with his magnanimity. Galehaut ends his conflict with Tristan with a generous pardon, performs other good deeds, and, toward the end of his short life, applies himself to eradicating the cruel custom of his ancestral home.

The Prose *Tristan* thus fleshes out the figure by setting him within a familiar social context while finding ways to preserve his exemplary nobility. At the same time, it all but eliminates his powerful challenge to Arthur's hegemony, diminishes his importance in relation to Lancelot, and effectively suppresses the extraordinary three-cornered love story of the Prose *Lancelot*.

Galehaut emerges soon afterwards in Italian literature, where he appears—Galeotto now—in a lyric composition, "Donna senza pietanza," by Lapuccio Belfradelli[9] and then, more tellingly, in a narrative text, as the protagonist of one of the brief tales in the late thirteenth-century *Conti di antichi cavalieri*. The tale blends the narrative strains developed in the two French prose romances. Thus Galeotto, in relation to Tristan, nobly undertakes to rid his paternal home of its evil custom. And, in relation to Lancelot, the same figure, valiant and magnanimous, though on a much reduced scale that permits no fine exploration of

---

of Per Nykrog (Amsterdam and Atlanta: Rodopi, 1999), 119-135; and Patricia Terry and Samuel N. Rosenberg, Lancelot and the Lord of the Distant Isles or, "The Book of Galehau"t Retold (Boston: David Godine, 2007).

[8] See Renée L. Curtis, ed., *Roman de Tristan en prose*, 2 vols. (Munich: Hueber / Leiden: Brill, 1963–1975; repr. Cambridge: Brewer, 1985), 1:206 (par. 414).

[9] Gardner, *The Arthurian Legend*, 33.

his career or affective life, is shown at the moment of his transformative encounter with the remarkable young knight: "Galeocto, vegendoli d'armi sì gran facti et valorosi fare, parlò a Lancelocto e, parlando, de lui innamoròe per la cortesia sua e bontà e gran cavallaria."[10] Of narrative development there is just enough to warrant the judgment of the story's final sentence: "Insomma esso ebbe el più alto e gentile e de bono aiere core ch'alcuno principe o re ch'al mundo fosse."[11]

It is this view of Galehaut—a model of chivalric greatness, and one divorced from amatory concerns—that became the norm in the Arthurian literature of Italy. The outstanding work, the anonymous *Tavola ritonda* of the second quarter of the fourteenth century, is at heart a version of the Prose *Tristan* and perpetuates the characterization found in that source. Thus Galeotto is identified as one of the last holdouts against a bellicose, imperial Artù; he is "l'alto prencipe [. . .] lo quale, per sua prodezza, signoreggiava diciotto reami."[12] The battle episode is briefly recounted in which he is impressed by Lancilotto's courage, wins him over to his side, and then agrees to yield to Artù.[13] But the much more weighty matter in this Italian tale is Galehaut's life before the advent of Lancelot, especially his relations with Tristan. Their conflict, detailed through chapters 38 and 39, allows the text to stress more than anything else Galeotto's generosity of spirit, for the episode ends with his magnanimous pardon of Tristano.[14] This is essentially all we hear of Galehaut in the *Tavola ritonda*.[15]

Of the other portrayals of Galehaut derived from Tristan material, Italian has several. What is never missing from them is the character's high stature as a knight and as a moral being. This is true, for example, of the predecessor of the *Tavola ritonda*, the *Tristano Riccardiano*, which, dating from the late thirteenth century, is the earliest Arthurian romance composed in Italian. Typically, the *Riccardiano* reports Galehaut's death with no disclosure of cause or description of circumstance; above all, the text makes no mention whatever of Lancelot in connection with it:

---

[10] Alberto Del Monte, ed., *Conti di antichi cavalieri* (Milan: Cisalpino-Goliardica, 1972), 151.

[11] Del Monte, *Conti*, 154.

[12] Marie-José Heijkant, ed., *La Tavola ritonda* (Milan: Luni, 1999), 78 (chap. 5).

[13] Heijkant, *La Tavola*, 91–95 (chap. 9).

[14] Heijkant, *La Tavola*, 183–190.

[15] At the beginning of chapter 40, Galeotto sends a letter to Artù in which he announces the end of the wicked ancestral custom that had led to his battle with Tristano: "ò disfatto lo castello dello Proro e tolta via ogni malvagia usanza" (190).

> E dappoi si ritorna nel suo reame con sua giente, e ppoco tenpo dimora dappoi ch'egli fue tornato in sua terra, ed egli sì si morio. Laonde ne fue grande damaggio nel suo reame di lui.[16]

The early fourteenth-century *Tristano Panciatichiano* is similar in its narrative treatment of Galehaut, maintaining the traditional focus on the figure as a knight of exemplary stature. Thus, when Tristan is informed that he is obliged to do battle with him, the text reports, in words closely echoing those of the *Riccardiano*:

> Et quando Tristano uditte queste parole, fu molto allegro perciò che "questi è lo più alto *prince* del mondo e lo più valente." E dice infra sé medesimo, "Ora sono io lo più aventuroso cavalieri del mondo, dapoiché io sono al campo con così alto sire." Molto si conforta Tristano di questa aventura.[17]

It is true that the *Panciatichiano* is no more detailed in its presentation of Galehaut's death than the *Tristano Riccardiano*.[18] However, his prestige is reflected a long while later in the valor of a descendant, the king of Sorelois, whom Tristan and his entourage encounter one day on the road:

> elli videro per la traversa della foresta venire une compagnia di cavalieri [...] Et intra loro era lo re di Sorlois, che Galiadis era appellato e è buono cavalieri e lo più valente che sia del lignaggio di Galeotto e è del suo corpo de' grandi cavalieri del mondo e molto gioioso. Et quelli di Sorlois li avieno data quella signoria novellamente, però ch'elli era del lignaggio di Galeotto.[19]

Then, at the end of the long romance, when it is time to bury Tristano and Ysotta, the long-dead high prince makes one final, oblique, appearance, the text here shedding light on a deeply significant tie that it had never before disclosed:

---

[16] E. G. Parodi, *Tristano Riccardiano*, rev. Marie-José Heijkant (Parma: Pratiche Editrice, 1991), 155 (par. 65).

[17] Gloria Allaire, ed. and trans., *Il Tristano panciatichiano* (Cambridge: Brewer, 2002), 200 (par. 124); compare Parodi and Heijkant, *Tristano*, 150 (chap. 63).

[18] Allaire, *Il Tristano*, 206 (par. 126).

[19] Allaire, *Il Tristano*, 564 (par. 350). As noted by various commentators, e.g., Gardner, *The Arthurian Legend*, 340, some texts confuse the name of Lancelot's son, Galahad, with that of Galehaut, translating both French names by the single Italian form Galeotto (whereas Galahad more commonly appears in Italian as Galasso or Galeazzo). The *Tristano Panciatichiano* is such a text. Context, however, normally makes correct identification clear. Nevertheless, there are two passages in Allaire where the English translation is in error, mistakenly substituting Galahad for Galehaut: first, the paragraph just cited, in which the king of Sorelois belongs without a doubt to the lineage of Galehaut and, second, the passage, cited next, which makes it absolutely certain that the Galeotto in question is Galehaut.

lo re Marco vi fece poi fare una sipoltura sì riccha [e sì m]eravigliosa che dinançi a quella nonn era nulla sì riccha [. . .] se non quella solamente di Galeotto, figliuolo dela gigantessa, che nacque in Lontane Ysoles. [. . .] Quella tomba era tutta piena d'oro e di pietre pretiose, [. . .] Et sappiate che quello Galeot fue princie e siri di .xxxviiij. reami e elli amava tanto messer Lancialotto di Lac come nullo potrebbe più ama[re] altrui e già non potrei contare lo bene ch'elli li voleva e ala fine moritte Galeot per Lancialotto.[20]

All of this brings us back to Dante, who clearly derived his Galeotto not from the tradition that had evolved in Italian retellings of the Tristan legend, but, in all likelihood, directly from the Prose *Lancelot*. That is, to be sure, the source identified in Canto V of the *Inferno*; the identification is, moreover, confirmed later in the *Commedia* by two other allusions to the same French work: *Inf.* 32: 61–62 and *Par.* 16: 13–15.[21] Dante's innovation must have impressed Boccaccio, who returned to Galehaut several times in his own writings. The early *Amorosa visione* (1342), for example, pictures a procession of Arthurian figures in which only the most highly placed characters precede him. King Arthur is there, with Perceval, Galahad, Lancelot, and Guenevere, who are followed immediately by Galehaut: "seguiva Galeotto, il cui valore / più ch'altro de' compagni si figura."[22]

Most strikingly, however, apparently inspired by Dante's metaphor equating Galehaut with a book, Boccaccio gave the name as a subtitle to his own *Decameron*: "Comincia il libro chiamato Decameron, cognominato Prencipe Galeotto."[23] That subtitle has, predictably, prompted no little discussion, but it is hard to imagine that Boccaccio would have chosen such a name had he intended disapproval or condemnation of the character.[24]

---

[20] Allaire, *Il Tristano*, 728 and 730 (par. 539). Cf. the burial of Tristano and Isotta in the *Tavola ritonda*, Parodi and Heijkant 512 (chap. 130), which makes no mention of Galeotto. The *Tristano Riccardiano* is incomplete, coming to a stop before the death and burial of the lovers.

[21] For these allusions, along with others in Dante, see Antonio Viscardi, "Arthurian Influences on Italian Literature from 1200 to 1500," in *Arthurian Literature in the Middle Ages: A Collaborative History*, ed. Roger Sherman Loomis (Oxford: Oxford University Press, 1959), 419–29, at 422–24.

[22] Boccaccio, *Tutte le opere*, 3: canto 11: 29–30. See, too, par. 272 of the *Corbaccio*, in Boccaccio, *Tutte le opere*, 5.2: 490–491.

[23] Boccaccio, *Tutte le opere*, 4:1.

[24] Consider, for example, Gardner, *The Arthurian Legend*, whose examination of the issue leads him to acknowledge "good reasons for holding that the sub-title is, in all probability, due to Boccaccio himself, and that the character of Galehaut, not as a 'turpe mezzano,' but as the 'cavalleresco messo d'amore,' the helpful friend of Lancelot in need, is thoroughly in accordance with the purpose that the writer himself professes in the *Decameron*" (237–39). See too, *inter alios*, Daniela Delcorno Branca, "Dante and the *Roman de Lancelot*," in *Text and Intertext in Medieval Arthurian Literature*, ed. Norris J. Lacy (New York: Garland, 1996), 133–45 (revised and translated into Italian as "L'alto

More telling of his view of Galehaut, however, is his elucidation of Dante's allusion in the commentary on the *Inferno* that Boccaccio wrote toward the end of his life, the *Esposizioni sopra la Comedia*. With no apparent disapprobation, he speaks there of a man exceptionally sensitive to love and motivated by the exceptional love he himself felt for Lancelot:

> Scrivesi ne' predetti romanzi che un prencipe Galeotto, il quale dicono che fu di spezie di gigante, sì era grande e grosso, sentì primo che alcuno altro l'occulto amor di Lancialotto e della reina Ginevra; il quale non essendo più avanti proceduto che per soli riguardi, ad istanzia di Lancialotto, il quale egli amava maravigliosamente, tratta un dì in una sala a ragionamento seco la reina Ginevra, e a quello chiamato Lancialotto, ad aprire questo amore con alcuno affetto fu il mezzano: e, quasi occupando con la persona il poter questi due esser veduti da alcuno altro della sala che da lui, fece che essi si basciarono insieme.[25]

The Dantean Galeotto seen by Boccaccio is a provider of comfort to others as they contend with the travails of amorous desire. The personage is far simpler than the original Galehaut and very different from the exemplary prince of other works, but it is strikingly benevolent.

After his long eclipse as a figure of nobility and moral worth—a phenomenon not explored in this essay (see note 1 above)—a prelapsarian Galeotto reappears in Italian literature in the early twentieth century. In a striking reconceptualization of the overlapping triangles of Lancelot-Guenevere-Arthur and Lancelot-Galehaut-Guenevere, Domenico Tumiati's verse play of 1925, *La Regina Ginevra*, brings him back as a singularly towering character in a collective tragedy that he alone has the strength, devotion, and intelligence to survive. Early in the play, Galeotto reassures a despairing Ginevra by pointing to the source and solidity of his determination to help:

> Fate cuore, chè tutta la mia vita
> è consacrata al vostro amore, poi
> che in voi soltanto vive Lancillotto,
> ed egli ed io siamo una vita sola.
> Potenza, gloria, tutto ho calpestato

---

principe Galeotto," in eadem, *Tristano e Lancillotto in Italia: Studi di letteratura arturiana* [Ravenna: Longo, 1998], 225–238); Robert Hollander, *Boccaccio's Two Venuses* (New York: Columbia University Press, 1977), 102–6, 225–27; and idem, *Boccaccio's Dante and the Shaping Force of Satire* (Ann Arbor: University of Michigan Press), 24, n.8.

[25] Boccaccio, *Tutte le opere*, 6:324. Cf. Vittorio Branca's reference to the line about Galeotto in the *Amorosa visione* (see n. 22 above): "Galeotto, la cui figura [. . .] è per il B[occaccio], come per Dante, non quella d'un turpe mezzano, ma di un cavalleresco messo d'amore" (*Tutte le opere*, 3:617), which echoes the statement in Gardner quoted in the preceding note.

dal giorno che mi balenò il suo cuore, *etc.*
. . . .
. . . . Tanto feci,
e pensate ch'io possa abbandonarvi?[26]

Of all the major characters in the play, Galeotto is the only one whose honesty and loyalty never flag. Lancillotto, torn between Christian duty and love for the queen, crumbles; the queen, an avowed heathen, recognizes no authority but that of passion; Arturo, weak and scheming, succumbs to an unkingly meanness. Galeotto never falters in the constancy of his self-sacrificing love.

This image of Galehaut would have been easily recognized by Italian readers many years earlier, in the Middle Ages, before the fall.

---

[26] Domenico Tumiati, *La regina Ginevra: tragedia* (Milano: Società Editrice Unitas, 1925), 45–46 (Act I, sc. 8).

Literary Afterlives in *Huon d'Auvergne*: "The Art of [Dantean] Citation"

Leslie Zarker Morgan

"La venue atendon do·u ch*eval*er alois
Que in ceste regne doit fare miracle ausis;
Ancor n'estoit il neç e a pieçe ni ert nasquis [. . .]"¹
(*Huon d'Auvergne* [Berlin], lines 7987–7989)

Dante's *Commedia* rapidly became authoritative upon its divulgation: its every aspect was imitated. Known from 1315, the *Inferno* was first used in *Huon d'Auvergne*, a chanson de geste dated to 1341 in the earliest manuscript.² Huon

---

¹ "We await the chosen knight / Who will do many miracles in this reign; / He is not yet born and will not be for a while. . ."

² All of the references to and quotes of line numbers here are to Berlin Kupferstichkabinett 78 D 8 (olim Ms. Hamilton 337), since it is the most carefully done of the three manuscripts containing the *Huon d'Auvergne* text. The Turin manuscript (Biblioteca nazionale N.III.19) follows the Berlin manuscript fairly closely, but was damaged in the fire of 1904. The Padua manuscript (Biblioteca del seminario vescovile 32) is much shorter than the Berlin and Turin manuscripts and is not illuminated. The Barbieri fragment in Bologna (Biblioteca dell'Archiginnasio B. 3429; ed. V. de Bartholomaeis, "La Discesa di Ugo d'Alvernia all'inferno secondo il frammento di Giovanni Maria Barbieri," *Memorie, Classe di Scienze morali, Sezione di scienze storico-filologiche e sezioni di scienze giuridiche, Reale accademia delle scienze dell'Istituto di Bologna*, Scr. 2, 10, Ser. 3, 3 [1929]: 3–54) contains only an initial short portion of the hell visit. Andrea da Barberino's *Ugone d'Alvernia* (ed. F. Zambrini [Bologna: Romagnoli, 1882; repr. Bologna: Commissione per i testi di lingua, 1968]) contains the entire story. For details of episodes, manuscript condition, and bibliography for the Padua manuscript see L. Zarker Morgan, "Nida and Carlo Martello: The Padua Manuscript of *Huon d'Auvergne* (Ms. 32 of the Biblioteca del Seminario Vescovile, 45ᴿ-49ᵛ)," *Olifant* 23 (2004): 65–114; for the Turin manuscript, see eadem, "Ynide and Charles Martel: Turin, Biblioteca Nazionale N III 19, Folios 72R-89R (I)," *Medioevo Romanzo* 29 (2005): 433–64. The transcriptions are my own, though reference is give to others' work where it exists. The manuscripts are unedited, though some lines are published, so numbering systems are not consistent. For the Berlin manuscript line numbers,

d'Auvergne's visit to hell to obtain tribute for King Charles Martel is well known.[3] Less well known are Huon's earlier travels, a form of purgatory through traditional romance trials (e.g., the land of the Utopian priest-king Prester John and battles with marvelous beasts), Old Testament lands (a garden around Noah's Ark where Adam, Noah, and other holy men gather for the octave of Easter), the Promised Land near where Huon encounters Enoch and Elijah,[4] and branches of afterlife geography deriving from various traditions.

Background and Methods

The descent into hell has a long and illustrious history. Greek and Latin literature contain examples, and from the second century AD on, visions more or less apocalyptic of the Christian afterlife appear.[5] These journeys provide much information about the times in which they were written, together with contemporary fears and hopes. However they were also widely circulated, contributing to subsequent literature. How then to distinguish sources? Direct quotes can point toward specific sources, permitting the modern reader thus to distinguish further structures and ideas that may have come from the quoted source.

To examine the anonymous redactor's use of Dante in *Huon d'Auvergne*, techniques developed by Christopher Kleinhenz to examine biblical citation in Dante model appropriate methods and results. In a series of five articles dating from 1986 to 1997,[6] Kleinhenz defines "poetics of citation" as "Dante's technique of

---

I number sequentially, not adding any line numbers for blank folios. For the reference of this being the first literary work to use the *Commedia*, see K. Busby, *Codex and Context: Reading Old French Verse Narrative in Manuscript* (Amsterdam: Rodopi, 2002), 2: 770. For a recent résumé of the dates of the *Commedia*, and the controversy surrounding them, see R. Hollander, *Dante* (New Haven: Yale University Press, 2001), 91–92.

[3] L. A. Meregazzi, "*L'Ugo d'Alvernia*: Poema Franco-Italiano," *Studi romanzi* 27 (1937): 5–87; E. Stengel, *Huons aus Auvergne Höllenfahrt nach der Berliner und Paduaner Hs.* (Greifswald: F. W. Kunike, 1908).

[4] E. Stengel, *Huons aus Auvergne Suche nach dem Hölleneingang nach der Berliner Hs.* (Greifswald: Emil Hartmann, 1912).

[5] Among recent publications are E. Gardiner, ed., *Visions of Heaven and Hell Before Dante* (New York: Italica, 1989), whose work contains English translations of some of the best-known visions, and J. Le Goff, *The Birth of Purgatory*, trans. A. Goldhammer (Chicago: University of Chicago Press, 1984), who discusses many of these in relation to his specific interest, the development of Purgatory. A. E. Bernstein (*The Formation of Hell: Death and Retribution in the Ancient and Early Christian Worlds* [Ithaca: Cornell University Press, 1993]), elaborates upon classical, Judaic, and early Christian afterworlds.

[6] The articles are, in chronological order, "Dante and the Bible: Intertextual Approaches to the *Divine Comedy*," *Italica* 63 (1986): 225–36; "Biblical Citation in Dante's *Divine Comedy*," *Annali d'Italianistica* 8 (1990): 346–59; "The Poetics of Citation: Dante's

evoking a particular word, verse, or passage in the Bible through the use of an exact or modified version of the Latin text or an Italian translation or paraphrase of the Vulgate within his own text," suggesting the six categories of exact, modified or incomplete citations in Latin or in vernacular, plus "imitative prophetic voice" for a total of seven.[7] As he points out, visual traditions are also thus evoked.[8] Kleinhenz demonstrates how the context of these quotes in the original assists in interpreting textual cruces. Subsequent writers cite Dante as "'new scripture',"[9] incorporating citations and techniques derived from the *Commedia*, and their use of it not only documents the reception of Dante's work but also illuminates those works in which it appears. Among the first works citing the *Commedia* is *Huon d'Auvergne*, an unedited Franco-Italian chanson de geste. There are three almost complete Franco-Italian manuscripts (two dated to 1341 and 1441), one fragment, and a prose version by Andrea da Barberino (these two last dated to the late fourteenth or early fifteenth century). *Huon d'Auvergne* furthermore partakes of earlier visionary literature as well as of the *Commedia* during Huon's travels, providing thus an intermingling of literary traditions. In *Huon d'Auvergne*, *Commedia* citation can be divided into several types by narrative level: first, the concept itself of salvational voyage; then the choice of episodes included; episodic structures calqued upon the *Commedia*; and finally, specific quotes. *Huon d'Auvergne* cites Dante's innovative, original text within a traditional format that prioritizes *matière de France* subjects and goals, in keeping with its origins. In it,

---

Divine Comedy and the Bible," in *Italiana 1988*, ed. Albert N. Mancini et al. (River Forest, IL: Rosary College, 1990), 1–21; "Dante and the Art of Citation," in *Dante Now: Current Trends in Dante Studies*, ed. Theodore J. Cachey, Jr. (Notre Dame: University of Notre Dame Press, 1995), 43–61 (as the reader will have noted, my title here calques this Kleinhenz title); "Dante and the Bible: Biblical Citation in the *Divine Comedy*," in *Dante: Contemporary Perspectives*, ed. A. Iannucci (Toronto: University of Toronto Press, 1997), 74–93. Others have treated issues of citation in the *Commedia*; for example, L. M. LaFavia, " '. . . Chè quivi per canti . . .' (*Purg.* XII, 113): Dante's Programmatic Use of Psalms and Hymns in the *Purgatorio*," *Studies in Iconography* 10 (1984–1986): 53–65, also speaks of psalms and hymns, A. Jacomuzzi, "La citazione come procedimento letterario. Appunti e considerazioni," in *L'arte dell'interpretare. Studi critici offerti a Giovanni Getto* (Cuneo: Arciere, 1984), 3–15, of the use of citations. For a summary up to the time of the article, see Kleinhenz, "Dante and the Bible," 235 n. 2. Citations here of Dante's *Commedia* are based upon Petrocchi's authoritative edition as it appears in R. M. Durling and R. L. Martinez's side-by-side translations *The Divine Comedy of Dante Alighieri: Inferno* (Oxford: Oxford University Press, 1996) and *The Divine Comedy of Dante Alighieri: Purgatorio* (Oxford: Oxford University Press, 2003). For *Paradiso*, A. Mandelbaum's side-by-side translation, *The Divine Comedy of Dante Alighieri: Paradiso* (New York: Bantam-Doubleday, 1984), similarly uses Petrocchi as its basis.

[7] Kleinhenz, "Biblical Citation," 347.
[8] Kleinhenz, "Dante and the Art of Citation," 55.
[9] Kleinhenz, "Biblical Citation," 348.

Huon links the *geste* of Guillaume d'Orange to the *Commedia*, evoking divine choice of government, demonstrated by Huon's anointment in holy places. We will briefly examine a few of the choices made in "citing" Dante and how they reverberate within the chanson de geste concerns of *Huon*.[10]

Episodic structure: the three-stage salvational voyage

At the highest level, in its episodic structure, *Huon d'Auvergne* combines chanson de geste national themes with individual adventure, as do many late chansons.[11] Where Dante's *Commedia* narrates a fictional personal voyage punctuated with (and underlined by) political commentary upon encountering personalities or in discussion with his guides, *Huon d'Auvergne* is a politically imposed journey; it is a feudal injustice forced upon an individual.[12] King Charles Martel orders Huon to hell for tribute from the devil so that he might seize Huon's wife. The motif

---

[10] See L. Zarker Morgan, "*Dirige gressus meos*: The Dialectic of Obedience in *Huon d'Auvergne*," *Neophilologus* 88 (2004): 19–32, for specific examples and demonstration of the use of psalms.

[11] See, for example, G. Doutrepont, *Les Mises en prose des épopées et des romans chevaleresques du XIVe au XVIe siècles* (Brussels: Palais des académies, 1939; repr. Geneva: Slatkine Reprints, 1969), esp. Chap. 7, "Genres et procédés de remaniement," 467–648, who speaks of additions, suppressions, abbreviations, and various alterations in referring to prose versions; W. W. Kibler, "La 'Chanson d'aventures'," in *Essor et fortune de la chanson de geste dans l'Europe et l'Orient latin*, Actes du IXe Congrès international de la Société Rencesvals (Padoue-Venise, 29 août-4 septembre 1982), ed. A. Limentani et al. (Modena: Mucchi, 1984), 509–15, who developed a term to describe the late chanson de geste; R. F. Cook, "'Méchants chansons' et épopée française: Pour une philologie profonde," *Esprit Créateur* 23 (1983): 64-74, who speaks of how the last chansons belie generic expectations; F. Suard, "L'Epopée française tardive (XIVe–XVe siècles)," in *Etudes de philologie romane et d'histoire littéraire offerts à Jules Horrent à l'occasion de son soixantième anniversaire*, ed. J. M. D'Heur et al. (Tournai: Gedit, 1980), 449–60, who lists five major types of development in late epic, and C. Roussel, "Le Mélange des genres dans les chansons de geste tardives," in *Les Chansons de geste*, Actes du XVIe Congrès International de la Société Rencesvals, Pour l'Étude des Épopées Romanes, Granada, 21–25 juillet 2003, ed. C. Alvar and J. Paredes (Granada: Universidad de Granada, 2005), 65–85, who demonstrates the variety of late chansons de geste.

[12] I do not wish to denigrate here the importance of political issues to Dante's work as a whole, merely to distinguish between functions in the literary pieces. See, for example, C. Kleinhenz, "Dante as Reader and Critic of Courtly Literature," in *Courtly Literature: Culture and Context*, Selected Papers from the 5th Triennial Congress of the International Courtly Literature Society, Dalfsen, The Netherlands, 9–16 August 1986, ed. K. Busby and E. Kooper (Amsterdam: Benjamins, 1990), 379–93, for a study of Dante's use of courtly literature and the links between language (especially poetry) and politics.

of "impossible message," typical of the chanson de geste, forms the entire plot instead of a single episode.[13]

After Huon departs from his castle in Auvergne, his travels can be divided into three parts, each of which in turn contains multiple events.[14] The first part of Huon's voyage takes him through the known world: Hungary, Rome (where he receives a flashlight-like cross from the pope), Greece, Jerusalem, and the Holy Land. During this segment of the voyage, fellow warriors and then two shipwrecked women accompany him. The second part of Huon's voyage begins with his visit to Prester John.[15] Prester John symbolically introduces Huon's literary adventures, during which Huon, compared to Galahad (lines 6226–6229), alone with his horse, encounters a series of literary horrors: female devils in a eerily beautiful city; awful birds (harpy-like creatures and mermen called *ocephali*);[16] a branch of hell; Noah's Ark; birds that are spirits who did neither good nor evil on their day off; the Promised Land with Elijah and Enoch; and finally, the last stretch during which his horse dies, leaving Huon entirely alone again. Death appropriately marks the division between second and third legs of his trip, since Huon there enters hell. In hell, he is guided by a trio: a devil, Aeneas, and Guillaume d'Orange. Thus Huon, like Dante's protagonist, passes through three progressively less earthbound regions, guided ultimately by three companions, before returning home to dispense justice on his temporal ruler.

---

[13] For motifs surrounding the messenger and embassy, see J.-P. Martin, *Les Motifs dans la chanson de geste: Définition et utilisation* (Lille: Université de Lille III, Centre d'Études Médiévales et Dialectales, 1992), 112, 148–50, etc.; J. Merceron, *Le message et sa fiction: La communication par messager dans la littérature française des XIIe et XIIIe siècles* (Berkeley: University of California Press, 1998); J.-C. Vallecalle, *Messages et ambassades dans l'épopée française médiévale: L'illusion de dialogue* (Paris: Champion, 2006). Perhaps the most frequently cited voyage to the afterworld in a chanson de geste cited by other critics is that of *Huon de Bordeaux* (see, for example, D. R. R. Owen, "The Principal Source of *Huon de Bordeaux*," *French Studies* 7 [1953]: 129–39)

[14] On Auvergne as a symbolic name as well as a place name, see G. Allaire, "Considerations on *Huon d'Auvergne / Ugo d'Alvernia*," *Viator* 32 (2001): 185–203, at 187 n.9.

[15] I divide the poem *Huon* into five episodes as it appears in the three different versions and the prose *Ugone d'Alvernia*; that is, not all manuscripts contain all five episodes. Each episode is then divided into segments. The Huon travel episode (the third) is itself divided by the narrator's recounting the trials of Ynide (Huon's wife) at home. The five episodes are: Sofia, Charles Martel's daughter, falling in love with Huon; Charles Martel's court where Charles Martel falls in love with Ynide; Huon's travels; Ynide's defense at Auvergne; and the siege of Rome. The Berlin manuscript does not contain episode 1.

[16] The *ocefali* derive from the *Roman d'Alexandre* (Meregazzi, "*L'Ugo d'Alvernia*," 20). The Harpy-like creatures evoke the *Aeneid* (3.211–218) but also Dante's circle of suicides (*Inf.* 13).

Encounters during the second third of Huon's voyage

Huon's adventures within the three portions of Huon's voyage themselves also parallel Dante's travels. But the order and emphasis differ, for in the second portion of *Huon*, Dante's worst sinners come first, followed by Noah's Ark; hell spirits on holiday; the Promised Land; and, before arriving at the third portion, a Dante-like hell. Hell alternates with paradise, instead of creating a narrative development through the worst bad to the greatest good, incorporating traditional visionary literature events such as those found in *St. Brendan's Voyage* and other visionary texts. Heavenly aid assists Huon during the first leg of his journey in battles against earthly opponents (from pirates to pagans). The second leg of his voyage, after seeing Prester John, initiates otherworldly encounters, each of which echoes portions of Dante's *Commedia* though based on earlier literary traditions. In his first encounter, upon meeting a group of singing females (who claim to be descendants of French people who came to see Alexander the Great—later revealed to be devils—) Huon laments his seven years of wandering.[17] While the encounter itself reflects an incident in the *Queste del sant Graal*, one cannot help thinking of Francesca in the overripe amorous environment evoked by the redactor when the queen says to him, "La grant beuteç qe ge ay en vos veue / Me torne en joie de ce q'avoy perdue, / De mon signor dont ge suy dechaue" (lines 6809–6811).[18] Yet other traditions are also involved, for the comment, together with the seven years of wandering, also evoke Aeneas and Dido: Aeneas mentions his seven years at the end of book 1 (*Aeneid* 1.755–756) just before Dido falls in love with him, and she soon thereafter says "agnosco veteris vestigia flammae" (4.24)—a theme picked up by Dante himself (*Purg.* 30: 48). Those evocations fit with the references to Alexander's leading people to the site, and the comparison of their queen with Medea (line 6790). The *Huon*'s negative assessment of these earlier literary works—both *matière de France* and *matière de Rome*—is typical of the chanson de geste. *Huon* similarly satirizes the use of courtly language and love triangle through Charles Martel's initial approach to Ynide and Charles' embassy to her.[19] Among other Franco-Italian texts, one recalls the *Entrée d'Espagne*'s denigrating reference to "flabes d'Artu," for here, Huon beats himself with a rock to reduce temptation, and calls upon God for

---

[17] For more about *Alexandre* and its links with *Huon*, see Meregazzi, "*L'Ugo d'Alvernia*," 19–22.

[18] "The great beauty that I have seen in you / Returns me to joy from that which I had lost, / From my lord, of whom I have been deprived." Dido, below, says, "I recognize the marks of an old fire": trans. R. Humphries: *The Aeneid of Virgil* (New York: Scribners, 1951), 88.

[19] See L. Zarker Morgan, "Passion of Ynide: Ynide's Defense in *Huon d'Auvergne* (Berlin, Kupferstichkabinett, Hamilton 337)," *Medioevo Romanzo* 27 (2003): 67–85, 425–62.

help.[20] The palace goes up in flames, and three angels descend to sing hymns as a lullaby (lines 6950–6953). Henceforth, fire becomes a leitmotif in Huon's otherworldly adventures to come, as fire was the image of Dido's torture and death. It furthermore appropriately prepares Huon for the afterlife: Le Goff notes that fire is typical of purgatorial passages, a part of "liminal rites."[21]

After passing through and around odd creatures, Huon comes to a fiery mountain that he believes to be hell (" [. . .] hore son venu a·l leu que desirons / Que cist ert l'Enfer [. . .]," lines 7402–7403). Mountains too are a staple of visionary literature,[22] yet here the mountain recalls more immediately Dante's initial obstacle (*Inf.* 1:13) and the mountain of Purgatory. Huon cannot understand how to approach the souls, and a young boy appears when he prays. The boy, a heavenly messenger in disguise, explains that this is a branch of hell, not the deepest, and that there are a number of these. Huon should believe in God and continue. It is later referred to as "le mont ardant" (line 8247). This fiery mountain parallels the volcanoes seen in pre-hell travels in *St. Brendan's Voyage*.[23] As one of a series of obstacles to be passed (like the hill at the beginning of the *Commedia*) it also evokes various tourist travels found in late chansons de geste, if not the top of Purgatory with its wall of fire.

Huon subsequently arrives at yet another hellish site, after passing over a fiery sea carried by griffons: a swamp of horrors. He progresses holding his cross received from the pope glowing in front of him, so that spirits avoid him. He continues through the fire ("lugo de·l feu," line 7727) until he comes to a mountain with spirits coming out, blocking his way and ignoring him. He conjures them in the name of the Trinity, until finally, one answers his queries:

"Laiseç aler nos voie, si fareç cum cortoy,
Que aseç some en tormant. Nos le dople, bien voy
Tiel çonse [a cross] as en main, garder non la poy,
Que en dople nos tormant; por ce mainir a toy." (lines 7757–7760)[24]

The passage with its doubled torment and references to justice can be compared to *Inferno* 14, where, in describing Capaneus, the fire causes the sand to "doppiar lo dolore" (14: 39). Huon asks the spirit who is present, and is told that there are Cain, Ham, Pharaoh, Esau, Herod, Judas, Ganelon, and others. The protagonists

---

[20] *L'Entrée d'Espagne*, ed. A. Thomas (Paris: Firmin Didot, 1913), l. 367.
[21] Le Goff, *Birth of Purgatory*, 8, citing Van Gennep.
[22] Le Goff, *Birth of Purgatory*, 27.
[23] Gardiner, *Visions*; A. Gurevich, *Medieval Popular Culture: Problems of Belief and Perception*, trans. J. M. Bak and P. A. Hollingsworth (Cambridge: Cambridge University Press, 1988).
[24] "Let us go our way, and you will do courteously ; / For we are tormented enough. You double it for us, I see well, / You have such a thing in your hand, I cannot look at it, / For it doubles our torment; for this reason, remain by yourself." Cf. Stengel, *Suche*, 22.

here are primarily biblical figures; only Ganelon stands out as being a vernacular villain. Huon comments that his spokesperson has "Cil qu'aveç meriç, justisse vos sermon" (line 7824 [What you deserve, justice speaks to you]). One thinks of Dante's "giustizia orribil arte" (*Inf.* 14: 6). However, the appearance of Judas and Ganelon here anticipates Dante's positioning of them (*Inf.* 32 and 34). Dante's fourteenth canto, evoked for justice and for the burning sands, echoes through this section of *Huon*; for it is also in *Inferno* 14 where the four rivers of the afterworld are evoked, and these too play an important role in Huon's voyage.

Noah's Ark, Huon's cousin, and relation to chanson de geste

On the other side of the mountain, the griffons again help Huon cross a sea, and the next afterlife event, Noah's Ark Mountain, begins. Huon explores near a spring, and comes to a cave where he discovers three men in Augustinian garb. They explain the site: this mountain is called "Noah's Ark."[25] All the animals in the world were here when God decided on the flood. All had offspring, but none can reproduce further, so the animals stay here on the mountain, sanctified. Every year on Good Friday, Adam, Noah, and other holy men come to visit the Ark. They stay for eight days, blessing the animals and anyone else present. Sinners cannot stay. The oldest hermit continues telling his own history, and he and Huon find that they are cousins (lines 7938–7947; 7993–8084). Huon recounts his adventures, and the cousin explains the earlier fiery mountain. His description of it and the noise it makes, comparing the racket to all the carpenters in the world at work, recalls *Inferno* 16, though the elements of comparison are different:

> Un raim e*st* de l'enfer, ou li dampné vo*nt*.
> Le g*ra*nt brait *et* le criç jusq*ue* ci s'intendro*nt* :
> Se il le fusent tot li carpentie*r* de·l mont,
> E carpentasent qua*nt* plus fort lavoro*nt*
> Tiel noixe no*n* fesent cum cil tot jo*r* en font. (lines 8025–8028)[26]

Huon d'Auvergne rarely makes use of the epic metaphor, unlike Dante, so when one does appear it forces the reader to search memory and finally concordances for like forms, in this case, only to find none. In *Inferno* 16, the water echoes as

---

[25] See Stengel, *Suche*, lines 8055–8090 (26–27); my lines 7900–7935.

[26] "It is a branch of hell, where the damned go. / The great cries and shrieks that can be heard all the way over here: / If all of the carpenters in the world were there, / And they hammered as when they worked the hardest / They would not make such a noise as these make the whole day long." Cf. Stengel, *Suche*, 30 (lines 8181–8185). The passage is on fols. 55Vb-56Ra.

it falls below, making it difficult for Dante to hear, in a comparison with the river of Acquacheta before Forlì, just before Dante's belt summons Geryon. Both texts use a lengthy comparison, but the effect of comparison with human noise (carpenters) contrasts with Dante's natural roar (water), and continues *Huon d'Auvergne*'s condemnation of things human. The noise again recalls the noise of volcanoes, believed to be diabolic.[27] The evocation of sound parallels the use of visual imagery in Dante as mentioned by Kleinhenz.

When the group arrives at Noah's Ark, the birds are singing as in Dante's Earthly Paradise:

Enç le ray do·u soleil quant il estoit leveç
Desus ceste montagne tot quant le vereç
Cum cant de melodie ni pas non levereç [. . .] (lines 8145–8147)[28]

These recall " [. . .] l'ore prime cantando ricevieno intra le foglie / che tenevan bordone a le sue rime" (*Purg.* 28: 16–18). These are not the same words, rather the same thought. Huon reads a message from the saints, "Tant *que* en memoire l'oit le quuen bien anoteç" (line 8219 [Until the count had it well noted in memory]; cf. "Bene ascolta chi la nota," *Inf.* 15: 99, referring to 10: 127–129), and he pays attention to his tour "Pur qu'il aige membrance quant il sera sortieç" (line 8222 [So that he would remember it when he left]), recalling the role of memory for Dante, especially in his relationship to Beatrice in Earthly Paradise.[29]

The water at the foot of the mountain is the Tigris, which Huon follows upon departing as Dante and Virgil, exiting hell, follow the "ruscelletto" (*Inf.* 34: 130). After resting under a tree, Huon awakes to find the tree full of birds. These sing and speak, quoting Psalm 132. A bird explains to him in Auvergnese that they are from hell: "[. . .] en forme d'oiselons / Nos que ci somes; ne bien ni mal feisons / Mes pur il ere la nostre entencions / De tenire sempre cum cil qi vencerons" (lines 8359–8361).[30] Their punishment is to fish all week, getting nothing. But they get Sunday off, when they must sing praises to God: "Ce estoit le nostre paradis qui clamons" (line 8374). Similar creatures are found in other accounts of the visionary afterlife.[31] The bird tells Huon, "Vestre voie ert mout longe [. . .]"

---

[27] Compare Gardiner, *Visions*, 115–16.

[28] "As soon as the ray of the sun when it is risen / You will see them on top of this mountain / How they sing melody nor do they move [arise]." Cf. Stengel, *Suche*, 34.

[29] For the role of memory, and evocations to the reader, see Durling and Martinez, *Inferno*, 137–38 and 94–96 n.8.

[30] "[. . .] in the form of birds / We are here; neither good nor evil did we do / But nonetheless it was our intention / To always stick with those who would win."

[31] Le Goff, *Birth of Purgatory*, 37, evokes the *Apocalypse of Saint Paul* as being the first appearance of the day of rest idea; see also Gardiner, *Visions*, 92–96; Meregazzi, "*L'Ugo d'Alvernia*," 26; Gurevich, *Medieval Popular Culture*, 134, calls it "typical of the Irish."

(line 8387), as the route through hell is for Dante (e.g., *Inf.* 4: 21; 33: 95, etc.). The theme is of those "sanza 'nfamia e sanza lodo" who "non furon ribelli / né fur fedeli a Dio, ma per sé fuoro" (*Inf.* 3: 36; 38–39). Though the idea of these souls as birds does not appear in Dante, birds as elements of comparison appear throughout *Inferno*: from Francesca and the *stornei, gru,* and *colombe* (5: 40, 46, 82) to the *spiriti lenti* of *Purgatorio* (2: 125). Huon's cruise on the Tigris too parallels earlier visionary literature; Le Goff mentions the "probative sauna" typical of medieval purgatories, where trial by water follows trial by flame.[32]

Finally, Huon sees a palace in the clouds, carved in Moses' time. The description—a palace of marble defending the passage, with a challenger to his purity—resembles the bridge crossings of earlier underworld accounts, though no bridge is mentioned. Huon is told that he cannot continue if he is not pure. With his cross in front of him, he passes through more marvels across into the Promised Land that he saw in the distance, full of excellent fruit and plants with no weeds: "'Terre de Promision' hom l'apelle et ot disue" (line 8468 ["'The Promised Land' men call it and had said"). After further travel, two men "d'antiquités," Enoch and Elijah, tell him that he will complete his quest this year and that his body will return safely home (lines 8511–8512). This is unlike Dante's voyage, since Dante is accompanied throughout by his guides; Dante's guides, of course, do reassure him regularly of his safety. Elijah and Enoch provide Huon with the magical fruits to enable him to survive until he reaches hell, and tell him Earthly Paradise is further on. Enoch, subject of the eponymous book recounting the apocalypse, together with Elijah, a father of the Judaeo-Christian tradition, then tell him that there are born the four streams that divide the earth, the Tigris, Euphrates, Jordan and Fison (adapted from Genesis 2: 10–14); Dante sees Tigris and Euphrates in Earthly Paradise as well (*Purg.* 33: 112).[33] Earthly Paradise is seen in other medieval versions of the afterlife; for example, at the end of seven years, St. Brendan finds it, forty days' journey to the west.[34] Le Goff says that it is found on medieval maps to the west of Gog and Magog.[35] *Huon*'s version of Earthly Paradise partially reduplicates the earlier Noah's Ark Mountain: it too uses biblical references, it too is fertile and attractive and populated with ancestral figures. However, no genealogical link here ties him personally to the site

---

[32] Le Goff, *Birth of Purgatory*, 9. Gregory the Great's sixth-century *Dialogues* is one example, and Le Goff offers others as well (Le Goff, *Birth of Purgatory*, 94; 107–22).

[33] See Le Goff, *Birth of Purgatory*, 2, for further discussion of the Earthly Paradise and its spatialization. It is interesting that Dante requires neither food nor drink, unlike other afterlife travelers; even Huon requires refreshment during his travels, a function prepared by a devil visiting him before his mission and carrying off a table of food.

[34] Gardiner, *Visions*, 124–26.

[35] Le Goff, *Birth of Purgatory*, 8.

or to the journey there. Rather, it is a sign of his being a chosen figure, specially selected and destined to succeed.[36]

Each of Huon's otherworldly encounters in the second leg of his voyage resemble otherworld events in earlier texts. From dancing seductresses to a branch of hell, followed by the fiery swamp, Noah's Ark, and the Promised Land leading to Earthly Paradise, the *Huon* redactor seems to have collected every possible rendition of afterlife description yet found it wanting. He replicates characters (Judas is seen twice) and geographical, environmental, or meteorological characteristics (horrendous beasts, mountains, water and storms are particularly popular), and echoes on occasion Dante's wording or ideas. Those echoes reverberate with even greater strength in the final pilgrimage event, hell itself.

Entrance to hell

Upon his horse's death, Huon's prayer *du plus grand péril* begins with a recall of the harrowing of Hell:[37] "En tenebrie aportas clere lux / A cil ch'erent a·u Limbe suspendus" (lines 8734–8735), and continues to the crucifixion, evoking John and Mary:

> "'Mulier,' dixis 'ecce ton filius',
> Et a Johann dixis puis cum a drus,
> 'Voy enci toe mere' [. . .] ." (lines 8750–8752)[38]

By using the *prière du plus grand péril*, the literary form emphasizes its chanson de geste origin, for in hell Dante does not evoke the Deity or pray.[39] Huon is in the New Testament, past the Garden of Eden and the ancient fathers of the Old Testament. Huon's extended family was revealed near Noah's Ark (where the

---

[36] On can compare Roland's experience with the hermit in the Franco-Italian *Entrée d'Espagne* (ed. Thomas; lines 14628–15286): there the mountain, the bridge, and the tree of life appear as garden motifs in a totally different context, a century earlier.

[37] For a brief résumé of the *prière du plus grand péril* bibliography and history, see Martin, *Les Motifs*, 298 n.40.

[38] "Into darkness you brought clear light / To those who were suspended in Limbo" and "'Woman', you said, 'here is your son' / And to John, you said, then, as to a beloved, / 'Here also is your mother' [. . .] "; cf. Vulgate, John 19: 26–27 (*Biblia Sacra juxta Vulgatam Clementinam*, ed. A. Colunga, O.P., and L. Turrado, 4th ed. [Madrid: Editorial catolica, 1965]).

[39] As Durling and Martinez point out, there is a lack of invocations of God in *Inferno*; only the centaur Chiron can do so (Durling and Martinez, *Inferno*, 196 n.119). Others speak of "another" (e.g., Ulysses). In *Paradiso* there are numerous prayers; one thinks of St. Bernard in particular praying to Mary on Dante's behalf (*Par.* 33). However, this particular biblical citation does not appear in the *Commedia*.

First Father, Adam, was one of those present). In hell Huon meets his literary fathers, for at the end of his prayer a series of guides present themselves. Behind these guides and the ultimate trip through hell lies Dante, even more clearly than elsewhere. Huon refuses the first guide when to his query, "Is home voir, o fantasme aparu?" (line 8781; cf. *Inf.* 1: 64, "[. . .] od ombra od omo certo"), and the spirit admits to being a *faus angle* (line 8808). This spirit mentions possible sights in hell as Cain and Judas (whom we know Huon has already seen). The second figure, armed, ten feet tall, mentions Marsille and Danebron, King Golias, Agolant and Helmont, as people to see in hell (all characters from the French epic that takes place in Italy, *Aspremont*).[40] Huon also asks him, "Is hom o ombre?" (line 8906), and the reply is much like Dante's Vergil: "De jant que sont ainç le bastisme née [. . .]" (line 8914) "Fil fuy Anchises, l'om m'apellent Enée [. . .]" (line 8940; cf. *Inf.* 1: 72–74, ". . . nel tempo de li dèi falsi e bugiardi [. . .] figliuol d'Anchise [. . .]"). Huon refuses him as well, thinking of Antenor and his betrayal (compare Dante's use of Antenora for the zone of *Inf.* 32: 88). From a fountain, the third candidate appears, "Un vieuç hermit" (line 9012). Aeneas here points out that Huon refused him because "non sui en l'aute compagnie / De li prophete et do·u sainct Jeremie" (9023–9024), but says that this third figure is a saint indeed. Huon tries to embrace this new figure, but "rien non trova mie" (line 9033 [(he) didn't find anything at all]), similarly to Dante and Casella in *Purgatory* 2: 76–81 (and of course to Aeneas and his mother in *Aeneid* 2.700–702).[41] The third spirit reveals that he is Guillaume d'Orange, and Huon thanks God: "De mon lignace estoit cestu la flor" (line 9084 [From my lineage this one was the best]). Thus, in major steps of his voyage, Huon is guided by family: a cousin and an ancestor.[42] Huon's coming was foretold, as was Christ's, and his way is sprinkled with miracles. Furthermore, Huon's voyage concludes with a third visit to the afterworld: he has seen other pieces in passing, but he spends time in three spots.

---

[40] See L. Zarker Morgan, "War is Hell (for Saracens): A Footnote to *Aspremont*'s Afterlife in Italy," forthcoming in *"Moult a sans et vallour": Studies in Medieval French Literature in Honor of William W. Kibler* (Amsterdam: Rodopi), ed. Monica Wright and Sarah Crisler, for *Aspremont* in *Huon d'Auvergne*, which includes bibliography about the popularity of *Aspremont* in Italy.

[41] There are two earlier times when an embrace encompasses no one: first Huon's wife, Ynide, in attempting to embrace her father's spirit (lines 5428–5430; see Zarker Morgan, "Passion," 73); the second, Huon in Earthly Paradise, attempting to embrace Adam and his companions (line 7913). The second clearly parallels Huon's attempt here to embrace Guillaume d'Orange.

[42] On family and genealogy in Italian tradition deriving from the chansons de geste, see G. Allaire, "Genealogy and Kinship as Unifying Device in Andrea da Barberino's *La Storia di Aiolfo dal Barbicone*," *Olifant* 21 (1996–1997): 47–69.

There are parallels between the different afterworld segments, as there are parallels in Dante's three realms.[43]

Dante encounters Cacciaguida in Paradise, and witnesses miraculous events, but in the *Commedia* the role of genealogy is subsumed into that of country; Cacciaguida, revered as ancestor, foretells Dante's exile, mixing his story with Florentine history. Guillaume d'Orange appears in Dante's heaven with his companion, Rainouart, as well as Charlemagne and Roland; it is fact in departing from Cacciaguida that Dante sees them (*Par.* 18: 43–48). The positive judgment of chanson de geste in the *Huon* text is reinforced by Dantean context and reference. Yet in contrast, Huon is led by and leads his family, chosen ones, for it is family—Huon's cousin and brothers-in-law—who defend his kingdom (and his wife) while he is away. It is they who lead him to biblical ancestors and to the devil to complete his mission. References to reading, writing, the harrowing of hell, the time period of Huon's visit to Noah's Ark (the week before Easter, the same time frame as Dante's journey), all recall the *Commedia*, though the events themselves—blessing and informational tours—differ and frequently echo other visionary literature of the twelfth and thirteenth centuries. The trip through hell might deceive the reader through direct quotes into thinking that it is the most Dantean borrowing, but Huon's entire tripartite voyage through the years, passing from earthly to progressively more ethereal sites, is in fact influenced by the *Commedia*, for it adapts wording, characters, and moral precepts to the chanson de geste tradition. Huon's careful note-taking is like that of *Huon*'s redactor, who borrows from numerous preceding works, concluding with Dante's *Commedia*. The fact that Dante himself is not mentioned, only quoted—like the Bible—signifies the authority to which the *Commedia* has already acceded.[44]

Conclusions

Dantean citation informs *Huon d'Auvergne*, but does not formulate it. The three *matières* of vernacular literacy—classical in evocations of the *Aeneid* and Alexander, courtly in the comparison with Galahad and in singular adventure, and that of France in participants from *Aspremont* and *Aliscans*—solidly link Huon to the vernacular tradition from which it derives. These in turn are placed within the genre of visionary literature, of which Dante is a part. Family and genealogy unite the episodes of *Huon d'Auvergne* in events that lead to the city of man, not of God. For Huon returns to the world, gives the devil's tribute to King Charles

---

[43] Compare A. Iannucci, "Autoesegesi dantesca: La tecnica dell'"episodio parallelo' nella Commedia," *Lettere Italiane* 33 (1981): 305–28.

[44] For more specific comparisons of *Huon d'Auvergne* quotes with the *Commedia*, see L. Zarker Morgan, "(Mis)Quoting Dante: Early Epic Intertextuality in *Huon d'Auvergne*," *Neophilologus* 93 (2008): 577–99.

Martel, and watches him be carried off to hell. The humdrum world of politics—electing a successor (weak William Capet), then running a distant war in Rome—evokes a creation neither optimistic nor visionary, but in keeping with chanson de geste tradition. It demonstrates constant combat between Christians and pagans, as well as between tribes of Christians. No one wins in the end, for Huon dies in combat for his "tribe," sainted, to be sure, but without leading the reader to a greater or deeper knowledge of the afterlife.[45] An "imitative prophetic voice" appears through Huon's journey alone,[46] not in the conclusion where the power of exemplum seeks to admonish the French monarchy for its errant ways in not going forth to crusade for the good of the church.

As Christopher Kleinhenz demonstrates, the context of citation reveals its relevance in *Huon d'Auvergne*: thrice repeated questioning of guides quoting Dante each time, thrice repeated attempts at embrace, thrice repeated visits to the afterworld where only the final one (the most Dantean) is successful, reveal the importance of Dante's vision to the redactor. The specific quotes and encounters lead us to see other factors—tone, triple structures, and pacing—as echoing Dante's *Commedia*. Together they reinforce, in Kleinhenz's words, the "new scripture" that the *Commedia* became in its time,[47] and the early date of the manuscript—1341—emphasizes the rapidity of that acceptance, demonstrating the progressive penetration of the *Commedia* into literary consciousness and its reception into extant traditions. As Dante uses the scriptures, writers used Dante's text for their own purposes, in connection with other texts and personal innovation to convey their own messages. The events briefly examined here—branches of hell, the Promised Land, Noah's Ark, and finally the gates of hell itself—demonstrate *Huon d'Auvergne*'s citation of Dante's *Commedia* in a different, though related, genre and context, that produces a differently nuanced, though again related, message to readers.

---

[45] Gurevich, *Medieval Popular Culture*, suggests that the chanson de geste from the twelfth century on became politicized, but one can argue that the *Chanson de Roland* is already in many ways a political poem. Certainly *Huon d'Auvergne* reflects the realities of the time, with Empire and France at odds.

[46] Kleinhenz, "Dante and the Bible: Biblical," 87.

[47] Kleinhenz, "Dante and the Bible: Biblical," 90.

Section II

Interpretations and Reception of Dante's Minor Works

The Formal Structure of the *Vita Nova*

Richard Lansing

That Dante's first book-length composition was the last of his works to appear in print is perhaps emblematic of its own somewhat quizzical status as a literary text.[1] Dante Gabriel Rossetti long ago called the *Vita Nova* an "enigmatic booklet," a view that has since been widely, if not universally, endorsed and repeatedly articulated in sundry ways. E.H. Strauch went so far as to characterize it as a "riddle" designed purposely to be taken as a riddle, since "it reflects Dante's mystical view of existence."[2] Maria Corti has underscored its ambiguous generic character, as has Luca Carlo Rossi for whom the specification of its primary literary identity escapes classification with any certainty.[3] Robert Hollander observes that these and similar assessments are, in fact, the common experience of virtually all readers.[4] Such a consensus developed over so long a period of time could only spawn endless further debate and reinterpretation, which at times produced readings nearly as puzzling as the issues they sought to resolve.[5] Most recently the topic of critical contention has shifted away from questions of genre to a reconsideration of the formal structure of the text, and, in particular, to its division into chapters. Working independently of each other, Guglielmo Gorni and Dino Cervigni almost simultaneously published

---

[1] The *Vita nuova di Dante Alighieri* was first printed by Bartolomeo Sermartelli, in Florence, in 1576.

[2] "Dante's *Vita Nuova* as Riddle," *Symposium* 21 (1967): 324–30. Quoted from *American Dante Bibliography*, 1967, at www.dantesociety.org/Publications/Bibliographies

[3] Dante Alighieri, *Vita Nuova* (Milan: Feltrinelli, 1993), 7; Dante Alighieri, *Vita Nova*, ed. Luca Carlo Rossi (Milan: Mondadori, 1999), 246.

[4] *Dante: A Life in Works* (New Haven: Yale University Press, 2001), 13. Stefano Carrai makes the same observation more recently in *Dante elegiaco: una chiave di lettura per la Vita nova* (Florence: Olschki, 2006), 15.

[5] Among the more successful and interesting of those approaches that have avoided this quandary is Ronald Martinez's suggestion in "Mourning Beatrice: The Rhetoric of Threnody in the *Vita nova*," *Modern Language Notes* 113 (1998): 1–29, that Dante models his text on the Book of Lamentations (Threni), creating a pattern expressive of a "dialectic of lament and future rejoicing" (3) to organize his commemorative praise of the beloved Beatrice.

rebuttals to Michele Barbi's longstanding division of the text into forty-two chapters, and indirectly as well to the edition in forty-three chapters published by Alessandro Torri in 1843, which Barbi had revised.[6] Emphasizing the fact that no extant manuscript reveals the presence of any chapter divisions, either by number or by rubric, both assert that the divisions which Barbi introduced into his edition of 1907 were not only unjustified in principle, but served, in fact, to impede a clear understanding of the text.

The practice of editorial partitioning in the west dates back at least to the scholiasts of Homer's epics, who divided both the *Iliad* and the *Odyssey* into twenty-four books as a pedagogic device to facilitate reference to individual portions of what were two very long narrative poems.[7] The specific number of divisions introduced later became itself a subject of interest. Each of the twenty-four parts of either epic was, originally, not really numbered but ascribed a letter of the Greek alphabet, which contained twenty-four letters. Subsequent writers of epic developed and hewed to a tradition of acknowledging their genealogical indebtedness to Homer frequently by dividing their works according to a factor, or aliquot part, of the number twenty-four. Once Vergil divided his *Aeneid* into twelve books to signal his indebtedness to Homer, the number twelve became the standard for epic poetry. Centuries later Boccaccio would take emulation of Vergil one step further in his *Teseida* by attempting to match the *Aeneid* not only book for book, but, according to one critic, verse for verse as well.[8] The partitioning of a text as a means of expressing hidden messages became commonplace from antiquity to the Renaissance and took the form of a variety of independent systems of numerical conceptualization. Augustine, for example, divides his *De civitate Dei* into twenty-two books to evoke a correspondence with the number of letters in the Hebrew alphabet, a correspondence he explicitly acknowledges in his text. And Dante's *Commedia*, of course, represents the pinnacle of the art of binding literary form to content through numerological symbolism. In view of the traditional authorial practice of meaningful partitioning, the critical

---

[6] Alessandro Torri, *La Vita nuova* di D. A. (Livorno: Vannini, 1843); Dino Cervigni and Edward Vasta, eds., *Vita Nuova* (Notre Dame: University of Notre Dame Press, 1995). Guglielmo Gorni has addressed the topic of chapter divisions in several essays, but chiefly in "'Paragrafi' e titolo della *Vita Nova*," *Studi di Filologia Italiana* 53 (1995): 203–22; "Per la *Vita nova*," *Studi di Filologia Italiana* 58 (2000): 29–48; and "Appunti sulla nuova *Vita Nova*," *Letture Classensi* 26 (1997): 7–20. His edition of the text was published by Einaudi (Turin) in 1996. This essay cites the Gorni text of the *Vita Nova* edited by Luca Carlo Rossi (n. 3 above).

[7] Well before Homer, biblical scholiasts commented on numerical schemas in the Hebrew bible. The 150 psalms of the Book of Psalms, for example, contained five sections, to reflect the five books of the Pentateuch.

[8] Edward Hutton, cited by Robert A. Pratt, "Chaucer's Use of the *Teseida*," *PMLA* 62 (1947): 598–621; see n. 3.

intervention performed by Barbi on the *Vita Nova* constituted an act of obfuscation that induced more than a few critics lacking familiarity with the text in its original form to devise numerical patterns based on his narrative structure of forty-two chapters. Both Gorni and Cervigni present arguments for identifying divisions based on a close adherence to the original textual form of the *libello* in multiple extant manuscripts. Nevertheless, the distance separating them from Barbi is less pronounced than might be expected, despite their different results, since each proposes an alternative model for dividing into chapters a text that in fact has none.

Gorni's conception, on the most basic level, centers on the premise that Dante's book contains thirty-one prose sections, or *paragrafi*, which in turn contain thirty-one lyrics, a number corresponding to, though not coincidental with, the prose sections.[9] On the next level of discrimination, events described in these *paragrafi* define the borders of larger thematic blocks of experience, which form three sets of nine chapters each, or *novene*, as Gorni christens them, followed by a coda of four chapters. The resulting pattern highlights both the Trinity and Beatrice's own number nine, of which three is its unique and therefore perfect (because self-identical) aliquot part.

Cervigni's breakdown into thirty *paragrafi* yields nearly the same number of divisions, but their parameters differ substantially from those in Gorni's sequence. Both schemas, however, mark a radical departure from the traditional view of the prose chapters and throw into question much of the previous interpretive work based on it. Yet they also raise significant questions of their own. What impact do the new narrative divisions have on the established reading of Dante's dramatization of his new life? In what way do they relate to the arrangement of the lyrics, which have long been thought to delineate an independent pattern of symmetry? Most importantly, do these schemas conform to or destabilize the commonly-held view that the *Vita Nova* registers a series of alternating advances and relapses in Dante's amatory quest to be united with Beatrice? If we

---

[9] Gorni borrows terminology that Dante himself employs in the first "chapter" as a metaphorical device he intends to use for identifying the major events in his amatory life that merit presentation to the reader: "verrò a quelle parole le quali sono scripte nella mia memoria sotto maggiori paragrafi" (*VN* 1.11). The term specifies the significant units of recollection selected for his *libello*, not the book's actual written chapters. This distinction, given Dante's analogical procedure, does not seriously weaken Gorni's claim that the poet means the reader to perceive the set of narrated events and lyrics as entailing individual "episodes" of his story. But different readers will, and do, delineate the divisions differently, which results in competing claims about the number of chapters or divisions in the book in totality. I would argue that there is no real need to attempt to specify formal divisions of any kind, in which one portion of the text could be said to separate itself from another portion. To assign divisions does not afford any measurable increase in our understanding of the work's meaning.

accept Gorni's judgment that the *libello* divides into two major parts, Beatrice *in vita* and *in morte*, as well as into three *novene* of nine *paragrafi* each, followed by a coda, is it still possible to speak of the work as having a true center in the classical sense of the term? Can so many narrative structures be simultaneously and mutually operative? Is it possible to identify any formal, organized narrative structure at all that can be said to illustrate the meaning of Dante's amatory experience? In simple terms, does the poet synchronize the form and content of the *Vita Nova* according to some structural principle?

Well before these issues gained currency, critics had long debated whether the lyrics could be said to define in some way the blueprint of Dante's amatory experience. The first to make such a claim was Charles Eliot Norton, who argued that the arrangement of the *Vita nova*'s 31 lyrics defines a symbolic pattern based on the number 3, organized by the three long canzoni around which the remaining lyrics fall into place.[10] He found, moreover, that the second and central canzone occupies the precise numerical center of the 31 lyrics and that the entire sequence reveals a chiastic correspondence between discrete and balanced groups of lyrics: 10 poems, 1st canzone, 4 poems, 2nd canzone, 4 poems, 3rd canzone, and 10 poems. This symmetrical arrangement had, he argued, the virtue of highlighting the number 3, the sign of the Trinity, while conferring a special importance on the middle canzone as its most dominant component. The formal center then marks what is central to and of prime significance for the book's overall meaning. For Norton, Dante's placement of his vision of Beatrice's death in the central canzone and at the precise "poetic" middle of his book therefore carries special meaning, one increased by the correlation of her envisioned death with that of Christ's death. Norton's pattern later underwent refinement in the hands of several critics, most famously C. S. Singleton, who conceived of the first set of 10 poems as 1+9 and the last as 9+1, with the first and last sonnets serving as prologue and epilogue. But Singleton, in fact, was not really the first to propose that schema. The credit must go to Giovanni Federzoni, for his essay on the *Vita Nova* published in *Studi e diporti danteschi* in 1902. Somewhat differently from Singleton, Federzoni had isolated the first and last sonnets on the basis that they were linked to the first and last of the poet's visions, a notion undermined by the text itself whose final lyric actually precedes the last vision. But the only difference between the two schemas lies in the reasoning behind separating the two frame-sonnets from the narrative whole, a distinction of negligible importance.[11]

---

[10] "On the Structure of the *Vita nuova*," in *The New Life of Dante Alighieri*, trans. Charles Eliot Norton (Boston and New York: Houghton, Mifflin and Company, 1867), 129–36.

[11] It will come as a surprise to many, as it did to this writer, to learn that "Singleton's" pattern of 1s and 9s is, in fact, not of his own making. Critics over time have credited Singleton with the discovery, and the continuous repetition of acknowledgment and praise, especially by prominent critics, coupled with Singleton's own celebrity as a critic,

The center panel of nine lyrics in the Federzoni-Singleton variation contains but demotes the second canzone by equalizing it with the four lyrics on either side. The final pattern, 1+9+1+9+1+9+1, may have an elegant simplicity and numerological relevance, but it is not clear why the frame lyrics should be considered as truly separable from the main body of poems. Moreover, the second canzone—arguably the most important of the three—loses its prominence as a longer lyric in this arrangement, being strangely collated among the minor lyrics. Singleton gives no formally coherent reason for revising the central lyrics from 4+1+4 to 9, other than finding his numerology more pleasing than Norton's, because it enhances Beatrice's relationship to Christ by virtue of a shared numerological identity.

In Dante's imagination, Beatrice owes her spiritual identity to the number 9 because her birth—"ne la sua generazione tutti e nove li mobile cieli perfettissimamente s'aveano insieme"—and her death—"ne la prima ora del non giorno del mese . . . nel nono mese dell'anno . . . del terzodecimo centinaio"—bear its imprint and express the miracle of her being. Its imprint is so profound that "questo numero fue ella medesima." And significantly Dante speaks of her as the product and creation of the number 3—"lo numero del tre. . .per sé medesimo fa nove"—, and the number 3 as the maker—"fattore"—and the root—"radice"—of her being. These two words are, of course, fundamental terms in the language of mathematics, but Dante clearly means to evoke the notion of a Trinitarian God who is the maker and creator of all things, and the origin and source from which all things are created. Beatrice is born of divinity itself. As a divine yet human creature, she shares an association with Christ in the commonality of their time of death, His at the ninth hour of the last day (the nones), hers on the ninth day of the ninth month in the ninth decade of the thirteenth century after His birth. The poet emerges from behind the symbolism he erects in paragraph 19 to explain its significance, but his real purpose is to suggest that Beatrice's

---

has had the effect of creating an assumption that further scrutiny of the matter was not required. The first to suggest the symmetrical pattern was Giovanni Federzoni. While Singleton does cite his name in an undocumented note at the end of *An Essay on the Vita nuova* (Cambridge, MA: Harvard University Press, 1949), there is no indication on page 79 of his text that there is any such note at all. Singleton approaches the topic of the symmetry by citing Kenneth McKenzie, "The Symmetrical Structure of Dante's *Vita Nuova*," *PMLA* 18 (1903): 341–55, noting that the latter believes Federzoni's pattern based on one and nine "to be mere ingenuity." Then Singleton remarks: "It had been suggested by Federzoni" (150). No source, no date, not even the critic's first name. Because Singleton's own brief discussion on page 79 led readers to think that the idea was his, it apparently never occurred to anyone that it was not. Federzoni, who published his idea in *Studi e diporti danteschi* (Bologna: Zanichelli, 1902, repr. 1935), is rarely given proper and due credit, but McKenzie does (350). John J. Guzzardo provides a useful analysis of Singleton's schema for the lyrics in "Number Symbolism in the *Vita Nuova*," in *Dante: Numerological Studies* (New York: Peter Lang, 1987), 15–39.

true identity is not an invention on his part, but a sacred truth communicated from above by the spheres themselves and by the sum of their revolutions about the earth, which is to say, by God. The Federzoni-Singleton schema might be the most perfect symbolic realization of Beatrice's identity, since the number 9 is featured in it exactly 3 times, but to arrive at such an ordering of parts requires subscribing to a subsidiary complex of contrary rules (somewhat ironically) based on addition and subtraction: merge these and those lyrics together as a set, while isolating the first and last from all other lyrics. However one reads the *Vita Nova*, the first poem is not a prologue, nor is the last an epilogue. Each crystallizes a single event in a series of events which as a whole defines the trajectory of Dante's amatory experience. They define a continuum, not one framed by an extra-narrational preamble and summary. What we have in the lyrics is a first moment and last moment, not preface and postscript. The last lyric, in fact, defies classification even according to the topos of constituting the "final word." It is the last, but not the final, word because Dante makes clear his intention to return to his project at a later time when he will have the artistic capability of continuing, and presumably, completing it. The *libello* lacks a classical closure, but so, in some sense, do all autobiographies. The real point here that bears stressing is that the two sequences, the lyric and the narrative, reach closure in different ways. While the narrative axis remains open, the lyrics possess a completeness of a kind created by the strong connection between the first and last sonnets expressed in the motif of the ascent into heaven. If death must one day remove Beatrice from his company on earth, as portended in the first vision ("mi parea che si ne gisse verso lo cielo," 1.18), at least Dante will learn how to collapse the distance that separates their spirits by going beyond the last sphere "che più larga gira" (31.1) to be with her, if only momentarily.

The lyrics may well be understood to illustrate a pattern, but the prose axis resists claims of a well-conceived, formal structure based on some notion of the sum of divided parts. Even less plausible, consequently, are theories of numerological properties. As best we know, Dante never formally divided this work into chapters, and any argument that he did would be at best mere conjecture. What has passed for chapter divisions for readers of the modern era developed out of an editorial practice first established by Boccaccio, who, moreover, also took the liberty of excising altogether Dante's digest of each poem's compositional properties which immediately preceded or followed it.[12]

Gorni bases his conception of the prose structure on the 31 paragraphs having a large initial letter that is illuminated in many manuscripts. Each paragraph

---

[12] Dante employs the term "divisione" (and the verb "dividere") to refer to this practice, one that Dante inaugurated in the Italian vernacular (as Gorni notes in his introduction to Luca Carlo Rossi's edition, *VN* 1, comment p. 20). It should not be confused with the critics' frequent use of the same term in English to refer to "chapters."

contains at least one lyric, with the exception of three (16, 19, 31).[13] Leaving aside the last paragraph, Gorni observes that paragraphs 16 and 19 both introduce digressions from the main narrative sequence: the first to justify the need for figural language in poetry, the second to interpret the symbolism of the numbers 3 and 9. The first, 16, proves significantly to be the centermost of the 31 "paragrafi" in his enumeration. The lyric center, by contrast, occurs in paragraph 14. This differential raises a host of questions: Must we then speak of a double middle, or duality of centers, one narrative and the other lyric? Could readers have grasped the idea of a prose center as well as a different lyric center? If they could, what kind of significance would they have attributed to such a dualistic positioning of important parts? The conception is excessively complex, not to say extremely uncharacteristic of a scholastic mentality like Dante's. And we must not forget the question raised earlier about Gorni's further partitioning into three *novene* plus coda, and, in a third and separate schema, into lyrics *in vita* and *in morte*.[14]

Cervigni, likewise subscribing to the notion that the text divides into *paragrafi*, based on a set of temporal expressions that introduce new events, counts only thirty, but the numerical proximity it shares with Gorni's thirty-one is deceptive since his divisions fall in altogether different places.[15] Medieval readers, however, would not necessarily have been prepared to detect new prose divisions introduced by temporal lexemes like "Apresso" or "Poi che," much less have been attentive to complex numerological structures "prophesied" by the number 9 that bespeaks Beatrice's identity. Gorni's architecture of three separate but interrelated models may well be simply too sophisticated to be fully convincing, and, despite a certain elegance in its logic, ultimately too artificial, in the sense of appearing to be a product designed to confirm some preconceived notion or truth, for us easily to suspend our disbelief.[16]

---

[13] Gorni's reasoning is sound and his argument for the number of divisions and their borders convincing, given the evidence he presents. His structuring of the narrative parts, call them *paragrafi* or chapters, has greater merit and justification than does Barbi's.

[14] Gorni focuses almost entirely on the prose *paragrafi* in his discussion of narrative structure, but he endorses Norton's pattern of symmetry for the lyrics, if somewhat hesitantly: "ormai appare anch'esso caduco, o almeno da ripensare a norma dell'originaria e ben documentata compagine in paragrafi" (Guglielmo Gorni, *Vita Nova* [Turin: Einaudi, 1996], xxv.

[15] See Dino Cervigni, "From Manuscript to Print: The Case of Dante's *Vita Nuova*," in *Dante Now: Current Trends in Dante Studies*, ed. Theodore J. Cachey, Jr. (Notre Dame: University of Notre Dame Press, 1995), 83–114, where he concludes that "These temporal expressions, therefore, together with the distinction between prose and poetry, provide the clearest patterns that create internal junctures within the text and the only patterns sufficiently extensive and consistent to provide an adequate number of divisions necessary for understanding and interpretation" (93).

[16] For example, Gorni's intriguing idea that Dante creates three sections of nine prose *paragrafi* to define three orders of experience does not accord with the traditional

Chapter 16, one of only three chapter-paragraphs lacking a lyric and also the prose centerpiece of the *Vita Nova* in Gorni's schema, suspends narration to deliver a meta-commentary on the topic of poetics, consisting of an apology on the use of the vernacular in love poetry, a brief history of the advent of love poetry in the West since the days of Ovid, and an explanation of the poet's need for employing figural language. The only other chapter having a similar digressive character is Gorni 19, which, after announcing Beatrice's death, proceeds to explicate the manifold relatedness of the number 9 to her earthly and as well her heavenly life. It marks the coordinates of her existence in historical time, defined by the calendar and the positions of the nine heavenly spheres, and also in eternity, by her relation to the nine hierarchies of angels and to the Trinity.[17] As angel, Beatrice possesses an identity analogous to that of the Trinity, which accounts for her miraculous power to confer beatitude on all those who gaze on her. Since Dante can only record the event of Beatrice's passing and not treat of it, the paragraph necessarily assumes a meta-narratological character. Despite the importance of these two didactic *paragrafi* on literary theory and number symbolism, their collocation in the narrative sequence does not appear to be designed to articulate any apparent symmetrical patterning. How could they serve to define two independent conceptual structures, narrative midpoint and dividing line between life and death, when the meta-content attaching to their narrative moments makes them interdependent, not independent? Perhaps, too, we cannot speak of these two chapters as being truly independent of the narrative despite their philosophical vein. When Dante observes the pilgrims passing through Florence on their way to Rome, he ruminates about their lack of awareness of Beatrice and indulges his reader with a brief digression on the various types of pilgrims, distinguishing among the Palmers, the Romers, and the pilgrims traveling to Galicia. Such explanations may not occur frequently in the *Vita Nova*, but neither are they entirely uncommon. Dante's thoughts, whether they explain lexical choices or describe physical or psychological events, remain a product of the poet's intellectual experience and cannot be conceived to stand apart as meta-commentary and hence stand out as markers defining the symbolic structure of

---

emphasis placed on the three major canzoni, so that the lyric structure functions independently of the prose paragraph structure.

[17] Chapter 19 contains, Gorni observes, exactly 9 instances of the word "nove"—if, that is, we omit one other instance that serves as a topical introduction, with Dante's listing of 9 explications (*ragioni*) of the meaning of the number 9 beginning at 19.4, "Io dico che . . ." There is also one instance of 9 in its adjectival form, "nono." As with the question of numerologically-based prose and lyric structures, "perfect," or perhaps more realistically, "almost perfect." Critics are very much like Dante himself, who confesses in this chapter that others might see more subtle meanings in the miraculous nature of the number, "ma questa è quella che io ne veggio, e che più mi piace" (19.7): They see what is most pleasing to their imagination.

the *Vita Nova*. The division of events according to Beatrice *in vita* and *in morte* appears not to have any particular significance in defining the *libello*'s structure.[18] Gorni's tripartite equation is shrewd, elegant, and very suggestive: 9 + 9 + 9 *paragrafi*, divided into two uneven but numerically related parts of 18 devoted to Beatrice *in vita*, the remaining 9 to Beatrice *in morte*—followed by the nettlesome odd set of 4 concluding *paragrafi*. His rationale for these divisions is somewhat weakened by the fact that the themes derive not from the individual sets of *paragrafi* but from the lyrics they contain. And since the *paragrafi* and lyrics are not coterminous by number in each group, the two structures generate a wrinkle. Why would Dante not have synchronized the *paragrafi* with the lyrics if he intended for readers to perceive a formal pattern? The first group contains not 9 but 10 lyrics, as does the second group. But thereafter even rough symmetry falls apart in the third group, which comprises 8 *paragrafi* and 8 lyrics, followed by the coda of 3 lyrics in the final 4 *paragrafi*. It is this discrepancy of complete and true symmetry, to my mind, which attenuates the validity of Gorni's schema. In the end, he gives us a variation of the old 1 + 9 + 1 + 9 + 1 + 9 + 1 pattern, which, while mapping out the lyrics and not the chapters, nevertheless stresses the number 9 in 3 panels of poems separated, again, by 4 single (though formally variable) poems. Gorni's structuring is both novel and yet still familiar, but its arcane and inherently overwrought character betray a certain artificial quality of order that the *libello* itself does not possess. If anything, the *Vita Nova* creates in the reader a sense of indirection, of emotional disequilibrium, of the poet's limited awareness of an inchoate and ever-changing amatory experience. Luca Carlo Rossi has aptly described this quality, calling the *libello* "un'opera dinamica, tumultuosa . . . [una] ricerca per tappe successive, senza un percorso tutto predeterminato né una meta finale già fissata" (*VN*, 247). Quite simply, the work is open-ended, progressive, and, perhaps most importantly for any consideration of narrative structure, incomplete. To be sure, the *Vita Nova* has an end, but the author leaves the story purposely unfinished. The abrupt announcement in the last lines of a *mirabile visione* whose retelling requires a skill as yet unavailable to the poet denies the work normative closure and suspends readers' expectations much in the same way as at the close of the *Commedia*, when Dante will experience the absolute peak of perceiving the divine nature in the *imago Dei* only to beg off with an apology for lacking sufficient memory of the event to be able to communicate it to others through language. There is no denouement in his *sacro poema*, only a sudden suspension of further utterance at the moment of greatest climax. In the case of the *Vita Nova*, we are promised a sequel of some kind and left with the sense that Dante's visions may not cease even once he is able to express the substance of the *mirabile visione* he has experienced. Without finality, the perfection of form must remain elusive because the poet's experience of Beatrice's love remains *in fieri*.

---

[18] The moment of Beatrice's death divides the work into 18 sections *in vita*, 13 *in morte*, and with respect to the lyrics, 20 before and 11 after her death.

It is another matter, however, to speak of patterns based solely on the number and arrangement of the lyrics, because taken together the lyrics can be said to reveal a pattern of events characterizing the significance of a period in Dante's love life leading up to and including the final lyric. As noted earlier, there is remarkable agreement among a majority of critics regarding the symmetrical pattern mapped out by the choice of poetic forms and their placement. Nevertheless I tend to regard with some skepticism even this pattern, which depends on more than one sleight of hand to work. Norton's pattern (10 + I + 4 + II + 4 + III + 10) and variations of it highlight Dante's vision of Beatrice's death as the central lyric and therefore the central event of Dante's amatory experience. But the first and last sets of ten lyrics are not all sonnets, nor are all of equal length: the Ballata, the sixth lyric, has forty-four verses, the two-stanza canzone *Quantunque volte, lasso, mi rimembra* twenty-four. They are not as long as any of the three major canzoni, of course, but not so short that we are justified in grouping them with the sonnets as a so-called "short" form. Moreover, the canzoni in fact number not three but five, as Dante himself indicates. Although in his edition Karl Witte declassified *Sì lungiamente m'à tenuto Amore* as a canzone on the basis that it was broken off by news of Beatrice's death and left as a mere fragment, Dante explicitly calls both it, as well as the *Quantunque volte* lyric, canzoni.[19]

What, then, can be considered a convincing and reliable measure of the structural properties of the *Vita Nova*? Certainly those which are designed to reinforce each other, and which capture our attention even in the absence of any rigid numerological arrangement of either prose *paragrafi* or the lyrics themselves. Since the interweaving of the prophetic "voice" against the chronological sequence of events is paramount to an understanding of Dante's amatory experience, the three *visioni* and four *ymaginationi* (or *fantasie*) would seem deserving of serious attention as structural markers. Here I would argue that their total number is less important than the fact that two of the seven occur back-to-back at the lyric center of the work. In the first vision (*ymaginazione*), recounted in the canzone *Donna pietosa e di novella etate*, Dante envisions the announcement of his own and Beatrice's death followed by the delirious spectacle of a deceased Beatrice lying inert on her deathbed (*VN* 14). In the second (also an *ymaginazione*), recounted in a sonnet, Dante observes Beatrice alive and well, strolling along a street in Florence accompanied by Giovanna, the beloved of his best friend and poet, Guido Cavalcanti. The shift in emotional register from one vision to the other is remarkably sudden, even shocking, and, like so much else in this work, bizarre: Dante seems to recover from his nightmare almost too quickly and too easily. But the sense of paradox created by the near conflation of these two visions is exactly what Dante, I believe, wants us to take note of. Together the two visions express the central paradox of Christian dogma, the death and resurrection

---

[19] *La Vita nuova di Dante Alighieri*, ed. Karl Witte (Leipzig: F.A. Brockhaus, 1876).

of Christ. Dante's prophetic subconscious conveys not only the double role of Beatrice, but his own *de profundis* as well. It is significant that this experience occurs at what almost all critics agree is the true center of the work, even aside from any consideration of numerically definable narrative parts or location of lyrics. The topos of descent into the underworld, or a metaphorical descent such as a meditation on the theme of death, or a visitation with dead souls to acquire special knowledge about the future, is an event traditionally placed at the center of a literary work, because of its potential to symbolize and thereby underscore the protagonist's central ruling experience, the turning point in a series of experiences, the defining moment of one's destiny. Dante was well aware of its importance, of course, for Aeneas' visit to the underworld in the central book of the *Aeneid* was already etched in his memory.

Dante's inspiration, of course, derives not from the epic tradition of nation-building, but from the culture of Christian theology, with its stress on ritualistic themes such as prophetic destiny, personal crisis, and individual lamentation. Despite the presence of many features of the liturgy of mourning which he finds in this model, Dante's *de profundis* motif derives generally from the Old Testament section of poetic works called the Writings (*Kethuvim*). For the Christian tradition—which is to say, for the realm of the New Testament—the most important books were Psalms, Proverbs, Job, Lamentations, the Song of Songs, and Daniel.[20] But of these, only in the book of Daniel do we find a broad range of significant thematic correspondences with the *Vita Nova*, even in spite of the absence of any specific citation or verbal echo of the book. The book of Daniel, in fact, is unique for containing the only apocalyptic vision in the Hebrew Bible. Its hero Daniel, renowned for his wisdom and piety, becomes a seer and interpreter of prophetic dreams. Like Dante, he is an exile from his homeland, and although Dante in the *Vita Nova* is an exile from Beatrice and not, as will later be the case, from Florence, he in fact explicitly characterizes his loss of Beatrice by her death as an exilic experience: "*Quomodo sedet sola civitas plena populo! Facta est quasi vidua domina gentium*" (*VN* 19.1). These words, borrowed from the opening of Jeremiah's Lamentations and recited in the Tenebrae rite of Holy Week, portray Florence as bereft of the miracle of Beatrice and the beginning of the poet's exile from her earthly presence, just as for the Hebrews they solemnize the destruction of Jerusalem in 586 BCE as the paramount event in Jewish history.[21] The

---

[20] Martinez, "Mourning Beatrice," has mapped out how the book of Lamentations serves as a principal literary model for the *Vita Nova*, convincingly showing how the *libello*'s many "plaintive passages" allude to Jeremiah's text. Especially important is his observation that the first and third full canzoni share the topos of lament, an aspect that complements their sibling relationship: Dante speaks of the first as "figliuola d'amore" and the third as "figliuola di tristizia" (14).

[21] Citing Daniel Grossberg in his introduction to the Book of Lamentations in the *Jewish Study Bible*, ed. Adele Berlin and Marc Zvi Brettler (New York: Oxford University

book of Daniel for its part ends with an eschatological vision of the end of history and the prophecy of the resurrection of the individual self. It is no wonder that this book became a fundamental source for Christian doctrine. These correspondences make Daniel an alter ego for Dante, not only at the time he was writing the *Vita Nova* but throughout his life. Dante could no doubt even take special delight in sharing with Daniel the first three letters of his name. But for his *libello*, the major connection would have been the experience of *de profundis*, of disaster averted on the basis of fidelity to and reliance on a divinity who provides the gift of resurrection.[22] Significantly, the *de profundis* episode appears at the very center in each work and depicts the theme of descent and return. In Daniel, the sixth and seventh chapters define the center of twelve and divide the whole into two symmetrically balanced sections, each articulating a separate thematic axis. The first group relates six court legends, including the story of Daniel's interpretation of Nebuchadnezzar's madness and culminating in Daniel's being cast into a pit with lions; the second, Daniel's four prophetic dreams, the last of which heralds the resurrection of the good souls. The very center, in chapter six, presents Daniel's miraculous escape from the pit and what seemed certain death, an event that will be interpreted allegorically by Christian theologians as a prefiguration of Christ's death on the cross and descent into Hell before his resurrection to everlasting life. In the *Vita Nova*, the parallel central event comprises Dante's hallucinatory vision of his own death and descent as a prelude to the envisioned death of Beatrice. Previous commentary on this *ymaginatione* has identified explicit allusions to the New Testament, in particular Matthew 27:45–52 (the ninth hour, the sky's darkening, the earthquake, the resurrection) and Luke 23:44–45 (the ninth hour, the darkened sky). Beatrice's ascent into heaven (*VN* 14.7) is seen to echo a set of biblical moments: the image of her as *una nebuletta bianchissima* ("et cum haec dixisset videntibus illis elevatus est et nubes suscepit eum ab oculis eorum," Acts 1:9) accompanied by a host of angels ("cum angelo multitudo militiae caelestis laudantium Deum," Luke 2:13–15) who cry out "Osanna in excelsis!", words that allude to the welcoming of Christ's into the city of Jerusalem (Mark 11:10 and elsewhere). Yet the book of Daniel adds something missing from all these passages, the connection between two figures sharing numerous attributes (Dante and Daniel), and the *de profundis* topos as the central narrative moment and pivotal experience of each protagonist followed by rebirth and

---

Press, 2004): "Lamentations is a form of mourning for a destruction that was to become a linchpin in Jewish history and Jewish religious thought. More than that, [it] eternalizes the destruction, thereby helping to make it a central event in the Jewish memory.... [It] is 'the eternal lament for all Jewish catastrophes, past, present, and future'" (1587).

[22] For perceptive remarks on Dante's shared identity with Daniel as prophet and his vision of the soul's resurrection, see Anna Chiavacci Leonardi, "'Le bianche stole': Il tema della resurrezione nel Paradiso," in *Dante e la bibbia*, ed. Giovanni Barblan (Florence: Olschki, 1988), 249–71, esp. 255–56.

promise of salvation under the aegis of God's angel ("Deus meus misit angelum suum et conclusit ora leonum," Daniel 6:22). The angel rescues Daniel and closes the mouths of the lions, as Beatrice, an angel by Dante's own definition, rescues Dante from despair over her envisioned death. She comes again, in the guise of Christ preceded by the figure of St. John, symbolizing the promise of resurrection, the promise that when her death on earth ultimately occurs Dante will not have lost her: her new life will become his new life.

Critics have of course been aware for some time that Dante fashions Beatrice as a Christ figure and that the second canzone plays a major role in establishing the "analogy of proportion" between the two figures, to use Singleton's terminology.[23] What I am suggesting here is that the book of Daniel supplied Dante in part with formal conceptions and thematic connections that became prototypes for structuring his own autobiographical narrative, the most important being the idea of a transformative central event. The idea of centrality, a point of maximal emotional tension, of death, even metaphorical death, at the midmost point of a work, does not derive from the standard repertoire of biblical citations (Matthew 27:45–51 and Luke 23:44–45). Vergil's use of the topos in the *Aeneid* 6 — Aeneas' descent to the underworld — is, while possible, an unlikely source. Dante's focus is on the Bible throughout the *Vita Nova*, not on epic struggle or nation building, but on the topos of lamentation, as Martinez has shown. Surely the book of Lamentations as well has contributed to Dante's notion of a structural center, for it too centralizes the *de profundis* moment of despair of the Hebrew people over the destruction of Jerusalem in 586 BCE in the first-person lament of an individual survivor forced into exile. Precisely in the middle chapter, the third of five, the narrator's sense of abandonment by God reaches its greatest degree of urgency:

> lapsa est in lacu vita mea et posuerunt lapidem super me
> inundaverunt aquae super caput meum dixi perii
> invocavi nomen tuum Domine de lacis novissimis.[24]

---

[23] Charles S. Singleton, *An Essay on the Vita Nuova* (Cambridge, MA: Harvard University Press, 1949), 114. The advantage of using the word "proportion" escapes me, since between the human and divine, as Dante says, there is no proportionality: "da lo mortale a lo immortale nulla sia proporzione" (*Convivio* 2.8.13). To say that Beatrice and Christ share the same identity is not to say they are the same person or being. The theological notion of shared human identity with Christ is explicit in Christian doctrine: He is the model to imitate, "the way and the truth and the life" (John 14:6), consubstantial with us as well as with God. Since the human is meant to reflect the divine, the idea of Beatrice reflecting Christ is simply an instance of theological ontology, and her instance, in Dante's view, an example of supreme correspondence. Her likeness to Christ is not so much "proportional" as it is conceptual, likeness not in degree but in conceptual nature.

[24] "They have ended my life in a pit / And cast stones at me. / Waters flowed over my head; / I said: I am lost! / I have called on Your name, O Lord, / From the depths of

Moreover, the book makes use of the topos of descent and return as elegiac lament yields, in the closing lines of chapter five, to pleas for a return to Jerusalem through divine favor and for Jerusalem herself to turn once again to God. In the Christian liturgical use each Lamentations lection ends with "Jerusalem, Jerusalem, convertere ad Dominum Deum tuum."

The two texts, of course, reveal no parallels between specific events or literary content, only analogous thematic motifs and narrative structures. The analogy between the book of Daniel and Dante's *libello* is, however, stronger, in my view, than that between it and Lamentations. When Dante comes to write the *Commedia* he will link the same *de profundis* topos to a crisis at a midpoint, only in this instance it will occur solely to designate the middle of the protagonist's life, "nel mezzo del cammin," not the midpoint in the narrative text. Only the *Vita Nova* fuses the crisis with the text's middle, elevating its significance above any other part of the amatory experience he records there. Its paramount importance rests in the envisioned double death of both beloved and lover, a unique event in the narrative. Moreover, together with the poet's day vision (*ymaginatione*) of Giovanna walking before Beatrice, which occurs in the very next *paragrafo*, it marks the center panel of two of his four revelations of Beatrice: the first occurs when Dante encounters his beloved a second time eighteen years after having first seen her (*VN* 1.12–19), and the last when, recovering his "Ragione" and overcoming the beguiling compassion of the *donna pietosa*, Beatrice returns to his mind in an image that recalls exactly the moment when he first saw her, dressed "con quelle vestimenta sanguigne" as a "giovane in simile etade in quale prima la vidi" (*VN* 28.1). The spacing between the first vision and the middle two is roughly the same as that between the middle and the final vision: 1, 14 || 15, 28. In fact, it may be better to speak of the movement from 1 to 14 as framing the elegiac lament of losing Beatrice to death, or the descent topos, and that from 15 to 28 as framing the theme of recovery and redemption. While each movement spans events clearly at odds with its larger thematics, the character and eventual result of each movement are epitomized by the second of the paired visions (*paragrafi* 1→14, 15→28). The *mirabile visione* of the last *paragrafo* (31) should be omitted from the group of Beatrice visions because its contents remain a mystery: we are not told how or even if Beatrice appears in that vision, only that it motivated him to defer speaking of her again until "io potessi più degnamente tractare di lei" (*VN* 31.1). Likewise, the other two *ymagination[i]* (*paragrafi* 4 and 5) concern the figure of Amore as subject, with Beatrice being entirely absent. With the *ymaginatione* in paragraph 28, we have come, as it were, full circle: we are back to Beatrice, as in the beginning, and from this point to the end that is not an end, there is no interruption of the protagonist's progress to achieve the greatest possible unity with Beatrice, which is recorded in the last lyric and serves as

---

the Pit" (Lamentations 3:53–55). The text is taken from the Tanakh translation in *The Jewish Study Bible*.

a completion of the heavenward trajectory mapped out in the first sonnet. Only here it is Dante who ascends to heaven, in spirit. If the narrative is made incomplete by the advent of a new and unrevealed vision, we can say at least that the last lyric *Oltre la spera* carries an aura of finality, by mimicking the neo-Platonic paradigm of the soul's return to its origin, by reaching the outer boundary of the universe, of presenting that beyond which there can be nothing further.

To speak of numerological patterns in the *Vita Nova* is to argue by degrees of plausibility. Some connections, in the last analysis, are more likely, more convincing than others, despite a wealth of suggestive, near-perfect correspondences. Perhaps "close enough" was an acceptable criterion for medieval thinkers employing the calculus of number symbolism. Perhaps, despite the formal heterogeneity of the "lesser" lyrics surrounding the three so-called "major" canzoni that carve out a center, the arrangement of lyrics first devised by Charles Eliot Norton remains convincing, at least "to a degree." Perhaps to "a lesser degree" regarding Giovanni Federzoni's (or the pseudo-Singleton) schema of ones and nines, and likewise Guglielmo Gorni's prose and lyric patterns, if simply because they are far more complex, hypothetical, and in some respects incompatible. Finally, to "some degree" regarding how many prose *paragrafi* may be said to exist: 43 (Torri), 42 (Barbi), 30 (Cervigni), or 31 (Gorni), or none.

In the end, any numbering must remain an imperfect index to the text's narrative structure. To be precise, we cannot truly speak of numbering if only because, to reiterate, there are no numbers! No written numerical indications for *either* the lyrics or the prose *paragrafi* exist. Whatever calculation is arrived at results from a reader's critical judgment of what constitutes a narrative segment or moment. The device of temporal incipits ("apresso ciò," "poi che," "avvenne poi") to begin many *paragrafi*, used at times in imitation of biblical incipits, is not systematically applied and, what is more important, characterizes Barbi's *paragrafi* as much as it does Gorni's. It does not, in other words, serve to underpin an argument in favor of any one particular structural schema over another.[25] I would argue that the most important notion of structure we should endorse is one that derives from the placement of the most significant events in the poet's amatory life, namely the phases of completed experience that define his continually changing relationship with Beatrice, the salient moments marked by a manifestation of symbolic signs or characterized by mythic, semi-liturgical, or pseudo-supernatural occurrences. Among these the paramount moment in the narrative continuum is its central event, the protagonist's *de profundis* experience, which announces the *Vita Nova*'s main theme of metaphoric death and resurrection, which occupies the central lyric component and its description in the preceding

---

[25] See Maria Corti, *Percorsi dell'invenzione: Il linguaggio poetico e Dante* (Turin: Einaudi, 1993), 41; G. Gorni, "'Paragrafi' e titolo della *Vita Nova*," in *Dante prima della Commedia* (Florence: Cadmo, 2001), 111–32; and, most recently, Carrai, *Dante elegiaco*, 54–56.

prose narrative. This is an approximate prose center and the actual lyric center. There is no need to count *paragrafi*, no need for there to be an exact numerically-defined center. The ideal formal presentation of the *Vita Nova* would be one that leaves out numbering and which least shows the presence of an editor's intervention. In this regard, Cervigni's text comes closer to the ideal than does Gorni's. But while suppressing paragraph numbering, Cervigni retains, in his edition, the division of the prose into paragraphs by supplying large capital initials for the initial word of a temporal expression. In the absence of a holograph, "paragraph divisions must be determined on some justifiable basis consistent not with extant manuscripts . . . but with the manuscript culture itself."[26] But must they? That is, must they be determined at all? Every *Vita Nova* that is not the holograph is only a necessarily imperfect copy and, consequently, an edition that reflects a concept of the image of the original text in the mind of a representer, that is, an editor. Perhaps, then, the simpler the better: no numbers, no large or colored initials, just the prosimetric text itself, prose followed by poem followed by the prose describing the poem's divisions, followed by prose, and so on. The real structure of this work is created by its events, the experiences that the poet relates sequentially, the nature, tenor, and symbolic significance of its episodes. The oneiric, mystical, and phenomenological quality of the narrative's moments, moreover, resists the very idea of an imposed formalism of the kind that a division into chapters or "paragraphs" would create. Any reflection on questions of numerology can pertain only to the lyrics and their arrangement, which, ironically, although perhaps fittingly, is where consideration of the *Vita Nova*'s formal structure first began.

---

[26] Cervigni and Vasta, *Vita Nuova*, 21.

Dream and Vision in Dante's *Vita Nova*

Ernesto Livorni

Dante's *Vita Nova* opens and ends with the distinctive marks of dream and vision, as though the entire narration were enclosed within these two terms. In chapter III (**1**) the young poet narrates the vision of Beatrice in the arms of Love as it appeared in a dream of his, whereas in the prose of chapter XLII, 1 (**31, 1**) he alerts the reader of "una mirabile visione, nella quale io vidi cose che mi fecero proporre di non dire più di questa benedecta infino a tanto che io potessi più degnamente tractare di lei" ("a miraculous vision in which I saw things that made me resolve to say no more about this blessèd one until I would be capable of writing about her in a nobler way"). The passage has often been interpreted as alluding to the writing of the *Divine Comedy*.[1] The *Vita Nova* cannot be ascribed to the

---

[1] All quotations are from Dante Alighieri, *Vita Nova*, ed. Guglielmo Gorni (Turin: Giulio Einaudi Editore, 1996); as is known, moving away from Barbi's 1907 critical edition of the *Vita Nova*, Gorni adopts a chapter division that aims at returning the text to its original order: see G. Gorni, "Paragrafi e simmetrie del testo" and "'Divisioni' e altri tecnicismi," sections in "La *Vita Nova* nell'opera di Dante," in *Vita Nova*, xxi–xxvii, xxvii–xxix. See also idem, "Saggio di lettura paragrafo per paragrafo" and "Nota al testo," in *Vita Nova*, 241–79, 287–349 (see the paper by Lansing in this volume). Quotations are given according to the Barbi division, followed by the Gorni division in bold numbers for the chapters. The English translation, unless otherwise specified, is from Mark Musa, *Dante's Vita Nuova: A Translation and an Essay*, 2nd ed. (Bloomington: Indiana University Press, 1973). The critical debate about the ending of the *Vita Nuova* is uncertain regarding the meaning to attribute to chapter XLII: see Maria Corti, "Quel rompicapo del finale della *Vita Nuova*," which is the sixth and last section of "L'amoroso uso di sapienza' nel *Convivio*," in *La felicità mentale: Nuove prospettive per Cavalcanti e Dante* (Turin: Giulio Einaudi Editore, 1983), 146–55; now in eadem, *Scritti su Cavalcanti e Dante: La felicità mentale: Percorsi dell'invenzione e altri saggi* (Turin: Giulio Einaudi Editore, 2003), 167–75; Roberto Leporatti, "'Io spero di dicer di lei quello che mai non fue detto d'alcuna' (V. N., XLII, 2): la *Vita Nuova* come *retractatio* della poesia giovanile di Dante in funzione della *Commedia*," in *La Gloriosa Donna de la Mente: A Commentary on the* Vita Nuova, ed. Vincent R. Moleta (Florence: Leo S. Olschki Editore, 1994), 249–91; Mario Marti, "Vita e morte della presunta doppia redazione della *Vita Nuova*," in *Studi in onore di Alfredo Schiaffini*, 2 vols., spec. no. of *Rivista di Cultura Classica e Medievale* 7 (1965): 2: 657–69;

tradition of the dream vision, a tradition that spans at least from Cicero's *Somnium Scipionis* to Boethius' *De Consolatione Philosophiae* and that will continue after Dante at least with Petrarch's *Trionfi* and Chaucer's *The House of Fame*.[2]

The *Vita Nova* does share with the dream vision the tension between two dimensions: the oneiric one of the dream and the apocalyptic one of the vision; the dream is understood as the narrative event, whereas the vision pertains to the realm of revelation. Thus the *Vita Nova* unfolds this tension and moves forward from the narrative event of the dream to the open-endedness of the vision. The dream as a narrative element presents at least the following characteristics: it is a message from the divinity, and as such it is an enigma that must be resolved and understood. In this respect, the first sonnet of the *Vita Nova* reflects Dante's attention to this tradition: the first dream Dante recounts in the *Vita Nova* presents a third character, besides Dante's self and his beloved: Love. Furthermore, it is so enigmatic that Dante first has to write a sonnet to make sense of the dream, and then he asks for interpretative support from his fellow poets. Thus, after the three chapters making the "proemio" and Dante's first two encounters with Beatrice, the *prosimetrum* of the "libello" ("little book") allows the first sonnet, "A ciascun'alma presa e gentil core" ("To every captive soul and loving heart") (III, 10–12: **1**, 21–23), to recount Dante's dream of Beatrice sleeping in the arms of Love, who wakes her up and forces her to eat Dante's heart. It is a self-enclosed

---

Bruno Nardi, "Dalla prima alla seconda *Vita Nuova*" and "Le figurazioni allegoriche e l'allegoria della 'donna gentile,'" in idem, *Nel mondo di Dante* (Rome: Edizioni di Storia e Letteratura, 1944), 1–20, 21–40; Luigi Pietrobono, "La *Vita Nuova*" and "Il rifacimento della *Vita Nuova* e le due fasi del pensiero dantesco," in idem, *Saggi danteschi* (Rome: Signorelli, 1936; repr. Turin: SEI, 1954), 1–24, 25–98; "Realtà e identità nella *Vita Nova*" and "Intorno alla data delle opere minori," in idem, *Nuovi saggi danteschi* (Turin: SEI, 1954), 1–12, 13–35.

[2] Of course, the tradition of the dream vision includes earlier and later texts than the two by Cicero and Boethius, but in those cases there are only episodes within a text rather than the entire work enclosed in the dream vision, which is indeed a situation closer to the *Vita Nova*. For an account of the tradition of the dream vision, see Carolly Erickson, *The Medieval Vision: Essays in History and Perception* (New York: Oxford University Press, 1976); Constance Hieatt, *The Realism of the Dream Vision: The Poetic Exploitation of the Dream-Experience in Chaucer and His Contemporaries* (The Hague: Mouton, 1967); Morton Kelsey, *God, Dreams, and Revelation: A Christian Interpretation of Dreams* (Minneapolis: Augsburg, 1968, rev. ed. 1974); Giuseppe Mazzotta, "Imagination and Knowledge," in idem, *Dante's Vision and the Circle of Knowledge* (Princeton: Princeton University Press, 1993), 116–34; J. Stephen Russell, "Meaningless Dreams and Meaningful Poems: The Form of the Medieval Dream Vision," *Massachusetts Studies in English* 7 (1980): 20–32; idem, *The English Dream Vision: Anatomy of a Form* (Columbus: Ohio State University Press, 1988); A. C. Spearing, *Medieval Dream-Poetry* (Cambridge: Cambridge University Press, 1978); Peter Dinzelbacher, *Vision und Visionliteratur im Mittelalter* (Stuttgart: Hiersemann, 1981).

episode, one that could make up (as it indeed does make up) a narrative of its own: the very fact that Dante sent the sonnet to his poet friends in order to understand the meaning of the dream shows that the episode may stand on its own. On the other hand, in a teleological and indeed providential understanding, the interpretation of that episode changes according to the development of the love story and the relationship the two characters have with Love. The *Vita Nova* ends with the negation of the narrative event of the first sonnet: in chapter XLII, 1 (**31**, 1) Dante claims that he has had "una mirabile visione." The circularity of such experience from vision to vision and yet the shift from dream, or to be exact dream vision, to vision is of primary importance, especially considering its crucial position at the end of the book; more importantly, it is a yet unsayable experience, so much so that Dante renounces the narrative and postpones it to a later time, thereby inevitably placing it outside of the textual specificity of the *Vita Nova*. In doing so, Dante leaves his book of youth open-ended.[3]

Dante's text, then, is distinctive in its movement from dream to its end in vision. In the dream vision tradition, in which dream and vision are one, the whole experience that is the dream vision moves towards apocalypse. Dante's text, with its postponement of closure in chapter XLII (**31**), redeems that ending with a distinctly Christian spin that opens the possibility of a yet again new life. If the title of the book refers exactly to that new life, which is "both a biological quality and a metaphor for the experience of spiritual conversion," the open ending proposes a further development of both dimensions.[4] Chapter XLII (**31**), with the promised unfolding of "a miraculous vision" hopefully destined to become a new narrative, ends one aspect of the *Vita Nova*, the biological and autobiographical one, and defers the other aspect, that of conversion: this strategy not only is powerful in rhetorical terms, but also avoids the apocalyptic risks implied in the dream vision. The apocalypse becomes the foundation of the narrative yet to come. The conversion, then, needs to take place in a further narrative: that is, the one presented in the *Divine Comedy*.

---

[3] In this respect, the *Vita Nova* falls into the pattern Giuseppe Mazzotta outlines in *Dante, Poet of the Desert: History and Allegory in the Divine Comedy* (Princeton: Princeton University Press, 1979), 8: "The structure of the poem [. . .] reflects Dante's sense of the paradox of history simultaneously closed and open-ended. [. . .] the poem is open-ended and [. . .] it is a mimetic representation of the totality of the world as well as a gloss on the book of creation." Although Mazzotta is referring to the *Divine Comedy*, later on he describes the *Vita Nova* as a text that already moves along these lines (8–9): "In this 'libello' the lover, one could infer, bent on snatching the elusive secret of the beloved, suspiciously reading the signs of love and fearful of betrayals, is the very figure of the interpreter." But see also Teodolinda Barolini, "'Cominciandomi dal principio infino a la fine' (V. N., XXIII, 15): Forging Anti-Narrative in the *Vita Nuova*," and Domenico De Robertis, "'Incipit vita nova' (V. N., I): Poetica del (ri)cominciamento," in *Gloriosa Donna*, ed. Moleta, 119–40 and 11–19 respectively.

[4] Mazzotta, *Dante, Poet of the Desert*, 39.

The visions in the *Vita Nova* have often drawn attention to their occurrence and their nature: critics have based their interpretations of Dante's "libello" according to their understanding of the visions and even to what constituted a vision in the text. There is not much agreement, however, on the specific connotations of the different dreams in which Love speaks either in Latin or in Italian. Dante considers visions only the events in chapters III (1–2, 1), XII (5), and XLII (31); of these occurrences, only the first two take place in a dream.[5] This remark carries weighty consequences for the understanding of the structure of the *Vita Nova* as well as for the claim about specific episodes that take place after chapter XII (5) and obviously before chapter XLII (31). It may be significant, of course, given Dante's fascination with a numerology openly based on the number three and its multiples, that the visions properly called so by the author are three and only three and that they take place in those specific chapters.[6]

The situation is further complicated by Dante's use of at least two more terms that tend to be assimilated, respectively, to "dream" and "vision": "fantasia" and

---

[5] Charles Singleton (*An Essay on the* Vita Nuova [Baltimore and London: Johns Hopkins University Press, 1949], 18), states that chapter XXIII as well must be considered a vision: "To deny to this vision the name of vision at the time it is narrated is simply to keep to the point of view of the protagonist who cannot yet know that it is a true vision. This is a protagonist upon whom the death of Beatrice is to break with the shock of a thing in no way expected. To call this vision a vision would be to point out its prophetic nature. [. . .] In this third vision, the death of Beatrice is actually experienced. To call it a vision would be to give away the secret so jealously kept up to now." Singleton's viewpoint is determined by the idea of structural centrality of Beatrice's death in the book; in fact, he adds (18): "The third is that vision which we observed at the outset to occupy the center of the *Vita Nuova* (chapter XXIII) and to be replete with meaning for the whole construction. That it comes on the ninth day of an illness suffered by the poet is a telling sign." While discussing the events of chapter IX, Musa repeats Dante's term and, as though the critic meant to highlight a somewhat embarrassment in his own use of the term "vision," he writes: "But if we turn next to the other 'imaginazione' (IX) among the four scenes, we will find the sharpest of contrasts" (Musa, "An Essay on the *Vita Nuova*," 110). Furthermore, he first defines as "The most vivid of the visions" the events in chapters III and XXIII (106), only to feel not so comfortable later in defining as vision the "vana ymaginatione" of chapter XXIII, justifying its function merely in relation to the episode of chapter XXIV, which is in turn considered a "visione" (125): "The 'vana imaginazione' mentioned in the opening line is the prophetic vision of Beatrice's death. That a connection exists between that vision, described in terms suggesting the Crucifixion, and this one in which Beatrice is indirectly compared to Christ, is obvious. In fact, the lover might not have been capable of having this last vision of Love until after having experienced the one prophetic of her death; this is surely suggested by the words of Love himself that describe the significance of the name of Beatrice's companion, Primavera."

[6] Of course, the numerology of the number three works only according to the chapter division in the Barbi edition: it is not validated according to the Gorni edition. See the paper by Lansing in this volume.

"ymaginatione." The most significant instance of Dante's desire to reach a closure in the little book is first marked by what he calls "una forte ymaginatione" (chapter XXXIX: 28), in which Beatrice appears to him in the same garments she wore that first time he saw her at the age of nine.[7] Finally, the term "apparimento" ("appearance") (III, 1: **1**, 12) completes an already intricate set of references that further enrich the semantic field in which dream and vision play opposite and complementary roles.

This is the overall sequence of occurrences of the several episodes: Dante describes as "apparimento" the first encounter with Beatrice as it takes place in chapter II, 2–3; after the second encounter with her, he has a "visione" in a dream (III, 3–7: **1**, 14–18), which is followed by a second dream vision (XII, 2–9: **5**, 9–16). If the third and last vision is announced, although not revealed in the narration, in chapter XLII, 1–2 (**31**, 1–2), the narration itself opens the spectrum of possibilities through the alternating dimensions of "fantasia" (XVI: 9; XXIII: 14) and "ymaginatione" (II, 7: **1**, 8; IX, 3, 7: **4**, 3–6; XXIII-XXIV: 14–15, XXXIX: 28). To be sure, "fantasia" is a term Dante employs only in a couple of chapters, whereas "ymaginatione" is much more pervasive. There is a standing disagreement among the critics about the substantially identical experience that "ymaginatione" and "visione" might be. Singleton, explaining that in the *Vita Nova* there are dreams and daydreams, states:[8] "There are other dreams in the *Vita Nova*. They are rather 'daydreams' and are not said to be visions, although

---

[7] Robert Pogue Harrison ("Approaching the *Vita nuova*," in *The Cambridge Companion to Dante*, ed. Rachel Jakoff [Cambridge: Cambridge University Press, 1993], 37) summarizes by saying that "Dante tells us that one day he had a vision of Beatrice in which she appeared to him in the guise in which he had seen her for the first time, at nine years of age, and that this image was overwhelming [. . .]." The translation by Musa also employs the term "vision" to describe a situation that Dante does not necessarily consider such.

[8] Singleton, "The Death of Beatrice," in *An Essay on the* Vita Nuova, 7–24: the citation is on 14. He, then, continues in the following manner, which will be relevant in the discussion (14–15):

At the end of the book we are told how a marvelous vision came to the poet in which he saw things which made him resolve to write no more of Beatrice until he could do so more worthily. No number nine occurs with this vision. But this last is the single exception. Of all the other dreams and daydreams and phantasies which come to the poet, only three are called visions. The rest are called 'imaginations', not visions. The difference is that a vision looks to the future, as an imagination does not. Moreover, the number nine occurs only with the first three (genuine) visions. And all three of these foretell the death of Beatrice. There are in the *Vita Nuova*, thus, four visions proper. But it seems more significant to see them as three visions plus one. The underscoring of the number nine which occurs only with the first three helps to set those off in this way, making them three against one. In such numbers there is a special meaning. They, like the number nine, express a mystery.

a casual reader might take them for such in a quite loose sense of the word. But in the *Vita Nova* the word 'vision' is not loosely used." For Musa the visions are in chapters III (**1**), IX (**4**), XII (**5**), and XXIV (**15**), whereas the vision of chapter XLII (**31**) is never mentioned.[9] Cervigni, on the other hand, separates the "ymaginatione" occurring in chapters IX (**4**), XXIV (**15**) (which he also defines as "apparimento"), and XXXIX (**28**), but he gives a pervasive role to the "apparimento" in the first part of the *Vita Nova*, until chapter XXIV (**15**); furthermore, he distinguishes between the properly called dream in chapter XII and the "delirious dream" in chapter XXIII (**14**), finally recognizing the vision, or rather a "higher vision," in the sonnet and in the prose, respectively, of the last two chapters, XLI-XLII (**30**–**31**).[10]

The temptation to yoke the two terms "fantasia" and "ymaginatione" to dream and vision is strong, especially in light of the important event that the vision is; yet, this temptation ought to be resisted and ultimately refused. Dante himself in chapter XIII, 4 (**6**, **4**), as he takes into consideration the four "pensamenti" ("thoughts") that busy his life, refers to a Latin phrase that has become proverbial: "lo nome d'Amore è sì dolce a udire, che impossibile mi pare che la sua propria operatione sia nelle più cose altro che dolce, con ciò sia cosa che li nomi seguitino le nominate cose, sì come è scripto: 'Nomina sunt consequentia rerum'" ("the name of Love is so sweet to hear that it seems impossible to me that the effect itself should be in most things other than sweet, since, as has often been said, names are the consequences of the things they name: *Nomina sunt consequentia rerum*" [Justinian, *Inst.* 2.7.3]). It is a sentence that Dante exploits several times: suffice it to say that Beatrice "fu chiamata da molti Beatrice li quali non sapeano che si chiamare" ("was called Beatrice even by those who did not know what her name was") (II, 1: **1**, **2**) and that the name of the "donna di questo primo mio amico" ("lady of my best friend") Cavalcanti "era Giovanna, salvo che per la sua bieltade, secondo che altri crede, imposto l'era nome Primavera" ("was Giovanna, but because of her beauty (as many believed) she had been given the

---

See also Jerome Mazzaro, "The *Vita Nuova* and the 'New' Poet," in idem, *The Figure of Dante: An Essay on the* Vita Nuova (Princeton: Princeton University Press, 1981), 3–26.

[9] Musa, "An Essay on the *Vita Nuova*," esp. 106–27.

[10] Dino Cervigni, *Dante's Poetry of Dreams* (Florence: Leo S. Olschki Editore, 1986), 13–70; see the schema on 56. On the vision see at least Ignazio Baldelli, "Visione, immaginazione e fantasia nella *Vita Nuova*," in *I sogni nel Medioevo*, ed. Tullio Gregory (Rome: Edizioni dell'Ateneo, 1985), 1–10; Marcello Ciccuto, "'Era venuta ne la mente mia' (V. N., XXXIV, 7): la visione nel libello e l'immagine in Dante," in *Gloriosa Donna*, ed. Moleta, 181–93; Egidio Guidubaldi, "Per una fenomenologia della visione dantesca," *Annali dell'Istituto di Studi Danteschi* 1 (Milan: Società Editrice Vita e Pensiero, 1967), 17–154; Giuseppe Mazzotta, "Language and Vision," in *Dante's Vision and the Circle of Knowledge*, 154–73.

name of Primavera, meaning Spring, and so she came to be called") (XXIV, 3: 15, 3). One is tempted to say that, by the same token, different names are a consequence of the difference of things, facts, situations that are under observation. In other words, different names are not necessarily synonyms, but signals of a different experience.[11]

In particular, it is helpful to consider that in chapters XXXIX, 1 (28, 1) and XLII, 1 (31, 1) there are an "ymaginatione" and a "visione," respectively; yet, the last "visione" is not depicted in the book, but it alludes to a future text that does not yet exist: that "visione" seems to be the theological leap after which literature is possible, whereas the "ymaginatione" is the very texture that clothes the literary text. It is not by chance that the two chapters in question propose two possible endings of the *Vita Nova*: Dante ends the little book of his life twice, so to speak, first with "una forte ymaginatione in me, che mi parve vedere questa gloriosa Beatrice con quelle vestimenta sanguigne co le quali apparve prima a li occhi miei" ("a powerful vision, in which I seemed to see that glorious Beatrice clothed in those crimson garments with which she first appeared to my eyes"), then with "una mirabile visione" ("a miraculous vision").

The episodes that Dante himself properly addresses with the term "visione" may be placed in the realm of theology, to which Dante's text looks forward; whereas the other episodes that generally Dante calls with the term "ymaginatione" fall in the realm of literature.[12] In this sense, "ymaginatione" appears to be an experience that is still fully wrapped in rhetorical discourse, whereas the "visione" alludes to a metaphysical discourse that Dante, as he states at least twice in the text, does not feel he is ready to utter yet. In doing so, he seems loosely to employ categories that may be traced back to Macrobius' *Commentarii* on Cicero's *Somnium Scipionis*,

---

[11] After all, an author such as Isidore of Seville in his *Etymologiae* draws very different settings for these terms: "Epilepsia autem in phantasia fit; melancholia in ratione; mania in memoria" ("De Chronicis Morbis," 4. 7. 9); "Nona species definitionis est, quam Graeci *katà ùpotúposin*, Latini per quandam imaginationem dicunt, ut: 'Aeneas est Veneris et Anchisae filius.'" ("De Divisione Definitionum ex Marii Victorini Libro Abbreviata," 2. 29. 10); "Lethargia a somno vocata. Est enim oppressio cerebri cum oblivione et somno iugi, veluti stertentis" ("De Acutis Morbis," 4. 6. 5); "Serum vocatum a clausis seris, quando iam nox venit, ut unusquisque somno tutior sit" ("De Diebus," 5. 30. 17); "Tertium genus est oppositorum habitus vel orbatio. Quod genus Cicero privationem vocat, qua ostendit aliquid quempiam habuisse, unde privatus est. Cuius species sunt tres: quarum prima est in re, secunda in loco, tertia in tempore congruo. In re, ut caecitas, visio. In loco, ut caecitatis et visionis in oculis locus est. In tempore congruo, ut infantem non dicere sine dentibus eum, cui dentes adhuc aetas parva negavit. Non enim est privatus dentibus, quos nondum habuit" ("De Oppositis," 2. 31. 6).

[12] See Giorgio Barberi Squarotti in his introduction to Dante, *Opere minori* (Turin: UTET, 1983), vol.1; now in idem, "Elevazione spirituale e affinamento poetico: introduzione alla *Vita nuova*," in *In nome di Beatrice e altre voci* (Turin: Genesi Editrice, 1989), 7–48.

to whom there are five types of dream:[13] "the enigmatic dream, in Greek *oneiros*, in Latin *somnium*; second, there is the prophetic vision, in Greek *horama*, in Latin *visio*; third, there is the oracular dream, in Greek *chrematismos*, in Latin *oraculum*; Latin *insomnium*; and last, the apparition, in Greek *phantasma*, which Cicero, when he has occasion to use the word, calls *visum*." Without setting strict correlations between Macrobius' classification and Dante's use of the terms "sogno," "visione," "ymaginatione," "fantasia," "apparimento," it is nevertheless interesting that the first three types Macrobius considers veridic ones correspond to the first four terms here listed that Dante employs, with a difficult distinction between "fantasia" and "ymaginatione." I would like to start the analysis of the passages in which Dante employs these terms by first taking into consideration the terms "fantasia" and "ymaginatione"; I will then move to the term "apparimento"; I will finally discuss the terms "sogno" and "visione."

The terms "fantasia" and "ymaginatione" have a long history in Italian and indeed in European culture at least from the Middle Ages until modernity. Although the meaning of the terms changed throughout the centuries, the dichotomy the two terms express has remained constant. For Dante himself, they undergo a quite different treatment according to the context in which they are employed and acquire a meaning that is not necessarily present in the *Vita Nova*. Thus, in the *Divine Comedy*, the poet never uses the term "ymaginatione," although there are abundant occurrences of the corresponding verb "ymaginare" and nouns "ymago" and "ymagine."[14] The term "fantasia," on the other hand, occurs a few times in the third canticle of the *Divine Comedy*.[15]

Dante highlights the strong link between "fantasia" and "ymaginatione" in the construction of chapters XXIII–XXIV (**14–15**). The two chapters are the

---

[13] Macrobius, *Commentarii in Somnium Scipionis*, 1. 3; the translation is quoted from Macrobius, *Commentary on the Dream of Scipio*, ed. and trans. William Harris Stahl (New York: Columbia University Press, 1952), 87–88. See also C. S. Lewis, *The Discarded Image* (Cambridge: Cambridge University Press, 1964), 63–66.

[14] Dante's sense of the faculty of the imagination derives from the medieval commentaries on Aristotle's *De anima*, especially 3, 427a3. For the use of the verb "imaginare," see at least *Inferno* XIV, 106; XXIII, 24; XXXI, 24; XXXIV 106; *Purgatorio* IV, 68; X, 62; XVII, 17, 43; *Paradiso* I, 89; X, 44; XIII, 1; XXXI, 137; much more frequent is Dante's use of the nouns "imago" or "imagine": see at least *Inferno* XV, 10, 83; XVII, 7; XX, 22, 123; XXIII, 26; XXV, 77; XXX, 68; *Purgatorio* IX, 142; X, 39; XVII, 7; XXV, 26; XXX, 131; *Paradiso* I, 53; II, 132; X, 44; XIII, 2; XIX, 2; XX, 76–77; XXII, 60; XXIV, 26; XXXI, 137; XXXIII, 138. Probably the closest Dante comes to the use of "ymaginatione" as he does in the *Vita Nova* is when he talks about the "imaginativa," that is, the imaginative faculty: see *Purgatorio* IX, 32; XVII, 13. Other occurrences of the term alluding to the imaginative faculty are in the following passages: *Quaestio* 82; *Convivio* II, ix, 4; III, v, 10–12; IV, vi, 4; xv, 15.

[15] For occurrences of the term "fantasia" in the *Divine Comedy*, see at least *Paradiso* X, 46; XIX, 9; XXXIII, 142. See also *Convivio* III, iv, 9–11; IV, xv, 15.

reversals of each other: one is the narration of a death experience that the poet feels is real, the other is the narration of a moment that the poet interprets allegorically.[16] Furthermore, in the experience narrated in chapter XXIII (14) there is an emphasis on the falsity and vanity of the experience, whereas real and true is the poet's voice addressing the soul of Beatrice; instead, in chapter XXIV, 2 (15, 2) the "ymaginatione d'Amore" needs no attribute to testify to the absolute truth of the experience. This ambivalent role of the two episodes is linked to the occurrence of the two terms "fantasia" and "ymaginatione" as though they were synonyms, which would explain the need to specify with the adjective the gnoseological value of the experience; the two terms may also generally refer to both the faculty of the mind and the object of that faculty. The faculties of the mind to which "fantasia" and "ymaginatione" refer are, respectively, the ability to organize the images and the ability to retain the images. According to this scheme, "ymaginatione" acts in order to retain images that then "fantasia" re-elaborates freely.

One finds confirmation of the risk of confusing the two mental activities already in chapter XVI, 1 (9, 1): while listing "quattro cose ancora sopra lo mio stato" ("four more things concerning my condition"), the poet remarks (XVI, 2: 9, 2): "La prima delle quali si è che molte volte io mi dolea quando la mia memoria movesse la fantasia ad ymaginare quale Amore mi facea" ("The first of these is that many times I suffered when my memory excited my imagination to reevoke the transformations that Love worked in me"). The "fantasia" is the faculty that triggers the process of imagination, in this particular case, with the help of memory.[17] However, in this passage the term "fantasia" connotes the faculty of the intellect rather than the outcome of that mental process.[18] In this respect, the confusion between "fantasia" and "ymaginatione," when the two terms indicate the faculty of the intellect, is a genuine one, which finds its justification also in a passage like the following in Thomas Aquinas' *Summa Theologiae* (I, 78, 4): "est

---

[16] Giuseppe Mazzotta ("The Language of Poetry in the *Vita Nuova*," *Rivista di Studi Italiani* 1 [1983]: 3–14) points out the use of "a grammatical future tense" in chapter XXIII, with death now being "the cutting edge that lays bare the precariousness of the correspondence" between words and things, and "the issue of figuration, which extends into the next chapter's discussion of metaphor" in chapter XXIV (8–9).

[17] In this sense, there is an allusion to the process of imagination in *Vita Nova* XV, 2.

[18] For further discussion of the topic, see at least E. T. H. Brann, *The World of Imagination* (London: Rowman-Littlefield, 1991); M. W. Bundy, *The Theory of Imagination in Classical and Medieval Thought* (Champaign: University of Illinois Press, 1927); G. Carchia, *Estetica ed erotica: Saggio sull'immaginazione* (Milan: Celuc, 1981); *Fantasia e immaginazione: phantasiaimaginatio*, ed. M. Fattori and M. Bianchi (Rome: Edizoni dell'Ateneo, 1988); Douglas Kelly, *Medieval Imagination: Rhetoric and the Poetry of Courtly Love* (Madison: University of Wisconsin Press, 1978); G. Watson, *Phantasia in Classical Thought* (Galway: Galway University Press, 1988).

enim phantasia sive imaginatio quasi thesaurus quidam formarum per sensum acceptarum."[19]

In chapter XXIII, 4–6 (**14**, 4–6), next to such a meaning, the term "fantasia" acquires yet another one:[20]

> [. . .] E però mi giunse uno sì forte smarrimento, che chiusi gli occhi e cominciai a travagliare come farnetica persona e a ymaginare in questo modo: che nel cominciamento de lo errare che fece la mia fantasia apparvero a me certi visi di donne scapigliate che mi diceano: "Tu pur morrai". [. . .] Così cominciando ad errare la mia fantasia, venni a quello che io non sapea ove io mi fosse; e vedere mi parea donne andare scapigliate piangendo per via, maravigliosamente triste; e pareami vedere lo sole oscurare, sì che le stelle si mostravano di colore ch'elli mi facea giudicare che piangessero; e pareami che gli uccelli volando per l'aria cadessero morti, e che fossero grandissimi terremuoti. E maravigliandomi in cotale fantasia, e paventando assai, ymaginai alcuno amico che mi venisse a dire: "Or non sai? la tua mirabile donna è partita di questo secolo." Allora cominciai a piangere molto pietosamente; e non solamente piangea nella ymaginatione, ma piangea con gli occhi, bagnandoli di vere lacrime.

Interestingly, Dante employs the term "fantasia," remarking "lo errare" of such faculty: since the start, the experience is described as a vanity, an emptying of the rational capability. When at the end of the quoted passage the term "ymaginatione" is employed, it refers to the mental location of that event, in order to stress

---

[19] Other important passages in the *Summa Theologiae* on this topic are I, 84, 7; I, 88, 1.

[20] The episode is often described as a dream, but it is not, as Dante himself specifies in XXIII, 12 (**14**, 12) ("Onde altre donne, che per la camera erano, s'accorsero di me che io piangea, per lo pianto che vedeano fare a questa; onde faccendo lei partire da me, la quale era meco di propinquissima sanguinità congiunta, elle si trassero verso me per isvegliarmi, credendo che io sognasse, e diceanmi: 'Non dormire più!', e 'Non ti sconfortare!'." "Then other ladies who were about the room became aware of my weeping because of her reaction to me. After sending away this lady, who was most closely related to me, they drew near to wake me, thinking that I was having a dream, and said to me: 'You must wake up' and 'Do not be afraid'."). The confusion is eased by the close resemblance of this situation and *Purgatorio* XVIII, 139–145, that is, the last lines of the canto describing Dante's falling into a state of sleep, which will favor the dream of the Siren in the following canto, *Purgatorio* XIX, 1–33, the second dream in that canticle: regarding this dream, see at least D. Cervigni, "'Nel Mezzo del Cammin': Demonic Interference and Divine Intervention in the Second Dream," in *Dante's Poetry of Dreams*, 117–52; Colin G. Hardie, "Purgatorio XIX: The Dream of the Siren," in *Lectura Dantis Internazionale*, ed. Vittorio Vettori (Milan: Marzorati, 1965), 217–49; Giuseppe Mazzotta, "The Dream of the Siren," in *Dante's Vision and the Circle of Knowledge*, 135–53; R. Stella, "L'expression symbolique dans les trois rêves du Purgatoire de Dante," *Revue des Etudes Italiennes* 25 (1979): 124–44.

how the act of crying is the only true situation ("bagnandoli di vere lacrime"), taking place both in the mind and in the body.

To be sure, later on and still in chapter XXIII, 8–10 (**14**, 8–10), the two terms in question are used to indicate again an experience that might resemble that of the vision, but it is again considered, no matter how "forte" ("wild"), "la erronea fantasia" ("the intensity of my hallucination"):

> [. . .] E per questo mi parea andare per vedere lo corpo nello quale era stata quella nobilissima e beata anima; e fue sì forte la erronea fantasia, che mi mostrò questa donna morta. E pareami che donne la covrissero, cioè la sua testa, con uno bianco velo; e pareami che la sua faccia avesse tanto aspetto d'umilitade, che parea che dicesse: "Io sono a vedere lo principio de la pace". In questa ymaginatione mi giunse tanta umilitade per vedere lei, che io chiamava la Morte, [. . .]. E quando io avea veduto compiere tutti li dolorosi mistieri che alle corpora de' morti s'usano di fare, mi parea tornare nella mia camera, e quivi mi parea guardare verso lo cielo; e sì forte era la mia ymaginatione, che piangendo cominciai a dire con verace boce: "Oi anima bellissima, com'è beato colui che ti vede!"

Beatrice's death is an erroneous datum of the "fantasia" that is followed by a second remark of the location of the error:[21] it is again "In questa ymaginatione," that is, in that place of the mind where the faculty of the "fantasia" has triggered the construction of a situation that does not find its truth in reality. Once again, then, the apparent synonymity of the terms "fantasia" and "ymaginatione" is dissolved when one considers the different semantic roles they play and the different activities they mark. Finally, this state is interrupted by the women in the room who start talking to him in order to take him out of that distress, until they succeed (XXIII, 13–15: **14**, 13–15): "[. . .] E parlandomi così, cessòe la forte fantasia

---

[21] To be sure, there are a few signals that allude to Beatrice's holiness: the poet opens the narration stressing the link with the number nine (XXIII, 1; **14**, 1: "Appresso ciò per pochi dì avenne che in alcuna parte della mia persona mi giunse una dolorosa infermitade, onde io continuamente sofferse per nove dì amarissima pena"; "A few days after this it happened that my body was afflicted by a painful disease which made me suffer intense anguish continuously for nine days"); the angels' words welcoming Beatrice in Heaven, which are the same as those in the Gospels (Matthew 21:9, Mark 11:10; Luke 19:38, John 12:13) welcoming Jesus Christ entering Jerusalem (XXIII, 7: "A me parea che questi angeli cantassero gloriosamente, e le parole del loro canto mi parea udire che fossero queste: 'Osanna in excelsis!'; e altro non mi parea udire." "It seemed to me that these angels were singing in glory, and the words of their song seemed to be: *Osanna in excelsis*; the rest I could not seem to hear." This reference is so important to Dante that he inserts it in the canzone "Donna pietosa e di novella etate," in this chapter XXIII, 25); Dante's own attempt at the end of his "fantasia" to address Beatrice with the words that the angel Gabriel uttered to Mary at the Annunciation included at the beginning of the Hail Mary (XXIII, 13; **14**, 13).

entro in quello puncto che io volea dicere: 'O Beatrice, benedecta sie tu!'; e già detto avea 'O Beatrice', quando riscotendomi apersi li occhi, e vidi che io era ingannato. [. . .] Onde io, essendo alquanto riconfortato, e conosciuto lo fallace ymaginare, rispuosi a lloro: 'Io vi diròe quello ch'i' òe avuto'." ("[. . .] And with these words of theirs my wild imaginings were cut off just when I was about to say: 'Oh, Beatrice, blessed art thou,' and I had already said: 'Oh, Beatrice,' when I opened my eyes with a start and realized that it had been only a dream. [. . .] Being somewhat comforted, aware that nothing was true of what I had imagined, I answered them: 'I will tell you what happened to me'.").

The experience narrated in chapter XXIII (**14**) seems at first to reach the same effect that will be achieved at the end of chapter XXXIX (**28**), where the "forte ymaginatione" ("powerful vision") takes place: in both instances, the poet composes a poem after recounting the event. The very fact that "la forte fantasia" of chapter XXIII (**14**) and the "forte ymaginatione" of chapter XXXIX (**28**) are described by the same adjective would invite a further reason for a parallel between the two episodes. Yet what Dante is experiencing in chapter XXIII (**14**) is at once false and true: it is false insofar as at the time of the experience Beatrice is alive; it is true as it is what will actually happen to Beatrice. In fact, she will die and ascend to Heaven, where she will be blessed among angels and saints, as it is predicted in the canzone manifesto "Donne ch'avete intelletto d'amore" (XIX: **10**; ll.15–46). In fact, Beatrice is destined to die in the canzone as well as in Dante's "fantasia" and "ymaginatione" in chapter XXIII (**14**), but Dante never recounts the actual death of the beloved, for reasons that he explains in chapter XXVIII (**19**).

To summarize, Dante attributes erroneous value to the experience of chapter XXIII (**14**): the mistaken wandering of "fantasia" in the "ymaginatione" is emphasized by Dante's own crying out "con verace boce" ("out loud") the beatitude of Beatrice's beholder now that she is in Heaven.[22]

Singleton includes the "vana ymaginatione" (XXIII: **14**) among the visions, although Dante never refers to this episode as a "visione." It is a vision, according to the American critic, of which Dante as character does not understand the true meaning; he adds that the function of the number nine, already highlighted

---

[22] The erroneous aspect is marked so often in the chapter, as we have seen. It is important to keep in mind that in the recounting of the event this characteristic is present since the beginning: "nel cominciamento dello errare che fece la mia fantasia," "cominciando ad errare la mia fantasia," "la erronea fantasia" (but also "la forte fantasia"), "lo fallace ymaginare." Even in the canzone the concept is repeated: "nel vano ymaginare," "Lo ymaginar fallace." Finally, at the time of the description of the "divisioni," Dante writes: "io fui levato d'una vana fantasia." As if that were not enough, at the beginning of chapter XXIV (**15**) he refers to the preceding chapter in eloquent terms: "Apresso questa vana ymaginatione"). The veracity of the voice, instead, is marked also in the canzone, but it is transferred to Beatrice who "avea seco Umiltà verace."

at the time of the first "visione" (III: **1**), and the central position within the little book of the episode of the "vana ymaginatione" of Beatrice's death would only confirm its value as "visione."[23]

The difficulty in establishing the value of the "fantasia" in chapter XXIII (**14**) as a vision is complicated by the fact that in chapter XXIV (**15**) Dante narrates (XXIV, 1–2: **15**, 1–2): "Appresso questa vana ymaginatione, avvenne uno die che sedendo io pensoso in alcuna parte, e io mi senti' cominciare un terremuoto nel cuore, così come se io fosse stato presente a questa donna. Allora dico che mi giunse una ymaginatione d'Amore: che mi parve vederlo venire da quella parte ove la mia donna stava, e pareami che lietamente mi dicesse nel cuor mio: 'Pensa di benedicere lo dì che io ti presi, però che tu lo dêi fare'." ("After this wild dream I happened one day to be sitting in a certain place deep in thought, when I felt a tremor begin in my heart, as if I were in the presence of my lady. Then a vi-

---

[23] Singleton, *An Essay on the* Vita Nuova, 18. Chapter XXIII (**14**) seems to mark the beginning of the second part of the book, the one in the sign of Beatrice's death. The second part would start with chapter XXII (**13**), where Dante recounts the death of the "genitore di tanta meraviglia quanta si vedea ch'era questa nobilissima Beatrice" ("the father of such a miraculous being as this most gracious Beatrice clearly was, [. . .]."). However, Dante himself seems to deny the hypothesis of the centrality of Beatrice's death, not only for the position assigned to that event in actuality (XXVIII, 2; **19**, 2) and for the lack of its narration, but especially for the justification that the poet offers of it:

E avegna che forse piacerebbe a presente tractare alquanto della sua partita da noi, non è lo mio intendimento di tractarne qui per tre ragioni. La prima è che ciò non è del presente proposito, se volemo guardare nel proemio che precede questo libello. La seconda si è che, posto che fosse del presente proposito, ancora non sarebbe sufficiente la mia lingua a tractare come si converrebbe di ciò. La terza si è che, posto che fosse l'uno e l'altro, non è convenevole a me tractare di ciò, per quello che tractando converrebbe essere me laudatore di me medesimo, la qual cosa è al postutto biasimevole a chi lo fa, e però lascio cotale tractato ad altro chiosatore.

The poet does not entertain the narration of his beloved's death because not only does he not want to risk praising himself by doing so, but also his language is not sufficiently apt to such a high endeavor and, after all, it is not the intent expressed in the "proemio." The second reason given by Dante returns in chapter XLII, at the time of the third and unrecalled "visione." Regarding the number nine, Dante points out in chapter XXIX, 3 (**19**, 6) its occurrence in the episode of the death of Beatrice and adds that "questo numero fue ella medesima" ("this number was she herself"): see at least Carlo Vecce, "'Ella era uno nove, cioè uno miracolo' (V. N., XXIX, 3): Il numero di Beatrice," in *Gloriosa Donna*, ed. Moleta, 161–79. After this chapter the number nine returns in the narration only in chapter XXXIX, to specify the hour when in "una forte ymaginatione" Dante sees Beatrice. Turning back to chapter XXIII, one can say that the presence of the woman dictates the presence of such a number.

sion of Love came to me, and I seemed to see him coming from that place where my lady dwelt, and he seemed to say joyously from within my heart: 'See that you bless the day that I took you captive; it is your duty to do so'."). After these words by Love, Dante witnesses first the passing by of Giovanna, Cavalcanti's beloved woman, also called Primavera, and then that of Beatrice herself. At this point, the poet receives another explanation provided by Love, who speaks in his heart and explains the allegorical meaning of the names Primavera and Giovanna.

Thus chapters XXIII-XXIV (14–15) present two situations, which are different insofar as one is considered erroneous and the other true and real; moreover, the first erroneous one seems to be so not only because Beatrice is at the time still alive, but also because it is not under the governance of Love. On the other hand, what makes the "ymaginatione d'Amore" revealing is the reality of the situation (the two women do go by the poet) and the truth about that reality revealed by Love's second utterance (XXIV, 4: 15, 4). As we saw, for the first episode there seems to be ambivalence in the terminology, as Dante oscillates between "fantasia" and "ymaginatione," marking the two terms with attributes that qualify the experience. However, there is no ambiguity in the definition of the "ymaginatione d'Amore," in which Love speaks the vulgar language and yet opens Dante's mind to a higher truth, in which the depiction of Beatrice as *figura Christi* is definitely stated: whereas Dante had been linking Beatrice since the beginning of the story to a variety of signs that indicates the metaphysical link, the number nine being the most telling of these signs, Love itself intervenes for the first time in chapter XXIV (15) to confirm the blessing of the lady. In fact, on two previous occasions, as we shall see, both in the visions narrated in chapters III (1) and XII (5), Love is either terrifying, or in dialogue with the lover, in the absence of the beloved: the former is the case of the first vision, where Love is holding Beatrice and forcing her to eat Dante's heart, whereas the latter occurs in the second vision.

To be sure, "ymaginatione" is a term that is ambiguously used already to describe what seems to be an apparition of Love to the lover. In chapter IX, 3 (4, 3) there is an instance of this: "E però lo dolcissimo signore, lo quale mi signoreggiava per la virtù della gentilissima donna, nella mia ymaginatione apparve come peregrino leggieramente vestito e di vili drappi" ("Therefore his very sweet lordship, who ruled over me through the power of that most gracious lady, took the shape in my mind of a pilgrim scantily and poorly dressed"). The prepositional phrase indicating the place where Love appeared immediately circumscribes the meaning of the term in question, which in fact seems to transform into topical the faculty to imagine, and to enclose it in a specific mental place. However, after Love has spoken to Dante, the poet concludes the episode with the following words: "E dette queste parole, disparve questa mia ymaginatione tutta subitamente per la grandissima parte che mi parve che Amore mi desse di sé; e, quasi cambiato nella vista mia, cavalcai quel giorno pensoso molto e acompagnato da molti sospiri" ("Having said these words, his image suddenly vanished from my mind, because Love had become so great a part of me, and as if transformed in my appearance, I rode on that day deep in thought, with my sighs for company") (IX, 7: **4**, 7). In this passage, it seems apparent that "ymaginatione" marks the aspect of the visualization of the lived experience, thus approaching the use of the term "visione." Yet "ymaginatione" is a term often employed with a possessive adjective (chapters II: **1**, XXIV: **15**) which stresses its extremely personal and subjective character; or it is accompanied by a demonstrative adjective (chapters IX: **4**, XXIII: **14**) which states its contingency, putting a limit on its impact; other times it is even marked by both possessive and demonstrative adjectives (chapters IX: **4**, XXIII: **14**), besides the rare occurrences in which there are no adjectives at all (chapters XXIII: **14**, XXIV: **15**). The only adjectives used with the term "ymaginatione" (chapter XXIV: "Appresso questa vana ymaginatione"; chapter XXXIX (**28**): "una forte ymaginatione") are never employed with the term "visione"; instead, as we have seen, they are used with the term "fantasia" (chapter XXIII (**14**): "la forte fantasia," "vana fantasia," "la erronea fantasia," which in this chapter is employed in the same semantic area as the adjectives "vano" and "fallace"; it is not by chance that the last two mentioned appear with "imaginare": "lo fallace imaginare" and, in the canzone "Donna pietosa e di novella etate," "nel vano imaginare" and "Lo imaginar fallace").

After the chapters just discussed, one has to wait until chapter XXXIX (**28**) to see the poet experiencing another "ymaginatione" after his interest in the "donna gentile" (XXXIX, 1: **28**, 1): "Contra questo adversario della Ragione si levòe un die, quasi nell'ora della nona, una forte ymaginatione in me, che mi parve vedere questa gloriosa Beatrice con quelle vestimenta sanguigne colle quali apparve prima agli occhi miei, e pareami giovane in simile etade in quale prima la vidi" ("One day, about the ninth hour, there arose in me against this adversary of reason a powerful vision, in which I seemed to see that glorious Beatrice clothed in those crimson garments with which she first appeared to my eyes, and she seemed young, of the same age as when I first saw her"). This chapter highlights the contradictions between the *Vita Nova* and the *Convivio*, which may be partly solved only by accepting the revision of the final chapters of the "libello":[24] in fact, this chapter represents a closure of its own because of the circularity in the text set by the "ymaginatione" here recounted. There is no further description or narration of the "ymaginatione" itself, as the reference to the time of the experience and, more importantly, to the appearance of Beatrice suffice to join this end of the story with its beginning. In fact, "quelle vestimenta sanguigne" that Beatrice wears in the "forte ymaginatione" are the same she wore at the beginning of the story. However, Beatrice is dressed in red clothes on two occasions: once when she and Dante meet for the first time (II, 3: **1**, 14: the same color "sanguigno" describes her garments) and a second time when Beatrice first

---

[24] See *Convivio* I, 1; II, 2, 12, for references to the *Vita Nova*.

appears as a vision in a dream (III, 4: **1**, 15).[25] Thus, the "forte ymaginatione" of chapter XXXIX (**28**) mediates between the first and the last vision, in chapters III (**1**) and XLII (**31**), respectively: on the one hand, it sets a returning circularity with the first vision, which justifies the silence over any further description of the "forte ymaginatione" itself; on the other, this silence prepares us for the silence covering the third and last vision. Therefore, the "forte ymaginatione" is not a vision, yet it partakes of important elements of the vision, whether they are explicit, as in the first vision, or implicit, as in the third and last.

At this point, one must look at the three visions in the *Vita Nova*, as they occur in chapters III (**1**), XII (**5**) and XLII (**31**). In doing so, we will touch upon "l'apparimento" as well, in its only occurrence in chapter III, although referring to the narration of chapter II (**1**). At the beginning of chapter III (**1**), Dante refers to the first encounter with Beatrice narrated in detail in chapter II (**1**); the reference to the first encounter is important to him also to calculate the time elapsed between the first and the second encounter (III, 1: **1**, 12):

> Poi che fuoro passati tanti dì che apuncto erano compiuti li nove anni appresso l'apparimento soprascripto di questa gentilissima, nell'ultimo di questi dì avenne che questa mirabile donna apparve a me vestita di colore bianchissimo, in mezzo di due gentili donne, le quali erano di più lunga etade; e passando per una via, volse gli occhi verso quella parte ov'io era molto pauroso, e per la sua ineffabile cortesia, la quale è oggi meritata nel grande secolo, mi salutòe virtuosamente tanto, che me parve allora vedere tutti li termini della beatitudine.

The effects of Love over the self that are shown are somewhat parallel to the events narrated in chapter II (**1**), with the important variants of the behavior of the lover and the apparition of Love to him. Given the iterative nature of the second encounter, we may infer that that episode is also an "apparimento." The two encounters, in fact, share some main features: the chronological calculation of the times in the respective lives of Dante and Beatrice, the description of the garments and especially the colors that the lady wears. As in chapter III, 1 (**1, 12**), so in chapter II, 2–3 (**1, 3–4**) Dante starts heavily employing the significant

---

[25] One must note that in *Purgatorio* XXX, 31–33, Beatrice appears again dressed in by now familiar colors: "sovra candido vel cinta d'uliva / donna m'apparve, sotto verde manto / vestita di color di fiamma viva" ("a woman showed herself to me; above / a white veil, she was crowned with olive boughs; / her cape was green; her dress beneath, flamered"). Toward the end of the same canto (133–135), Beatrice seems to allude to moments of *Vita Nova* such as the one in chapter XXXIX: "Né l'impetrare ispirazione mi valse, / con le quali e in sogno e altrimenti / lo rivocai: sì poco a lui ne calse!" ("Nor did the inspirations I received — / with which, in dream and otherwise, I called / him back — help me; he paid so little heed!"). Quotations of the *Divine Comedy* are from the verse translation with an introduction by Allen Mandelbaum (New York: Bantam Books, 1982).

verb "apparve," as he does throughout the narration:[26] "Ella era già in questa vita stata tanto, che nel suo tempo lo Cielo Stellato era mosso verso la parte d'oriente delle dodici parti l'una d'un grado, sì che quasi dal principio del suo anno nono apparve a me, e io la vidi quasi dalla fine del mio nono. Apparve vestita di nobilissimo colore umile e onesto sanguigno, cinta e ornata alla guisa che alla sua giovanissima etade si convenia" ("She had been in this life long enough for the heaven of the fixed stars to be able to move a twelfth of a degree to the East in her time; that is, she appeared to me at about the beginning of her ninth year, and I first saw her near the end of my ninth year. She appeared dressed in the most patrician of colors, a subdued and decorous crimson, her robe bound round and adorned in a style suitable to her years"). Whereas the second encounter adds the important element of Beatrice's greeting, the first one focuses on the dramatic effects that "l'apparimento" causes in the beholder (II, 4–8: 1, 5–8):[27]

> [. . .] In quel puncto dico veracemente che lo spirito della vita, lo quale dimora nella secretissima camera del cuore, cominciò a tremare sì fortemente, che apparia nelli menomi polsi orribilmente; e tremando disse queste parole: 'Ecce deus fortior me, qui veniens dominabitur michi!'. In quel puncto lo spirito animale, lo quale dimora nell'alta camera nella quale tutti li spiriti sensitivi portano le loro perceptioni, si cominciò a maravigliare molto, e parlando spetialmente alli spiriti del viso, disse queste parole: 'Apparuit iam beatitudo vestra'. In quel puncto lo spirito naturale, lo quale dimora in quella parte ove si ministra lo nutrimento nostro, cominciò a piangere, e piangendo disse queste parole: 'Heu, miser, quia frequenter impeditus ero deinceps!'. D'allora innanzi, dico che Amore segnoreggiò la mia anima, la quale fu sì tosto a·llui disponsata, e cominciò a prendere sopra me tanta sicurtade e tanta signoria per la virtù che li dava la mia ymaginatione, che me convenia fare tutti li suoi piaceri compiutamente. [. . .]

The passage is built according to a ritualistic repetition that highlights the pervasive effect of the invasion of the self by Love, as the last quoted sentence remarks at the peak of the climax. For the time being, one must also notice the exchange between Love, which has power over the self, and imagination, which belongs to the self and yet is what gives power to Love itself. There is no presence of Love otherwise stated, that is, Love does not appear to the lover; in fact, the specified

---

[26] On the use of this verb, see at least Gianfranco Contini, "Esercizio d'interpretazione sopra un sonetto di Dante," in idem, *Un'idea di Dante* (Turin: Einaudi, 1970), 21–31.

[27] On this first dream vision, see at least Michele Scherillo, "La prima visione," in Dante, *La Vita nuova e il Canzoniere*, ed. Michele Scherillo, 3rd rev. ed. (Milan: Ulrico Hoepli Editore, 1930), 458–77; Robert Pogue Harrison, "Dante's Dream," in idem, *The Body of Beatrice* (Baltimore and London: The Johns Hopkins University Press, 1988), 17–30.

role of imagination suggests a power of Love that after all still answers to the higher power of the imagination of the self. Instead, there is the introduction of a dynamics that will appear three times in the little book and that involves the spirits of sight. In fact, in chapter XI, 1–2 (5, 4–5), while Dante is describing the benefic effects of Beatrice's greeting on him, he writes:

> Dico che quando ella apparia da parte alcuna, per la speranza della mirabile salute nullo nemico mi rimanea, anzi mi giugnea una fiamma di caritade, la quale mi facea perdonare a chiunque m'avesse offeso. E chi allora m'avesse domandato di cosa alcuna, la mia risponsione sarebbe stata solamente 'Amore', con viso vestito d'umiltà. E quando ella fosse alquanto propinqua al salutare, uno spirito d'amore, distruggendo tutti gli altri spiriti sensitivi, pingea fuori li deboletti spiriti del viso, e dicea loro: 'Andate a onorare la donna vostra', ed elli si rimanea nel luogo loro.

The ambiguity of the term "viso," in the first occurrence referring to the face of the lover and in the second to sight, contributes to the ambivalence of the entire situation in chapter XI (5). Also, the apparent dichotomy between "salute" and "saluto," which are indeed one embodied in Beatrice, returns in chapter XIV, 5 (7, 5), when Dante accompanies a friend to a wedding party, unaware of the fact that Beatrice will be there as well:[28] "Allora fuoro sì dructi li miei spiriti per la forza che Amore prese veggendosi in tanta propinquitade alla gentilissima donna, che non ne rimasero in vita più che li spiriti del viso; e ancora questi rimasero fuori delli loro strumenti, però che Amore volea stare nel loro nobilissimo luogo per vedere la mirabile donna" ("Then my spirits were so disrupted by the strength Love acquired when he saw himself this close to the most gracious lady, that none survived except the spirits of sight; and even these were driven forth, because Love desired to occupy their enviable post in order to behold the marvelous lady") What is a consequence of this moment is the lover's transfiguration to which Dante refers twice, once pointing out that many women were aware "della mia transfiguratione" ("the transformation I had undergone") (XIV, 7: 7, 7), and then again, when he is back in his room and plans to write a sonnet on "la cagione del mio trasfiguramento" ("the reason for the change in my appearance") (XIV, 10: 7, 10).[29] In both episodes in chapters XI (5) and XIV (7), the term "viso" is

---

[28] For a similar experience, see *Convivio* III, ix, 15.

[29] At the beginning of XV, 1 (8, 1), Dante refers to the experience as "la nova transfiguratione" ("that strange transformation"); see also in the sonnet in *Vita Nova* XIV, 11–12, the mentions of "figura nova" ("so laughable a figure") and "figura d'altrui" ("I have been changed") (ll.3, 12). Another moment that seems to be a transfiguration is the one described in the sonnet "Oltre la spera che più larga gira" ("Beyond the sphere that makes the widest round") (XLI, 10–13). In a movement of tension toward "una mirabile visione" in chapter XLII, 1, this transfiguration is an important step toward that final and unsayable episode.

employed in its double reference to face and sight, therefore retaining the main semantic references of the Latin term *visum*. In the passages in question, there is a further invitation never to forget the Latin meaning of crucial terms employed: the use of the term "obumbrare" ("tempering") in chapter XI (5), and the double lexicalization of the same fact as "trasfigurazione" and "trasfiguramento" in chapter XIV (7), in which again the Latin semantics of the suffix plays a crucial role.[30] By the same token, the term "viso," as the vulgar rendition of the Latin term, seems to be taking upon itself the role Macrobius assigns to "visum" in the division of five kinds of dream that he presents in *Somnium Scipionis*.

To return to the discussion of the first vision in chapter III, 3–8 (1, 14–18), the narration of the dream is quite elaborate. As known, this dream also prompts the poet to write a sonnet, "A ciascun'alma presa e gentil core" (III, 10–12: 1, 21–23), to which "fu risposto da molti, e di diverse sentenzie; tra li quali fu risponditore quelli cui io chiamo primo delli miei amici, e disse allora uno sonetto, lo quale comincia *Vedesti, al mio parere, omne valore*. E questo fu quasi lo principio dell'amistà tra lui e me, quando elli seppe che io era quelli che li avea ciò mandato" ("was answered by many, who offered a variety of interpretations; among those who answered was the one I call my best friend, who responded with a sonnet beginning: *I think that you beheld all worth*. This exchange of sonnets marked the beginning of our friendship") (III, 14: 2, 1). The dream, then, and the sonnet that it inspires mark the beginning of the friendship between Dante and Guido Cavalcanti, which is also on Dante's part a process of distancing himself from the poetics of the second Guido:[31]

> [. . .] E pensando di lei, mi sopragiunse uno soave sonno, nel quale m'apparve una maravigliosa visione. Che mi parea vedere nella mia camera una

---

[30] Regarding "obumbrare," the verb used by Gabriel to Mary in Luke 1:35 (Vulg.), see Giovanni Pascoli, "L'angiolo e la donna," in *La mirabile visione: Abbozzo d'una storia della Divina Commedia*, 2nd ed. (Bologna: Zanichelli, 1913), pp. 155-56.

[31] Regarding the poetic friendship between Dante and Guido Cavalcanti, see at least Maria Luisa Ardizzone, *Guido Cavalcanti: The Other Middle Ages* (Toronto: University of Toronto Press, 2002); M. Corti, *Scritti su Cavalcanti e Dante* (Turin: Einaudi, 2003); Domenico De Robertis, "Cavalcanti ovvero la non-beatrice," in *Il libro della Vita nuova*, 2nd expanded ed. (Florene: G. C. Sansoni, 1970), 71–85; Guido Favati, *Inchiesta sul dolce stil nuovo* (Florence: Felice Le Monnier Editore, 1975); Alberto Gessani, *Dante, Guido Cavalcanti, e l'"amoroso regno"* (Macerata: Quodlibet, 2004); R. Harrison, *The Body of Beatrice*; Enrico Malato, *Dante e Guido Cavalcanti: Il dissidio per la* Vita nuova *e il "disdegno" di Guido*, 2nd ed. (Rome: Salerno Editrice, 2004); Mario Marti, *Storia dello Stil Nuovo* (Lecce: Milella, 1973); Bruno Nardi, "Dante e Guido Cavalcanti," in idem, *Saggi e note di critica dantesca* (Milan and Naples: Ricciardi Editore, 1966), 190–219; Rinaldina Russell, *Tre versanti della poesia stilnovistica: Guinizelli, Cavalcanti, Dante* (Bari: Adriatica, 1973); J. E. Shaw, *Guido Cavalcanti's Theory of Love* (Toronto: University of Toronto Press, 1949).

nebula di colore di fuoco, dentro alla quale io discernea una figura d'uno signore, di pauroso aspecto a chi la guardasse; e pareami con tanta letitia quanto a·ssé, che mirabile cosa era; e nelle sue parole dicea molte cose, le quali io non intendea se non poche, tra le quali io intendea queste: 'Ego Dominus tuus'. Nelle sue braccia mi parea vedere una persona dormire nuda, salvo che involta mi parea in uno drappo sanguigno leggieramente; la quale io riguardando molto intentivamente, conobbi ch'era la donna della salute, la quale m'avea lo giorno dinanzi degnato di salutare. E nell'una delle mani mi parea che questi tenesse una cosa la quale ardesse tutta; e pareami che mi dicesse queste parole: 'Vide cor tuum!'. E quando elli era stato alquanto, pareami che disvegliasse questa che dormia; e tanto si sforzava per suo ingegno, che le facea mangiare questa cosa che in mano li ardea, la quale ella mangiava dubitosamente. Appresso ciò poco dimorava che la sua letitia si convertia in amarissimo pianto; e così piangendo si ricoglica questa donna nelle sue braccia, e con essa mi parea che si ne gisse verso lo cielo. Onde io sostenea sì grande angoscia, che lo mio deboletto sonno non poteo sostenere, anzi si ruppe e fui disvegliato.

The role that in chapter II (1) is given to "la secretissima camera del cuore" now properly belongs to the "solingo luogo d'una mia camera" (III, 2: **1**, 13), which is in turn duplicated in the dream when the dreamer seems to see "nella mia camera" a red cloud.[32] This is a strategic device often adopted in the dream vision tradition, although the duplication of the room, which works as a sort of *incunabulum*, is quite unique. Furthermore, the reference to the cloud of the color of fire resonates with similar episodes in the Bible, the most relevant of which may be the pillar or cloud of fire in Exodus 14:19–24: this cloud is God's manifestation to the Israelites during their captivity in Egypt and on the way to the Land of Canaan. Love, then, appears to Dante in his sleep also to remind him, although in a still confused way, of his exilic condition, the understanding of which fully takes place in the last three chapters of the *Vita Nova* (XL-XLII: **29–31**), after Dante sees the pilgrims going through Florence on their way to Rome. The most striking aspect, however, is the presence of the heart, Dante's heart,

---

[32] It must be noted that at the beginning of the narration the term adopted by Dante is "sonno," which is replaced at the end of chapter II (1) by the more precise "sogno" (III, 15; **2**, 2): "Lo verace iuditio del detto sogno non fu veduto allora per alcuno, ma ora è manifestissimo alli più semplici" ("The true meaning of the dream I described was not perceived by anyone then, but now it is completely clear even to the least sophisticated"). As is known, the two terms come from the Latin *somnium*: for observations on the transformation of the Latin term into the two in question, see at least Gerhard Rohlfs, *Historische Grammatik der Italienischen Sprache und ihrer Mundarten, I: Lautlehre* (Bern: A. Francke AG, 1949): # 282, 268. The critical need for a distinct definition of dream and vision is prompted by the actual occurrence of the terms in the description of some specific episodes: it is Dante himself who suggests the fine boundaries that separate the two realms.

in what appears to be at once a paradoxical and parodic presence of the sacrament of communion and of what will become the devotion of the Sacred Heart of Jesus.[33] In fact, Beatrice, not yet a *figura Christi*, performs the cannibalistic ritual of eating Dante's heart, as Love forces her to do. No matter how horrific the details of this vision are, it is still "una maravigliosa visione," as Dante calls it before recounting it: the adjective alludes to the one that accompanies the last and unsaid vision, "una mirabile visione." But before then, Dante experiences a vision in chapter XII (5).

To be sure, Dante defines the vision in chapter XII (5) only in the last paragraph before the ballad "Ballata, I' voi" ("I want you to go, ballad"), besides confirming that he had described a "visione" of "Amore" at the beginning of chapter XIII (6). When the vision disappears, he wakes up and considers that the hour of the experience confirms the link of the vision to Beatrice through the number nine, according to a dynamic already present at the end of the first vision in chapter III (1). The vision itself, however, shows no sign of Beatrice, but it is only Love that appears to the lover. This may also be due to a number of facts: Beatrice has just denied her greeting, as we are told at the very beginning of the chapter, which triggers Dante's desire to withdraw "in solinga parte" ("to a solitary place") (XII, 1: 5, 8) and finally "misimi nella mia camera" ("I went to my bedroom") (XII, 2: 5, 9); when in the room, Dante invokes Love to help him. The recognition of Love is attributed to the poet's familiarity with this figure acquired "assai fiate nelli miei sonni" ("many times before in my sleep") (XII, 4: 5, 11). The attitude of Love, this time, is much more compassionate than it was in the first vision in chapter III (1): Love's cry remains enigmatic and the lover is in the same situation in which the reader is, unable to understand whether Love cries because of Dante's loss of Beatrice's greeting or because Love foresees suffering in the future, given the allusions in the Latin phrases Love addresses to the lover.

To summarize, the *Vita Nova* is an autobiographical tale of Dante's love for Beatrice as it moves from eros to agape, from a sensual appreciation to a spiritual understanding of love. In this process of knowledge, the dream vision plays a crucial role, as it is placed at the beginning and at the end of the book. However, there are a few facts that show the elaboration on the dream vision motif: not only is the third and last vision not told, but there is no indication that it is a dream vision. If that vision is the one narrated in the *Divine Comedy*, one can infer that it is still taking place in a dream: at the beginning of that narration (*Inferno* I, 10–12), Dante makes a disclaim: "Io non so ben ridir com'i' v'intrai,

---

[33] As is known, in the twelfth and thirteenth centuries there were the first expressions of the devotion that will culminate only in the seventeenth century with the revelations to Margaret Mary Alacoque, whereas the consecration was a long process throughout the nineteenth century that culminated in 1856, when Pope Pius IX extended the feast, by then popular in France, to the universal Church, and finally in 1899, when Pope Leo XIII formulated the consecration.

/ tant'era pien di sonno a quel punto / che la verace via abbandonai" ("I cannot clearly say how I had entered / the wood; I was so full of sleep just at / the point where I abandoned the true path"). What in theological terms still holds true (the *Divine Comedy* may be considered, in turn, a dream vision and, as such, aiming at its apocalypse in the final vision of God), in literary terms is undermined in an act of reticence that does not allow the identification of the third vision as a dream vision. This movement of that motif within the text is necessary because of the nature of the text itself, which is not only the text of an autobiography, but also the text of a conversion, as the title suggests as well. In this process of conversion, there are several steps and degrees that are taken along the way: the episodes described as "fantasia" and "ymaginatione" refer to the conquests and the obstacles on the path toward a knowledge that is finally enlightened by a metaphysical vision.

Re-Configuring the Self through Suffering, Violence, and Death in Dante's *Vita nuova* and *Comedy*

Dino S. Cervigni

1. The Notion of Sacrifice

At the core of Christianity resides the belief that Christ, God incarnate, willingly accepted death, wrongfully imposed upon Him by humankind, in order to bring a corrupt humanity to a state of renewed innocence. A Christian poet and thinker, Dante, in his two closely intertwined works, the *Vita nuova* and the *Comedy*, exploits this fundamental Christian notion of sacrifice.[1] Accordingly, in the *Comedy*, much more so than in the *Vita nuova*, Dante the poet presents Christ's Redemption, especially His death on the cross, as that act of violence wrongfully perpetrated upon Him by others, and willingly accepted by Him, that enables Dante the protagonist to hope of reaching Beatrice in heaven in his youthful autobiographical work and then fulfill this goal in his masterpiece.

The need of sacrifice to appease the divinity and/or to attain a lofty goal finds support also outside Christian theology. In addition to the findings by anthropologists of religion, take for instance the theory proposed by René Girard, who endorses the function of sacrifice as it emerges from Dante's *Comedy*. For Girard, as for Christianity, in fact, "[s]acrifice has often been described as an act of mediation between a sacrificer and a 'deity'."[2] At the same time, however, in Girardian theory, "[o]nly an arbitrary victim can resolve the crisis" that has emerged within a community;[3] it follows that the Christian sacrifice, precisely

---

[1] Fundamental in the *Comedy* are Beatrice's explanations of Christ's redemptive act in *Par.* 7, primarily vv. 52–120. References to Christ's sacrifice can be found in most works of Dante, e.g.: *Monarchia* 2.11.1–6; 2.11.5; *Epistola* 2.13.21; *De vulgari eloquentia* 1.6.6.

[2] René Girard, *Violence and the Sacred*, trans. Patrick Gregory (Baltimore: Johns Hopkins University Press, 1977), 6.

[3] René Girard, *Things Hidden Since the Foundation of the World*, trans. Stephen Bann and Michael Metteer (Stanford: Stanford University Press, 1987), 25.

because its innocent and willing victim descended to earth and was born for this eternally planned role, dismisses the millenary custom of the unwilling, arbitrary, and substitute victim.

The fact remains that the first and only Christian sacrifice, Christ's death on the cross, constitutes an act of violence perpetrated on an innocent victim. Furthermore, according to Christianity, all human beings must believe in that act of violence and must also somehow participate in it in order to be saved. On the one hand, therefore, Christ preaches meekness, tolerance, and forgiveness; on the other, He Himself, stretched out on the cross, conveys to everyone that salvation comes through undergoing suffering, even violence, which no human being can avoid and which every Christian believer must patiently embrace. Dante's *Comedy*, and to a much lesser extent also the *Vita nuova*, portray such a Christian notion of the willing and innocent victim, Christ, together with that of the protagonist, who, although guilty, is at times reluctant, but ultimately becomes a willing participant in His sacrifice. By contrast, all those who refuse to participate in that foundational act of violence are condemned to eternal punishment, hell, which cannot but be seen as a parody of Christ's sacrifice.[4]

Because of the magnitude of the topic, the purpose of this essay is necessarily limited. I first intend to analyze the language of violence Dante employs in presenting Christ's sacrifice in the *Comedy* and, second, the transforming effects deriving from the participation of the *Vita nuova*'s characters in Christ's death. I will then conclude with some fundamental considerations on the ultimate and dilemmatic resolution of violence in the *Vita nuova* and the *Comedy*. For the Christian believer, and thus also for Dante, in fact, the fate of all those who refuse Christ's violent death and perpetrate violence is to be themselves condemned to eternal violence in the afterlife, as is the case with the souls condemned to Dante's hell; by contrast, all those who accept Christ crucified will see their sufferings transformed into a glorious and eternal state.

2. Christ's Sacrifice in the *Comedy*

The all-pervasive presence of Christ's Redemption in Dante's *Comedy* can hardly be summarized in just a few words.[5] In brief, Christ's Redemption—His death on the cross and His Resurrection—constitutes the *sine qua non* for Dante the

---

[4] For an example of a punishment that parodies Christ's crucifixion, see Caiaphas, nailed on Hell's floor and walked upon by all those condemned to the same bolgia of the hypocrites (*Inf.* 23.109–22).

[5] Two textual elements, strategically posited at the first cantica's beginning and ending, respectively, emblematize the pervasive presence of Christ crucified in Dante's hell: the "sign of victory" with which Christ triumphantly descended into hell (*Inf.* 4.54) and the representation of Lucifer as the mock-Verbum or mock-Logos in *Inferno* 34.

Pilgrim to journey through hell, climb Mount Purgatory, and ascend to heaven ultimately to obtain the beatific vision. The justice brought about by Christ's Redemption is visible in a horrific manner throughout hell, where the rebellious souls are being punished for refusing Christ and where Christ's suffering is parodied through the souls' torments. By contrast, the suffering souls in purgatory, justly punished for their earthly shortcomings, patiently and lovingly atone in order to ascend to paradise, modeling themselves on the innocent victim on the cross. As Dante the Pilgrim witnesses the torments of the souls in hell and the purification of those in purgatory, he also learns to repudiate the sins of the rebellious and join the sufferings of the purifying souls. At the end of his heavenly journey, as we shall see, Dante the Pilgrim will be granted the privilege of contemplating God through the glorified Christ crucified (*Par.* 33.127–141).

In addition to this pervasive presence of Christ—and Christ crucified—which ranges from *Inf.* 4 to the very last lines of *Par.* 33, a series of important statements help the reader understand the way in which Dante the poet conceived that central act of violence that brought about humankind's redemption.

First of all, Adam and Eve's primordial transgression is in itself viewed as an act of violence. In paradise Adam himself refers to his disobedience as "il trapassar del segno," that is, "the trespassing or transgressing of the sign" (*Par.* 26.117), which is not unlike the mythical Remus's trespassing that brought about Romulus's vengeance and his twin brother's murder. Adam and Eve's initial trespassing the boundaries set by God, together with all of humankind's sins, causes God's *ira* or wrath, according to the words spoken by Justinian in *Par.* 6.90 and iterated by Beatrice in the following canto. God's wrath, a typical biblical expression, is not like human anger.[6] The word's etymology can help understand this biblical

---

Concerning the former, as we hear from Virgil's description of the harrowing of hell, Christ descended into the netherworld "con segno di vittoria coronato" (*Inf.* 4.54). That sign of victory is arguably the cross itself which, according to the apocryphal gospel of Nicodemus, was placed by Christ in the middle of hell as a sign of triumph over Satan ("posuitque Dominus crucem suam in medio inferni, quae est signum victoriae": Tischendorf, *Evang. Apoc.* 430, qtd. in *La divina commedia*, comm. G. Vandelli [Milan: Hoepli, 1989]). Concerning Lucifer as the parody of the Verbum or Logos, I would like to refer to Dino Cervigni, "Dante's Lucifer: The Denial of the Word," *Lectura Dantis* 3 (1988): 51–62, and idem, "The Muted Self-Referentiality of Dante's Lucifer," *Dante Studies* 107 (1989): 45–74. For its focus on sacrifice, albeit from a different perspective, see Ricardo J. Quinones, *Foundation Sacrifice in Dante's Commedia* (University Park: Pennsylvania State University Press, 1994).

[6] E.g.: John 3:36, "sed ira Dei manet super eum"; Rom. 1:18, "Revelatur ira Dei"; Eph. 5:6, "ira Dei in filios." All quotations from the Bible are from *Biblia sacra iuxta vulgatam clementinam* (Madrid: BAC, 1982). Saint Thomas Aquinas explains the biblical image of divine wrath as an act of the will and not as a passion (e.g. *Summa Th.* 1 q. 3 ad 2).

notion. The word's root, in fact, suggests passion, even madness, but it also denotes the power present in a divine manifestation.[7]

Dante the poet's employment of the term *ira* to describe God's attitude toward humankind as a consequence of sin is modeled on the same biblical term. More so in the Old than in the New Testament, two contrasting passions characterize the biblical God: wrath and mercy, as we read, for example, in Isaiah 54:8 and in Psalm 30:6.[8] In brief, God's wrath — a form of violence, indeed even bloody violence — is brought about by humankind's sin; thus His indignation reveals itself through various forms of violent punishment inflicted upon humankind, including famine (2 Sam. 24:13), plague (Numbers 17:11), disease (Numbers 12:9), and even death (Gen. 3:19). When man returns to God, however, God's wrath ceases; otherwise God's anger becomes everlasting, as the case is in Dante's hell. In fact, the torments of Dante's *Inferno*, which range from a perennial storm to incessant rain, and from unendingly burning fire to crippling disease and freezing ice, graphically represent the manifestations of the biblical notion of God's wrath caused by man's obstinacy in his transgressions.

Just as Dante employs the biblical image and notion of wrath, he also adopts another image that is consequent upon that of wrath; namely, God's vengeance.[9] Thus Dante the poet views humankind's history marked by God's wrath, on the one hand (*Inf.* 2.94–96), and God's just revenge, on the other (*Par.* 6–7); at the same time, human history is and will always be traversed by divine mercy from beginning to end, as Dante the pilgrim experiences in his own life and as Beatrice clearly states in explaining the Pilgrim's privilege to Virgil: "*Donna è gentil nel ciel che si compiange / di questo 'mpedimento ov'io ti mando, / sì che duro giudicio là sù frange*" (*Inf.* 2.94–96; emphasis added).

---

[7] The English word *ire* (derived from the Latin *ira*) is connected with the Greek word *hieros*: "filled with the divine," "holy." Even medieval etymologers were aware of this meaning of *hieros*; e.g. Uguccione, "GERA [hiera] grece, latine interpretatur sacrum vel sanctum" (*Derivationes*, ed. Enzo Cecchini et al. [Florence: Galluzzo, 2009]), 1.527). This anthropomorphic manifestation of the divine bears out a form of violence, implicit in another word connected with "ira": the English term *iron*, which has a corresponding term in Old High German with the meaning of "holy metal," arguably the metaphoric instrument by which God forcefully exercises his justice (*American Heritage Dictionary* [Boston: Houghton Mifflin, 1996], "eis-," 2102).

[8] "In momento indignationis abscondi faciem meam parumper a te; et in misericordia sempiterna misertus sum tui" (Is. 54:8); "Quoniam ira in indignatione eius, et vita in voluntate eius; ad vesperum demorabitur fletus, et ad matutinum laetitia" (Psalm 29:6). Cf. also Hab. 3:2: "Cum iratus fueris, misericordiae recordaberis."

[9] Precisely as Paul writes in the letter to the Romans: "Non vosmetipsos defendentes charissimi, sed date locum irae. Scriptum est enim: Mihi vindicta: ego retribuam, dicit Dominus" (Rom. 12:19). Uguccione distinguishes between *vindicare* and *ulcisci*: "[. . .] vindicat aliquis cum a periculo liberat, ulciscitur cum ille iam mala passus est [. . .]" (2.1280).

In the Bible, God, confronted by humankind's transgressions, becomes irate in order to bring believers and unbelievers alike to the right path. According to Saint Paul, in fact, man is sinful (Rom. 1:18–32) and is consequently deserving of death (Rom. 3:20); becoming the object of divine wrath, humanity is being likened to a vase filled with divine anger, a vase which can nevertheless be filled also with divine mercy (Rom. 9:22–23).[10]

One should read the words of Justinian in *Par.* 6 and those of Beatrice in *Par.* 7 precisely within this context of the biblical notion of divine wrath and vengeance. The eagle, the symbol of the Roman Empire, during and within which Christ's Redemption took place, was granted the glory of avenging God's wrath (*Par.* 6.88–90); then Emperor Titus hurried to avenge the revenge of the ancient sin (*Par.* 6.92–93).[11] Beatrice reiterates Justinian's language, while explaining how it is possible for God's just revenge to be afterward avenged by a just court.[12]

And yet, even within the biblical context that lies at the origin of these Dantean expressions, Justinian's and Beatrice's words sound shocking. For, in fact, the sinless and guiltless Son of God becomes the object of His own Father's wrath and revenge in order to redeem humankind. To appease His own wrath and bring about justice, God the Father opted for His own Son to die on the cross, a mysterious decision that is hardly understandable to anyone who has not matured in God's love, as Beatrice explains to Dante the Pilgrim in one of her longest speeches (*Par.* 7.52–120).[13] Thus the ultimate violence, Christ's death on the cross, and thus also Christ's Redemption, remains an inscrutable mystery (*Par.* 7.55–57).

The first murder ever perpetrated in humankind's history—that is, the violence carried out by a brother against his brother: Cain killing Abel—is thus surpassed by another act of violence: the one that God the Father allowed to be carried out against His own Son, who becomes the object of His own wrath and revenge. Although this specific image has, to my knowledge, no exact equivalent in scriptural writings, the Bible proposes a related notion and image. For Paul,

---

[10] For some of these biblical notions I am indebted to related entries (*colère, vengeance*) in the *Vocabulaire de théologie biblique*, ed. X. Léon-Dufour et al. (Paris: Cerf, 1964).

[11] In the *Comedy* the word *vendetta* occurs 22 times, six of which signify human revenge (*Inf.* 12.69; 14.57; 18.96; 32.80; *Purg.* 10.83; 17.122); in most instances, therefore, *vendetta* stands for God's revenge, in hell (*Inf.* 7.12; 11.90; 14.16; 24.120; 26.57), purgatory (*Purg.* 20.47; 20.95; 21.6; 33.36), and primarily in paradise (*Par.* 6.90; 6.92; 6.93; 7.20; 7.50; 17.53; 22.14).

[12] "Non ti dee oramai parer piú forte, / quando si dice che giusta vendetta / poscia vengiata fu da giusta corte" (*Par.* 7.49–51).

[13] "Questo decreto, frate, sta sepulto / a li occhi di ciascuno il cui ingegno / ne la fiamma d'amor non è adulto" (*Par.* 7.58–60).

in fact, Christ becomes Himself sin, in order to defeat sin;[14] Christ also becomes God's curse, in order to bring about God's justice.[15]

Just as in the Bible God's wrath is not in vain, for His revenge brings about His justice, so also Christ's violent death on the cross as the innocent victim leads to His glorification in both the Bible and the *Comedy*. This notion needs emphasizing: in both works violence has no purpose in itself, is brought about by a human transgression, and is ultimately intended for a specific goal. Consequently, unlike the souls condemned to hell, those who accept Christ crucified will experience, with Christ glorified in heaven, eternal glory.

Paul's words to the Philippians help us understand God the Father's glorification of His Son, whose triumph in heaven will be proclaimed by every one in heaven and in hell as well (Phil. 2:5–11). To represent Christ's glory in heaven Dante the poet resorts to one of his most intriguing and symbolic images precisely when the Pilgrim's vision comes to a close and the Poet's masterpiece reaches its end. Like the *Comedy*, also the *Vita nuova* concludes with a vision and hope of eternal glory. Before focusing on Dante's representation of Christ's glory, however, I would like briefly to analyze the function of Christ's death on the cross in Dante's novel of the youthful self, the *Vita nuova*, and the extent to which its two main characters share in Christ's sacrifice.

3. The *Vita nuova* and Christ's Sacrifice

A main character in both the *Vita nuova* and the *Comedy*, Beatrice plays a fundamental role in the salvation history of the male protagonist. In the *Vita nuova*, Beatrice, a Christlike figure, is the miracle descended from heaven upon earth, who through her gaze, word, and smile is empowered, like Christ, to transform everything and everyone who is willing to accept her, especially the unnamed male protagonist of the *Vita nuova*. Through her presence, when she is alive, and through her remembrance, when she is dead, she guides the Dantean hero through his youthful life, who thus hopes of joining her in the glory of heaven (*VN* 42). In the *Comedy*, listening to Mary's and Lucia's solicitations, she summons Virgil to guide Dante the Pilgrim through hell and purgatory and she herself leads him from the top of Mount Purgatory to the highest heaven, leaving to St. Bernard and the Blessed Virgin the ultimate task of obtaining God's beatific vision for the Pilgrim. As we have seen, Dante the Pilgrim is empowered to jour-

---

[14] "Eum, qui non noverat peccatum, pro nobis peccatum fecit, ut nos efficeremur iustitia Dei in ipso" (2 Cor. 5:21); "Deus Filium suum mittens in similitudinem carnis peccati et de peccato, damnavit peccatum in carne, ut iustificatio legis impleretur in nobis, qui non secundum carnem ambulamus, sed secundum spiritum" (Rom. 8:3).

[15] "Christus nos redemit de maledicto legis, factus pro nobis maledictum. quia scriptum est, Maledictus omnis qui pendet in ligno" (Gal. 3:13) (quoting Deut. 21:23).

ney through hell, purgatory, and paradise through the salvific grace of Christ's Redemption. Accordingly, the *Comedy*'s hero is also saved from God's wrath and revenge, because God's Son Himself becomes humankind's sacrificial victim. At the same time, in order to share in Christ's salvation, Dante the Pilgrim must join him in his sufferings and undergo a sort of deathly experience.[16]

Concerning the *Vita nuova*, the question at hand is: To what extent is this notion of Christ's sacrifice, which pervades the *Comedy* from beginning to end, also present in Dante's youthful work? And to what extent does the male protagonist of the *Vita nuova* become also a co-participant in the sufferings of Christ's Redemption, as Dante the Pilgrim does in the *Comedy*? The answer to these questions will help us understand the extent to which the author of the *Vita nuova*, who wrote this autobiographical narrative at the approximate age of twenty-eight,[17] is aware of the importance of Christ's Redemption, which entails His violent death, in configuring the lover's journey toward conversion and salvation.

To begin with, no violent death occurs in the *Vita nuova*; and yet, death is present and each narrative concerning death is marked, in the narrator's mind, by the will or pleasure of God (*VN* 8.1; 22.1; 28.1). More precisely, the text presents the death of three characters, one man and two women, according to the following narrative order: first, that of a young lady, whom the lover had seen in the company of Beatrice (*VN* 8); second, the death of Beatrice's father (*VN* 22); and, third, the death of Beatrice herself (*VN* 28–29).

Dante the poet describes the death of the young lady through the eyes of the male protagonist, who grieves and weeps because his Beatrice also grieves and weeps:

> Appresso lo partire di questa gentile donna fue piacere del segnore de li angeli di chiamare a la sua gloria una donna giovane e di gentile aspetto molto, la quale fue assai graziosa in questa sopradetta cittade; lo cui corpo io vidi giacere sanza l'anima in mezzo di molte donne, le quali piangeano assai pietosamente.
>
> (*VN* 8.1)[18]

---

[16] For instance, through the Pilgrim's two deathly swoons, for which I would like to refer to Dino Cervigni, *Dante's Poetry of Dreams* (Florence: Olschki, 1986), 165–80, and in my two essays quoted above on *Inf.* 3 and *Inf.* 34.

[17] According to most critics, the *Vita nuova* was written between 1292 and 1295 ("*Vita nuova*," in *Enciclopedia dantesca*).

[18] Quotations of the *Vita nuova* come from *Vita nuova*, trans. and ed. Dino S. Cervigni and Edward Vasta (Notre Dame: University of Notre Dame Press, 1995). All quotations of the *Comedy* follow *La Commedia secondo l'antica vulgata*, ed. Giorgio Petrocchi, 4 vols. (Milan: Mondadori, 1966–1967).

The death of a young person cannot but be seen as an act of violence perpetrated on nature and life. Consequently, the poet-lover accuses death, violently attacking it by means of the rhetorical figure of *improperium*:

> Morte villana, di pietà nemica,
> di dolor madre antica,
> giudicio incontastabile gravoso,
> poi che hai data matera al cor doglioso
> ond'io vado pensoso,
> di te blasmar la lingua s'affatica.
> (*VN* 8.8, vv. 1–6)

The second occurrence of death affects Beatrice (and thus also the poet-lover) more closely, since it fells her father:

> Appresso ciò non molti dì passati, sì come piacque al glorioso sire lo quale non negoe la morte a sé, colui che era stato genitore di tanta meraviglia quanta si vedea ch'era questa nobilissima Beatrice, di questa vita uscendo, a la gloria etternale se ne gio veracemente.
> (*VN* 22.1)

Thus the story in *Vita nuova* 22 focuses first on the death of Beatrice's father, which is situated in a peculiar relation to that of Christ, and second on the daughter's grief, which is so deep as to transform her into a *filia dolorosa*: the grieving daughter patterned after Christ's *mater dolorosa*.

Beatrice's grief becomes the central motif of the story to such an extent as to cause the compassion (likened to death) not only of all onlookers but especially of the protagonist, who, without ever seeing her amidst her sorrow, joins the grieving women in mourning together with Beatrice. Thus, partaking in Beatrice's daughterly grief, the hero is being cured of his continuous self-pity caused by his failed attempts (*VN* 5–14) to obtain from Beatrice a response to his misdirected love, of which she had earlier disapproved (*VN* 10) and for which she had even mocked him, at least from the perspective of the lover (*VN* 14). Now the lover, freed from self-pity and even transformed in his external aspect, experiences true love for his lady by sharing her sorrow for the loss of her father.

God's decision to have Beatrice's father leave this world and attain eternal life is viewed as an act of benevolence ("piacque").[19] Although no explicit reason is giv-

---

[19] This expression ("sì come piacque") finds its model in the Bible. See especially Ecclesiasticus 44:16, where to God's act of benevolence corresponds God's decision to take up to heaven the just Enoch: "Enoch placuit Deo, et translatus est in paradisum, ut det gentibus poenitentiam"; see also. Matt 12:18: "Ecce puer meus, quem elegi, dilectus meus, in quo bene complacuit animae meae." Further examples can be found in the baptism of Christ (Matt. 3:17; Mark 1:11; Luke 3:22).

en for such benevolence, God's love toward the father may be explained through the father's goodness "in alto grado" ("in a high degree") and his close relation, by blood and love, to Beatrice, upon whom God has bestowed the "grace" to save anyone who speaks to her (*VN* 19.10, vv. 41–42), and thus her own father before anyone else.[20] Ultimately, therefore, God's benevolence, which manifests itself in willing her father's death, is mysterious, since it counters all humans' desire to live and also breaks nature's innate tendencies toward survival; at the same time, the death of the father and later of the daughter brings these two characters closer to Christ, who willingly accepted death as the most appropriate, albeit mysterious (*Par.* 7.55–60), way to redeem humankind. By joining Beatrice in her grief for her father's death and then by being transformed by her own death, the hero is also associated with the transforming effects of Christ's death.

The sentence that precedes the announcement of the death of Beatrice's father ("glorioso sire [. . .] non negoe la morte a sé," *VN* 22.1) constitutes the first clear reference to Christ's Redemption in the *Vita nuova*.[21] It also constitutes the

---

[20] Apart from any historical considerations (which are not easily verifiable and lie outside Dante's work) concerning the death of the members of the Portinari family, if one is willing to pursue this critical direction proposed by Boccaccio, what is striking is that Dante the author (who in Augustine's *Confessions* read the narrative of the death of a mother, Monica, in front of her son, Augustine) here establishes a female (Beatrice) to male (her father) mourning relationship. Later he develops a male (the lover) to female mourning relationship (according to the Augustinian model) when Beatrice's death is first announced and then it actually occurs. Insofar as Monica's death may have played a sacrificial role in her son's conversion, Dante may have had that narrative in mind in constructing the story of his lady, whose focus is her redemptive death (*VN* 23 and *VN* 28).

[21] Another important reference to Christ's death occurs in *Vita nuova* 40: "[. . .] quella imagine benedetta la quale Iesu Cristo lasciò a noi per essemplo de la sua bellissima figura." That "blessed image" is the so-called Veronica: the imprint of the face of Jesus that, according to the legend, was left on the kerchief offered to him by a woman called Veronica. Most legends concerning Veronica derive from the so-called apocryphal writings of Pilate. Accordingly, the name of the woman suffering from a hemorrhage and healed by Christ (Matt. 9:20–22; Mark 5:25–34; Luke 8:43–48) was called *Bernike* or *Beronike*, in the Greek apocrypha of Pilate, or *Veronica*, according to the apocryphal writings of Pilate in Latin, Coptic, or Syriac. According to the *Mors Pilati*, Christ left the imprint of his face on the veil on which that woman wanted an artist to reproduce Christ's semblance. Later in the Middle Ages, it was believed that Christ, on the road to Calvary, left the imprint of his face on the kerchief offered to him to wipe his sweat by a woman called Veronica. Since the 12th century, this relic was kept in St. Peter's in Rome and became the destination of many pilgrimages (*Par.* 31.104–08; Petrarch, *Rhymes* 16; *Familiarium rerum lib.* 9.13.34). In a 1289 papal letter by Nicholas IV (1288–1292), the kerchief ("praetiosissimi vultus imaginem, quam *Veronicam* fidelium vox appellat," "the image of the most precious face, which the voice of the faithful calls *Veronica*") was listed among the most precious relics of the Vatican Basilica, ahead of St. Peter's body and all the other sacred objects (*Enciclopedia cattolica*, "Veronica"). An important textual detail thus far left

text's first attempt, in close conjunction with the death of Beatrice's father, to see human death within a providential plan.[22] Gradually, therefore, Dante the author creates for Beatrice a co-redemptive role: anticipated first by the death of a lady friend (*VN* 7) and then by that of her father, Beatrice's death seems to be required for the salvation of the protagonist (and others as well. *VN* 19.9, vv. 29–42), thus sharing in the function of Christ's death.

Thus, finally, Beatrice also dies:

> *Quomodo sedet sola civitas plena populo! facta est quasi vidua domina gentium.*
> Io era nel proponimento ancora di questa canzone, e compiuta n'avea questa soprascritta stanzia, quando lo segnore de la giustizia chiamoe questa gentilissima a gloriare sotto la insegna di quella regina benedetta virgo Maria, lo cui nome fue in grandissima reverenzia ne le parole di questa Beatrice beata.
> (*VN* 28.1)

Several elements characterize the narrative that announces Beatrice's death: first, the narrator's refusal to describe her death, a narrative strategy for which the text provides an explanation; and second, the poet-lover's statement that Beatrice did not die because of disease or any other natural cause; rather, she was called to heaven because Paradise, being without her, lacked some goodness. Beatrice was thus summoned to heaven by God, who listened to the prayers of the angels and saints.

In fact, the programmatic canzone of *Vita nuova* 19 reads: "Madonna è disiata in sommo cielo" (*VN* 19.9, v. 29). Therefore, she leaves the earth not because of any disease but because, like Enoch, she pleases God, as we read in the first canzone after her death:

> Ita n'è Beatrice in l'alto cielo,
> nel reame ove li angeli hanno pace,
> e sta con loro, e voi, donne, ha lassate;
> no la ci tolse qualità di gelo
> né di calore, come l'altre face,
> ma solo fue sua gran benignitate;
> ché luce de la sua umilitate
> passò li cieli con tanta vertute,
> che fé maravigliar l'etterno sire,
> sì che dolce disire
> lo giunse di chiamar tanta salute;

---

unnoticed by critics, this kerchief or *imagine benedetta*—a concrete and specific object that Dante and his contemporaries believed to be authentic—constitutes the only physical and historical document and/or monument clearly identified within the *Vita nuova*, together with St. James's sepulcher, which is mentioned in *Vita nuova* 40.7.

[22] Christ's decision to accept death is a fundamental theme in St. Paul's letters, e.g., Philipp. 2:6–9.

> e fella di qua giù a sé venire,
> perché vedea ch'esta vita noiosa
> non era degna di sì gentil cosa.
> (*VN* 31.10, vv. 15–28)

If the *Vita nuova* contained no further salvific elements, then it would certainly lack almost completely the fundamental presence of Christ's Redemption, which characterizes the *Comedy* and which is also essential for the transformation of the poet-lover-protagonist.

And yet, immediately after the death of Beatrice's father, because of which she becomes a *filia dolorosa* (while the lover participates in her grief), a series of ordinary and extraordinary events affect the life of the protagonist. He first becomes ill, verging almost on death. Then, after a nine-day illness, he enters a peculiar visionary state, which cannot be better defined than a dreamlike and nightmarish condition. Accordingly, totally transformed by his illness, and concerned less by his serious condition than about the awareness that Beatrice too might one day succumb to death, he imagines an apocalyptic scene:

> Così cominciando ad errare la mia fantasia, venni a quello ch'io non sapea ove io mi fosse; e vedere mi parea donne andare scapigliate piangendo per via, maravigliosamente triste; e pareami vedere lo sole oscurare, sì che le stelle si mostravano di colore ch'elle mi faceano giudicare che piangessero; e pareami che li uccelli volando per l'aria cadessero morti, e che fossero grandissimi terremuoti.
> (*VN* 23.5)

Within this apocalyptic context, he imagines people approaching him and telling him first: "'Tu pur morrai'"; and then "'Tu se' morto'" (*VN* 23.4). And finally, he sees Beatrice dead and surrounded by weeping ladies, and then her soul, in the form of a little white cloud, ascend to heaven while being surrounded by angels, who sing "'*Osanna in excelsis*'" (*VN* 23.6–8).

The narrative of the imagined death of Beatrice contains many intriguing elements. On the one hand, the overall context associates the story of her death with that of Christ, because of the apocalyptic elements characteristic of Christ's crucifixion, as well as with that of the biblical end of time; on the other hand, Beatrice's peaceful demise, which is accompanied by no suffering and no disease, clearly likens her death to Mary's *dormitio* or *transitus*: that is, a departure and a transition rather than a human death, as one can determine from legends, Christian beliefs, and iconography concerning Mary's *transitus*.[23] Where then is the sacrificial participation of the Christian hero in Christ's Redemption that is essential for one's salvation and is so pervasive in the *Comedy*?

---

[23] The iconography of Mary's departing soul can resemble a small white cloud: in Byzantine-influenced art it is a small figure like an infant.

During the second half of the twentieth century, especially after the publication of Charles S. Singleton's essay on the *Vita nuova* (originally 1949), the Beatrice of the *Vita nuova* has almost invariably been understood as a Christlike figure. Her death—Singleton writes—stands "at the center"—obviously, to be understood metaphorically, rather than literally—of the protagonist's new life; Singleton further adds that heaven could be attained only "through the death of Beatrice."[24]

And yet, Singleton, although he sees the relationship of Beatrice's death to that of Christ as an analogy (*An Essay*, 114), does not elaborate on Beatrice's participation in Christ's Redemption, and even less on the participatory role that the lover-protagonist plays in the Christlike function of Beatrice. For Singleton, in fact, there are two salvific actions in the *Vita nuova*: "At the center of one is Christ on the cross, dying on the ninth hour. At the center of the other is Beatrice, dying in a vision which came on the ninth day of a fever" (*An Essay*, 113).[25] More intriguingly, Singleton states that Beatrice does not "die in order to save him [the lover], as Christ did for all men," although "it is nonetheless true that without her removal through death from the scene of this world, her lover's love would not have attained to the place of its perfection and rest" (*An Essay*, 113). By contrast, I see both beloved and lover more intimately involved in the sacrificial and violent death of Christ.

In fact, at the beginning as well toward the end of Beatrice's involvement with the Dante-persona, the story contains an element that, according to my reading, can be associated with her sacrificial role: the color of her clothes, "sanguigno"; that is, that of blood. The story's emphasis on the color of blood occurs at three crucial moments: first, when Beatrice enters the life of the protagonist at the age of nine, "vestita di nobilissimo colore, umile e onesto, sanguigno [. . .]" (2.3); second, in the prose narrative that, according to many critics, anticipates her death: "una persona nuda, salvo che involta mi parea in uno drappo sanguigno leggeramente [. . .]" (3.4);[26] and, third, when Beatrice, already in heaven,

---

[24] The two quotations come from Charles S. Singleton, *An Essay on the Vita nuova*, 2nd ed. (Baltimore: Johns Hopkins University Press, 1977), 24, 96. Singleton further adds that heaven could be attained only "through the death of Beatrice" (96) and that Beatrice's death is fundamental also for the development of a new poetics of love (100).

[25] Theologically correct, the first part of Singleton's statement—Christ's death on the cross constitutes the *sine qua non* for humankind's salvation—needs clarification in terms of its role in the *Vita nuova*, for nowhere does the *Vita nuova* text state the necessity of Christ's redemption except indirectly in a passage already quoted ("sì come piacque al glorioso sire lo quale non negoe la morte a sé," *VN* 22.1).

[26] For some critics, likely the majority, "gir verso lo cielo" announces Beatrice's death—a reading that was proposed, according to Margherita De Bonfils Templer (*Itinerario di amore: Dialettica di amore e morte nella* Vita nuova, University of North Carolina Studies in Romance Languages and Literature (Chapel Hill: University of North Carolina Press, 1973), 30–31 n. 1, by Norton, Barbi, Grandgent, and Shaw, to whom I

appears in the lover's imagining "con quelle vestimenta sanguigne co le quali apparve prima [. . .]" (39.1). Since the text no longer refers *explicitly* to any other appearance of Beatrice after this last one, her explicitly stated presence in the story is therefore enclosed within that initial appearance and this final one, while wearing the same "blood-red garments." Is the reader supposed to dismiss as totally insignificant this threefold presence of the adjective *sanguigno* in reference to Beatrice's garments? Or, instead, would it be possible to situate, as I am suggesting, this emphatic reference to the color of blood precisely within the sacrificial role of Beatrice? The color *sanguigno* is in fact universally associated with blood and, within the context of Dante's works, with the blood that Christ shed for the salvation of humankind. Might not the text point specifically to Beatrice's sacrificial role for the salvation of the lover through the color of her garments, *sanguigno*, at these three crucial moments of the story? As I have pointed out above, and will also pursue below, Beatrice's figure is associated with Christ's Redemption and with Mary's participatory role in it.

In fact, the presence of Christ's death on the cross is clearly stated shortly before the death of Beatrice's father and thus of her overwhelming grief: The "glorioso sire [. . .] non negoe la morte a sé" (*VN* 22.1). Thus the *Vita nuova* presents Christ's Redemption as a voluntary submission to the principal physical consequence of humankind's sin—death—without elaborating on the violence of such an action. Most interestingly, the text offers no clue (arguably either old age or illness) as to the cause of the father's death.

Beatrice's sorrow is also comparable to that of the *mater dolorosa*, Mary, who stands in front of her crucified son.[27] In fact, the words that most distinctly describe Beatrice's grief ("amarissimamente piena di dolore") recall Jeremiah's words characterizing the desolate Jerusalem, a figure of the suffering Church, the grieving Mary, and also Beatrice's city after her death (*VN* 28.1).[28] Transformed into a *filia dolorosa*, Beatrice therefore experiences suffering, the first and also the only time in the story. Thus the unexplained death of the father and Beatrice's filial grief can be viewed as an inexplicable act of violence perpetrated upon both

---

can add: D'Ancona, Casini, and Federzoni in their commentaries; G. Bárberi Squarotti, "'L'ambiguità' della *Vita nuova*," in *Psicoanalisi e strutturalismo di fronte a Dante*, 3 vols. (Florence; Olschki, 1972), 1: 38–39; D. De Robertis, *Il libro della* Vita nuova (Florence: Sansoni, 1970), 39; M. Musa, *Dante's* Vita nuova: *A Translation and an Essay* (Bloomington: Indiana University Press, 1973), 119–20; etc. This reading has also been proposed most vigorously by Singleton, for whom that sentence ("gir verso lo cielo") is "the most significant detail of the whole vision" and "the very sign which made it prophetic and disclosed its true meaning" (*An Essay*, 13–14).

[27] See *VN* 5.1 and 28.1 for Beatrice's devotion to Mary.

[28] "Quoniam amaritudine plena sum [. . .] et domi mors similis est" (Lam. 1:20). Also: "Replevit me amaritudinibus" (Lam. 3:15), as sung in Holy Week; "implet me [Deus] amaritudinibus" (Job 9:18).

of them, since (according to the text) her father was good "in a high degree" and she was "in altissimo grado di bontade" (*VN* 22.2). Death, suffering, and weeping, in fact, are the consequences of sin and not of goodness.

As an observer of Beatrice's grief through the accounts of the ladies who leave the mourning site and describe the daughter's countenance, the lover too becomes totally transformed by her grief, in which he wholly participates. A few days afterward, he becomes seriously ill. Then, at the end of a seven-day illness, as we have seen, during an apocalyptic scene produced by a nightmarish and dreamlike visionary experience, he sees Beatrice dead and witnesses her assumption to heaven.

Next to the violence perpetrated on human nature by death, no greater violence can be imagined than that exercised on the universe by the end of time, the biblical apocalypse. During the protagonist's nightmarish vision, the sun darkens, the stars become discolored (Rev. 6:12–13), and the birds fall. Although the violence of Beatrice's death is somewhat softened by her peaceful countenance (*VN* 23.8) and by her immediate assumption to heaven (*VN* 23.7), the entire scene's violence affects the seer most forcefully. Already verging on death in reality because of his serious illness, during the nightmarish vision he is approached by disheveled women and then by horrifying faces who announce to him, respectively, "Tu pur morrai" and "Tu se' morto" (*VN* 23.5)—words launched at him arguably at the same time Beatrice dies. After her grief for her father's death, Beatrice no longer suffers, not even because of her real death, which is caused by no illness (*VN* 28–29; 31.10, vv. 15–30). The protagonist, by contrast, after joining her in her grief at the time of her father's death, further experiences suffering because of her imagined death (*VN* 23) and then also and foremost because of her real death (*VN* 28–34). After her death, turning somewhat into self-pity and going momentarily astray (*VN* 35–38), the lover's grief focuses again on the dead Beatrice after her appearance in his imagination (*VN* 39). Feeling remorse (*VN* 39) for his misdirected love (*VN* 35–38), he then painfully longs for Beatrice and suffers because she no longer walks the streets of the desolate city (*VN* 40). Finally, after seeing her in her heavenly glory (*VN* 41–42), his grief turns into a hopeful desire to join her (*VN* 42).

Thus, starting at about the middle point of the story (*VN* 22), the protagonist's suffering is so pervasive as to make him a true participant in the redemptive role that the father's death and Beatrice's sorrow and death play in the story through their association with Christ's death (*VN* 22.1).[29] The death of Beatrice, a Christlike sacrifice, is the *sine qua non* for the male protagonist not to become

---

[29] Seeking to recreate iconographically the scene in its essential traits, one would situate the father's figure at the center, next the mourning Beatrice, then the grieving ladies, and finally, at a greater distance, the weeping male protagonist. Thus the scene's essential iconography imitates that of Christ's crucifixion or deposition from the cross, in front of which stood several ladies, including the Blessed Virgin, but also John.

lost on earth and to hope for life eternal, and for Dante the author the *sine qua non* for his narrative to continue its unfolding beyond the youthful narrative into the masterpiece of his maturity, the *Comedy*. The violence implicit in every death gradually transforms the protagonist, because he accepts it and even invokes it (*VN* 23.9). Therefore, becoming an active participant in its transforming powers, he hopes to "gire a vedere la gloria de la sua donna, cioè di quella benedetta Beatrice, la quale gloriosamente mira ne la faccia di colui *qui est per omnia saecula benedictus*" (*VN* 42.3).

Therefore, as I have announced at the beginning of this essay, although violence is the necessary way toward salvation, it does not constitute an end in itself, since, when accepted, it leads to glory. At the very end of the *Comedy*, in fact, Dante the poet glorifies not only God Incarnate but also the Pilgrim as the latter seeks to understand human beings' impossible challenge; namely, to contemplate God Triune and understand how it is possible for man, Christ, to be God.

4. The Glory of Christ Crucified

At the end of the *Comedy*, through the image of the circle Dante the poet seeks at first to represent God, One and Triune, occupying three circles of the same "contenenza" and of three different colors, the first circle reflected by the second, the third being like a fire equally breathing from those two, and all three engaged in an infinitely active life represented by their own circular motion:

> Ne la profonda e chiara sussistenza
> de l'alto lume parvermi tre giri
> di tre colori e d'una contenenza;
> e l'un da l'altro come iri da iri
> parea reflesso, e 'l terzo parea foco
> che quinci e quindi igualmente si spiri.
> (*Par.* 33.115–20)[30]

Then, as the Pilgrim first sees the vision of the three rotating circles, his eyes fix themselves on the reflected circle, representing the second person of the Trinity, within which another mystery is perceived:

> Quella circulazion che sí concetta
> pareva in te come lume reflesso,
> da li occhi miei alquanto circunspetta,
> dentro da sé, del suo colore stesso,

---

[30] For a recent essay on this last canto, focusing on what the author calls "prova glorificante," see Georges Güntert, "La 'prova glorificante': *Paradiso* 33," *Cuadernos de filología italiana* 9 (2002): 33–48.

mi parve pinta de la nostra effige
per che 'l mio viso in lei tutto era messo.
(*Par.* 33.127–32)

At the very end of his voyage through the afterlife, the Pilgrim sees a human figure: *la nostra effige*. This human effigy is "pinta" ("painted" or "depicted") within itself (*dentro da sé*), namely, within the reflected circle, of which the same human effigy shares the same color: that is, while becoming human, the second Person of the Trinity is and remains always God.

Where is "our human effigy" and why does Dante the poet say that it is "pinta"? Is this effigy of ours painted on the indivisible line forming the circle, arguably an absolute impossibility? or is it painted on the space contained within the circle? The text proposes that "our effigy" is painted—that is, present in its human form and appearance—within the second circle, which occupies the same space of the other two. Thus our effigy occupies the space contained by the three circles, representing the *verbum caro factum* (John 1:14).[31]

It is precisely through "our effigy" that the seer finally is empowered to see and understand also the other two persons of the Trinity. In fact, as we read in the Gospel according to John, whoever sees Him—Christ says—sees also the Father, for He is in the Father and the Father is in Him ("[. . .] qui videt me, videt et patrem [. . .] ego in Patre, et Pater in me est [. . .]": John 14:9–10). Furthermore, and even more importantly, nobody can know the Father and thus accede to Him except through Christ (John 14:6).

But what is it then that Dante the Pilgrim sees in the form of our effigy within the circle, and what is the relationship of the effigy to the circle that contains it? The text offers no explanation. I would like to propose that the effigy within the circle cannot be but that of Christ crucified, and yet glorious and

---

[31] Concerning the meaning of the adjective *pinta*, one should bear in mind several elements: 1) the topos of "deus pictor": God painter of the universe and the molder of man in his own image (E. R. Curtius, *European Literature and the Latin Middle Ages*, trans. W. R. Trask, 2nd ed. [Princeton: Princeton University Press, 1973], 562); 2) God as the father of Christ (see the hymn formerly ascribed to Ambrose, *Caeli deus*, for which see Curtius, *European Literature*, 562, and also 544, *Deus artifex*). See *pingere* and *dipingere* in *Enciclopedia dantesca*, according to which the two verbs have mostly a figurative meaning and convey the idea of representation. The term *effigie* derives from the Lat. *effigies* < *ex* + *fingo*: "propr. 'esprimere (*ex*) modellando con l'argilla (*fingere*)'" (*Dizionario etimologico della lingua italiana*, ed. M. Cortelazzo and P. Zolli, 5 vols. [Bologna: Zanichelli, 1979–1988], s.v.); the Latin *fingere* carries a broad semantic area, which includes *to shape, sculpt, make, create, imagine, represent, imitate, simulate*. The It. *effige*, recurring twice only in the *Comedy*, refers to Beatrice (*Par.* 31.77) and then Christ; in both instances the term means the human semblance, whether it refers to the whole person or just to the face as a part for the whole, as implied by medieval etymologers (Isidore, *Etymologiae* 11.1.33: "Facies dicta ab effigie. Ibi est enim tota figura hominis et uniuscuiusque personae cognitio").

resurrected, who, as we hear from Virgil's description of the harrowing of hell, was "con segno di vittoria coronato" (*Inf.* 4.54): crowned with the sign of victory, the cross, as a fundamental passage in *Paradise* evinces most clearly:

> Qui vince la memoria mia lo 'ngegno;
> ché quella croce lampeggiava Cristo,
> sì ch'io non so trovare essempro degno;
> (*Par.* 14.103–105)

Completely overtaken by the vision in the heaven of Mars, Dante the Pilgrim had already offered himself up wholly, as the term *olocausto* (wholly burned) means, thereby becoming a martyr by desire, and joining Christ himself in His sacrifice:

> Con tutto 'l core e con quella favella
> ch'è una in tutti, a Dio feci olocausto,
> qual conveniesi a la grazia novella.
> (*Par.* 14.88–90)[32]

The fact is that the cross of the martyrs is no longer a sign of ignominy and in fact shines through Christ, or on it Christ shines through.[33] The cross thus

---

[32] On the Pilgrim's sacrifice (holocaust), see Quinones, *Foundation Sacrifice*, esp. 123–35.

[33] For line 104 Petrocchi prefers "ché quella croce lampeggiava Cristo"—"for that cross shone forth Christ"—over the other variant, chosen by the 1921 critical edition of the Società Dantesca Italiana (followed also by Antonio Lanza): "ché 'n quella croce lampeggiava Cristo", "for Christ shone forth on that cross." In her commentary, A. M. Chiavacci Leonardi points out correctly that this second variant "ci sembra tuttavia dare senso migliore: risplendeva 'a modo di lampo,'" in agreement "con l'espressione usata più avanti" (*La divina commedia: Paradiso* [Milan: Mondadori, 2005], 404 n. 104); namely, "vedendo in quell'albor balenar Cristo" (*Par.* 14.108). Chiavacci Leonardi points out correctly that the text does not specify whether "l'immagine del Redentore appare [. . .] in quella croce di stelle: forse al suo centro, come nella croce di Ravenna; forse in tutta la sua estensione" (404 n. 104). In note 100–102 of the same canto, she remarks that the face of Christ appears at the center of a Greek cross in the apse of St. Apollinare in Classe in Ravenna, adding further that many were "le figurazioni di tal genere nelle chiese di allora," making reference to G. Fallani, "Il canto XIV del *Paradiso*," *Nuove letture dantesche* 6 (1973): 147–62 (esp. 160). The latter, connecting the resplendent Christ of *Par.* 14 with the "nostra effige" of *Par.* 33, adds that in the second circle of the Trinity "vi appare l'immagine del Redentore" (161), arguably the whole person of the Redeemer. On the complex issue of the squaring of the circle and its poetic implications in Dante, I refer to R. B. Herzman and G. W. Towsley, "Squaring of the Circle: *Paradiso* 33 and the Poetics of Geometry," *Traditio* 49 (1994): 95–125; on the final vision, see K. Foster, *The Two Dantes and Other Studies* (Berkeley: University of California Press, 1977), 66–85.

foregrounds the glorious Christ on a Greek cross, the only kind of cross, and thus of Christ crucified, that can fit within a circle, as we read in *Par.* 33:

> ....
> veder voleva come si convenne
> l'imago al cerchio e come vi s'indova;
> ma non eran da ciò le proprie penne:
> (*Par.* 33.137–139)

Contrary to what happens in *Par.* 14.103–105, where the Pilgrim-turned-writer remembers but cannot describe, at the end of the journey he declares his inability to understand how and where the image—namely, "la nostra effige": in my opinion, the glorious Christ on a Greek cross—fits perfectly within the second circle representing God Incarnate.[34] The impossibility of the human endeavor, brought forth by the simile of the squaring of the circle, that Dante the author deploys here (*Par.* 33:133–35) points up, on the one hand, the human inadequacy to understand God Incarnate and Triune, and, on the other, the need of God's Redemption for the Pilgrim, and all humans, to ascend to Heaven and contemplate God. In fact, as the seer seeks in vain to penetrate the inscrutable mystery, he, only through Christ and Christ crucified, satisfies his ultimate desire and attains to the highest truth and vision:

> ....
> se non che la mia mente fu percossa
> da un fulgore in che sua voglia venne.
> (*Par.* 33.140–41)

J. T. Schnapp, *The Transfiguration of History at the Center of Dante's* Paradise (Princeton: Princeton University Press, 1986) (to whom I refer for a rich analysis of the complex imagery of the cross) points out in a note a relationship between the cross in *Par.* 14 and the three circles in *Par.* 33.116–117 (81n).

[34] Accordingly, "our effigy"—in my opinion, the glorious Christ on a resplendent cross, as in *Par.* 14.104–105—may be visualized to touch, with the cross on which He is stretched—or with His arms and feet, if we reject the image of the cross —, the four opposite points of the circle. Thus Christ lies at the center of the triune circle representing the Trinity, just as He lies at the center of the Christian universe, as shown by the medieval maps, where Christ stood at the center of the known universe (Hereford map; T maps; I would also like to refer to the Vitruvian figure, inscribed in a square and a circle, for which see M. Praz, *Mnemosyne* [Princeton: Princeton University Press, 1970], 79–105, esp. 83; also Schnapp, *Transfiguration of History*, Index, 263, s.v. "Cross"). In fact, Chiavacci Leonardi points out the cross of *Par.* 14 recalls "la divisione del cielo secondo i quattro punti cardinali nella quale gli antichi cristiani riconoscevano appunto la croce di Cristo" (*Paradiso*, 404 n. 100–102).

Thus the highest glorification of Christ crucified and, because of Him, also of the Pilgrim who has followed him, marks the end of the poem:

> A l'alta fantasia qui mancò possa;
> ma già volgeva il mio disio e 'l *velle*,
> sí come rota ch'igualmente è mossa,
> l'amor che move il sole e l'altre stelle.
> (*Par.* 33.142–145)

Thus with this last image—one of violence ("la mia mente fu percossa / da un fulgore") and thus of sacrifice —[35] the motif of sacrifice begun in Dante's youthful autobiography comes full circle, attaining its highest manifestation precisely at the moment that describes the Pilgrim's beatific vision.

Works Cited

Alighieri, Dante. *La commedia*. Nuovo testo critico secondo i più antichi manoscritti fiorentini. Ed. Antonio Lanza. Anzio: De Rubeis Editore, 1995.
———. *La commedia secondo l'antica vulgata*. Ed. Giorgio Petrocchi. 4 vols. Milan: Mondadori, 1966–67.
———. *La divina commedia. Paradiso*. 1994. Comm. Anna Maria Chiavacci Leonardi. Milan: Oscar Mondadori, 2005.
———. *La divina commedia:* Testo critico della Società Dantesca Italiana col commento scartazziniano rifatto da G. Vandelli. Milan: Hoepli, 1989.
———. *Vita nuova*: Italian Text with Facing English Translation. Trans. and ed. Dino S. Cervigni and Edward Vasta. Notre Dame: University of Notre Dame Press, 1995.
The American Heritage Dictionary of the English Language. Boston: Houghton Mifflin, 1996.
Augustine, Saint. *Oeuvres de Saint Augustin*, 13 and 14: *Les Confessions*. Vol. 1, Livres 1–7; Vol. 2, Livres 8–13. Ed. M. Skutella, introd. and notes A. Solignac, trans. E. Tréhorel and G. Bouissou. Paris: Desclée de Brouwer, 1962.
Bandera, Cesáreo. "Tasso and the Epic. A Girardian Reading." *Annali d'Italianistica* 15 (1997): 109–24.

---

[35] The phrase that Dante the author employs here to describe the Pilgrim's illumination—"percossa / da un fulgore"—is fairly common in patristic writings (the electronic search of Migne's *Patrologia Latina* yields several hits), while the verb itself (Italian, *percuotere*; Latin, *percutere*) is employed by St. Augustine, in referring to John 19:34 ("[. . .] unus militum lancea latus eius aperuit, et continuo exivit sanguis et aqua"), to describe the ultimate act of violence inflicted upon Christ (my emph.): "[. . .] mortuo Christo lancea *percutitur* latus (Joan. XIX, 34), ut profluant sacramenta, quibus formetur Ecclesia" (PL 35. 1463: *In Ioannis Evangelium Tractatus CXXIV,* IX, Cap. II, V. 1–11).

Bárberi Squarotti, Giorgio. "'L'ambiguità' della *Vita nuova*." In *Psicoanalisi e strutturalismo di fronte a Dante: Dalla lettura profetica medievale agli odierni strumenti critici*. Atti dei mesi danteschi 1969–1971, 3:7–55. 3 vols. Florence: Olschki, 1972.

Biblia sacra iuxta vulgatam clementinam. Madrid: Biblioteca de autores cristianos, 1982.

Casini, T., comm. *La vita nuova*. Florence: Sansoni, 1885.

Cervigni, Dino S. "L'Acheronte dantesco: morte del Pellegrino e della poesia." *Quaderni d'Italianistica* 10 (1989): 71–89.

———. "Dante's Lucifer: The Denial of the Word." *Lectura Dantis. A Forum for Dante Research and Interpretation* 3 (1988): 51–62.

———. *Dante's Poetry of Dreams*. Florence: Olschki, 1986.

———. "The Muted Self-Referentiality of Dante's Lucifer." *Dante Studies* 107 (1989): 45–74.

Cortelazzo, Manlio, and Paolo Zolli. *Dizionario etimologico della lingua italiana*. 5 vols. Bologna: Zanichelli, 1979–1988.

Curtius, Ernst Robert. *European Literature and the Latin Middle Ages*. 1948. Trans. Willard R. Trask. Princeton: Princeton University Press, 1973.

D'Ancona, Alessandro, comm. *La vita nuova*. Pisa: Galileo già ff. Nistri, 1884.

De Bonfils Templer, Margherita. *Itinerario di Amore: Dialettica di Amore e Morte nella* Vita nuova. University of North Carolina Studies in Romance Languages and Literature. Chapel Hill: University of North Carolina Press, 1973.

De Robertis, Domenico. *Il libro della* Vita nuova. Florence: Sansoni, 1970.

Enciclopedia cattolica. 11 vols. Vatican City, 1948–1953.

Enciclopedia dantesca. 6 vols. Rome: Istituto della Enciclopedia Italiana fondata da Giovanni Treccani, 1970–78.

Fallani, Giovanni. "Il canto XIV del *Paradiso*." *Nuove letture dantesche* 6 (1973): 147–62.

Federzoni, G., and G. Carducci, comm. *La vita nuova*. Bologna: Zanichelli, 1910.

Foster, Kenelm. *The Two Dantes and Other Studies*. Berkeley: University of California Press, 1977.

Girard, René. *Things Hidden Since the Foundation of the World*. Trans. Stephen Bann and Michael Metteer. Stanford: Stanford University Press, 1987.

———. *Violence and the Sacred*. Trans. Patrick Gregory. Baltimore: Johns Hopkins University Press, 1977.

Güntert, Georges. "La 'prova glorificante': *Paradiso* 33." *Cuadernos de filología italiana* 9 (2002): 33–48.

Herzman, Ronald B., and Gary W. Towsley. "Squaring of the Circle: *Paradiso* 33 and the Poetics of Geometry." *Traditio* 49 (1994): 95–125.

Isidori Hispalensis Episcopi *Etymologiarum sive originum libri XX*, ed. W. M. Lindsay. 2 vols. Oxford: Clarendon Press, 1911.

Melodia, G., comm. *La vita nuova.* Milan: Vallardi, 1905.

Musa, Mark. *Dante's* Vita nuova: *A Translation and an Essay.* Bloomington: Indiana University Press, 1973.

Petrarca, Francesco. *Canzoniere.* Ed. and comm. Marco Santagata. Milan: Mondadori, 1996.

———. *Opere. Canzoniere. Trionfi. Familiarum Rerum Libri.* Florence: Sansoni, 1975.

Praz, Mario. *Mnemosyne: The Parallel between Literature and the Visual Arts.* Bollingen Series 35.16. Princeton: Princeton University Press, 1970.

Quinones, Ricardo J. *Foundation Sacrifice in Dante's* Commedia. University Park: The Pennsylvania State University Press, 1994.

Uguccione da Pisa. *Derivationes.* Ed. Enzo Cecchini et alii. 2 vols. Florence: Edizioni del Galluzzo, 2004.

Scherillo, Michele, comm. *La vita nuova.* Milan: Hoepli, 1911.

Singleton, Charles. 1949. *An Essay on the* Vita nuova. 2nd ed. Baltimore: Johns Hopkins University Press, 1977.

Schnapp, Jeffrey T. *The Transfiguration of Hostory at the Center of Dante's* Paradise. Princeton: Princeton University Press, 1986.

Strummiello, Giusi. *Il Logos violato: La violenza nella filosofia.* Bari: Dedalo, 2001.

Thomas Aquinas. *Summa theologiae.* 5 vols. Madrid: Biblioteca de autores cristianos, 1956–1962.

Vocabulaire de théologie biblique. Ed. Xavier Léon-Dufour et al. Paris: Editions du Cerf, 1964.

Sixteenth-Century Criticism of Dante's *Tenzone* with Forese Donati: Vincenzio Borghini's "De' poeti antichi toscani"[1]

Fabian Alfie

It is impossible to say exactly when the tradition of scholarship on Dante's *tenzone* with Forese Donati began. The great poet himself adopted a critical stance towards the literary exchange when he cast Forese as a character on the terrace of gluttony in *Purgatorio* XXIII and XXIV and seemingly recollected with regret their previous spurious verse.[2] As a personal and artistic statement, the episode in *Purgatorio* is impressive, but when read as criticism of the poetic correspondence, it is less than satisfying. Thanks in part to the poet's palinodic intentions therein, he casts in a different light the experience of his literary correspondence in his magnum opus; he reinscribes the insulting *tenzone* with a signification perhaps not originally intended and thereby alters subsequent readers' comprehension of it.[3] Dante, the young poet who slandered Forese Donati in the early 1290s, had radically different aims from those of Dante, the author of *Purgatorio*, who recalled the literary exchange in his maturity. During the 1350s Giovanni Boccaccio cited verses of the *tenzone* in his prose works, twice in the *Decameron*

---

[1] I would like to thank the staff at the Biblioteca Nazionale Centrale of Florence for its assistance in consulting Vincenzio Borghini's manuscripts, and for information about Firenze II, i, 39. I would also like to thank the staff at the Biblioteca Riccardiana for its assistance in determining information about the "Anonimo Fiorentino" (Riccardiano 1016).

[2] Ciro Tribalza, "Canto XXIII," in *Letture dantesche*, vol. 2, *Purgatorio* (Florence: Sansoni, 1965), 1148.

[3] For representative examples of scholars who speak of the passage in *Purgatorio* XXIII and XXIV as the poet's subsequent repudiation of the *tenzone*, see Umberto Bosco, "Forese," in *Dante vicino* (Rome: Caltanissetta, 1985), 170; Tommaso Giuffreda, *Dante e Forese* (Bari: Danisi, 1952), 6.

(IV.10 and VII.8) and once in the *Corbaccio* (l. 319).[4] As with the reminiscence of the *tenzone* in *Purgatorio*, Boccaccio has artistic purposes for citing the *tenzone* other than that of allowing readers to understand the six poems more fully; he tends to quote writing by other individuals ironically, putting the citations in contexts which force a reinterpretation of their texts.[5] Boccaccio's reminiscences of the poetic exchange between Dante and Forese indicate only his own artistic interpretation of it, which is freighted with his own literary intentions and not necessarily those of Alighieri and Donati. To be sure, the intertextualities of other literary works with the *tenzone* convey to a degree the great authors' critical perspectives on the correspondence, but they only partially assist readership in the interpretation of the sonnets.

Additionally, three commentaries on Dante's *Commedia* mention the *tenzone* with Forese Donati when explicating *Purgatorio* XXIII and XXIV. These works advance the scholarly understanding of the exchange although their primary thrust is that of clarifying the *Commedia* and not the poetic correspondence. In the marginalia to Dante's masterpiece found in manuscript Firenze II i 39,[6] a codex most likely penned by the notary Andrea Lancia ca. 1343,[7] the commentator explains that Forese Donati was renowned as a glutton, a vice for which Dante

---

[4] The *Decameron* is cited from Giovanni Boccaccio, *Decameron*, ed. Vittore Branca (Turin: Einaudi, 1992). The *Corbaccio* is cited from Vittore Branca, ed., *Tutte le opere di Giovanni Boccaccio*, 5.2 (Milan: Mondadori, 1994).

[5] J. H. Whitfield characterizes Boccaccio's appropriation of Alighieri's poetry as "misuse," and Robert Hollander observes that the literary aims of the two authors frequently lie at odds with one another. See J. H. Whitfield, "Dante in Boccaccio," *Italian Studies* 15, Supplement (1960): 1–48, here 26; and Robert Hollander, "Boccaccio's Dante," *Italica* 63 (1986): 278–89, here 284.

[6] For a succinct description of the manuscript, see Barbara Banchi and Alessandra Stefanin, *La 'Commedia': I codici della Biblioteca Nazionale Centrale di Firenze* (Florence: Società Dantesca Italiana, 1998), 40; see also Gabriella Pomaro, "Analisi codicologica e valutazioni testuali della tradizione della *Commedia*," in *"Per correr miglior acque. . .": Bilanci e prospettive degli studi danteschi alle soglie del nuovo millennio. Atti del Convegno internazionale di Verona-Ravenna, 25–29 ottobre 1999* (Rome: Salerno, 2001), 1: 1055–67. For an in-depth description of the codex, see Luca Azzetta, "Le chiose alla *Commedia* di Andrea Lancia, *l'Epistola a Cangrande* e altre questioni dantesche," *L'Alighieri* 44 (2003): 5–76.

[7] Regarding the attribution of the manuscript to Andrea Lancia, see Azzetta, "Le chiose alla *Commedia* di Andrea Lancia," 5–11. Azzetta acknowledges that Gabriella Pomaro had also suggested that the manuscript was Andrea Lancia's working copy. See Pomaro, "Analisi codicologica e valutazioni testuali della tradizione della *Commedia*," 1065. Regarding the dating of the manuscript, see Azzetta, "Le chiose alla *Commedia* di Andrea Lancia," 19–23.

addressed poetry to him.[8] His knowledge of the *tenzone* appears incomplete because he speaks of Dante having written about Forese's gluttony in one sonnet ("uno sonetto"); in fact, Dante treats the topic of Forese's overeating in two extant sonnets of the correspondence. Sadly, Lancia breaks off the discussion midsentence, providing little more than biographical information about Forese that can be derived from the text of the *Commedia*.

More substantially, the commentary known as "anonimo fiorentino" (ca. 1380–1420) contained in the manuscript Riccardiano 1016 (fol. 284v) refers to the insulting poetry of the *tenzone* but also provides the earliest known citation of four verses of one of the sonnets:

> Questa anima che introduce qui l'Auttore a parlare, sì fu Forese, fratello di messer Corso Donati da Firenze, il quale fu molto corrotto nel vizio della gola, e nella prima vita fu molto dimestico dell'Auttore; per la qual dimestichezza egli fece festa a Dante, et molti sonetti et cose in rima scrisse l'uno all'altro; e fra gli altri l'Auttore riprendendolo di questo vizio della gola, gli scrisse uno sonetto in questa forma:
>
> Ben ti faranno il nodo Salomone,
> Bicci novello, i petti delle starne,
> Ma peggio fia la lonza del castrone,
> Ché 'l cuoio farà vendetta della carne, ecc.
> Questo Forese Donati fu chiamato per soprannome Bicci.[9]

The anonymous Florentine commentator explicitly mentions the poetic correspondence and cites a portion of it, as well as providing a considerable amount of pertinent information. In addition to the biographical data about Forese, his friendship with Dante, and the Donati family, the unidentified Florentine offers a succinct critical analysis of the *tenzone*. When writing that Dante reproves Forese for his vice ("riprendendolo di questo uitio"), the "anonimo fiorentino" adopts a critical stance to the exchange as evidenced by his use of key terms from medieval literary scholarship. According to Paul Miller, the medieval vulgate definitions of satire—frequently conflated to those of comedies in general—explain that the purpose of satire is to censure ("reprehendere") and its subject matter is vice ("vitium").[10] Thus the unknown Florentine commentator interprets

---

[8] The marginalium reads literally: "qui finge lautore un suo noto nome forese de donati di fire(n)ze il quale peccoe i(n) questo uitio onde lautore fece uiue(n)te forese uno sonetto che comi(n)cia" (fol. 110v).

[9] The "Anonimo Fiorentino" is cited from Pietro Fanfani, ed., *Commento alla Divina Commedia d'Anonimo Fiorentino del Secolo XIV, ora per la prima volta stampato* (Bologna: Presso Gaetano Romagnoli, 1868), 2: 378–79.

[10] Paul Miller, "John Gower, Satiric Poet," in *Gower's Confessio Amantis: Responses and Reassessments*, ed. A. J. Minnis (Cambridge: D. S. Brewer, 1983), 79–105, here 80–81.

the six sonnets by situating them within the commonplace moral framework for medieval satires and comedies of reprehending sin.[11] By employing recognizable literary terminology, the commentator all but asserts that the *tenzone* is an example of comic satire, as the genre was understood during the Middle Ages. The "anonimo fiorentino" subtly furnishes an interpretation of the sonnets in accordance with medieval definitions of comedies; in effect, the poems between Dante and Forese played the social role of enforcing morality by publicly shaming and deriding vice.

In his commentary on the *Commedia*, Giovanni da Serravalle (1416–1417) alludes to the *tenzone* saying only that the two young men had made accusations about one another ("fecerunt invicem et insimul").[12] Serravalle only suggests the poetic correspondence when he speaks of the reciprocal insults between Dante and Forese. In keeping with the personal poetics of *Purgatorio* XXIII and XXIV, Giovanni presents the *tenzone* primarily as a biographical event—the interpersonal exchange of accusations—rather than as a literary phenomenon like the "anonimo fiorentino." Taken together, the commentaries by Andrea Lancia, the anonymous Florentine, and Giovanni da Serravalle comprise the entire critical tradition on the *tenzone* between Dante and Forese of the late Middle Ages and Renaissance.

Given the relatively slight critical history of the *tenzone* in the fourteenth, fifteenth, and sixteenth centuries, the unfinished treatise found in Firenze II x 105 marks an important achievement in Dante scholarship. Composed by the Florentine philologist Vincenzio Borghini (1515–1580), the passage, entitled "De' poeti antichi toscani" by subsequent librarians, treats several medieval slanderous *tenzoni*, not just that between Dante and Forese, although references to the latter recur throughout the text. Despite not being a systematic writer—having left many texts unfinished owing in part to his work as the director of the Florentine hospital—Borghini is considered by many to be an important sixteenth-century scholar on medieval literature.[13] He composed some forty manuscripts, many of which are his notebooks now housed in the Biblioteca Nazionale Centrale of Florence, and he was a member of the team that "corrected"

Regarding the conflation of the definitions of satire and comedy, see Judson Boyce Allen, "Hermann the German's Averroistic Aristotle and Medieval Poetic Theory," *Mosaic* 9 (1976): 67–81, here 68.

[11] Judson Boyce Allen, *The Ethical Poetic of the Later Middle Ages: A Decorum of Convenient Distinction* (Toronto: University of Toronto Press, 1982), 19–20.

[12] Cited from *La Divina Commedia nella figurazione artistica e nel secolare commento*, vol. 2, *Purgatorio*, ed. G. Biagi, G. L. Passerini, and E. Rostagno (Turin: UTET, 1931), 487.

[13] Giancarlo Mazzacurati, "Borgini, Vincenzio," in *Enciclopedia dantesca* (Rome: Istituto della Enciclopedia Italiana, 1970), 1: 685–86.

the *Decameron* for approval by the Inquisition.[14] He was part of the movement that left the Accademia Fiorentina, attacking the linguistic theories of Giovan Battista Gelli,[15] who believed that Florentine was derived from ancient Aramaic.[16] Borghini's reaction against Pietro Bembo's linguistic and literary theories inspired to an extent his interest in the history of the Florentine language.[17] He published several defenses of Dante, including an affirmation of the author's Catholic orthodoxy,[18] and an attack on the practices of the Venetian printer Ruscelli, who rewrote works into modern Italian.[19] In the 1550s, he wrote *Lettera intorno a' manoscritti antichi*, about reconstructing ancient texts by collating various codicological exemplars.[20] During the same decade, he began work on an unfinished essay about literary polemics, *Dello scrivere contro altrui*,[21] in which he tried to distinguish between public debates and trivial private slanders;[22] as Gino Belloni and Riccardo Drusi observe, he aimed therein to find the boundaries between humanistic enterprises and merely bestial diatribes.[23] By writing the text, he hoped to discourage the simple defamation of other people's texts.[24] In short, Borghini was thoroughly engaged in the literary and linguistic debates of the high sixteenth century.

Yet Vincenzio Borghini's groundbreaking work as a philological linguist accounts for his stature among modern Dante scholars. As Benedetto Croce writes, Vincenzio reacted against the Renaissance fashion of interpreting Dante

---

[14] Michele Barbi, "Degli studi di Vincenzio Borghini sopra la storia e la lingua di Firenze," in *Vincenzio Borghini dall'erudizione alla filologia: Una raccolta di testi*, ed. Gino Belloni (Pescara: Libreria dell'Università Editrice, 1998), 191–259, here 243.

[15] Giuseppe Guido Ferrero, "Dante e i grammatici della prima metà del cinquecento," *Giornale storico della letteratura italiana* 105 (1935): 52.

[16] Domenico Zanrè, *Cultural Non-Conformity in Early Modern Florence* (Aldershot: Ashgate, 2004), 104.

[17] Riccardo Scrivano, "La posizione di Vincenzio Borghini nella critica cinquecentesca," *Rassegna della Letteratura Italiana* 62 (1958): 22–37, here 29.

[18] Scrivano, "La posizione di Vincenzio Borghini," 35.

[19] Brian Richardson, *Print Culture in Renaissance Italy: The Editor and the Vernacular Text, 1470–1600* (Cambridge: Cambridge University Press, 1994), 124.

[20] Gino Belloni and Riccardo Drusi, *Vincenzio Borghini: Filologia e invenzione nella Firenze di Cosimo I* (Florence: Olschki, 2002), 354. See also Gino Belloni, ed., *Vincenzio Borghini: Lettera intorno a' manoscritti antichi* (Rome: Salerno Editore, 1995), xiii.

[21] For a complete edition of the treatise, see *Dello scrivere contro ad alcuno, discorso inedito di V. Borghini*, ed. Giuseppe Aiazzi (Florence: Tipografia di Luigi Pezzati, 1841).

[22] Gino Belloni, "Borghini, *Dello scrivere contro altrui*: Un abbozzo di Galateo per la polemica letteraria," in *Bufere e molli aurette: Polemiche letterarie dallo Stilnovo alla "Voce"*, ed. Maria Grazia Pensa (Milan: Guerini, 1996), 53–65.

[23] Belloni and Drusi, *Vincenzio Borghini*, 351.

[24] Gino Belloni, "Introduzione," in *Vincenzio Borghini dall'erudizione alla filologia*, ed. idem, XII.

allegorically, insisting instead on the need to understand his work historically.[25] Michele Barbi asserts that he was perhaps the first scholar to study the fourteenth-century Florentine idiom in its entirety, reading not just the exalted works of Dante, Boccaccio, and Petrarch, but also the poetry of Cino, Lapo, Gianni, Guinizzelli, and Cavalcanti, and the prose texts of Franco Sacchetti, Giovanni Villani, the anonymous *Novellino*, and the commentary on the *Commedia* known as "ottimo commento."[26] In his glosses to medieval writers, he strove to remain faithful to the historical grammar and vocabulary of the works at hand, locating other similarly dated writings to elucidate their language.[27] Indeed, Michele Barbi claims that, by using texts to explicate texts, Vincenzio Borghini figures among those who initiated modern philological studies of the Middle Ages.[28]

The manuscript containing "De' poeti antichi toscani," Firenze II x 105, constitutes an incomplete miscellany of several writings.[29] The first ten pages are unnumbered and were clearly intended as a type of index; each page is divided into three columns, and the names of individuals are listed alphabetically. After two blank leaves the numeration begins, but the first actual text appears on page 5. From page 5 through 8 there is found the commentary to a poem by Monte Magno; pages 9 through 12 contain "De' poeti antichi toscani," followed by four blank sheets. Pages 17 through 44 hold a thesis on the family of Berlingaccio, followed by another fifty-two blank pages. Page 97 is dedicated to a grammatical piece on the use of the gerund, preceding seven more blank pages. From page 105 to 107 there appears the letter "Quante cose si potrebbon dire," after which the rest of the codex, some fifty-six pages, is left blank.

The literary treatise under examination is clearly an unfinished work. It begins with several stylistically polished paragraphs but quickly transforms into little more than a series of notes. Given its relevance to the history of Dante scholarship, the entire work will be transcribed below in its entirety in spite of its length. In the transcription below, I strive to be as faithful as possible to the manuscript source. The punctuation, including capitalizations, is Borghini's except for the following: parentheses indicate the spelling-out of scribal abbreviations; square brackets denote editorial corrections or interventions in the text; quotation marks have been placed around the citation of poetic verses to

---

[25] Benedetto Croce, "Un critico di poesia: Vincenzio Borghini," in *Poeti e scrittori del pieno e del tardo rinascimento* (Bari: Laterza, 1958), 2: 139–41.

[26] Barbi, "Degli studi di Vincenzio Borghini sopra la storia e la lingua di Firenze," 229–33.

[27] Aldo Vallone, *L'interpretazione di Dante nel Cinquecento* (Florence: Olschki, 1969), 219.

[28] Barbi, "Degli studi di Vincenzio Borghini," 229.

[29] For a brief description of the manuscript, see Giuseppe Mazzatinti, *Inventari dei manoscritti delle biblioteche d'Italia* (Forlì: Tipografia Sociale [Successori Bordandini], 1902–1903), 12: 57.

differentiate them from Borghini's remarks. In addition, for the sake of clarity the letters "v" and "u" have been distinguished, the accent marks have been regularized to follow contemporary usage, and the titles of literary works have been rendered in italic letters. Borghini's work reads:[30]

> [p. 9] Fra i componimenti de' poeti antichi sono mescolate molte canzonette ballate et sonetti, et io no(n) credo pu(r) vi sono di q(uei) tali autori: indicio me ne par ched una cagione et al sicuro ci è di mezzo l'esperienza et in alcuni testi delle canz. di Da(n)te, et in canzonetti poi ve ne sono dietro assai, et [illegible strikethrough] al certo si fa(n)no a dir di detti autori [illegible] hanno il proprio loro ce li fa dir: ma di q(ue)lle il facitore delle quali no(n) è noto, si rimangono a loro spesso a torto: pur nel l(ibr)o del Brevio et di Be(m)bo: ne sono fra q(ue)lle di D. et Guido Cavalc. specialmente delle molto deboli et bassi, et sto p(er) dire sciocche et quanto a me, credo esserci appiccate per quella via, et è quella CAGIONE ch[e] io intendo et in q(uei) tempi di haver un suo libro di questi sone[tti] come uscivan fuor nuove co(m)posizioni, p(er) esser o sonetti o canzoni, l'aggiugnella [sic: aggiungerla] a quel suo libro: fatto et ordinato p(er) quel tale p(er) q(ue)llo effetto: cosa ch(e) et p^{er} [sic] et anchora è in uso ch(e) un d(eve) far un libro per una sorte di scrittori, ve ne mette tutte q(ue)lle ch(e) gli vengono alle mani a quella materia come è quel libro stampato di' Agennio d(e) fini' constitutione ch(e) si vede esser stato di alcuno di quella professione dove haveva per sua co(m)modità ragunato insieme i [sic] tutto quello che haveva trovato di q(ue)lla materia o ch(e) facea p(er) lui et si vede ch(e) vi è fino al titolo del digesto et di codice fini' regundorum. Così di queste tali co(m)posizioni [p. 10] avveniva et d(e)ll' alcun(o) anchora, ch(e) già mi capitò un libro ove era la profetia ch(e) si dice di S. Brigida composta in serventese "Destate o fier leoni" poi dietro ce n'era da XV o XVI di diversi sorti in versi o in prosa de' più strani nomi ch'io sentissi mai. Così q(u)i è et la similitudine fa accozzar insieme le materie. Et spesso ond(e) interveniva che era un tal libro pogniam caso che canzoni di Dante in una casa: ch(e) di mano in mano età p(er) età vi s'aggiugnieva q(ue)lla cosa come dava la sorte, et di q(ue)llo credo io, che sia in q(ue)l libro del Brevio e Bem. q(uell)a mescolanza.
>
> Hora il mettergli p(er) di que' la' poeti et fra lor, inde no(n) ci è da far': gittargli via inde anch(e) bene perche si sono a(n)tichi, et almeno si conosce dalla q(ua)lità della ma(n) et più dal modo d(e)l dir: almeno vi sono parole usanze et notizie, ch(e) possono esser talhora buoni a qualch(e) proposito. Ch(e) credo fussi in q(uei) tempi com[c] ne' n(ostri) è stato, et andavan fuor certi sonetti piacevoli e in burla, et p(er) u(n) pezzo correano et gli voleva ognuno, come già mi ricordo di q(ue)l d(e)ll'Asino l'accidio et p(er) q(ue)llo

---

[30] For another *lectio* of the passage at hand, see Michele Barbi, *Studi di manoscritti e testi inediti*, vol. 1: *La raccolta bartoliniana di rime antiche e i codici da essa derivati* (Bologna: Zanichelli, 1900), 42–44.

"Lorenzo Strozzi, ha' titolo."[31] Hora io noterò alcune color a q(uell)o proposito.

Fra q(uelli) di D. ne sono alcunj contro a Forese Donati d(e)l quale fu gra(n)dis(sim)o amico: se in verità sono [p. 11] voglio sia giudizio d'altri: mordaci sono et quasi simili a q(ue)lli di Franco et di Pulci—quello ch(e) cominc[ia] "Bicci novel figliuol di no(n) so cui." Et q(uell)o fu il sopranome di Forese. Ha q(ue)l verso "Giù per la gola tanta Roba hai messa": et fa molto aproposito p(er) la historia et p(er) che lo mette D. fra Golosi in *purg*. Ch(e) si vede che D. mise in quella sua opera Persone publicamente in quei ta' vitij—
"Piange la madre ch' ha piu d'una doglia
Dicendo lassa me p(er) fichi secchi
messa l'havrej in casa il conte Guido." Era motto di q(uei) tempi, di far gran parentado di poca spesa e l'usò il Bocc. "la poteva allogar in casa i con Guidi p(er) un pezzo di pane"

[Marginalium alongside previous paragraph, atop p. 11]: Forese morì man(co) il 1300 cinq[ue] anni come dice D. o meno. Erano dunq(ue) Giovani se lor pur sono

Èvvenne un d'un Ser Giovanni Simonj [strikethrough: Quel da co]
"Quel da Cammin ed coraggio gentile
Non credo ch(e) sciogliessi piu vile parte
Quando a servigi dar voleva Marte
Che l'acca(m)pò nel bel fiume di Sile
Così l'animo è sempre esile." Et credo intenda quegli Buon Gherardo da Cammino, del quale in esempio di nobiltà parla Dante nel suo *Co(n)vivio* et forse nel *Purgatorio*.

Fra que' di Guido Cavalc. ve n'è uno d'incerto autore
"Una figura della Donna mia"
"S'adora Guido a S. Michele in orto" [illegible] A la quale rispose un Guido Orla(n)di co(n) q(ue)l sonetto e par ballato "S'havessi detti Amico di Maria." "Gratia l'hora et pia" et dichiara benissimo [p. 12] Al luogo del Villani che parla d(el) Miracolo et comi(n)cia a far la figura di N(ostra) Donna, ond(e) ci cominciò q(ue)lla compagnia di anchora in essere dei Capitani di Ors. M. et d(e)lle dispute et allhor ne funno di certi frati.

Sonvi alcune voci da notar come in q(ue)llo "Se non ti caggia," "E 'l tramazzar d(e)ll' altra sua famiglia." Credo sia nel *Novellino* "il tramazzo

---

[31] Michele Barbi treats this statement as an incipit verse; see Barbi, *Studi di manoscritti e testi inediti*, 42. However, no reference to such a sonnet appears in the following editions: *Rime inedite di Lorenzo Strozzi*, ed. Pio Ferrieri (Pavia: Premiata tipografia fratelli Fusi, 1885); "Lorenzo di Filippo Strozzi" in *Canti carnascialeschi del rinascimento*, ed. Charles S. Singleton (Bari: Laterza, 1936), 246–49; Lorenzo di Filippo Strozzi, *Commedie: Commedia in versi, La pisana, La Violante*, ed. Andrea Gareffi (Ravenna: Longo, 1980).

di q(ue)lla notte." In q(ue)llo "Guarda Manetto q(ue)lla scrignatuzza" vi è q(ue)l verso "Con cappellina et coi veli soggolata": onde sono anchor detti (per) soggoli come bende ma no(n) credo gli ab[b]ino più se no(n) le monache. Et sono queste voci nel *Corb*.

[Marginalium appears alongside previous paragraph]: Le pittur[e] antiche mostra che l'usasser anch(e) le donne secolari, et io mi vo' ricordar haverne vedute in mia fanciullezza

In que' di D. "La mal fatata" cioè graziata et avventurata et fata [above line: o fatto] haveano p(er) destino.

"Merce del copertoio ch'è cortonese." "Merce del popol tuo" Detti nell'op(er)a gra(n)de. Et quel cortonese, et vile e basso modo di metaphora è d(el) volgo ch(e) la parola vuol dir da Cortona et significa corto. La similitudine sola d(e)lle voci è usata p(er) altra proprietà. Et è debol modo.

"Per gir a guadagnar—ove che fossi"—e di Forese è detto ove che fosse, come ove che sia. "La vendetta che facesti di lui si bella et netta" di Forese. Così hoggi usiamo anchora quel netta et netto in que(sto) modo.

D'un Lippo Paschi dei Bardi "ch(e) mostra a dito que' che vanno a bere": mostrar a dito è accusar cola mano. Ve' là colui: già s'usava a not(are) un bene hoggi per villano costume.

Despite its rhetorical flourishes typical of Renaissance prose, as a study of Dante's *tenzone* with Forese Vincenzio's passage is remarkably modern. Borghini writes of his source material and attempts to explain its derivation. Throughout the treatise, he studies the correspondence between Dante and Forese from a generic point of view, associating it with other similar insulting exchanges of the age. He then glosses some of its language and that of the other works by referring to other medieval texts. Further, he attempts to reconstruct not only the language of thirteenth-century Florence but also its culture, mentioning some of the practices of the times. Although unfinished, it unambiguously strives to clarify the sonnets of the *tenzone* between Dante and Forese along with other similar medieval texts.

In "De' poeti antichi toscani," Borghini gives compelling evidence about the source of his information therein. In a letter written during the carnival of 1573, Vincenzio claimed to possess a copy of the manuscript compiled by Lorenzo Bartolini between 1527 and 1533.[32] The so-called "raccolta bartoliniana," now identified as Crusca 53,[33] was indirectly derived from four primary codices: Vatican 3214; Biblioteca Universitaria Bolognese 1289; the "raccolta aragonese"

---

[32] Barbi, *Studi di manoscritti e testi inediti*, 2.
[33] Giorgio Petrocchi, "Bartolini, Lorenzo," in *Enciclopedia dantesca*, 1: 524.

purportedly compiled by Angelo Poliziano and commissioned by Lorenzo de' Medici ca. 1476, now lost; and Chigiano L.VIII.305.[34] Thus the "raccolta bartoliniana" represents the continued reception of medieval literature during the Florentine Renaissance.[35] Importantly, the codex Crusca 53 explicitly mentions its direct sources as being two manuscripts, that of the canon of Ceneda and occasional author Giovanni Brevio (ca. 1500 – ca. 1549),[36] and that of Pietro Bembo. When Vincenzio Borghini speaks of the book by Brevio and Bembo in "De' poeti antichi toscani," therefore, he very clearly points to Crusca 53 or a copy as his source manuscript. Furthermore, all the texts discussed in the treatise are found in the "raccolta bartoliniana": the *tenzone* between Dante and Forese (fols. 3r-3v); Guido Cavalcanti's "S'e' non ti cagia la tua santalena" (fol. 14r), "Guarda [*sic*] Manetto, quella scrignatuzza" (fol. 15v), and "Una figura della Donna mia" (fol. 12r), and Guido Orlandi's response to the latter "S'avessi detto, amico, di Maria" (fol. 114r);[37] Lippo Paschi de' Bardi's "Io vorrei k'un segno avvenenato" (fol. 119r);[38] and Ser Giovanni Simoni's "Quel da Cammino col coraggio gentile" (fol. 132v).[39] According to Barbi, the latter poem is found only in Crusca 53 and its derivative manuscripts.[40] Regarding the *tenzone* between Dante and Forese, Crusca 53, like its indirect source Chigiano L.VIII.305 and two other manuscripts,[41] contains only four sonnets of the exchange, "Chi udisse tossir la mal fatata," "L'altra notte mi venn'una gran tosse," "Bicci novel, figliuol di non so cui," and "Ben so che fosti figliuol d'Allaghieri."[42] In "De' poeti antichi toscani," Vincenzio cites or discusses all four sonnets. Borghini's treatise, therefore, offers further proof of the importance of the "raccolta bartoliniana" for Italian literature, and illustrates the continuing relevance of the medieval poetry therein for the influential figures of the Florentine Renaissance.

Vincenzio dedicates his opening paragraphs to addressing the question of the authenticity of the poems he will discuss in the rest of the passage. In the

---

[34] Barbi, "La raccolta bartoliniana e le sue fonti," 122.

[35] Petrocchi, "Bartolini, Lorenzo," 524.

[36] Sabrina Trovò, ed., *Le novelle di Giovanni Brevio: Edizione critica* (Padua: Il Poligrafo, 2003), 15–24.

[37] The poetry of Guido Cavalcanti and Guido Orlandi is cited from Guido Cavalcanti, *Rime*, ed. Letterio Cassata (Rome: Donzelli, 1998).

[38] Lippo's poetry is cited from "Lippo Pasci dei Bardi" in *Poeti del Duecento*, vol. 2, ed. Gianfranco Contini (Milan–Naples: Ricciardi, 1960), 781–86.

[39] For a complete summary of the contents of Crusca 53, see Michele Barbi, "La raccolta bartoliniana e le sue fonti," in *Studi sul canzoniere di Dante, con nuove indagini sulle raccolte manoscritte e a stampa di antiche rime italiane* (Florence: Sansoni, 1965), 133–53.

[40] Barbi, *Studi di manoscritti e testi inediti*, 45.

[41] The two other manuscripts containing the four sonnets of the *tenzone* are Trivulziano 1058 and Banco Rari 69.

[42] The poetry of the *tenzone* between Dante and Forese is cited from Domenico de Robertis, ed., *Dante Alighieri: Rime*, vol. 3, *Testi* (Florence: Le Lettere, 2002).

process, he draws upon his experience as a philologist as laid out in his *Lettera intorno a' manoscritti antichi*. He recognizes that manuscript rubrics can frequently be unreliable ("indicio me ne par ched una cagione") and insists that the scholar needs to be judicious and depend upon other related criteria ("ci è di mezzo l'esperienza"). He then puts forth a theory as to how the manuscript was assembled, explaining that as the poems were made public, the scribes simply added them to the book ("come uscivan fuor nuove co(m)posizioni [. . .] l'aggiunella a quel suo libro"). He imagines a privately owned manuscript, to which generations of a family continually introduced works by Dante as they located them. To support his hypothesis, he refers to another unidentified manuscript besides Crusca 53 in which he found the prophetic poem attributed to Saint Birgitta, "Destati o fiero leone," alongside some fifteen or sixteen unrelated compositions. According to Domenico Pezzini, the writings of Saint Birgitta circulated widely in Italy during the fifteenth and sixteenth centuries,[43] and the poem mentioned by Borghini, which was comprised of 103 tercets in *terza rima*, was particularly popular during the Florentine Renaissance.[44] Of the six extant codices for the poem, none fits Borghini's description, for the only miscellany among them contains primarily authors well known among the humanists (e.g. Petrarch, Antonio da Ferrara, and the classical authors Seneca, Cicero, and Horace).[45] Undoubtedly the source manuscript for "Destati o fiero leone" cited by Borghini has been lost, but it serves as an example that many codices warranted a skeptical attitude. Alluding to the prevalence of untrustworthy published editions during the high Renaissance,[46] Vincenzio also mentions the volume of *De finium constitutione*, under the name of the classical author Agennius, which was similarly compiled in a haphazard manner. As Barbi states, Borghini was well aware of the weaknesses of the printed editions of vernacular literature, frequently emending them by referring to the source manuscripts.[47]

Just as Vincenzio cannot fully accept the sonnets as part of the authors' literary productions, he makes it plain that he cannot justify discarding these questionable poems either. The texts, he states, contain terminology and historical references that may prove invaluable to his scholarly endeavors ("vi sono parole usanze et notizie, ch(e) possono esser talhora buoni a qualche proposito"). Thus

---

[43] Domenico Pezzini, "The Italian Reception of Brigittine Writings," in *The Translation of the Works of St. Birgitta of Sweden into the Medieval Vernaculars*, ed. Bridget Morris and Veronica O'Mara (Turnhout: Brepols, 2002), 186–212, here 185–90; regarding the fame of the poem under discussion, see 203–4.

[44] Pezzini, "The Italian Reception of Brigittine Writings," 203–4.

[45] For a description of the humanistic miscellany that contains "Destati o fiero leone," Firenze II ix 125, see Giuseppe Mazzatinti and Fortunato Pintor, *Inventari dei manoscritti delle biblioteche d'Italia*, 12: 12–14.

[46] Richardson, *Print Culture in Renaissance Italy*, 1–7.

[47] Barbi, "Degli studi di Vincenzio Borghini," 238–39.

he substantiates the *raison d'être* of the present work as an attempt at understanding the language of the lyrics without having to attribute them definitively. Paradoxically, however, nothing in Crusca 53 gives any indication of doubt about the authenticity of the verse discussed by Borghini. On the contrary, it treats all the poems as legitimate, and few modern-day editors question their validity.[48] In addition, Lorenzo Bartolini's codex displays few traits of the disorganized assembly described by Vincenzio: it plainly lists its sources and those sources are generally trustworthy, and groups the poems together according to author. It may be that his distrust of Pietro Bembo's linguistic notions induced Borghini to suspect his manuscript as well.[49] Yet closer examination of Borghini's misgivings about the attribution of the poetry may illuminate some of his rationale for questioning its provenance. Throughout the passage, he reiterates his uncertainties only in two cases: in relationship to Guido Cavalcanti ("ve n'è uno d'incerto autore") and to the *tenzone* between Dante and Forese ("se in verità sono voglio sia giudizio d'altri"; "se lor pur sono"). Regarding the latter, however, he uses the sonnets to explicate Forese's presence in *Purgatorio*, stating that Dante clearly chose people publicly known for their vices—in this case, gluttony—and observing that

---

[48] Regarding those scholars who question the authenticity of Dante's *tenzone* with Forese Donati, see the following: Domenico Guerri, "Dante e Forese?" and "Le fosse, il guadagno e l'amor di Dante," chaps. 7 and 8 in *La corrente popolare nel rinascimento: Berte burle e baie nella Firenze del Brunellesco e del Burchiello* (Florence: Sansoni, 1931), 104–20, 121–48; idem, "Dal 'gagno' d'Alighiero a fra Timoteo," in *Scritti danteschi e d'altra letteratura antica*, ed. Antonio Lanza (Rome: De Rubeis, 1990), 331–8; idem, "Ancora il 'gagno' d'Alighero," in *Scritti danteschi e d'altra letteratura antica*, 339–54; idem, "Per la storia di Monna Tessa," in *Scritti danteschi e d'altra letteratura antica*, 355–65; idem, "Elementi del Decamerone nel primo sonetto d' 'Alighiero' con Bicci," in *Scritti danteschi e d'altra letteratura antica*, 367–78; Antonio Lanza, "Una volgare lite nella Firenze del primo quattrocento: la cosiddetta tenzone di Dante con Forese Donati—nuovi contributi alla tesi di Domenico Guerri," in *Polemiche e berte letterarie nella Firenze del primo quattrocento* (Rome: Bulzoni, 1971), 396–409; Mauro Cursietti, *La falsa tenzone di Dante con Forese Donati* (Rome: De Rubeis, 1995); idem, "Nuovi contributi per l'apocrifia della cosiddetta tenzone di Dante con Forese Donati ovvero la tenzone del Panìco," in *Bibliografia e critica dantesca: Saggi dedicati a Enzo Esposito*, ed. V. De Gregorio (Ravenna: Longo, 1997), 53–72; Antonio Lanza, "A norma di filologia: ancora a proposito della cosiddetta 'Tenzone tra Dante e Forese'," *L'Alighieri* 10 (1997): 43–54; Mauro Cursietti, "Una beffa parallela alla falsa Tenzone di Dante con Forese Donati: la berta di Cavalcanti 'cavalcato,'" *L'Alighieri* 13 (1999): 91–110; idem, "Dante e Forese alla taverna del Panìco: Le prove documentarie della falsità della tenzone," *L'Alighieri* 16 (2000): 8–22. The only one who questions the attribution of the sonnet to Guido Cavalcanti is Mauro Cursietti, "I doppi sensi del sonetto 'S'e' non ti caggia la tua santalena'," *La parola del testo* 3 (1999): 75–83.

[49] It should be noted that Pietro Bembo acknowledges Forese Donati as a poet, including him in a list of authors who were predecessors to, or contemporaries with, Dante. See Pietro Bembo, *Prose della volgar lingua* II, ii; cited from *Prose e rime di Pietro Bembo*, ed. Carlo Dionisotti (Turin: UTET, 1966).

Forese died prior to 1300. In other words, he seemingly accepts that the sonnets were directed to, and hence rebutted by, Forese Donati. Rather, he apparently questions only Dante's participation in the slanderous exchange. It may be, therefore, that the marked dissimilarity of these lyrics to the majority of works by Dante and Cavalcanti, two authors with whose work he was familiar, caused Borghini to wonder about the accuracy of the manuscript rubrics.

After the first two paragraphs, much of "De' poeti antichi toscani" follows Borghini's literary approach of using ancient texts to explicate other works. Thus he initiates the discussion of the *tenzone* with Donati in order to rationalize Forese's presence on the terrace of gluttony in *Purgatorio*. He then notes the textual similarity between the final verses of "Chi udisse tossir la mal fatata" and *Decameron* VII.8. In Boccaccio's *novella*, the protagonist's mother hurls abuse at her good-for-nothing son-in-law Arriguccio, exclaiming: "che [i miei figli] ti potevano così orrevolmente acconciare *in casa i conti Guidi con un pezzo di pane*" (l. 47; emphasis added). Given Borghini's presuppositions, he elucidates the resemblance as a common linguistic usage, although owing to Boccaccio's pattern of citation of the *tenzone*, discussed above, it now appears more likely to constitute a case of deliberate intertextuality. Vincenzio similarly explicates Ser Giovanni Simoni's poem as dealing with Gherardo da Cammino, recalling Dante's praise of the nobleman in *Convivio* and his reference to "buon Gherardo" in *Purgatorio* XVI (v. 124);[50] like many other commentators, the "ottimo commento," of which Vincenzio had knowledge, asserts that the passage in *Purgatorio* refers to Gherardo da Cammino.[51] And when discussing Cavalcanti's works, Borghini acknowledges the use of the term "tramazzo" in *Novellino* (49.19).[52] In short, Vincenzio brings to bear his familiarity with other important texts to the discussion of the slanderous poetry.

In his analysis of the verse, Vincenzio also proclaims that Boccaccio employs the word "soggolo" in the *Corbaccio*. While Boccaccio repeatedly mentions veils in that work ("benda" or "velo"), the specific term "soggolo" does not appear therein.[53] Importantly, however, Borghini shows himself to be interested not only in linguistic practices, but in historical customs as well, indicating that ancient paintings portray even secular women wearing veils; hence, in this light

---

[50] In the *Convivio* Dante writes: "Pognamo che Gherardo da Cammino fosse stato nipote del più villano che mai bevesse del Sile o del Cagnano [. . .] chi sarà oso di dire che Gherardo da Cammino fosse vile uomo?" (IV, xii, 6).

[51] *L'ottimo commento della Divina Commedia: Testo inedito d'un contemporaneo di Dante*, vol. 2, *Purgatorio*, ed. Alessandro Torri, rev. Francesco Mazzoni (Bologna: Forni, 1995), 292.

[52] The *Novellino* is cited from *Il Novellino*, ed. Alberto Conte (Rome: Salerno, 2001), 231.

[53] For references to "benda" or "bende," see *Corbaccio*, ll. 92, 287, and 310. For references to "velo" or "veli," see *Corbaccio*, ll. 239 and 240.

the reference to *Corbaccio* supports his reading of Cavalcanti's lyric. Similarly, in treating Lippo Pasci dei Bardi's sonnet Borghini explains the cultural difference in pointing out someone, which in contemporary times denotes only reprehension but in the past also implied praise ("già s'usava a not(are) un bene hoggi per villano costume"). Borghini comments that Cavalcanti's sonnet "Una figura della Donna mia" speaks of the miraculous powers of an image of the Virgin Mary in the church of Orsanmichele. In his examination, he cites the historian Giovanni Villani who discusses not only the icon's miracles, but also the resistance to accepting its power on the part of the Dominicans and the Franciscans: "Ma i frati predicatori e ancora i minori per invidia o per altra cagione non vi davano fede, onde caddono in grande infamia de' Fiorentini" (VIII, clv, [367]).[54] From the information gleaned from Villani, Vincenzio interprets the closing tercet of Cavalcanti's sonnet historically,[55] overlooking the traditional anticlericalism of the poem and referring instead to the actual debates of the friars ("d(e)lle dispute et allhor ne funno di certi frati").[56] Thus, in addition to clarifying the idiom of the fourteenth century, Borghini behaves as a cultural historian, attempting to use different sources to reconstruct the life and mores of the past.

Elsewhere in "De' poeti antichi toscani," Vincenzio simply glosses terms and expressions. He elucidates the expressions "ove che fossi" from Forese's sonnet "L'altra notte mi venn'una gran tosse" as being nearly identical to contemporary usage, as is the phrase "la vendetta [. . .] si bella e netta" from Forese's "Ben so che fosti figliuol d'Allaghieri." He explicates "mal fatata" from Dante's sonnet "Chi udisse tossir la mal fatata" as derived from the word "fata" — the modern-day "fato" — which in the Duecento meant "destiny." From the same sonnet, he explains the use of the word "mercè" by citing *Purgatorio* IV. 129 ("Mercè del popol tuo").[57] Vincenzio then clarifies Dante's statement, "copertoio c'ha cortonese," as denoting provenance from Cortona but connoting short ("corto"); in accordance with the current interpretation by Gianfranco Contini and Domenico De

---

[54] Giovanni Villani is cited from *Giovanni Villani*, ed. Giuseppe Edoardo Sansone and Giulio Cura Curà (Rome: Istituto Poligrafico e Zecca dello Stato, 2002). It should also be noted that Borghini annotated his copy of Giovanni Villani's history; for further information, see Vincenzio Borghini, *Annotazioni sopra Giovanni Villani*, ed., Riccardo Drusi (Florence: Presso l'Accademia, 2001).

[55] The final verses of Cavalcanti's sonnet read: "La voce va per lontane camina; / ma dicon ch'è idolatra i fra' minori, / per invidia che nonn è lor vicina."

[56] Regarding the anticlericalism of the sonnet, Ronald L. Martinez writes: "Guido Cavalcanti's sonnet gives a mischievously anti-clerical account of the miracle-working Madonna." See Ronald L. Martinez, "Guido Cavalcanti's 'Una figura della donna mia' and the Specter of Idolatry Haunting the *Stilnovo*," *Exemplaria* 15 (2003): 297–324, here 303.

[57] The *Commedia* is cited from *La Divina Commedia di Dante Alighieri nobile fiorentino ridotta a miglior lezione dagli Accademici della Crusca* (Florence: Domenico Manzani, 1595; repr. Florence: Accademia della Crusca, 2002).

Robertis,[58] Borghini interprets "cortonese" as Dante's suggestion that Forese had a small penis. Yet Borghini seems incensed at the implications of the adjective, calling it a vile and low type of metaphor ("vile e basso modo di metaphora"); he underscores his low opinion of the *double-entendre* later, calling it weak ("Et è debol modo"). By describing it as vile and low ("vile e basso") he interprets the expression as strictly insulting, cutting off other possible connotations to Dante's language.

Borghini's disdain for Dante's insulting pun on the word "cortonese" may open a window on the deeper awareness of his understanding of the literature of affront. It may further explain his repeated attempts throughout his lifetime to make sense of the poetry of vituperation. He describes the sonnets of the *tenzone* between Dante and Forese as "mordaci," reiterating a commonplace characterization of the literature of insult during the Middle Ages and Renaissance.[59] He then compares it to the fifteenth-century *tenzone* between Luigi Pulci and Matteo Franco.[60] Elsewhere, he relates the derisive poetry in the "raccolta bartoliniana" in general to the literary exchange between Lorenzo Strozzi (1482–1549) and Asino l'accidio.[61] In other words, he comprehends the literary phenomena found in Crusca 53 by the light of seemingly similar derisive exchanges of more recent decades. In fact, in the very same sentence in which he mentions Lorenzo Strozzi and Asino l'accidio, he reveals his accidental assumption that thirteenth-century *vituperationes* must perforce be like fifteenth- and sixteenth-century *tenzoni* when he characterizes the poetry under examination as "sonetti piacevoli e in burla." In his description of the poetry, Vincenzio's lexicon is extremely precise: by describing the sonnets with the term "burla," he calls to mind the sixteenth-century critical understanding of the verse of Francesco Berni. The term "burlesco" was first used by Antonfrancesco Grazzini to praise Berni's poetry,[62] and it quickly became synonymous with his poetics and that of his followers.[63] Yet Berni's literary praxis was the parodic deflation of texts and individuals, a literature of mockery that praised humble objects such as animals, foodstuffs,

---

[58] Gianfranco Contini and Domenico de Robertis, eds., *Dante Alighieri: Opere minori* 1: 1, *Vita Nuova, Rime* (Milano–Naples: Ricciardi, 1995), 369.

[59] Franco Suitner, *La poesia satirica e giocosa nell'età dei comuni* (Padova: Antenore, 1983), 17.

[60] For examples of the *tenzone* between Pulci and Franco, see Luigi Pulci, *Morgante e opere minori*, ed. Aulo Greco (Turin: UTET, 1997), 1383–1423.

[61] Biographical information about Lorenzo Strozzi is derived from Lorenzo di Filippo Strozzi, *Commedie: Commedia in versi, La pisana, La Violante*, ed. Gareffi, 31. No information is available about his opponent, Asino l'accidio.

[62] Silvia Longhi, "Francesco Berni," in *Poeti del Cinquecento*, vol. 1, *Poeti lirici, burleschi, satirici e didascalici*, ed. Guglielmo Gorni e Silvia Longhi (Milan–Naples: Ricciardi, 2001), 629.

[63] Salvatore Battaglia, ed. *Grande dizionario della lingua italiana*, vol. 2 (Turin: UTET, 1962), 457.

and household utensils in an ornate Latinate style.⁶⁴ Berni satirized the very language of encomium by praising that which was least worthy of praise.⁶⁵ Unlike medieval comedies, which as mentioned above fit inside a moral framework of chastising the sinful, burlesque literature is born from a humoristic impulse; it "criticizes [. . .] but not to scold, only for a laugh."⁶⁶ Borghini apparently agrees with the definition of Bernesque poetics, for he calls such poetry not just mocking ("in burla") but intended to provide pleasure ("piacevoli"). Elsewhere in 'De' poeti antichi toscani" he implies the vacuity of the poetics of slander ("molto deboli et bassi, et sto p(er) dire sciocche"). He does not appear to conceive of the poetry in Crusca 53 in a manner similar to that of "anonimo fiorentino," that is to say, of serving a crucial social function by castigating the sinful, but instead by the more recent practice of mockery for the sake of provoking laughter in others. Indeed, by composing the unfinished treatise on literary debates, *Dello scrivere contro altri*, he hoped to differentiate between useful public debates and empty personal slanders—the latter constituting the very definition of Bernesque vituperation. In short, he seems inadvertently to apply the sixteenth-century critical understanding of literary insult to thirteenth- and fourteenth-century examples of it. And perhaps this unintentional blurring of the two styles may further account for his resistance to accept the sonnets as authentic.

In conclusion, despite its flaws and unfinished nature, Vincenzio Borghini's "De' poeti antichi toscani" represents an important milestone in the critical tradition of Dante's *tenzone*. He seems to be the first to gloss some of the terminology therein with citations from texts of a similar age. He situates it among other similar slanderous verse, such as the poems by Guido Cavalcanti, thereby illustrating its participation in a recognizable genre. He indicates the intertextualities of the poetic correspondence with *Purgatorio* XXIII and XXIV, and with *Decameron* VII 8. Many of Borghini's observations anticipate, and have been confirmed by, those by twentieth-century scholars of the *tenzone* between Dante and Forese. Yet while Vincenzio Borghini's treatise has relevance to the history of the scholarship of Dante's lyric poems, his anachronistic application of the concept of burlesque literature to medieval slanderous verse also has a cautionary function for contemporary literary scholars. Ever since the eighteenth century, and cemented by the publication of Aldo Francesco Massèra's anthology entitled *Sonetti burleschi e satirici dei primi due secoli*,⁶⁷ the term "burlesque" has appeared frequently in the scholarship of the defamatory poetry of the Middle Ages. Due

---

⁶⁴ Benedetto Croce, *Poeti e scrittori del Rinascimento*, vol. 1 (Bari: Laterza, 1958), 78.

⁶⁵ Patrizia Bettella, "Discourse of Resistance: The Parody of Feminine Beauty in Berni, Doni and Firenzuola," *Modern Language Notes* 113 (1998): 192–203, here 194.

⁶⁶ "Burlesque," in *Cassell's Encyclopedia of World Literature*, ed. S.H. Steinberg (New York: William Morrow & Company, Inc. 1973), 1: 84–85.

⁶⁷ Aldo Francesco Massèra, *Sonetti burleschi e satirici dei primi due secoli* (Bari: Laterza, 1920).

to the sixteenth-century origins of the word "burlesque," it unwittingly distorts the modern understanding of medieval literature by speaking of it in Renaissance terms; medieval literary theorists consistently portrayed comedies as the socially relevant castigation of vice, not as simple entertainments, and the poetics of *vituperium* must be critically read with that definition in mind. Not to do so is as wrong as the anachronistic allegorical readings of the *Commedia* so prevalent in the Renaissance and so vehemently argued against by Borghini himself. This is not to say that no medieval authors ever composed poetry with the intent of inspiring pleasant humor in a burlesque manner, but scholars should first rule out the more typically medieval ethical purposes to comedies and satires before arriving at such a conclusion. Despite the fact that several decades ago Luigi Russo warned against the use of the lexeme "burlesque" in medieval contexts,[68] it has not disappeared from critical discourse. Just as the critically-laden term affected Borghini's conception of the poetry of Cavalcanti, Dante, and others, so too will the careless use of it continue to influence negatively the contemporary scholarly understanding of medieval *vituperium*.

---

[68] Luigi Russo, "La letteratura 'comico-realistica' nella Toscana del Duecento e Rustico di Filippo," in *Studi sul Due e Trecento* (Rome: Edizioni italiane, 1946), 131–57, here 136.

Section III

Interpretations and Reception of Dante's *Commedia*

Dante Equestrian

Gloria Allaire

Studies of Dante's *Commedia* typically refer to a dichotomous persona: Dante Poet and Dante Pilgrim. This essay will suggest another aspect of the great author which emerges in various passages that appear throughout the *Commedia*: Dante as an accomplished equestrian. My intent here is to closely examine the allusions to horses and horsemanship, the details of which show that Dante understood these things thoroughly. Beyond the picturesque realism, Dante's descriptions of the horse and ways of managing it become an important allegory for the way in which God directs the progress of the human soul.

The ownership of horses has always been an expensive proposition. Through the centuries, to possess a stable of fine horses has been a luxury permitted only to the wealthy. Still today, horses and their accoutrements—riding clothes, country estates with ample pasturage, the stately nobility of the creatures themselves—denote prestige and luxury unattainable for most people. Long before Dante Alighieri walked this earth, the horse had become firmly associated with the landed aristocracy: being a knight and serving in a cavalry were privileges reserved to the noble class.

Carol Lansing has discussed the changing nature of Italian knighthood in the twelfth and thirteenth centuries, an argument I will not rehearse here. Lansing has shown that in medieval Florence, "the character of . . . urban knighthood changed as the commune began to bestow the title on men of lower social origins." By the late Duecento, "[t]he military vocation did not automatically imply nobility."[1] Since Dante belonged to the lower nobility of Florence, his social rank was never in question; as a result, he was eligible to serve his Commune as one of the "feditori," the hand-picked members of the cavalry.[2] Although solid documentary evidence attesting to his participation in that role at the Battle of Campaldino is now lost, Barbara Reynolds points out that "in *Inferno* he mentions being present at the siege of the fortress of Caprona"; in addition, one of

---

[1] Carol Lansing, *The Florentine Magnates: Lineage and Faction in a Medieval Commune* (Princeton: Princeton University Press, 1991), 149–50.

[2] Lansing, *Florentine Magnates*, 153.

his sonnets refers to the time he spent in masculine pursuits like hunting—presumably on horseback—with hounds, a particularly dangerous medieval "sport" which rivalled warfare for its perils.[3] In short, "che Dante cavalcasse non fa meraviglia. Il cavallo era il mezzo normale di viaggio."[4]

In his biography of Dante, the humanist Leonardo Bruni had no trouble accepting a valiant Dante "young but well esteemed, who fought vigorously, mounted and in the front rank" at Campaldino. Such an image was fully concordant with Bruni's ideal of an active life, and Bruni even takes Boccaccio to task for omitting to discuss this aspect of Dante in his own *Vita di Dante*.[5] In any age, a scholar's attention will be drawn to arguments which seem most poignant to his or her own world view; eliding a particular topic may be pardoned when one better understands the ideology of a writer and the context in which a given study was produced. Thus we find that for scholars and writers in the second half of the twentieth century, the loss of daily contact with horses has erased them and their accoutrements from our vocabulary. Since roughly the end of the Second World War, industrialized countries no longer depend on literal horsepower for travel, transportation, and warfare. This has led to a loss of comprehension among the general public about equestrianism, and a lack of appreciation for the literary representation of horses. A citation from Allen Mandelbaum's translation of Dante's *Comedy*[6] will demonstrate:

> And at the name of noble Maccabeus,
> I saw another flame wheel round itself,
> and gladness was the whip that spurred that top.
> (Par. XVIII. 40–42, trans. Mandelbaum)
> Original: . . .e letizia era ferza del paleo.

Here, the lack of even the most rudimentary understanding of riding equipment has led to a horribly mixed metaphor: "gladness was the whip that spurred that top." Both whip and spur can be used to urge a horse forward, to get the horse's attention, to ask for greater speed, or for disciplinary purposes; whereas of the two, the spur can precisely control lateral motion or influence direction.

Except for a slim body of criticism on the centaurs,[7] little has been said about Dante's realistic or figurative observations concerning the nature of horses and

---

[3] Barbara Reynolds, *Dante: The Poet, the Political Thinker, the Man* (Emeryville, CA: Shoemaker Hoard, 2006), 9–10.

[4] Piero Bargellini, *Vita di Dante* (Florence: Vallecchi, 1964), 82. That the young Dante saw action as a knight, see also 83–85.

[5] *The Earliest Lives of Dante*, trans. James Robinson Smith (New York: Henry Holt, 1901), 83–84.

[6] *Paradiso*, trans. A. Mandelbaum (Berkeley: University of California Press, 1982).

[7] Steven Botterill, "Inferno XII," *Lectura Dantis* 6 (1990): 149–62, at 150, and 161 n. 1 provides a bibliographical summary.

equitation in the *Commedia*. The nuances within these references reveal more than the art of a great poet: they indicate the sensibility of a true *conoscente*. From such passages, we can deduce that Dante clearly understood the behavior and nature of the horse, and that he was familiar with the proper use of the rider's "aids": rein, whip, spur, and bit.[8] Although centuries have passed since Dante lived and wrote, the essential nature of the horse—both physiological and psychological—has not changed. Artefacts displayed in museums reveal a remarkable similarity to their modern-day counterparts. Although we now have synthetic materials and new metal alloys, bridle and saddle construction, farriers' tools and shoeing methods, the functioning of bits and reins remain fundamentally the same due to the unchanging nature of the horse's body.

While we do not know how extensive Dante's combat experience may have been, as a practicing knight he would have needed to possess reliable equestrian skills and a solid knowledge of horses. In the opening of *Inferno* XXII, he catalogues various maneuvers of *cavalieri* in battle or in jousts:

> Io *vidi* già cavalier muover campo,
> e cominciare stormo e far lor mostra,
> e talvolta partir per loro scampo;
> corridor *vidi* per la terra vostra,
> o Aretini, e *vidi* gir gualdane,
> fedir torneamenti e correr giostra; (*Inf.* XXII. 1–6)

The formula "io vidi" here and elsewhere further suggests that Dante the man had actual expertise in the world of horses.[9]

If Dante had been a knight, he would have had to serve some sort of apprenticeship as a youth, perhaps even working in his mentor's stables. There is perhaps no more pertinent image for scratching the scabby skin of the falsifiers than that of a stable boy hurrying to clean his lord's horse with a currycomb:

> e non vidi già mai menare stregghia
> a ragazzo aspettato dal segnorso . . . (*Inf.* XXIX. 76–77)

When horses roll in a wet pasture or traverse muddy roads, they become splattered with filth. From late fall to early spring, the muck which encrusts their

---

[8] These are the artificial aids. The natural aids are any part of the rider's body and the voice.

[9] Emphasis added above. For other evidence that Dante has watched knights in battle, see Forese Donati's hasty departure: "Qual esce alcuna volta di gualoppo / lo cavalier di schiera che cavalchi, / e va per farsi onor del primo intoppo" (*Purg.* XXIV. 94–96). All citations in Italian are taken from Dante Alighieri, *La Divina Commedia*, ed. C.H. Grandgent, rev. Charles S. Singleton (Cambridge, MA: Harvard University Press, 1972).

long winter coats is especially difficult to remove: it can take forty-five minutes to an hour to do this task. Areas where tack goes must be cleaned to prevent sores or skin rashes. On joints and delicate parts of the body which do not have much hair, horsemen frequently resort to using their own fingernails to loosen the caked layer, difficult to remove even with modern-day grooming tools. Anyone who rides on a regular basis quickly becomes familiar with this pre-ride ritual, whether doing the grooming oneself or having the mount prepared by a groom. Even if Dante had not been a groom and never rode in actual combat, given the heavy reliance on the horse for transportation in previous centuries, he surely would have witnessed this sort of scene many times.

The first extended reference to equids, in *Inferno* XII, describes the centaurs who guard the violent:

> Io vidi un'ampia fossa in arco torta,
> come quella che tutto 'l piano abbraccia,
> secondo ch'avea detto la mia scorta;
> e tra 'l piè de la ripa ed essa, in traccia
> corrien centauri, armati di saette,
> come solien nel mondo andare a caccia. (*Inf.* XII. 52–57)

To medieval readers familiar with Ovid's battle of the Lapiths and centaurs (to which Dante alludes in *Purg.* XXIV), there could be no more fitting image of unopposable violence: the physical strength and power of a stallion combined with the cunning intellectual powers of the human brain. The vision of a running herd immediately conjures to the horseman's mind the accompanying thunder of hooves. The earthquake that accompanied Christ's Harrowing of Hell, "da tutte parti l'alta valle feda / tremò" (*Inf.* XII. 40–41) ("on all sides the steep, filthy valley trembled") is a majestic prelude to the trembling ground which would result from the centaurs' galloping. When even a small herd of horses charges across a pasture or slope, one *feels* their presence before the ear can actually distinguish the sound or the direction. A vast herd such as Dante portrays could produce a sensation very similar to an earthquake's tremor.

Scholars have noted the centaurs' double nature, articulated in the famous "doppi petti" (double breasts) verse of *Purgatorio* XXIV: they are both rational and bestial.[10] Even the normal horse can be dangerously deceptive, at one moment a child's gentle mount or a mare nuzzling her foal, in the next a furious combination of snapping teeth, writhing torso, and lashing hooves. Even while acknowledging this double nature, modern commentators tend to privilege one set of attributes at the expense of the other.

---

[10] Giuseppe Izzi, in *Enciclopedia Dantesca* (Rome: Istituto della Enciclopedia Italiana, 1976), 1:909.

In a rare article on equitation in the *Commedia*, Robert Hollander has a hard time believing that Dante actually rode Nessus at the end of *Inferno* XII.[11] Other modern commentators express similar "hesitance or confusion" about interpreting the passage. Hollander laments the lack of details concerning how Dante mounted and crossed the river, claiming that Dante intended an ellipsis to challenge the reader. Yet for a medieval reader, there could have been no more banal act than to mount and travel upon a beast, and certainly no reason for Dante to be "self-conscious" about describing it. It would be like explaining to a modern reader how to enter and start a car. The omitted details are hardly central to the episode. However, from Virgil's request to Chiron

che porti costui in su la groppa . . . (*Inf.* XII. 95)

it is clear that Ovid's cunning, murderous centaur Nessus is here transformed into a trustworthy palfrey to assist Dante Pilgrim to ford the boiling river, a pragmatic necessity so that he is not burned.[12] Anyone who has ever taken a recreational trail ride can appreciate the quiet nature of a reliable, unflappable "packer": a horse that takes care of even beginning riders. Horses by nature are extremely wary of where they place their feet and do not willingly enter a body of water or step on a dark shadow because these appear to be dangerous bottomless pits. Given the boiling river and the shrieks of the damned in the *Inferno* XII passage, Dante's designation of the Nessus as "la scorta *fida*" (the trusted escort) is a great compliment. In the real world, such sights and sounds and the accompanying smells of burning flesh and boiling blood would have sent most horses spinning into reverse to flee the area as quickly as possible. Two lines later Dante pays Nessus another compliment, referring to him as " 'l gran centauro." Dante's portrayal of the centaur has now softened from the violent one of Ovid's *Metamorphoses* to a representation of the horse's nobler side and high intelligence as lauded by Pliny, Solinus, Albertus Magnus, and Brunetto Latini.

The next time we see Dante mounted is during his flight on Geryon's back (*Inf.* XVII. 83–95), described with great abundance of detail. The medieval reader acquainted with horses would easily have understood the anatomy of a centaur, but this strange hybrid monster merits a detailed description. Although Geryon is not a horse, the nuances in the passage illuminate the psychology of both rider and mount. Part of Dante Pilgrim's amazement stems from the strange feeling of being astride such a creature and experiencing its unusual way of going.

During Dante's ride on Geryon, he compares his own fear to that of Phaethon who could not control Apollo's horses:

---

[11] Robert Hollander, "Dante on Horseback?" *Italica* 61 (1984): 287–96.
[12] As Botterill notes, "*Inferno* XII," 160.

Maggior paura non credo che fosse
quando Fetonte abbandonò li freni,
per che 'l ciel, come pare ancor, si cosse ... (*Inf.* XVII. 106–108)

Dropping the reins for any reason is a sure sign of an inexperienced rider, a dangerous gesture that surrenders complete control to the horse. The *freno* (meaning both the rein and, by extension, the bridle which holds the bit in the horse's mouth) is the primary means of controlling the horse. Learning to hold and activate the reins effectively, causing least resistance from the horse while obtaining maximum obedience, takes much practice. The issue is not merely a matter of controlling behavior in the crudest terms, but extends to proper, skillful control.

Of fourteen occurrences of the word *freno* in the *Commedia*, some are literal, but most are metaphorical and stress proper guidance,[13] especially the apostrophe to Italy in the political canto, *Purgatorio* VI:

Che val perché ti racconciasse il freno
Iustinïano, se la sella è vòta?
Sanz' esso fora la vergogna meno.
Ahi gente che dovresti esser devota,
e lasciar seder Cesare in la sella,
se bene intendi ciò che Dio ti nota,
guarda come esta fiera è fatta fella
per non esser corretta da li sproni,
poi che ponesti mano a la predella. (*Purg.* VI. 88–96)

Justinian "adjusted the bridle," in effect serving as a good trainer for a difficult mount. Dante clearly indicates that the proper rider for this horse (Italy) is the emperor, and that clergy have no business trying to ride a spirited, disobedient horse. The invective brilliantly concludes with the word *predella* which can signify either part of an altarpiece or the portion of the bridle close to the bit.[14] The feminized reading of *Italia* as servant, whore, and *fiera* carries special resonance for horsemen: mares, despite cozy scenes of broodmares and foals, can be especially difficult due to their unpredictable moods. In modern equestrian parlance, a special adjective—"mareish"—indicates this; many riders prefer stallions. The difficulty that a poor rider (the Church) would have in controlling this recalcitrant horse (Italy) is due in part to its gender. (There are additional sexual implications

---

[13] Dante always uses the word *freno* to mean both reins and the entire bridle; the term "briglia"—apparently rare in the Trecento—came into use later. See Salvatore Battaglia, ed., *Grande dizionario della lingua italiana* (Turin: Unione tipografico-editrice torinese, 1961–), 2: 378–79.

[14] See "briglia" in Ottorino Pianigiani, *Dizionario etimologico della Lingua Italiana* online at: www.etimo.it.

in the metaphor of riding: a real man/rider is needed to control the whorish/mareish female Italy. The clergy have no business "in the saddle.")[15]

Horse/rider imagery proliferates throughout *Purgatory*. In the extended Lord's Prayer, our weak human "virtue" easily submits to the devil's spurring:

> Nostra virtù che di legger s'adona,
> non spermentar con l'antico avversaro,
> ma libera da lui che sì la sprona. (*Purg.* XI. 19–21)

By contrast, God is the proper rider of the soul in *Purg.* XIV, where Virgil speaks words inspired by Psalm 32 (Vulgate 31):

> [. . .] "Quel fu 'l duro camo
> che dovria l'uom tener dentro a sua meta.
> Ma voi prendete l'esca, sì che l'amo
> de l'antico avversaro a sé vi tira;
> e però poco val freno o richiamo." (*Purg.* XIV. 143–147)

In *Purgatorio* XVI, the rein signifies the Law which restrains citizens and makes them behave properly.[16] In *Purgatorio* XX, Hugh Capet holds the rein of government.

> ". . . trova'mi stretto ne le mani il freno
> del governo del regno . . ." (*Purg.* XX. 55–56)

The former butcher's son expresses his surprise at finding himself in the position of command. His ill ease does not bode well for his kingship: as in the apostrophe to Italy, Dante contends that only the aristocrat trained in the arts of war and equitation can be the proper "rider," i.e. ruler, of a country. That *trova'mi* speaks volumes, as does the adjective *stretto* to modify *freno*: not only does Hugh suddenly "find" himself on the back of a horse, but the tight rein indicates the horse is pulling strongly against his hands. A non-horseman finding himself on the back of a powerful horse can only experience great fear and trepidation, as with Phaethon in the sun chariot or Dante on Geryon's back. In modern parlance, a beginning rider on such an inappropriate mount is termed "overhorsed." Such a combination is ripe for disaster, precisely what happens in Dante's account of the Capetian kings whose improper use of power (their mount) caused a series of political and ecclesiastical disasters which had great impact on the fate of Italy. An

---

[15] In medieval literature, the horse was frequently a metaphor for sexuality, and riding imagery could suggest sexual coupling. See Andreas Capellanus, *On Love*, trans. P.G. Walsh (London: Duckworth, 1993), 31, 233; and V.A. Kolve, *Chaucer and the Imagery of Narrative: The First Five Canterbury Tales* (Stanford: Stanford University Press, 1984), 244–45.

[16] "Onde convenne legge per fren porre" (*Purg.* XVI. 94).

amateur rider who cannot control his horse is the worst potential menace to riding and horse handling, for such a person compromises the safety of other, more experienced riders and horses.

As noted, the rein is used to control direction or to slow and stop the horse. The spur is used to urge the horse forward or to move its body sideways. On the threshold of Hell, Virgil gives Dante a preview of the infernal torments and their cause.

> ". . . pronti sono a trapassar lo rio,
> ché la divina giustizia li sprona,
> sì che la tema si volve in disio." (*Inf.* III. 124–126)

God is the rider who spurs the fearful souls forward to their punishment. The damned souls in hell represent the complete failure to restrain unruly human passions and desires.[17] This failure is how Adam brought damnation upon himself and on his seed, the only reference to *freno* in *Paradiso*:

> Per non soffrire a la virtù che vole
> freno a suo prode, quell'uom che non nacque,
> dannando sé, dannò tutta sua prole . . . (*Par.* VII. 25–27)

The preponderance of rein and spur references occurs in *Purgatorio*.[18] Here, affection spurs the sinners to move now faster, now slower, but always forward "secondo l'affezion ch'ad ir ci sprona" (*Purg.* XX. 119) ("according to the sentiment that spurs us forward . . .") By contrast, the rein can restrain all the human's dangerous inclinations: *freno a tutti orgogli umani* (*Purg.* XXVIII. 72). The allegories of whip and rein articulated in *Purg.* XIII. 39–40 are fundamental to expressing the lessons found in that canticle, in which issues of steering the "horse" (soul) in the proper moral direction and urging it forward toward the ultimate good are crucial.

In a passage based on historical fact, Forese Donati prophesies the horrible death of his brother Corso, already condemned for treason:

> ". . . quei che più n'ha colpa,
> vegg' ïo a coda d'una bestia tratto
> inver' la valle ove mai non si scolpa.
> La bestia ad ogne passo va più ratto,
> crescendo sempre, fin ch'ella il percuota,
> e lascia il corpo vilmente disfatto." (*Purg.* XXIV. 82–87)

---

[17] "Oh cieca cupidigia e ira folle, / che sì ci sproni ne la vita corta . . ." (*Inf.* XII.49–50) ("O blind cupidity and insane madness, that so spurs us in our short life . . .")

[18] Numerous references to "cavallo" occur only in *Convivio* and in *Inferno*, the canticle written in the more realistic, literal key (see *Enciclopedia Dantesca*, 1:899).

Although the versions of the story differ, this sort of accident is any horseman's worst nightmare.[19] Whether Corso's foot was caught in the stirrup or he was tied to the horse's tail (a means of executing traitors), the result would be the same. The frightened horse would perceive the human body below as a predator and would react by fleeing and kicking at it until it was lacerated and destroyed.

Given the less tactile, more philosophical texture and content of *Paradiso*, equine references in the third canticle are scarce. A noteworthy passage in canto XXI features Peter Damian denouncing the clergy and contains the humorous image of fat prelates who ostentatiously ride instead of humbly walking:

"Or voglion quinci e quindi chi rincalzi
li moderni pastori e chi li meni,
tanto son gravi, e chi di rietro li alzi.
Cuopron d'i manti loro i palafreni,
sì che due bestie van sott' una pelle:
oh pazïenza che tanto sostieni!" (*Par.* XXI. 130–135)

Their horsemanship is as compromised as their spirituality since they can barely stay astride a gentle palfrey, "tanto son gravi." Ironically, here the *gravitas* expected of a true pastor of the church has taken a turn for the corporeal. Excessive appetite extends to other excesses in lifestyle: the copious yardage in the fabric of their cloaks drapes over the mount as well, creating a grotesque monster with two bodies under one skin—man above and beast below—a grotesque echo of the majestically fit centaurs of *Inferno* XII. These clergymen require additional servants to hold them aboard. In riding, an overweight, out-of-shape body is anathema and can actually be dangerous, causing unnecessary falls and more serious injury than a fit rider would experience. Furthermore, the weight of a corpulent man and his garments combined with the draperies inundating the small palfrey would hinder its natural movement and waste its energy. More waste: the mantle would become soiled during the ride, covered with horsehair and sweat from the perspiring beast, either ruining the garment or entailing more work to clean it.

To conclude, the context of horsemanship in the *Commedia* may even furnish the key to interpreting two perplexing tercets in St. John's examination of Dante on Love:

"Ma dì ancor se tu senti altre *corde*
tirarti verso lui, sì che tu suone
con quanti denti questo amor ti morde." [. . .]

---

[19] Singleton observes that Dante's version of Corso's death is not found elsewhere (*Commedia*, ed. Grandgent, 523).

[...] "Tutti quei *morsi*
che posson *far* lo cor *volgere* a Dio,
a la mia caritate son concorsi . . ." (*Par.* XXVI. 49–51, 55–57)

Scholars have puzzled over the strangeness of the metaphors and the apparent clumsiness in the poetry; attempts at glossing and translating have proven unsatisfactory. What are the cords which pull the soul toward God? What do cords have to do with teeth? What do teeth have to do with Love? A mixed metaphor indeed! The confusion grows two tercets later. What exactly are "tutti quei morsi"? "Things?" "Teeth?" "Urgings, promptings?" "Motivations?"[20]

In speaking of this canto, Kevin Brownlee has stated: the "two principal themes are love and language. Both are treated in terms of the key question of authority." The various horse/rider metaphors in the *Commedia* aptly symbolize the question of proper control of potentially dangerous inclinations. With the rein held by a skilled horseman, even the most unruly horse's energy can be channeled toward a useful purpose. By bringing to bear on this passage the equestrian images of authority outlined above, I would propose the following equicentric reading of the difficult metaphor: the "morso" is the bit and the "corde" are the reins which work together to control the direction of the horse. Such a reading perfectly explains the second tercet: "All those *bits* that can make the heart turn to God." God is the good rider who skillfully steers the horse (heart) toward the highest good. But how then do we account for the "denti" of the earlier tercet?

One must realize the importance then as now of being able to steer, slow, and stop a horse. There is no more frightening feeling than being an unwilling "passenger" on the back of a galloping runaway! (Ariosto's *cavallo sfrenato* comes to mind immediately.) For a strong-willed horse with a "hard mouth," a harsh bit is in order: "Quel fu '*l duro camo* / che dovria l'uom tener dentro a sua meta." Throughout the *Commedia*, human nature presents a tough challenge to God's divine plan. Allegorically, the heart is a difficult horse which needs a strong bit.

---

[20] *The Divine Comedy of Dante Alighieri, III: Paradiso*, trans. John D. Sinclair (New York: Oxford University Press, 1961), 375: "All those *things* whose bite can make the heart turn to God . . ." (emphasis mine); *The Paradiso*, trans. John Ciardi (New York: New American Library, 1970): "All those *teeth* with power enough to turn the heart of any man to God . . .," glossed in his note (on 294) as "Urgings, promptings." Mandelbaum, 3:237, follows Cardi's translation almost verbatim. Bruno Nardi ("Il canto XXVI del *Paradiso*," *L'Alighieri* 26 [1985]: 28) offers this solution: "[T]utti quei *motivi* . . . ." Tommaseo (cited in Giancarlo Rati, "Il canto XXVI del *Paradiso*," *L'Alighieri* 32 [1991]: 25 n. 21) laments the word choice: "'*Corde* dell'amore di Dio è alquanto grosso . . . e peggio il mordere de' denti . . .'." Singleton, *Commedia*, 861 n.: "An odd combination of metaphors." And finally, "The third question [of St. John] is couched in a language that sounds strange in this context to modern ears . . ." (Joseph Cremona, "*Paradiso* XXVI," in *Cambridge Readings in Dante's* Comedy, ed. Kenelm Foster and Patrick Boyde [Cambridge: Cambridge University Press, 1981], 174–90, on 179).

The nature of the horse has not changed since Dante's day. Hard-mouthed horses will always be the plague of riders' existence; two medieval citations by later Florentine writers will suffice:

"O signor mio, perdonami, che non per mio difetto questo è avvenuto, né per malizia ho contro la tua signoria offeso: la dura bocca del mio cavallo di questo m'ha colpa."[21]

A me parrebbe che, considerando la natura di questo cavallo ne la sua magrezza, sia forte da dubitare quando fia rifatto e rimesso ne le pristine carni. E però farei di metterli uno *freno* con *uno morso a piè di gatta o a piè di leone* che debba essere ancor più forte.[22]

To control the difficult "horse," Arezzo, Sacchetti recommends a "cat's-paw bit" or the even stronger "lion's-paw bit." These descriptions can refer only to sharp points affixed on the mouthpiece, smaller points in the case of the "morso a piè di gatta" and larger ones for the "morso a piè di leone." Then as now there would have been a wide variety of styles according to the behavior, size, and strength of the beast. The "teeth" in Dante's metaphor, therefore, refer to the literal features of the mouthpiece on a very strong bit designed to control a difficult horse.

Actual bits with multiple biting "teeth" can be seen in a fifteenth-century manuscript, the present-day Ashburnham MS. 1309. In this modern description, the manuscript cataloguer—obviously not a horseman—finds the "dozens and dozens of types according to the character of the horse" humorous and the codex "witty." However, similar series of bit designs appear in the various *trattati di mascalcia* preserved in Landau Finaly MS. 127, and in printed equestrian manuals of the sixteenth century. Six pages of bits in a single modern tack catalogue display a total of 406 styles suitable for English-style riding; curb bits and those used in other disciplines are not shown.[23] This number does not include the different length mouthpieces: there are, in addition, normally two or three sizes available for each of the 406 discrete designs.

By taking real-world horse management as a subtext, St. John's question in *Paradiso* XXVI may therefore be interpreted quite logically as follows: "But tell me again if you feel other *reins* pulling you toward him, so that you acknowledge

---

[21] Boccaccio, *Il Filocolo*, ed. Antonio Enzo Quaglio ([Verona:] Mondadori, 1967), 480–81.

[22] Sacchetti, quoted in Battaglia, *Grande dizionario*, 10: 934.

[23] For illustrations from Ashb. MS. 1309, see Biblioteca Medicea Laurenziana, *Disegni nei manoscritti laurenziani sec. X-XVII: Firenze, ottobre 1979-febbraio 1980*, ed. Francesco Guerrieri (Florence: Leo S. Olschki, 1979), 160. For Landau Finaly MS. 127 bit designs, see Biblioteca Nazionale Centrale, Firenze, *Le grandi biblioteche d'Italia* (Florence: Nardini, 1989), 88. For modern bits, see Libertyville Saddle Shop, *English Equestrian 2000* (n.p.), 39–51; (for examples, see website: www.saddleshop.com).

with how many *teeth* this love is biting[24] you," and Dante's response: "All those *bits* that can make the heart turn to God have joined together to [create] my charity." God the good rider/trainer has exhausted his repertoire of bits on the stubborn horse Dante, turning him at last in the right direction. In horse training, using a series of different bits or alternating bits on different days can be beneficial in helping the horse to progress to a desired goal. Thus, it is not at all unreasonable to imagine Dante's allegory as referring to the wide range of bits needed to accomplish God's divine plan: that the heart desire good.

[24] It may even be that medieval horsemen used the verb "mordere" to indicate teaching the horse to accept the bit, for "bitting" or selecting the proper bit.

"Quanto si convenia a tanto uccello" (*Inf.* 34.47): Dante's Satan as Winged Phallus

Madison U. Sowell

Proin, viator, hunc deum vereberis
manumque sursum habebis: hoc tibi expedit,
Parata namque crux stat ecce mentula.
Virgil, *Priapea* 2.16–18[1]

The description of the poets' emergence from the body of Hell has an anatomical character and features hints of ingestion, defecation, ejaculation and birth.
Tom Phillips[2]

Scholars invariably discuss Dante's hideous and turgid Satan, described formally in *Inferno* 34.28–67, in terms of parody.[3] Tom Phillips, in an imaginative and

---

[1] Virgil, *Aeneid VII-XII, The Minor Poems.*, trans. H. Rushton Fairclough, rev. ed. (Cambridge, MA: Harvard University Press, 1986), 2:482. This Loeb Classical Library translation reads thus: "Therefore, O wayfarer, thou shalt fear this god [Priapus], and hold thy hand high: this is worth thy while, for lo! there stands ready *thy cross, the phallus*" (emphasis mine).

[2] Tom Phillips, trans. and illus., *Dante's Inferno* (London: Thames and Hudson, 1985), 310.

[3] In fact, this essay was first presented in an abbreviated version as a paper read on 26 May 2006, in a session on "Dante and Parody" organized by Professor Dino Cervigni for the joint meeting of the American Association of Teachers of Italian and the American Association for Italian Studies held in Genoa, Italy. Professor Christopher Kleinhenz, my longtime friend and esteemed colleague, attended the session, and we enjoyed a hearty meal thereafter. For these reasons I have chosen to dedicate this essay to him on the occasion of his retirement. All citations of the *Commedia* come from Charles S. Singleton, trans. and comm., *The Divine Comedy* (Princeton: Princeton University Press, 1970–1975).

shockingly Freudian illustration of the *Inferno*'s final canto, pushes this parody to the limit by depicting an ithyphallic Satan—that is, a giant, erect, ejaculating *membrum virile* raping Mother Earth. While appreciating Phillips' brilliance in imagining Satan as the ultimate degradation, serious readers and sentient viewers of the illustrated poem may question the textual basis or historical context for such a sexually charged interpretation of Satan. The illustrator in his "Iconographical Notes and Commentary on the Illustrations," cited above and at the end of this essay, does not pretend to adduce hard evidence; rather he simply asserts his artistic beliefs regarding Satan as an archetypal icon lodged in the earth's womb.[4] Consequently, a question naturally arises in the mind of any trained Dantist: To what extent might such a twentieth-century artistic credo actually be grounded in the fourteenth-century text of the *Commedia* and in the artistic traditions predating and surrounding the allegorical epic? In this essay I propose to address that question by exploring textual and iconographical evidence that Dante intended to re-present Satan, *inter alia*, as a parody *ne plus ultra*: a winged phallus that can beat its wings but cannot fly because it is ironically grounded in the earth's core.[5]

By definition, parody thrives on imitation or exaggeration, and it naturally presumes a literate or informed audience. In the case of the *Commedia*, if readers wish to fathom the multiple layers not only of the poem's allegory but also of its parody, they must be well versed in classical and medieval culture, informed as to allegorical modes of discourse, and sophisticated in deciphering iconography. Furthermore, as prominent literary critics such as Northrop Frye have long noted, parody derives its inspiration from criticism as well as comedy. When a parodist highlights the comedic, laughter naturally follows, "but when the element of critical mimicry is stressed, the humor may be slight."[6] In the case of Dante's parodic depiction of Satan, critical mimicry proves so extreme as to make any humor the blackest and foulest of the *Commedia*. For, as Dante-Poet exclaims in attempting to capture in word-images the *pozzo scuro* of Hell's ninth circle, ". . . non è impresa da pigliare a gabbo / discriver fondo a tutto l'universo"

---

[4] Phillips is hardly alone in making Freudian archetypal connections within texts that preceded Freud by several centuries. See, for example, Joseph Campbell, *The Hero with a Thousand Faces*, 2nd ed. (Princeton: Princeton University Press, 1968), 154–65, for a discussion of what he terms the "penis womb."

[5] Paradoxically, Satan's minions—for example, the horned demons with phallic whips or pizzles in *Inferno* 18 and the winged devils with sharp phallic hooks presided over by Malacoda ("evil tail") in *Inferno* 21–22—have the power of movement, even though they also are restricted to their respective abodes in the First Bolgia and Fifth Bolgia of the Eighth Circle.

[6] Northrop Frye, Sheridan Baker, and George Perkins, *The Harper Handbook to Literature* (New York: Harper & Row, 1985), 337.

(*Inf.* 32.7–8). In other words, the mimicry of Satan hardly represents mere sport; rather it attempts to represent, allegorically and iconographically, evil incarnate.

So how does Dante depict Satan in linguistic and iconographic terms in the relatively few tercets allotted to this towering monster? Given Dante's preoccupation with names, easily traceable to his celebrated *Vita nova* dictum that "names are the consequences of things" (*Nomina sunt consequentia rerum*), we turn first to the *Commedia*'s formal naming of the Devil for a shadow of things to come. In *Inferno* 34 the poet writes of this evil figure employing three proper nouns—*Dite* (v. 20, "Dis," a pagan designation), *Lucifero* (v. 89, "Lucifer," an Old Testament appellation), and *Belzebù* (v. 127, "Beelzebub," a New Testament reference). The title of "Satan," which is the Devil's most commonly ascribed cognomen in Dante commentaries, actually occurs only in the untranslatable double reference that Plutus utters in Upper Hell: "*Pape Satàn, pape Satàn aleppe!*" (*Inf.* 7.1). From a strictly etymological viewpoint, none of these four names carries phallic denotations. (This is true despite popular medieval depictions of Satan with a pointed phallic tail and sharp phallic horns.) Nevertheless at least one name portends the subsequent presentation of the Devil as a parody of Christ's cross. It is the name of Dis. Dante employs this term to refer both to Satan (*Inf.* 11.65 and 12.39) and to Lower Hell (*Inf.* 8.68). It derives from Virgil's references in *Aeneid* 6.127 and 541 to the underworld as Dis. But placed by our Christian poet in Virgil the Guide's mouth in the phrase "Ecco Dite" (*Inf.* 34.20), the two words (each of two syllables) subtly echo and parody Pilate's infamous bisyllabic words, "Ecce homo" (John 19:5), referring to the presentation of the scourged and bleeding Christ to the assembled Jews.[7] The poet's simple introduction to Dis immediately invites readers to connect Satan and the sanguinary Word Made Flesh in parodic fashion.

For better clues to how Satan functions as parody we must turn to other epithets and circumlocutions employed by Dante. Forever confined to the last circle of Hell's pit and frozen eternally at the farthest point from God's Empyrean, "Lo 'mperador del doloroso regno" (*Inf.* 34.28) clearly represents the antithesis of "quello imperador che là sù regna" (*Inf.* 1.124). Precisely because the poet employs the word *imperador* only twice in the *Commedia*'s initial canticle and because these appearances occur like bookends in the first and last cantos of the *Inferno*, the contrast between God ruling majestically in the heavens and Satan reigning terrifyingly in the netherworld could hardly be more dramatic. Lucifer, once so beautiful and glorious that this biblical name signifies "bearer of light," now personifies ugliness and hideousness (*Inf.* 34.34: ". . . el fu sì bel com'

---

[7] As in the case of the other names, *Satan* comes from the Hebrew word for "adversary"; *Lucifer* appears as a *hapax legomenon* not only in the *Commedia* but also in St. Jerome's translation of Isaiah 14:12, where it literally refers to the king of Babylon but was interpreted by early Christians as a reference to a fallen angel (i.e., the Devil); and *Belzebub* is the "the prince of the devils," according to Matthew 12:24–27.

elli è ora brutto"). In sum, Satan appears to be, in the words of Virgil the Guide, little more than an "evil worm" piercing—i.e. violating or raping—the world (*Inf.* 34.108: "... vermo reo che 'l mondo fóra"). In highly dramatic fashion Satan symbolizes the perverse incarnation of what Vanni Fucci foreshadows when the damned thief raises both his hands in an obscene gesture aimed at God: "... il ladro / le mani alzò con amendue le fiche, / gridando: 'Togli, Dio, ch'a te le squadro!'" (*Inf.* 25.2–3).[8]

That Dante wishes to highlight the parodic aspects of his encounter with Satan now appears retrospectively evident from the opening salvo of *Inferno* 34.1: *Vexilla regis prodeunt inferni*. The poet's insertion of the word *inferni* at the end of the first line of Venantius Fortunatus's celebrated processional hymn—so that the verse reads, in translation, "the banners advance of the king *of hell*"—packs powerful irony and adumbrates the parodic depiction of a winged Dis later in the canto. As is well known, Fortunatus wrote his hymn to celebrate the arrival of a fragment of the so-called True Cross, and it was traditionally sung at the Saturday vespers before Passion Sunday (the second Sunday before Easter). Saturday night corresponds to the time of the Pilgrim's encounter with Satan.[9] Many critics see, therefore, the erect and imprisoned Satan, who drips bloody froth from three mouths, as a living parody of Christ's blood-stained cross, a *crux diaboli* or a *diabolus in patibulo*.[10] Others view him more simply and primarily as a parodic Trinity. In Satan's three faces in one head, Natalino Sapegno states succinctly, we see an "apparente analogia, e in reale antitesi, al concetto dell'unità e trinità di Dio."[11] Certainly the symbolic colors of Satan's faces—black (ignorance), red (hate), and yellow-white (impotence)—stand in direct contrast to God the Son's wisdom or omniscience, God the Holy Ghost's love, and God the Father's power or omnipotence. Martinez and Durling interpret even the wind from Satan's wings, which freezes Cocytus and thus entombs the treacherous, as "a parody of the Spirit of God, which in Gen. 1.2 'moved over the face of the waters'."[12]

The figure of Dante's Satan has, of course, been interpreted in various other, even more imaginative, ways over the years. For example, Anthony Cassell

---

[8] It goes almost without noting that, like Malacoda's highly suggestive name, such images as a penetrating worm or the thumb thrust between the index and middle fingers are ageless in their phallic suggestiveness.

[9] *The Divine Comedy*, trans. and comm. Singleton, *Inferno* 2:626–27.

[10] John Freccero, *Dante: The Poetics of Conversion*, ed. Rachel Jacoff (Cambridge, MA: Harvard University Press, 1986), 175–76.

[11] Dante Alighieri, *La Divina Commedia: Inferno*, ed. Natalino Sapegno (Florence: La Nuova Italia, 1971), 375.

[12] Dante Alighieri, *The Divine Comedy: Inferno*, intro. and annot. Ronald L. Martinez and Robert M. Durling (New York: Oxford University Press, 1996), 544.

interpreted Lucifer's tripartite iconography as inverted baptism.[13] Without a doubt, Satan frozen in ice and visible only from the waist up and with batlike wings behind his head blatantly parodies medieval mosaics and paintings of Christ standing in baptismal waters with a dove hovering overhead. On the other hand, Robert McMahon has read Satan as an infernal, self-absorbed Narcissus.[14] Sarah Spence, in her reading of *Inferno* 34, focused on two ampullae that depict the crucifixion to establish a connection between Christ's cross and the myrrh tree, between the depiction of the crucified Christ and the rooted Satan.[15] Dino Cervigni has suggested that Lucifer's three names by which he is addressed in *Inferno* 34 (the above-cited *Dite*, *Lucifero*, and *Belzebù*) represent a perversion of the Holy Trinity.[16] Most recently, Mary Watt has suggested that "Satan himself is the antithesis of the Eucharist," eating men in contrast to men partaking of the Host.[17]

In a seminal essay John Freccero posited that the image of Satan as a *vexillum* or banner should not be interpreted merely as a *res*, an object or a thing, but that it should be seen as a *signum*, a sign pointing to a process embodied in Satan himself.[18] That process details the act of conversion that Dante himself undergoes as the pilgrim. Freccero argues that Satan's similarities to the mulberry tree and the cross of Christ reinforce that position: the colors of Satan's faces do not represent static sinful states, but stages in the mulberry's process of ripening or the soul's penitential journey. He focuses on the off-white and not-quite-black faces, arguing that their non-absolute color suggests motion from the extremes of sin's blackness through penance's redness and towards the sanctification of white. He also argues that Dante as a figure of Zacchaeus, who climbed the sycamore tree in the New Testament (Luke 19:2–6), points the way to salvation by climbing the *crux diaboli*.[19]

In a second, much shorter essay Freccero further clarifies the role of Dante's Satan as a *crux diaboli*. Just as the Christian who would be saved must embrace and metaphorically climb *up* the cross of Christ, so Dante the Pilgrim must

---

[13] See Anthony K. Cassell, *Dante's Fearful Art of Justice* (Toronto: University of Toronto Press, 1984), chap. 8.

[14] Robert McMahon, "Satan as Infernal Narcissus: Interpretative Translation in the *Commedia*," in *Dante and Ovid: Essays in Intertextuality*, ed. Madison U. Sowell, MRTS 82 (Binghamton: MRTS, 1991), 65–86.

[15] Sarah Spence, "Myrrha, Myrrha in the Well: Metonymy and Interpretation in *Inferno* XXXIV," *Dante Studies* 103 (1985): 15–36.

[16] Dino S. Cervigni, "*Inferno* XXXIV," *Lectura Dantis* 6 (1990): 428–38.

[17] Mary Alexandra Watt, *The Cross That Dante Bears: Pilgrimage, Crusade, and the Cruciform Church in the "Divine Comedy"* (Gainesville: University Press of Florida, 2005), 114. For a positive assessment of Professor Watt's study, see the review by Madison U. Sowell in *Speculum* 83 (2008): 250–51.

[18] Freccero, *Poetics of Conversion*, 179.

[19] Freccero, *Poetics of Conversion*, 167–79.

climb *down* the devil's cross (referred to in *Inferno* 34.82 as *scale* or stairs and in 34.119 as *scala* or ladder) in order to escape Hell and ascend towards God.[20] Other reversals are also taking place at the topsy-turvy center of the universe. For example, to exit the icy depths of Hell, Dante-Pilgrim, who has been a figure of Aeneas up to this point, climbs on the back of Virgil, the wise father figure who mirrors Anchises. In this context the act of climbing on the back recalls the reverse image of Aeneas shouldering Anchises when father and son had to abandon burning Troy.[21] Such ladder and climbing imagery, in particular, parallels medieval notions not only of the ladder as an instrument of the Passion (used in removing Christ's body from the cross) but also of Christ's cross as a ladder itself, with rungs that the penitent soul seeking salvation must climb in order to flee sin and find salvation.[22]

I have summarized Freccero's two essays more extensively than those of other critics because it is precisely upon this notion of Satan as the personification of the devil's cross that I should like to build. In the remainder of this essay I shall detail why Dante's Satan, in one of the poet's most syncretistic moments, also embodies and parodies the classical phenomenon of the flying phallus. I have published elsewhere that Dante's introduction of the unique term *perizoma* in *Inferno* 31.61, where it describes the bank that hides the giants' nether regions or genitals, is an allusive and highly suggestive tour de force.[23] Dante's *hapax* derives from the singular Vulgate use of *perizomata* in Genesis 3:7 (a transliteration of the Septuagint word) for the aprons of fig leaves fashioned by the fallen Adam and Eve to hide their nakedness. In the case of Dante's *perizoma*, the allusion, falling as it does between the penultimate and final circles, proleptically prepares the reader for what the dark and womblike last circle entombs in ice: the horrible figure of a swollen and winged Lucifer, instigator of the Fall of humankind's first parents. Certainly the apron-like bank, which recalls Edenic events and hides shameful sights, presages many other sacred images that will be re-presented *in*

---

[20] Freccero, *Poetics of Conversion*, 180–85.

[21] Dante may have known the iconographic portrayal of the Aeneas group, which includes father Anchises and son Ascanius, from the Forum of Augustus in Rome. What is interesting for our argument is that parodies of the Aeneas group existed from classical times, including one showing the three males "as apes with dogs' heads and huge phalloi." See Paul Zanker, *The Power of Images in the Age of Augustus*, trans. Alan Shapiro (Ann Arbor: University of Michigan Press, 1988), 209, for both the quotation cited and an illustration (figure 162) of the dog-headed apes with prominent phalluses.

[22] Note, for example, the medieval crucifix (Venetian school, c. 1420–1425) in the Torcello basilica near Venice. The vertical bar of the cross displays seven horizontal rungs of a ladder, each of which presumably corresponds to a virtue needed to ascend the cross and embrace the crucified Lord.

[23] Sowell, ed., *Dante and Ovid: Essays in Intertextuality*, 9–11.

malo in the "rime aspre e chiocce" (*Inf.* 32.1) of Hell's pit, from the perverted eucharistic imagery of Count Ugolino's tale to the parodic three faces of Satan.

In medieval paintings of Christ's crucifixion, there often appears at the base of the cross a skull upon which the blood of Christ often drips. This skull symbolizes at least three ideas: first, like all skulls it represents a *memento mori*, a reminder that life is brief and the viewer will someday die and should prepare for the eternities; second, it highlights that Golgotha, the hill upon which Christ was crucified, was identified scripturally as the place of the skull (Matthew 27:33, Mark 15:22, John 19:17); and third, it stands for Adam's skull, an allusion to the medieval legend that Adam was buried on the spot where Christ was crucified and that the tree of the cross grew out of a seed or branch from the tree of life that was buried with Adam.[24] Given the centrality of the skull to pictorial representations of Christ's crucifixion and the connection of Satan to a *crux diaboli*, it is not surprising to locate a skull near the base of Satan's parodic cross. It is, of course, the *teschio* that appears in *Inferno* 32.132, the skull of Archbishop Ruggieri upon which Count Ugolino is gnawing. In fact, the word *teschio* more or less frames Ugolino's account, not only appearing in the initial image of the two damned souls but also reappearing in *Inferno* 33.77, after Ugolino concludes his tale: "Quand'ebbe detto ciò, con li occhi torti / riprese 'l teschio misero co' denti, / che furo a l'osso, come d'un can, forti" (*Inf.* 33.76–78). To underscore the importance of this image, the word *teschio* does not reappear in any other episode of the entire *Commedia*.

A logical next question relates to why, if Satan doubles as a parodic cross, does he have wings? After all, he has not one, not two, but three *pairs* of wings. From *Inferno* 34.46–51 the description of the wings that emerge from behind Satan's faces reads as follows: "Sotto ciascuna uscivan due grand' ali, / quanto si convenia a tanto uccello: / vele di mar non vid'io mai cotali. / Non avean penne, ma di vispistrello / era loro modo; e quelle svolazzava, / sì che tre venti si movean da ello." The image of the *vele di mar* ("sails at sea") recalls and clarifies the image of the *vexilla* ("banners") in the opening line of the canto. The beating bat-like wings represent flapping banners. In the context of the iconography of Satan, who like Farinata (not to mention Pope Nicholas III, the upside down simonist of *Inferno* 19) emerges only halfway from his entombment, these banners contrast sharply with Christ's resurrection banner, white with a red cross, which He carries triumphantly upon emerging from His tomb. Christ, upon His resurrection, left the tomb and ascended to heaven. Satan's banner-wings, by contrast, serve only to create frigid winds that ensure that he will never leave the confines of hell but will remain there frantic and frozen for all time. While Christ proffers "living waters" that refresh, heal, and save (John 4:10–11, 14), the parodic Satan has only a frozen, polluted, and deadly lake to offer.

---

[24] J. C. J. Metford, *Dictionary of Christian Lore and Legend* (London: Thames and Hudson, 1983), 76.

To explicate the more obvious significance of the wings, the commentary tradition proves helpful but hardly exhaustive. A survey of approximately 60 commentaries on the question of Satan's wings reveals that nearly all commentators arrive at the same conclusion, which is that Lucifer belonged to the order of Seraphim before he was cast out of heaven.[25] Here we may cite Robert Hollander's recent gloss on *Inferno* 34.46–51: "The six wings of Satan are his six wings as one of the angelic order of Seraphim (Isaiah 6:2); they are now not glorious in color but the wings of a giant bat." Hollander goes on to suggest that the wings and their "resemblance to sails on a great ship are parodic, since Satan proceeds nowhere, but connect with images associated with Ulysses (*Inf.* XXVI) and the ship bringing the saved souls to the shore of purgatory (*Purg.* I)." As for Satan being branded a large *uccello*, almost all of the examined commentaries read the allusion simply as a straightforward reference to Dante's Satan having wings: "Appella **uccello** Lucifero per essere alato," writes Lombardi in the Settecento. In the next century Gregorio di Siena comments, "**Uccello**, sì per relazione alle **ali**, come perchè Lucifero fu angelo, e agli angeli si attribuiscono le ali, per significare ch'ei sono nunzi di Dio." Only two of the scores of reviewed commentaries suggested, both in very vague terms, that something else might be at play here. Gioachino Berthier, writing in the 1890s, comments on the word *uccello*: "Questa parola è qui per disprezzo." And Charles Singleton states dryly that "tanto uccello" is "Plainly ironical and derisive." But nothing else is offered in either case, which leaves to me the dubious honor of explaining the irony, the parody, and the derision.

The use of the term *uccello* as slang for the *membrum virile* is not only common in modern Italian but is also attested in the language of the Tuscan Trecento. Two *novelle* by Boccaccio in which the image of the bird doubles as the male sexual organ unquestionably demonstrate this fact. In the *Decameron*'s fourth tale of the fifth day, Caterina cites the coolness of the balcony and the sweetness of the nightingale's song as excuses to sleep outside. There she rendezvous with Ricciardo and, as Boccaccio narrates, together they succeed in "molte volte faccendo cantar l'usignolo" (making the nightingale sing several times).[26] To make sure that the reader understands what the *usignolo* signifies, the narrator explains that after their love-making Caterina takes in her left hand "quella cosa che voi tra gli uomini piú vi vergognate di nominare" and then falls asleep.[27] The next morning her father discovers the couple naked and asleep in this position and informs his wife that "tua figliuola è stata sí vaga dell'usignolo, che ella è stata tanto alla

---

[25] For the convenience of the reader, Dante commentaries cited in the remainder of this article (e.g., Berthier, Gregorio di Siena, Hollander, and Lombardi) derive from the useful Dartmouth Dante website: http://dante.dartmouth.edu.

[26] Giovanni Boccaccio, *Decameron*, ed. Cesare Segre (Milan: Mursia, 1974), 344.

[27] *Decameron*, 344.

posta che ella l'ha preso e tienlosi in mano."[28] Clearly the bird in Caterina's hand is Ricciardo's reproductive organ.

In the ninth tale of the seventh day, Lidia slays her husband's hawk in an act of symbolic castration. In doing so, she revenges Nicostrato's failure to satisfy her sexual needs. She then berates her male audience by employing a remarkable double entendre that explicitly employs the word *uccello*: "Voi dovete sapere che questo uccello tutto il tempo da dover esser prestato dagli uomini al piacere delle donne lungamente m'ha tolto" (You must know that this bird, which should always be loaned by men for women's pleasure, has taken from me just that).[29] In truth, the bird as phallic symbol is traceable to classical antiquity. J. N. Adams in his study devoted to *The Latin Sexual Vocabulary* details that "Various bird-names are recorded with the metaphorical sense 'penis' in Latin."[30] He then provides a variety of examples. In parallel fashion, Venus and carnal love were represented in antiquity by a pair of cooing doves desirous to mate—hence the appropriateness of the allusion to *colombe dal disio chiamate* in Dante's Paolo and Francesca episode of carnal love (*Inf.* 5.82). Similarly, when the bossy devil Barbariccia yells at the demon Farfarello, he calls the latter a most derogatory name: "malvagio uccello" (*Inf.* 22.96). Singleton translates the phrase as "villainous bird"; however, in the context of the coarse language of the devils, Phillips' much livelier translation—"misbegotten prick"—seems more apropos.

But if Satan himself is being derided as a phallus, the ultimate insult to one who was once so beautiful that he was compared to the morning star (Isaiah 14:12), how does this allusion relate to his image, so long and widely accepted, as a *crux diaboli* and why do his wings receive such emphasis, both for their number and for their image as *vexilla*?

To answer the first question, one must realize that the cross has a history that predates not only Christianity but also the Roman era. From ancient times this artifact was widely regarded as having a talismanic value and was held by occultists to represent the joining of the male principle (phallic verticality) and the female principle (vaginal horizontality) in its crossed bars.[31] Over time it came to be associated more clearly with what was perceived as the dominant male force. The anonymous author of *The Masculine Cross*, for instance, writes that "amongst some ancient Etruscan remains, a cross formed of four phalli of equal length, their narrow end point inwards . . . in which the phallus was made of inordinate

---

[28] *Decameron*, 344.
[29] *Decameron*, 459.
[30] J. N. Adams, *The Latin Sexual Vocabulary* (Baltimore: Johns Hopkins University Press, 1982), 31.
[31] Count Goblet D'Alviella, *The Migration of Symbols* (Westminster: Archibald Constable, 1894), 45.

length . . . was probably [also] used by the Phoenicians."[32] One may extrapolate from this archeological finding that these phallic Etruscan crosses were the precursors of the Roman variety, upon which the more offensive criminals in the Empire were hung while stripped naked with their own phalluses exposed to the derision of the gaping public. Interestingly enough, it is the author Virgil, in his three-part poem devoted to the god Priapus, cited in our epigraph, that perhaps most clearly associates the cross with the phallus in his bold declaration: "namque crux stat ecce mentula" (*Priapea* 2.18, "there stands ready thy cross, the phallus"). In the Virgilian poem, Priapus's erect phallus provides a cudgel or club that a wayfarer (*viator*) might grab for his defense, much as a Christian pilgrim (e.g. Dante) might cling to the cross for his or her protection.

Phallic or priapic symbols discovered set in walls at intersections in Pompeii were used to ward off the evil eye, much as crosses are used today. As Catherine Johns explains, "phalluses were displayed [in antiquity] not only as personal good-luck charms but also in a more public way, on walls, floors, buildings and so on. These are not casual graffiti, but carefully executed apotropaic devices."[33] An apotropaic—a word of Greek derivation that etymologically refers to "turning away" evil—often depicts the symbol of what is feared, whether it is the evil eye or some other type of harm. In fact, Virgil the Guide's reference to Satan as a *vermo reo* calls to mind the parallel image found on the phallus amulet. Such a talisman was worn, according to Varro, by Roman boys to keep evil from coming to them: "Potest vel ab eo quod pueris turpicula res in collo quaedam suspenditur, ne quid obsit" ("Perhaps it is from this that a certain indecent object [a *membrum virile*] . . . is hung on the necks of boys, to prevent harm from coming to them."[34] Its use in Italy today is no less widespread, and often a piece of pink, apotropaic, phallic coral is seen in conjunction with a gold cross hanging around a man's neck.

What is curious but rarely (if ever) noted in Dante scholarship is that early medieval paintings of Christ on the cross, especially those based on Greek models or produced in what is called the Byzantine style, often cause modern viewers to do a double-take because of a visual double-entendre. For example, Coppo di Marcovaldo, the same artist who executed the magnificent mosaic of the *Last Judgment* in the pyramidal vault of Florence's Baptistry, painted a notably phallic crucifix. Located today in the Museo Civico of San Gimignano, this work depicts a Byzantine-style Savior with an elaborately folded white cloth (somewhat

---

[32] *The Masculine Cross, or, A History of Ancient and Modern Crosses and Their Connection with the Mysteries of Sex Worship: Also an Account of the Kindred Phases of Phallic Faiths and Practices* ([London?: n. p.], 1904), 35–36.

[33] Catherine Johns, *Sex or Symbol: Erotic Images of Greece and Rome* (Austin: University of Texas Press, 1982), 64.

[34] Varro, *On the Latin Language* [*De lingua latina*], trans. Roland G. Kent, vol. 1 (Cambridge, MA: Harvard University Press, 1977), 7.97.

resembling wings) wrapped around his loins, presumably to hide his genitalia.[35] Christ's abdomen and rib cages, however, are stylized in such a pointed and tapered way that a giant erect phallus appears to emerge from the loincloth. A second example, by an unknown Sienese painter of the Duecento, is found in the same museum, and other examples may be multiplied.[36] What is clear is that vestiges of the pagan Greek and Roman connections of cross and phallus—what the scholar Alexandre Leupin calls *phallophanies* ("phallic epiphanies")—remained in many of the Italian thirteenth-century depictions of the crucified Savior. Presumably Dante and his contemporaries would have had first-hand knowledge of these images.[37]

As to the question of why wings may be associated with the phallus, once again we turn to classical antiquity for at least part of the answer. (The other part may be traced to the physiology of the rising and falling phallus itself.) As Johns notes, the phallus in ancient art "is often accompanied by some other motif, to make its apotropaic function even more explicit."[38] Because the male member was generally used to ward off the evil eye, a common association is with an eye or a pair of eyes painted on the head or glans. It will be recalled that Dante's Sa-

---

[35] These and assorted images of the phallic crucified Christ may be found in a number of on-line sources, including Alexandre Leupin's website: www.alexandreleupin.com. See also Alexandre Leupin, *Phallophanies: La chair et le sacré* (Paris: Editions du Regard, 2000). I am indebted to Professor Ilona Klein for the comment on the loincloth's possible resemblance to wings.

[36] For a variety of classical examples of phallic idols and images, see the illustrations in Sanger Brown, II, M.D., *Sex Worship and Symbolism, with Illustrations* (Boston: Gorham Press, 1922), and in Hodder M. Westropp and C. Staniland Wake, *Ancient Symbol Worship: Influence of the Phallic Idea in the Religions of Antiquity* (New York: J. W. Bouton, 1875). For a scholarly analysis related to the sexual way in which Christ is depicted in post-medieval (i.e. Renaissance) art, see Leo Steinberg, *The Sexuality of Christ in Renaissance Art and in Modern Oblivion* (New York: Pantheon/October Books, 1983). His pages dealing with the theology of Christ's circumcision (50–65) and the erection motif of the dead Christ (82–108) are especially pertinent to the discussion of the crucified Lord's stylized phallus.

[37] Following the formal presentation of this essay to Christopher Kleinhenz at the AATI annual convention in Washington, DC, on 13 October 2007, Professor Kleinhenz drew my attention to a remarkable discovery, made in 2000, of a medieval Tuscan mural, dating from the late 13th century, which depicts a tree adorned with phalluses. The tree is surrounded by eagles and a group of women who are plucking the unusual "fruit." See George Ferzoco's bilingual book on the subject: *Il murale di Massa Marittima / The Massa Marittima Mural* (Florence: Consiglio Regionale della Toscana, 2004). For a color reproduction (also readily available on-line) of this extraordinary mural—which brings together a tree, phalluses, and flying birds—see George Ferzoco, "The Penis in Pre-Modern Western Culture," in *The Gazette* (Society for the Social History of Medicine) 40 (December 2006): 2–3.

[38] Johns, *Sex or Symbol*, 66.

tan, who personifies the Evil Eye, has three pairs of eyes: "Con sei occhi piangëa" (*Inf.* 34.53). Johns marshals evidence that adding "legs and wings to phalluses may express two or three different concepts," including associating the *membrum* with certain licentious animals (such as birds) or deities (such as Priapus).[39] From the River Mosel in Trier has been recovered a polyphallus displaying both wings and bells, the latter making it a tintinnabulum.[40] And in Naples at the Museo Nazionale are found a terracotta drinking-bowl mask decorated with winged phalluses and another example of a tintinnabulum with a winged phallus.[41]

These archeological examples, which also may be multiplied with citations of various Greek vases, go a long way toward explaining the iconographical tradition of the flying phallus, so reminiscent of the parallel tradition in pre-Columbian American of the flying serpent. Certainly Dante in the Middle Ages would have known at the very least of the phallic figure of the biblical serpent, both as found in the Garden of Eden (Genesis 2) and also as raised by Moses on a brass pole to save the Israelites (Numbers 21:8–9). Ultimately, in penetrating syncretism Dante drew on the legends of his time — classical cross-phallus allusions, parodies of the Trinity, and the Byzantine-inspired iconography of the crucifixion — to show the state of degradation of Satan. The cross *in bono* points to the redemptive act of Christ, who bleeds for others; it has the potential to save mankind from the Fall. Satan, the cross *in malo* that causes others to bleed, exists only to distance humanity from Christ's atoning sacrifice.

To conclude, I cite the remainder of the description that accompanies Phillips' illustration of Satan. It will be recalled that this artist boldly depicts Satan not as a flaccid phallus but as a spurting one raping Mother Earth. Phillips' own commentary on why he chose to present an ithyphallic Satan is illuminating and is, I believe, supported by Dante's textual allusions to Satan as *vermo* and *uccello* as well as by contemporary Tuscan depictions of the crucified Christ and pre-existing archeological evidence of the classical phenomenon of the winged phallus. The artist-commentator makes these points regarding his illustration of Satan:

> [A]ny penetration into the Underworld is an image of a rape of Mother Earth. The pilgrims enter through a bushy orifice into a great enclosure: they progress through tracts and ducts and chambers in which the Humours and the Elements have their place and in which blood and tears form canals and rivers and cataracts. Eventually, they emerge through a narrow channel, released into the open air from their first purging and ready to face the Mountain of Redemption that is denied to the world's pilgrim without some equivalent of this process of rebirth. Outside this abbreviated anatomy (reminding us that the genitals of Satan are exactly at the Earth's

---

[39] Johns, *Sex or Symbol*, 68.
[40] Johns, *Sex or Symbol*, 68.
[41] Antonia Mulas, *Eros in Antiquity: Photographs* (New York: Erotic Art Book Society, 1978), 118, 126.

centre) we see the pilgrims in various orientations, to indicate their change of hemisphere as they pass this point, climbing through the forest of hair on the skin of Beelzebub. They are seen again in a chamber within this scrotal or anal fiction and again ejaculated from the penis above.[42]

While Phillips may be writing and illustrating post-Freud, the images of the phallic cross and the winged phallus undeniably predate not only Phillips and Freud but also Dante Alighieri. Fortunately, when choosing how to interpret the *Commedia*, postmodern readers of the twenty-first century no longer have to limit themselves to a single interpretation. My intent in this excursus has been to demonstrate that Phillips' reading of Dante's Satan is not only reasonable but probable.

---

[42] Phillips, *Dante's Inferno*, 310.

Dal tema del "pellegrinaggio" alle icone della musica: per una rivisitazione di *Purgatorio* II

Emilio Pasquini

Non di grande complessità, ma ritmato in cinque segmenti di ampiezza disuguale, la struttura del canto. Dopo i primi dodici versi dedicati all'indicazione astronomica dell'ora, in chiave diurna, come di norma nel *Purgatorio* (in opposizione a quelle infernali, tutte in chiave lunare o notturna), e allo stato d'animo dei due viaggiatori, i vv. 13–51 sono addetti alla descrizione dell'arrivo dall'oceano sulla spiaggia delle anime dei purganti e all'uscita di scena dell'angelo nocchiero; i vv. 52–75 allo stato d'animo e al comportamento dei nuovi arrivati; i vv. 76–117 al colloquio con Casella; i vv. 118–133 al ritorno in scena di Catone e al suo rimprovero per la perdita di tempo causata da quell'incontro.

Uno "stilizzato abbraccio cosmico"[1] la connessione Sole-Gerusalemme-montagna del Purgatorio, ripresa ai vv. 55–57 per il nesso Sole-Capricorno. Scontata, già per Buti e Landino, la prosopopea dell'Aurora; un po' meno la precisazione cromatica (le *guance* di lei, *bianche* e *vermiglie*, che divengono *rance*), non solo per il possibile richiamo alle *cappe rance* degli ipocriti (*Inferno* XXIII 100). Non superflua la nota del Tommaseo, in polemica implicita con Landino e Vellutello:[2] "*rance* in antico non sonava punto 'rancide', ma rammentava l'origine 'aurantius' (. . .) Virg. *Eneide* VI 'roscis Aurora quadrigis.'" In merito alla terna *Aurora alba-rubea-lutea*, richiamata dal Mattalia, non è inutile rileggere la chiosa

---

[1] Così la definisce Antonio Enzo Quaglio nel commento garzantiano (in collaborazione con Emilio Pasquini); vedi Emilio Pasquini e Antonio Enzo Quaglio, edd., *Dante Alighieri Commedia: Purgatorio* (Milano: Garzanti, 1992), 29. S'avverta che per semplicità i commenti alla *Commedia* vengono citati col solo nome dei commentatore; e che i riferimenti all'esegesi antica, quando è possibile, chiamano in causa il secondo tomo della *Divina Commedia nella figurazione artistica e nel secolare commento*, ed. Guido Biagi, Giuseppe L. Passerini, e Enrico Ristagno (Torino: UTET, 1931).

[2] Fuori strada soprattutto quest'ultimo: "viete e vecchie per troppa etate; et è similitudine da le cose che si gustano, quando per essere troppo invecchiate, hanno perduto il suo buono e natural sapore, e che diciamo 'saper di rancio.'"

di Benvenuto: "gene Aurore, que fuerunt primo albe, postea rubre, nunc fiebant subrufe *per troppa etate*, idest moram, quia nimis steterant ante conspectum solis venientis cum splendore magno."

Su questa miniatura astronomica prevale però il motivo del "pellegrinaggio," all'origine di un'ampia area metaforica in Dante, avviatasi con la *Vita nova*: "come colui che non sa per qual via pigli lo suo cammino, e che vuole andare e non sa onde se ne vada" (XIII 6) e "in largo, in quanto è peregrino chiunque è fuori de la sua patria; in modo stretto non s'intende peregrino se non chi va verso la casa di sa' Iacopo o riede" (XL 6). Si tratta di un vero e proprio *Leitmotiv* nella seconda cantica, a partire da I 118–120 ("Noi andavam per lo solingo piano / com'om che torna a la perduta strada, / che 'nfino ad essa li pare ire invano"), con altri agganci in questo canto ai vv. 61–63 ("...ma noi siam peregrin come voi siete") e 132 ("com'om che va, né sa dove riesca") e un'eco nel III, al v. 72 ("com'a guardar, chi va dubbiando, stassi").

In questo clima di pellegrinaggio foriero di sorprese, non stupisce che la seconda sequenza, tutta improntata al movimento e all'evento (l'arrivo delle nuove anime), sia introdotta dal nesso *Ed ecco...*, calco di *Et ecce...*, modulo scritturale e virgiliano,[3] replicato al v. 119, per la ricomparsa improvvisa di Catone. *Difficilior*, senza dubbio, la lezione "sorpreso dal mattino" (v. 14), "colto dall'avvento della prima luce," addetta al pianeta Marte che funge[4] da termine di paragone per il *lume* del duo angelo-vasello, rispetto a "sul presso del mattino": ciò fin dall'acuto Castelvetro, contro la filiera Landino-Cesari.[5] Forse troppo sottile la chiosa di Benvenuto: "Et declarat ipsum angelum per unam comparationem nobilem vel propriam (...). Sicut mars, planeta calidus, rubeus de sua natura, accendit homines ad bella, ita Angelus, splendens et ardens, inducit homines et inclinat hic ad bellandum contra vitia."

Di maggior interesse, proprio per la sua incidenza nel repertorio espressivo di Dante, la gradualità della visione per quella sua straordinaria capacità di cogliere la realtà in movimento, che sembra preannunciare gli argomenti del *Laocoonte* di Lessing sull'arte del tempo antitetica a quella dello spazio:[6] già il vecchio Benvenuto citava, a riscontro di questa graduale apparizione angelica, il

---

[3] Erich Auerbach, *Mimesi: Il realismo nella letteratura occidentale*, trad. Aurelio Roncaglia (Torino: Einaudi, 1956), 184–88.

[4] Forse nella scia di *Convivio* II xiii 21: "lo suo calore è simile a quello del fuoco; e questo è quello per che esso pare affocato di colore, quando più e quando meno, secondo la spessezza e raritade de li vapori che 'l seguono...".

[5] Si veda ora il riepilogo di Anna Maria Chiavacci Leonardi, ed., *Dante Alighieri: Commedia*, vol. 2, *Purgatorio* (Milano: Mondadori, 1994), 67–68.

[6] Emilio Pasquini, *Dante e le figure del vero: La fabbrica della "Commedia"* (Milano: Mondadori, 2001), 18–23. Vedi anche Gotthold Lessing, *Laocoonte* (Palermo: Aesthetica, 2007).

progressivo rivelarsi dei Giganti infernali. È interessante[7] che anche Virgilio, come Dante personaggio, nel *Purgatorio* scopra poco alla volta la realtà mentre gli si manifesta: diversamente avveniva nell'Inferno di cui Virgilio era ben edotto.[8]

Inoltre, anche in questo canto, come del resto in molti altri, si verifica la convivenza fra Virgilio- personaggio e Virgilio-autore: dietro le *ali* (v. 33) e le *etterne penne* (v. 35) stanno il *remigium alarum* di *Eneide* VI 19 e le *praepetibus pennis* di *Eneide* VI 15 (sintagmi, entrambi, adibiti per Dedalo). Alla tradizione latina, dove "la *vela* appellavasi *velum*," secondo il Lombardi, si richiama anche il *velo* del v. 32.

A tutt'altre radici si rifà invece il *vasello snelletto e leggiero* del v. 41, che sembra risultare da un incrocio fra il *vasel* di *Guido, i' vorrei*, la *nave piccioletta* di Flegiàs (*Inferno* VIII 14), in un canto dove al v. 17 ricorreva già il lessema *galeotto*, qui (sempre in rima) al v. 27,[9] e il *vasello* marchigiano di *Inferno* XXVIII 79. Verso aure paradisiache orienta invece il *celestial nocchiero* del v. 43, che al tempo stesso si configura come contromodello di Caronte, il "nocchier de la livida palude" (*Inferno* III 82 ss.); il quale peraltro aveva preannunciato a Dante: "più lieve legno convien che ti porti"[10] (Daniello, da cui Venturi). Quanto all'alternativa di lezione fra "tal che parea beato per iscripto," da Sapegno spiegato con riferimento ai cartigli che nell'iconografia pittorica si associano a figure di santi,[11] e "tal che faria beato pur descripto" cioè "che, descritto solamente, anche senza essere contemplato, renderebbe felice ogni uomo,"[12] io non saprei uscire da una diagnosi di adiaforia, del resto nella scia di Giorgio Petrocchi.

Fondamentale per l'intera concezione della *Commedia*, specie nella prospettiva di un Charles S. Singleton,[13] è l'inizio del Salmo 113, intonato *ad una voce* (v. 47), "all'unisono,"[14] dai nuovi arrivati: è "la prima delle molte preghiere che

---

[7] L'osservazione è adombrata nel commento Rossi-Frascino, i quali però non ne deducono un giudizio di ordine generale, tanto meno nella prospettiva di un Lessing.

[8] Si ricordi *Inferno* IX 22–23: "ver è ch'altra fiata qua giù fui, / congiurato da quella Eriton cruda...."

[9] Ma già Tommaseo l'aveva contrapposta al battello angelico, non certo carico del corpo di Dante, come implicitamente osserva Benvenuto: "non mergebatur (. . .) infra aquam, quia navis erat levis, et anime sedentes in navi erant leves sine pondere carnis."

[10] Così il Daniello, da cui il Venturi e molti fra i commentatori moderni.

[11] Solo apparentemente più banale la glossa "sembrava che la beatitudine gli fosse scritta in volto," condivisa da Torraca, Rossi-Frascino, Chimenz, e Petrocchi.

[12] Pasquini e Quaglio, edd., *Purgatorio*, 23.

[13] Charles S. Singleton, *La poesia della Divina Commedia* (Bologna: Il Mulino, 1999), 37–50, 495–520.

[14] Anche questo particolare è importante, in quanto "prima nota di quella poesia corale che domina nel Purgatorio": Natalino Sapegno, *La Divina Commedia*, vol. 2, *Purgatorio* (Firenze: La Nuova Italia, 1968), 17.

echeggiano nel mondo dell'espiazione."[15] Già citato nel *Convivio*[16] e poi sottoposto ai quattro sensi dell'esegesi biblica nell'*Epistola a Cangrande* (*Epistola* XIII 21), esso è qui utilizzato non tanto perché si cantasse nella liturgia cristiana durante l'accompagnamento dei defunti al camposanto (anche nella Vigilia Pasquale), e neppure come canto della liberazione degli Ebrei dalla schiavitù d'Egitto, anche se questo significa il ritorno alla Terra Promessa. Che è il primo senso investigato da Dante nell' *Epistola* XIII:[17]

> Nam si ad litteram solam inspiciamus, significatur nobis exitus filiorum Israel de Egipto, tempore Moysis; si ad allegoriam, nobis significatur nostra redemptio facta per Christum; si ad moralem sensum, significatur nobis conversio anime de luctu et miseria peccati ad statum gratie; si ad anagogicum, significatur exitus anime sancte ab corruptionis servitute ad eterne glorie libertatem.

> Infatti, se guardiamo alla sola lettera del testo, il significato è che i figli d'Israele uscirono d'Egitto, al tempo di Mosè; se guardiamo all'allegoria, il significato è che noi siamo stati redenti da Cristo; se guardiamo al significato morale, il senso è che l'anima passa dalle tenebre e dalla infelicità del peccato allo stato di grazia; se guardiamo al significato anagogico, il senso è che l'anima santificata esce dalla schiavitù della presente corruzione terrena alla libertà dell'eterna gloria.

Nel contesto di cui ci occupiamo, intensamente polisemico, risulta dunque che il senso allegorico vale per le nuove anime degli espianti; quello morale e l'anagogico per Dante pellegrino nell'oltretomba.

Passando alla terza sequenza, dopo quello straordinario endecasillabo dattilico, per lo svanire dell'angelo, "ed el sen gì, come venne, veloce" (v. 51), che non manca di riscontri nel poema,[18] l'obiettivo si sposta sulla "turba (. . .) selvaggia (. . .) del loco" (vv. 52–53), cioè "inesperta, imperita," come già glossava Serravalle ("silvestris, idest peregrina"), sviluppato un po' ingenuamente dal Lombardi,[19] "selvaggio per inesperto, proprietà essendo del selvaggio di non esser pratico

---

[15] Pasquini e Quaglio, edd., *Purgatorio*, 30.

[16] "Spiritualmente s'intende (. . .) che nell'uscita dell'anima del peccato, essa si è fatta santa e libera in sua podestate" (*Convivio* II i 7).

[17] Cito dall'edizione a cura di Giorgio Brugnoli, in Dante Alighieri, *Opere minori*, vol. 2 (Milano-Napoli: Ricciardi, 1979), 610–11.

[18] Si pensi soltanto a un verso come "si dileguò, come da corda cocca" (*Inferno* XVII 136) e si ricorra fruttuosamente a Gian Luigi Beccaria, *L'autonomia del significante: Figure del ritmo e della sintassi: Dante, Pascoli, D'Annunzio* (Torino: Einaudi, 1975).

[19] Ben altra finezza nella postilla del Sapegno sulla condizione spirituale di "incertezza esitante" che accomuna Dante alle anime. Vedi Natalino Sapegno, *La Divina Commedia*, vol. 2, *Purgatorio*, 17.

di altro luogo che della sua selva."[20] Quanto al dardeggiare del sole, ormai alto sull'orizzonte (vv. 55 ss.), occorre subito sgombrare il campo dall'impossibile intertesto addotto dal Cesari (e sulla sua scorta dall'Andreoli): "dovette D. averlo preso da Lucrezio, che "lucida tela diei" usò ben cinque volte." È opportuno sottolineare, col Toraca e col Sapegno, che le *saette conte* valgono "esperte, infallibili" (da COGNITAE), come, per le *parole*, a Inferno X 39[21] e XXXIII 31, secondo quanto aveva già proposto il Buti ("certe, perché sempre percuotono in un certo luogo"), seguito dal Landino ("vere e certe, perché e raggi del sole non mutano mai ordine nel ferire"); e non "adorne" o simili (da COMPTAE), come suggerivano il Serravalle ("promptis, vel ornatis et manifestis"), il Cesari ("famose, celebrate, ecc., accennano al Pitone dal Sole ucciso") e l'Andreoli ("chiare, luminose," con richiamo al Lucrezio chiamato in causa dal Cesari).

Senza storia l'alternanza "siamo spirti"/"siamo esperti";[22] fin troppo evidente che per alludere alla via già percorsa attraverso l'Inferno Virgilio adoperi la dittologia "aspra e forte," che ripete esattamente *Inferno* I 5. Più significativo è che il tema del riconoscimento di Dante come persona viva, non estraneo alla prima cantica, trovi nella seconda modalità diverse, mai agonistiche, e invece improntate a quella solerte curiosità che spesso sfocia in una carità solidale. Qui, l'agnizione si manifesta come una meraviglia che produce pallore: *smorte* è così glossato da Buti: "lo smortore procede da paura (...) e le cose meravigliose aduceno paura." Tommaseo cita dal VI dell' *Eneide* "Adrasti pallentis imago"; mentre l'Anonimo fiorentino coglie uno straordinario nesso intratestuale, con la canzone *Così nel mio parlar voglio esser aspro*, vv. 45-47: "e 'l sangue, ch'è per le vene disperso, / fuggendo corre verso / lo cor, che 'l chiama, ond'io rimango bianco." Iper-razionalista al solito, quanto alla causa del riconoscimento, il Castelvetro, per il quale non è verosimile che, "essendo l'aer temperato, e non freddo, e levato il sole, che altri vegga il fiato di persona, il quale non si suole vedere se non d'inverno, quando l'aere è grosso." Giustamente il Cesari: "Quello spirare appariva nel levarsi delle coste e abbassarsi che il petto fa respirando (...) od anche nel movimento ed *atto de la gola*, al qual segno e' fu già (*Inferno* XXIII 88) da altri riconosciuto"; e il concetto viene ribadito dal Tommaseo, proprio in polemica col Castelvetro.

Al tempo stesso l'incontro col vivo va correlandosi al tema medievale del "messagger che porta ulivo" (v. 70). Un possibile ipotesto classico è il Virgilio

---

[20] Si veda la voce del *Grande Dizionario della Lingua Italiana*, che cita—oltre a questo—esempi di Francesco da Barberino e Giovanni Villani, poi di Monti e Gioberti in età moderna.

[21] L'accostamento era già nel Tommaseo, il quale chiosava sagacemente: "qui può anche valere: "che fa conoscer con la sua luce le cose." Di qui probabilmente la perifrasi addotta da Rossi-Frascino: "che sanno tutte le plaghe del cielo."

[22] Giorgio Petrocchi, nell'introduzione all'edizione della *Commedia secondo l'antica vulgata* (Milano: Mondadori, 1966), 193.

dell'*Eneide* (8.116 e 11.101), per la prima volta chiamato in causa dal Lombardi (poi dall'Andreoli); mentre Benvenuto ci dà un ennesimo referto in tema di similitudini: "Nota quantum comparatio sit propria ad propositum: nam Poeta (. . .) erat novus nuntius portans bona nova"; e a proposito del *quasi obliando* suggerisce una sorta di giustificazione: "imaginabantur non perdere tempus et operam, si videbant hominem constitutum tanta gratia vivum ire per Purgatorium." A sua volta il Torraca allega il *Convivio* (IV xxviii 5): "E sì come a colui che viene di lungo cammino, anzi ch'entri ne la porta de la sua cittade, gli si fanno incontro li cittadini di quella. . . ."

Esplicita la contrapposizione fra queste "anime fortunate" e le dannate dell'Inferno; tanto più significativa la pausa di questo incontro col vivo che esse si concedono "quasi obliando d'ire a farsi belle" (v. 85). Di là dalla "maliosa e intraducibile vaghezza" di questi versi (Mattalia), notevole è il riscontro intratestuale con XVI 31–32 ("O creatura che ti mondi / per tornar bella a colui che ti fece"). Una spontanea levità connota ancora la voce dell'autore, nel passaggio alla quarta sequenza, persino al cimento di un motivo topico come l'abbraccio vano ad un'ombra. Sul piano intertestuale, il debito richiamo a *Eneide* VI 700 ss. (per l'incontro di Enea col padre Anchise) si deve a Pietro Alighieri, seguito dall'Anonimo Fiorentino; forse più interessante, sul versante intratestuale, il nesso con *Inferno* VI 36 e con le spiegazioni date a *Purg.* III 19–33 e soprattutto XXV 79–117. Di fatto, di fronte alla corpulenza e plasticità dei paesaggi e personaggi della prima cantica, ci dimentichiamo di queste "ombre vane, fuor che ne l'aspetto" (v. 79). Giova ricordare come il Landino riferisca l'opinione di alcuni che vedevano contraddizione fra questo passo e la "palpabilità" delle anime nell'Inferno, col memorabile "Allor lo presi per la cuticagna"; e come egli la risolva col buonsenso: "in Inferno poeticamente attribuì quello all'anima che naturalmente non ha." Viceversa Castelvetro insisteva nel suo razionalismo antipoetico, citando il luogo di *Inferno* VI 35–36 "e ponavam le piante / sopra lor vanità che par persona," allegato assai più tardi anche dal Tommaseo.

L'agnizione scatta però grazie alla voce, come avverrà con Forese Donati: ed è questo in Dante il primo anello del recupero, distribuito per tutta la seconda cantica, dell'avventura della propria giovinezza, il suo personale "portrait of the artist as a young man." Non ci soffermiamo sulle notizie biografiche relative a Casella, artista ben noto anche ai musicologi d'oggi, morto assai prima del 1300.[23] Una volta acquisito il significato di *sciolta* (da SOLUTA, ovviamente dal corpo), come già intendevano Lana ("desligada dal corpo") e l'Ottimo ("dislegata dal corpo suo"), nella battuta iniziale di Forese, in discorso diretto, è importante rilevare, come la prima risposta di Dante-personaggio alluda a un viaggio con ritorno al Purgatorio piuttosto che in terra fra gli uomini, prefigurando il saluto iniziale di Cacciaguida al suo lontano discendente: "sicut tibi cui / bis

---

[23] Vedi il paragrafo relativo nella *Letteratura italiana*, dovuto a F. Alberto Gallo, *Teatro, musica, tradizione dei classici* (Torino: Einaudi, 1986), 245.

unquam celi ianua reclusa?" (*Paradiso* XV 29–30). Meno chiara la seconda battuta del musicista, di fronte alla meraviglia di Dante per il suo arrivo in Purgatorio a distanza di mesi dalla morte: una risposta un po' misteriosa, nonostante l'aggancio storico alla data della proclamazione del Giubileo con la relativa amnistia (22 febbraio 1300, non senza effetto retroattivo a partire dal 25 dicembre 1299). Forse una sorta di "sciopero" di Casella, per il rifiuto delle indulgenze di Bonifacio VIII? Torraca ricorda come Caronte in Virgilio cacci via le anime degli insepolti, ma la soluzione a lui come a Rossi–Frascino non risulta appagante; Chimenz ricorda anche Palinuro, che chiede invano ad Enea di fargli traversare l'Acheronte; Sapegno infino sta con lo Zingarelli ("non tutte le assoluzioni sono irreprensibili").[24]

Simbolicamente notevole la scelta del luogo per l'imbarco delle anime alla volta di una meta oceanica (la stessa sospirata da Ulisse), "dove l'acqua di Tevero s'insala":[25] il fiume sacro a Roma antica, ma soprattutto alla Chiesa e all'Impero. L'aveva ben inteso Benvenuto ("omnis anima salvanda transit per passum illum, scilicet per precepta romane Ecclesie"), seguito da Landino e Vellutello. Il vertice poetico dell'episodio coincide però con la preghiera di Dante, in nome della comune passione per quella musica "che mi solea quetar tutte mie voglie" (v. 108), di sentirlo ancora eseguire un brano musicale, nella speranza che i decreti celesti non gli avessero tolto "memoria o uso a l'amoroso canto" (vv. 106–108). È la riconferma di un culto per questa arte a cui allude anche Boccaccio nella sua biografia dantesca:

> Sommamente si dilettò in suoni e in canti nella sua giovinezza, e a ciascuno che a que' tempi era ottimo cantatore o sonatore fu amico e ebbe sua usanza; e assai cose, da questo diletto tirato, compose, le quali di piacevole e maestrevole nota a questi cotali facea rivestire...[26]

così sviluppato da Benvenuto:

> cum enim usus musice naturaliter sit amicus omnibus etatibus et omnibus moribus, maxime iuvenes et melancholici indigent delectatione. Hic Poeta fuit valde melancholicus a natura et a studio, sicut communiter fuerunt viri sapientes...

Ma il miglior commento a questo incontro viene dal *Convivio* (II xiii 24):

> la Musica trae a sé li spiriti umani, che quasi sono principalmente vapori del cuore, sì che quasi cessano da ogni operazione: sì e l'anima intera,

---

[24] Sapegno, *La Divina Commedia*, vol. 2, *Purgatorio*, 20.
[25] Neologismo coniato sulla metonimia *sale* per "mare", a *Paradiso* II 13.
[26] Nell'edizione del *Trattatello in laude di Dante*, ed. Pier Giorgio Ricci, in *Tutte le opere*, ed. Vittore Branca, vol. 3 (Milano: Mondadori, 1974), 466.

quando l'ode, e la virtù di tutte quasi corre a lo spirito sensibile che riceve lo suono.

Non sappiamo con certezza se Casella abbia mai musicato *Amor che ne la mente mi ragiona*, che oggi si legge in capo al III libro del *Convivio* e di cui qui si cita solo il capoverso. L'Anonimo fiorentino, forse edotto da chi avvicinò direttamente l'Alighieri, non mostra di ritenere che questa canzone rientrasse fra le rime dantesche musicate da Casella, dubitando della musicabilità delle "canzoni morali" e ipotizzando che questo inizio appartenesse anche a una ballata o a un sonetto.[27] Val la pena di rileggere il passo dell'Anonimo:

> fu molto dimestico dell'A., però che in sua giovinezza fece Dante molte canzone e ballate che questi intonò; et a Dante dilettò forte l'udirle da lui, e massimamente al tempo ch'era innamorato di Beatrice o di Pargoletta, o di quella altra di Casentino...

Dove va messo in primo piano il rinvio alla stagione giovanile dominata da Beatrice rispetto alla chiamata in causa degli altri due amori. Se poi l'ultima allusione concerne, come sembra, il prosimetro costituito dalla canzone "montanina" e dall'epistola a Moroello, va detto che nel 1307 Casella era già morto da un pezzo: evidente, dunque, la confusione, a meno che l'Anonimo non si riferisca a una versione giovanile della "montanina" stessa.[28] In ogni caso, la sua testimonianza conferma l'esistenza—proclamata da Boccaccio—di una donna casentinese amata da Dante: solo implicita, la sua distanza dai tempi di Beatrice e della Pargoletta.[29] Non arbitrariamente, dunque, Quaglio parla di un "revival stilnovistico," nel *Purgatorio*, legato anche alla presenza di tanti amici della giovinezza: *Amor che ne la mente mi ragiona* fu infatti composta negli anni della *Vita nova* e poi "assunta e commentata nel *Convivio*" in una chiave morale.[30] Viene quindi a

---

[27] Il Chimenz se la cava con una chiosa generica ("canti d'amore"); vedi Siro A. Chimenz, ed., *La Divina Commedia di Dante Alighieri* (Torino: UTET, 1966), 337. Per Sapegno, invece, con *amoroso canto* si designerebbe, "tecnicamente, il canto monodico, strettamente legato alla lirica di alto stile." Vedi Sapegno, *La Divina Commedia*, vol. 2, *Purgatorio*, 20. Ma si veda anche Luigi Peirone, "Casella," nell' *Enciclopedia dantesca* (Roma: Istituto della Enciclopedia Italiana, 1970), 1: 856–58.

[28] Supposta di recente da Guglielmo Gorni, "La canzone 'montanina'," *Letture classensi* 24 (1995): 129–50 e sulla sua scia da Paola Allegretti, *La canzone montanina* (Verbania: Tararà, 2001). Ma sia consentito un rinvio al mio contributo su *Un crocevia dell'esilio: la canzone "montanina" e l'epistola a Moroello*, in corso di stampa nella miscellanea in onore di Gennaro Barbarisi.

[29] Guglielmo Gorni, *Il nodo della lingua e il verbo d'amore* (Firenze: Olschki, 1981), 57, e idem, *Metrica e analisi letteraria* (Bologna: Il Mulino, 1993), 221.

[30] Pasquini e Quaglio, edd., *Purgatorio*, 32. Vedi la voce dovuta a Vincenzo Pernicone nell' *Enciclopedia dantesca*, 219–21; e si veda anche l'edizione critica delle *Rime*

rappresentare le due principali stagioni della lirica dantesca: "l'onore del suo passato artistico viene consacrato dal trapianto nella *Commedia*."[31]

Questo dato storico sembra allo stesso studioso prevalente rispetto a una generica "catarsi artistica attribuita alla musica"; e l'insistenza sul tema della *dulcedo* ("dolcemente... dolcezza"), costitutivo dell'ideale melodico dello Stilnovo,[32] sembrerebbe dargli ragione. Eppure, se rileggiamo i vv. 113–117 sullo sfondo del passo già citato del *Convivio*, non possiamo ignorare la magia di questa estasi musicale, riassunta in un solo verso, il 117, "come a nessun toccasse altro la mente" (un verbo che al Tommaseo suggeriva l'ipotesto di *Eneide* 1: 462, "mentem... tangunt"). Del resto, anche Quaglio è indotto ad ammettere che qui prevale quel desiderio di "placare con la musica dell'antica poesia l'ansia smarrita del presente".[33] E un'utile integrazione viene offerta dalla Chiavacci Leonardi nel suo richiamare—nella scia di Poletto e Freccero - il luogo di Boezio dove il personaggio-autore "resta rapito dal dolce canto della Filosofia, chiamata "summum lassorum solamen animorum."[34] Ma soprattutto non mi sottraggo alla tentazione di richiamare qui un passo straordinario di Benvenuto da Imola in calce ai vv. 48 ss. del canto XXVIII:[35]

> Et hic nota (...), lector, quam pulcros rythmos Poeta noster fabricavit in tam pulcra materia. Ex quo apparet verum esse illud quod festive dixit quidam in commendationem eius: dicebat enim quo quando Dante primo parabat se ad tam nobile poema, omnes rythmi mundi presentarunt se compsectui eius tamquam pulcerrime domicelle suppliciter rogantes singule, ut dignaretur admittere illas libenter in opere tanto. At ille cepit vocare nunc istam nunc illam, et unamquamque in ordine secundum exigentiam materie collocare: tandem, libro ad felix complemento producto, nulla remanserat extra: sub hoc curiali dicto volens ostendere, quod videtur impossibile extorquere rhythmum Danti.

Una favola commovente e gentile, con i ritmi personificati in fanciulle affascinanti, quasi innamorate di quel creatore; una favola però che mira nella sostanza

---

di Dante a cura di Domenico De Robertis, introduzione (Firenze: Le Lettere, 2002), 723–54.

[31] Pasquini e Quaglio, edd., *Purgatorio*, 34.

[32] Vedi da ultimo Emilio Pasquini, "Il 'dolce stil novo'," nella *Storia della letteratura italiana*, vol. 1, *Dalle origini a Dante* (Roma: Salerno, 1995), 649–721.

[33] Pasquini e Quaglio, edd., *Purgatorio*, 33.

[34] Chiavacci Leonardi, ed., *Purgatorio*, 43.

[35] Vedi Mario Pazzaglia, "Benvenuto da Imola lettore della 'Commedia,'" nel miscellaneo *Benvenuto da Imola lettore degli antichi e dei moderni: Atti del Convegno internazionale di Imola, 26–27 maggio 1989*, ed. P. Palmieri e C. Paolazzi (Ravenna: Longo, 1991), 257–58, e la mia recente lettura di quel canto del *Purgatorio* in corso di stampa nella *Lectura Dantis Metelliana 32* (a parare).

ad allogare Dante sotto la costellazione del ritmo (o dei ritmi), quasi archetipo di un universo musicale, detentore miracoloso dell'armonia del mondo. E che dunque implicitamente suggerisce analoga soluzione fiabesca per il repertorio delle rime (rime e ritmi, ma non nell'accezione tecnica di Carducci), collocando quindi la genesi della *Commedia* al crocevia dell'invenzione del metro, quella terzina (nata probabilmente allo spartiacque fra i due secoli) che incatena in un mirabile congegno di rime e ritmi concetti ed immagini, un'idea complessa, o meglio totalizzante, del mondo terreno visto dalla specola dell'oltremondo.

Geniale il passaggio dalla sospensione nell'estasi musicale all'urgenza concreta del presente; dal "Noi eravam tutti fissi e attenti / a le sue note..." (vv. 117 ss.) all'*et ecce* del brusco intervento di Catone, quasi inviato dal cielo a spezzare un incanto troppo terreno. Immediato e senza attenuanti il rimprovero di fronte a quell'indebita evasione, bollata come "lentezza" o negligenza:[36] soprattutto pigrizia imperdonabile per chi avrebbe subito dovuto "correre" alla montagna per liberarsi dello "scoglio" che li separa ancora da Dio.

Su questo termine *scoglio* (nella *iunctura* col verbo "spogliare"), col valore di "scorza, involucro" (del peccato), unico esempio nel *Grande Dizionario della Lingua Italiana* di estensione metaforica del lemma, occorre soffermarsi un attimo. L'acquisizione semantica procede dal Lana ("'l peccato, che oscura sì omne cognizione d'anima, che la somma felicità per quella no po essere cognosciuda"), da cui dipende alla lettera l'Ottimo, per arrivare a Buti ("la macchia del vizio e del peccato, la quale si spoglia co la penitenzia"), fonte di Landino, Vellutello e Daniello, questi ultimi due orientati più genericamente verso "impedimento." Benvenuto invece va per altra strada ("saxum et onus vitiorum, quod pergravat animam ad ima"), tale da consentire ironie razionalistiche al solito Castelvetro: "lo scoglio si rimuove, si spezza, si rompe, si fora, ecc., ma non si spoglia." L'altra linea (non "masso", ma "integumento, scorza") è però quella vincente, grazie anche al preciso rinvio di Lombardi a Paolo, *Colossesi* 3:9 ("expoliantes vos veterem hominem cum actibus suis") e al consenso del Tommaseo. Più specificamente in polemica con Castelvetro, il Cesari ("la pelle che il serpente suole mutare"), rifluito nell'Andreoli, in Chimenz e nel Torraca (il quale cita un esempio di Bono Giamboni); conciliante, invece, la glossa del Sapegno: "la pelle dei rettili o d'altri animali, la scorza dei frutti e simili."

La conclusiva similitudine coi "colombi adunati alla pastura," messi in fuga da qualche stimolo esterno (vv. 123 ss.), è giudicata da Benvenuto una felice *comparatio domestica*, mentre il Cesari precisa trattarsi dei colombi selvatici ("palombi") e non dei domestici: in ogni caso lontanissima dalla fissità dei bestiari; Rossi-Frascino suggeriscono in aggiunta come la similitudine rispecchi la concordia delle anime, connotato precipuo del *Purgatorio*. Più importante rilevare il valore del sintagma "usato orgoglio" (v. 126): per Tommaseo, un po' asciuttamente,

---

[36] Il doppio sintagma interrogativo del v. 121 appare modellato su *Eneide* 6:373–374: "Festinate, viri: nam quae tam sera moratur segnities?"

"lieta vivacità," ma per un moderno come Mattalia, con eccessivo antropomorfismo (temperato nel Torraca), "il loro usuale starsene impettiti che li fa parere uccelli orgogliosi e presuntuosetti." Quanto all'altro sintagma "masnada fresca" (v. 130), nessun dubbio per la resa "compagnia o brigata giunta da poco" (già Benvenuto: "turbam novam illarum animarum"), dato che in antico il sostantivo non aveva significato negativo (ciò sia detto anche alla luce di *Inferno* XV 41).

Assai più aderente allo stato d'animo sia delle anime sia dei due viaggiatori la similitudine, contratta in un solo verso (132), "com'uom che va, né sa dove riesca,"[37] in quanto si connette col tema conduttore del pellegrinaggio, essenziale e quasi endemico nella seconda cantica. Che poi Catone, già definito da Lucano (*Pharsalia* IX, per la prima volta allegato da Tommaseo) "durae (...) virtutis amator," si prospetti quasi come un anti-Casella, si puo ammettere a condizione però che non si perda di vista la complementarità dei due personaggi nel loro rispecchiare "la condizione psicologica di tutti gli espianti, sospesi fra il ricordo della terra e l'attesa del cielo."[38] Insomma l'itinerario ascetico di Dante "pellegrino" si va delineando attraverso un contrappunto quasi ossimorico, che sfocerà nella radiosa formula, messa in bocca a Forese (*Purgatorio* XXIII 86), "lo dolce assenzo de' martìri." Qui, vada detto conclusivamente, la dolcezza della musica o dell'arte[39] sembra prevalere sull'amaro rimprovero di Catone, vincitore sì, ma in certa misura solo in apparenza. Non dimentichiamo che Stazio confesserà (*Purgatorio* XXI 100–102) di essere disposto a stare un anno in più fra le pene del Purgatorio, pur di conoscere Virgilio. E dunque anche questa "eretica" vittoria della musica terrena sull'ansia della salvezza celeste si accrediti alla non mai abbastanza benedetta laicità del nostro poeta.

---

[37] Si richiami il già citato passo di *Vita nova* XIII 6.
[38] Pasquini e Quaglio, edd., *Purgatorio*, 35.
[39] Definito bene da Chiavacci Leonardi "il più alto, e quindi pericoloso, degli incanti terreni": *Purgatorio*, 68.

Philomela: The "Civic" Rape of the Empire

Margherita Pampinella-Cropper

Dante's passage from Ante-purgatory to Purgatory proper is marked by the first prophetic dream experienced by the pilgrim in this canticle. Having fallen asleep in the Valley of the Princes at the end of canto 8, in the next canto Dante awakens at the gate of Purgatory after dreaming of an eagle with golden feathers that seizes him, just like Ganymede when he was hunting on Mt. Ida, and carries him there. Dante mentions the swallow, which sings in a melancholy way in memory of her ancient sufferings, to designate the time of his dream, i.e. just before dawn when dreams are true:

> Ne l'ora che comincia i tristi lai
> la rondinella presso a la mattina,
> forse a memoria de' suoi primi guai
> e che la mente nostra, peregrina
> più da la carne e men da' pensier presa,
> a le sue visïon quasi è divina, . . . (*Purg.* 9.13–18)

Swallow and nightingale were traditionally connected to the classical myth of the two daughters of the Athenian king Pandion, Philomela and Procne.[1] The

---

[1] Although in the Greek tradition Philomela is the swallow and Procne the nightingale, in the Latin tradition Hyginus (2nd century AD) offers the first attestation of the switching of the birds. In Hyginus' *Fabulae*, 45 Philomela is changed into a nightingale and the paradox of her sweet singing is avoided by the omission of her mutilation. In the western tradition Philomela, because of the Greek etymon, usually represents the nightingale which symbolizes the regaining of the voice through the tapestry sent to Procne. For a complete overview of the ancient variants of the story and the switching of the birds see Franz Bömer, *P.Ovidius Naso: Metamorphosen*, 7 vols. (Heidelberg: Carl Winter Universitätsverlag, 1969–1976), 6–7: 115–19; 177.

In Ovid's *Metamorphoses* it is not clear what species of birds the two sisters became. The only details Ovid provides the readers are the red marks on their breasts and the opposite direction of their flight: one takes refuge in the woods, the other to the roof-top: "quarum petit altera silvas, / altera tecta subit, neque adhuc de pectore caedis / excessere notae, signataque sanguine pluma est" (*Met.* 6. 668–670). Bömer, *Metamorphosen*, 6–7:

ancient sufferings of the swallow are interpreted in all medieval commentaries on the *Comedy*[2] as an obvious reference to Philomela's rape and mutilation by her brother-in-law Tereus, although most of the commentators identify Philomela's sister Procne as the swallow and Philomela herself as the nightingale. Modern commentators, however, agree on Philomela being the swallow, since the nightingale appears in *Purg.* 17.19–21, as a vision of punished wrath, thus referring to Procne's cruelty in the murder of her own son.[3]

The story of the swallow, whether Philomela or Procne is to be understood, refers to a very violent myth of abduction, rape, potential incest, mutilation, deceit, infanticide, and cannibalism. Nevertheless, Dante alludes to it in the solemn and miraculous context of his dream of the eagle with golden feathers, which is a figure of St. Lucy who is responsible for his ascent to the gate of Purgatory, as Virgil explains to Dante later. Moreover, he evokes the swallow to sanction the truth of his experience. The mere mention of the swallow would evoke in the mind of the reader the whole gruesome story of the two unlucky sisters. Dante is well aware of the power of intertextuality, it being one of the most powerful techniques of the *Comedy*.

Whether Dante is referring to Procne or Philomela, this is the only mention of this myth and that of Ganymede as well. He compares himself to Ganymede seized by the eagle, either sent by Jove or Jove himself in disguise, when he was hunting on Mt. Ida. When he awakens from the dream, he finds himself at the gate of Purgatory and learns that it was St. Lucy who had brought him there. Medieval and modern commentators see Ganymede in a direct figural relationship to Dante, the myth of Ganymede being interpreted *in bono* by Dante, and

---

115–19; 177: "Bei Ovid sind beide Schwestern an der Bluttat beteiligt (VI 641 f. 643 ff. 658); es ist also *von hier aus* kein Schluß möglich, welche der beiden Schwestern hier die Schwalbe sein soll." Frederick Ahl, *Metaformations* (Ithaca: Cornell University Press, 1985), 230, argues that Ovid "probably assumes that we will recognize in the tongueless Philomela the garrulous swallow." James C. McKeown, *Ovid: Amores*, 4 vols. (Liverpool: Francis Cairns, 1988), 3: 115, argues that "in many of Ovid's frequent references to the myth, it is unclear which version he is following, but specific details are occasionally given: the swallow is Itys' mother at *Ars* 2.383 and *Trist.* 3.12.9; Procne is Itys' mother at *Met.* 6.424 ff.; the swallow, named as Procne, is Itys' mother at *Fast.* 2.853 ff.; the raped sister is Philomela at *Rem.* 61, probably a nightingale (swallows are conspicuously not woodland birds) at *Pont.* 1.3.39 ff. Here [*Amores* 2.6], as elsewhere, it may be that Ovid is showing his awareness of the variants in the tradition by declining to commit himself firmly to any particular version."

[2] Medieval and modern commentaries on Dante's *Divine Comedy* from the Dartmouth Dante Project. (http://dante.dartmouth.edu)

[3] Edward Moore, *Studies in Dante, First Series: Scripture and Classical Authors in Dante* (New York: Haskell, 1896; repr. New York: Greenwood Press, 1968), 209–10: "The 'primi guai' far more appropriately refer to the cruel outrage and sufferings of Philomela than to the wrongs of Procne."

largely stripped of any sexual undertones. Dante alludes to the grim destiny of Philomela with the mere mention of the sorrowful song of the swallow which remembers its sad past, while he explicitly draws a parallel between his own experience of ascending to the threshold of Purgatory and Ganymede's abduction.

Even though it does not apply directly to the content of the dream, the reference to the swallow still plays an important role in determining the propitious time, that particular time of the night, just before dawn, when the mind, free of material concerns, can receive truthful visions. Dante discusses the prophetic skills of the mind revealed in dreams in the *Convivio*,[4] where he considers this power of divination to be proof of the immortality of the soul. In fact, he argues, how could the mind foresee the future if there were no immortal parts in ourselves? Thus, while not bearing any direct relation to the content of the dream, the swallow still attests to the truth of the dream itself. The credibility of the dream and therefore of Dante's transformative experience relies on the reference to the swallow.

It may seem inappropriate to link the violence of the myth of Philomela to Ganymede's apotheosis, yet the fact that this is the only mention of these myths in the *Divine Comedy* would argue in favor of Dante's intentional linking of the two. Dante must have seen a meaningful connection between the two characters and wanted to underscore it, thus adding an additional value to the entire episode: both mortals, both desired, both abducted, both connected to bird imagery (Philomela becomes a swallow, Ganymede is carried to the gods by an eagle).

However, there is also a crucial difference between Philomela and Ganymede. In the Ovidian version, reported by many medieval commentators on the *Comedy* as well,[5] Tereus is described as an eagle when he carries Philomela away on his ship. The eagle, a bird of prey, can bring the mortal down, depriving him/her of human nature, or can raise him/her up giving him/her divine stature (=apotheosis). Philomela, contaminated by Tereus-eagle, is imprisoned in a bird's body, able to sing only sorrowful songs, while Ganymede, carried by Jove-eagle, relies on the bird as a means of transportation to the gods.

Is the reference to the swallow a device to emphasize the difference between the animal nature of Philomela, contaminated by carnal and bestial desire, and the divine nature of Ganymede, touched by the sublimated love of God? Or is Dante recuperating the figure of Philomela, an innocent victim of the basest male desire? The metamorphosis into a bird could be seen through the filter of the Platonic and Neoplatonic idea of the wings of the soul and therefore understood not as a punishment, but rather as a form of escape from the wretched human condition. Because Dante uses this image of the swallow to underline the truth of his dream, it seems likely that he wanted to grant Philomela a kind of

---

[4] *Convivio*, 2.8.13. See also *Inferno* 26.7.
[5] Both L'Ottimo (1333) and Benvenuto (1380) offer the version of the myth closest to Ovid's *Metamorphoses*. Benvenuto preserves the simile of Tereus as an eagle.

supernatural stature. Thus the swallow (Philomela) could indicate an intermediate state between human and divine, a sort of penitent phase of the soul. In fact, Dante is moving upwards in the realm of Purgatory where souls are grooming themselves, as it were, fashioning their wings for their eventual flight to Paradise, with a final metamorphosis from worms into angelic butterflies ("vermi / nati a formar l'angelica farfalla" [*Purg.* 10.124–125]).

Considering the political connotation of the eagle in the imperial imagery of the *Comedy*[6] and the political context of the valley of the princes, where Dante spent the night and received the prophetic dream that marks his entrance in Purgatory proper and finally his access to the earthly Paradise, we are led to believe that the dream concerns a vision of the ideal empire on earth after the sad acknowledgment of the political failures in the valley of the negligent rulers. The myths of Philomela and of Ganymede contribute to the definition of this dream, with their political undertones. In the myth of Philomela and Procne, the political and the sexual overlap: Tereus abuses his power over the city of Athens just as he forces himself on his sister-in-law and mutilates her. Tereus' confusion of family roles and rules is an immediate and more horrifying reflection of his po-

---

[6] John A. Scott, *Dante's Political Purgatory* (Philadelphia: University of Pennsylvania Press, 1996), 133, notes that out of the twelve references to eagles in the *Comedy*, "in no fewer than five instances, the eagle clearly stands for the Roman Empire (*Purg.* XXXII.125; XXXIII. 38; *Par.* VI. 1) and its ideal of Justice (*Par.* XVIII.107; XX.26). [. . .] Outside the *Comedy*, the eagle symbolizes the universal Empire of Rome in *Monarchia* II.ix.15, xi.6, and in *Epistles* V.iv.II (*sublimis aquila*), VI.iii.12 (*aquila in auro terribilis*), VII.i.5 (*signa Tarpeia*—the imperial eagle is associated with the very heart of Rome, the Capitol's *Tarpeius mons* mentioned just after Dante's dream, *Purg.* IX.136–38). Beside these five instances, we must add the highly significant allusion to Emperor Henry VII as *Iovis armiger* ("Jove's armiger") in Giovanni del Virgilio's First Eclogue to Dante (I.26). This is the term used to designate the eagle in Virgil's reference to the rape of Ganymede (*Aen.* 5.252–55): "inwoven thereon the royal boy [Ganymede], with javelin and speedy foot, on leafy Ida tires fleet stags, eager, and like to one who pants; him Jove's swift armor-bearer [*Iovis armiger*] has caught up aloft from Ida in his talons." Giovanni del Virgilio evidently took it for granted that Dante would grasp the equation *Iovis armiger* = Eagle → the Emperor. Moreover, two of the contexts outside the *Comedy* are of particular importance. The first has been noted by a number of scholars. It is the passage already indicated in *Ep.* V.iv.II, in which Dante speaks of the Emperor's arrival in Italy as that of an "eagle from on high, swooping down like a thunderbolt" (*sublimis aquila fulguris instar descendens*). The image of the thunderbolt is repeated in the Pilgrim's dream: "mi parea che... terribil come folgor discendesse" (*Purg.* IX.28–29). The second passage is found in *Ep.* VI.iii.12, when Dante warns the most wicked Florentines who have rebelled against Henry that the Emperor will arrive and "terrible in gold, the eagle shall swoop down" (*cum advolaverit aquila in auro terribilis*). Here, two details are given: one is the fact that the eagle is *terribilis*, the other that it is *in auro*, in other words it is the heraldic eagle, symbol of the Empire. Both details are given in Dante's dream: "an eagle poised in the heavens *with wings of gold*" (l. 20), "*terrible* like thunder" (l. 29)".

litical wrongdoing. Philomela's *raptus* does not end on a happy note as does that of Ganymede, because Tereus' actions are not guided by the light of prevenient St. Lucy;[7] his ruling is a false image of righteous political behavior: behind his appearance as an eagle lies the heart of a wolf. The allusion to Ganymede, however, takes us back to the very beginning of the Empire and to Troy, which derived its name from Ganymede's father Tros, and which gave birth to Aeneas.[8] Ganymede's *raptus* thus concludes not only in his being cupbearer of the Gods, but also in the Empire's being the instrument of Divine Will.

There is yet another tale of abduction alluded to in the opening lines of canto 9. While the sorrowful song of the swallow is used as a temporal indicator for the onset of morning in the realm of Purgatory, dawn on earth is described through the reference to Aurora rising from the bed of ancient Tithonus:

> La concubina di Titone antico
> già s'imbiancava al balco d'oriente,
> fuor de le braccia del suo dolce amico (*Purg.* 9.1–3)

Although this mythological allusion had become traditional as a temporal indicator since the Homeric poems and throughout Latin poetry, in this canto the very sensual image of Aurora as her sweet friend's concubine calls to mind the abduction of Tithonus. In a nuanced, indirect way, the myth of Aurora opens a series of different *raptus*,[9] forming what we might call a hierarchical progression leading up to the perfection of Dante's own ascent.

---

[7] Dante learns from Virgil that St. Lucy is responsible for carrying him to the gate of Purgatory proper. As Scott (*Dante's Political Purgatory*, 134–35) rightly notes, "the polysemy of Dante's poem allows to accept the eagle as a symbol both of God's grace and of the Empire." St. Lucy is a symbol of enlightening grace, needed by the empire to reach the goal of temporal happiness on earth for humanity.

[8] http://dante.dartmouth.edu/. Carroll (1904) suggests that "it is the poet's way of connecting his dream with the Empire. Rome was through Aeneas the descendant of Troy.[. . .] The allusion therefore carries us back to the very source of the Empire, from which alone the Eagle deigns to bear up any in its feet."

[9] In tracing the historical semantic development of the Latin *rapere*, Kathryn Gravdal, *Ravishing Maidens: Writing Rape in Medieval French Literature and Law* (Philadelphia: University of Pennsylvania Press, 1991), 4–11, points out the original ambiguousness inherent in the verb, whose more common meanings were to carry off, snatch, rob, and finally to abduct (a virgin). From *rapere* derived the popular **rapire*, which gives the Old French *ravir*. Gravdal notes the shift toward a sexual meaning in the words *rap* (c. 1155) or *rat* (c. 1235), which designate "abduction by violence or by seduction, for the purpose of forced coitus." The word *ravissement*, appearing in the thirteenth century, introduces a new etymological spin, assuming a spiritual or religious sense in the fourteenth century: the action of carrying a soul to heaven. Hence the meaning of a state of emotional exaltation, and through psychological troping the meaning shifted to the sexual trope of rapture. Gravdal underlines how "the shift reveals the assumption that

In order to evaluate how these meaningful connections might have developed and what response Dante might have expected from his audience, we must go back to the original narrations of the myths and to their corresponding medieval allegorizations. In so doing we will attempt to establish what tradition of these myths was available to Dante and his readers in order to understand whether the poet was drawing on a traditional, long-established link between the myths or whether he was inviting the reader to make a connection that would give new meaning to them.

The Rape of Philomela

The most complete ancient version of the myth was supposedly offered by Sophocles in his tragedy *Tereus*.[10] In Latin literature the most detailed account of the story is given by Ovid in the *Metamorphoses* (6.423–672). The metamorphoses

---

whatever is attractive begs to be ravished: carried off, seized or raped. The ideas of a woman's attractiveness and a man's desire to rape are conflated in *ravissant*." In Italian the verb *rapire* keeps the meaning of snatching, seizing, and kidnapping. English *rape*, deriving from Latin *rapere*, corresponds instead to Italian *stupro* (from Latin *stuprum*, 'defilement, dishonor, disgrace').

[10] Sophocles, *Fragments*, ed. and trans. Hugh Lloyd-Jones (Cambridge, MA and London: Harvard University Press, 1996). It was first presented in 415 BC, but unfortunately only a few fragments of it are extant. From them we can gather that Tereus underwent a metamorphosis, becoming a hoopoe, although it is not clear which birds the two sisters became. In fragment 595, Philomela, who managed to reveal her sad destiny to her sister, became a symbol of the regaining of the power to communicate by silenced women: the voice of the shuttle (κερκίδος φωνή). Philomela, in fact, deprived of her tongue by Tereus to prevent her from accusing him, embroiders the savage deed on a robe and has it delivered to Procne. In the *Poetics* (16.6–7) Aristotle mentions the Sophoclean voice of the shuttle as an example of discovery scenes manufactured by the poet and therefore inartistic. This mention attests to the popularity of the tragedy, but fails to show any true appreciation of the brilliant metaphor. Patricia Klindienst, "The Voice of the Shuttle is Ours," *Stanford Literature Review* 1 (1984): 25–53 (also available on-line: http://www.english.ucsb.edu/faculty/ayliu/research/klindienst.html), offers a very interesting analysis of the power of this metaphor from the perspective of feminist poetics, seeing Philomela as "the sign of what threatens the woman's voiced existence in culture." References to the myth of Philomela and especially to the metamorphosis into a nightingale of Procne, the cruel and, at the same time, pitiful mother, who killed her son Itys and then lamented his loss, were common in Greek literature. In *The Suppliant Maidens* Aeschylus refers to the voice of Tereus' wife, although he identifies her with Metis, as the hawk-chased nightingale. Aeschylus, *Supplices*, 58–67: "And if some neighbor here knows bird cries, / Hearing our bitter passion he will think / He hears the hawk-chased, sad bird Metis, / The wife of Tereus, who weeps with passion / Barred from rivers, and the countryside; / Who sang a child's death-dirge, whom she killed, / Perverse her wrath" (*The Complete*

of Tereus and the two sisters into birds are just the *culmen* of a long story that stretches for over 250 verses in the sixth book of the poem. The scene opens with Athens besieged by barbarians, and thus the story begins with an image of violence. Although the violation of the city is prevented by the intervention of Tereus, king of Thrace, the threat of civic "rape" sets the tone for the rest of the story. The overlapping of the political and sexual spheres in the civic realm of the city is evident when Pandion, king of Athens, offers his daughter Procne as a bride to Tereus out of gratitude for his military help, thus exchanging sexual favors for defense in battle. The political power achieved by Tereus through acts of violence in war translates into sexual power over a woman, Procne, who as the king's daughter represents Athens. Although both acts are sanctioned by law and find their own legitimacy in the political definition of war and in the civil institution of marriage, there is an inherent violence to them which will explode and taint the whole story.

Tereus and Procne's wedding is not at all blessed, nor is the birth of their son Itys, although both events are celebrated by the unaware couple and the whole of Thrace. At Procne's request, Tereus goes to fetch Philomela in Athens, and at the sight of the virgin he is immediately overcome by sexual desire. Ovid uses natural similes to describe Tereus' passion in order to show the baseness of his desire. Besides Philomela's beauty, Ovid gives the additional reason for Tereus' ardor that all the Thracians are all too quick at loving. Tereus' individual *libido* is closely tied to the nature of his whole nation, drawing again a parallel between land and woman, both to be conquered with violence in order to satisfy male desire for power. The strategy of seduction follows the unspoken rules of political transactions:[11] the leaders attempt to bribe the opposing leaders before resorting to open war.

Greek Tragedies, ed. David Grene and Richmond Lattimore, 4 vols. [Chicago: University of Chicago Press, 1956]). According to this version of the story Tereus was transformed into a hawk, forever chasing the wife-nightingale who killed his son. The metamorphosis of Tereus into a hoopoe seems to be an innovation introduced by Sophocles (frag. 581). The chorus in the *Rhesus,* attributed to Euripides, also identified the nightingale with the mother who slew her child: [Euripides,] *Rhesus,* 546–550: "I hear. But perched above Simois / the nightingale, / the own-child-slayer in vociferous chant / sings her murderous marriage, sings her song and her sorrow" (*The Complete Greek Tragedies*).

[11] The same overlapping of political and sexual spheres characterizes Jason's seduction and abandonment of Hypsipyle and later of Medea, as presented by Dante in *Inferno* 18.82–99. The poet places the mythical leader of the Argonauts in the first pouch of the eighth circle, also called Malebolge, where ordinary fraud is punished. The seductions of Hypsipyle and Medea had been instrumental to the retrieval of the golden fleece from Colchis, and eventually to Jason's victorious return to his homeland as the king. Medea, just like Procne, takes her revenge on the husband responsible for the family's destruction, by killing his own son.

Finally everything is ready for the departure, and Philomela is carried away on Tereus' painted ship. Although Philomela agreed to go of her own free will, the scene is very much that of an abduction. Tereus, called *barbarus*, emits a warlike cry of victory at the realization of having Philomela at his mercy. He is also described as a *praedator* and *raptor* by means of the simile with the eagle, the bird of Jove, when it brings the hapless prey to his nest. Once reaching the shore, Tereus takes Philomela to a ramshackle hut in the woods and rapes her, but beforehand he describes what is going to happen to her. Nothing can help her, not calling her father or her sister, nor appealing to the great gods. The bestiality of the act, which is underlined by the frequent animal imagery throughout the entire episode, is too much for Philomela to bear, and she loses her senses. Tereus has already been described as an eagle, a bird of prey, and now Philomela is first compared to a frightened lamb attacked by a gray wolf, then to a dove with her own blood all over her feathers.

In the dramatic picture drawn by Ovid, colors acquire metaphorical meaning in depicting Philomela's virginity through the white wool and feathers of the lamb and the dove respectively. Although Philomela is innocent, the mere contact with evil degrades her, even if only temporarily, to animal status. When she recovers, she regains her rationality and the human faculty of speech. She accuses Tereus of breaking every human law, from the respect due to his father-in-law and her virginity to the love for his wife. Nevertheless, she seems more concerned about the rupture of social conventions, considering her sister as Tereus' wife, her father as the ruler, and her virginity as a forbidden land, rather than addressing the violence itself as a rupture of any natural law.[12] Through his wicked deed Tereus, according to Philomela, confused and mixed up everything,[13] making her and him outlaws and "living oxymorons":[14] she is the rival of her own sister Procne, who will be her enemy from now on, and mistress of Tereus, who is now a bigamist.[15]

---

[12] Bömer, *Metamorphosen*, 6–7: 145: "*nefas* als Verstoß gegen die (ungeschriebenen) Gesetze der Familie z.B. auch [. . .] Cic. *Cluent*. 12 *generi sui, contra quam fas erat, amore capta*: Unrechte Liebe zum Schwiegersohn. Verg. Aen. II 585 personate: Helena als *nefas*. [. . .] Hor. carm. III 24, 21 ff. *Dos est magna parentium virtus et metuens alterius viri certo foedere castitas, et peccare nefas*. [. . .] vgl. auch Komm. zu fast. II 140 und met. VIII 86 *praeda nefanda*, von Scyllas Vergehen gegen ihren Vater."

[13] Leonard Barkan, *The Gods Made Flesh: Metamorphosis and the Pursuit of Paganism* (New Haven and London: Yale University Press, 1986), 91, defines Philomela's accusation "a metamorphic assertion," able to spread the contagion of confusion in the metamorphic world. "If things turn into other things, then so do individuals, concepts, rules, emotions."

[14] Barkan, *The Gods Made Flesh*, 61.

[15] Bömer, *Metamorphosen*, 6–7: 148: "Diesen Vorwurf hat bei Ovid sicher nicht nur Tereus verdient; trotzdem ist er singulär."

Again it is clear how Philomela identifies herself within an extremely gender-conditioned social frame rather than being aware of her autonomous self. In appreciating death as a better option than life in her situation, she evidently views her virginity and compliance with the social expectations of her gender as the reason and essence of her life. The rape had the power to make her guilty and to taint her soul, while murder would have left her an innocent ghost.

The first sign of her metamorphosis is her blasphemous doubt about the existence of gods, whom she calls upon—should they really exist and have witnessed the wicked deed—for revenge. Her revenge will consist in telling everybody about the rape. What was before described as *nefandus* (*Met.* 6.540) is now going to be shouted out loud. Philomela is irremediably changed by the rape. Not only her body, but also her soul has been shaken, and she defies the social convention of woman's silence by claiming her right to speak up. Nonetheless, she doesn't regard her voice as a right: rather it is all that is left to her, after losing her *pudor* (*Met.* 6.544–545), which allowed her rightful membership in the human community. It is interesting that she includes, among her goals, the desire to move to pity even the very woods and rocks. The ability to tame wild animals and to move even inanimate objects is always attributed to mythological figures such as Orpheus, who traditionally embodies the archetypal poet. Is she simply referring to her right to vengeance, or is she claiming a voice for traditionally silenced women?[16] There is in any event a clear link between poetry and marginalization in this passage. Poetry is described by Philomela as the last resource to make oneself heard, for anyone who has been cast aside by society, which is thus responsible for assigning blame and therefore shame upon one. Nonetheless, poetry, much like vengeance, can destabilize institutionalized power but does not necessarily result in demarginalization and subsequent reintegration within acceptable social orders.

Tereus is obviously frightened by this threat to his position as a ruler, and rips out Philomela's tongue to prevent her from speaking and to reaffirm his power; the mutilation is in fact followed by several rapes.[17] Despite depriving the woman of her tongue, he doesn't succeed in silencing her. On the contrary, the

---

[16] Ahl, *Metaformations*, 229, links Philomela's choice of weaving her story, in order to be understood by her sister, with the intention to convey "one woman's message to another in woman's language—a language that excludes man." We could see in Philomela's words, before her mutilation, an attempt at creating a woman's public spoken language.

[17] Barkan, *The Gods Made Flesh*, 61, considers Tereus too as a victim of transformation. "Tereus' attempt to 'shut up' Philomela becomes a paradigmatic opposition to the very process of change he has set in motion. The mutilation that he inflicts upon her, the cutting of her tongue, is an attempt to cancel the consequences of his acts."

Elissa Marder, "Disarticulated Voices: Feminism and Philomela," in *Language and Liberation*, ed. Christina Hendricks and Kelly Oliver (New York: State University of New York Press, 1999), 149–72, defines the cutting off of the tongue as an act of "raping

mutilation contributes to marginalize her even further and therefore to enhance her will to communicate.[18] The tapestry on which Philomela weaves her gruesome fate becomes the living metaphor for her voice. Any effort to suppress the voice of poetry results in empowering its message.[19]

The discovery of Tereus' wicked deed leaves Procne literally speechless.[20] Unlike Philomela, who is able to understand and analyze the confusion of reality and hold Tereus responsible for that degeneration, Procne is assailed by such confusion: *fas* and *nefas* (*Met.* 6.585) cross each other in her mind. She has already rejected words for action. Wrath overcomes her just as passion overcame Tereus; reason abandons her, and she is ready for a crime neither more nor less cruel than Tereus' rape of Philomela: the murder of her own son Itys, whose flesh is later served to his father Tereus in a banquet.[21] Although not promoting the infanticide, Philomela plays an active role in the crime both physically, by hurling Itys' severed bloody head at his grieving father, and emotionally, by rejoicing in the deed. Nonetheless, she regrets the loss of her tongue which would have allowed her to express her feelings more properly. Surely she doesn't regret her crime, but

---

speech" which occurs after the act of speaking rape. In between these two acts comes the sexual rape.

Lynn Enterline, *The Rhetoric of the Body from Ovid to Shakespeare* (Cambridge: Cambridge University Press, 2000), 3–4, analyzes how "Ovid uses stories of bodily violation to dramatize language's vicissitudes. [. . .] Violated bodies also provide Ovid with the occasion to reflect on the power and limitations of language as such." Enterline thus interprets Tereus' mutilation of Philomela as a literalization of his unspeakable act, giving her a speechless mouth.

[18] According to Amy Richlin, "Reading Ovid's Rapes," in *Pornography and Representation in Greece and Rome*, ed. eadem (New York and Oxford: Oxford University Press, 1992), 158–79, here 162–65, the cutting out of the tongue turns Philomela from the object of violence into the perpetrator. Richlin seems to identify the transformative point in the mutilation rather than in the rape. The tongue murmuring on the dark earth, compared to a snake, offers a new view of Philomela as a snake rather than a lamb or a dove. Not only is Philomela changing but also the text is apparently shifting its sympathies.

[19] Enterline, *Rhetoric of the Body*, 4: " 'Great pain' begets in her the very 'talent' to which Ovid elsewhere often lays claim as a poet. [. . .] The work that Philomela produces, moreover, amplifies the problems raised by her 'moving' tongue: her tapestry takes up where her tongue left off, telling us that in this story, presumed distinctions between language and action, the speakable and the unspeakable, aesthetics and violence verge on collapse."

[20] Ahl, *Metaformations*, 229, stresses the difference between Philomela's forced silence and Procne's "beastlike silence leading to an act of more than beastlike vengeance."

[21] Ahl, *Metaformations*, 127, notes a wordplay in the verses describing Tereus' passion for Philomela (6.480–481): "omnia pro stimulis faCIBUSque CIBOque furoris / accipit." The more or less hidden reference to food would anticipate the cannibalism resulting from Procne's revenge.

Ovid is here clearly comparing the revenge to be achieved with words, which Philomela had wished for initially, and the revenge staged by Procne, which Philomela abetted. She now wishes for her power to speak, not realizing that she had it despite the loss of her tongue: in fact, she had found her voice in the art of weaving. She lost it, though, when she succumbed to wrath.

The metamorphosis into birds is the result of the confusion of social and human law and marks Philomela's, as well as Procne's and Tereus', exile from human life and society.[22] Philomela's metamorphosis bears the mark of a double destiny. Her transformation into a bird signifies her estrangement from human society which she achieved as an accomplice in her nephew's murder, while as the victim of a bird of prey she enjoys an intermediate position which does not completely cut her off from human relations, but definitely degrades her to a lower status characterized by the lack of communication with human beings, other than through sounds of grief. She manages to escape on wings, fleeing Tereus' sword, but her metamorphosis provides only temporary salvation from murder, and involves the punishment of being forever chased by the hoopoe's warlike beak and forever remembering her sad past. She is trapped in mourning for eternity.[23]

In the short version of the myth given by *Vatican Mythographer*[24] *I*, Philomela (4) uses her own blood to describe her rape and mutilation on a tapestry for her sister, a gruesome detail which further enhances the tragedy of the girl's destiny. Moreover, there is no mention of Philomela's participation in the infanticide; Procne is the only one responsible for killing and serving the son to the father Tereus. Philomela is thus freed from every charge. Nevertheless, she is still changed into a bird, *luscinia*, the nightingale.

---

[22] Barkan, *The Gods Made Flesh*, 58–59: "It is not the hero's or heroine's change of physical shape (that will come too, but it is later and less important) but rather the discovery that what seemed like such rigid categories of family and society can dissolve, just as physical categories dissolve in metamorphosis. [. . .] From that point it is a short step to literal metamorphosis, a condition that merely serves as the final punctuation mark for a narrative experience whose crucial metamorphosis has amounted to the dissolution of assumptions we live by."

[23] Barkan, *The Gods Made Flesh*, 66: "[Metamorphosis] proves that the moral freak is a physical freak, for a human being who has become a bird is still a figure outside all clear categories. Yet at the same time it is a kind of triumph. [. . .] The mutilated Philomela sings. [. . .] While metamorphosis typifies the crime and reflects the terrible extremes to which the victim is driven, it also provides an escape from entrapment into a higher condition where the blurred categories are no longer meaningful."

[24] *Mythographi Vaticani I et II*, ed. Peter Kulcsár, CCSL 91C (Turnhout: Brepols, 1987); trans. Ronald E. Pepin, *The Vatican Mythographers* (New York: Fordham University Press, 2008).

Tereus rex Thracum fuit. Qui quum Pandionis, Athenarum regis, filiam, Procne nomine, duxisset uxorem, et per aliquantum tempus ab ea rogaretur, sibi Philomelam sororem videndam accerseret, profectus Athenas, dum adduxit puellam, eam vitiavit in itinere, et ei linguam, ne facinus indicaret, abscidit. Illa tamen querelam, in veste suo cruore descriptam, misit sorori. Qua cognita, Procne Ityn filium interemit et patri epulandum apposuit. Postea omnes in aves mutati sunt; Tereus in upupam, Itys in phasianum, Procne in hirundinem, Philomela in lusciniam.

Tereus was king of the Thracians. He married Procne, the daughter of Pandion, king of Athens. After a short time she asked him to fetch Philomela, her sister, for a visit. He proceeded to Athens, and while he was bringing the girl back, he violated her on the way and cut out her tongue so that she would not tell of his wicked deed. Yet the girl sent the true story to her sister depicted in her own blood on a tapestry. When this accusation became clear, Procne killed her son, Itys, and set him before his father to be eaten. Afterward, all were changed into birds: Tereus into a hoopoe, Itys into a pheasant, Procne into a swallow, Philomela into a nightingale.

Arnulf d'Orléans[25] (VI, 18) underlines the historicity of the myth, except for the metamorphosis itself which is strictly allegorical. The interpretation applies in fact just to the transformation: both birds have red marks on their breasts as a sign of the ancient crime, though it is not clear whether the crime is the infanticide or the wounds received from Tereus chasing them with his sword. Furthermore, according to Arnulf's commentary, Procne turned into the swallow as she still lives in the city where she used to be the queen, and Philomela is turned into the bird bearing her name, namely *philomela*, the nightingale which lives in the woods. Neither a commentary nor a summary is given for the events preceding the metamorphoses:

Quod de Tereo et Progne et Philomena dicitur totum est historicum. De mutatione vero allegoricum. Tereo eas sequente quia cito aufugerunt in aves mutate dicte sunt, sed in philomenam et in hirundinem pocius quam in alias quia ille aves pectora habent rubore notata quod est signum cedis antique. Que clausa fuerat in silvis ideo in philomenam, quia avis illa pocius in silvas habitat quam hirundo. Progne in hirundinem que domos habitat et urbes sicut solebat dum regina erat. Thereus quia velociter eas sequebatur, fingitur in avem esse mutatus sed in hupupam pocius quam in aliam quia avis illa videtur irata sicut Thereus dum sorores insequeretur.

The entire story of Tereus, Procne, and Philomela is historical. The metamorphosis is however an allegory. Procne and Philomela are said to have

---

[25] Fausto Ghisalberti, "Arnolfo d'Orléans: Un cultore di Ovidio nel secolo XII," *Memorie del Reale Istituto Lombardo di Scienze e Lettere* 24 (1932): 157–234.

been transformed into birds, because they quickly escaped when Tereus was chasing them, but they turned into a nightingale and a swallow rather than other birds, because the breasts of those birds are marked with redness, which is a sign of the old bloodshed. The woman who had been confined in the woods turned then into a nightingale, because that bird, rather than the swallow, lives in the woods. Procne turned into a swallow, which lives in the houses and in the city, as she used to do when she was the queen. As Tereus was quickly following them, he is supposed to have turned into a bird, but into a hoopoe rather than any other bird, because that bird seems angry as Tereus was when he was chasing the two sisters.

John of Garland's *Integumenta* [26] (VI, 289–292) devotes just two couplets to the myth of Philomela, without shedding much light on the actual plot of the story, but stressing its historical truth and interpreting the metamorphosis with a parallel between love and birds, both of whom seek wilderness:

> Historiam tangit describens Terea de quo
> Musa sophocleo carmine grande canit.
> Commentatur aves doctrina poetica quippe
> Devia poscit avis, devia poscit amor.

> He mentions the story describing Tereus, about whom the Muse sings in an important tragedy by Sophocles. The poetic discipline treats them as birds since both birds and love seek wilderness.

The last line identifying lovers as birds in their desire for wilderness underscores either a sinful connotation of love, if we are to understand wilderness as opposed to civilization, or more probably a romantic vision of love which raises the lovers above the crowd, though it doesn't really apply to Tereus' lust for Philomela.

Giovanni del Virgilio[27] (VI, 32) focuses on the metamorphoses of all the characters, included Itys, into birds. Following the tradition of the *Vatican Mythographers* and Arnulf d'Orléans, he reports Procne as the swallow which bears red stains of blood from the infanticide on her breast and Philomena as the nightingale which forever laments her lost virginity. Even in Giovanni del Virgilio's version Philomela is not responsible for the killing of her nephew: instead, she is depicted as the only real victim:

> Trigesima secunda est de Tereo, Progne, Philomena et Ythi mutatis in aves. Nam Ovidius describit hanc hystoriam, que vera tamen, modo poetico i. ficticio. Posset tamen ad mores aptari. Unde per hoc quod Prognes conversa

---

[26] John of Garland, *Integumenta Ovidii*, ed. Fausto Ghisalberti (Messina and Milan: Principato, 1933).

[27] Fausto Ghisalberti, "Giovanni del Virgilio espositore delle *Metamorfosi*," *Giornale dantesco* 34 (1933): 3–110.

fuit in avem et Philomena etiam intellige velocitatem quam habuerunt in fugiendo a manibus Terei. Sed in speciali Progne conversa dicitur in yrundinem propter duo quia sicut yrundo habet rubicundum pectus ad modum sanguinis, ita Prognes rubuit cede filii sui, et sicut yrundo manet in tectis ita Prognes etiam in civitate mansit. Sed quia Philomena fugit extra civitatem in nemora et quia non habebat linguam ideo conversa in Philomenam avem, que non habet linguam et nemora tantum inhabitat, et quia toto tempore conquesta fuit de virginitate amissa. Sed Thereus quia fetidissimum peccatum commisit ideo dicitur conversus in upupam cristatam et stercoribus manentem quia ille cum esset rex et coronam gereret, sicut upupa, incestuosa libidine usus est violata uxoris sorore. Unde metrice d.e.:

Naso per historiam incestum condemnat amorem
    Et notat obscenus quam male finit amor.
Pectore rubra trucem matrem designat hirundo
    Ampla velut quondam nunc quoque tecta colens.
Et veterem renovat cantu Phylomena querelam
    Quodque latens coluit pergemit illa nemus.
Tereus incesto turpi fit spurca volucris
    Upupa, quod signat crista tyrannis erat.

The thirty-second metamorphosis is about Tereus, Procne, Philomela, and Itys turned into birds. For Ovid describes this story, that is in fact true, in a poetical style, that is fictitious. Yet it can be adapted to morals. Therefore consider Procne and Philomela's speed in fleeing from Tereus' hands as the reason why they were transformed into birds. In particular Procne is said to have turned into a swallow for two reasons, namely because just as the swallow's breast is red as blood, so did Procne turn red with the murder of her son, and as the swallow stays in the housetops, so did Procne remain in the city too. But since Philomela escaped out of the city into the woods and had no tongue, she was transformed for these reasons into a nightingale, which does not have a tongue and lives only in the woods, and also because she complained all the time about her lost virginity. Tereus, on the other hand, who committed the most fetid sin, was transformed for this reason into a crested hoopoe living in dung, because when he was a king and wore the crown, just like the hoopoe, he consumed his incestuous passion, violating his wife's sister.

With the story Ovid condemns incestuous love and shows how badly obscene love ends. The red-breasted swallow indicates the savage mother who inhabits powerful houses now just like before. Philomela reaffirms the old grievance with her song and, because she lived in hiding in the woods, now she fills the woods with her sighs. Because of the indecent incest, Tereus becomes a dirty bird, the hoopoe, its crest representing the king.

Although Procne's cruelty in murdering her son is evident, Tereus' sin is more heavily stressed. His actions are guided, or rather misguided, by incestuous love. The moral comment focuses on incest as the cause of the tragedy that led to the metamorphoses. This prominence of the notion of incest (mentioned in the first and the last hexameters) not only shows a deep moral concern about this specific sexual behavior,[28] but also contributes to the further victimization and marginalization of Philomela. Besides losing her virginity through violence, she becomes unwillingly involved in a crime against God and society.

The analysis of the versions of the Philomela myth offered by different medieval authors shows the consolidated tradition of Philomela as the nightingale and seems to indicate a shift of focus from the series of tragic events leading up to the metamorphoses, to the metamorphoses themselves, which in Ovid were just the *culmen* of the story. This abridgement of the narration entails a weakening, if not a complete loss, of the psychological analysis offered by Ovid. Consequently, characters are reduced to one clear function in the myth, serving the purpose of the moral interpretation. Philomela has clearly become the victim, the prototype of the virgin raped, who laments the violence she suffered.

Almost all medieval commentaries on the *Comedy* follow this tradition of Procne as the swallow and Philomela as the nightingale. Almost all of them (Lombardus, 1322; Lana, 1324–1328; Pietro di Dante, 1340–1341; Cassinese, 1350–1375) also hold Procne as the one solely responsible for the infanticide, while L'Ottimo (1333) and Benvenuto (1380), who seem to follow Ovid's original version more closely, report Philomela's involvement in the murder of Itys. Nonetheless, L'Ottimo interprets the red marks on Philomela/the nightingale's breast as the sign of her lost virginity, thus carrying no memory of the murder. Lombardus' interpretation (1322) is the most interesting, although it shows a confused knowledge of the myth. It is the only one to consider the swallow as the raped sister, who is never given a name in the narration. Lombardus also

---

[28] Although according to classical Roman law the union of second grade collateral in-laws (such was the relation between Tereus and Philomela) wasn't considered incest, imperial Roman law prohibited such unions as incestuous. Apostolic councils in the fourth century sanctioned harsh punishments for people guilty of incest. The Council of Elvira in the fourth century proclaimed that a man marrying his wife's sister could not take Communion, along with the new wife, for five years. The Council of Neocaesarea excommunicated a woman who married two brothers in succession. The Trullan Council in 692 invalidated incestuous marriages and excommunicated those who contracted them. The Council of Worms in 888 prohibited incestuous marriages. The Fourth Lateran Council in 1215 removed the prohibition for third and second grade in-laws (see Giuseppe Sirna, "Incesto," in *Enciclopedia Cattolica*, 12 vols. [Florence: L'Impronta, 1951], 6: 1759). Thus, according to this latest council, the union of Tereus and Philomela would not be considered incestuous. In any event incest was definitely an important religious issue in the Middle Ages, and ascribing this sin to Tereus, although not accurately from a technical point of view, would enhance the blasphemy of his action.

transforms Itys into a girl and adds the shocking detail of the raped sister's pregnancy, but it is not clear whether it is the result of the rape:

> In parte ista dicit autor, quod Ovidius ponit quod Philomena fuit uxor Terei regis Tracie et filia Pandionis regis Athenarum: occisit Ictu[m] filiam suam, et partem fecit coqui et dedit in cibum Tereo patri puelle et marito suo. Et dum discumberet Tereus et peteret ab uxore sua perveniente, quid esset de filia, respondit ei uxor: tu comedisti partem, et partem accipe. Et capud puelle proiecit per faciem mariti discumbentis. Et hoc dicitur fecisse pre nimio dolore et furore, eo quod dictus eius maritus violaverat pregnam sororem dicte Filomene, et deinde asciderat linguam eius, ne scelus hoc propalare posset; quod notum fuit Philomene ex contentu literarum in quodam opere facto per dictam pregnam, hoc scelus continente. Et ob hoc mutata fuit ipsa pregna in rondinella; et ideo dicit in testu:
>
> Fosse a memoria de' suo' primi guai, (15)
>
> idest primum recordatur sui pristini doloris, et hoc circa mane. Et dicta Philomena mutata fuit in philomenam avem.

> In this section the poet says that Ovid states that Philomena was the wife of Tereus, king of Thrace, and the daughter of Pandion, king of Athens: she killed her daughter Ictus, had part of her cooked and gave it to the father of the girl and her husband to eat. When Tereus was going to bed and asked his wife, who was arriving, where her daughter was, his wife answered him: you ate part of her, now take the rest. And she threw the girl's head in the face of her husband who was lying in bed. She is said to have done it because of excessive pain and anger, since her husband had raped the pregnant sister of the said Filomena, and then he had cut off her tongue, lest she could reveal the crime; Philomena learned about it from the content of an inscription in some composition made by the pregnant sister, which contained the crime. For this reason the pregnant sister was transformed into a swallow; and therefore it reads in the text:
>
> Fosse a memoria de' suo' primi guai, (15)
>
> that is, she recalls the beginning of her previous sorrow, and this happens around early in the morning. The said Philomena was transformed into a nightingale.

While according to most medieval commentaries Dante would refer to Procne when mentioning the sad song of the swallow, Lombardus seems to be the only one to think that Dante is referring to the raped sister as the swallow who laments her previous sorrows. Since Lombardus' poor knowledge of the mythological tradition concerning the two unlucky sisters is evident, we may argue that his reconstruction of the story is based only partially on the sources available at the time, and instead greatly influenced by his perception of Dante's employment of the myth in the context of the *Comedy*. Although Lombardus cannot name the raped sister turned into the swallow, what is important is that she is an innocent victim, finally able to reveal the crime which stained her for eternity.

The Abduction of Ganymede

According to the oldest literary versions of the story,[29] the Trojan prince Ganymede, being the most handsome among mortals, was taken to heaven by Zeus and made the cupbearer of the gods. The details of the abduction become clear only in the later versions by Apollodorus (*Bibliotheca* 3.12.2), where the eagle is mentioned for the first time, and in the *Aeneid* (5.252–255), where Ganymede is snatched while hunting on Mt. Ida by the eagle of Jove. In Ovid's *Metamorphoses* it is Jove himself, disguised as an eagle, who carries away the young boy. The Ovidian version alludes to the definite erotic undertone of the myth.[30] In fact, Orpheus, who tells this story among others, prefaces his song with an invocation to the Muse that she may begin from Jove and announces one of the themes: boys loved by the gods. The first episode is appropriately devoted to the abduction of Ganymede, a boy loved by Jove himself. The theme of metamorphosis is already introduced by Jove's passion for Ganymede: love is described as the ultimate desire not only to be with the loved one, but rather to be the loved one. Jove compensates his frustrated urge for this impossible metamorphosis (into the object of his passion) with one of his usual transformations into an animal, but the most noble of animals, the eagle. The erotic relationship between Jove and Ganymede is further underscored by Juno's anger at her husband's betrayal. Moreover, in Ovid's version, Ganymede is not generally the cupbearer of all the gods, but rather Jove's personal attendant, to whom he serves the nectar of his sexual favors.

---

[29] *Iliad* 20.232 ff., Pindar, *Olympian* I.44, 10.105. For a more detailed discussion of the myth's tradition, see W. H. Roscher, *Ausführliche Lexicon der griechischen und römischen Mythologie*, 6 vols. (Leipzig: Teubner, 1902–1909), 1: 4595–4603. See Harvey Alan Shapiro, "Eros in Love: Pederasty and Pornography in Greece," in *Pornography and Representation in Greece and Rome,* ed. Richlin, 53–72, for the erotic evolution of the myth in classical Greece.

[30] A sexual connotation is first to be found in Ibycus, frag. 289 (*Greek Lyric*, ed. and trans. David A. Campbell, 5 vols. [Cambridge, MA: Harvard University Press; London: Heinemann, 1982–1993], 3: 259). According to the scholiast on Apollonius of Rhodes, Ibycus' song to Gorgias contained an account of the rape of Ganymede and also included how Eos carried off Tithonus.

Bernard Sergent interprets mythological homosexuality as the literary expression of rites of initiation.[31] These rites were institutional in early Indo-European societies and marked the passage from boyhood to adulthood with ceremonies and trials of various sorts. Just as in rites of initiation, in the mythological episodes of homosexuality the loved one achieves a promotion of his status through service to the lover: in the case of love between mortals, the change of status results in entrance to adult society; in the case of love by a god, the initiated boy leaves the society of mortals and gains access to heaven. The lover is always the master, the educator, and the loved one is the student, the apprentice. Through the sexual relationship the student learns what he needs to raise his status, and this increase in knowledge is represented by a gift: Ganymede's gift is the cup symbolic of his service to his master.

Ganymede's destiny makes him different from and superior to any other man loved by a god. He's one of the few loved by Jove and the only one to enjoy his company forever, being by his side in heaven. While there are stories about Jove's love for Priam and Euphorion, they are not as popular as that of Ganymede, and the gifts they received did not include their elevation from the earth.

Vatican Mythographers I, 181, *II*, 226, and *III*, 15 recount the myth of Ganymede's ascent to heaven as cupbearer for Jupiter and offer an original reason for his abduction:

> Juppiter ne infamiam virentis, id est masculini, concubitus subiret, versus in aquilam ex Ida monte Ganymedem rapuit, et fecit eum pincernam in caelo. (I.181)

> So that Jupiter might not subject himself to the disgrace of sexual union with a youth, that is, a male, he changed into an eagle. He snatched Ganymede from Mount Ida and made him the cup-bearer in heaven.

> Ganymedes, Troili regis Trojanorum et Callirrhoae filius, propter corporis pulchritudinem, ne infamiam connubii masculini subiret, dum in Ida silva venaretur, ab aquila in caelum raptus, est constitutus pincerna deorum, remota Hebe, Junonis filia. (II.226)

> Ganymede was the son of Troilus, king of the Trojans, and Callirrhoe. So that he might not suffer the shame of male intercourse because of the beauty of his body, an eagle snatched him up to the sky while he was hunting in the forest on Mount Ida. He was made cupbearer to the gods after Hebe, Juno's daughter, was removed [from that office].

---

[31] Bernard Sergent, *L'homosexualité dans la mythologie grecque* (Paris: Payot, 1984), 11–14.

Apparently Jupiter lifts him to the sky in order to save him from the corruption of a homosexual rape. There is a clear intent on the part of the mythographers to desexualize the myth: the overwhelming concern with the danger of a sexual intercourse 'against nature' serves the purpose of freeing Jupiter from any possible sexual charge, which was latent in Ovid even though not spelled out. The attempt to set the myth in a mystical light is attested by the *Vatican Mythographer III*, 15.1, where Ganymede is called "dilectus a Jove,"[32] which recalls God's words referring to Jesus,[33] especially to a Christian reader accustomed to find correspondences with the Holy Scriptures (e.g. Song of Songs 2:10, "En dilectus meus loquitur mihi"), although the same adjective, "dilectus," is also used by Ovid in a sexual context.

Arnulf (VI, 7) does not give any reason for Ganymede's rape, but instead focuses on Jove's metamorphosis. Following Fulgentius' interpretation,[34] Arnulf explains how the eagle was the symbol chosen by Jove as a standard in battle. Inserting the episode into a war context and shifting the focus from the rape to the eagle imagery are other ways of depriving the myth of its sexual connotations:

> Idem Iupiter Asteriem in specie aquile rapuit i. bellando aquilis preeuntibus sicut Ganymedem. Nam ut Anacreon refert, dum Iupiter adversus Titanas, Titani filios, qui frater Saturni fuerat, bellum assumeret et sacrificium in caelo fecisset, in victorie auspicium aquile prosperum sibi vidit adesse volatum. Pro quo tam felici omine, et quia victoria consecuta est, in signis bellicis sibi auream fecit aquilam tuteleque sue virtuti deputavit. Unde et apud romanos huiuscemodi signa tractata sunt.

> Jupiter, in the guise of an eagle, seized Ganymede, that is just like when eagles lead the way in battle. In fact as Anacreon reports, while Jupiter was fighting against the Titans, sons of Titan, who was brother of Saturn, and had offered a sacrifice in the sky, he saw an eagle flying close to him as a lucky sign of victory. For such a fortunate omen, and because victory was obtained, he chose a golden eagle for his standards and considered it protection for his virtue. Therefore also among the Romans these kind of standards have been carried.

The myth of Ganymede is not even mentioned by John of Garland in his *Integumenta*, while Giovanni del Virgilio follows Arnulf's version, and ultimately

---

[32] *Scriptores rerum mythicarum Latini tres Romae nuper reperti*, ed. Georg Heinrich Bode, 2 vols. (Cellis: Schulze, 1834; repr. Hildesheim: Olms, 1968), III.11.28.

[33] Matthew 3:17 from the Vulgate: "et ecce vox de caelis dicens hic est Filius meus dilectus in quo mihi conplacui": "And lo a voice from heaven, saying, This is my beloved Son, in whom I am well pleased."

[34] Leslie George Whitbread, *Fulgentius the Mythographer* (Columbus: Ohio State University Press, 1971), 1.20. The same interpretation is to be found in the *Vatican Mythographers*.

Fulgentius and the *Vatican Mythographers*, in associating the eagle with the military standards. With regard to the rape, while tending to agree with his sources on their interpretation *in bono* of the myth, he sticks to Augustine's version (*De civitate Dei* VII.26), apparently out of respect for the great author. Augustine accuses Jove of being a pedophile, calling him *stuprator puerorum*. As Giovanni del Virgilio points out, though, Augustine considers the myth literally and thus gives no interpretation:

> Sexta mutatio est de Ganimede converso in Aquarium signum. Ista transmutatio possumus ad bonum reduci. Sed quia Augustinus dicit ad litteram de hoc in libro de Civitate Dei, ideo ne videar dicere contra eum, dico sicut ipse. Dicit enim quod Jupiter fuit rex cretensis, qui captus erat amore Ganimedis filii Trois. Ivit ergo circa civitatem in qua erat cum exercitu et cum aquilis depictis, ideo dicitur conversus in aquilam. Et rapuit eum vi, et convertit eum ad malos usus. Unde Augustinus appellat eum stupratorem puerorum ut increpet adorantes tales deos et fecit eum servitorem sciphi ut delectaretur eo. U.:

> Iupiter in bellis aquilarum signa ferendo
>   Arripuit puerum cuius amator erat.

> The sixth metamorphosis concerns Ganymede transformed into the zodiacal sign of Aquarius. We can interpret this metamorphosis *in bono*. On the other hand, as Augustine interprets it literally in *De Civitate Dei*, I do the same, lest I appear to speak against him. He says, in fact, that Jupiter was king of Crete and he was in love with Ganymede son of Tros. Therefore he surrounded the city where Ganymede was, with the army and with eagles on the standards; for this reason they say he turned into an eagle. He seized him by force and put him to bad uses. Therefore Augustine calls him a pedophile, as he rebukes those who worship such gods, who made him the cupbearer in order to take pleasure in him.

> Jupiter snatched the boy whom he was in love with, while carrying standards with eagles in battle.

Giovanni del Virgilio's presentation of the episode as the metamorphosis of Ganymede into the zodiacal sign of Aquarius also attests the intention of elevating the myth and interpreting it *in bono*.

The Abduction of Tithonus

Tithonus was famous for his beauty, and Eos/Aurora, the goddess of the dawn, abducted him and made him her husband. The Homeric *Hymn to Aphrodite* gives us a detailed account of Tithonus' sad fate. After the rape, Aurora went to Zeus and asked for immortality for her husband, but forgot to add eternal youth. Thus Tithonus grew older and older until he could no longer move. Eventually Aurora turned him into a cicada so that she might enjoy his voice forever, since his voice was all that was left of him.[35] The motif of Aurora rising from the bed of ancient Tithonus became traditional as a temporal metaphor for the dawn.[36]

Tithonus wasn't the only man loved by Aurora; indeed, he was also not the only one whom she abducted. Having fallen in love with Cephalus, a grandson of Aeolus and recently married to Procris, Aurora carried him away while he was hunting on Mt. Hymettus.[37] The abduction was not successful, though, since Cephalus wanted to go back to his wife (*Met.* 7.702–714). Another hunter was the victim of Aurora's love: Orion, who was killed by Artemis who was jealous of his relationship with the goddess.[38] It seems that Aurora's passions and consequent abductions are likely to result in failure for her, as she becomes a victim of her own desires.

The myth of Tithonus' abduction, absent from Ovid's *Metamorphoses*, appears only in *Vatican Mythographers I*, 136 and *II*, 221. The version in book I is slightly different from the other. In book I it is Tithonus who begs his lover Aurora for immortality ("Qui quum adamatus fuisset ab Aurora, petiit ab ea longitudinem vitae"), while in book II Aurora lifts him to the sky ("Hunc Aurora amatum in caelum levavit"). In both versions, though, Tithonus is not granted eternal youth and eventually turns into a cicada, thus degraded to the lower animal state as an indirect result of his love affair with Aurora. Although not associated with Tithonus, Aurora is mentioned in connection with other myths by the *Vatican Mythographers*. In book I, 44 Aurora has an illicit love affair with the married Cephalus and in II, 65 Aurora appears again as the lover of one of the Giants, Astraeus. In this last episode the verb "concubuit" contributes to conveying the idea of an illicit love, outside the bond of marriage. Aurora definitely appears to be promiscuous, her sexual behavior not conforming to acceptable social and moral standards.

---

[35] McKeown, *Ovid: Amores*, 2: 356, comments on *Amores* 1.13 that "in saying that Tithonus has no opportunity to tell tales about Aurora, Ovid recalls that detail of the legend, with the cynical implication that Tithonus is a prisoner and that his endless chatter consists of impotent complaints against Aurora's infidelities. Contrast Prop. 2.18 A.7 ff. where with a sentimental interpretation of that same passage in the Homeric hymn, Aurora's tender care for her husband is presented as a model of conjugal devotion."

[36] Virgil, *Aeneid* 4.585.

[37] Hesiod, *Theogonia* 986 ff.

[38] *Odyssey* 5.121 ff.; Apollodorus, *Bibliotheca* 1.4.4, according to which version Venus made Aurora fall in love with Orion because she was her rival for Mars' love. Also see Roscher, *Ausführliche Lexicon der griechischen und römischen Mythologie*, 1: 1267–68 and 3: 1020–28.

Dante, *Purgatory* 9

The series of different *raptus* which opens canto 9 of Dante's *Purgatory* is structured according to a hierarchical progression leading up to the perfection of Dante's own ascent. The first image of Aurora rising from the bed of ancient Tithonus represents the first and basest example of abduction, structured as the exact opposite of Ganymede's.[39] Whereas Ganymede's abduction is here free of any sexual allusion,[40] the relation between Aurora and Tithonus is very highly sexually charged. The medieval mythographic tradition contributed to this understanding of the two myths. Aurora's behavior doesn't conform to acceptable moral standards not only because of her promiscuity, but also for her sexual initiative. The myth of Tithonus and Aurora is alluded to in canto 9 of *Purgatory*, where dawn in the inhabited world (the northern hemisphere) corresponds to sunset in Purgatory, the two land masses being at the antipodes.[41] The geographical/astronomical detail adds a further element of inversion to the perception of the myth.

The allusion to Philomela stands between those to Tithonus and to Ganymede. Dante seems to follow the contemporary mythographic tradition in the victimization of Philomela, freed from the charge of murder. Nevertheless, he

---

[39] Robert Hollander, *Allegory in Dante's "Commedia"* (Princeton: Princeton University Press, 1969), 145–49, focuses on the myths of Philomela, Ganymede, and Achilles (which follows right after) but views the three narrations as examples of "destructive rapes, which turn out to be negative versions of the actual and positive event," the positive event being Dante's ascent to the gate of Purgatory. He sees Ganymede's abduction as very fitting for the first terrace Dante will visit after entering Purgatory, where the sin of pride is purged, since Ganymede is "a mortal who is singled out from his fellows and carried up to heaven to be among the immortals." According to Hollander, the three classical allusions would apply to "to the uneasy internal state of the Pilgrim," of which he gives a figural interpretation: "as Philomela was raped by the husband of Procne; as Ganymede was raped by Zeus; and as Achilles was carried off by his mother, apparently to safety but actually to his death; so Dante was *not* to be raped, but borne safely by Lucia towards his vision of God."

[40] According to Rachel Jacoff and Jeffrey T. Schnapp (Introduction, *The Poetry of Allusion: Virgil and Ovid in Dante's "Commedia"*, ed. eidem [Stanford: Stanford University Press, 1991], 1–15), the treatment of Ganymede's myth is an exception to Dante's practice of "allusive neutrality" in Purgatory, with regard to Ovidian myths. "Dante revises the equation of eros and death by superimposing a Christian narrative of sublime and sublimated love that underscores the distance between the Ovidian original and its Dantesque reworking."

[41] On the dispute caused by these opening lines (whether the reference is to sunrise in Italy or moonrise in Purgatory) see Robert Hollander, " 'La concubina di Titone antico': *Purgatorio* IX, 1," in Electronic Bulletin of the Dante Society of America: http://www.princeton.edu/~dante/ebdsa/index.html. July 2001.

distances himself from that tradition in the interpretation of the metamorphosis.[42] Dante recuperates the *littera* of the metamorphosis, whereas medieval moralizations and allegorizations would undermine the credibility of the literal sense stressing the hidden meaning behind it, and turns it into a symbolic reality of the spiritual transformation, thus creating a new figure.[43] Furthermore, he refers to Philomela as the swallow, going against the established tradition of her metamorphosis into the nightingale. As Wendy Pfeffer notes, the Romance languages coined a masculine noun, *usignolo* in Italian, for the Latin *luscinia*, the nightingale,[44] whereas the Latin *hirundo*, the swallow, maintained the feminine gender, *rondine* in Italian. By identifying Philomela with the swallow, Dante can call her *rondinella* and preserve, along with the grammatical gender of the noun, the feminine focus of the original myth. Distancing his Philomela from the traditional one also involves metapoetical issues.

The bird imagery is a very fertile metaphor for the soul and its ability to fly either downwards or upwards.[45] Philomela, forced to earth by Tereus' rape, manages to find temporary salvation. Her wings are symbolic of her sorrowful songs, "lai" (which is also the anagram of the word "ali"). Philomela becomes a symbol

---

[42] For the different interpretations of the Ovidian metamorphosis by medieval commentators and by Dante, see Michelangelo Picone, "L'Ovidio di Dante," in *Dante e la "bella scola" della poesia: Autorità e sfida poetica*, ed. Amilcare Iannucci (Ravenna: Longo, 1993), 107–44.

[43] Christopher Kleinhenz, "Notes on Dante's use of Classical Myths and the Mythographical Tradition," *Romance Quarterly* 33 (1986): 477–84, points out that "virtually all of the mythological figures present in the *Comedy* are different from their classical prototypes. [. . .] Dante mythographer and Dante poet merge in the figure of Dante mythmaker."

Madison U. Sowell, "Dante and Ovid," in *Dante and Ovid: Essays in Intertextuality*, ed. idem, MRTS 82 (Binghamton, NY: Medieval and Renaissance Texts and Studies, 1991), 9–14, views Dante's ability to recontextualize, represent, and metamorphose into something else any image he may seize, as Dante's assimilation of Ovid's art: "Ovid's appeal to Dante is also one of style, not simply one of subject."

[44] Wendy Pfeffer, *The Change of Philomel: The Nightingale in Medieval Literature* (New York: Lang, 1985), 158.

[45] Barkan, *The Gods Made Flesh*, 141: "In the various medieval responses to classical mythology we observed a process of translation, from the concrete details of the Ovidian stories to a whole range of moral abstractions. That persistent hermeneutic impulse produced a system of metaphor by which physical conditions were yoked to spiritual meaning. Dante is the first to cross the bridge in the other direction: that is, to begin with the moral condition of man, degraded from *imago dei*, and to translate that abstraction back into a myth of metamorphosis, at once Ovidian and yet indubitably Christian."

According to Lavinia Lorch and Maristella Lorch, "Metaphor and Metamorphosis: *Purgatorio* 27 and *Metamorphoses* 4," in *Dante and Ovid*, ed. Sowell, 99–121, here 101, "Ovid teaches Dante the art of metaphor[. . .] and how to use metaphorically." Ovid's metamorphosis becomes metaphor in Dante.

of poetry, an earthly poetry, though, that doesn't lead to heaven. There is only one other occurrence of the word "lai" in the *Comedy*, also rhyming with "guai": in *Inferno* 5 the sinners of carnal love are compared first to starlings and then to cranes who sings their "lai":

> E come i gru van cantando lor lai,
> faccendo in aere di sè lunga riga,
> così vid'io venir, traendo guai,
> ombre portate da la detta briga . . . (*Inf.* 5.46–49)

The word "lai" used to define poems accompanied by music and was popular in French medieval courtly poetry. Provençal troubadours used the word to describe the songs of birds.[46] Although "lai" ended up meaning simply 'laments' after the semantic shift derived from Dante's usage in the *Comedy*,[47] to Dante's medieval readers the word still referred to a poetic genre consisting of words and music, and could be associated with the song of birds.

The most famous author of *lais* was Marie de France, who wrote in the twelfth century and was known among medieval poets and most likely also to Dante. The main theme of her *lais* was love lamented by abandoned and victimized women. The connection with the "lai" in *Inferno* 5 is easy to draw: the damned souls, among whom a woman, Francesca da Rimini, stands out, lament the love that overwhelmed them in life and caused their eternal damnation. Furthermore, poetry is central in this canto and is indicated as being responsible for leading Paolo and Francesca into temptation. Interestingly enough, one of Marie de France's most famous poems is *Laüstic*, in Breton "the nightingale," describing a triangle of two knights and a woman, where the bird acts as go-between for the lovers (nightingale as *galeotto*?). The nightingale is at once a masculine and feminine symbol, according to very intricate sexual imagery. As Wendy Pfeffer notes, "there is no question that the nightingale image has sexual connotations in medieval lyrics."[48] By associating the swallow/Philomela with the poetic genre of the *lais*, which recalls medieval lyrics in general and Marie de France's literary production in particular, in which a poem about the nightingale stands out, Dante is acknowledging the tradition of Philomela as the nightingale in courtly poetry but, at the same time, he is distancing himself from that tradition, creating a new Philomela, unwillingly linked to earth and sexual violence and still trying to lift her soul upwards.

---

[46] Ferdinando Neri, "La voce *lai* nei testi italiani," *Atti della Reale Accademia delle Scienze di Torino* 72 (1937): 105–19.

[47] Bruno Migliorini, "Dante nella storia della lingua italiana," in *Dante nella critica d'oggi* (Florence: Le Monnier, 1965), 138–42.

[48] Pfeffer, *The Change of Philomel*, 168.

In *Purgatory* 9 Philomela laments the wicked love of Tereus which contaminated her. Although her metamorphosis into a bird allowed her to flee from her rapist, nevertheless it kept her in the position of being forever chased by him as a hoopoe. Her psychological resistance to the rape doesn't exonerate her completely from the taint of sexual contamination. Medieval views of rape involved shame for the person raped as much as for the rapist. Kathryn Gravdal analyzes the sexual plot of female saints' legends in order to arrive at the patristic understanding of female sexuality. What is characteristic of these narratives is that no rape is ever completed. The hagiographic tradition thus legitimizes sexual violence as a test of the saintly female.[49] We can't assume that Dante is legitimizing Tereus' sexual assault, but we can definitely see a correspondence between Philomela's fate and the traditional pattern of female saints' lives, both marked by sexual threat and mutilation.[50] Contrary to female martyrs, Philomela is unable to keep her virginity. Therefore, even though she regained her voice as a singing bird, her song is one of eternal mourning linked to the rape, to Tereus' carnal love, and ultimately to earth.

The uplifting power of poetry is central in Purgatory where the souls still feel earthly ties, yet they are purging themselves of their human burdens to prepare themselves to enter Heaven; thus spiritual transformation is very important. Dante will undergo—symbolically—the same process of cleansing in order to eventually reach God. His *raptus* by the eagle—albeit in his dream—represents a further step upwards and marks his entrance into Purgatory proper. On a poetic level Dante is purifying himself of his earthly poetry in order to write his divine poem. In this regard, bird imagery is often used by Dante when referring to himself, playing on the double meaning of the word "penne" as pens and wings. In *Purgatory* 24.58–59 the poet Bonagiunta da Lucca comments on Dante's poetic inspiration using the metaphor of the "penne" that follow closely behind Love who dictates:

> Io veggio ben come le vostre penne
> di retro al dittator sen vanno strette,
> che de le nostre certo non avvenne. (*Purg.* 24.58–60)

Finally, Beatrice rebukes Dante's straying after Lady Philosophy:

> Ben ti dovevi, per lo primo strale
> de le cose fallaci, levar suso
> di retro a me che non era più tale.
> Non ti dovea gravar le penne in giuso,
> ad aspettar più colpo, o pargoletta
> o altra novità con sì breve uso. (*Purg.* 31.55–60)

---

[49] Gravdal, *Ravishing Maidens*, 21–41.
[50] For example, the removal of Saint Lucy's eyes and of Saint Agatha's breasts.

It is here clear how Dante uses this image: the wings may represent human capability to ascend to heaven, distancing oneself from deceptive earthly goods.[51] Dante's love for Beatrice is refined, purified of any sexual drive. Since Beatrice leads Dante to God and appears herself as a type of Christ-figure, Dante's love for her is a divine love, and this, in turn, inspires divine poetry. The progression of *raptus* leading up to Dante's ascent is, in fact, also characterized also by a progressive physical detachment from earth expressed through a gradual weakening of the vibrant sensuality of the first image to the complete purity of Ganymede-Dante's abduction.

The reference to Philomela, central in the progression of mythological *raptus*, marks a very meaningful intermediate stage of the soul, linked to both the sensuality and degradation of Tithonus, irremediably fastened to the earth with his condemnation to unnatural earthly immortality, and the elevation of Ganymede. In his re-reading and re-presenting of the Ovidian myth, Dante selects the rape as the origin of both contamination and regained voice and represents in the swallow the condition of the repentant souls in Purgatory,[52] who are developing wings to fly upward to heaven, but at the same time he maintains the tragedy of the eternal mourning of the swallow/Philomela.

The new vision of Philomela offered by Dante not only involves metapoetical issues, but also, and most important for our analysis, the political context of the myth is recuperated. Philomela with her eternal mourning becomes a symbol of the family and of the society violated and corrupted by a negligent leader. Although Tereus, whose name should be added to the list of evil rulers, should be the one to be blamed, Dante decides instead to make Philomela the focus of his allusion. The horror of her destiny is more powerful than the mention of Tereus and his terrible deeds, just as the degeneration of the family and of the society deserves more concern than the ruler who is himself responsible for such corruption.

The focus on Philomela, the female character, reveals Dante's intent to underscore the importance of the feminine principle of society, holder of the power of procreation and growth. Women are responsible for the continuation of the family and of society along with their moral values. The contamination of Philomela symbolizes the destruction of such values, thus jeopardizing the chances of continuity for society on earth and of happiness for the individuals in the

---

[51] The wings may also lead men to self-destruction if guided by an ill-oriented will, as in the case of Ulysses and his companions' last journey: ". . . e volta nostra poppa nel mattino, / de' remi facemmo ali al folle volo / sempre acquistando dal lato mancino" (*Inf.* 26.124–126).

[52] Concerning the swallow, Hugh of Fouilloy (1132–1152) in his *Aviarium: The Medieval Book of Birds*, trans. Willene B. Clark, MRTS 80 (Binghamton, NY: Medieval and Renaissance Texts and Studies, 1992), 46, writes "Si nosti clamorem hirundinis, nisi fallor, questum designat animae poenitentis" [If you are familiar with the cry of the swallow, unless I am mistaken, it symbolizes the lament of the penitent spirit].

afterlife. Quite differently, Ganymede as well as Dante, lifted by the eagle above the worldly affairs, represents the individual led to happiness in heaven by prudent leaders on earth who are inspired by divine grace.

Appunti su Guglielmo Maramauro, sull'*Auctoritas* e sulla Lettura di Dante nel Trecento

Zygmunt Baranski

La fortuna di Dante nell'Italia del Trecento fu straordinaria. La *Commedia* e la fama del suo autore penetrarono tanto nelle scuole quanto nelle strade, nei luoghi sacri quanto nelle sedi governative. Non tutti i lettori reagivano con approvazione o con sensibile intelligenza; ma, una cosa è certa: il poema fu letto, riletto, e utilizzato larghissimamente. Soltanto la Bibbia godette di maggior popolarità; e come aumentavano i copisti, i lettori, e gli ascoltatori della *Commedia*, cosí cresceva l'"autorevolezza" del suo *auctor*—poeta volgare non solo giudicato da molti alla pari dei *magni poetæ regulares*, ma tale, secondo alcuni dei suoi primi estimatori, che riusciva persino a sorpassare i grandi dell'era classica.[1] Il Trecento, c'è poco da dire, fu una vera e propria *ætas Dantis*. Particolarmente a Firenze, il poeta—o meglio, la *Commedia* assieme ai miti ed agli interessi che rapidamente si unirono al poema e alla figura del suo autore—costituiva sempre piú il fulcro chiave della vita della città,[2] come, per esempio, ha dimostrato Christian Bec, illuminando uno degli angoli piú oscuri ma anche piú suggestivi del variegato interesse trecentesco per Dante. Lo studioso francese è riuscito a gettar luce sui rapporti di un intero gruppo sociale col poema dantesco, chiarendo, con una ricca messe di prove, che, fra il Tre- e il Quattrocento, Dante deve il suo successo

---

[1] Sulla fortuna di Dante nel Trecento, si vedano almeno Zygmunt G. Baranski, *"Chiosar con altro testo": Leggere Dante nel Trecento* (Fiesole: Cadmo, 2007); Corrado Bologna, *Tradizione e fortuna dei classici italiani*, 2 voll. (Torino: Einaudi, 1993), 1:157–99; Steven Botterill, "The Trecento Commentaries on Dante's *Commedia*," in *The Cambridge History of Literary Criticism*, vol. 2: *The Middle Ages*, ed. Alastair Minnis e Ian Johnson (Cambridge: Cambridge University Press, 2005), 590–611; Simon Gilson, *Dante and Renaissance Florence* (Cambridge: Cambridge University Press, 2005), 1–93; Bruno Sandkühler, *Die frühen Dantekommentare und ihr Verhältnis zur mittelalterlichen Kommentartradition* (Monaco: Max Hueber Verlag, 1967); Aldo Vallone, *Storia della critica dantesca dal XIV al XX secolo*, 2 voll. ([Milano:] Vallardi, 1981), 1:51–230.

[2] Si veda Gilson, *Dante and Renaissance Florence*.

fiorentino non solo ad intellettuali di professione ma pure ai *marchands écrivains* della città.³ Allo stesso modo, non furono solo le zone a cui l'Alighieri fu piú legato, la Toscana, il Veneto, ecc., che riconobbero l'importanza della sua esperienza culturale. Nel corso del Trecento, anche luoghi in cui Dante non mise mai piede sentirono sempre di piú la forza del suo fascino. Ciò è vero, per esempio, se si pensa al Meridione,⁴ e, specificamente, a Napoli,⁵ dove i primi sviluppi di una prosa in vernacolo napoletano si immedesimano coll'esegesi della *Commedia*.⁶ Ed è su qualche aspetto di questa *lectura* partenopea che vorrei fermare l'attenzione: in particolare, sui modi in cui il poeta fiorentino e la sua opera divennero coinvolti nei tentativi di un maestro napoletano di fissare la propria fisionomia intellettuale—questioni intrecciate di *auctoritas* poetica e di autorità accademica.⁷

La figura di Guglielmo Maramauro, destinatario di due *Senili* petrarchesche (11.5 e 15.4), è emersa con un certo spessore solo negli ultimi anni dopo l'uscita, nel 1998 per i tipi dell'Editrice Antenore, della bella edizione della sua *Expositione sopra l'"Inferno" di Dante Alligieri* a cura di Pier Giacomo Pisoni e Saverio Bellomo—evento di prima importanza per chiunque si interessi della ricezione trecentesca di Dante.⁸ Prima di questa data, non si sapeva molto dell'attività di

---

³ Christian Bec, *Cultura e società a Firenze nell'età della Rinascenza* (Roma: Salerno, 1981); *Les Livres des Florentins (1413–1608)* (Firenze: Olschki, 1984); *Les Marchands écrivains: affaires et humanisme à Florence 1375–1434* (Parigi: Mouton, 1967); si veda anche Bologna, *Tradizione e fortuna*, 1:187–88.

⁴ Giorgio Petrocchi, "Vulgata e tradizioni regionali," in *La critica del testo: Problemi di metodo ed esperienze di lavoro* (Roma: Salerno, 1985), 113–26.

⁵ Andrea Mazzucchi, "Introduzione," in *"Chiose filippine,"* ed. idem, 2 voll. (Roma: Salerno, 2002), 2:9–17; Mario Rotili, *I codici danteschi miniati a Napoli* (Napoli: Libreria Scientifica Editrice, 1972); Francesco Sabatini, *Napoli angioina: Cultura e società* (Napoli: Edizioni Scientifiche Italiane, 1975), 63, 65, 94–95, 126–27, 240–42, 253–54, 263–64.

⁶ Sabatini, *Napoli angioina*, 101–3, 108–10.

⁷ Spero che questi appunti di carattere "seccamente" storico-filologico non dispiacciano all'amico Chris, il quale, lungo tutta la carriera di storico della letteratura medievale—come ha giustamente riconosciuto un maestro dell'autorevolezza di Mario Marti—si è rivelato uno studioso dotato di "connaturate esigenze di concretezza e di precisione," stendendo lavori "privi di superflui abbandoni descrittivi e d'ogni oratorio e retorico compiacimento, e seccamente ricchi, al contrario, di sudati e faticosi dati di fatto, tanto utili quanto incisivi": Mario Marti, ["Presentazione,"] in Christopher Kleinhenz, *The Early Italian Sonnet: The First Century (1220–1321)* (Lecce: Milella, 1986), 1–2.

⁸ Su Guglielmo Maramauro, si vedano Saverio Bellomo, "Da Napoli al Lago Maggiore: Schede sul commento dantesco di Guglielmo Maramauro," *Verbanus* 13 (1992): 63–73; idem, *Dizionario dei commenti danteschi: L'esegesi della "Commedia" da Iacopo Alighieri a Nidobeato* (Firenze: Olschki, 2004), 325–29; idem, "Introduzione," in Guglielmo Maramauro, *Expositione sopra l'"Inferno" di Dante Alligieri*, ed. Pier Giacomo Pisoni e Saverio Bellomo (Padova: Antenore, 1998), 3–43; idem, "Un sonetto su Dante da restituire al napoletano Guglielmo Maramauro," in *Bibliologia e critica dantesca: Saggi dedicati a Enzo Esposito*, vol. 2: *Saggi danteschi*, ed. Vincenzo De Gregorio (Ravenna: Longo, 1997),

"dantista" del Maramauro.⁹ Dai dati a noi pervenuti, Maramauro—membro di un'importante famiglia napoletana, ben inserito negli ambienti culturali e politici della sua città, in contatto con intellettuali ed artisti del calibro di Petrarca e di Boccaccio, senatore romano, *eques* del "sovrano militare ospedaliero Ordine di San Giovanni di Gerusalemme, detto di Rodi, detto di Malta,"¹⁰ uomo di interessi eclettici, viaggiatore entusiasta¹¹—sembra aver avuto i primi contatti con l'opera dantesca, quasi sicuramente incoraggiati dalla forte presenza fiorentina a Napoli, attorno alla metà del Trecento, come testimoniano i quattro sonetti, probabilmente scritti in quest'epoca, i quali rivelano, assieme ad echi stilnovistici, petrarcheschi, e boccacciani, l'influsso dell'Alighieri.¹² Anche nelle tre restanti poesie superstiti (un sonetto e due canzoni), scritte dopo il 1374, Dante svolge un ruolo importante.¹³ Anzi, la presenza dantesca è di gran lunga più massiccia in questi ultimi testi, dato che furono composti dopo la stesura del commento alla *Commedia*, il quale, come è detto nel Prologo (10), fu eseguito tra il 1369 e il 1373. Ed è sul Prologo che vorrei principalmente concentrare l'attenzione in

---

329–33; Rosario Coluccia, "Due nuove canzoni di Guglielmo Maramauro, rimatore napoletano del sec. XIV," *Giornale storico della letteratura italiana* 160 (1983): 161–202; idem, "L'edizione dei documenti e i problemi linguistici della copia (con tre appendici un po' stravaganti) intorno a Guglielmo Maramauro," *Medioevo romanzo* 24 (2000): 237–55; idem, "Tradizioni auliche e popolari nella poesia del Regno di Napoli in età angioina," *Medioevo romanzo* 2 (1975): 51–54, 82–83, 86–89; Pier Giacomo Pisoni, "Guglielmo Maramauro commentatore di Dante e amico del Petrarca," *Studi petrarcheschi* 1 (1984): 253–55; Sabatini, *Napoli angioina*, 90, 95, 124–27, 253–54, 263, 267. Inoltre, specificamente sull'*Exposizione*, si vedano Claudia Di Fonzo, "Noterella relativa alla fenomenologia della copia dei commenti antichi della *Commedia*," *Italian Studies* 63 (2008): 11–13; Mazzucchi, "Introduzione," 37–41.

⁹ Secondo Bellomo (annotazione in Maramauro, *Expositione*, 167), la più antica attestazione del termine "dantista" si troverebbe nell'*Expositione*; e si vedano anche Saverio Bellomo, "'Parvi Florentia mater amoris': Gli epitafi sul sepolcro di Dante," in *Vetustatis indagator: Scritti offerti a Filippo Di Benedetto*, ed. Vincenzo Fera e Augusto Guida (Messina: Università degli studi di Messina-Centro interdipartimentale di studi umasitici-Biblioteca Medicea Laurenziana, 1999), 19–33; idem, "Prime vicende del sepolcro di Dante," *Letture classensi* 28 (1999): 55–71. Si vedano, però, anche Gilson, *Dante and Renaissance Florence*, 61 e 255; Gioacchino Paparelli, "Dante e il Trecento," in *Dante nel pensiero e nell'esegesi dei secoli XIV e XV* (Firenze: Olschki, 1975), 32 e 34.

¹⁰ Coluccia, "Edizione," 251.

¹¹ Bellomo, "Introduzione," 3–5, 9–12, 28–31, 34–39; Coluccia, "Edizione," 240–41, 249–52.

¹² Bellomo, "Introduzione," 17–21; Coluccia, "Edizione," 237; idem, "Tradizioni," 86–89; Sabatini, *Napoli angioina*, 126–27.

¹³ Bellomo, "Introduzione," 17–21; Coluccia, "Due"; "Edizione," 241. Un ulteriore sonetto, "Vostro sí pio officio," che si collega alla tradizione degli epitafi per la tomba di Dante, è stato attribuito, ma con debita cautela, a Maramauro; si vedano Bellomo, "'Parvi'"; idem, "Prime."

questo breve saggio, per offrire qualche riflessione sulla natura del commento e del suo autore, che rivelano ambedue dei tratti alquanto inconsueti nei riguardi della tradizione dei *commentaria* trecenteschi alla *Commedia*.[14]

Il commento si lega ad un momento chiave della vita di Guglielmo Maramauro: "La qual opera cominciai io in Napoli ne li anni de mia età de cinquantadoi e ne li anni de l'incarnatione de Cristo miletrecentosexantanove, con la conduta del venerabile doctore miser san Tomaso d'Aquino" (Prologo 10). Gli inizi della *Expositione*, quindi, si associano strettamente con l'incarico accademico recentemente conferito al suo autore: "una cattedra di teologia, o piú precisamente [. . .] un lettorato dell'opera di san Tommaso" presso lo Studio di Napoli, specificamente "presso i frati predicatori, che risiedevano nel convento di San Domenico Maggiore."[15] Non può non colpire il fatto che, subito dopo aver accettato la nomina di *lector* dell'Aquinate, Maramauro si metta a commentare un poeta secolare, sia pure della statura di Dante. È curioso non tanto perché ci si aspetterebbe che egli si fosse impegnato in un lavoro di esegesi tomistica o almeno di stampo teologico, ma piuttosto perché sembra una scelta molto poco appropriata date le ben note riserve dei domenicani nei riguardi di Dante e dei suoi scritti, e di Tommaso e di altri suoi confratelli nei riguardi della poesia e della cultura secolare in generale.[16] Inoltre, l'apparente mancanza di diplomazia e di sensibilità che Maramauro sembra dimostrare nei confronti della facoltà teologica dell'ordine aumenta notevolmente se si rammenta che il novello lettore non apparteneva ai domenicani e, addirittura, neanche al clero. Ci troviamo di fronte ad un groviglio di problemi che mi pare che gli studiosi di Maramauro non solo non abbiano risolto, ma non abbiano neppure riconosciuto—problemi, però, che lasciano un marchio indelebile sul commento.

Non direi che la decisione di Maramauro di commentare Dante costituisca una manovra volutamente polemica nei riguardi dei suoi colleghi domenicani. Il tono di orgoglio con cui egli fa riferimento alle sue responsabilità didattiche verso il "venerabile doctore," assieme ad altri aspetti del commento su cui tornerò, militano contro una tale interpretazione. Malgrado i rapporti con due grandissimi difensori della poesia quali Petrarca e Boccaccio, ed il ricorso alla loro autorità nel Prologo (13), la decisione di Maramauro di glossare Dante mentre "leggeva" Tommaso non ha scopi, almeno esplicitamente, filo-poetici. L'*Expositione*, dunque, non è da annoverare tra i contributi di coloro che, lungo tutto il

---

[14] Per un'analisi approfondita, corredata con una bibliografia piú ampia, di alcuni dei problemi sollevati in questo studio, si veda Baranski, "*Chiosar*," 117–52.

[15] Bellomo, "Introduzione," 8–9.

[16] Roberto Antonelli, "L'Ordine domenicano e la letteratura italiana nell'Italia pretridentina," in *Letteratura italiana*, vol. 1: *Il letterato e le istituzioni*, ed. Alberto Asor Rosa (Torino: Einaudi, 1982), 681–728; Anthony K. Cassell, *The Monarchia Controversy* (Washington: Catholic University Press of America, 2003); Nevio Matteini, *Il più antico oppositore politico di Dante: Guido Vernani da Rimini* (Padova: Cedam, 1958).

Trecento, da un lato, si opponevano alla gerarchia delle scienze e delle arti fissata e difesa dai domenicani (gerarchia in cui, alla teologia, si assegnava il primato e, alla poesia, l'ultimo posto) e, dall'altro, in maniera volutamente antagonistica, sostenevano invece il connubio tra le due *artes* particolarmente nella figura del *poeta-theologus*.[17] Non si trovano tracce effettive di tale prospettiva nel commento di Guglielmo; in verità, ciò che vi si scopre è un chiaro senso della distinzione tra la poesia dell'aldilà ridotta a *fictio* — "a dare bene intendere che esso [Dante] non vide mai V[irgilio] [. . .]. E però [. . .] in questo so poema alegoricamente lo figura" (1.88–89; e si veda anche Prologo 3; 1.93) — e la teologia che tratta "scientificamente" delle cose piú alte: "Teologia non è altro a dire che scientia la qual tracta de Dio e de sua lode" (2.74). La posizione conservatrice presa da Maramauro sulla questione, cosí fondamentale, dei rapporti tra le "arti" obbliga a ridimensionare l'ipotesi che egli fosse in stretta sintonia con sviluppi culturali di punta;[18] e, come si vedrà, anche altri elementi suggeriscono di trattare con cautela l'idea che, da un punto di vista ideologico, il commentatore fosse legato armonicamente con intellettuali vicini a Petrarca; allo stesso tempo, ciò non dovrebbe portare ad escludere che, in pratica, egli avesse contatti con alcuni di loro.[19]

Se non fu uno spirito polemico ad ispirare l'*Expositione*, quali potrebbero essere state le ragioni che spinsero Maramauro ad intraprendere un lavoro potenzialmente cosí pieno di tranelli per un *lector* legato ad ambienti domenicani? Paradossalmente, l'ipotesi che vorrei qui proporre è che fu giusto il desiderio di rivendicare l'opportunità della sua nomina al lettorato tomistico che cova dietro la decisione maramauriana "a volere exponere questa altissima opera" (Prologo 12).

Né il commento né le poesie né altri documenti pervenutici offrono prove che Guglielmo Maramauro fosse competente in materia filosofica e teologica, e, dunque, che avesse le carte accademiche in regola come esegeta dell'Aquinate. In effetti, le prove offerte dalla *Expositione* testimoniano esattamente l'opposto. Delle sette citazioni tomistiche, sei sono prese dalla redazione ashburnhamiana del commento di Pietro Alighieri (4.4; 7.41; 8.7; 9.20; 10.43; 29.68), testo che — come Bellomo ha definitivamente dimostrato[20] — costituisce una delle fonti principali dell'opera di Maramauro. La settima, che è allegata alla spiegazione del termine "ipocrita," non trova riscontri in altri commenti danteschi

---

[17] Salvatore Battaglia, "Teoria del poeta teologo," in *Esemplarità e antagonismo nel pensiero di Dante*, 2 voll. (Napoli: Liguori, 1967), 1:271–301; Robert Hollander, "Dante theologus-poeta," in idem, *Studies in Dante* (Ravenna: Longo, 1980), 39–89; Claudio Mesoniat, *Poetica theologia: La "Lucula noctis" di Giovanni Dominici e le dispute letterarie tra '300 e '400* (Roma: Edizioni di storia e letteratura, 1984); Ronald Witt, "Coluccio Salutati and the Conception of the *poeta theologus* in the Fourteenth Century," *Renaissance Quarterly* 30 (1977): 538–63.

[18] Bellomo, "Introduzione," 14, 25–27, 28–31, 34–35.

[19] Bellomo, "Introduzione," 26–31, 34–39.

[20] Bellomo, "Da Napoli"; annotazioni in Maramauro, *Expositione*.

a me noti: "E cossí prova san Tomaso in libro *De regno* alegando Isaia: 'Regnare fecisti ypocritam propter peccata populi' " (23.3). Il passo, quindi, potrebbe essere frutto di una lettura diretta del *De regimine principum* (6); ma potrebbe ugualmente esser stato preso da un'opera di compilazione quale un lessico, una *summa* od uno dei tanti trattati sui peccati. In ogni caso, il rinvio ad Isaia è erroneo; il brano proviene da Giobbe 34:30. Il commento di Maramauro, come avrò occasione di mostrare con maggior precisione, è strapieno di errori—elemento ulteriore che mette in forse le sue doti e conoscenze intellettuali. Una delle sviste peggiori tocca proprio San Tommaso. Nell'elucidare il contrapasso dei falsatori di metalli, Maramauro osserva: "E però san Tomaso, $2^a\ 2^e$, dice: 'Nam alchimiste die noctuque laborantes, falso modo volentes corrumpere metalla, dicuntur "leprosi" ' " (29.68). In sé, non c'è niente di strano che il commentatore si appoggi sull'autorità dell'Aquinate; solo che le parole non sono del santo ma della fonte di Maramauro, Pietro Alighieri: "alchimiste, die noctuque laborantes cum manibus, et nichil ultimo acquirentes, nisi furfur, ut faciunt gractantes et fricantes se a scabia, dici possunt leprosi, ut fingit auctor hic. [. . .] quomodo enim alchimia possit fieri vel fiat vitiose et non vitiose, curiosus videat Tomam de Aquino in secunda secunde, questione lxx^a, articulo primo" (394). Le nove *auctoritates* aristoteliche presenti nel commento confermano le debolezze filosofiche ed intellettuali di Maramauro già messe a fuoco dai passi tomistici: tre sono prestiti da Pietro (11.34; 11.39; 15.55); una provviene quasi di sicuro dal commento, ora perduto, ma che si ipotizza circolava a Napoli prima del 1369, da cui dipendono l'*Exposizione* e il secondo strato di chiose (B; della prima metà del Quattrocento) presenti nel Filippino,[21] altro *commentarium* saccheggiato da Maramauro (6.49);[22] due sono generiche (6.3; 32.3); due hanno l'aria di essere topiche (9.35;

---

[21] "Se, come argomenta Bellomo, 'si esclude perentoriamente dal confronto dei testi' ["Introduzione," 41 e n.] che il Filippino abbia copiato da Maramauro, l'evidenza paleografica, insieme con altre minori considerazioni (Maramauro, ad esempio, ignora totalmente le chiose vergate da A), induce a scartare l'alternativa ipotesi che sia stato quest'ultimo a servirsi del manoscritto dell'Oratoriana. Prescindendo dunque da una reciproca diretta conoscenza, non resta, per razionalizzare i contatti tra i due testi, che ammettere l'esistenza di un *corpus* di chiose alla *Commedia*, oggi perduto, ma presente a Napoli prima del 1369 e ancora diffuso nei primi decenni del XV secolo, dal quale abbiano attinto informazioni indipendentemente Maramauro e il secondo anonimo chiosatore del Filippino" (Mazzucchi, "Introduzione," 37). I dati che Bellomo presenta per dimostrare la dipendenza di Maramauro dal Filippino devono ora essere visti come prove della dipendenza di Guglielmo dal glossatore napoletano cosí intelligentemente ipotizzato da Mazzucchi. Dunque, dove Bellomo parla del Filippino, dobbiamo ora sostituire questo commento misterioso. Per ciò che riguarda la mia tesi, non è tanto l'identità del commento che è importante, ma il fatto che Maramauro dipenda in maniera imponente da chiose presenti a Napoli.

[22] Si veda Bellomo, "Da Napoli"; e annotazioni in Maramauro, *Expositione*; ma ora corretto da Mazzucchi, "Introduzione," 37–41.

12.48); mentre una, sorprendentemente, associando *Inferno* 2.88–90 con *Etica Nicomachea* 3.6.1115a-b, offre, per la prima volta nella critica dantesca, un preciso riscontro filosofico per le parole di Beatrice: "E questo concorda col testo de Aristotile ne l'*Etica*, ove tracta de la virtú de la forteza, la quale dice che è forteza contra la viltà de l'animo; e dice che forteza è virtú per la qual se dee temere le cose che ragionevelmente se debono timere, ma l'altre non, como dice qui el testo" (2.63). Il riscontro è indubbiamente pertinente; ma, da solo, non dimostra una conoscenza profonda dell'*Etica* da parte di Maramauro. La spiegazione piú probabile è che, come l'altro rinvio alle "parole de Aristotile, libro *De etica*" (13.34), introdotto nel corso dell'esegesi di *Inferno* 13, il passo sulla "forteza" provenga da una fonte intermedia.

Se, da un punto di vista strettamente accademico, Maramauro non sembra essere stato il candidato ideale per il posto di lettore di San Tommaso, quali possono essere state le ragioni della sua nomina? Direi che Saverio Bellomo è sulla via giusta quando mette a fuoco il ruolo che la famiglia ha potuto avere in questo processo:

> Aveva [. . .] fatto carriera accademica, in ciò forse facilitato—senza per questo volergli togliere merito alcuno—dalla famiglia, le cui sorti in piú occasioni si intrecciarono con quelle dello Studio: il nonno Guglielmo tesoriere del giustizierato degli scolari e Pietro Maramauro professore di diritto canonico e persino rettore. [. . .] Ma non credo di peccare di troppa malizia se pongo in relazione la sua nomina con il legame di parentela con un domenicano di grande prestigio come Guido, che [. . .] forse gli fu zio.[23]

Nel contesto del filo argomentativo che qui sto seguendo, la proposta di Bellomo mi sembra del tutto plausibile (anche se, ovviamente, non posso condividere la sua opinione circa i "meriti" di Maramauro). Inoltre, vorrei aggiungere che ci potrebbe essere stato anche altro appoggio potente in favore della candidatura di Guglielmo. Esistono prove inconfutabili che egli fu vicino alla corte di Giovanna I;[24] e, come si sa, anche se le facoltà di teologia avevano una certa libertà di manovra, lo Studio napoletano fu largamente sotto il controllo della corona.[25] Non è difficile immaginarsi come la doppia pressione esercitata da Giovanna e dagli illustri Maramauri, da lungo legati, anche loro, al potere regale, potesse avere come risultato la nomina del nostro "dantista" ad un posto che non avrebbe dovuto spettargli.

Sospetto che Guglielmo fosse piú che conscio di quanto poco egli fosse adatto a svolgere l'incarico che aveva accettato. Il commento alla *Commedia*, dunque, avrebbe avuto la funzione di dimostrare ai suoi protettori laici che avevano

---

[23] Bellomo, "Introduzione," 8–9. Sui tre parenti di Guglielmo qui menzionati, 4–5.
[24] Bellomo, "Introduzione," 12–13; Coluccia, "L'edizione," 240.
[25] Sabatini, *Napoli angioina*, 55–65, 238–42.

sostenuto una persona degna del loro appoggio—in altre parole, un addetto ai lavori. Da questo punto di vista, si spiegano benissimo sia la scelta di Dante come autore da commentare sia quella del volgare come lingua per il suo lavoro di esegesi. "Esporre" la *Commedia*, nella seconda metà del Trecento a Napoli, aveva risvolti culturali molto precisi. Confermava l'adesione—anche se tale adesione, come nel caso di Guglielmo, fosse del tutto superficiale od illusoria—al partito maggioritario di coloro che, sotto l'influsso di Petrarca e di Boccaccio, privilegiavano la poesia; rivelava anche l'adesione a quella toscanizzazione della cultura napoletana che rappresentava la linea culturale dominante, entro la quale Dante godeva di particolare prestigio; mentre l'uso del volgare napoletano permetteva a Maramauro sia di dare un contributo notevole alla nascente letteratura scritta nella lingua locale sia di raggiungere lettori di non altissima preparazione scolastica, tra cui è da annoverare quasi sicuramente anche Giovanna I, la quale "fu ignara di latino e abbastanza distaccata ormai dalla lingua francese."[26] È chiaro che Maramauro, grazie al suo commento, sperava di raggiungere un grosso pubblico cittadino e di corte di fronte al quale dispiegare le proprie credenziali di intellettuale degno di insegnare presso lo Studio, ma anche aperto ad altre iniziative culturali—da qui nascono anche l'intento di spiegare i significati letterali del fiorentino di Dante a lettori di madrelingua napoletana, ed i rinvii a fatti di cronaca e ad altri dati di interesse generale che hanno poco a che fare con la *Commedia* (per esempio, 9.60; 11.3; 12.53; 14; 16.15 e 55; 31.72). Guglielmo si dimostra molto abile, dunque, a sintetizzare ed a riconciliare correnti diverse nella sua opera: egli si sforza di parlare tanto a parenti-professori quanto a persone di poca o minima preparazione scolastica. L'unico gruppo—come spieghero meglio di seguito—a cui il suo commento avrebbe detto ben poco sarebbero stati i "dantisti" di professione. Le abilità tattiche di Maramauro sono anche da riconoscere nei modi in cui egli sembra voler evitare di offendere i domenicani. Quindi, malgrado la decisione di elucidare il massimo poeta volgare, egli ebbe cura—come si è visto—di mantenere un chiaro distacco gerarchico tra la teologia e la poesia, a favore della prima. Ugualmente, lungo tutto il corso del commento, Maramauro sottolineò il carattere etico dell'opera dantesca ed i suoi vincoli con il problema della salvezza dell'anima—temi, ovviamente, che avrebbero dovuto riscuotere un certo consenso tra i santi padri.

Se, da un lato, Guglielmo si dimostra sensibile tanto a tendenze quanto a tensioni culturali dell'epoca, dall'altro, rivela una notevole superficialità intellettuale e di cultura. Paradossalmente, il commento a Dante che doveva confermare le sue doti di *lector*, finisce solo—come si è già iniziato a mostrare—col rivelare le sue mancanze.

Che si debba prendere l'*Expositione* come una sorta di "carta da visita," è ovvio tanto dal modo ossessivo con cui Maramauro parla di sé, quanto dalle

---

[26] Bellomo, "Introduzione," 24.

strategie retoriche che egli adotta, il cui fine è di associarlo con la grandezza di Dante, introducendo corrispondenze suggestive tra il poeta ed il suo "espositore" napoletano. Per tutto il commento, Maramauro fa cenno, in prima persona, non solo alle proprie opinioni critiche, ma anche alla propria vita. Le allusioni a viaggi che egli intraprese in luoghi esotici—nelle isole greche, in Ungheria, in Germania, forse persino in Inghilterra (4.84; 14.40; 32.15; 33.36; per l'episodio inglese, 12.64)—servono a creare l'immagine di un uomo di mondo, ricco di conoscenze pratiche ed intellettuali; un uomo le cui parole sono degne di fede perché nascono da esperienze dirette;[27] un uomo ricco di autorità, quindi. In piú, l'enfasi che Maramauro pone sul fatto che egli vide realmente le cose notevoli che descrive—da qui la cura con cui correda le sue reminiscenze di date precise e di rimandi storici (per esempio, 4.84; 12.64; 14.40)—non solo mette a fuoco la sua veridicità e la forza tenace della sua memoria, ma anche implica una sottile *deminutio* di Dante nei propri confronti, almeno al livello delle esperienze vissute, dato che il poeta viaggiò e "vidde per alteza de inzegno" (Prologo 3), mentre lui, Guglielmo, affrontò i fastidi del viaggiatore per offrire testimonianze oculari ai suoi lettori.

Si possono notare, lungo tutto il corso dell'*Expositione*, tali processi di auto-promozione—processi che dipendono fondamentalmente dall'*auctoritas* dantesca. Comunque, è nel Prologo che tale strategia è messa in atto per la prima volta e raggiunge, come ci si può aspettare in un luogo testuale tanto altamente privilegiato dalla cultura letteraria medievale,[28] la sua estrinsecazione piú sostenuta. Per esempio, Maramauro mette a fuoco con energia la propria unicità e quella dell'*Expositione*, che egli collega in maniera calcolata con le straordinarie esperienze dantesche. Prendiamo come punto di partenza il paragrafo con cui il Prologo si chiude:

> E posso bene dir che questo se pò chiamare "expositione", e "scripto", e "comento", però che troveriti in esso exposto con vocabulo, e dichiarata l'intentione de l'autore, e aprovato che esso dice e difeso con boni e chiari rasone e argumenti, excusandolo iustamente contra colloro che 'l vogliono calupniare. (18)

Colpisce il fatto che sia Dante sia Guglielmo sono scrittori ingiustamente "calunniati": "So bene certo che io non porria passare senza morso de alcuni" (Prologo 16), cioè, che non può sottrarsi alle accuse di inadeguatezza ermeneutica lanciategli da coloro che non vogliono riconoscere le difficoltà esegetiche che

---

[27] Jeanette M. A. Beer, *Narrative Conventions of Truth in the Middle Ages* (Ginevra: Droz, 1981); Ruth Morse, *Truth and Convention in the Middle Ages* (Cambridge: Cambridge University Press, 1991).

[28] Ernest A. Gallo, "Matthew of Vendôme: Introductory Treatise on the Art of Poetry," *Proceedings of the American Philosophical Society* 118 (1974): 51–92, qui 59–60.

egli ha dovuto affrontare. Si era già osservato come, pure altrove, Guglielmo si fosse immedesimato con Dante; e, in effetti, questa strategia caratterizza, sin dall'inizio, l'autodefinizione maramauriana. Quindi, al punto chiave nel Prologo, al momento in cui il commentatore lascia di parlare di Dante per parlare di sé (10), interessanti legami uniscono il poeta ed il glossatore. L'ultimo rinvio a Dante si ferma sul suo ruolo di "maestro" di Giovanni del Virgilio e su "la doctrina de sí excellente doctore come fo esso" (Prologo 7), cioè, sulle doti didattiche ed intellettuali, piuttosto che poetiche, dell'Alighieri. Maramauro inizia la propria presentazione sottolineando in se stesso esattamente i medesimi tratti: egli fissa il proprio valore di intellettuale alludendo sia alla propria maturità ("mia età de cinquantadoi") sia all'incarico universitario. Inoltre, dichiarandosi esperto "del venerabile doctore miser san Tomaso d'Aquino" (Prologo 11), egli si rivela *lector* ideale anche dell'altro "excellente doctore"—fatto confermato subito dopo dalla presunta vastità della sua *scientia*, frutto di amicizie autorevolissime e di letture sterminate che egli elenca nome per nome, titolo per titolo (Prologo 12–15).[29] È interessante riconoscere il nodo stretto che Maramauro allaccia tra Dante e Tommaso. Ciò confermerebbe, come ho accennato prima, che, attraverso l'*Expositione*, per soddisfare ambizioni personali e legittimare la sua posizione presso lo Studio, il commentatore napoletano volesse stabilire un rapporto tra l'esegesi dei due grandi del Medioevo italiano. Dimostrarsi esperto nel commentare l'uno confermava la sua idoneità a "dichiarare l'intenzione" dell'altro. Piú specificamente, avere successo nell'interpretazione di Dante, era il modo migliore per creare l'impressione del successo che egli, "inevitabilmente," stava anche raggiungendo presso la facoltà teologica.

Dante è sfruttato. La scelta della *Commedia* da parte di Maramauro come testo da elucidare è dettato—a mio parere—da ragioni di vantaggio personale piuttosto che di impegno di studioso. Dato il culto a Napoli per Dante, riuscire ad associarsi con il poeta, sino al punto di suggerire connessioni tra sé e l'Alighieri, era tra i modi piú efficaci per creare l'idea della propria autorevolezza. È ovvio che sia la lista dei libri sia le dichiarazioni dell'aiuto venutogli da altri commentatori danteschi e dai suoi quattro imponenti sostenitori dovevano svolgere la stessa funzione autopromozionale:

> E bene che io sollo da me stesso non sia messo a volere exponere questa altissima opera: io vidi lo scripto de Iacomo de la Lana, el qual è assai autentico e famoso, e quel de miser Gratiolo Bambaioli da Bologna, el quale è in gramatica, ed ebi el comento intitolato <. . .>. E tanto con l'aiuto de questi expositori, quanto con l'aiuto de miser Zoan Bocacio, e de miser Francesco

---

[29] La lista è difatto copiata dall'epistola di dedica che accompagna il commento a Valerio Massimo di Dionigi da Borgo San Sepolcro. Su questo elenco, si veda Baranski, "*Chiosar*," 136–47, 150–52.

Petrarca, e del pivan Forese e de miser Bernardo Scanabechi, io me mossi a volere prendere questa dura impresa. (Prologo 12–13)

La scelta del quartetto è ben calibrata. L'autorità di Petrarca e di Boccaccio, particolarmente a Napoli, fu assoluta;[30] mentre l'amicizia con il toscano Forese Donati e con il veneto Bernardo Scannabecchi, ambedue figure di spicco e noti come cultori di Dante,[31] serviva a dimostrare quanto Guglielmo fosse ben inserito negli ambienti intellettuali della penisola. Era un luogo comune del mondo culturale medievale quello di costruire la propria autorità tramite l'associazione con figure e testi la cui autorevolezza era indiscutibile.[32] Ma la sfacciataggine con cui Maramauro svolge tale operazione non può che lasciare un senso di disappunto. Il ringraziamento pubblicamente espresso nei riguardi di Jacopo, Graziolo e l'anonimo commentatore è volutamente fuorviante. Come Bellomo ha incontrovertibilmente dimostrato, Guglielmo ha debiti di poco peso verso di loro[33] — cosa che è resa ancor piú chiara se si riconosce quanto sia enorme il debito che egli deve a Pietro Alighieri ed all'ormai svanito commentatore napoletano tracce del cui *commentarium* sono sopravvissute tanto nell'*Expositione* quanto nella parte B del manoscritto Filippino della Biblioteca Oratoriana di Napoli (C.F. 2. 16), ambedue mai menzionati nel corso dell'*Expositione*.[34] Maramauro occulta deliberatamente i due testi su cui il suo commento si basa in modo massiccio.[35] Ci troviamo di fronte un caso strapotente di "plagio", di abuso di "diritti d'autore"; persino in una cultura in cui la *compilatio* fu una forma del tutto legittima, il fare maramauriano, particolarmente in clima proto-umanistico, è altamente problematico. In piú, costituisce uno dei punti deboli nella sua strategia di autopromozione. C'era il pericolo costante per Guglielmo che le sue fonti "segrete" potessero essere scoperte, e che, quindi, venisse alla luce l'effettiva povertà della sua preparazione intellettuale. Sospetto che la ragione principale per cui, normalmente, l'*Expositione*

---

[30] Francesco Sabatini, "Lingue e letterature volgari in competizione," in idem, *Italia linguistica delle origini*, 2 voll. (Lecce: Argo, 1996), 2:524–32.

[31] Bellomo, "Introduzione," 27–28, 31–34.

[32] Rita Copeland, *Rhetoric, Hermeneutics, and Translation in the Middle Ages* (Cambridge: Cambridge University Press, 1991).

[33] Si vedano, nell'edizione dell'*Expositione*, l'Indice delle fonti e dei luoghi paralleli s.vv. *Bambaglioli, Graziolo* e *Lana, Jacopo della*.

[34] Bellomo spiega, con ragionamenti assolutamente convincenti, che non è possibile che Pietro e, per lui (si veda la n. 21), il "Filippino" si celino dietro l'anonimo "commento intitolato <. . .>": "Ora, è pensabile che volesse indicare uno di questi due commenti, quantunque appaia strano che designasse sia l'uno che l'altro con il titolo, come se ne ignorasse l'autore. [. . .] Tanto meno pare credibile che Maramauro ignorasse il nome del napoletano che, poco tempo prima aveva apposto la maggior parte delle chiose sul manoscritto Filippino" ("Introduzione," 39–40).

[35] Si veda, nell'edizione dell'*Expositione*, l'Indice delle fonti e dei luoghi paralleli s.vv. *Alighieri, Pietro* e *Filippino*.

ha un carattere alquanto spento, banalizzante e poco rivelatorio—non per niente i passi piú interessanti e vivaci sono quelli in cui Maramauro parla di sé—provenga dal fatto che il commentatore stesse ripetendo, non di rado solo con lievi cambiamenti, idee altrui. Però, se non avesse avuto il lavoro degli altri su cui appoggiarsi, dati i propri limiti, non avrebbe potuto stendere l'*Expositione*, e, dunque, non avrebbe potuto mettere in atto un programma di promozione personale. Tutto sommato, non poteva che aprirsi ai rischi a cui, potenzialmente, lo esponeva la forza delle sue ambizioni inesorabili.

Bisogna ammettere che Maramauro fa del suo meglio per allontanare tali pericoli insistendo vigorosamente non solo sulle proprie abilità ma anche, come ho acennato di passaggio prima, sulle caratteristiche speciali del suo commento. Allo stesso modo in cui egli sembra distinguersi dagli altri "dantisti" a causa delle similarità che, singolarmente, lo associano a Dante, Maramauro presenta l'*Expositione* come un *unicum* se messa in raffronto con gli altri commenti alla *Commedia*. Se torniamo un'ultima volta al paragrafo conclusivo del Prologo, troviamo una definizione di largo respiro del *commentarium* maramauriano: "questo se pò chiamare 'expositione', e 'scripto', e 'comento', però che troveriti in esso exposto con vocabulo, e dichiarata l'intentione de l'autore, e aprovato che esso dice e difeso con boni e chiari rasone e argumenti" (18). Non è qui il caso d'indagare i possibili significati dei tre termini che Maramauro adopera per descrivere il proprio *comentum* (tentativo—sospetto—ingrato data la flessibilità semantica della terminologia nel Medioevo), né i possibili rapporti fra i tre termini ed i tre scopi esegetici che il commentatore propone di soddisfare con il suo lavoro. Ciò che è importante riconoscere, nel contesto della presente analisi delle strategie apologetiche di Guglielmo, è che, in contrasto con l'*Expositione*, gli altri commenti danteschi a cui si accenna nel Prologo sono fregiati di un singolo termine descrittivo: Jacopo e Graziolo sono autori di "script*i*", mentre l'anonimo glossatore ha prodotto un "comento" (12). La superiorità dell'esegesi di Maramauro è garantita dal fatto che essa riesce ad abbracciare non uno ma tre sottogeneri ermeneutici, cosa che gli permette di spiegare la lettera e i significati traslati della *Commedia* e di dar appoggio alle posizioni sostenute dall'Alighieri.

Stiamo, quindi, per leggere un caso preminente non solo del commento a Dante ma anche del commento in assoluto. Solo che, se si considera l'*Expositione* dal punto di vista delle forme del *commentarium* medievale, essa si rivela sorprendentemente mancante. Il Prologo, che dovrebbe dimostrare l'*auctoritas* del *commentator* e del suo *comentum*, è, invece, un vero pasticcio. Guglielmo non sembra essere in grado di seguire le piú banali convenzioni dell'*accessus*.[36] Basta fermarsi sulla parte piú ovviamente tecnica del Prologo:

---

[36] Richard William Hunt, "The Introductions to the *artes* in the Twelfth Century," in *Studia medievalia in honorem R.M. Martin* (Bruges: "de Tempel", 1948), 85–112; *Medieval Literary Theory and Criticism c.1100–c.1375*, ed. A. J. Minnis e A. B. Scott (Oxford:

Io faria la divisione de questo libro: de la materia, e de la forma, e del titolo del libro, e a che parte de filosofia se sotomete, e ancora de la forma del tractato, e ancora de la forma del tractare. Ma, per non fare prolixità de parole, io lo pretermeto e solo a la parte de filosofia morale io reduco questa opera, però che segondo el mal operare omo merita pena e segondo el bene operare omo merita premio de salute. (4)

Maramauro qui confonde diversi aspetti del lavoro critico che l'*accessus* organizzava in modo preciso e discriminante. "La divisione de questo libro," cioè la *divisio textus*, non aveva niente a che fare con la "materia," con la "forma" in senso lato, con il "titolo" e con la dimensione filosofica di un'opera. La *divisio textus* era uguale alla *forma tractatus* ed all'*ordinatio partium*, tutte e tre si riferivano all'organizzazione formale di un testo, ciò che, oggi, si direbbe "struttura."[37] Maramauro, dunque, subordina alla "divisione" un aspetto, "la forma del tractato," che è, in realtà, il suo preciso equivalente! E c'è di peggio. Egli sottomette alla *divisio textus* "la forma del tractare"—in latino la *forma tractandi*, ciò che, oggi, chiamiamo "stile"—, caratteristica testuale e critica che fu mantenuta ben distinta dalla *forma tractatus*.[38] Ma, la confusione non finisce qui. La materia, la forma, il titolo e la "parte de filosofia," che, per Guglielmo, costituiscono le questioni da analizzare "dividendo" un'opera, sono, in realtà, quattro delle rubriche standard attorno alle quali si organizzavano gli *accessus*: la *materia libri*, il *modus agendi*, il *titulus libri*, e il problema *cui parti philosophiae supponitur*.[39] Ciò che è cruciale ricordare riguardo a queste rubriche è che ognuna godeva di una condizione di indipendenza rispetto alle altre—ognuna chiariva elementi diversi di un testo—, esattamente la cosa di cui Maramauro, confondendole, si dimentica.[40]

La spiegazione che Guglielmo offre della concisione del suo *accessus*, il desiderio di non voler essere prolisso, e, quindi, la decisione di concentrarsi unicamente sulla "parte de filosofia morale," è una scusa poco convincente. Rivela, piuttosto, come un po' tutta la presentazione della "divisione de questo libro," quanto poca familiarità egli debba aver avuto con le convenzioni esegetiche medievali. Da un lato, non elucidando le questioni tipiche dell'*accessus*, egli non fa che dimostrare le proprie inadeguatezze quale commentatore—precisamente la cosa che, ad ogni costo, gli premeva nascondere. Dall'altro lato, nasce il sospetto che la decisione di sorvolare sulla maggioranza delle rubriche dell'*accessus* indichi una incapacità di fondo nel maneggiare il genere e nel rispondere alle sue esigenze.

Clarendon Press, 1988), 12–36; Alastair J. Minnis, *Medieval Theory of Authorship* (Aldershot: Scolar Press, 1988), 9–72.

[37] Minnis, *Medieval Theory*, 29, 145–59.
[38] Minnis, *Medieval Theory*, 29, 118–45.
[39] Minnis, *Medieval Theory*, 19–25.
[40] Minnis, *Medieval Theory*, 19.

I limiti di Maramauro come *commentator* sono veramente schiaccianti; e questi sono confermati dall'enorme numero di errori che sfigurano il commento — errori che confermano pure le insufficienze di Guglielmo come intellettuale. Gli errori sono di ogni tipo: di designazione (Maramauro si riferisce ad ognuna delle tre parti principali della *Commedia* col termine "comedia" (Prologo 17.4, 13.32 e 13)); di latino (per esempio, si confonde tra "oratio", preghiera, e il poeta "Oratio": 5.47); di fonte (per esempio, nel citare un passo biblico scambia Isaia con "David profeta": 1.8); di volgare (usa e capisce parole in maniera impropria: per esempio, 1.29); di interpretazione del testo della *Commedia* (a volte, data la debolezza in latino, non comprende il commento da cui sta copiando: per esempio, 1.50); di personaggi (per esempio, scambia Sara con Lia: 2.73); di dati storici (per esempio, 3.40), letterari (per esempio, 15.15), filosofici (per esempio, 12.18), mitologici (per esempio, 9.24) e geografici (per esempio, 26.45); di citazione (per esempio, 21.62); di informazioni retoriche (9.5). Una volta che si riconoscano i piú di cento errori presenti nell'*Expositione*, a cui bisogna aggiungere le altre carenze di Maramauro quale *lector* e le sue esagerate pretese di *auctoritas*, è difficile non trattare tutto il suo commento con molta cautela. Forse già i lettori tre- e quattrocenteschi avevano avuto la medesima reazione, da cui deriverà il fatto che l'*Expositione* sembra aver avuto una fortuna limitatissima.

La storia di Guglielmo Maramauro il "dantista-tomista" è affascinante. Ci permette di percepire qualcosa del mondo aggrovigliato dei rapporti culturali e di potere a Napoli nella seconda metà del Trecento. Ci permette anche di riconoscere la centralità che Dante aveva assunto nella città partenopea, particolarmente, per ciò che riguarda la nascente letteratura in volgare e nella mente di persone di cultura non troppo alta. L'*Expositione* non fu un lavoro scritto per specialisti, i quali avrebbero trovato ben poco di utile tra gli errori, le scopiazzature e le pedestri annotazioni morali del Nostro. Anzi, i "dantisti," specificamente quelli napoletani, alcuni dei quali sicuramente avrebbero avuto l'occasione di leggere il commento latino ipotizzato da Mazzucchi, erano coloro dai quali, prima di tutti, Maramauro doveva allontanare il commento, siccome essi potevano con facilità smascherare l'operazione che egli aveva compiuto. Ugualmente, non è credibile che Guglielmo pensasse ad altri intellettuali partenopei ben preparati quali potenziali lettori. Anche questi, con non troppa difficoltà, avrebbero riconosciuto le debolezze dell'*Expositione*.[41] Come si è cercato di dimostrare, il commentatore napoletano voleva colpire favorevolmente ben altro pubblico. Anche molti degli

---

[41] La mia conclusione circa il pubblico dell'*Expositione* differisce da quella sostenuta da Bellomo: "l'*Expositione è* destinata a un pubblico colto, e che anzi gli impliciti interlocutori di Maramauro *sono* gli 'adetti ai lavori', quelli che egli chiama [. . .] 'i dantisti' " ("Introduzione," 24). Anche su altri punti mi allontano dalle posizioni di Bellomo. Però, malgrado il divario tra le nostre interpretazioni di Maramauro, desidero sottolineare il valore del lavoro di Bellomo, senza le cui ricerche questo studio sarebbe stato molto piú povero.

altri commentatori danteschi nel Trecento scrissero i loro *commentaria* per ragioni che non furono unicamente dettate da interessi strettamente di studio. Comunque, nessuno di loro ha sfruttato, come Guglielmo, l'*auctoritas* di Dante per scopi altrettanto personali. Il *lector* neofita ci teneva molto a stabilire le proprie credenziali; il poeta offriva un mezzo effettivo con cui realizzare questo scopo. In maniera emblematica, Guglielmo Maramauro ci ricorda, particolarmente a noi dantisti, quanto dobbiamo al nostro poeta. Ci ricorda pure—e ciò costituisce, per dirla medievalmente, il "senso morale" della sua esperienza—il bisogno fondamentale di rispettare le responsabilità che tali debiti ci impongono—cosa che, dispiace ammetterlo, il commentatore napoletano non tenne in sufficiente considerazione.[42]

---

[42] Vorrei ringraziare Giulio Lepschy per i suoi commenti ad una versione precedente di questo studio.

"Quella Dolce Terra Latina": The Dantesque Landscape of Alberto Moravia's *La Ciociara* ("Two Women")

Mary Watt

One of the most frequently noted features of Dante's *Divine Comedy*[1] is the attention its author pays to describing the landscape of the three realms through which the pilgrim protagonist journeys. Dante uses a variety of devices to ensure that his reader can visualize every rough crag and barren plain of the *Inferno*, to ensure that that the reader can imagine the rocky face of Mount *Purgatorio* and envision the starry sky and tranquil garden of *Paradiso*. The end result is a well-constructed *iter* in which the pilgrim reader's road is punctuated with recognizable landmarks that signal not only the direction but also the meaning of the journey. Just as the downward trajectory of *Inferno* signifies the soul's descent into sin, for example, so too do the pitch-filled swamps of the *malebolge* demonstrate literally the true filth that lies behind the apparent glamour of evil.

Given the effectiveness of this strategy and the fact that Dante equates his experience with that of war,[2] it ought not to be surprising that its key components also provide the foundation for the hermeneutic strategy of Alberto Moravia's wartime novel *La Ciociara*. On its literal level, *La Ciociara* tells the story of Cesira, who leaves Rome with her daughter Rosetta to take refuge in the mountains of the Ciociaria as the Allied forces move up the Italian peninsula in the last days of World War II. Like the *Commedia*, *La Ciociara* pays close attention to the interplay of narrative and landscape, and it eventually becomes evident to the reader that Cesira's odyssey, like that of Dante's pilgrim, contains a deeper significance. Moreover, *La Ciociara*'s landscape is constructed in such a way that the

---

[1] Margaret Grimes has suggested, for example, that Dante's life is rarely far removed from the geography of the poem, that no matter how richly symbolic the *selva oscura* may be, "it is also a thicket in Italy of the fourteenth century, not too far from Florence": Margaret Grimes, "The Sunlit Hill of *Inferno* I," *Romance Notes* 28 (1987): 28.

[2] "e io sol uno / m'apparecchiava a sostener la guerra": *Inferno*, 2.3–4. Citations are from Dante Alighieri, *La Divina Commedia*, ed. Natalino Sapegno, 3 vols. (Florence: La Nuova Italia, 1985).

careful reader cannot help recalling the *Commedia*, and as such, the reader also becomes aware that this significance is also closely linked to that of the *Commedia*. Cesira's war, like Dante's "guerra," involves an initial descent followed by a purgatorial climb and, ultimately, a return to Rome. Indeed, a closer inspection reveals that Moravia's purportedly modern tale bears many of the hallmarks of Dante's *capolavoro*. More specifically, the basic hermeneutic strategy of *La Ciociara* relies on its successful and, quite often, evident absorption and adaptation of some of the most fundamental narrative structures of the *Commedia*. More specifically, it is Moravia's choice of setting that facilitates his project of absorption. As Cesira's Ciociaria and Dante's "dolce terra latina"[3] both represent synechdochically a greater *iter* of damnation, purgation, and hope for salvation, both landscapes also serve a significative purpose well beyond that of simple backdrop. More importantly, however, the subtle yet insistent affinities that Moravia creates between the two landscapes link Cesira's journey with Dante's and thus imbue Moravia's text with an even greater allegorical significance, expanding it beyond a personal account of triumph over adversity to a story of national redemption.

Besides the obvious framing metaphor of the journey that is, logically, linked to the landscape, three other distinct structures rely on the creation of a Dantesque landscape to connect *La Ciociara* to the *Commedia*. The ascent / descent pattern of Cesira's and Rosetta's journey recalls the same trope in the *Commedia*[4] both in terms of the pilgrim's journey and in respect of the narrative models to which it connects itself, the journeys of Aeneas and of St. Paul. The dual nature of Rome, as abyss and apex, as Babylon and Jerusalem,[5] informs the journey of the two women, Cesira and Rosetta, as much as it did Dante's own journey, providing both a point of departure and a terminus of return. Finally, the pseudo-autobiographical aspects of both works adopt a common paradigm, as the narration creates an opposition of then and now, of pre- and post-conversion, a

---

[3] *Inferno*, 27.26–27.

[4] Ascent / descent as a traditional pattern of conversion familiar in Christian doctrine and its application to the narrative structure of the *Commedia* was considered at length by Charles Singleton, "In Exitu Israel de Aegypto," *78th Annual Report of the Dante Society* (1960): 1–24. See also John Freccero, "Dante's Pilgrim in a Gyre," *PMLA* 76 (1961): 168–81.

[5] Charles T. Davis has written extensively on this duality. In "Rome and Babylon in Dante," in *Rome in the Renaissance: The City and the Myth*, ed. P.A. Ramsay, MRTS 18 (Binghamton, NY: Medieval & Renaissance Texts and Studies, 1982), 19–40, he explores both the negative figure of Rome as the corrupt and evil "Babylon" of pagandom and the positive figure of Rome as the eventual new Jerusalem. For an even more extensive treatment of Rome in the *Commedia* see also idem, *Dante and the Idea of Rome* (Oxford: Clarendon Press, 1957). Similarly, Rocco Montano notes that for Dante the earthly ideal represented by "Rome," or the earthly city with its *humana civilitas*, and the heavenly Jerusalem are not inconsistent: Rocco Montano, "Italian Humanism: Dante and Petrarch," *Italica* 50 (1973): 205–21.

structure adapted by Dante from the *nunc et tunc* model of St. Augustine's *Confessions* and, just as likely, from the story of St. Paul.

Before turning to the ascent-descent pattern, it should be noted as well that in many respects these structures interact in *La Ciociara* as in the *Commedia* in such a way that the binary opposition inherent in each becomes typologically linked to the others. Not only then does Moravia absorb many of the emblematic significative paradigms of the *Commedia*, but he also absorbs its hermeneutic methodology; that is, the use of types to explicate a larger allegorical significance. Accordingly, we shall see that as the ascent-descent pattern serves as a catalyst for conversion, it is at the same time intimately linked to the autobiographical stance of then and now, and provides, as well, the physical setting for the spiritual journey away from a Rome that has become Babylon, and back to a "Rome where Christ is a Roman,"[6] a New Jerusalem.

Structurally Dante's journey and that of *La Ciociara* both start with a species of proem, an overture as it were, in which the basic elements of the journey are set out, almost as a foreshadowing or a "mini-commedia" that will educate the reader as to the structure of the journey to come. In this way, the opening cantos of the *Commedia* function much in the same way as the prose introductions and explications that surround the poetry of *La Vita Nuova* inasmuch as Dante sets up the poem by telling us what inspired it and what it means, *vida* and *razon* all wrapped up into one. So too do Cesira's opening chapters function almost as a "mini-*La Ciociara*." Cesira describes her earlier youth and transformation, her youthful journey from Ciociaria to Rome. But now, like Dante, she is thirty-five years old, therefore in "the middle of the road of our life."[7] This midpoint functions as a fulcrum or turning point, as Cesira descends into a coal cellar with an acquaintance and there suffers a sexual indignity. This event is presented as a species of *discesa agli inferi*,[8] as, reflecting on it, Cesira makes the statement "e una volta che si cambiano le abitudini, la vita diventa un inferno e noialtri tanti diavoli scatenati."[9] Still later, thinking about the encounter in the coal cellar she further states, "quel giorno soffrii le pene dell'inferno." [10]

In the opening chapters there is still another prefiguration of descent as Cesira and Rosetta descend into the darkness of an air raid shelter and hear premonitions of sexual indignity to be suffered by Rosetta. In light of this

---

[6] "quella Roma onde Cristo è romano": *Purgatorio* 32.102.

[7] "Nel mezzo del cammin di nostra vita": *Inferno* 1.1.
Psalm 90:10 states "The days of our lives are seventy years." Dante, in following this tradition, identifies his age by placing himself in the middle of that span.

[8] For the structural significance of the *discesa* in the narrative of the *Commedia*, see especially Amilcare Iannucci, *Forma ed Evento nella Divina Commedia* (Rome: Bulzoni, 1984), chap. 2, "La discesa di Beatrice agli inferi."

[9] Alberto Moravia, *La Ciociara* (Milan: Bompiani, 1957), 26.

[10] Moravia, *La Ciociara*, 27.

degradation and its possibility, Cesira talks of escaping, of ascending the slopes of her native Ciociaria, of how she and Rosetta will climb its terraced landscape and escape the war and find respite before safely returning to Rome, not that Rome that has become a Babylon, but rather a Rome cleansed and safe from war. Only then does the real story start.

The descent proper then begins as Cesira and Rosetta board a train to leave Rome. Like the sinners of the *Inferno*, they are crammed together, not, however, into boats but rather into train carriages, but the imagery is the same, as masses of people are crammed together like beasts being taken to slaughter: "Stavano ammucchiati nei corridoi e negli scompartimenti, come bestie che vengono portate al macello."[11] Just as Dante uses the trope of sleep or unconsciousness to effect some of his most substantial transitions, so too does Moravia employ this conceit. As the train pulls out of Rome to take her and her daughter to the countryside, as the Germans on board the train sing their national anthem, Cesira is overcome by an intense desire to sleep. And she does. The first chapter closes with a simple statement, "Quindi mi addormentai."[12] When Cesira awakens at the beginning of the next chapter, it is in an *inferno* that she finds herself: "Dentro il vagone, adesso, dal caldo quasi non respirava."[13] The train, however, will go no farther. The passengers must get out even though they have not yet reached their desired destination. The trainman functions like Charon forcing the sinners out onto a hostile shore: "Dovete scendere."[14] The women are thirsty but the drinking fountain doesn't work. Exhausted and speechless, "la gola arsa, stanche e ammutolite,"[15] they finally arrive on foot in Fondi. The town is empty, as if decimated by plague: "Sembrava di camminare per una città in cui tutti gli abitanti fossero morti per qualche epidemia."[16] And there is, worst of all, no one to take them up into the mountains. Instead they fall into the company of a family of thieves, Vincenzo and Concetta. Here they are lied to, threatened, bitten by insects, fed half-rotten swill, and made to live surrounded by human waste. As Thomas Erling Peterson has pointed out, "those encountered in the mountains are often reminiscent of the *Divine Comedy*, in which the eternal landscapes feature isolated individuals who reveal, for better or worse, their moral identities and destinies."[17] Yet while the infernal similarities are rather obvious to a reader of Dante, Moravia ensures that such affinities are explicit as Cesira observes, "La guerra è dappertutto,"[18] reminding the reader of Dante's characterization of Hell

---

[11] Moravia, *La Ciociara*, 42.
[12] Moravia, *La Ciociara*, 44.
[13] Moravia, *La Ciociara*, 45.
[14] Moravia, *La Ciociara*, 48.
[15] Moravia, *La Ciociara*, 50.
[16] Moravia, *La Ciociara*, 50.
[17] T.E. Peterson, *Alberto Moravia* (New York: Twayne, 1996), 77.
[18] Moravia, *La Ciociara*, 75.

as war.[19] For Dante Hell is war, and for Cesira war is Hell. Finally, though, there seems to be an end to this hell as Cesira decides she must leave. What happens as Cesira and Rosetta start their ascent is a fascinating fusion of a number of images culled from, or at very least evocative of, the opening cantos of *Purgatorio*. As Dante and Virgil arrive in Purgatory in the first rays of morning, so too do Cesira and Rosetta start out at morning's first light. Suddenly an airplane appears, as Cesira says, "con una velocità da non si dire."[20] It comes straight at the women as Cesira throws herself and her daughter to the ground into a ditch. The moment is eerily like that of *Purgatorio* 2 as the angel boatman arrives "un lume per lo mar venir sì ratto."[21] So too does the quick dive into the ditch recall the quick genuflection of Dante and Virgil as they are forced to their knees, but the image is revised by Moravia; this is no celestial *nocchiero*. Instead the pilot shoots at Cesira and her daughter. They survive, certainly, but the reader now realizes that the purgatorial process of *La Ciociara* may be considerably more fraught with danger than Dante's was. Moreover, in Moravia's hands the start of purgation is fused also with the last moments of Dante's *Inferno*, suggesting that it is difficult to say where one experience ends and the other begins. This fusion also prepares us for the lack of the easy compartmentalization seen in Dante's narrative structure, suggesting—as we shall see later—that it is not such a simple thing to leave the war completely behind. The moment with the airplane is also suggestive of the nadir of the *Inferno*. As Cesira and Rosetta dive into the ditch we see they have descended as low as they can and now must take a new direction, just as Dante's pilgrim had to turn on Satan's hairy haunch before starting his purgatorial ascent. Moravia confirms the new direction as his pilgrims reach a fork in the road. It seems they might actually be able to start on a new trajectory and ascend the mountain with its terraced landscape to which Moravia makes specific reference. The start of the Purgatorial climb is also confirmed by the appearance of a Cato-like figure. While Cesira's gatekeeper bears considerably less resemblance to Moses[22] than did Dante's *portiere*, Moravia does allude to this aspect of Cato's presence in describing Tommasino:

---

[19] *Inferno*, 2.3–4.

[20] Moravia, *La Ciociara*, 74.

[21] *Purgatorio*, 2.17.

[22] Robert Hollander notes this resemblance, stating, "Cato the guardian of Purgatory, is presented (cantos I and II) in ways that portray him as the pagan antitype of Moses": Robert Hollander, *Dante: A Life in Works* (New Haven: Yale University Press, 2001), 102. Dante's description of Cato, "un veglio solo, / degno di tanta reverenza in vista" (*Purgatorio* 1.31–33), recalls Moses the patriarch in its insistence on his venerability. More particularly, Dante's description of Cato bears a striking resemblance, in particular, to the biblical descriptions of Moses after his ascent of Mt. Sinai ("Lunga la barba e di pel bianco mista / portava, a' suoi capelli simigliante, / de' quai cadeva al petto doppia lista. / Li raggi de le quattro luci sante / fregiavan sì la sua faccia di lume, / ch'i' 'l vedea come

Alla fine, ecco, all'angolo della strada spuntare un uomo che camminava piano mangiando un'arancia. Riconobbi subito Tommasino che rassomigliava tale e quale un ebreo del ghetto, con il viso lungo, la barba di una settimana, il naso ricurvo, gli occhi a fior di pelle e il passo strasciato coi piedi in fuori. [23]

Like Dante and Virgil,[24] Rosetta and Cesira are pilgrims who admit they do not know where to go, "non sappiamo dove andare,"[25] and the festive atmosphere that pervades Rosetta's and Cesira's first encounter with the other refugees and mountain folk equally recalls that moment in the opening cantos of *Purgatorio* where Dante, Casella, and the new arrivals sing and linger on the shores. But the lighthearted mood is short-lived and the arduous days soon begin.

Indeed, the next portion of the book deals with the seemingly endless days and the genuine purgation of the various sins of the refugees. They are hungry. They are tired. And they are afraid. The process does work, however, as they eventually do learn what things have value. The purgatorial aspects of the sojourn are signaled by the textual cues sprinkled throughout the narrative. As a plundered family screams, their groans are described as "come da un Purgatorio." Similarly, the starving *contadini* stooped over and picking chicory weed for survival are described as "gente che se ne andava a testa curva, passo passo come tante anime di purgatorio,"[26] recalling the souls of the prideful in *Purgatorio* 11.

This purgation, however, is not followed by a further and more immediate ascent, as in the case of the *Commedia*. Cesira does backslide, figuratively, and venture back down into the valley. Such descents recall Dante's own occasional backward glances in *Purgatorio* and the continual warning against such retrospection. Indeed, as Janice Kozma points out, whenever Cesira "descends that mountain, bad things happen to her."[27] Rather the final ascent, the journey to a celestial Rome, the reward for the purgative process, is not yet fulfilled. The dome of St. Peter's beckons, but we, the readers, are not privy to what this new heaven may be, of what this post-apocalyptic City of God is constituted. The city of Rome and its dual capacity as heaven and hell, Babylon and Jerusalem, both prison and Promised Land, are nonetheless deeply entrenched in the narrative of

---

l sol fosse davante": *Purgatorio* 1.34–39. *Cf.* Exodus 34:30: "Now it was so, when Moses came down from Mount Sinai (and the two tablets of the Testimony were in Moses' hand when he came down from the mountain,) that Moses did not know that the skin of his face shone, and they were afraid to come near him."

[23] Moravia, *La Ciociara*, 78.

[24] "Voi credete / forse che siamo esperti d'esto loco; / ma noi siam peregrin come voi siete": *Purgatorio*, 2.61–63.

[25] Moravia, *La Ciociara*, 78.

[26] Moravia, *La Ciociara*, 257.

[27] Janice M. Kozma, *The Architecture of Imagery in Alberto Moravia's Fiction* (Chapel Hill: University of North Carolina Press, 1993), 82.

Moravia's classic. For Cesira, Rome is the city that she came to as a young girl. Rome for Cesira is not necessarily her first home, just as for Dante it was not, but once she is up in the mountains suffering her purgation, Rome becomes idealized in her mind and, as the war ends, so too can she return to Rome. Now, however, it is not the Rome of shopkeepers and black markets to which she returns but rather Rome of the martyrs, Christian Rome, again to quote Beatrice: "quella Roma onde Cristo è romano."[28] As she and Rosetta finally approach Rome after their ordeal, Cesira says:

> Finalmente, ecco apparire in fondo alla pianura distesa e verde, una lunga striscia di colore incerto, tra il bianco e il giallo; i sobborghi di Roma. E dietro questa striscia, sovrastandola, grigia sullo sfondo del cielo grigio, lontanissima, eppure chiara, la cupola di San Pietro. Dio sa se avevo sperato durante tutto l'anno di rivedere, laggiù all'orizzonte, quella cara cupola, così piccola e al tempo stesso così grande da potere essere quasi scambiata per un accidente del terreno, per una collina o una montagnola; . . . Laggiù, in fondo all'orizzonte quella cupola mi diceva che io potevo ormai tornare fiduciosa a casa.[29]

And while the return is presented as prospective, the refugees have been made ready for the final ascent by the purgation process. The process is directly linked to the paradigm of the *Commedia*. As Cesira and Rosetta start to walk again along the path of their own life ("avevamo ripreso a camminare nella nostra vita")[30] the reader cannot help thinking of the "cammin di nostra vita." Cesira refers to this path as "full of obscurities and errors" ("piena di oscurità e di errore")[31] but notes that she has a new confidence, and that she and Rosetta, turned into a thief and a prostitute by the horrors of war, had been saved by "dolore," pain or sorrow, and now could return to Rome, cleansed and transformed.[32]

The agent of this transformation, however, is not simply *dolore*, the pain of purgation. Rather both women have had a guiding hand along the way. Rosetta, the childlike daughter, puts her faith in the Madonna and continually attributes their salvation to her intervention. For Cesira, who is admittedly not very

---

[28] *Purgatorio*, 32.102.
[29] Moravia, *La Ciociara*, 413.
[30] Moravia, *La Ciociara*, 414.
[31] Moravia, *La Ciociara*, 414.
[32] "e per qualche tempo eravamo state morte anche noi due, Rosetta e io, morte alla pietà che si deve agli altri e a se stessi. Ma il dolore ci aveva salvate [. . .] poiché, grazie al dolore, eravamo alla fine, uscite dalla guerra che ci chiudeva nella sua tomba di indifferenza e di malvagità ed avevamo ripreso a camminare nella nostra vita, la quale era forse una povera cosa piena di oscurità e di errore, ma purtroppo la sola che dovessimo vivere, come senza dubbio Michele ci avrebbe detto se fosse stato con noi": Moravia, *La Ciociara*, 414.

religious, the guide is the enigmatic asexual intellectual Michele. Michele "constantly berates the various characters for their deliberate moral blindness to the implications of war, a blindness which results in them being dead"[33] and reinforces the Dantesque nature of the landscape when on two occasions he specifically refers to Dante.[34] Moreover, Michele's narrative significance is not confined to the literal level but extends into the allegorical, as he is revealed, after his execution by Nazi soldiers, as (befitting his name) a species of archangel. His power to save souls even from the depths of Hell is made clear when Michele appears to Cesira in a vision as she attempts to end her own life. Just as Beatrice descends into Hell to save Dante, revealing her special role in his salvation, so too is Michele's salvific role revealed by his own trajectory of ascent and descent.

It is Michele, but more importantly, the death of Michele that spurs the conversion recounted in the first-person narrative of *La Ciociara*. Cesira's story is rife with examples of temporal indicators that make it clear to the reader that the narrator knows how the story will end, that this is a recollection of events that have already seen their culmination. Cesira, the Roman shopkeeper, talks continually about then and now: before and after the death of her husband, before she came to Rome, before the war happened and before the war ended, but it is clear that the story is over before Cesira begins narrating it. It is this detachment from the past that is essential to the narrative stance that Moravia, in the person of Cesira, assumes. In many respects this stance reflects Moravia's own temporal detachment from his wartime experiences[35] and at the same time links it also to Dante's narrative stance. The existence and importance of this temporal detachment is expressed through Cesira's frequent addresses to the reader. Cesira understands the importance of explaining the "tunc" so as to properly contextualize the "nunc."

> Ho voluto raccontare questa preghiera soprattutto per dare un'idea del carattere di Rosetta chi finora no ho descritto. Poiché, in seguito, a causa della guerra, questo carattere cambiò dal giorno alla notte, voglio adesso dire come'era Rosetta allora. . .[36]

---

[33] Jan Kozma-Southall, "Omen and Image: Presage and Sacrifice in Moravia's *La Ciociara*," *Italica* 61 (1984): 207–19, here 217.

[34] In his encounters with both English and German soldiers, Michele makes reference to Dante. In the latter encounter Michele specifically cites Dante (sic): "E cortesia fu in lui esser villano," (Moravia, *La Ciociara*, 228) (N.B.: The actual quotation is "e cortesia fu lui esser villano," *Inferno* 33.150.)

[35] Soon after Moravia's return to Rome following his exile in Ciociaria, he began to write. "I invented the character of Cesira and typed out about eighty pages, I believe, then I stopped because I didn't seem to have enough contemplative distance, let us say, from the events which I wanted to narrate." It was ten years before he returned to complete the novel: Peterson, *Alberto Moravia*, 75.

[36] Moravia, *La Ciociara*, 112.

And while the "nunc et tunc" is not invasive to the extent of becoming overly obvious in its foreshadowing,[37] it points to a hermeneutic strategy common to the *Commedia* in which early events will be made clear by subsequent events. In particular, the eventual rape of Rosetta creates a death of sorts, a cataclysmic event that signals, shockingly, a death of the innocence of the past. An innocence that is now revealed as myopic reminds the reader of the blindness of Dante's sinners and penitents who were blind but now can see. In service of this trope Moravia uses a device that is disturbing to his readers, for whom it is difficult to imagine a rape as having any possible positive circumstances, but to understand the impact of this we can look to several classical sources. In the myth of Demeter and Persephone, the daughter's maturation and independence has its genesis in her rape and descent into the underworld. Dominique Fernandez also notes the rebirth signaled by the rape in *La Ciociara*, observing that "[l']esperienza del sesso si confonde con l'esperienza cosmica, ancestrale della natura, e fa di Rosetta un essere umano completo, compiuto."[38] Within the political allegory of *La Ciociara* (which quite properly provides the basis for a study in itself) Rosetta may be seen as representative of the next generation, forced through violence to relinquish the blindness and apathy of the past, but also for whom innocence has been replaced with knowledge.[39] Within the history of Rome, it is the rape of Lucretia that spurs the overthrow of the Tarquin kings. Similarly, the rape and the subsequent conversion it occasions is also reminiscent of the events recounted in Augustine's *City of God* in which the destruction of Rome, in many ways, paves the way for the Babylon of Revelation to become the New Jerusalem. *Ex malo bonum* indeed! It is not then insignificant that a seventeenth-century book of emblems represents the notion of *ex malo bonum* by a rose being plucked.[40] Within this context

---

[37] Kozma-Southall traces the deft foreshadowing of the rape of Rosetta, pointing to the construction on Moravia's part of an extended metaphor in which Rosetta is likened to a goat, preparing the reader for the sacrificial role that she assumes as a victim of sexual violence: Kozma-Southall, "Omen and Image, 207–19.

[38] Dominique Fernandez, *Il romanzo italiano e la crisi della coscienza moderna* (Milan: Lerici, 1960), 92.

[39] Joan Ross and Donald Freed see the pre-rape Rosetta as symbolizing "modern Italy before she was ravished by the fascists and subjected to the terrors of war": Joan Ross and Donald Freed, *The Existentialism of Alberto Moravia* (Carbondale: Southern Illinois University Press, 1972), 140.

[40] Georgette de Montenay's *Cent emblemes chrestiens* shows a woman picking up her skirt as a rose is plucked, with the following accompanying text:

Spina rosam educit placido durissima vere / Cùm trahit incuruo taurus aratra iugo: / Quod peccant homines, iustisque pijsque saluti, / Nomen & est semper auctius inde Dei. / On tire bien des espines poignantes / Rose tres bonne & pleine de beauté. / Des reprouvez & leurs œuures meschantes / Dieu tire aussi du bien par sa bonté, / Faisant seruir leur fausse volonté / A sa grand' gloire & salut des esleuz, / Et par iustice, ainsi qu'a decreté, / Dieu fait tout bien: que nul n'en doute plus.

it is possible also then to see the moment as linked to an even earlier moment in Roman history, the so-called "rape of the Sabines," a violent event comprised of theft and sexual assault that nonetheless allowed a city to grow. It is not, however, so much that Moravia explicitly cites these traditions so much as that his setting, Lazio, is also suggestive of the beginnings of Rome, a Rome that Virgil, Dante's own guide, knew well. Cesira's story takes place within a context that is not only personally relevant but also one with substantially broader significance, a charged background as it were. The Dantesque landscape thus fuses with the Virgilian as "quella dolce terra" and provides a polysemous backdrop, one that constantly recalls the many traditions and the literary heritage that give significance to the shape and events of Cesira's voyage. Moravia thus uses a backdrop already associated with journeys of salvation and regeneration. As the Dantesque landscape encompasses both Aeneas' and Paul's journeys, Moravia is able to exploit these paradigms as well as the violent history of Rome to paint Cesira and Rosetta as pilgrims on their way to Rome, pioneers forging a new foundation[41] and martyrs whose suffering will give way to conversion.

At the same time, Moravia's first-person narrative lends immediate authenticity to the war experience, but it also provided a larger link to the Dantesque project of exile and wandering and the perspective such experience engenders. In Dante's case the pronouncement of exile creates a narrative stance that allows him to look back and survey that which was and distinguish it from that which is. The cataclysm of his expulsion from Florence effects a reassessment of his former life not only spiritually and politically but also in terms of his literary project. Like Dante's story, the story of the two women presents a travelogue of the author's own journey of purgation and a highly personal record of the changes wrought by the challenges and suffering engendered by that journey. In 1943 Alberto Moravia tried to escape to Naples, but, unable to cross the frontier, fled with his wife Elsa Morante into the mountains of Ciociaria.[42] For Moravia, his exile in the mountains marked the end of one literary period and the start of another, and shaped his own view of the collective suffering of his fellow Italians.

Georgette de Montenay, *Cent emblemes chrestiens* (Heidelberg: Lancellotti & Cambieri, 1602), 66.

[41] This regenerative aspect has been noted by Peterson, who proposes that Moravia's major works of the 1950s including *La Ciociara* "were based on a representation of an Italy whose hopes for national rebirth lay in the people": Peterson, *Alberto Moravia*, 57.

[42] Moravia had written in 1941 a comic parody of the Mussolini government, *La Mascherata*, and attacked fascism in his articles in *Il Popolo di Roma*, and was in danger of being arrested. Banned from publishing under Mussolini, he emerged after World War II. He went into hiding in the peasant community in Fondi, near Cassino, until the Allied liberation. In 1944 he started to write *Two Women*, but returned to the work ten years later, when he had gained more distance from his own experiences.

While the experience could not help coloring his postwar writing,[43] it is his absorption of the Dantesque model with its echoes of a Virgilian national mythology that is most effective in extending the significance of one woman's (or rather Moravia's story) story to that of an entire generation. The pseudo-autobiographical function of *La Ciociara* then is similar to that of the *Commedia* as it links the pilgrim's story to a larger collective. Just as Dante claims he is neither Paul nor Aeneas, but is, in essence, a fusion of both, Cesira and Rosetta also become both, retracing in many ways the journeys of Paul from blindness to a more enlightened sight and eventually to Rome, and like Aeneas, traversing a landscape over which his shipwrecked survivors trod.[44] Rome, the eternal city and paradigm of conversion, the goal of both Paul's and Aeneas's journeys, is ultimately the terminus of both journeys: Cesira's, whose name evokes, if only like a distant whisper, Rome of the Caesars, and of Rosetta whose name recalls the purity of the Christian rose. These two women encapsulate both the ancient imperial and the converted Christian Rome. But both cities are damaged, and the women return to a Rome anxious to be remade once more, to go further still beyond Dante's celestial Rome where Christ is a Roman. This is still another Rome—not the Rome of Aeneas, not the Rome of Paul, but one that sits in the future, a distant chimera on an ancient hill.

What then is the point of this absorption? Kozma has noted that Moravia consistently uses metaphors and similes pivotal to his plot structure in such a way that without some awareness of the centrality of the metaphor we cannot fully understand the story. She concludes, "The figurative and the literal are one for Moravia."[45] Moravia thus uses the Dantesque landscape of Ciociaria to create an extended metaphor the centrality of which is essential to understanding that the story of *La Ciociara* is not only one of purgation and the conversion it effects but also one of regeneration on a grander national scale. In adopting the Dantesque landscape as the central motif, Moravia has also absorbed all that Dante's

---

[43] About the effects of this exile, Ross and Freed conclude: "A putative social critic, he was forced to flee Rome and the Fascists, not underground as his French colleagues, not into politics, but into exile, into the primitive Italian mountains. In this moral fastness he lived with the poorest of the poor, and his body of work since those days is never untouched—disguised in a hundred ways though it is—by that season of danger": Ross and Freed, *The Existentialism of Alberto Moravia*, 5–6.

As Peterson points out, "Alberto and Elsa had been poor and persecuted during the war; though the success of *The Woman of Rome* began to remedy this, the reality of that experience was transferred into the novels they now wrote": Peterson, *Alberto Moravia*, 56.

[44] Jan Kozma observes both the conversional and regenerative aspects of the journey but does not draw a link to any particular literary or hagiographical source when she states "*La Ciociara* is the story of Cesira's journey from blindness and 'death' to enlightenment and 'rebirth'": Kosma-Southall, "Omen and Image," 218.

[45] Kozma, *The Architecture of Imagery*, 81.

landscape had in turn absorbed, that is, its associations with the Virgilian mythologies of Rome and the Pauline conversion from pagan to Christian capital.

Moreover, the appropriation of the Dantesque landscape and its exploitation as the central vessel of meaning in Moravia's novel underline the enduring significative potential of the *Commedia*. It is tempting to suggest that Moravia has merely looked to archetypal imagery in his creation of Cesira's mountain, or even that the mountain setting is merely logical in a story about a "Ciociara." But such a response is facile and ignores the many indications in Moravia's narrative strategies that we are to link Cesira's story to Dante's. It also ignores that great tradition of Italian intertextuality and contextuality that pervades the national corpus, and more specifically the enormous presence of the *Commedia* throughout Italian literature and in Moravia's own literary project.[46] Put more succinctly, as an Italian author, Moravia "knows where he comes from and he feels deeply his continuity with Dante."[47] As Peterson has pointed out, Moravia's postwar literature looked more to the literature of Dante than it did to modern writers in his quest for a new "national popular literature."[48] Indeed, the *Commedia's* empathetic treatment of those displaced by political conflict and its attempt to make sense of the exile's suffering, moreover, makes it an ideal source for the extended metaphor of *La Ciociara*. But more importantly, Dante's story, like Cesira's, is the story of one but also the story of many,[49] of those who know how salt is the taste of another man's bread and how hard is the way up his stairs.[50]

It is a testament then to the enduring quality of the *Commedia* that in this modern era, in which the global community witnesses mass migrations as a result of wars and political conflict, the story of Everyman continues to provide an adaptable paradigm for purgation and an apt template for reconciliation, not only for two women but for entire nations.

---

[46] Peterson notes that Moravia has made "countless references" in his fiction to the inherited Italian literary tradition, particularly that of the poets Dante, Petrarch, Tasso, and Leopardi: Peterson, *Alberto Moravia*, 147.

[47] Ross and Freed, *The Existentialism of Alberto Moravia*, 10.

[48] "Myths—as used by the decadents and postdecadents—were irrational and destructive. Yet could not one counter the myths of a Nietzsche, a d'Annunzio, or a Pavese—with their incumbent 'neonaturalism'—with a myth of the nations whose oppressed citizens sought to regain their dignity? Might not a search of the past avoid the atavistic drives of regressive passion so as to recover a material culture and language long suppressed (as found in Dante and Boccaccio, for example)?": Peterson, *Alberto Moravia*, 58.

[49] Peterson notes that Moravia's postwar novels attest to "a sense of common struggle undertaken in the face of war, a calamity of universal proportions": Peterson, *Alberto Moravia*, 57.

[50] In *Paradiso* 17, Dante's ancestor Cacciaguida prophesies Dante's exile thus: "Tu proverai sì come sa di sale / lo pane altrui, e come è duro calle / lo scendere e 'l salire per l'altrui scale": *Paradiso*, 17.58–60.

Section IV

Studies on the Italian Middle Ages (Thirteenth and Fourteenth Centuries)

The Portrayal of Falconry in Encyclopedic Literature: The Sport Meets the Scholar

Teresa Gualtieri-Clark

Although keeping tamed hawks for recreational hunting is a practice that goes back thousands of years in the Middle East and the steppes of Eastern Europe, and although falconry was practiced for food hunting on occasion in the Greco-Roman world, it truly finds its niche as a typical pastime of the nobility of Western Europe under the conditions of the feudal system.[1] The feudal nobility have capital, leisure time, and land in abundance—exactly the qualities needed for recreational hunting.[2] In addition, during the Crusades, the contact of Western nobility with the Islamic world brings the expertise, practices, and treatises of Arab falconers to Europe. The westerners, who enthusiastically embrace this hobby, write many treatises of their own, culminating in the *De arte venandi cum avibus* written by Emperor Frederick II.[3]

---

[1] This article is a re-edited excerpt from the first chapter of my dissertation, written under the aegis of our esteemed honoree Dr. Christopher Kleinhenz. The chapter in its entirety covers the appearance of birds of prey and the sport of falconry in literature from the ancient world, medieval encyclopedias and bestiaries, falconry manuals, Arabic texts, and English, French, and Provençal vernacular literature: Teresa Gualtieri, "Birds of Prey and the Sport of Falconry in Italian Literature through the Fourteenth Century: From Serving Love to Served for Dinner" (Ph.D. diss., University of Wisconsin-Madison, 2005), 14–28.

[2] See Robin Oggins, "Falconry and Medieval Social Status," *Medievalia* 12 (1989): 43–55: "In modern sociological terms, . . . falconry was an almost perfect example of conspicuous consumption: it was expensive, time-consuming, and useless (as its purpose was not for acquiring food), and in all three respects it served to set its practitioners apart as a class."

[3] An edition with excellent notes and commentary is Frederick II, *The Art of Falconry, Being the De Arte Venandi Cum Avibus of Frederick II of Hohenstaufen*, ed. Casey A. Wood and F. Marjorie Fyfe (Stanford: Stanford University Press, 1943). From slightly

The growth of the special role that falcons and hawks have in society can be seen in their increasing inclusion in types of texts whose earlier incarnations omitted them or had merely cursory comments. Such is the case with encyclopedic literature and bestiaries, whose sections on falcons and hawks grow and multiply with the parallel growth of popularity in the sport and its accompanying how-to treatises.[4] This paper examines the treatment of birds of prey in encyclopedic literature with a view towards determining the position of falconry in the intellectual and literary culture of medieval Italy. I will also make reference to falconry treatises and bestiaries because of their involvement with encyclopedic literature in the area of falconry; however, for reasons of space, I omit a detailed discussion here. Falconry treatises and bestiaries are treated in full in the dissertation from which the bulk of this paper derives.[5]

Although they begin as two separate genres, in the later Middle Ages encyclopedic works and bestiaries see their boundaries blur. By the time of the appearance of bestiaries in vernacular languages, in the late twelfth and early thirteenth centuries, encyclopedic text relating to animals has found its way into bestiary material, and vice versa. In the particular case of birds of prey, a third genre of instructional text, falconry treatises, is also involved in this cross-contamination. Prompted by the emergence of falconry as a sport for the nobility, the existence of this last genre causes entries in late encyclopedic works for falcons and hawks to be quite different from those for other animals, in that they include instructions for care.

By far the most influential encyclopedic source of material on hawks is Isidore of Seville's *Etymologiae*, copied often by authors of late medieval bestiaries. This seventh-century bishop's information on the *accipiter*, or hawk, is derived largely from the classical tradition. His account is as follows:

> Accipiter avis animo plus armata quam ungulis, virtutem maiorem in minore corpore gestans. Hic ab accipiendo, id est a capiendo, nomen sumpsit.

---

later we now have Egidius of Aquino (attr.), *Liber avium viventium de rapina*, ed. F. Capaccioni (Tumhout: Brepols, 2008).

[4] Robin Oggins has found that that falcons and hawks start to make their presence felt in bestiaries and encyclopedic works around the time of the Crusades, owing to the increased contact with the Arab world, where the sport had been popular for centuries. Oggins has done extensive research on the development of falconry as a noble sport in England, and on its place in European society in general. See Oggins, "Albertus Magnus on Falcons and Hawks," in *Albertus Magnus and the Sciences* (Toronto: Pontifical Institute of Mediaeval Studies, 1980), 441–62; idem, "Falconry and Medieval Social Status" and "Falconry and Medieval Views of Nature," in *The Medieval World of Nature*, ed. Joyce E. Salisbury (New York and London: Garland, 1993), 47–60; and idem, *The Kings and Their Hawks: Falconry in Medieval England* (New Haven and London: Yale University Press, 2004).

[5] See Gualtieri, "Birds of Prey and the Sport of Falconry," 14–17, 28–33.

> Est enim avis rapiendis aliis avibus avida, ideoque vocatur accipiter, hoc est raptor. Unde et Paulus Apostolus dicit: "Sustenetis enim, si quis accipit"; ut enim diceret "si quis rapit", dixit "si quis accipit". Fertur autem accipitres circa pullos suos impios esse; nam dum viderint eos posse tentare volatus, nullas eis praebent escas, sed verberant pinnis et a nido praecipitant atque a tenero compellunt ad praedam, ne forte adulti pigrescant.[6]

Hrabanus Maurus, in his ninth-century *De naturis rerum*, repeats Isidore's statements, but adds to them Christian allegorical significance:

> Accipiter interdum sanctum virum significat, utpote rapiens regnum dei. De quo scriptum est in Job: *Nunquid in sapientia tua plumescit accipiter expandens alas suas ad austrum?* (*Job.* XXXIX) id est, nunquid cuilibet electo tu intelligentiam contulisti, ut flante sancto Spiritu cogitationum alas expandat, quatenus pondera vetustae conversationis abjiciat, et virtutum plumas in usum novi volatus sumat. Potest etiam per hunc accipitrem renovata gentilitas designari.[7]

This type of interpretation of animal behavior is typical of the *Physiologus* and its related bestiaries;[8] however, Hrabanus's commentary is unique among Latin allegorizing texts of his era in including hawks.

Encyclopedic literature of the twelfth century and later often includes hawks and falcons, with anecdotes about the birds' behavior, regularly

---

[6] Isidore of Seville, *Etymologiae* 12.7 55–56 (PL 82. 466–467). Florence McCulloch provides this translation: "The hawk is armed more with determination than with claws, having great courage in a small body. Its name comes from *accipiendo*, 'taking', related to *capiendo*, 'seizing', for it is a bird which snatches greedily from other birds. On that account they call it *accipiter*, that is, a 'robber'. . . . The hawk is said to be harsh with its young for when it sees them able to fly, it gives them no food, but beats them with its wings and pushes them out of the nest. It thus forces them while young to seek prey lest by chance they become lazy adults": Florence McCulloch, *Mediaeval Latin and French Bestiaries* (Chapel Hill: University of North Carolina Press, 1960), 123.

[7] Rabanus Maurus, "De universo libri XXII," in PL 111. 253–54; translation mine: "The hawk sometimes symbolizes a holy man, such as one that steals the kingdom of God. In fact, it is written in Job XXXIX: *Doth the hawk fly by thy wisdom, and stretch her wings toward the south?* Which means: Did you perhaps give intelligence to someone you chose so that under the inspiration of the Holy Spirit he may expand the wings of his thoughts while shedding the weight of the old way of life and take the feathers of virtue for a new flight? Also, the hawk may symbolize renewed gentility."

[8] The originator of the bestiary genre, the *Physiologus*, was written in Greek, most likely in Alexandria, around the third or fourth century A.D. The oldest extant Latin manuscripts of this work date to the eighth century, and can be divided into families according to their variations in content. See McCulloch, *Medieval Latin and French Bestiaries*, for a detailed discussion of the families into which the *Physiologus* descendants may be divided.

anthropomorphized, or information incorporated from falconry treatises. Three thirteenth-century texts that saw wide distribution are the encyclopedias of Thomas of Cantimpré, Vincent of Beauvais, and Bartholomaeus Anglicus.[9] Their entries on hawks and falcons are greatly expanded compared to those of the earlier encyclopedists. They include naturalist passages from Aristotle and Pliny,[10] and advice on caring for tame birds taken from various hunting manuals. However, here I would like to highlight the texts of four other encyclopedists who take diverse approaches to their treatment of birds of prey, thereby shedding light on the variety of ways in which these birds were viewed and used as exemplars in the late Middle Ages.

A twelfth-century text that takes a unique angle is the *De Naturis Rerum* of Alexander Neckam. His encyclopedia is distinguished by its lengthy fables, nearly to the exclusion of other manners of description. It lacks any allegorization of animal behavior, interpreting it instead in ways that teach everyday secular morality. He includes seven chapters (chapters twenty-four through thirty) on hawks and falcons, each of which tells a tale in which the birds act like humans, and from which humans can learn moral values.[11]

The first of these fables is of particular interest because it bears a clear relationship to a story that appears a century later in the anonymous Italian *Novellino*.[12] Neckam's human protagonist is an anonymous British king; in the *Novellino*, it is the famously falconry-crazed emperor Frederick II. In Neckam's version, the king is out hawking one day when one of his hawks is suddenly threatened by an eagle. The hawk escapes into a large basket full of lambs, but the eagle chases it, and gets its head stuck between the weaving of the basket. The hawk takes this opportunity to kill the eagle. A debate is had among the nobles and other dignitaries to decide what is to be done with the victorious hawk: should it be recognized for bravery or should it be punished? While others determine that the hawk should be rewarded, the king declares that the hawk should be hanged for having killed its own master, the eagle, a "royal" bird, as an example of what might happen to traitors among his own people. The moral of this story,

---

[9] Thomas Cantimpratensis, *Liber de natura rerum* (Berlin and New York: Walter De Gruyter, 1973); Vincentius Bellovacensis, *Speculum naturale* (Graz: Akademische Druck- und Verlagsanstalt, 1964); Bartholomaeus Anglicus, *De genuinis rerum coelestium, terrestrium et inferiarum proprietatibus, libri XVIII* (Frankfurt: Wolfgang Richter, 1650); ed. B. van den Abeele, 6 vols. (Turnhout: Brepols, 2007).

[10] Aristotle, *Historia animalium*, ed. and trans. D. M. Balme (Cambridge, MA: Harvard University Press, 1991), 8. 36. 309; Pliny, *Natural History*, trans. J. Bostock and H. Riley (London: H. G. Bohn, 1855), 10. 10.

[11] The following tales may be found in Alexander Neckam, *De naturis rerum*, ed. Thomas Wright (London: Longman, Green, Longman, Roberts, and Green, 1863), 75–82.

[12] *Novella* XC, in Joseph Consoli, ed., *The Novellino or One Hundred Ancient Tales* (New York and London: Garland Publishing, 1997), 116.

according to Neckam, is that it is necessary for the powerful to instill fear in their subjects, in order to hide the fear that they themselves have of their subjects.

This story makes several interesting cultural assumptions: first, that falconry is a typical noble pastime, a fact that would not have been true a couple of hundred years earlier; second, that there is a perceived hierarchy of birds that mirrors the hierarchy of feudal Europe, in which the ranking of an eagle above a hawk parallels the difference in status between the king and his nobles; third, that birds acting in ways really quite normal for their species—attack and defense—can be interpreted as having anthropomorphic emotions and motivations for their actions which permit them to be judged as if they were humans; and fourth, that this anthropomorphizing allows humans to learn moral truths from the birds' actions.

The *Novellino*'s version reflects exactly the same view of the role of hawks as exemplars in feudal society. Again, the hawk is hanged for killing its master, the eagle. The text is as follows:

> Lo'mperadore Federigo andava una volta a falcone et avevane uno molto sovrano kell'avea caro più d'una cittade. Lasciollo a una Grua quella montò alta. Il falcone si mise alto molto sopra lei. Videssi sotto una Guglia giovane percossella a terra e tanto la tenne kell'uccise. Lo'mperadore corse credendo ke fosse una Grua trovò come era. Allora con ira chiamò il Giustitiere e comandò kal falcone fosse tagliato il capo perkè avea morto lo suo Singniore.[13]

Instead of seizing the crane, as expected, the falcon attacks the eagle. To Frederick, who views both raptors according to their figurative significance, the eagle outranks the hawk. The bird hierarchy mirrors that in his own society, in which he himself is of the highest rank, like the eagle. He carries the image logically to its most extreme conclusion, executing the falcon as if it were a human traitor to its lord. Frederick uses the episode as an opportunity to provide an example of the sort of treatment that those who betray him might expect.

In Neckam's following tales, hawks and falcons are positive models for human morality and behavior. The next tale is a simple anecdote: in the cold season, Neckam tells, a hawk will catch a bird at night and keep it close in order to keep warm. In the morning, the hawk releases it unharmed, in return for its services.

---

[13] *The Novellino*, novella XC, translation mine: "The Emperor Frederick was out hunting with his falcon one day, and had a very fine one that he treasured more than a city. He flew it at a crane that ascended high into the sky. The falcon positioned itself even higher than the crane. Seeing a young eagle far below, the falcon attacked it, striking the eagle to the earth and holding it until it was dead. Believing that his falcon had caught the crane, the Emperor ran to the scene and found what had truly happened. Angry, he called the executioner and commanded that the falcon should be beheaded because it had killed its lord."

Neckam provides a few different interpretations for this action, contrary to the nature of a bird of prey; the one he prefers is that the hawk's deed derives from its sense of generosity and fairness. Nor does the hawk go to recapture the bird after releasing it, because of "memor nobilitatis propriae": its awareness of its own nobility.

Neckam also includes two instances in which humans are inspired to imitate the actions of falcons. He begins Chapter 26 by recognizing the useful role of both hawks and falcons in filling the larders of the upper class; he is the first encyclopedist to do so. Then he tells of a type of human entertainment that is derived from watching falcons: he states that the practice of jousting in tournaments was inspired by watching falcons pursue and catch their prey with marvelously agile dives.

In Chapter 27, he again tells of military maneuvers learned from birds. It is a story about two falcons, friends, who fight over territory with an eagle. Eventually, the eagle catches one of them alone and kills it. Depressed and defeated, its companion leaves the area. Elsewhere, it finds a wooden bridge with a falcon-sized hole in it that would make an excellent defense against the eagle. It plans revenge, practicing swooping into the hole until it is able to achieve great accuracy. It returns to harass the eagle that killed its companion. Unable to defeat the eagle and finding it necessary to flee, the falcon retreats cleverly into its wooden refuge where the eagle cannot reach.

Neckam praises the ties of friendship that bound the two falcons, comparing them to Patroclus and Achilles, and other legendary friends. He also relates that this occurrence was witnessed by a people that he calls the Rotomagi, who learned from it ideas on how to avoid the attacks of the Franks.[14]

Neckam's stories show that the interweaving of the lives of humans and those of hunting birds in both a literal and a figurative sense is very strong in the cultural fabric of his time. Indeed, the surge in popularity of the use of animals as human exemplars as well as the beginning of the writing of fables in vernacular languages can be traced to the twelfth century.[15] According to Joyce Salisbury, the twelfth century also provides the origin of the assignment to the animal kingdom of a social structure that mirrors that of human feudal society.[16] This association is quite clear in Neckam's text, and is evidence of the evolution of the late medieval view of hunting birds. Because they are fierce predators, they are representative of the ruling class, though still below the eagle; they represent

---

[14] The Rotomagi lived in Rotomagus, the ancient Roman name for the modern city of Rouen: S. A. Cook et al., eds., *Storia del mondo antico* (Cambridge and Milan: Cambridge University Press/Garzanti, 1974), 9: 635.

[15] For the history of the use of animals as human exemplars, see Joyce Salisbury, *The Beast Within* (New York and London: Routledge, 1994), esp. Chap. 4.

[16] Marie de France is cited as a particular innovator: see Salisbury, *The Beast Within*, 117 ff.

nobility also because they are partners in life with that class as well, central to the nobility's recreational activities. Because of this association, the actions of the birds of prey are seen as showing their strength of character, or inner nobility: hawks release birds that keep them warm, because *noblesse oblige*.

The association of falcons and hawks with the upper classes is taken to a new level by Hugh de Fouilloy, a twelfth-century Augustinian canon and the author of a work known as the *Aviarium*,[17] which is distinctive in that it treats only the characteristics of birds, excluding other animals. It was a popular text; there are seventy-eight extant manuscripts, more than half with a standardized program of illustration, two of these of early fourteenth-century Italian origin. Because of falconry's popularity in medieval life, Hugh, ever practical, endows the hawk with an exceptional spiritual significance.

The *Aviarium* is unique also in its structure. It is divided into two parts, the second of which is organized like a typical bestiary—one bird is discussed per chapter, with allegorical interpretation. The first part, however, consists of multi-chapter allegorical treatments of birds of particular interest, as well as of two trees, the cedar and the palm. The hawk receives seven chapters of attention, second only to the dove's eleven.

Hugh begins his book with two prologues in which he states his intention of structuring his work symbolically around the dove and the hawk. To understand why he did this it is helpful to know the circumstances under which the book was written. It was written for and on the prompting of a brother Rainier, surnamed *Corde Benignum*, who had been a knight before conversion to a religious life, where he would have been a lay-brother. Hugh may have written the text as a guide, both verbal and visual, to assist Rainier in the teaching of religion and morality to other, less educated lay-brothers.[18] Hugh compares himself to a dove, and Rainier, the former knight, to a hawk.[19] One represents the contemplative, the other the active life. Rainier's conversion to the religious life is likened to the taming of a hawk: Rainier has progressed from being a wild hawk that hunts domestic fowl into being a domesticated one that seizes wild birds, i.e. laymen, and brings them to conversion:

> Ecce in eadem pertica sedent accipiter et columba. Ego enim de clero, tu de militia. Ad conversionem venimus ut in regulari vita quasi in pertica

---

[17] Willene B. Clark, ed., *The Medieval Book of Birds: Hugh of Fouilloy's Aviarium*, MRTS 80 (Binghamton, NY: Medieval & Renaissance Texts and Studies, 1992).

[18] See Clark, *Aviarium*, as well as eadem,"The Illustrated Medieval Aviary and the Lay-Brotherhood," *Gesta* 21 (1982): 63–74.

[19] Clark notes that the dove and hawk as symbols of monk and knight are not exclusive to this text but are found in others as well (*Aviarium*, 2, n.1).

sedeamus; et qui rapere consueveras domesticas aves, nunc bonae operationis manu silvestres ad conversionem trahas, id est saeculares.[20]

In addition to the intriguing notion of the lay-brother/hawk doing good works by "capturing" sinners, the very idea of seeing the domestication of a hawk caught in the wild as a metaphor for the enlightenment and conversion of the sinner is quite rare.[21] Although in Provençal poetry, Italian poetry of the Duecento, and German poetry as well, the training of the hawk is used to indicate the acquiring and "training" of a lover,[22] only Dante in Italian literature truly exploits the mystical religious potential of this image.[23]

---

[20] Clark's translation: "See how the hawk and the dove sit on the same perch. I am from the clergy and you from the military. We come to conversion so that we may sit within the life of the Rule, as though on a perch; and so that you who were accustomed to seizing domestic fowl, now with the hand of good deeds may bring to conversion the wild ones, that is, laymen."

[21] Daniela Boccassini finds this concept also in concurrent literature from the Arab world: see *Il volo della mente. Falconeria e sofia nel mondo mediterraneo: Islam, Federico II, Dante* (Ravenna: Longo, 2003), 239.

[22] This metaphor can be found discussed throughout Chaps. 1 and 2 of Gualtieri, "Birds of Prey and the Sport of Falconry."

[23] Gualtieri, "Birds of Prey and the Sport of Falconry," Chap. 3, 96–98: In *Purgatorio* XIII, the envious undergo what is essentially a stage of falconry training: their eyes are sewn up as those of sparrowhawks are "seeled" to remove undesirable distractions and stimuli; this accustoms the falcons, or the sinners, to respond only to the stimuli provided by the falconer—or God—and to hunt only appropriate things.

Even more interestingly, throughout the *Commedia*, Dante is like a falcon under instruction; in his entire progression through the afterlife, he is learning to pay attention to what he ought, learning to direct his mind to the greatest good, and learning to be a servant of God. In Canto XIX of *Purgatorio*, Dante the pilgrim is overtly identified for the first time as a falcon. Having just been bemused by his dream of the Siren, he keeps his eyes on the ground. Virgil reminds him where he ought to direct his eyes—to his divine master, who is luring him:

> "Vedesti" disse "quell'antica strega
> che sola sovra noi omai si piagne;
> vedesti come l'uom da lei si slega.
> Bastiti, e batti a terra le calcagne:
> li occhi rivolgi al logoro che gira
> lo rege etterno con le rote magne." (*Purgatorio* XIX. 58–63)

The lure that God uses is indeed impressive—the celestial spheres. Dante responds as a properly trained falcon ought:

> Quale il falcon, che prima a' piè si mira,
> indi si volge al grido e si protende

Hugh's chapters on the hawk consist primarily of allegorical interpretations of various aspects of the lives of domesticated hawks, some of them quite original, based on real-life falconry practices. Hugh parallels the life of the domestic hawk to the life of the monk, including God as the "falconer," in ways that are sometimes rather uncomfortable to read. Note his seventeenth chapter, which continues the contrast between wild and domesticated hawks:

> Duae sunt species accipitris, domesticus scilicet et silvestris. Idem tamen, sed diversis temporibus potest esse silvestris et domesticus. Silvestris rapere consuevit domesticas aves, et domesticus silvestres. Silvestris quas rapit continuo devorat; domesticus captas domino suo relinquendas servat. Porro dominus eius captarum volucrum ventres aperit, et earum corda accipitri in cibum tribuenda sumit. Interiora ventris cum fimo eicit, qui intus remanens putredinem carnium cum fetore gignit. Moraliter silvestris accipiter captas volucres et rapit et devorat, quia quilibet perversus actus et cogitationes simplicium dissipare non cessat. Domesticus vero accipiter est quilibet spiritualis pater, qui totiens silvestres volucres rapit quotiens saeculares ad conversionem praedicando trahit. Captas occidit dum saecula mundo mori per carnis mortificationem cogit. Dominus autem eius, id est, Omnipotens Deus ventres earum aperit quia mollitiem carnalium per Scripturas increpando solvit. Corda vero extrahit dum cogitationes saecularium per confessionem manifestas facit. Interiora ventris cum fimo eicit quando memoriam peccati fetentem reddit. Ad mensam itaque Domini captae volucres veniunt, dum in corpus ecclesiae peccatores doctorum dentibus masticati sese convertunt.[24]

> per lo disio del pasto che là il tira;
> tal mi fec'io. (64–67)

The way to train a falcon to go after live prey was to first drag meat over its feet, while making a yelling or a whistling noise. When the falcon connected the idea of food with the sound, the trainer would use the lure in the air to attract the bird, still yelling, and get it to fly after prey. Its reward would be a portion of what it caught. Here we have Dante being instructed to watch the heavenly lure, the ultimate lure in the universe, the spheres swinging around him, giving him the desire for God. Virgil reminds him that as a falcon and as a pilgrim he is past looking at his feet; he has gone beyond that phase of training and is ready to hear the *grido* which leads him to the *pasto* of heaven. God is the ultimate falconer: he spins the ultimate lure which all pilgrims must heed.

[24] *Aviarium*, 143, Clark trans.: "There are two forms of the hawk, namely, the tame and the wild. Nevertheless, they are the same, but sometimes the bird can be wild, and sometimes tame. The wild one is accustomed to prey on tame fowl, and the tame hawk on wild birds. The wild one immediately eats its prey; the tame one preserves the birds taken to be relinquished to its master. Afterwards its master opens the belly of the captured birds and takes their hearts to offer to the hawk as food. He throws away the gut with the excrement, which, if it <the gut> remains within, produces a stinking rot of tissues. Interpreted allegorically the wild hawk both seizes and eats the birds taken, because any

Indeed it was common practice to give the hawk the heart of the bird it had caught as reward, but to see that and the rest of the butchering of the prey as symbolizing the conversion of sinners is unusual to say the least. Hugh continues in this allegorical vein in the rest of the chapters on hawks. He discusses the method of carrying the hawk (on the left hand so that it may fly towards the right—from worldly goods towards the spiritual good). The hawk's perch and the cord that tethers it to the perch have meaning as well: the perch symbolizes the monastic life, and it is sustained by two walls—the active and contemplative life. The cord that tethers the hawk to the perch is the mortification of the flesh, which holds lay-brothers to the monastic life.[25]

If indeed Hugh wrote this text to instruct lay-brothers in the ways of living a Christian life by monastic rules, it stands to reason that he would employ images from contemporary life, to which these new brothers could easily relate, to achieve his goal. Falconry is an excellent source from which such examples could be mined, since it is highly likely that its practices were familiar to those brothers coming out of the secular world.

Another clerical writer who demonstrates a very close familiarity with the sport of falconry is Albert the Great. His work, *De animalibus*,[26] written in the mid-thirteenth century, is not spiritual, but a voluminous encyclopedic opus intended as a commentary on Aristotle's books about animals. Books 22 through 26 of his text, however, are written in the naturalist vein, providing descriptions of many different animals from various sources and also his own observations. Book 23 in this series is devoted to birds, and a solid half of this text is reserved for discussion of hawks and falcons, from both a naturalist's and a falconer's point of view. Along with dividing the birds of prey into species, he discusses in depth the birds' appearance, habits, coloration, bird-calls, classification, care and training, their preferred geographical area, and their relative usefulness for hunting. He also gives veterinary advice. His sources are his own personal experience, along with information he has received from consulting falconers, and the

---

wicked person continually disturbs the actions and thoughts of simple folk. But the tame hawk is any spiritual father, who seizes the wild birds whenever he draws laymen to conversion through preaching. It kills the prey while he compels laymen to die to the world through the mortification of the flesh. Moreover, the <hawk's> master, that is, Almighty God, opens the stomachs of <the prey>, because He does away with the weakness of carnal men by rebuking them through Scripture. Indeed, He extracts their hearts when through confession He makes manifest the thoughts of laymen. He throws away the gut with the excrement while he causes the memory of a sinner to stink. And the birds seized come to the table of the Lord while sinners, chewed by the teeth of the teachers, are converted into the body of the Church."

[25] *Aviarium*, chaps. 19–22.

[26] Albertus Magnus, *Man and the Beasts (De Animalibus Books 22–26)*, trans. James J. Scanlan, MRTS 47 (Binghamton, NY: Medieval and Renaissance Texts and Studies, 1987).

authoritative texts of the time: an apocryphal letter from Aquila, Symmachus, and Theodotion to Ptolemy, king of Egypt, and treatises by Guillelmus falconarius and Gerardus falconarius.[27] He also uses material from the magnum opus of his contemporary, Frederick II.[28] In total, Albertus Magnus is practical, thorough, and knowledgeable, and he clearly appreciates the importance of falconry to the culture of his time.

Falconry treatises are integral parts of other thirteenth-century encyclopedic works as well. Brunetto Latini's *Tresor* has a section on falconry, by far the most extensive description of birds of prey to be found in an encyclopedic text in the French or Italian vernacular.[29] The information that he provides about the birds emphasizes the perspective of their usefulness in hunting, as is shown by his first statement: "Ostours est uns oiseaus de proie, si come sont faucons et esperviers et autres oiseaus que l'en tient par delit a penre autres oiseaus."[30] He has two chapters on the goshawk, one on the sparrowhawk, one on the falcon, and one on the merlin. In the goshawk entry, he repeats Isidore's description of its character and its behavior towards its offspring. Then he continues, here and in the rest of the chapters, with tips on selecting and keeping a bird. He describes the physical characteristics that one should search for (i.e. long head, yellow nostrils, etc.) when looking for a good hunting bird, and gives advice on keeping the hawk healthy.[31] He stays with this theme in the sparrowhawk entry. Here we find his comment that is of the most interest in a literary context, since literary mentions of hawks and falcons make this distinction as well:

> E sappiate, che tutti gli uccelli feditori sono di tre maniere, cioè nidacie, ramacie, e grifagni. Il nidacie è quello, che l'uomo cava di nido, e che si nutrica e piglia sicurtade dale gente che l'hanno. Ramacie è quello, che già è volato, e ha preso alcuna preda. Grifagni son quelli che son presi all'entrata di verno, che son mudati, e che hanno gli occhi rossi come fuoco.[32]

---

[27] For the latter two, a version is available in Francesco Zambrini, ed., *Libro delle nature degli uccelli fatto per lo re Danchi* (Bologna: Gaetano Romagnoli, 1874). Also see Charles Homer Haskins, "Some Early Treatises on Falconry," *Romanic Review* 13 (1922): 18–27.

[28] For detailed discussion of Albert's sources, see Oggins, "Albertus Magnus on Falcons and Hawks."

[29] Francis J. Carmody, ed., *Li Livres dou Tresor de Brunetto Latini* (Berkeley and Los Angeles: University of California Press, 1948), 1: 146–150; ed. S. Baldwin and P. Barrette, MRTS 237 (Tempe: ACMRS, 2003), 117–21. Also P. Chabaille, ed., *Il tesoro di Brunetto Latini volgarizzato da Bono Giamboni* (Bologna: Gaetano Romagnoli, 1877).

[30] My translation: "The goshawk is a bird of prey, as are falcons and sparrowhawks and other birds that one keeps for the sport of hunting other birds."

[31] Bono Giamboni omits the section on goshawk maladies in his translation.

[32] Chabaille, ed., *Il tesoro*, 155–56.

This is Bono Giamboni's translation, quoted here instead of the French because of the Italian falconry vocabulary that it includes; these are words found in literary mentions of falcons and hawks: *nidace, ramace, grifagno*. These terms are well-known among Italian poets; consider Dante's description in *Inferno* of "Cesare armato con gli occhi grifagni."[33] A *sparviere grifagno* is an adult and experienced hunter several years of age. Taken from the wild and tamed when already grown, it is considered fiercer than one that was taken to train when younger. It would be logical to conclude here not that Caesar has red eyes, but simply that Dante gives Caesar the penetrating eyes of a hawk, the word *grifagno* effectively conveying the idea of Caesar's fierceness. It will be noted that in *Paradiso* it is the military leaders and rulers that are associated with falcons in a favorable manner;[34] the bird is of course emblematic of the ruling or military class, and Caesar, though in Limbo, fits in well with this group.

Latini's writings on animals are a compendium of many types of sources. In the particular case of birds of prey, he has a wide variety of literature from which to choose, and he seems to have picked through all of it. From the usual encyclopedic moral exempla, to expository naturalist descriptions, to veterinary advice, he paints a picture of a kind of bird that has great symbolic and actual relevance to his world. His text and that of Albertus Magnus, both of the thirteenth century, demonstrate serious interest in falcons and hawks as birds central to recreational life at their time. The twelfth-century works of Alexander Neckam and Hugh of Fouilloy demonstrate instead the symbolic potential of hawks and falcons. They are exempla from which humans may learn noble behavior, they are symbolic of the status of knights in the feudal hierarchy, and their process of domestication is an allegory for the spiritual training of the human mind.

The textual popularity of these birds extends of course beyond didactic literature. They appear throughout Europe as symbols of those nobles who practice the lifestyle of which the birds are a part—an idealized world in which knights pursue ladies by showing off with lavish spending, good manners, feats of arms, and the writing of poetry. All the connotations of courtly nobility are transferred to these falcons and hawks, to such a point that their mere appearance in literature or art[35] evokes the entire world to which they belong. The chivalric way of life that revolves around hunting and loving often combines the two, resulting in a particularly apt adaptation of birds of prey to the hunt of love; in poetry they may represent the lover, the lady, or merciless Love itself. In addition, the

---

[33] Dante Alighieri, *La divina commedia*, ed. Luigi Scorrano and Aldo Vallone (Napels: Editrice Ferraro, 1990), *Inferno* IV. 123.

[34] *Paradiso* XVIII. 45.

[35] An excellent treatment of the subject of falconry in art and medieval love is Mira Friedman, "The Falcon and the Hunt: Symbolic Love Imagery in Medieval and Renaissance Art," in *Poetics of Love in the Middle Ages*, ed. M. Lazar and N. J. Lacy (Fairfax: George Mason University Press, 1989), 157–80.

domestication or training of the falcon is an image used to symbolize many different levels and types of love, from sublimated courtly love, to erotic carnal love, to divine love and spiritual enlightenment.[36] In all, the falcon and hawk are ubiquitous in the late Middle Ages in life and literature, both as a symbol and as an integral part of the noble lifestyle.

---

[36] An examination of the role of falcons and hawks and the sport of falconry in medieval love literature is of course central to Gualtieri, "Birds of Prey and the Sport of Falconry."

"VENITE A LAUDARE":
REFLECTIONS OF THE MARIAN CULT IN
IL LAUDARIO DI CORTONA

Alan R. Perry

In Italy during the thirteenth century, the cult of the Virgin Mary permeated all aspects of religious thought and culture. From Latin hymns sung in her honor through the recitation of the Angelus to paintings and statues bearing her image, Mary influenced the rhythm of everyday life. Since she had humbly born the Savior and was present at His crucifixion, the faithful intimately associated her with the risen Christ. Mary was the supreme Queen, the Mother of the Church, and, as we shall see in this study, she also embraced many other roles and identities. Indeed, according to the late Yale historian Jaroslav Pelikan, it "is impossible to understand the history of Western spirituality and devotion without paying attention to the place of the Virgin Mary."[1]

Scholarly attention to the Virgin Mary has grown immensely over the last decades, but, as Pelikan stresses, the biggest challenge in Marian historiography has been for scholars to discover "a methodology that would get beyond the dominance of 'high culture' to discover the beliefs and practices of simple and illiterate people."[2] One method of investigation might involve the study of religious documents the common folk knew intimately and used on a regular basis. In the Italian context, a collection of vernacular hymns of praise—the *laude* in the *Laudario di Cortona*—written and chanted by the lay penitents in praise of the Blessed Mother provides such an example.[3] In this inquiry, we will trace the major lines of historical development of the Virgin's cult in order to help us grasp many of the most prevalent Marian allusions in the *laude*. Through this process,

---

[1] Jaroslav Pelikan, *Mary Through the Centuries: Her Place in the History of Culture* (New Haven: Yale University Press, 1996), 215.

[2] Pelikan, *Mary Through the Centuries*, 215.

[3] For a succinct review of the *lauda*, as a form of music understood in its late medieval social context, see Blake Wilson, "Lauda," in *New Grove Dictionary of Music* (London: Macmillan, 2001), 14: 367-74, esp. 367-68.

we will come to understand better what ordinary people believed of arguably the most famous woman in the Middle Ages.

II. An Overview of the Blessed Virgin's Cult

What we have come to know and believe of Jesus' mother has its roots mainly in tradition, for the Bible says precious little about the life of Mary. Although several Marian tales abound in various apocryphal gospels, most official textual information we do have comes from the infancy narratives in Luke 1–2 and Matthew 1–2. Emphasis here is given to her virginal conception, her identification as a favored one, and her faith in God.[4] In John's Gospel she is identified as "the mother of Jesus," and after her request at Cana and brief appearance at Capernaum (John 2:12), she does not appear again until she stands under the foot of the cross.[5] In Mark, Mary is not conspicuous in any particular way and is mentioned in differentiating Jesus' natural and eschatological families (Mark 3: 34–35; 6: 1–6).[6]

Although up until the fifth century Marian piety was not particularly prevalent, some miracles were attributed to her and debate over her virgin birth occupied a few theological circles.[7] At this time there was no well-developed theological position on her Assumption into heaven. But, even in the first centuries after Jesus' birth, Mary was always considered special for her role in the birth of Christ.[8]

In the fifth century, Marian devotion began to expand in large part because of the decree issued at the Council of Ephesus stating that Mary was the Mother both of God (*Theotokos*) and of Christ (*Christotokos*). Feast days dedicated to the Virgin began to multiply, and the belief that she was bodily assumed into heaven became more and more accepted.[9] As the theologian Richard McBrien, S.J., notes:

---

[4] Karl Rahner, *Mary, Mother of the Lord*, trans. W.J. O'Hara (New York: Herder and Herder, 1963), 17.

[5] In this study, for all biblical references, I use *The New American Bible* (New York: P. J. Kenedy & Sons, 1970).

[6] Raymond E. Brown, Karl P. Donfried, et al., *Mary in the New Testament: A Collaborative Assessment by Protestant and Roman Catholic Scholars* (Philadelphia: Paulist Press, 1978), 51–72.

[7] Richard P. McBrien, *Catholicism* (San Francisco: Harper & Row, 1981), 871–72.

[8] John Macquarrie, *Mary for All Christians* (London: Collins, 1990), 3.

[9] Luigi Gambero, *Maria nel pensiero dei padri della Chiesa* (Milan: Edizioni Paoline, 1991), 264–68; see also G. Podskalsky, "Virgin Mary," in the *Oxford Dictionary of Byzantium*, 3 vols. (New York: Oxford University Press, 1991), 3: 2173–74.

The belief originated not from biblical evidence, nor even patristic testimony, but as the conclusion of a so-called argument from convenience or fittingness. It was "fitting" that Jesus should have rescued his mother from the corruption of the flesh, and so he "must have" taken her bodily into heaven. By the middle of the seventh century four separate Marian feasts were observed in Rome: the Annunciation, the Purification, the Assumption, and the Nativity of Mary.[10]

In the eighth century, Marian piety received a boost from Germanus, the patriarch of Constantinople who popularized the belief that Mary was humankind's *mediatrix* with God. Because of her special relationship to God, she could avert His wrath and intercede on behalf of the faithful.[11] In one of his sermons, Germanus directly addressed Mary and captured this philosophical drift concerning the Virgin:

> But you, having maternal power with God, can obtain abundant forgiveness even for the greatest of sinners. For He can never fail to hear you, because God obeys you through and in all things as His true mother. [. . .] You turn away the just and the sentence of damnation, because you love the Christians. [. . .] therefore the Christian people trustfully turn to you, refuge of sinners.[12]

A popular legend that conveyed Mary's special ability to appease God's anger had tremendous influence upon Marian devotion. The story of Theophilus, translated into Latin by a Benedictine monk at Monte Cassino, recounts a man's travails after he sold himself to the devil in order to acquire employment. He later repents and prays to the Blessed Virgin, asking her to ask God to forgive him. Mary does obtain forgiveness for him, and the devil has to give up his control.[13] The legend "had a very wide distribution [. . .] and was one of the most powerful influences in the spread of an ever increasing belief in the never-failing efficacy of Mary's intercession."[14]

Perhaps the most influential factor on the development of the Marian cult came through the twelfth-century Cistercian monk Bernard of Clairvaux. As the French historian Henri Daniel-Rops indicates, devotion to Mary in the late Middle Ages was inseparable from him.[15] The medieval Christian belief in

---

[10] McBrien, *Catholicism*, 873.

[11] Hilda Graef, *Mary: A History of Doctrine and Devotion*, vol. 1 (New York: Sheed and Ward, 1963), 146–47.

[12] Graef, *Mary*, 147.

[13] McBrien, *Catholicism*, 874.

[14] Graef, *Mary*, 171.

[15] Henri Daniel-Rops, *Cathedral & Crusade*, trans. John Warrington (New York: E.P. Dutton & Co, 1957), 91.

the Virgin's all-encompassing power found an anchor in Bernard's sermons "In Praise of the Virgin Mary." In them, he extols the notion that God wills humans to have everything through Mary, and while not rejecting Jesus' place as the prime mediator, he felt that men and women may fear Him because He would one day come to judge them.[16] Thus, Bernard believed that humans needed another mediator with more gentle qualities, and there was none more effective than God's mother.[17] Once, for example, he told his congregation:

> Needest thou an advocate with Jesus? Fly, then, to Mary. I say without hesitation, Mary will be heard because of due consideration due to her. The Son will hear His mother, and the Father His son. Confidence, unflinching confidence, is the stairway; that is the foundation of my hope.[18]

By the mid-thirteenth century, the laity had a fervid belief that asking Mary to pray for them brought special rewards. Twice in the *lauda* "Venite a laudare" the Virgin's powers as intercessor are mentioned in asking forgiveness for sins. In the third stanza, we find: "Cortese che fai grandi doni, / l'amor tuo mai non ci abbandoni: / pregante che tu ne perdoni / tutta la nostra villania."[19] Four stanzas later we come upon a more dramatic echo of St. Bernard's idea of flying back to the Virgin in asking pardon: "Retorni a tua grande fidanza / l'omo con grande speranza / che tu li farai perdonanza / più ch'adomandar non sapria."

A tradition holds that Bernard was the first to call Mary "Our Lady" and provided the final words to the "Salve Regina" when, moved by the chanting of the antiphon, he is said to have leapt up and shouted, "O clemens! O dulcis! O pia!"[20] As Marina Warner indicates, Bernard's passion for Mary became

---

[16] An excellent, well-documented text on St. Bernard's devotion to the Virgin Mary may be found in Michel Aubron, *L'Oeuvre Mariale de Saint Bernard* (Paris: Institut d'Etudes du Massif Central, 1935). One can find a more recent publication of all of St. Bernard's sermons on the Virgin Mary, translated into English from the original Latin, by Ailbe John Luddy, *St. Bernard's Sermons on the Blessed Virgin Mary* (Chumleigh: Augustine, 1984).

[17] Eileen Power, Introduction to *Miracles of the Blessed Virgin Mary*, trans. and ed. C.C. Swinton Bland (London: Routledge & Sons, 1928), xiii.

[18] Daniel-Rops, *Cathedral & Crusade*, 91. Christians can find succinct references of Bernard's words in the present form of the prayer known as the "Memorare": "Remember, oh Most Blessed Virgin Mary, that never was it known that anyone who fled to thy protection, implored thy help, or sought thy intercession was left unaided. Inspired by this confidence, we fly unto thee, oh Virgin of Virgins, our Mother. Unto you do we come, before thee do we stand, sinful and sorrowful. Oh, Holy Mother of the Word Incarnate, despise not our petitions, but in thy mercy, hear and answer us. Amen."

[19] Reference made to all the *laude* found in the *Laudario di Cortona* may be found in Gianfranco Contini, *Poeti del Duecento*, vol. 2 (Milan: Ricciardi, 1960), 10–58.

[20] Daniel-Rops, *Cathedral & Crusade*, 91.

a benchmark for the Cistercian order: monks wore white robes in honor of her purity, and the seals of the abbey contained Bernard's image. His intense love for the Virgin "was thus carried all over Europe, where during the next hundred and fifty years cathedrals rose in her honor, lay confraternities were founded, and altar pieces commissioned to sing her praise."[21]

St. Bonaventure was also instrumental in Marian devotion, and many of his sermons focused on Mary's role in the "redemptive act of the cross." To the laity, no other person could have acutely felt Jesus' pain and agony as His mother. Mary's own sorrow and pain served as a model for Christians to better comprehend the mystery of the Passion.[22] Because Mary consented to the sacrifice of her Son and compassionately participated in His death by suffering under the cross, she was seen as helping to assure humankind's redemption.[23] The growing, multilayered nature of her identity thus acquired a new notion: she became the Co-Redemptrix of the human race.

Several of Jacopone da Todi's *laude*, especially "Donna di Paradiso," have the Mater Dolorosa as a central theme; however, the *Laudario di Cortona* does not focus on the Virgin along these lines. These *laude* instead aim more to praise and uplift the Virgin's glorious qualities rather than lament a tragic element. In a few *laude*, Jesus' passion is central, but Mary does not weep for Him at this moment. Rather, we usually find a penitent's exhortation to approach the cross personally, as with verses forty-eight through fifty-one: "Oime lasso e freddo lo mio core": "Vienne, cor mio, andiamone a la croce; / sospira e piange e lassa si gran boce, / che fende el polmone enfine a lo foce, / e transmortise."

During the twelfth century, through her association as a Co-Redemptrix with Jesus, the Virgin solicited greater awe among the laity. Marian antiphons grew in popularity and the "Hail Mary" became a simple prayer to be learned by all Christians who would recite them together in groups of fifty called *rosarium* after Mary's title "rosa mystica." This practice became a popular substitute for the Liturgy of the Hours in the West while at the same time Christians in the Byzantine, Syriac, Coptic, and Armenian churches developed elaborate hymns to the Virgin.[24] Medieval Christians also developed the custom of reciting the Angelus, a group of Marian prayers repeated three times each day.[25]

---

[21] Marina Warner, *Alone of All Her Sex: The Myth and Cult of the Virgin Mary* (New York: Knopf, 1976), 132. More than thirty years later, Warner's exhaustive study is still fundamental to contemporary Mariology.

[22] Daniel-Rops, *Cathedral & Crusade*, 16–17.

[23] McBrien, *Catholicism*, 876.

[24] *The Catechism of the Catholic Church* (New York: Catholic Book Publishing Co., 1994), 644.

[25] McBrien, *Catholicism*, 876.

As we mentioned, the majority of churches built during the twelfth and thirteenth centuries, especially in France, took the Blessed Mother as their patron.[26] Salvatore Accardo indicates that the number of Florentine churches that bear the Virgin's namesake gives testament to "quanto il culto mariano fosse sentito in Firenze [. . .] da Santa Maria Maggiore alla Santissima Annunziata, da Santa Maria Novella a Santa Maria del Fiore per citare le più note."[27]

The rising interest in the Virgin during the late twelfth century was also reflected in art. As the artistic representations of Mary increased, the Romanesque image of the seated Virgin and Child slowly gave way to the Gothic image of the Triumph of the Virgin that shows Mary and the adult Jesus seated next to each other in heaven.[28] This image then developed into both the Coronation of the Virgin and the Standing Virgin and Child. Essentially, the Madonna gained in stature and importance as an artistic theme. Mosaics, altarpieces, statues, and bas-reliefs above church portals also show how the Virgin acquired much more equality with Jesus in artistic representations and expression.

Written collections of her miracles began in the late eleventh century and knowledge of the Virgin's powers became quite common and spread quickly.[29] One such miracle reportedly occurred near Turin at the Abbey of the Sagra of San Michele. A young monk "dropped the consecrated wine on a white towel when he was serving Mass, and after a moment of intense misery prayed earnestly to Mary; the stain disappeared."[30]

Along with an interest in her miracles, the faithful often desired to obtain objects that supposedly belonged to her. Because she was assumed into heaven, earthly relics belonging to her person were hard to find, but nevertheless, "pieces of her veil and the like—even drops of her milk—were to be found in many places; and Chartres claimed to possess the nightdress she was wearing when she gave birth to Jesus."[31]

Marian devotion found a vibrant expression even in vernacular literature. As the medieval historian Eileen Power states, notions about the Virgin were

---

[26] Geoffrey Ashe, *The Virgin* (London: Routledge & Kegan Paul, 1971), 217.

[27] Salvatore Accardo, "La Vergine nel pensiero e nella poesia di Dante," *Studium* 84 (1988): 540–56, here 548.

[28] Penny Schine Gold, *The Lady & The Virgin* (Chicago: University of Chicago Press, 1990), 46–49.

[29] Power, *Miracles of the Blessed Virgin Mary*, ix. Scholars will find an excellent source of Marian miracles with Michael S. Durham's *Miracles of Mary: Apparitions, Legends, and Miraculous Works by the Blessed Virgin Mary* (San Francisco: HarperSanFrancisco, 1995). Furthermore, Michael P. Carroll's *The Cult of the Virgin Mary* (Princeton: Princeton University Press, 1986) offers psychological insight to the widespread popular veneration of Mary throughout the centuries.

[30] Christopher and Rosalind Brooke, *Popular Religion in the Middle Ages: Western Europe* (Leipzig: Thames and Hudson, 1984), 32.

[31] Brooke and Brooke, *Popular Religion in the Middle Ages*, 32.

tinged with chivalrous romance, which appears in the songs of the troubadours and in the great epics of the day. In later Provencal poetry, all the chief characteristic formulas of the love lyric are used to celebrate the Virgin and it has even been held by some critics that Rudel's *princesse lointaine* was no lady of Tripoli but the Virgin herself on whom the mystical devotion was lavished.[32]

Pier Cardinal wrote one of the first Provencal hymns to the Virgin in which he asks for her intercession with Jesus: "Vera maire, ver'amia / Ver'amors, vera merces / Per la vera merce sia / Qu'estend'en me tos heres."[33] Lanfrac Cigala, an Italian troubadour, wrote that the "Virgin was the only woman he could praise without fear of contradiction."[34]

Monte Andrea's sonnet *Si come i marinar' guida la stella* also shows the influence of the cult of Mary upon a secular work. Since the ninth century, a very popular Marian hymn, the *Ave Maris Stella*, circulated widely in Europe. In it, as Graef says, Mary "appears as the loving helper of men who frees prisoners from their fetters, brings light to the blind, drives away our ills and asks for all good things, exercising the prerogatives so often attributed to her [. . .] in the position of mother."[35] Like the Virgin of the hymn, Andrea's *donna* guides him along the safer path of life:

> Voi, gentile ed amorosa pulzella
> di cui m'ha mess'Amore in segnoraggio
> che' troppo è scura la mia via e fella
> a gir, se vostra lumer non aggio.[36]

As we will later investigate, when Andrea uses the term "pulzella," he also reflects upon the keen attention the Church gave to Mary's chastity and the value placed upon a woman's virginity during this time.

Mary's association with a heavenly star is constantly reinforced in the *laude* where she is referred to as a guiding star, "altissima luce," or more often than not,

---

[32] Power, *Miracles of the Blessed Virgin Mary*, xiv–xv.

[33] Joseph Anglade, *Anthologie des Troubadours* (Paris: E. de Boccard, 1927), 167.

[34] Warner, *Alone of All her Sex*, 151.

[35] Graef, *Mary*, 174. The seven stanzas of the *Ave Maris Stella*, as found in Ruth E. Messenger, *The Medieval Latin Hymn* (Washington, DC: Capital Press, 1953), 215–16, are as follows: "1.) Ave maris stella, / Dei mater alma / Atque semper virgo, / Felix caeli porta. 2.) Sumens illud Ave / Gabrielis ore / Funda nos in pace, / Mutans nomen Evae. 3.) Solve vincla reis, / Profer lumen caecis, / Mala nostra pelle, / Bona cuncta posce. 4.) Monstra te esse matrem, / Sumat per te preces, / Qui pro nobis natus, / Tulit esse tuus. 5.) Virgo singularis, / Inter omnes mitis, / Nos culpis solutos / Mites fac et castos. 6.) Vitam praesta puram, / Iter para tutum, / Ut videntes Iesum / Semper collaetemur. 7.) Sit laus Deo Parti, / Summo Christo decus, / Spiritui Sancto: / Tribus honor unus."

[36] Piero Cudini, ed., *Poesia Italiana: Il Duecento* (Milan: Garzanti, 1993), 108.

the morning star, as is the case in "Venite a laudare": "Diana stella lucente / letizia de tutta la gente / tutto lo mondo è perdente / senza la tua vigoria" (v. 56–59). In "Ave Maria gratia plena" she is called "stella de dia, luce serena" and "stella lucente." In another *ballata*, "O maria—d'omelia" we find her beseeched as "Chiara sposa, gran lumera, dà conforto." Finally, in "Ave, Vergene gaudente" three references are made to this sidereal aspect of Mary: "tu se' via de salvamento, / chiara stella d'oriente, " "Stella [che] corra la luna / più resplende che neuna," and "Li rai de la tua lumera / [i]splendente se smera: / de te ['l] sol prende la spera, / può che se' relevente" (v. 71–74). All of these images of the star, according to the music historian Franco Mancini, point to the saving power of Christ in terms of the Living God and Light of the World.[37]

Several historians and literary scholars see strong influences of the Virgin's cult upon the Dolce Stil Nuovo. In Dante's *Commedia*, the undisputed masterpiece of medieval literature, the Blessed Virgin "emerges from the poem as the cornerstone of the architecture of the Christian salvation, the instrument of the Incarnation and the merciful intercessor for sinners, including Dante himself."[38]

Religious orders also reflected the passion for Mary in the late Middle Ages in how they dedicated a great number of new houses to her. Almost by default a founder of an order chose the Virgin as a patron. Even St. Francis' devotion to the Blessed Mother inspired a group of pious laymen in Florence to found *i Servi* or "The Order of the Servants of the Blessed Virgin Mary."[39]

The penitential movement likewise had a deep Marian strain, and many confraternities were likewise named in her honor.[40] Such is the case with the group of penitents in Cortona, the Fraternity of Santa Maria, that wrote the famous and well-preserved *laudario*. As with their religious counterparts in various orders, they too chanted popular Latin hymns to Mary, but they more importantly gave rise to a great interest and production of religious lyric poetry in the vernacular.[41] Indeed, according to Mancini, an analysis of the *laudario* reveals

---

[37] Franco Mancini, *Il tempo della gioia: Un' interpretazione del Laudario di Cortono con appendice di not esegetiche* (Rome: Archivio Guido Izzi, 1996), 43–45.

[38] Warner, *Alone of All her Sex*, 161.

[39] Brooke and Brooke, *Popular Religion in the Middle Ages*, 31. See also Blake Wilson, *Music and Merchants: The Laudesi Companies of Republican Florence* (Oxford: Oxford University Press, 1992).

[40] Michael Goodrich, *Vita Perfecta: The Ideal of Sainthood in the Thirteenth Century* (Stuttgart: Hiersemann, 1982), 156.

[41] Andre Vauchez, *The Laity in the Middle Ages*, trans. Margery J. Schnieder (Notre Dame: University of Notre Dame Press, 1993), 125. Trying to reconstruct how the penitents actually chanted the hymns has proved challenging because various manuscripts diverge in regards to musical notes and tones. Theodore Karp investigates this situation and offers his own reading of the hymns in "Editing the Cortona *Laudario*," *Journal of Musicology* 11 (1993): 73–105.

several thematic links with the prevalent Sicilian school of love poetry in the thirteenth century. He states:

> [. . .] il Cortonese rappresenta—attraverso la rivisitazione francescana della materia cortese effettuata all'insegna della conformità a Cristo—un importante esempio di recupero o, meglio, dei riappropriazione analogica—ma soprattutto anagogica (anagogica mediatrice comunque fra il terreno e il celeste)—di temi e di moduli, che la poesia d'amore dei siciliani aveva a sua volta esemplato sulla lirica dei provenzali [. . .].[42]

In observing the *laudario,* we have already discussed the Virgin's role as intercessor and her identification with a guiding star. We have also noted that the Mater Dolorosa theme does not really appear here. We shall now explore the significance of other symbols and qualities related to the Virgin, continuing to use "Venite a laudare" as our primary reference.

II. Multifaceted Aspects of the Virgin as Seen in "Venite a laudare"

Before we begin to analyze other Marian references, let us look at the actual structure of this *lauda,* the first of the forty-six Cortona *laude* that were set to music.[43] The form is that of a ballad, more precisely a *ballata minore,* comprised, as Contini states, "di tutti novenari, con alternanza di qualche ottonario."[44] Indeed, as Cyrilla Barr notes, the alternation of the refrain and stanzas of a ballad "causes the *ballata* to be very well suited to group singing and consequently makes it adaptable to the evangelizing purpose of the *lauda.*"[45]

---

[42] Mancini, *Il tempo della gioia,* 5.

[43] An accessible critical edition of these *laude* can be found in Anna Maria Guarnieri's *Laudario di Cortona: Edizione critica* (Spoleto: Centro Italiano di Studi sull'Alto Medioevo, 1991). Fernando Luizzi in *La lauda e i primordi della melodia italiana,* 2 vols. (Rome: Libreria dello Stato, 1935) lists forty-six *laude* that comprise the *laudario* while Giorgio Veranini et al., in *Laude Cortonesi dal secolo XIII al XIV,* 4 vols. (Florence: Olschki, 1985) list forty-seven.

[44] Contini, *Poeti del Duecento,* 2:12. As the musicologist Hans Tischler indicates, however, in *The Earliest Laude: The Cortona Hymnal* (Ottawa: The Institute of Mediaeval Music, 2002), xv, while the *lauda* and ballad are poetically similar in form, their usage and social roles differed greatly. The *lauda* was very similar to a hymn and was created by the simple folk, while the ballad belonged to high society and was expressed in games and dance; furthermore, the *lauda* was primarily chanted slowly and plainly while the ballad was animated, accompanied by instruments, and placed emphasis on meter and rhythm.

[45] Cyrilla Barr, *The Monophonic Lauda and the Lay Confraternities of Tuscany and Umbria in the Late Middle Ages* (Kalamazoo: Medieval Institute Publications, 1988), 82.

Here the refrain consists of two *settenari* and one *endecasillabo*. Each stanza is connected to the following through the use of *coblas capfinidas* (e.g., Virgo pia / Pietosa / Cortesia / Cortese / balia / Balia). In the last stanza we even find a form of *congedo* where Mary is addressed directly and told that the *lauda* is meant for her: "Vigorosa, potente, beata, / per te è questa laude cantata: / tu se' la nostra avocata, / la più fedel che mai sia" (v. 60–63).[46] Thus, "Venite a laudare," as with other *laude* in the form of ballads, contains many stylistic elements found in secular poetry. As Contini states:

> L'assottigliamento del corpo delle più antiche ballate non consente se non per congettura un raffronto stilistico al paradigma profano, che sarà sempre da introdurre idealmente in filigrana: qui basti sottolineare, coi non rari echi siciliani, la presenza frequente del collegamento, usuale nella poesia provenzale e nella siciliana, anzi in vigore fino al Stil Nuovo, e nelle laude del culto mariano il tema della cortesia, che del resto viene a essere in qualche modo un ritorno del motivo alla sua sede sacra.[47]

One of the Virgin's common Latin names—*Regina Caeli*—communicates the theme of Marian *cortesia* to which Contini refers. By the sixth century Mary had acquired her identity as Queen of the Heavens in large part through the belief in her Assumption, for in it she was seen as triumphing over human weakness and evil. Like Jesus, albeit in a different way, she too conquered death. Thus, the faithful saw her as having special powers and gave her a special place next to the risen Christ. They had no problem projecting the social hierarchy of their own world into heaven, and ordered the heavenly host to resemble the earthly society.[48] In figurative representations from the very first centuries, the Virgin acquired a crown and was seated on a throne with the Christ-child.[49] God was supreme and unique, the only King of heaven, and Mary was Queen, often so

---

[46] In this last stanza, we find the grouping of three adjectives—"Vigorosa, potente, beata"— to describe the Virgin. Several other medieval prayers have a same pattern of triple repetition to describe either God or the Vigin, such as "Il Cantico delle Creature"—"Altissimu, omnipotente, bon Signore"—or the "Salve Regina"—"O dulcis, o pia, o clemens!" The overarching spiritual importance of the Trinity in the collective conscience of the faithful could possibly help to explain the common repetition of three adjectives in prayers.

[47] Contini, *Poeti del Duecento*, 2:12.

[48] Brooke and Brooke, *Popular Religion in the Middle Ages*, 32.

[49] According to Pietro Romanelli and Per Jonas Nordhagen, *Santa Maria Antiqua* (Rome: Istituto Poligrafico dello Stato, 1964) the first image of Maria Regina was depicted on the wall of the church Santa Maria Antiqua, the oldest Christian building in the Roman Forum. The Virgin Queen sits in majesty on a throne and is arrayed in the regalia of a secular monarch (46).

represented in the scene of the coronation by her Son.[50] In time, the honor usually paid to an earthly queen was extended to Mary.[51]

In the *ballata*, the Virgin is the "Pietosa regina sovrana" who watches over and heals the world: "conforta la mente ch'è vana: / grande medicina che sana, / aiutan' per tua cortesia" (v. 9–11). Humanity thus yearns to do the Queen's will—"volemo a te fare ubidienza / e stare a la tua signoria" (v. 22–23)—and always sing her praises: "per sempre sia molta laudata / [. . .] / Siate a piacere, gloriosa, / chi canta la tua laude amorosa, / de farli la mente studiosa / che laudi be notte e dia" (v. 5, 52–55). The Virgin in turn serves her faithful as their heavenly representative—"tu se' la nostra avocata / la più fedel che mai sia" (v. 62–63). The faithful thus know that without her guidance, all the world would be lost: "tutto l[o] mondo è perdente / senza la tua vigoria" (v. 58–59).

Other *laude* also refer to Mary as Queen, and often we find her named "regina potentissima," "regina gentilissima," or again as "avocata nostra" just as she is called in the "Salve Regina":

> Salve, Regina, mater misericordiae: vita, dulcedo, et spes nostra, salve. Ad te clamamus exsules filii Hevae. Ad te suspiramus, gementes et flentes in hac lacrimarum valle. Eja, ergo, advocata nostra, illos tuos misericordes oculos ad nos converte. Et Jesum, benedictum fructum ventris tui, nobis post hoc exsilium ostende. O clemens, o pia, o dulcis Virgo Maria.[52]

Of course, Dante also specifically identifies the Virgin as queen: "[. . .] la regina / cui questo regno è suddito e devoto" (*Par.* 31. 116–117).[53] Later, he prays to her as such: "Ancor ti priego, regina, che puoi / ciò che tu vuoli, che conservi sani / dopo tanto veder, li affetti suoi, / Vinca tua guardia i movimenti umani" (*Par.* 33. 34–37).[54]

When the Virgin is identified in the *laude* as a queen who helps her religious subjects, we gather a sense of *nobiltà* and *gentilezza* present in a feudal or royal court so often evoked in the secular poetry of this time.[55] From the Sicilians to Guinizelli and Dante, Italian poets of the Duecento praise the *donna gentile* for her refined and noble qualities. As their most cherished goal, they seek her requited love.

Although Mary is Queen of heaven and earth, she has never really remained at an unapproachable distance from humankind because while she reigns sovereign, she nurtures as Mother. The importance of the motherhood of Mary grew in appreciation

---

[50] Brooke and Brooke, *Popular Religion in the Middle Ages*, 32–33.
[51] Power, *Miracles of the Blessed Virgin Mary*, xiv.
[52] www.domcentral.org/life/salve.htm.
[53] Dante Alighieri, *Commedia*, ed. Emilio Pasquini and Antonio Quaglio (Milan: Garzanti, 1987), 1113.
[54] Dante, *Commedia*, 1135.
[55] Power, *Miracles of the Blessed Virgin Mary*, xiv.

in the late Middle Ages because St. Francis preached the value of remembering Mary's humble role in rearing humankind's Savior. As Warner explains:

> The impact of the friars' new ethic on the cult of the Virgin was profound, for they remodeled her to their revolutionary ideals. In Italy and France, the Virgin left her starry throne in the heavens and laid aside her robes and insignia and diadem to sit cross-legged on the bare earth like a peasant mother with child.[56]

In artistic representations, Mary was more often depicted as the Madonna kneeling in adoration before the newborn Savior, and people came to glorify her because of her humanity.[57]

"Venite a laudare" refers to the Virgin Mary three times as mother, and in two instances her identity is closely linked to her regal role: "Balia ne dona e potenzia / O madre, de far penitenza: / [. . .] / Signoria d'affranchi lo core / è la tua, madre d'amore" (v. 20–21, 24–25). In the tenth stanza, her identity as mother is qualified by the adjective "sweet" ("dolze madre") a notation present, as we have seen, in the "Salve Regina." In other *laude* we find references constantly made to the Virgin's motherhood: "madre nostra nodice," "di te naque Dio ed omo,", "Madre, non mi saria grave," "Da' mi conforto, madre de l'amore," "Madre di Cristo, piena di scienza," "Onerata sei del Padre / di cui s' figlia e madre."

An interesting aspect of Mary's maternal role reveals itself in "Venite a laudare," and refers to the Virgin's act of suckling the baby Jesus. From the early Middle Ages, artists had always represented Mary nursing her child. In time, Christians began to associate her milk, which gave life to the Savior, with their own spiritual nourishment, and they further believed that since Mary assured human salvation by feeding Jesus, she could do the same with humans.[58] Figuratively, this belief took the form of Mary offering her breasts that trickled or sprayed her healing milk to countless sickly people. Mary thus nourished the Holy Church and provided an echo for Isaiah's God, described in feminine fashion, who fed Jerusalem, His holy city: "For thus says the Lord: Lo, I will spread prosperity over her like a river, and the wealth of the nations like an

---

[56] Warner, *Alone of All her Sex*, 182.

[57] Over the past decades, several feminist scholars have explored the cult of the Madonna in relation to humankind's view of women. For example, Simone de Beauvoir in *The Second Sex*, trans. H.M. Parshley (New York: Knopf, 1971) states that the representations of the Madonna kneeling before her Son reflect how in medieval society the second-rate position of women continued to be solidified: "For the first time in human history, the mother kneels before her son: she freely accepts her inferiority. This is the supreme masculine victory. Consummated in the act of the Virgin—it is the rehabilitation of women through the accomplishment of her defeat" (86).

[58] Warner, *Alone of All her Sex*, 194.

overflowing torrent. As nurslings, you shall be carried in her arms, and fondled in her lap" (Isaiah 66: 12).

Many miracle stories depict the Virgin coming to the aid of a dying man or woman and offering her breast. In one case of the twelfth century, the Virgin came to the bedside of a Cistercian monk who was dying of a putrid disease of the mouth. After giving him her nipple, she withdrew it, showering him with her milk. The monk, of course, was immediately healed.[59] Furthermore, medieval artists often portrayed St. Bernard with outstretched arms near the uncovered breast of the Virgin, his thirst soon to be quenched. One such "Lactation of St. Bernard" may be viewed in the window of the church of Laines-au-Bois in the diocese of Troyes, France.[60]

In the eighth stanza of "Venite a laudare," the terms "breast" and "milk" are not directly mentioned; however, the image of the lactating Virgin is present, cloaked in terms of a "dolze fontana," which alludes to her breasts spouting milk. Anyone who tastes of the Virgin will come to love and have greater thirst for her: "Sapesse la gente cristiana, / ch'è sconoscente e villana, / gustar de te, dolze fonanta, / d'amarte più gran sete avria" (v. 32–35).

Mary's glorification as Mother is problematic, in part, because tradition holds that, after Jesus' miraculous virgin birth, she abstained from sex with Joseph and bore no other children of her own. According to Michael Carroll, Mary's total disassociation from sex is the central element in the Christian cult of Mary that clearly distinguishes her from other Mother-Earth goddesses who have dominated Mediterranean religions for the past thousand years.[61]

The Gospels do not clearly establish her own sinless birth, but early Christians thought that in order for God to become man, He had to choose the purest of creatures to bring Himself into the world. For them, therefore, Jesus' mother had to have been conceived free of the human corruption of original sin, then perpetually kept in a virginal state. In 451, the Council of Chalcedon officially gave Mary the title *Aeiparthenos* (ever-virgin) and thus affirmed her virginity both *in partu* and *post-partum*.[62] Pope Martin I declared two hundred years later

---

[59] Warner, *Alone of All her Sex*, 195.

[60] Henri Focillon in *Le Peinture des Miracles Notre Dame* (Paris: P. Hartmann, 1950) details many illustrations of the lactation theme in European art.

[61] Carroll, *The Cult of the Virgin Mary*, 5–9.

[62] *The Catechism of the Catholic Church* further elaborates, explaining that although the Bible mentions that Jesus had brothers and sisters, the "Church has always understood these passages as not referring to other children of the Virgin Mary. In fact James and Joseph, 'brothers of Jesus,' are the sons of another Mary, a disciple of Christ, whom St. Matthew significantly calls 'the other Mary.' They are close relations of Jesus, according to an Old Testament expression" (126).

that Mary's perpetual virginity was a dogma of the church.[63] In the twelfth and thirteenth centuries, however, great debates still took place over her Immaculate Conception, how her hymen was restored after Jesus' birth, and whether or not her Son had biological brothers and sisters.[64]

Mary's virginity became a focal point because the laity saw in it a paradigmatic social value. From its earliest times, the church cultivated a keen interest for the pureness of spirit seen in not having sexual relations because it meant renouncing human feelings tied to earthly matters for the greater glory of God and the afterlife.[65] In Corinthians, St. Paul writes:

> A man is better off having no relations with a woman. [. . .] To those not married and to widows I have this to say: It would be well if they remain as they are, even as I do myself; but if they cannot exercise self-control, they should marry. It is better to marry than to be on fire. [. . .] The virgin—indeed, any unmarried woman—is concerned with things of the Lord, in pursuit of holiness in body and spirit. The married woman, on the other hand, has the cares of this world to absorb her and is concerned with pleasing her husband (1 Corinthians 7:1, 8–9, 34).

In the *Summa Theologica*, Aquinas discusses the values of virginity at length, drawing upon previously postulated positions:

> Virgins are 'the more honored portion of Christ's flock and their glory more sublime' [quoting St. Cyprian] in comparison with widows and married women. The hundredfold fruit is ascribed to widowhood, to which the sixtyfold fruit is ascribed, and to marriage, to which is ascribed the thirtyfold fruit.
>
> The error of Jovinian consisted in holding virginity not to be preferable to marriage. This error is refuted above all by the example of Christ who both chose a virgin for His mother and remained Himself a virgin.[66]

The historical anthropologist Julia O'Faolain believes that medieval men saw the opposite of their own "lust" and "carnality" in virgin women, and in seeking and attaining a chaste wife as property, they could acquire honor and virility for

---

[63] Warner, *Alone of All her Sex*, 160. St. Augustine also preached that Mary was "a virgin in conceiving her Son, a virgin in giving birth to him, a virgin carrying him, a virgin in nursing him at her breast, always a virgin" (*Sermones* 186, qtd. in *Catechism*, 128).

[64] Graef, *Mary*, 250–60.

[65] See P. R. L. Brown, *The Body and Society: Men, Women, and Sexual Renunciation in Early Christianity* (New York: Columbia University Press, 1988).

[66] Thomas Aquinas, *Summa Theologica*, trans. and ed. A.M. Fairweather (Philadelphia: Westminster Press, 1954), 18:118.

themselves.[67] Women nurtured by this mystification of virginity found a security in remaining chaste for they had something that men prized upon entering a marriage alliance.

In "Venite a laudare" we have one major reference to Mary's chastity: "preghiam che ne si avocata / al tuo figliuolo, Virgo pia" (v. 6–7). Several of the other ballads focus more intently upon the virginity theme. Such is the case with "Altissima luce col grande splendore" where we find "Verginitade—a Dio prommetesti;" "Vergene pura—con tutta bellezza;" "Virgene santa—son tutta onoranza;" and "Ave, regina—pulzella amorosa," that, through the term "pulzella," may recall the value of virginity in Monte Andrea's sonnet *Si come i marinar' guida la stella*.

As we noted earlier, prayers said to Mary in groups of fifty were called rosaries, a name derived from "rosa mystica," another name the Virgin acquired from the rising fervor of her cult. Although this is one Marian symbol that does not appear in "Venite a laudare," it occurs several times in other *laude*. As Barbara Seward indicates in *The Symbolic Rose*, the identity has its roots in the pagan worship of a goddess of earthly love whose chief symbol as the queen of flowers was the rose. Throughout the Middle Ages, Christians quite naturally assimilated this symbol and gave it to their own Queen:

> Surprising only is the fact that the rose was granted its most popular religious meaning comparatively late in the Catholic era. [. . .] Whatever the reasons, the fact remains that Mary, who had long been identified with Isaiah's rod of Jesse blossoming in the holy flower of Christ, did not herself become a rose until the advent of her twelfth-century devotee, St. Bernard of Clairvaux. Then, as if to make up for lost time and lost analogies, both Bernard and the Catholic writers who followed him established Mary as the most elaborate of ecclesiastical roses to date.[68]

From religious sermons to secular poetry and literature, conventional associations were developed between Mary and her identity as Rose. For example, troubadours and minnesingers often praised the women that they esteemed as roses, and in "Rosa fresca aulentissima," Ciclo d'Alcamo stands out among countless poets of the Duecento who refer to the *donna* as a rose or other flower.[69] The same may be said for Guido Cavalcanti with "Fresca rosa novella" and Lapo Gianni with "Questa rosa novella."

Dante brought the rose to its fullest development in the *Commedia*, expanding the Virgin's role to encompass a multi-leveled "symbol of perfection, grace, paradise, Christ's triumph, and the eternal love in which all temporal things find their

---

[67] Julia O'Faolain and Lauro Martines, eds., *Not in God's Image* (San Francisco: Harper & Row, 1973), 137.
[68] Barbara Seward, *The Symbolic Rose* (New York: Columbia University Press, 1960), 22.
[69] Seward, *The Symbolic Rose*, 24.

fulfillment and their end.[70] In the *Paradiso*, the poet describes the entire company of the Church triumphant as a rose: "In forma dunque di candida rosa / mi si mostrava la milizia santa, / che nel suo sangue Cristo fece sposa" (*Par.* 31. 1–3).[71]

In all the *laude* where we find praise for the Virgin as a central theme, Mary is referred to as a Rose at least once. In "Ave, donna santissima," she is called "rosa freschissima." In "Fa' mi cantar l'amor di la beata," we note "fior sov'r ogni cosa." Mary is praised as "Ros'aulente, splendiente" in "O Maria—d'omelia" and in "Ave, Vergene gaudente," we have, "rosa bianc[a] e vermiglia / Sovr'ogni altro fiore aulente."

III. Final Observations

The penitents who composed these *laude* no doubt drew upon Latin Marian antiphons so prevalent in the thirteenth century. They were not hymns per se, but prayers chanted at specific times during the Mass and Office.[72] Indeed, both the *laudesi*—confraternities that formed expressively to chant—and the *disciplinati*—groups whose statutes also espoused self-flagellation—employed the *laude* as paraliturgical exercises during processions, prayer meetings, funeral services, personal devotions, and Holy Week observances.[73] We have already mentioned the "Ave Maris Stella" and the "Salve Regina." Others included "Ave Regina Caelorum," "Regina Caeli Laetare," and the well-known "Ave Maria."[74] The faithful also hailed the Virgin with litanies of her own, and, because she had come to dominate so many of the lists of saints, the clergy separated her from the other saints and addressed her uniquely. Indeed, the oldest known text of the most important litany—the Litany of Loreto—was composed around 1200 and contains seventy-three invocations to the Madonna.[75]

Both the clergy and the laity were very familiar with these antiphons and litanies because of the Mass and Office. But Christians knew them also in the general

---

[70] Seward, *The Symbolic Rose*, 24.

[71] Dante, *Commedia*, 1103.

[72] Messenger, *The Medieval Latin Hymn*, 79.

[73] Barr, *The Monophonic Lauda*, 17–57. As Wilson, "Lauda," 367, notes: "Throughout the 14th and 15th centuries relatively unbroken traditions of *lauda*-singing were maintained by both types of confraternity, but the paraliturgical services of the *laudesi* confraternities provided the *lauda's* primary context."

[74] Joseph Connelly, *Hymns of the Roman Liturgy* (London: Longmans, Green and Co., 1957), 44–47. See also Bonnie J. Blackburn, "*Te Matrem Dei Laudamus*: A Study in the Musical Veneration of Mary," *Musical Quarterly* 53 (1967): 53–76, and Nino Pirotta, *Music and Culture in Italy from the Middle Ages to the Baroque* (Cambridge, MA: Harvard University Press, 1984).

[75] Ashe, *The Virgin*, 218.

context of the overriding, religiously sensitive culture of the Middle Ages.[76] That is, because the hymns were tied to so many other Marian cultural aspects, they became a natural part of the social fabric of daily life. We find in them, just as we do in the *laudario*, that Mary is called "queen," emphasis is placed on her virginity, and reference is made to her as Star of the Sea. Actual hymns to the Blessed Mother on her various feast days stress more or less the same elements.

We should not be too amazed to find Mary at the center of most of the Cortonian religious *laude*, for the penitents who composed them were literally bombarded with signs and symbols of Mary. They lived at a time when Marian culture was ultra-present and important in everyday life. [77]

In analyzing the structure of "Venite a laudare," we observed that it is in the form of a *ballata* where secular stylistic elements such as *coblas capfinidas* abound. We can infer then that the *penitenti* were artistically inclined to draw upon vernacular poetic forms that helped them better express their love for the Virgin. The songs they sang to the Madonna naturally grew out of a long Latin tradition that came into contact with the secular poetry of the Italian Duecento. At times, an opposite form of borrowing would occur because of the pervasiveness of the religious cult: reference to the Virgin Mary would occur in secular poetry.

Other religious themes are present in the *laudario di Cortona*, from the suffering Christ to the mortification of St. John at seeing his master's crucifixion.[78] But a Marian emphasis specially marks the *laude*, and as we have seen, it does not speak of the Virgin in terms of one identity alone. Rather, we have a splendid amalgamation and consolidation of her various identities. She is not just Queen, she is Mother. She is not just Virgin, she is Star, Rose, and Advocate.

In this study, we have investigated many of her multifaceted signs and symbols in order to fathom what lies behind the attention given to her in the *laude*. Furnished with this knowledge about the cult of Mary, we can more fully appreciate, comprehend, and demonstrate its manifestations in other medieval ballads, songs, and poems, both religious and secular.

---

[76] R.W. Southern, *Western Society and the Church in the Middle Ages* (Harmondsworth: Penguin Books, 1970), 16–17.

[77] As Blackburn in "*Te Matrem Dei Laudamus*," 76, reminds us, we "tend to forget just how fervent devotion to Mary was" in the 13th through the 16th centuries. "For it was Mary, Mother of Mercy, rather than Christ, the Judge, in whom people had put their hope — *in te dulcis Maria speramus: ut nos defendas in aeternum*."

[78] As Barr in *The Monophonic Lauda* lists (68–69), the number of the specific arguments within the forty-six *laude* set to music is as follows: Praise of Mary (13); the Annunciation (3); Catherine of Alexandria (1); Mary Magdalene (2); the Nativity of Christ (2); the Epiphany (1); the Passion of Christ (4); the Holy Cross (1); the Resurrection (1); the Resurrection and Ascension (1); the Holy Spirit (2); Pentecost (1); the Holy Trinity (1); the love of Christ (2); Admonition to Penance (2); Death (1); St. Francis (2); St. Anthony of Padua (1); Michael the Archangel (1); All Saints (1); John the Baptist (1); St. John the Evangelist (1); and the Apostles (1).

IL VI PROMETTO — VE LO INTENDO DIMOSTRARE: VARIABLE DOUBLE OBJECT CLITIC CLUSTERS IN THE *DECAMERON* AND MEDIEVAL FLORENTINE*

JANICE ASKI

L'ordine di successione di più pronomi atoni è uno dei non molti fenomeni che, nella sostanziale staticità dell'italiano, consentono di delineare un'evoluzione dall'antico al moderno.[1]

I. Introduction

In several medieval Florentine texts of the mid- to late fourteenth century, such as Boccaccio's *Decameron*, the order of clitic pronouns in double object clitic clusters was variable, in that the third person singular and plural accusative (Acc) clitics (*lo, la, li, le*) could precede or follow the second person singular and plural dative (Dat) clitics (*mi, ti, ci, vi*). Similarly, clitic combinations with a locative (Loc), *ci* or *vi*, and a third person singular or plural Acc clitic were unstable. This variation signals the transition from consistent placement of the Acc clitic in the first slot (Acc-Dat, Acc-Loc), which was typical prior to this period. Rohlfs reports that only Acc-Dat (or ILLUM MIHI) is found in the Novellino (1281–1300) and, in Dante's *Divina Commedia* (1314–1321) the opposite construction, Dat-Acc (or MIHI ILLUM), is rare.[2] Melander finds 14 cases of ILLUM MIHI and only one example of MIHI ILLUM in the *Vita Nuova* (1294–1295). His

---

* I express my sincerest gratitude to Thomas D. Cravens, Christopher Kleinhenz, Michele Loporcaro, Martin Maiden, Scott Schwenter, Dieter Wanner, and Antony Shuttleworth for their helpful comments and suggestions. I, however, take full responsibility for the contents of this paper.

[1] Alfredo Stussi, *Storia linguistica e storia letteraria* (Bologna: Il Mulino, 2005), 102.

[2] Gerhard Rohlfs, *Grammatica storica della lingua italiana e dei suoi dialetti: Morfologia* (Turin: Einaudi, 1968), 176–78.

examination of several other Florentine texts from the end of the thirteenth century (*La Disciplina Clericalis, La Distruzione di Troia, Le Rime di Rustico Filippo, Il Fiore*, and *Le Cento Novelle Antiche*) reveals consistent use of ILLUM MIHI.[3] The transition to the Dat-Acc, Loc-Acc order found in modern Standard Italian, which is derived essentially from late medieval Florentine, was complete by the sixteenth or seventeenth centuries.

Hetzron considers the possibility that alternation in clitic order reflects a "hesitation between an older and newer system," while Lombard, Melander, and Castellani describe the alternation between the two clitic orders as a period of variation between two fixed order types. However, Weinreich, Labov, and Herzog's examination of synchronic linguistic variation, which revealed that ". . . the key to a rational conception of language change — indeed, of language itself — is the possibility of describing *orderly* differentiation in a language serving a community" (my emphasis), encourages research to move beyond pure description of linguistic phenomena or the identification of internal influences in language change, in order to uncover the external motivations for linguistic patterns.[4]

The goal of this paper is to demonstrate that the variation found in the *Decameron*, as well as in several other texts from the same period, is not free; rather, the relative order of clitic pronouns has a pragmatic function in the discourse. The data indicate that the Dat-Acc order is triggered by the speaker's empathy for, or identification with, one of the two interlocutors. The reverse, Acc-Dat, construction appears when the antecedent of the Acc clitic undergoes left dislocation as the sentence theme, or when — due to its critical, often urgent, role in the situation — it can be identified as the discourse topic. These results demonstrate that despite the atonic, non-emphatic, and non-contrastive nature of clitics, in medieval Florentine clitic order was functional and iconic. The order was functional in that the first slot was reserved for, and thus marked, clitics whose antecedents were the focus of the speaker's empathy, the sentence theme or the discourse topic. The combination was iconic in that it mimicked the relative prominence of one referent over the other in the previous discourse. Lastly, we will see that empathy was only one of several factors that triggered the use of MIHI ILLUM in the medieval documents examined, and that these factors ultimately conspired to eliminate the ILLUM MIHI cluster altogether.

---

[3] Jacques Melander, "L'origine de l'italien *me ne, me lo, te la*, etc.," *Studia Neophilologica* 2 (1929): 169–203, here 177.

[4] See Robert Hetzron, "Clitic Pronouns and their Linear Representation," *Forum Linguisticum* 1 (1976): 189–215; Alf Lombard, "Le groupement de pronoms personnels en italien," *Studier Modern Sprakvetenskap* 12 (1934): 21–76 ; Melander, "L'origine," 181; Arrigo Castellani, *Nuovi testi fiorentini*, vol. 1 (Florence: Sansoni, 1952), 92; Uriel Weinreich, William Labov, and Marvin Herzog, "Empirical Foundations for a Theory of Language Change," in *Directions for Historical Linguistics*, ed. Winfred P. Lehmann and Yakov Malkiel (Austin: University of Texas Press, 1968), 100–1.

The paper is organized as follows. In Section 2 the texts consulted and the structures that are examined in (and excluded from) this study are presented and discussed. Section 3 explores the primacy of discourse participants, as manifested in the empathy hierarchy (also known as the animacy, person, or topicality hierarchy), and how this primacy can influence language structure. Examples of how empathy triggers MIHI ILLUM in medieval Florentine texts are provided beside others, in which the discourse salience of the referent of the Acc clitic results in the ILLUM MIHI order. This is followed by an investigation of the role of empathy, as well as other dialectal and structural pressures, in the shift from ILLUM MIHI to MIHI ILLUM.

II. The Medieval Florentine Texts Consulted and the Structures Examined

Boccaccio's *Decameron*, written between 1348 and 1353, is the main focus of this study because it has significant variation in the order of double object clitic constructions. For example, MIHI ILLUM clusters, as in (1), appear beside ILLUM MIHI clusters, as in (2).

(1) volentieri **te la** donerei (I,9:6)[5]
(2) io **la t'**insegnerei (II,4:13).

In the *Decameron*, Boccaccio sought to portray the sociopolitical environment of the period. Given this desire, this variation might have mirrored the actual usage in the community. Wanner states that "[t]he suspicion is high that the extended medieval Romance typology of ILLUM MIHI mainly is a literary phenomenon, well documented in the appropriate manuscripts, but never an exclusive solution in the actual speech community."[6] It appears that this variation was not limited

---

[5] All citations from the *Decameron* are referenced by day, story, and paragraph number according to Giovanni Boccaccio, *Decameron*, ed. Vittore Branca (Florence: Accademia della Crusca, 1976).
  After a thorough analysis of the characteristics of the manuscript, such as the handwriting, drawings, and corrections, Branca concludes that "[q]ueste caratteristiche riflettono senza possibilità di dubbio . . . le abitudini del Boccaccio trascrittore nell'ultimo periodo della sua vita . . ." (XXIX).

[6] Dieter Wanner, "Clitic Clusters in Romance: A Modest Account," in *Grammatical Analyses in Basque and Romance Linguistics*, ed. Jon Franco, Alazne Landa, and Juan Martín (Amsterdam: John Benjamins, 1999), 257–77, here 269. Similarly, the exclusive use of MIHI ILLUM in late 14th-century Florentine texts may be a stylistic choice. Giovanni Fiorentino and Franco Sacchetti, known to be from Florence, each wrote a series of *novelle*: the *Pecorone* (1378) and *Trecentonovelle* (1385), respectively. An analysis of Fiorentino's first six stories in Esposito's edition and Sacchetti's first 64 stories in Lanza's edition

to Florentine. Variation is documented during this period and earlier in other areas of Tuscany as well as in Umbria and the Marche, which suggests that Florentine may have been the last stronghold of ILLUM MIHI in literary texts. Rohlfs states that the earliest texts from Pistoia, Siena, and Arezzo show a preference for (not exclusive use of) MIHI ILLUM, and Melander identifies variable usage in thirteenth-century documents from Lucca and Pisa, in Pistoia from the thirteenth century to Cino da Pistoia (1347), as well as in late thirteenth-century to early fourteenth-century Umbrian texts and early fourteenth-century texts from the Marche.[7]

Supporting evidence for the patterns uncovered in the *Decameron* are taken from Paolo da Certaldo's *Il Libro di Buoni Costumi* (first decades of the second half of the fourteenth century), Francesco da Barberino's *Reggimento e Costumi di Donna* (1318–1320), and *Il Libro dei Sette Savj di Roma* (end thirteenth century–beginning of fourteenth century) written by an anonymous author.[8] The editions

---

shows exclusive use of MIHI ILLUM in the clusters examined in this study, despite the fact that the 16th-century Florentine grammarian Varchi (1520) still accepts both order types in his discussion of the Florentine language. See Giovanni Fiorentino, *Il pecorone*, ed. Enzo Esposito (Ravenna: Longo, 1974); Franco Sacchetti, *Il trecentonovelle*, ed. Antonio Lanza (Florence: Sansoni, 1984).

[7] Rohlfs, *Grammatica storica*, 178; Melander, "L'origine."

[8] The editor of this edition of *Costumi* insists that this is the original manuscript: "... ma nessun dubbio può correre che qui non si abbia l'autografo del compilatore, perché non mancano correzioni che si debbono dire d'autore, e giunte, sia in fine ai capitoletti sia negli interlinei, e richiami formati non solo con postille marginali, ma anche per entro il contesto, e con riferimento alle pagine di questo esemplare": *Il libro di buoni costumi*, ed. Salomone Morpurgo, *Atti della Reale Accademia della Crusca* 1919–1920, (Florence: Galileiana, 1921), XXXIII. All citations are by page number.

The editor of Barberino's text guarantees the authenticity of this edition: "A tenore adunque di tali prinicipii, ci siamo proposto in questa edizione di rappresentare esatamente la lezione dell'antico ed unico manoscritto Barberiniano ... Avviene quindi, che chi faccia studi sull'antica nostra lingua, pronunzia od ortografia, potrà con sicurezza fondare le sue ricerche sul testo da noi publicato ...": Francesco da Barberino, *Del reggimento e costumi di donna*, ed. Claudio Baudi di Vesme (Bologna: Gaetano Romagnoli, 1895), XXXII – XXXIII. All citations are by paragraph number. The variation found in Barberino's text has been attributed to influence from dialects in which MIHI ILLUM has been the norm from the earliest documents. Castellani states that "Francesco da Barberino scrive in una lingua composita, che abbonda di tratti certamente non fiorentini ... Anche gli esempi del tipo *me lo, ne lo* vanno senza dubbio compresi in questo filone dialettale" (Castellani, *Nuovi testi*, 91). Although contact phenomena probably played a role in introducing MIHI ILLUM to the Florence area (see Section IV for discussion), the focus of this analysis of these texts is to identify a pattern of distribution of the two order types once they were both available.

Il Libro dei Sette Savj di Roma has been translated into many languages. The text examined is a translation by an anonymous author of the French version. Old French was

are the same as those examined by Melander, who catalogues the variable clitic pronoun order in these texts as evidence of variation in Florentine.[9]

The scope of this investigation is limited to preverbal double object clitic constructions composed of first and second person singular and plural Dat clitics (*mi, ti, ci, vi*) and third person singular and plural Acc clitics (*lo, la, li, le*). Loc (*ci, vi*) combined with third person singular and plural Acc clitics are also examined. Since combinations with the third person Dat were invariable and consistently appeared as *gliele*, *lili*, or *lele* during this period, it is not clear whether the Acc was perceived as the first element of the cluster and this cluster is, therefore, excluded from this study.[10]

Postverbal clitic combinations are not considered, since evidence indicates that clitic order in this position was relatively stable. Compare the number of postverbal Acc-Dat and Dat-Acc constructions in the *Decameron* (80% to 20%) in Table 1 to the number of the same constructions in preverbal position (50% to 50%). In preverbal position there is an even number of both constructions, while in postverbal position the Acc-Dat order predominates and is nearly systematic. A similar pattern is also found in the *Reggimento* and the *Savj*.[11]

	Postverbal		Preverbal	
	ILLUM MIHI	MIHI ILLUM	ILLUM MIHI	MIHI ILLUM
Decameron	20	5	22	22
Costumi	1	2	2	2
Reggimento	1	0	6*	7
Savj	2	0	16	7

Table 1. Double object clitic pronoun constructions in pre- and postverbal position. *According to Melander the following construction shows hesitation between the two clitic orders, and is not counted: dir no**l vel** potrei (97–98). The pre- or postverbal position is also unclear in the following: io dar **la ti** porrei (*Reggimento*, 390). See "L'origine," 180.

---

similar to Old Florentine in that it also had exclusively the ILLUM MIHI clitic order and underwent an order change in the mid-13th century. See *Il libro dei sette savj di Roma*, ed. Francesco Zambrini (Pisa: Fratelli Nistri, 1864); Melander, "L'origine"; and Dieter Wanner, "The Evolution of Romance Clitic Order," in *Linguistic Studies in Romance Languages*, ed. R. Joe Campbell et al. (Washington, DC: Georgetown University Press, 1974), 158–77. All citations are by page number.

[9] Melander, "L'origine."

[10] Rohlfs states that the invariable 3p Dat + Acc cluster was considered acceptable by grammarians until the 16th century. See *Grammatica storica*, 168.

[11] The postverbal constructions from the four texts are presented in Appendix A.

The data suggest that the transition from ILLUM MIHI to MIHI ILLUM began in preverbal position and later extended to postverbal position.[12] In fact, it appears that this complementary distribution may have persisted as late as the fourteenth or early fifteenth century in some authors. Gregorio Dati's *Il Libro Segreto* contains the memoirs of a Florentine silk merchant who describes his business transactions and domestic affairs between the years 1384 and 1434.[13] In the text, six occurrences of the Dat-Acc order are found beside three instances of Acc-Dat. The forms are distributed systematically between pre- and postverbal position; the Dat-Acc order appears preverbally while constructions with the Acc in the first slot are postverbal.

Preverbal Dat-Acc: perché io non **ve li** avea (28), e io **ve lo** lasciai (34), non so se **me li** potrò mai ritrarre (120), che Idio **ce li** conceda diritti e buoni (21), e quando **mel** disse (89), Idio **cel** facci buono uomo (103)

Postverbal Acc-Dat: e lascià**lovi** (33), piaccia far**lici** riuscire (50), Piaccia a Dio prestar**loci** (77)

Since evidence from thirteenth- to fifteenth- century texts demonstrates that clitic order in postverbal position is nearly consistent, and that the transition from ILLUM MIHI to the reverse construction most likely postdated that of preverbal constructions, postverbal clusters are not examined. However, it is consistent with the analysis presented that the change lagged in postverbal position, in part due to the relative salience of the two positions. Research on urgency, clitic climbing, and left dislocation, which is discussed in Section III B below, has found that salient elements appear earlier in the utterance than less significant information. There is evidence that the relative salience of earlier positions at the utterance level may be reflected at the phrase level. For example, Maiden notes the tendency in some southern Italian varieties to place finite verbs at the end of their clause, after objects, infinitives, gerunds, and participles.[14] In the case of gerunds and participles, the gender and number markers occur after the verb root, which carries the semantic content of the phrase (e.g. *arrivato sono* 'arrived I have,' *parlando sto* 'speaking I am'). In addition, in Standard Italian noun phrases, adjectives normally occur in postnominal position. However, certain adjectives can acquire a different meaning or create a rhetorical effect only

---

[12] Elizabeth Pearce examines the first two *novelle* of the *Decameron* and also concludes that the transition from Acc-Dat to Dat-Acc occurred first in preverbal position. See "On Comparing French and Italian: The Switch from *illum mihi* to *mihi illum*," in *New Analyses in Romance Linguistics*, ed. Dieter Wanner and Douglas A. Kibbee (Amsterdam: Benjamins, 1991), 253–69.

[13] Giorgio Dati, *Il libro segreto in scelta di curiosità letterarie*, ed. Carlo Gargiolli (Bologna: Commissione per i Testi di Lingua, 1968).

[14] Martin Maiden, *A Linguistic History of Italian* (London: Longman, 1995), 264.

if placed before the noun. Compare the meaning of *grande* 'big, large' in the following phrases: *l'uomo grande* 'the (physically) big man' and *il grande uomo* 'the great man.' These phenomena support the relative salience of prenuclear (preverbal) position, and suggest that speakers may have directed more attention to preverbal, rather than postverbal, clitics during the transition from ILLUM MIHI to MIHI ILLUM.[15]

Combinations with *ne*, a clitic with a variety of usages/meanings (see below), are also not considered. Rohlfs reports that in Old Florentine, as found in the Novellino, *ne* appears in the second slot, but things begin to change with the *Decameron*. Constructions with the first and second person Dat consistently appear as Dat-*ne* (e.g. *me ne, te ne, ce ne, ve ne*), but Melander observes that in the *Decameron*, *ne gli* predominates.[16] He notes that *ne* also occupies the first slot when combined with the third person Acc pronouns (e.g. *ne lo, ne la*, etc.).[17] The data from the first five days of the *Decameron* shown in Table 2 indicate that in pre- and postverbal position *ne* indeed predominates in the first slot when combined with a third person Dat or Acc clitic.[18]

	3p ne + Acc	3p Acc + ne	ne gli	gli ne	total ne-Acc/gli	total Acc/gli-ne
Decameron	23	5	9	4	32	9
Costumi	1	0	0	3	1	3
Reggimento	6	1	0	2	6	3
Savj	2	3	0	3	2	6

Table 2. Dative and accusative combinations with *ne*.

Lombard suggests that *ne* + *gli* is a *certaldisme*, but Castellani objects and points out that also the Florentines Velluti and Goro Dati "... hanno *ne gli* per *glie ne* ...Nella *Cronica domestica* del Velluti s'incontra due volte *ne gli* (65, 221) e mai *glie ne*, nel *Libro segreto* del Dati una volta *ne li* (58) e mai *glie ne*."[19]

The patterns found in the three other texts are less consistent than those of the *Decameron*. The difficulty with *ne*-constructions may be due to the fact that, unlike the Dat or Acc pronouns, *ne* has a variety of meanings/usages. It may function as a locative:

---

[15] Maiden, *Linguistic History*, 176–77. See section IV for further discussion.
[16] Rohlfs, *Grammatica storica*, 178; Melander, "L'origine," 181.
[17] In modern Italian the combination *ne* + *lo/la/li/le*, in which *ne* refers to removal from a person or place, may occur, but it is extremely rare.
[18] See Appendix B for citations from the Medieval texts examined.
[19] Lombard, "Le groupement des pronomes," 30; Castellani, *Nuovi testi*, 1: 87.

(3) a casa   **ne** le   recasse
    to home   **there** them   bring (3ps, past)
    he brought them home (*Decameron* III, 1:15)

or as a partitive:

(4) più che tre rimase non   le   **ne**   erano (II, 7:22)
    more than three left   neg   to her   **of them**   were (3ppl, past)
    there were not more than three of them left to her (*Decameron* II, 7:22)

Its referent may be a prepositional phrase (with *di*):

(5) E in brieve de' così fatti   **ne**   gli   disse   molti.
    and in brief of these facts   **about it**   to him   said (3ps, past) many
    and in brief he said many things of this sort about it to him (*Decameron* I, 1:65)

or it may indicate removal of an object from a person or a place:

(6) andò   all'altare ...; e levon**ne**   quell'incienso
    went (3ps) to the altar ...; and took (3ps) **from there** that incense
    he went to the altar ...; and took that incense (*Reggimento*, 59).

The variegated semantic load that *ne* carries may contribute to the prolonged textual confusion over its position in double object clitic constructions, which was resolved by Boccaccio by his (nearly) consistent placement of *ne* in the first slot in clusters with third person clitics, and in the second slot with first and second person clitics (see Section IV for a discussion of the outcome of clusters with *ne* in modern Italian).[20]

III. Pragmatic/Discourse Constraints Governing Clitic Pronoun Order

A. MIHI ILLUM: Empathy

The equal distribution of preverbal Dat-Acc and Acc-Dat clusters in the stories of the first five days of the *Decameron* suggests that the choice of order could be motivated rather than random. An investigation of the contexts suggests that empathy dictates the use of MIHI ILLUM.

---

[20] Similarly, in this study constructions with *si* are not taken into consideration given the varying content of this pronoun (impersonal, reflexive, passive).

The notion of empathy was developed by Kuno in the 1970s (and further elaborated in 1987)[21] to account for a variety of syntactic properties in English and Japanese. For Kuno empathy is characterized as the speaker's varying identification with a person or thing participating in the event. He develops several hierarchies in which empathy is the operative factor, such as the Topic Empathy Hierarchy, which predicts that it is easier for the speaker to empathize with the discourse topic (or the object or person that has already been discussed) rather than a non-topic (which has been introduced for the first time), and the Speech Act Empathy Hierarchy, by which the speaker empathizes more with himself than with the hearer or a third person.

The same principles are applied in Silverstein's animacy hierarchy (also known as the empathy hierarchy), which was introduced to explain split-ergative marking systems. A slightly simplified version of Silverstein's hierarchy is presented in Deane as

> 1st person pronoun > 2nd p.pr. > 3rd p. anaphor > 3rd p. demonstrative > proper name > kin-term > human + animate > concrete object > container > location > perceivable NP > abstract NP. [22]

This hierarchy ranks NPs according to their lexical content. At the top are highly context-dependent forms, while abstract entities occupy the bottom. Deane points out that the Silverstein hierarchy is essentially a hierarchy of markedness as topic, since "[t]he more salient the referent is likely to be within the situation of speaking, and the more tightly the NP's reference is determined by the situation of speaking, the higher it will be on the Silverstein hierarchy, and the likelier it will be construed as topical in the absence of indications to the contrary." [23]

---

[21] See, for example, Susumu Kuno, "Subject, Theme and the Speaker's Empathy—A Reexamination of Relativization Phenomena," in *Subject and Topic*, ed. Charles N. Li (New York: Academic Press, 1976), 417–44; idem, "The Speaker's Empathy and its Effect on Syntax: A Reexamination of Yaru and Kureru on Japanese," *Journal of the Association of Teachers of Japanese* 2/3 (1976): 249–71; idem and Etsuko Kaburaki, "Empathy and Syntax," *Linguistic Inquiry* 8 (1977): 627–72; Susumu Kuno, *Functional Syntax: Anaphora, Discourse and Empathy* (Chicago: University of Chicago Press, 1987).

[22] M. Silverstein, "Hierarchy of Features and Ergativity," in *Grammatical Categories in Australian Languages*, ed. R. M. W. Dixon (Canberra: Australian Institute of Aboriginal Studies, 1976), 112–71; Paul Deane, "English Possessives, Topicality, and the Silverstein Hierarchy," in *Proceedings of the Thirteenth Annual Meeting of the Berkeley Linguistics Society*, ed. James Aske et al. (Berkeley: Berkeley Linguistics Society, 1987), 65–76, here 67.

[23] Deane, "English Possessives," 73.

During the same period, Givón introduced the universal hierarchy of topicality, or the likelihood that various NP arguments could be the topic of sentences:[24]

a. HUMAN > NON-HUMAN

b. DEFINITE > INDEFINITE

c. MORE INVOLVED PARTICIPANT > LESS INVOLVED PARTICIPANT

d. 1ST PERSON > 2ND PERSON > 3RD PERSON

His hierarchy reflects the tendency for (a) humans to speak more about humans than non-humans (the ego/anthropocentric nature of discourse), and for (b) old information to be the topic and new information an assertion. Factor (c) predicts the following case hierarchy of topicality: agent > dative > accusative, since agents are usually the most involved participants, appearing as subjects, and accusatives are the least involved. The last factor, referred to as the 'Hierarchy of Persons' by Yamamoto, also expresses the egocentric nature of discourse, since the speaker tends to be the point of reference.[25]

Langacker gives topicality an interpretation in cognitive grammar.[26] He identifies four topicality factors regarding the conception of the clausal participants, one of which is the empathy hierarchy.[27] His empathy hierarchy "reflects an egocentric assessment of the various sorts of entities that populate the world. It ranks them according to their potential to attract our empathy, i.e. on the basis of such matters as likeness and common concerns. . .:

> speaker > hearer > human > animal > physical object > abstract entity"
> (*Foundations*, 2:306–7) .

---

[24] Talmy Givón, "Topic, Pronoun and Grammatical Agreement," in *Subject and Topic*, ed. Li, 149–88. Givón continued to elaborate upon and apply the hierarchy. See, for example, idem, *Topic Continuity in Discourse* (Amsterdam: John Benjamins, 1983); idem, "The Pragmatics of Word Order: Predictability, Importance and Attention," in *Studies in Syntactic Typology*, ed. Michael Hammond, Edith Moravcsik, and Jessica Wirth (Amsterdam: John Benjamins, 1988), 243–84; idem, "The Grammar of Referential Coherence as Mental Processing Instructions," *Linguistics* 30 (1992): 5–55.

[25] Mutsumi Yamamoto, *Animacy and Reference* (Amsterdam: John Benjamins, 1999).

[26] Ronald W. Langacker, *Foundations of Cognitive Grammar*, vol.2: *Descriptive Application* (Stanford: Stanford University Press, 1991), 306–8.

[27] The other factors are semantic role, definiteness, and figure/ground organization.

Yamamoto points out that the concept of 'empathy' plays a significant role in the perception of animacy, and that what Langacker has called the 'empathy hierarchy' has been labeled an 'animacy hierarchy.'[28] She gives examples of how animacy affects word order and concludes that "[e]ntities with strong animacy trigger special linguistic markings and occupy salient positions in clauses and discourse; it seems reasonable to argue that the concept of animacy strongly influences our mind in the process of language use" (67).[29]

Regardless of the conceptual overlap and terminological confusion, each of these hierarchies highlights the primacy of the interlocutors in discourse, since Dat animates rank higher than Acc inanimates, and the first and second person are higher than the third person. There is evidence of the effect of these hierarchies on the structures of a variety of languages,[30] and there are indications that

---

[28] Yamamoto, *Animacy;* Langacker, *Foundations.*

[29] For a discussion of the role of animacy in topicalization see John Myhill, *Typlogical Discourse Analysis: Quantitative Approaches to the Study of Linguistic Function* (Oxford: Blackwell, 1992), 189–92.

[30] Deane applies Silverstein's empathy hierarchy to English possessives and finds that the higher the possessor NP is on the hierarchy, the more acceptable are possessives with the suffix –*'s* or a pronoun, and the less acceptable are possessives with *of*. As pointed out by Yamamoto, the results of Leech, Francis, and Xu's investigation of English genitives also demonstrates that animacy of the possessor is one of the most crucial factors responsible for the preference for the suffixed possessive rather than for the construction with *of*. Delancey explores the role of empathy in the split ergativity pattern in Australian languages. Cienki employs the animacy hierarchy and its relation to empathy in his discussion of possessive marking in Russian. Cook investigates the role of empathy in cliticization and the appearance of the *–cia* suffix in Samoan. Yamamoto gives several examples from the literature that demonstrate the effect of animacy, empathy, and person on word order. For example, in an Australian language, Gunqinggu, Siewierska (following Oates) shows that first or second person bound pronouns always precede third person noun phrases, so that in the phrases equivalent to "I'll hit them" and "They'll hit me," the first person pronoun always precedes the third, regardless of its role. Croft reports that in Navajo, the argument that encodes higher animacy always precedes a lower animacy argument, so that in the phrase "The horse kicked the man," it would be ungrammatical for "the horse" to precede "the man." Ertel provides an example of empathy influencing word order. He found that in write-ups of football matches in (English) newspapers by local reporters, the home team players occupied subject position more often than opposing team players. Schwenter and Silva demonstrate that the interaction of the dimensions of animacy and specificity dictate the variable form of anaphoric direct objects in Brazilian Portuguese. Finally, Gerlach provides an interpretation of Dat–Acc clitic order in Optimality Theory that is based on similar hierarchies: person and argument hierarchies. See Deane, "English Possessives"; Yamamoto, *Animacy,* 50–52; Geoffrey Leech, Brian Francis, and Xunfeng Xu, "The Use of Computer Corpora in the Textual Demonstrability of Gradience in Linguistic Categories," in *Continuity in Linguistic Semantics,* ed. Catherine Fuchs and Bernard Victorri (Philadelphia: John Benjamins, 1994), 57–76. Scott

these concepts can also account for phenomena in Italian. For example, Parry reports that:

> [f]irst and second person clitic pronouns, in view of their salience, are particularly topical and hence liable to be included early in the discourse. In fact, a significant number of the examples of 'clitic splitting' show instances of a first or second person clitic raising to the finite verb, leaving a third person clitic on the lower verb.[31]

Berretta refers to the topicality hierarchy in her interpretation of the tendency for Dat rather than Acc clitics to be raised from the infinitive to the main verb in speech.[32]

(7) <u>mi</u> voglio fare una bella dormita, stanotte

Here the Dat is clause-initial, instead of clause-final and attached to the infinitive (*voglio far<u>mi</u>* . . .). The same is true in the following example, in which the Dat + Acc cluster appears before the finite verb instead of being attached to the infinitive (*vorrei dar<u>gliela</u>* . . .).

(8) <u>Gliela</u> vorrei dare io, la risposta, se permette

Delancey, "An Interpretation of Split Ergativity and Related Phenomena," *Language* 57 (1982): 626–57. Alan Cienki, "Experiencers, Possessors, and Overlap between Russian Dative and *u* + Genitive," in *Proceedings of the 19th Annual Meeting of the Berkeley Linguistics Society, February 12–15, 1993*, ed. Joshua S. Guenter, Barbara A. Kaiser, and Cheryl C. Zoll (Berkeley: Berkeley Linguistics Society, 1993), 77–89. Kenneth William Cook, "The Empathy Hierarchy and Samoan Clitic Pronouns," *Cognitive Linguistics* 4 (1994): 57–75. Yamamoto, *Animacy*. Anna Siewierska, *Word Order Rules* (London: Croom Helm, 1988). Lynette F. Oates, *A Tentative Description of the Gunwinggu Language (of Western Arnhem Land)* (Sydney: Oceania Linguistics Monographs, 1964). William Croft, *Typology and Universals* (Cambridge: Cambridge University Press, 1990), 114. Suitbert Ertel, "Where do the Subjects of Sentences Come From?" in *Sentence Production: Developments in Research and Theory*, ed. Sheldon Rosenberg (Hillsdale, NJ: Lawrence Erlbaum, 1977), 141–68. Scott Schwenter and Glaucia V. Silva, "Anaphoric Direct Objects in Spoken Brazilian Portuguese: Semantics and Pragmatics," *Revista Internacional de Linguistica Iberoromanica* 1 (2003): 99–123. Birgit Gerlach, *Clitics between Syntax and Lexicon* (Amsterdam: John Benjamins, 2002), chap. 4.

[31] Mair M. Parry, "Preverbal Negation and Clitic Ordering," *Zeitschrift für romanische Philologie* 113 (1997): 243–70, here 261.

[32] Monica Berretta, "Struttura informativa e sintassi dei pronomi atoni: condizioni che favoriscono la 'risalita'," in *Tema-rema in italiano*, ed. Harro Stammerjohann (Tübingen: Narr, 1986), 71–83, here 78.

Instances of clitic raising (or climbing) in the medieval texts demonstrate the propensity for leftward movement of the Dat in Old Florentine. Although clitic climbing with *convenire* 'to be advisable' + infinitive is not acceptable in modern Italian, it occurs throughout the medieval texts examined.[33] In each of the following examples, the Acc argument of the infinitive is raised to either pre- or postverbal position on the first verb of the complex, but the Dat argument of *convenire* occupies the first slot:[34]

(9) **me la** conviene in questa guisa tanti anni seguitar (V,8:26)

(10) convien**tela** dare (*Costumi*: 376)

(11) **tel** conviene pur fare (*Savj*: 39 and 48)

(12) **mel** conviene sofferire (*Savj*: 83)[35]

The nearly consistent use of MIHI ILLUM in this raising environment reflects the priority given to the discourse participants, as predicted by the empathy hierarchy. In the medieval texts examined, the priority of the interlocutors is also found in non-raising contexts, in which the speaker's empathy for, or preoccupation with, the addressee or him/herself triggers placement of the Dat in the leftmost slot.[36] Preoccupation for the listener is frequently reflected in the speaker's deference to the addressee when asking a favor, and in the speaker's politeness toward a group of listeners when asking for their attention.[37] By preposing the Dat, whose referent is the source of preoccupation for the speaker, the relative order of clitics is an iconic representation of the pragmatic structure of the dis-

---

[33] Napoli hypothesizes that *convenire* might have been less semantically full for Boccaccio than for present-day speakers. See Donna Jo Napoli, "Semantic Interpretation vs. Lexical Governance: Clitic Climbing in Italian," *Language* 57 (1981): 841–87, here 873.

[34] In the medieval texts examined, clitic climbing occurs in verb + infinitive constructions with *volere* 'to want,' *potere* 'to be able to,' *osare* 'to dare,' *intendere* 'to intend,' and the causative construction with *fare* 'to make.' The Acc and Dat arguments of the infinitive are both raised to the finite verb, and the distribution of MIHI ILLUM (60%) and ILLUM MIHI (40%) orders is in favor of the former.

[35] There is one exception: "Non vedete voi, diss' ella, come catun dì i vostri cani guastano *i panni nostri e il letto*, che non passa mai due dì che non **li ci** convenga canbiare?" (*Savj*, 45).

[36] The examples provided for each cluster (MIHI ILLUM and ILLUM MIHI) are from the *Decameron*, and additional examples from the supporting Medieval texts are found in Appendices C and D respectively. In each citation the antecedent of the clitic occupying the first slot appears in italics, and the cluster is in bold.

[37] The speaker's focus on the addressee is also expected when reprimanding or giving advice, commands, or instructions. Examples of MIHI ILLUM in these contexts from the supporting texts are shown in Appendix C.

course. For example, in 13–15, when a speaker asks a favor of a socially superior individual, the Dat clitic in first position indicates deference for the listener, with the desired goal of getting the wish granted.

> 13. " . . .'*O signor mio*,' diss'io 'io *vi* priego che voi mi perdoniate.' E egli allora disse: 'E io ti perdono per tal convenente, che tu a lei vadi come tu prima potrai e faccisi perdonare: e dove ella non ti perdoni, io ci tornerò e darottene tante, che io ti farò tristo per tutto il tempo che tu ci viverai.' Quello che egli poi mi dicesse, io non <u>ve l'</u>oso dire, se prima non mi perdonate." (IV,2:19)

> 14. "*Signor mio*, io non vengo nella tua presenza per vendetta che io attenda della ingiuria che m'è stata fatta; ma in sodisfacimento di quella *ti* priego che *tu* m'insegni come *tu* sofferi quelle le quali io intendo che *ti* son fatte, acciò che, da *te* apparando, io possa pazientemente la mia comportare: la quale, sallo Idio, se io far lo postessi, volentieri <u>te la</u> donerei, . . ." (I,9:6)[38]

> 15. . . . e essa dopo la confession disse: "*Padre mio*, a me conviene ricorrere a *voi* per aiuto e per conseglio di ciò che *voi* udirete. Io so, come colei che detto <u>ve l'</u>ho, che *voi* conoscete i miei parenti e 'l mio marito, . . ." (III,3:9)

A similar use of deference is found in the third story of the third day, in which a woman goes to confession and induces a solemn friar to unwittingly send her way a young man whom she has been admiring from a distance. The respect that she shows to the friar as she manipulates him is reflected in the Dat-Acc clitic order in 16:

> 16. ". . . il che io ho avuto e ho sì forte per male, che io credo, se io non avessi guardato al peccato, e poscia per *vostro* amore, io avrei fatto il diavolo; ma pure mi son rattemperata, né ho voluto fare né dire cosa alcuna che io non <u>vel</u> faccia prima assapere. . . ." (III,3:26)

The woman's obsequious manner with the friar is also found in the exchange between Zima and the nobleman and future governor of Milan, Messer Francesco Vergellesi. Zima has just tricked Vergellesi into letting him talk privately with his wife in exchange for Zima's horse. Vergellesi thinks he has outwitted Zima by instructing his wife not to say a word during the conversation, but instead Zima is able to use the encounter to convince the woman to meet with him when Vergellesi is away.

---

[38] Examples 13 and 14 also contain contextual triggers for the opposite, Acc-Dat, order. Conflicts of this type are discussed in Section IV.

17. "Omai è ben mio il pallafren che fu tuo." A cui il Zima rispose: "*Messer sì, ma se io avessi creduto trarre di questa grazia ricevuta da voi tal frutto chente tratto n'ho, senza domandarla*vi **ve l**'avrei donato: . . ." (III,5:27)

In 18 the speaker is married to a spiritual man who, because he strives for eternal paradise, has chosen celibacy. Consequently, the woman has become more of a servant than a wife and has sought carnal pleasure elsewhere. In the following example, the woman is in bed with another man and is trying to placate her suspicious husband who is in an adjacent room:

18. "Come ti dimeni? che vuol dir questo dimenare?" La donna ridendo. . .rispose: "Come non sapete voi quello che questo vuol dire? Ora io **ve l'** ho udito dire mille volte: . . ." (III,4:26)

Being gracious to the listener is particularly important when addressing an audience. In four of five cases Boccaccio's storytellers use the Dat-Acc order when addressing the entire group before or after telling their story.

19. —*Giovani donne*, spesse volte già addivenne che quello che varie riprensioni e molte pene date a alcuno non hanno potuto in lui adoperare, una parola molte volte, per accidente non che *ex proposito* detta, l'ha operato. Il che assai bene appare nella novella raccontata dalla Lauretta, e io ancora con un'altra assai brieve **ve lo** intendo dimostrare:. . . (I,9:3)

20. —*Carissime compagne*, quantunque Pampinea, per sua cortesia più che per mia vertù m'abbia di voi tutte fatta reina, non sono io per ciò disposta nella forma del nostro vivere dover solamente il mio giudicio seguire, ma col mio il vostro insieme; e acciò che quello che a me di far pare conosciate, e per conseguente aggiugnere e menomar possiate a vostro piacere, con poche parole **ve lo** intendo di dimostrare. (I, Concl.:6)

21. E per ciò che la fatica, la quale altra volta ho impresa e ora son per pigliare, a niuno altro fine riguarda se non a dover*vi* torre malinconia, e riso e allegrezza porger*vi*, quantunque la materia della mia seguente novella, *innamorate giovani*, sia in parte men che onesta, però che diletto può porgere, **ve la** pur dirò. (V,10:4)

22. Per che così vi vo' dire, *donne mie care*, che chi **te la** fa, fagliele; e se tu non puoi,. . . (V, 10:64)

There is only one exception in which the Acc precedes the Dat in this context.

—Graziose donne, voi non udiste forse mai dire come il diavolo si rimetta in Inferno; e per ciò, senza partirmi guari dall'effetto che voi tutto questo dì ragionato avete, io **il vi** vo' dire:. . .(III,10:3)

In this case, the Acc clitic may be preposed because of the scatological nature of its referent, which the speaker knows will be disturbing to the listeners. The referent of the Acc is the story of how the devil was put back into hell, in which the devil is a euphemism for the penis, and hell for the vagina of a naïve young woman.

The empathy hierarchy predicts that the speaker will empathize more with him/herself than with a hearer or a third participant. In contexts in which the speaker is concerned with his/her own state of affairs, s/he discusses his/her own actions, which often results in verbs conjugated in the first person throughout the discourse. The subject, especially if it persists in the discourse, is identifiable as the discourse topic. Givón's topicality hierarchy highlights the connection between the subject and discourse topic, which he identifies as

> the participant most crucially involved in the action sequence of the paragraph; it is the participant most closely associated with the higher-level "Theme" of the paragraph; and finally it is the participant most likely to be coded as the primary topic—or grammaticalized subject—of the vast majority of sequentially-ordered clauses/sentences comprising the thematic paragraph.[39]

He also points out that topic persistence is the factor that most directly reflects a topic's importance in the discourse, and, thus, is considered a measure of the speaker's intent. He accepts as self-evident the assumption that "[m]ore important discourse topics appear more frequently in the register, i.e. they have a higher probability of persisting longer in the register after a relevant measuring point" (15).

The speaker's empathy for his/her own state of affairs is reflected in the Dat-Acc clitic order in the following examples. In 23, the antecedent of the Dat is the subject of the main verb in the preceding clause:[40]

---

[39] Givón, *Topic Continuity*, 8.

[40] In the following example the woman is in confession discussing her dismal situation with her half-wit husband. Although in this context the first person (*io*) does not appear as the subject, the speaker's frustration with her situation is reflected in the Dat-Acc order: "Messere, se Idio m'avesse dato marito o non **me l'**avesse dato, . . ." (III,8:8). Focus on the speaker is also demonstrated in two cases in which the dative clitic may be interpreted as contrastive, and thus appears in the first slot. In the following example, Guillaume de Roussillon kills his wife's lover, removes his heart, and instructs the cook to prepare it for their evening meal. He tells the cook to bring the heart to him while he and his wife are both at the table (so that he can pass it on to his wife and, once she has finished eating, tell her what/who she ate): "Prenderai quel cuor di cinghiare e fa che tu ne facci una vivandetta la miglioe e la più dilettevole a mangiar che tu sai; e quando a tavola sarò, **me la** manda in una scodella d'argento" (IV,9:16). In the next exchange, two fishermen claim that the carpenter sold a chest to them. The carpenter responds that they

23. "... *Io* non ho queste cose sapute da' vicini: ella medesima, forte di te dolendosi, **me l'**ha dette...." (III,3:18)

In 24, the speaker suffered greatly from the death of her lover and insists that no one can take him from her heart. She is also concerned about her unkind behavior toward him prior to his departure. The antecedent (*io*) of the dative clitic (*me*) persists as the subject of one or more verbs in the discourse preceding the clitic cluster:

24. "*Io* veggio che Idio vi dimostra tutti i segreti degli uomini, e per ciò *io* son disposta a non celarvi i miei. Egli è il vero che nella mia giovanezza *io* amai sommamente lo sventurato giovane la cui morte è apposta al mio marito: la qual morte *io* ho tanto pianta, quanto dolent'è a me, per ciò che, quantunque *io* rigida e salvatica verso di lui mi mostrassi anzi la sua partita, né la sua partita né la sua lunga dimora né ancora la sventurata morte mai **me l'**hanno potuto trarre del cuore." (III,7:26)

In 25 the woman's preoccupation with her own distress over the loss of her lover is signaled by her opening comment, "What did I do?", and by her concern over wasting the last six months of her life.

25. "Che fo io? perché perdo io la mia giovanezza? Questi se ne è andato a Melano e non tornerà di questi sei mesi; e quando **me gli** ristorerà egli giammai?..." (III,5:30)

In the fourth story of the first day, a monk sneaks a woman into his cell and realizes that an abbot has witnessed his transgression. To avoid punishment, he lures the abbot to commit the same violation so that he can blackmail him. In 26 the monk is asking the abbot for forgiveness, while at the same time letting him know that he is aware that the abbot is also guilty. The preposed Dat signals the speaker's preoccupation with his predicament as he asks to be pardoned:

26. "Messere, *io* non sono ancora tanto all'Ordine di san Benedetto stato, che *io* possa avere ogni particularità di quello apparata; e voi ancora non *m'*avavate monstrato che' monaci si debban far dalle femine premiere come da' digiuni e dalle vigilie; ma ora che mostrato **me l'**avete,..." (I,4:21)

---

are lying, and that he didn't sell it *to them*, but rather that they must have stolen it *from him*. "... 'Non è così, anzi l'hai venduta alli due giovani prestatori, sì come essi stanotte mi dissero quando in casa loro la vidi allora che fu preso Ruggieri.' A cui il legnaiuolo disse: 'Essi mentono, per ciò che mai io non la vendei loro ma essi questa notte passata **me l'**avranno imbolata;...'" (IV,10:37). Additional examples from the supporting texts, in which the speaker's arrogance or preoccupation with his/her own affairs produce the MIHI ILLUM order, are provided in Appendix D.

As predicted by the empathy hierarchy, the majority of clusters with the first person dative pronoun (9/11 or 82%) have the MIHI ILLUM order in the *Decameron*.[41] These data demonstrate that empathy may play a role in the leftward movement of the Dat clitic, or the MIHI ILLUM order. However, the evidence is not conclusive unless contrasted with the contexts in which the reverse order appears. The next section demonstrates that use of the ILLUM MIHI order is inextricably linked to the discourse structure, such that the Acc clitic is preposed when its antecedent functions as the sentence theme or discourse topic.

B. ILLUM MIHI: Sentence Themes and (Urgent) Discourse Topics

Vanelli contrasts Old Italian (the language of Tuscany between 1200–1300) and modern Italian by comparing the elements permitted in phrase-initial position. While in modern Italian this position seems to be strongly linked to the function of subject, in Old Italian it could also be associated with the sentence theme. She defines the theme as "il punto di partenza per lo sviluppo successivo del discorso, ciò su cui verte la predicazione (rema)." In cases in which an adverbial of place or time occupies initial position, she generalizes her definition (based on Chafe) to setting "a spacial, temporal, or individual framework within which the main predication holds."[42] The following examples from the *Decameron* demonstrate a few of the elements that could undergo left dislocation (LD) in Old Italian.

Dislocation of the direct object (which is still common in modern Italian):

(27) Ma **questo** come si può fare? (III,7:56)

Dislocation of the indirect object:

(28) l'amore il quale **a Efigenia** portava (V,1:19)

Dislocation of other nuclear complements:

(29) se egli **dieci anni o sempre mai** fuori di casa dimorasse (II,9:10)

---

[41] The predominance of the first person Dat in the first slot is not as striking in the supporting texts. The *Reggimento* has MIHI ILLUM in 3/7 cases and, in the *Savj*, the first person Dat occupies the first slot in 2/3 cases. The first person Dat does not appear in clusters in the *Costumi*.

[42] See Laura Vanelli, "Strutture tematiche in italiano antico," in *Tema-rema in italiano*, ed. Stammerjohann, 249–74, here 270, n. 2; Wallace L. Chafe, "Givenness, Contrastiveness, Definiteness, Subjects, Topics, and Point of View," in *Subject and Topic*, ed. Li, 25–55, here 50.

(30) **per lo salvatico luogo** s'andò (V,3:20–21)

(31) ché **di pervenire infino al corpo santo** troverò io ben modo (II,1:8)

According to Vanelli, Old Italian had several strategies for focusing on the theme in a sentence. One possibility was LD without a pronominal copy of the theme, as shown above.[43] Another strategy was left dislocation of the theme to phrase initial position followed by a pronominal copy, which is a form of thematization still found in modern Italian, as in the example:

(32) Carlo, l'hanno fermato i carabinieri[44]

Berretta offers support for the propensity for leftward movement of the sentence theme in modern Italian when she reports that in informal speech, some verbs, such as *cercare di* 'to try', *provvedere a* 'to make provisions', *permettere di* 'to permit', *aiutare a* 'to help', *fare a* 'succeed', trigger clitic climbing, as in

(33) cercate**le** di sentire, queste rime

instead of Standard written *cercate di sentir**le**, queste rime*.[45] She suggests that this raising phenomenon may be due, at least in part, to a greater tendency in the spoken language to place the theme as far to the left in the utterance as possible.[46] Berretta also states that in cases of LD, it may be coreferencing with the displaced, tonic element that renders the clitic maximally thematic and therefore results in raising to the first verb of the complex.[47]

---

[43] The result is a surface structure similar to modern topicalized constructions, in which, rather than given information that is present in the consciousness of the listener being dislocated, new or contrastive information moves leftward. The following example is from Vanelli, "Strutture tematiche," 253: I carabinieri hanno fermato Paolo. No! CARLO, hanno fermato i carabinieri (non Paolo).

[44] Vanelli, "Strutture tematiche," 251.

[45] Berretta, "Struttura informativa," 72.

[46] She also suggests that other contributing factors may be the tendency to transform verbs with prepositional infinitives into auxiliaries as a result of frequent usage that leads to semantic erosion, and/or syntactic simplification. She adds that the two hypotheses can coexist, since: "che il comportamento dei pronomi sia spesso collegato ad esigenze più late di sinistra e testualità è del resto ampiamente noto" ("Struttura informativa," 72).

[47] She notes that this raising context is very similar to that in Portuguese main clauses described by Wanner. He finds that when the verb is preceded by a constituent different from the clitic + verb group (that is rhythmically joined with the verb into one unit, especially barring a pause between the two elements), proclisis indicates that the preceding element is the focus, while enclisis indicates non-focus. In all other cases enclisis is the norm. Berretta concludes with Wanner that this raising phenomenon must be due to a combination of pragmatic and intonational factors. Wanner also sees a link

Benincà points out that in Old Italian the dislocated element could be separated from its host verb by other constituents, in which case the use of a pronominal copy was obligatory.[48] She adds that relative pronouns, when separated from the verb, had a pronominal copy. She compares the following examples from the *Decameron*. In the first the preposed element (*la quale*) is separated from the verb (*donerei*) by a clause (*se io farlo potessi*) and has a pronominal copy, while in the second, the same type of object is next to the verb (ignoring the adverb, *agramente*) and a clitic does not appear:

(34) (...ingiuria...) **la quale**, sallo iddio, se io farlo potessi, volentieri **te la** donerei (*Decameron*, I,9:6)[49]

(35) (...ingiuria...) **la quale** agramente vendicò.

In the *Decameron* the Acc-Dat order is used in clusters in which the referent of the Acc is dislocated to the left as in 36–38. In 39 and 40, the relative pronoun is separated from the verb by one or more clauses, and its pronominal copy appears in the first slot of the double object cluster. Placing the Acc in the first or left-most slot mimics and is iconic of the leftward movement and thematization of the referent in the text:

36. *quello che non si dee pote fare* non so perché bisogni che io **il vi** prometta. (III,7:56)

37. Io ti richeggio per Dio che *le condizion postemi per li due cavalieri che io ti mandai*, tu **le mi** osservi (III, 9:58)

38. *Questo, s'el* ti piace, io **il ti** prometto (V,5:10)

---

between clitic placement in European Portuguese and LD: "The strange encliticizations of EP, dependent on the topic nature (or other lower or absent emphasis) of the preceding constituent appears as an extension of the widely attested structures with extracted, left dislocated and 'topicalized' elements, also known in EP." See Berretta, "Struttura informativa"; Dieter Wanner, "Pragmatics and Syntax in Portuguese Clitic Placement," in *Current Research in Romance Languages*, ed. James P. Lantolf and Gregory B. Stone (Bloomington: Indiana University Linguistics Club, 1982), 194–206, here 202–3.

[48] She also remarks that, although the types of constituents that separate the dislocated element from the verb and trigger an obligatory clitic must yet be investigated, she finds that clitics, some adverbs and negation do not require a pronominal copy. See Paola Benincà, "Il lato sinistro della frase italiana," *Association of Teachers of Italian Journal* 47 (1986): 57–85.

[49] This example corresponds to 14 above. Because of LD, one would expect the order Acc-Dat. This conflict is discussed in Section IV.

39. *il quale*, poi ch'avendo*lo* avuto continuamente con voi e non *l*'avete conosciuto, io **il vi** voglio mostrare (III,7:88)

In 40, although the relative pronoun is omitted, the second phrase can be interpreted as a relative clause. The relative pronoun (*la quale*) would be separated from the verb by other constituents, which results in a pronominal copy:

40. assagliamo *la nave*; [la quale] Idio, alla nostra impresa favorevole, senza vento prestarle

la ci tien ferma (IV,4:17)

In the following examples the referent of the Acc clitic appears in a preceding clause as a relative pronoun that is separated from the verb and followed by a pronominal copy (41), or it is a dislocated element (42–43). In the latter, the Acc clitic appears in the first slot of the cluster as a marker of its referent's thematization even though it is not a pronominal copy in the LD construction:

41. *le quali* acciò che tu *l*'avessi, pose Idio nell'animo al mio dispietato padre che a me ti mandasse, e io **le ti** darò (IV,1:52–54).[50]

42. da me *un picciol don* vogliate...io donar no **l vi** possa (V,9:34)

43. io vi promisi di *niuna cosa* farne che io prima no**l vi** dicessi (III,3:39)

Vanelli points out that adverbials of space and time can also be dislocated, in which case the dislocation serves to set the spacial framework for the discourse.[51] In medieval Italian the unmarked order for clitic clusters with a Loc is Acc + Loc, as demonstrated by the following examples: **il vi** traesse (I,5:10) , veduta non **la ci** ho (V,3:37), io **la vi** mandassi (III,6:20), io **la ci** farò dipignere (II,8:17), **la**

---

[50] In this citation the speaker is addressing the heart of her slain lover, which has been placed in a chalice and given to her. Earlier in the monologue, her lover's heart, or the addressee, is the topic, as signaled by *Tu* 'you' as the subject of the clause preceding the Dat-Acc cluster: "... *Tu* hai il tuo corso fornito, e di tale chente la fortuna **tel** concedette ti se' spacciato:..." (IV,1:52). The Acc-Dat order in 41 signals the topic shift, as she bemoans that fact that her lover's death lacked the tears of the woman he loved.

[51] Vanelli, "Strutture tematiche."

<u>vi</u> confermò sù (III,6:22), la sua fortuna <u>il vi</u> guidò, in un pratello (V,1:7).[52] However, when the locative is dislocated left, the order is reversed:[53]

44. *dentro* <u>vel</u> potrem mettere (IV,10:19)

45. *dentro* <u>vel</u> misero (IV,10:20)

46. *a casa* <u>ne le</u> recasse . . .più giorni <u>vel</u> tenne. . .(III,1:15).

47. *Quivi* parendogli esser sicuro, ringraziando Idio che condotto <u>ve lo</u> avea (II,4:29)

48. non aveva *in inferno* messo diavolo. . .ché ancora *al ninferno*, non che altrui, duole . . . <u>vel</u> rimisero,. . . (III,10:20–22).

By placing the clitic whose referent is thematized by LD in the left-most slot, clitic order is dictated by the structure of the preceding discourse. This sensitivity of clitic order to sentence structure can be extended to the discourse as a whole, in that the antecedent of the clitic in the first slot can often be identified as the discourse topic.[54] However, determining the discourse topic empirically is not straightforward.[55] Gómez-González reviews the findings of research based on semantic interpretations of the topic, which view it as a phrase representing the object or matter about which text is written. She finds that "aboutness

---

[52] In the last two examples the Loc is a cataphor, so its appearance in the second slot may be indexical/deictic. This is also the case in: "Ma quanto tutti coloro che così credono sieno ingannati, mi piace, poi che la reina comandato <u>me l'</u>ha, non uscendo della proposta fattaci da lei, *di farvene più chiare con una piccola novelletta*." (III,1:5). There is one case in which the Loc is cataphoric but its clitic does not appear in the second slot: ". . . io ho tante borse e tante cintole che io <u>ve l'</u>afogherei *entro*. . . ." (III,3:27). However, the referent of the Acc clitic (l') is unclear, and is translated as "myself."

[53] There are two exceptions in which the referent of the locative is dislocated but the clitic is not: ". . .per la qual cosa la donna, sappiendo *lui* la notte non dovere tornare a casa, come usata era, occultatamente si fece venir *Ruggieri* e nella sua camera *il* mise e *dentro* <u>il vi</u> serrò infino a tanto che certe altre persone della casa s'andassero a dormire." (IV,10:12) ". . .per che, senza alcuno indugio pigliare, *accostatosi* a Giacomino che ancora era quivi, *il* pregò che *in casa sua il* menasse e veder *gli* facesse questa giovane. Giacomino <u>il vi</u> menò volentieri. . ."(V,5:33).

[54] Bertuccelli Papi reports that there is confusion in the literature between the meaning of theme and topic, and for that reason identifies the theme as "what the sentence is about" and the topic as "what the text is about." This distinction is adopted here. See Marcella Bertuccelli Papi, "On the Relationship between Sentence Themes and Text Topics," *Studi italiani di linguistica teorica e applicata* 1 (1994): 127–40, here 128.

[55] Gillian Brown and George Yule, *Discourse Analysis* (Cambridge: Cambridge University Press, 1983).

cannot be regarded as an objectively identifiable *unique* category, but as a clearly *intuitive*, and therefore, subjective concept, since 'what is being talked about' may be judged differently at different points in discourse, and participants themselves may not have identical views of 'what is being talked about'. . ." (original emphasis).[56]

Literary texts pose a particular challenge. Lotfipour-Saedi and Rezai-Tajani point out that the lack of topics in theme positions or the occurrence of intervening secondary themes unrelated to the text topic may be employed by the author to divert the attention of the reader to create a particular effect (e.g. imagination). They compare modes of thematization in literary and scientific texts and find that in scientific texts the relation between the individual sentences and the central topic is indicated explicitly by many direct and indirect references to the topic. Since this is often not the case in literary texts, they observe that identification of the central topic in a literary text may involve inferences.[57]

Although 'aboutness' is an elusive and subjective notion, the concept of 'empathy' predicts that the interlocutors often take a predominant role in the discourse. However, the centrality or importance of an element other than the discourse participants may be highlighted by the element's urgency, or importance, to the plot and/or interlocutors. Urgency has been found to play a role in word order, and may account for the clitic, whose antecedent is the object or information desperately sought (the discourse topic), appearing in the first slot of clitic clusters. After examining languages with variable word order, Givón reports that urgent information tends to be preposed as a means of attracting the attention of the readers/interlocutors.

> . . .the unifying factor in the pre-posing of urgent information—urgent for whatever reason—is *attention*. . .The pre-posing of more urgent information is simply a reflection of the *temporal ordering of priorities* by the task-driven organism. Given [the principle 'attend first to the most urgent task'], one could expect the following consequences in attending to and storing linearly-ordered information: . . . 'The string-initial position invites the hearer to pay more attention, and thus to store and retrieve the information more efficiently' (original emphasis).[58]

To support his position, Givón cites research in psychology that demonstrates that paragraph-initial clauses and sentence-initial words are processed more slowly, or receive more attention, than non-initial elements. Moreover, accounts focusing on the linear quality of language identify clause-initial position as the

---

[56] Maria Gomez-Gonzalez, *The Theme-Topic Interface: Evidence from English*, (Amsterdam: John Benjamins, 2001), 31.

[57] Kazem Lotfipour-Saedi and Forouzan Rezai-Tajani, "Exploration in Thematization Strategies and their Discoursal Values in English" *Text* 6 (1996): 225–49, here 234.

[58] Givón, "Pragmatics of Word Order," 276.

location of the theme or topic. Gómez-González cites research in psycholinguistics and text linguistics that shows the functional relevance of clause or message initial position and thus supports its saliency.[59]

In the medieval texts examined there are many cases in which a person, object, or certain information is desperately sought, and it is this sense of urgency that marks these elements as the discourse topic. Although the discourse topic does not move to phrase or paragraph initial position, the clitic whose antecedent is the critical element appears in the first slot, thus reflecting its topicality. In 49 the young woman, Gostanza, is dragged to the side of the ship by Saracens who slaughter her and throw her into the sea before the eyes of her lover, who has come to save her. The repeated references to the woman and the clitic order reflect that she is the focus of attention.

> 49. Il che veggendo i saracini e conoscendo sé di necessità o doversi arrendere o morire, fatto sopra coverta *la figliuola del re* venire, che *sotto coverta piagnea*, e *quella* menata alla proda della nave e chiamato il Gerbino, presente agli occhi suoi *lei gridante mercé e aiuto*[60] svenarono, e in mar gittando*la* disson: "Togli, noi **la ti** diamo qual noi possiamo e chente la tua fede l'ha meritata." (IV,4:23)

In the story of Federigo degli Alberighi (V,9), the protagonist is in love with a widow whose son adores Federigo's only prized possession, a falcon. The son falls ill and tells his mother that the only way he will be cured is if she goes to Federigo and asks him for his falcon. Biagini, Lapini, and Tortorizio point out the falcon's centrality in the text when they state that "L'elemento chiave...nella novella di Federigo è costituito dal falcone. Esso torna costantemente nelle varie parti della novella e crea una serie di rapporti più complessi tra i protagonisti..."[61] This centrality of the falcon is reflected in his owner's admiration of it and the child's desire for it.

> 50. "Figliuol mio, confortati e pensa di guerire di forza, ché io ti prometto che la prima cosa che io farò domattina, io andrò per *esso* e sì **il ti** recherò." (V, 9:16)

In the following example, the king promises to give the woman a husband if she cures him of his ailment, but the woman objects and states that she wants a husband of her own choice. The antecedent of the Acc in the first slot is the future husband being discussed:

---

[59] Gomez-Gonzalez, *Theme-Topic Interface*, 49–50.

[60] This instance of the discourse topic has undergone left dislocation, or thematization.

[61] Luca Biagini, Lia Lapini, and Maria Bianca Totorizio, "Seminari fiorentini sul 'Decameron'," *Studi sul Boccaccio* 7 (1973): 159–77, here 172.

51. "Monsignore, veramente mi piace che voi mi maritiate, ma io voglio *un marito tale quale* io **il vi** domanderò, . . ." (III,9:16)[62]

In 52 the importance of *le cose* 'the things,' the antecedent of the accusative clitic, is indicated by the fact that it is the subject of both phrases preceding the cluster, and that the speaker insists that the things are his and that he does not want to sell them:

52. "Messer, *le cose* son mie e non *le* vendo; ma s'*elle* vi piacciono, io **le vi** donerò volentieri." (II, 9:49)

In 53, the speaker, Don Felice, wants to sleep with the wife of Brother Puccio, who is living a spiritual and celibate life and is desperate to go to Paradise. To occupy Puccio, Don Felice invents a penance for him that requires that he leave the house every night. Don Felice claims that the penance, which is the referent of the Acc clitic, is so important that it is known only by the pope and his closest advisors:

53. "Io ho già assai volte compreso, fra Puccio, che tutto il tuo disidero è di divenir santo; alla qual cosa mi par che tu vadi per una lunga via, là dove ce n'è *una ch'è molto corta, la quale* il Papa e gli altri suoi maggior prelati, che *la* sanno e usano, non vogliono che *ella* si mostri; per ciò che l'ordine chericato, che il più di limosine vive, incontanente sarebbe disfatto, sì come quello al quale più i secolari né con limosine né con altro attenderebbono. Ma per ciò che tu se' mio amico e haimi onorato molto, dove io credessi che tu a niuna persona del mondo l'appalesassi e volessi*la* seguire, io **la t'**insegnerei." (III,4:12)

In the following exchanges one interlocutor desperately seeks information from another, and this information becomes their primary concern. The accusative clitic referring to this information appears in the first slot:[63]

---

[62] The notion of empathy, discussed in Section III A, may also play a role in the prominence of the animate antecedents of the accusative clitic in 49–51. The speaker's empathy for the woman who is sent to her death in 49 and the speaker's interest in the woman's future mate in 51 override empathy for the listener. Empathy may be felt for the falcon in 50, even though it is an animate non-human. Yamamoto notes that the empathy one feels toward an entity can sometimes be quite idiosyncratic, such that a cat-lover may rank cats higher on the hierarchy than would a person who despises animals. In other words, humans may not rank highest on every person's hierarchy. See Yamamoto, *Animacy and Reference*.

[63] The prominence of desired or important information is also found with verbs such as *credere* "to believe," *disdire* "to refuse," *promettere* "to promise," *giurare* "to swear," *garantire* "to guarantee," in which the clitic referring to the information occupies the first slot: La donna rispose: "Monsignore, in buona fé ella m'è piaciuta molto." "Se m'aiuti

54. Al quale ser Ciappelletto sospirando rispose: "Padre mio, di questa parte mi vergogno io di dirvene *il vero* temendo di non peccare in vanagloria." Al quale il santo frate disse: "Dì sicuramente, ché *il vero* dicendo né in confessione né in altro atto si peccò giammai." Disse allora ser Ciappelletto. "Poiché voi di questo mi fate sicuro, e io <u>il vi</u> dirò: . . ."(I,1,37)

55. Disse allora ser Ciappelletto sempre piagnendo forte: "Oimè, padre mio, *il mio è troppo gran peccato*, e appena posso credere, se i vostri prieghi non ci si adoperano, che egli me debba mai da Dio esser perdonato." A cui il frate disse: "Dil*lo* sicuramente, ché io ti prometto di pregare Idio per te." Ser Ciappelletto pur piagnea e nol dicea, e il frate pure il confortava a dire; ma poi che ser Ciappelletto piagnendo ebbe un grandissimo pezzo tenuto il frate così sospeso, e egli gittò un gran sospiro e disse: "Padre mio, poscia che voi mi promettete di pregare Idio per me, io <u>il vi</u> dirò: . . ."(I,1:69)

56. Frate Puccio, divenuto disideroso di *questa cosa*, prima cominciò a pregare con grandissima instanzia che glie*le* insegnasse e poi a giurare che mai, se non quanto gli piacesse, a alcun nol direbbe, affermando che, se tal fosse che esso seguir *la* potesse, di mettervisi. "Poi che tu così mi prometti," disse il monaco "e io <u>la ti</u> mostrerò. . . ." (III,4:14)

57. "Io vi diceva ben, frate Alberto, che le mie bellezze eran celestiali; ma, se Dio m'aiuti, di voi m'increscie, e infino a ora, acciò che più non vi sia fatto male, io vi perdono, sì veramente che voi mi diciate *ciò che l'angelo poi vi disse*." Frate Alberto disse: "Madonna, poi che perdonato m'avete, io <u>il vi</u> dirò volentieri; . . ." (IV,2:20)

Similarly, when a speaker begins the response to a question with the equivalent of modern Standard Italian *te lo dirò* "I will tell you (it)," the clitic referring to the desired information, or the answer to the question, appears in the first slot, as in 58–59:[64]

58. Disse allora donna mestola: "E chi ve ne gastigò così?" Disse frate Alberto: "Io <u>il vi</u> dirò. . . ." (IV,2:16)

59. A cui la gentil donna disse: "Madonna, se il conte ama mia figliuola io nol so, ma egli ne fa gran sembianti; ma che posso io per ciò in questo

Idio," disse il cavaliere "io <u>il vi</u> credo . . ." (IV,9:19). Examples from the supporting texts are found in Appendix D.

[64] In the following example, the speaker is pointing out that the listener did not understand what she has just said. The Dat-Acc order in this particular utterance reflects her concern with the addressee rather than the information (despite the fact that the referent of the Acc clitic undergoes LD. (For a discussion of this type of conflict, see Section IV): A cui frate Alberto disse: "Madonna, . . .quello che il mio corpo si divenisse, io non so." "Non <u>vel</u> dich'io?" disse la donna . . . (IV,2:35).

adoperare che voi disiderate?" "Madonna," rispose la contessa, "io il vi dirò; . . ."(III,9:43)

The Acc-Dat clitic order in this particular construction appears to be significant, since in the *Savj* seven of eight occurrences of this type follow the ILLUM MIHI order: il vi dirò (19, 22, 33, 56, 73), il vi direi (22), no l vi dirò (66).[65] In addition, in the expression equivalent to English "I told you so" (io il ti diciea bene [*Savj*:49]), the clitic whose antecedent is the information, rather than the clitic whose antecedent is the addressee, appears in the first slot.

The data presented demonstrate that the two orders of clitics, Dat-Acc and Acc-Dat, have a complementary distribution, the former governed by empathy and the latter by the discourse structure. The sentence theme can be identified objectively as the dislocated element. However, identifying the speaker's empathy and isolating the discourse topic require an exploration of the dynamics of the context in which the clusters are used. To render this analysis as objective as possible, the contexts that provoke the speaker's empathy are limited to those in which the speaker is deferential to the addressee or is overly preoccupied with his/her own state of affairs, while the discourse topic is identified as the element that generates a sense of urgency or immediacy. Given the restrictions placed on the concepts of 'empathy' and 'discourse topic' in this analysis, the creative expression in literary texts is bound to result in a certain number of exceptions. However, an overwhelming majority of citations from the medieval texts examined fall into one of these categories, which indicates that during the transition from ILLUM MIHI to MIHI ILLUM, clitic pronoun order was not random, but rather highly regulated by the pragmatic/discourse context.

The relatively consistent division of labor between the two order types was eventually abandoned in favor of the unmarked, invariable cluster, MIHI ILLUM. An indication of the bleaching of the pragmatic/discourse functions of the two clusters is already found in the *Decameron*, where MIHI ILLUM appears in a fixed construction — the exclamation: "As God tells you" (come Dio vel dica (I, 1:53)). The next section explores the factors that contributed to the bleaching of the functional distribution of clitics in double object clusters, and resulted in the selection of one, invariable cluster, MIHI ILLUM.

---

[65] There is one exception from the *Decameron* and one from *Savj*: "Questo è vero: ma perché t'ha per ciò questa parola commosso?" "Messer," rispose il buono uomo, "io vel dirò. . . ." (I,6:18); E che gli avvenne della sua gazza?. . .io vel dirò. . . (*Savj*: 56).

IV. The order change

Galambos argues that ILLUM MIHI was the original pre-Romance order and that the Romance languages that did undergo the change to MIHI ILLUM did so at variable rates.[66] This hypothesis conforms to Wanner's observation that the Dat-Acc order predominates in the Romance languages and that documentation of the inverse evolution away from MIHI ILLUM does not exist.[67] Like medieval Florentine, other languages, such as Catalan, Occitan, Northern French,[68] and dialects in parts of Northern and Central Italian underwent a change in double object clitic order from ILLUM MIHI to MIHI ILLUM that was complete by the sixteenth or seventeenth centuries. Certain local dialects of Northern Italy, Occitan, as well as Catalan and Aragonese (Balearic Islands, Val de Hecho) did not undergo the change and thus retain the Acc-Dat construction,[69] while the MIHI ILLUM order is attested in the rest of the Romance languages (Portuguese, Spanish, Sardinian, some Northern and Central, and most Southern Italian dialects) from the medieval period.[70]

The distribution of clitic clusters in medieval Italian texts indicates that empathy played a role in the initial uses of MIHI ILLUM, which restricted the use of ILLUM MIHI and ultimately influenced its loss. Berretta points out that it is not accidental that the Dat-Acc order of clitic clusters is extremely frequent in the languages of the world, which could be due to the egocentric nature of discourse. Her data lead her to conclude that

---

[66] Sylvia Joseph Galambos, "Mechanisms of Change in the Position of Object Pronouns: From Classical Latin to Modern French," in *Selected Papers from the 13th Linguistic Symposium on Romance Languages, Chapel Hill, N.C., 24–26 March 1983*, ed. Larry D. King and Catherine A. Maley (Amsterdam: John Benjamins, 1985), 99–116.

[67] Wanner, "The Evolution," 161; idem, "Clitic Clusters in Romance," 262.

[68] This transition is incomplete in modern Standard French, in which the accusative precedes the third person dative (e.g. *le leur, le lui* etc.) and the accusative occupies the first slot after positive imperatives (e.g. *donne - le - moi!*). See note 72 for discussion.

[69] Although one can only speculate as to why the order did not change in these dialects, it may be related to a preference for textual, rather than 'extratextual,' deixis. In his discussion of the ILLUM MIHI order in Old French, Meyer-Lübke states that "[l]a raison d'être de cette disposition, c'est peut-être que, dans la grande majorité des cas, le pronom-accusatif se rapporte à une énonciation antérieure . . . et que le pronom-datif ne représente très souvent que la personne qui parle, celle à qui l'on s'adresse ou une troisième personne sur laquelle parfois on peut par un geste attirer l'attention." See Wilhelm Meyer-Lübke, *Grammaire des langues romanes*, trans. Eugène Rabiet (New York: Stechert, 1923), 835–36.

[70] Wanner reports that there is not enough information to report reliably on the developments in Romanian (in a broad sense), Raeto/Alpino-Romance, and Dalmatian. See Wanner, "Clitic Clusters," 262.

> ... si tende a parlare più spesso e più a lungo di persone (e fra queste soprattutto dei partecipanti all'interazione), e le persone si configurano in genere come dativi, piuttosto che come accusativi; ne consegue che dativi animati saranno più 'tematici' (o: prevedibili come temi) degli accusativi, e ... tenderanno a stare più a sinistra di questi ultimi.[71]

Galambos employs the topicality hierarchy to account for the order change in French. She states that the motivating force behind the shift to the MIHI ILLUM order was the discourse-pragmatic tendency to place the dative, usually a first or second person, in the first slot because it "is more topical than the accusative and less essential to the process," and to place the accusative next to the verb, "since it is less topical than the dative and semantically more closely associated with the verb."[72]

The increasing influence of empathy in clitic ordering in the *Decameron* is identifiable in environments in which there are contextual cues for both order types but MIHI ILLUM wins out. For example, MIHI ILLUM is motivated in 13, 14, 18, and 20 by the speaker's deference to the listener. However, in each case the referent of the accusative clitic has undergone LD, which should trigger the opposite order. In two of these four citations (13, 20) the role of empathy is reinforced by the fact that these clusters appear in a verb + infinitive construction and have undergone clitic climbing from the infinitive to the first verb of the complex. Clitic climbing has been demonstrated to be symptomatic of the propensity for leftward movement of the dative (see Section III A), and the data from the medieval texts examined reveal nearly consistent placement of the Dat in the first slot in this construction.

The influence of animacy and empathy is also indicated by the outcome in modern Standard Italian of clusters with a Loc pronoun. In medieval Italian, third person direct object clitics preceded the Loc. *Mi* also preceded the Loc, most likely due to the psychological prominence of the speaker, while *ti* and *ci* usually occupied the second slot.[73] However, in modern Standard Italian, the first slot is reserved for *mi* and *ti* (with animate referents), while third person Acc pronouns (*lo, la, li, le*), the referents of which are frequently inanimate, occupy the

---

[71] Berretta, "Struttura informativa," 78–79.
[72] See Galambos, "Mechanisms of Change," 102, 106. Galambos argues that the postverbal ILLUM MIHI order is preserved due to rhythmic constraints. The anteposed ILLUM MIHI in third person clusters occurred because during the change to MIHI ILLUM third person accusatives were usually omitted when combined with the third person dative. Once the third person accusative was reintroduced in the 16th century, it occupied the second slot, as it did in postposition to the verb.
[73] See Maiden, *A Linguistic History*, 174.

second slot.[74] A similar pattern is found in clusters with *ne*: in medieval Italian, *ne* always occupied the second slot. In modern Italian, *ne* follows all but the third person accusative clitics (*lo, la, li, le*). Although this combination is rare in the modern language,[75] it was more frequent in Old Italian. Evidence of the readjustment of *ne* clusters is found in the *Decameron* (see Section II).

While empathy played a role in the shift away from ILLUM MIHI, the shift and ultimate change to the invariable Dat-Acc cluster, devoid of its pragmatic/discourse functions, may have also been encouraged by structural pressures and contact phenomena. Pearce, Antinucci and Marcantonio, and DeKock interpret the order change as a shift from syntactic enclisis to syntactic proclisis. Syntactic enclisis presupposes that preverbal clitics are enclitic to the constituent to the left, while in proclisis they are attached to the following verb, and attachment to the host corresponds to the order in which the arguments appear in relation to the verb in the VP.[76] The accusative, being the sister of the V, appears closer to the verb, while the dative occupies a more peripheral position. Thus, the earlier stage of enclisis generates ILLUM MIHI and the later, proclisic phase results in MIHI ILLUM. In a similar vein, Russi slightly modifies Maiden's approach by suggesting that the IO-DO order became the canonical (unmarked) order for clitic sequences as a result of the predominance of proclisis and a preference for keeping the DO, which is the more central argument, next to its host.[77] Eventually, this pattern was extended to the more marginal enclitic sequence. According to these interpretations, clitic order is iconic of the structure of the VP constituent. These structural solutions are not antithetical to the pragmatic interpretation presented in this essay. Rather, the shift from enclisis to proclisis or the preference for proclisis could have been an additional motivation for the Dat-Acc order, and so the shift to structural iconicity would have accompanied the shift to pragmatic iconicity during the order change.[78]

Phonotactics may have also played a role in the Dat-Acc order. Lombard suggests that the *me lo* pattern may have been related to the high incidence of

---

[74] Combinations of *vi* and *ci* generally have the order *vi ci* regardless of their functions. See Martin Maiden and Cecilia Robustelli, *A Reference Grammar of Modern Italian* (Lincolnwood [Chicago], IL: NTC Publishing Group, 2000), 102.

[75] Maiden and Robustelli, *Reference Grammar*, 102.

[76] See Pearce, "Comparing French and Italian"; Francesco Antinucci and Angela Marcantonio, "I meccanismi del mutamento diacronico: Il cambiamento d'ordine dei pronomi clitici in italiano," *Rivista di grammatica generativa* 5 (1980): 3–49; Ans DeKock, *La place du pronom personnel régime conjoint en français: Une étude diachronique* (Amsterdam: Rodopi, 1985).

[77] Cinzia Russi, *Italian Clitics: An Empirical Approach* (Berlin: Mouton, 2008), 82–83; Maiden, *Linguistic History*.

[78] These structural approaches to the order shift accounts for Dat + Acc constructions, but cannot account for clusters with a Loc, since Acc *mi* and *ti* precede the Loc.

words ending in the sequence V + [l] + V, such as *cavolo* 'cabbage,' *angelo* 'angel,' etc. Maiden finds this argument convincing in light of Tuttle's observations that these endings may have influenced the reorganization of the Tuscan atonic vowel system.[79]

Lastly, the change may have been encouraged by dialectal pressure. The Old Florentine Acc-Dat order does not correspond to medieval usages throughout the rest of the peninsula. According to Rohlfs, the earliest documents from Pistoia, Siena, and Arezzo have a preference for (not exclusive use of) the Dat-Acc order, and both clitic orders can be found in later texts from Pistoia and Lucca.[80] In northern Italy, the Dat-Acc construction appears almost everywhere from the earliest texts,[81] as is the case in Southern Italy from Abruzzo to Sicily. Based on this data, Rohlfs concludes that

> è facile supporre che il particolar tipo toscano sia stato, per influsso settentrionale e meridionale, schiacciato dall'altro, tanto più diffuso; specie considerando il fatto che nella stessa Toscana c'erano zone (Pistoia, Siena, Arezzo) che sin dai più antichi documenti ci mostrano aver dato la preferenza al tipo panitaliano (*te lo porto*). Nell'inversione d'ordine accaduta nel toscano sarebbe dunque da vedere l'azione di forze centripete.[82]

Since the Dat-Acc order predominated in surrounding Tuscan dialects while Florentine had the reverse construction (Acc-Dat), Rohlfs argues that contact with these dialects resulted in the new construction infiltrating Florentine, slowly supplanting the previously invariable ILLUM MIHI. Melander supports the borrowing thesis by arguing that the forms *me* and *te* (instead of *mi* and *ti*) in clusters indicate borrowing from dialects in which atonic [e] was raised to [i].[83]

---

[79] See Lombard, "Le groupement"; Maiden, *Linguistic History*, 176; Edward Tuttle, "*Sedano, senero, prezzemolo* and the Intertonic Vowels in Tuscan," *Romance Philology* 27 (1974): 451–65.

[80] Rohlfs, *Grammatica storica*, 176–77.

[81] Alternation is found in Medieval Bolognese poets. Although research on the alternations in these dialects may shed light on the same variation in Florentine, they are not examined in this essay.

[82] Rohlfs, *Grammatica storica*, 178. Castellani provides a similar perspective when he states that "[l]'adozione dell'ordine MIHI ILLUM, INDE ILLUM. . .è probabilmente dovuta ai dialetti vicini. Se il fenomeno fosse spontaneo, infatti, ci aspetteremmo un'evoluzione graduale (come quella di ILLUM MIHI a MIHI ILLUM nel francese e nel provenzale). Inoltre bisogna tenere presente che dopo i primi decenni del Trecento i dialetti toscani hanno esercitato una pressione notevole sul fiorentino (vedi, nella seconda metà del secolo, *el, fussi* ed *arò*; e vedi *dia, stia*, che ben difficilmente potrebbero essere forme indigene)" (*Nuovi testi*, 104).

[83] Melander, "L'origine." However, Russi reconstructs the vowel change based on phonological processes that occurred during the development of Italian from Latin. See *Italian Clitics: An Empirical Study*, 90.

Variation in medieval texts indicates that empathy for, or preoccupation with, the interlocutors provoked the use of the MIHI ILLUM, which, in turn, limited the use of ILLUM MIHI to contexts in which the referent of the Acc clitic carried discourse salience. Other pressures, such as contact with neighboring dialects with invariable MIHI ILLUM, analogy to a phonotactic pattern already in the system, and syntactic restructuring, may have also provoked the use of MIHI ILLUM and conspired to finally oust the Acc clitic from the first slot.

V. Concluding Remarks

In the modern Romance languages clitic pronouns are non-emphatic, non-contrastive atonic elements associated with a host (verb), and when they appear in clusters, the clusters have rigid ordering. The nature of clitics prompts Wanner, in his discussion of the alternation of clitic order in the *Decameron*, to state that it is not very convincing to argue that variable clitic order was utilized for stylistic purposes, since ". . . clitic elements constitute a rather unexpressive area of syntax to carry stylistic information in their mutual order."[84]

Wanner points out that there are cases in which a particular pronoun may achieve more prominence than the other, but this secondary effect is achieved only because the clitic carries stress.[85] In Modern Greek postverbal clitic combinations with imperative verbs the last clitic is more prominent because of the independently required clitic accent on the second syllable from the anchor's word stress, as in *pés-mu-tó!* "tell-imp-sg me it" and *pés-to-mú!* "tell-imp-sg it me."[86] This is similar to the slight differentiation reported in modern spoken French,[87] in which *donne-le mói!* (standard) and *donne-moi-lé* (non-standard) appear to put the last element in relief due to the independent phrasal stress on this position.[88]

Liddicoat reports that in the Norman French dialects on the Channel islands of Jersey and Sark variation is found only where the pronouns are enclitic to positive imperatives, as in the French example above, and the most frequent

---

[84] Wanner, "The Evolution," 165. See also idem, *The Development of Romance Clitic Pronouns from Latin to Old Romance* (New York: Mouton, 1987), 31–32; idem, "Clitic Clusters," 275; Pearce, "Comparing French and Italian," 257.

[85] See Dieter Wanner, "Modern Greek Clitics: Placement, Order and Function," in *Proceedings of the Fourth Annual Meeting of the Berkeley Linguistics Society*, ed. Jeri J. Jaeger et al. (Berkeley: Berkeley Linguistics Society, 1978), 268–82; and Wanner, "Clitic Clusters in Romance."

[86] Wanner, "Clitic Clusters in Romance," 270.

[87] See Yves-Charles Morin, "La morphophonologie des pronoms clitiques en français populaire," *Cahiers de Linguistique* 9 (1979): 1–36; idem, "More Remarks on French Clitic Order," *Linguistic Analysis* 5 (1979): 293–312.

[88] Wanner, "Clitic Clusters in Romance," 270.

enclitic order is direct object + dative/reflexive.[89] However, an examination of counter-examples reveals that when the direct object is less topical and less accessible, in that it is considerably distant from the last mention of its referent, "... the stress/intonation pattern is such that the final element receives the most emphasis and as such is the place where the element requiring the most work on the part of the hearer will be found."[90]

The evidence presented could be taken to suggest that clitic order can reflect discourse dynamics only if the pronouns are stressed. However, it is possible that clitic order may carry meaning in the absence of stress. Wanner points out that in modern Standard Italian clusters consisting of *si* (third person reflexive, non-specified human subject 'Pro') and *lo, la, li, le* (third person accusative, non-reflexive) have two possible orders that are functionally differentiated. *Se lo* is reserved for reflexive + Acc clusters, while *lo si* is exclusively employed for Acc + impersonal *si* (non-specified human subject).

> [t]here is nothing surprising in the need to differentiate between the two situations. The unexpected aspect is only that it is precisely the non-emphatic, non-contrastive forms of clitic pronouns that carry the burden of differentiation in their respective linear order. Clitic pronouns thus can be seen as potentially serving wider functions than simple place marking for a given constituent type (DO of specific reference, or similar). In this, clitic pronouns are directly connected to the productive processes of Italian syntax which allow functional difference to be signaled by differential sequence of elements, a > b ≠ b > a, e.g. for normal focus assignment in *un grosso errore* vs. *un errore grosso*.[91]

As in modern Italian, medieval clusters were atonic, non-emphatic, and non-contrastive. Similar to modern clusters with *si*, the sequence of clitics in medieval Florentine double object clitic clusters, ILLUM MIHI versus MIHI ILLUM, signals a functional difference. However, in order to uncover this difference, this analysis has explored external, pragmatic pressures, rather than internal, structural factors. The data reveal that despite the fundamentally unexpressive nature of atonic clitics, the relative order of clitics in medieval Florentine clusters was governed by the pragmatics of the discourse and was an iconic representation of the discourse structure.

---

[89] Anthony J. Liddicoat, "The Function of Pronoun Order in Imperative Verb Phrases in the Dialects of Jersey and Sark," *Linguistische Berichte* 131 (1991): 24–36. According to Liddicoat "[t]he variation in word order in modern French appears to be stylistic rather than pragmatically motivated. The two word orders communicate social [i.e. class] rather than discourse information" (34).

[90] Liddicoat, "Jersey and Sark," 31.

[91] Dieter Wanner, "Clitic Pronouns in Italian: A Linguistic Guide," *Italica* 64 (1987): 410–42.

Appendix A: Postverbal clusters

ILLUM MIHI

Decameron: tien<u>loti</u> (V,10:64), Diro<u>lti</u> (V,10:32), osservar<u>lomi</u> (V,7:20–21), vedete<u>lvi</u> voi (III,3:41), dil<u>lami</u> (V,4:11), conceder<u>lami</u> / date<u>lami</u> (V,1:30–32), date<u>leti</u> (IV,1:54), contar<u>levi</u> (III,7:68), traggo<u>gliti</u> (III,6:38), domandar<u>lavi</u> (III,5:27), dir<u>lovi</u> (III,6:18), Dico<u>lti</u> (II,1:10), voler<u>lami</u> (II,10:20), donar<u>lomi</u> / aver<u>loti</u> (V,9:32), dite<u>lmi</u> (III,7:23), mostrar<u>lovi</u> (I,Concl.:10), dir<u>lovi</u> (III,6:11–12), impon<u>lomi</u> (V,1:60); *Reggimento*: Dite<u>lmi</u> (280); *Savj*: dite<u>lmi</u> (26), date<u>lmi</u> (8), *Costumi*: pensa<u>lti</u>! (249)

MIHI ILLUM

Decameron: voglian<u>telo</u> aver detto (V,3:28), dic<u>celo</u> (II,9:51), vedendo<u>tel</u> (IV, 6:40), rendendo<u>mela</u> (II,6:59), ritener<u>celo</u> (III,1:16); *Costumi*: convien<u>tela</u> (376), aiuta<u>tele</u> (336); *Reggimento*: dite<u>lmi</u> (280)

Appendix B: Clusters combining *ne* and an Acc or *gli*

ne + Acc: *Decameron*: tratto<u>nelo</u> (II,4:24), volendo<u>negli</u> (II,8:82), mandar<u>nelo</u> (III,3:45), portar<u>nela</u> (V,6,369:18–19), menaron<u>nelo</u> (II,1:22), portar<u>nela</u> / <u>ne la</u> portarono (IV,10:20), <u>nel</u> portasse (IV, 9:13), <u>ne la</u> dovea (IV,4:11), <u>ne la</u> portò (V,5:28), <u>ne le</u> recasse (III,1:15), <u>ne la</u> portò (V,2:13), <u>ne la</u> menò (V,2:25), <u>ne la</u> portava (V,3:11), <u>ne la</u> menò (V,5:38), <u>ne la</u> mandò (V,7:23), avendo<u>nela</u> (IV, 5:0), richieder<u>nelo</u> (IV,1:5), voler<u>nela</u> (III,1:18), <u>ne la</u> dee (III,3:28), <u>ne la</u> potea (V,9:33), <u>ne la</u> prese (III,5:27), <u>nel</u> gastigò (IV,8:7); *Costumi*: <u>nel</u> pagho (307); *Reggimento*: portò<u>nelo</u> (59), <u>nel</u> levi (319), <u>nel</u> possa (176), menon<u>nela</u> (402), <u>nel</u> pagò (248), <u>Nel</u> pagò (248); *Savj*: mandon<u>nela</u> (85), <u>nel</u> meneremo (36)

ne-gli/le: *Decameron*: <u>ne gli</u> avvenisse (II,10:3), <u>ne gli</u> manderò (III,1:10), <u>ne gli</u> poteron (II,10:42), <u>ne gli</u> ho (III,3:41), <u>ne le</u> prese (V,2:20), <u>ne le</u> fu (IV,10:6), <u>ne gli</u> disse (IV,8:7), <u>ne gli</u> piacquero (II,5:3), <u>ne gli</u> disse (I,1:65)

Acc-ne: *Decameron*: far<u>lene</u> (I,4:11), trar<u>lone</u> (III,8:31), <u>la ne</u> menerebbe (V,6:18–19), <u>la ne</u> portava (V,3:17–20), <u>la ne</u> menasse (II,6:23); *Reggimento*: <u>la ne</u> fe'(215); *Savj*: menado<u>lne</u> (21), portar<u>lone</u> (20), portar<u>lone</u> (43)

gli/le-ne: *Decameron*: comportar**gliene** (III,3:40–41), **le ne** erano (II,7,:22–24), **gli ne** potrebbe (III,3:30), **le ne** donò (III,9:53); *Costumi*: **glie ne** favelasse (307), dona**gliene** (113), **glie ne** (266); *Reggimento*: fal**gliene** (323), **glie n'** àn portati (130); *Savj*: **glie n'** è adivenuto (40), **gliene** trovassono (42), trovaron**gliene** (42)

Appendix C: MIHI ILLUM in the supporting texts

Deference to addressee: sì ch'io **vel** posso dare (*Reggimento*:13), i' **vel** posso mostrare (*Reggimento*: 104)

Giving advice or a command / instructions:[92] e' **tel** farà valere. (*Reggimento*), E elgliono **tel** daranno (*Costumi*: 323), e anche **tel** gita in grado (*Costumi*: 376), io **tel** comando (*Savj*: 39), ch'io non **tel** direi altrimenti (*Reggimento*: 371), Io **tel** dirò, disse la madre (*Savj*: 44)[93]

Arrogance or preoccupation with one's own state of affairs: voglio **me lo** diate (*Savj*: 1–2), ch' ella **me l'**avea promessa (*Reggimento*: 170)

Antecedent is the subject of the main verb in the preceding clause: in segreto **me le** diede Iddio (*Reggimento*: 135)

Appendix D: ILLUM MIHI in the supporting texts

Left dislocation in a previous clause: perchè **la vi** dirrei io (*Savi*: 60–61).

Cataphor: Perchè **mel** desti (*Reggimento*: 207).

Antecedent of Acc clitic is urgent information/discourse topic: perchè **la mi** menasti tu? (*Reggimento*: 40), Se **'l mi** dovevi così tosto torre? (*Reggimento*:

---

[92] The following examples with the Acc-Dat order are exceptions, since the speaker is giving advice. However, *i fatti tuoi* "your business" and *l'arme tue* "your weapons" are the focus of the discussion: "Non fidare *il tuo avere né tuoi fatti* in persona che non ami l'anima sua, però che chi non amerà l'anima sua, non amerà *i fatti tuoi* e no**gli ti** farà a buona fede..."(*Costumi*: 92); "Mai non prestare *l'arme tue* a persona che **la ti** domandi,..." (*Costumi*: 105).

[93] Although the listener is anxious for the information, which should trigger the reverse order (see Section III B), the mother is giving instructions and is preoccupied with her daughter's behavior.

207), <u>lo vi</u> darò quanto che voi vorrete (*Savj*: 52), E io <u>il vi</u> dono (*Savj*: 61) no <u>gli ti</u> farà a buona fede (*Costumi*: 84).

Listener is desperate for information: Priego che <u>'l mi</u> dica (*Reggimento*: 428), io voglio che voi <u>il mi</u> diciate (*Savj*: 27, 61), io no<u>l vi</u> dirò punto (*Savj*: 77).

Antecedent to Acc clitic is the answer to a question: Tu, Iddio, <u>la mi</u> mostra; (*Reggimento*: 282), E io <u>il vi</u> dono (*Savj*: 61)

credere 'to believe,' *disdire* 'to refuse,' *promettere* 'to promise,' *garantire* 'to guarantee': no<u>l vi</u> credo. (*Savj:* 55), i' no<u>l ti</u> crederia. (*Reggimento*: 323), no<u>l ti</u> disdirà (*Costumi*: 98), <u>lo ti</u> prometto e giuro (*Reggimento*: 134), E io <u>il vi</u> guarento. (*Savj*: 66).

Works Cited

Antinucci, Francesco, and Angela Marcantonio. "I meccanismi del mutamento diacronico: Il cambiamento d'ordine dei pronomi clitici in italiano." *Rivista di grammatica generativa* 5 (1980): 3–49.
Benincà, Paola. "Il lato sinistro della frase italiana." *Association of Teachers of Italian Journal* 47 (1986): 57–85.
Berretta, Monica. "Struttura informativa e sintassi dei pronomi atoni: condizioni che favoriscono la 'risalita'." In *Tema-rema in italiano*, ed. by Harro Stammerjohann, 71–83. Tübingen: Narr, 1986.
———. "I pronomi clitici nell'italiano parlato." In *Gesprochenes Italienisch in Geschichte und Gegenwart*, ed. by Günter Holtus and Edgar Radtke, 185–224. Tübingen: Narr, 1985.
Bertuccelli Papi, Marcella. "On the Relationship between Sentence Themes and Text Topics." *Studi italiani di linguistica teorica e applicata* 1 (1994): 127–140.
Biagini, Luca, Lia Lapini, and Maria Bianca Totorizio. "Seminari fiorentini sul 'Decameron'." *Studi sul Boccaccio* 7 (1973): 159–177.
Boccaccio, Giovanni. *Decameron*. Ed. Vittore Branca. Florence: Accademia della Crusca, 1976.
Brown, Gillian, and George Yule. *Discourse Analysis*. Cambridge: Cambridge University Press, 1983.
Castellani, Arrigo. *Nuovi testi fiorentini*. Vol. 1. Florence: Sansoni, 1952.
Chafe, Wallace L. "Givenness, Contrastiveness, Definiteness, Subjects, Topics, and Point of View." In *Subject and Topic*, ed. Charles N. Li, 25–55. New York: Academic Press, 1976.
Cienki, Alan. "Experiencers, Possessors, and Overlap between Russian Dative and *u* + Genitive". In *Proceedings of the 19th Annual Meeting of the Berkeley Linguistics Society, February 12–15, 1993*, ed. Joshua S. Guenter, Barbara A. Kaiser, and Cheryl C. Zoll, 77–89. Berkeley: Berkeley Linguistics Society, 1993.
Cook, Kenneth William. "The Empathy Hierarchy and Samoan Clitic Pronouns." *Cognitive Linguistics* 4 (1994): 57–75.
Croft, William. *Typology and Universals*. Cambridge: Cambridge University Press, 1990.
da Barberino, Francesco. *Del reggimento e costumi di donna*. Ed. Claudio Baudi di Vesme. Bologna: Gaetano Romagnoli, 1895.
da Certaldo, Paolo. *Il libro di buoni costumi*. (Atti della Reale Accademia della Crusca 1919–1920). Ed. Salomone Morpurgo. Florence: Galileiana, 1921.
Dati, Gregorio. *Il libro segreto in scelta di curiosità letterarie*. Edited by Carlo Gargiolli. Bologna: Commissione per i Testi di Lingua, 1968.

Deane, Paul. "English Possessives, Topicality, and the Silverstein Hierarchy." In *Proceedings of the Thirteenth Annual Meeting of the Berkeley Linguistics Society*, ed. James Aske et al., 65–76. Berkeley: Berkeley Linguistics Society, 1987.

DeKock, Ans. *La place du pronom personnel régime conjoint en français: Un etude diachronique*. Amsterdam: Rodopi, 1985.

Delancey, Scott. "An Interpretation of Split Ergativity and Related Phenomena." *Language* 57 (1981): 626–57.

Ertel, Suitbert. "Where do the Subjects of Sentences Come from?" In *Sentence Production: Developments in Research and Theory*, ed. Sheldon Rosenberg, 141–168. Hillsdale, NJ: Lawrence Erlbaum, 1977.

Fiorentino, Giovanni. *Il pecorone*. Ed. Enzo Esposito. Ravenna: Longo, 1974.

Galambos, Sylvia Joseph. "Mechanisms of Change in the Position of Object Pronouns: From Classical Latin to Modern French." In *Selected Papers from the 13th Linguistic Symposium on Romance Languages, Chapel Hill, N.C., 24–26 March 1983*, ed. Larry D. King and Catherine A. Maley, 99–116. Amsterdam: John Benjamins, 1985.

Gerlach, Birgit. *Clitics between Syntax and Lexicon*. Amsterdam: John Benjamins, 2002.

Givón, Talmy. "Topic, Pronoun and Grammatical Agreement." In *Subject and Topic*, ed. Li, 149–188.

———. *Topic Continuity in Discourse*. Amsterdam: John Benjamins, 1983.

———. "The Pragmatics of Word Order: Predictability, Importance and Attention." In *Studies in Syntactic Typology*, ed. Michael Hammond, Edith Moravcsik, and Jessica Wirth, 243–84. Amsterdam: John Benjamins, 1988.

———. "The Grammar of Referential Coherence as Mental Processing Instructions." *Linguistics* 30 (1992): 5–55.

Gomez-Gonzalez, Maria. *The Theme-Topic Interface: Evidence from English*. Amsterdam: John Benjamins, 2001.

Hetzron, Robert. "Clitic Pronouns and their Linear Representation." *Forum Linguisticum* 1 (1976): 189–215.

Il libro dei sette savj di Roma. Ed. Francesco Zambrini. Pisa: Fratelli Nistri, 1864.

Kuno, Susumu. "Subject, Theme and the Speaker's Empathy—A Reexamination of Relativization Phenomena." In *Subject and Topic*, ed. Li, 417–44.

———. "The Speaker's Empathy and its Effect on Syntax: A Reexamination of Yaru and Kureru on Japanese." *Journal of the Association of Teachers of Japanese* 2/3 (1976): 249–71.

———. *Functional Syntax: Anaphora, Discourse and Empathy*. Chicago: University of Chicago Press, 1987.

———, and Etsuko Kaburaki. "Empathy and Syntax." *Linguistic Inquiry* 8 (1977): 627–72.

Langacker, Ronald W. *Foundations of Cognitive Grammar; Volume 2: Descriptive Application*. Stanford: Stanford University Press, 1991.

Leech, Geoffrey, Brian Francis, and Xunfeng Xu. "The Use of Computer Corpora in the Textual Demonstrability of Gradience in Linguistic Categories." In *Continuity in Linguistic Semantics*, ed. Catherine Fuchs and Bernard Victorri, 57–76. Philadelphia: John Benjamins, 1994.

Liddicoat, Anthony J. "The Function of Pronoun Order in Imperative Verb Phrases in the Dialects of Jersey and Sark." *Linguistische Berichte* 131 (1991): 24–36.

Lombard, Alf. "Le groupement de pronoms personnels en italien." *Studier Modern Sprakvetenskap* 12 (1934): 21–76.

Lotfipour-Saedi, Kazem, and Forouzan Rezai-Tajani. "Exploration in Thematization Strategies and their Discoursal Values in English." *Text* 6 (1996): 225–49.

Maiden, Martin. *A Linguistic History of Italian*. London: Longman, 1995.

———, and Cecilia Robustelli. *A Reference Grammar of Modern Italian*. Lincolnwood (Chicago), IL: NTC Publishing Group, 2000.

Marcantonio, Angela. "Un aspetto dell'ordine delle parole nell'italiano del Due-Trecento." *Rivista di grammatica generativa* 1 (1976): 57–77.

Melander, Jacques. "L'origine de l'italien *me ne, me lo, te la*, etc." *Studia Neophilologica* 2 (1929): 169–203.

Meyer-Lübke, Wilhelm. *Grammaire des langues romanes*. Trans. Eugène Rabiet. New York: Stechert, 1923.

Morin, Yves-Charles. "La morphophonologie des pronoms clitiques en français populaire." *Cahiers de Linguistique* 9 (1979): 1–36.

———. "More Remarks on French Clitic Order." *Linguistic Analysis* 5 (1979): 293–312.

Myhill, John. *Typlogical Discourse Analysis: Quantitative Approaches to the Study of Linguistic Function*. Oxford: Blackwell, 1992.

Napoli, Donna Jo. "Semantic Interpretation vs. Lexical Governance: Clitic Climbing in Italian." *Language* 57 (1981): 841–87.

Oates, Lynette F. *A Tentative Description of the Gunwinggu Language (of Western Arnhem Land)*. Sydney: Oceania Linguistics Monographs, 1964.

Pearce, Elizabeth. "On Comparing French and Italian: The Switch from *illum mihi* to *mihi illum*." In *New Analyses in Romance Linguistics*, ed. Dieter Wanner and Douglas A. Kibbee, 253–69. Amsterdam: Benjamins, 1991.

Parry, M. Mair. "Preverbal Negation and Clitic Ordering." *Zeitschrift für romanische Philologie* 113 (1997): 243–70.

Perlmutter, David. "Surface Structure Constraints in Syntax." *Linguistic Inquiry* 1 (1970): 187–255.

Rohlfs, Gerhard. *Grammatica storica della lingua italiana e dei suoi dialetti: Morfologia*. Turin: Einaudi, 1968.

Russi, Cinzia. *Italian Clitics: An Empirical Study*. Berlin: Mouton, 2008.

Sacchetti, Franco. *Il trecentonovelle*. Ed. Antonio Lanza. Florence: Sansoni, 1984.

Schwenter, Scott, and Glaucia V. Silva. "Anaphoric Direct Objects in Spoken Brazilian Portuguese: Semantics and Pragmatics." *Revista internacional de linguistica iberoromanica* 1 (2003): 99–123.

Siewierska, Anna. *Word Order Rules*. London: Croom Helm, 1988.

Silverstein, M. "Hierarchy of Features and Ergativity." In *Grammatical Categories in Australian Languages*, ed. R. M. W. Dixon, 112–71. Canberra: Australian Institute of Aboriginal Studies, 1976.

Stussi, Alfredo. *Storia linguistica e storia letteraria*. Bologna: Il Mulino, 2005.

Tuttle, Edward. "*Sedano, senero, prezzemolo* and the Intertonic Vowels in Tuscan." *Romance Philology* 27 (1974): 451–65.

Yamamoto, Mutsumi. *Animacy and Reference*. Amsterdam: John Benjamins, 1999.

Vanelli, Laura. "Strutture tematiche in italiano antico." In *Tema-rema in italiano*, ed. Harro Stammerjohann, 249–74. Tübingen: Narr, 1986.

Wanner, Dieter. "The Evolution of Romance Clitic Order." In *Linguistic Studies in Romance Languages*, ed. R. Joe Campbell et al., 158–77. Washington, D C: Georgetown University Press, 1974.

———. "Modern Greek Clitics: Placement, Order and Function." In *Proceedings of the Fourth Annual Meeting of the Berkeley Linguistics Society*, ed. Jeri J. Jaeger et al., 268–82. Berkeley: Berkeley Linguistics Society, 1978.

———. "Pragmatics and Syntax in Portuguese Clitic Placement." In *Current Research in Romance Languages*, ed. James P. Lantolf and Gregory B. Stone, 194–206. Bloomington: Indiana University Linguistics Club, 1982.

———. *The Development of Romance Clitic Pronouns from Latin to Old Romance*. New York: Mouton, 1987.

———. "Clitic Pronouns in Italian: A Linguistic Guide." *Italica* 64 (1987): 410–42.

———. "Clitic Clusters in Romance: A Modest Account." In *Grammatical Analyses in Basque and Romance Linguistics*, ed. Jon Franco, Alazne Landa, and Juan Martín, 257–77. Amsterdam: John Benjamins, 1999.

Weinreich, Uriel, William Labov, and Marvin Herzog. "Empirical Foundations for a Theory of Language Change." In *Directions for Historical Linguistics*, ed. Winfred P. Lehmann and Yakov Malkiel, 95–195. Austin: University of Texas Press, 1968.

Literary Imagination and Mercantile Pragmatism in Goro Dati's *Sfera*

Dario Del Puppo

Writing on 1 January 1403, Goro Dati, a prominent Florentine businessman and civic intellectual,[1] declares in his *Libro segreto* that he is turning over a new leaf: "questo dì propongo e dilibero una cosa da qui inanzi osservare, cioè che in perpetuo mai in alcuno dì di festa solenne e comandata dalla Santa Chiesa io non debo stare a bottega, né andarmi a fare alcuno esercizio, né consentire o comandare che altri per me il faccia d'opera di guadagno o utile temporale . . ."[2] Promising to donate one gold florin to the poor each time he breaks his resolution, he asserts: "E questa scrittura ò fatta per tenere meglio a mente, e per mia confusione se contro a ciò facessi."[3] As the title of his *ricordi* suggests, Dati's is a book of intimate writings, quite likely intended for his heirs and most certainly useful to its writer as a mirror of his spiritual and emotional development. He was also the author of two other very public writings, the *Istoria di Firenze dal 1380 al 1405*[4] and the *Sfera* that reveal him to be an *écrivain marchand*, as Christian Bec aptly called the Florentine writers of the merchant class.[5]

---

[1] See Paolo Viti, "Dati, Gregorio (Goro)," in *Dizionario biografico degli italiani*, vol. 33 (Rome: Istituto dell'Enciclopedia Italiana, 1987), 35–40.

[2] The English translation of Dati's diary is taken from Gene Brucker, ed., and Julia Martines, trans., *Two Memoirs of Renaissance Florence: The Diaries of Buonaccorso Pitti and Gregorio Dati* (Prospect Heights, IL: Waveland Press, 1991), 124: "I resolve from this day forward to refrain from going to the shop or conducting business on solemn Church holidays, or from permitting others to work for me or seek temporal gain such days." The original edition is *Il libro segreto di Gregorio Dati*, ed. Carlo Gargiolli (Bologna: Romagnoli, 1869).

[3] *Two Memoirs of Renaissance Florence*, ed. and trans. Brucker and Martines, 124: "I have written this down so that I may remember my promise and be ashamed if I should chance to break it."

[4] Gregorio Dati, *Istoria di Firenze di Goro Dati dall'anno 1380 all'anno1405*, ed. Giuseppe Manni (Florence: G. Manni, 1735).

[5] Christian Bec, *Les marchands écrivains: affaires et humanisme à Florence, 1375–1434* (Paris and The Hague: Mouton, 1967).

Dati promises to make amends for his past transgressions and to safeguard against backsliding behavior in the future. He does more than simply make a pious oath, however; he asserts control over his life. Every memoir or work of literature is arguably about identity. Yet we sense in this particular *ricordo* and in his other writings that Dati constantly wrestled with issues of personal and social identity in a world where fortunes were made and lost on a daily basis.[6] This might not seem extraordinary to us today, so used to theorizing about writing and the self; but Dati's doubts and hope for change are lodged between the *Santa Chiesa* and the *bottega*, and they underscore the impact of the changing spiritual paradigm on the consciousness of many intellectuals of the time. Like his contemporaries, Dati lived on the cusp of a major shift when empirical knowledge, technology, and science were challenging existing beliefs and when commercial practices threatened the dominant religious ideology.

Personal and social identity is also tied to literary imagination, the ability to represent the world based on experience and creativity. Perhaps more than any of his other works, Dati's *Sfera* illustrates best his understanding of the physical world in the age before the great explorations that were driven by mercantile and political interests. To analyze his geographical and didactic poem as a representation of its author's worldview therefore is to examine the interplay among epistemology, ontology, and aesthetics on the part of intellectuals who were rooted in the merchant class. As Raymond Clemens has explained, "The astronomical and cosmological parts of Dati's book have excited little interest and little research, despite the fact that his work was the first in western Europe designed to convey such information, often believed to be unnecessary or even dangerous, to the 'common man.'"[7] From his writings, we can say that Dati never meant to challenge the church's teachings. He was deeply moralistic, if not pious, and given

---

[6] These issues in Dati and other *diaristi* in the Quattrocento have long been of interest to scholars. For a recent and insightful analysis of Dati's moral and political attitudes and behavior, see Ionut Epurescu-Pascovici, "Gregorio Dati (1362–1435) and the Limits of Individual Agency." *Medieval History Journal* 9 (2006): 297–325. Much of what Epurescu-Pascovici says about Dati's individual agency, as expressed in the *Libro segreto*, is applicable to our reading of the *Sfera*. In brief, according to Epurescu-Pascovici, Dati approached his political life using two complementary strategies: he de-emphasized his involvement in Florentine politics as a means of coping with risky or sensitive matters, or he avoided action because of his attachment to an ideal model or form (301). My reading is that the former is a strategy by which Dati counteracts the possibility of failure and addresses his own political and financial vulnerability, whereas with the latter he "negotiates" his real and ideal selves.

[7] Raymond Clemens, "The Newberry *Sfera* and the Study of Renaissance Geography," *Mapline* 94/95 (2002): 1–4, and http://www.newberry.org/smith/Mapline/94–95/94–95feature.html. See also idem and Tmothy Graham, *Introduction to Manuscript Studies* (Ithaca: Cornell University Press, 2007), chap. 15, "Maps," 240–49, esp. here 245–46 with pls. 15–18.

his family background he wrote the *Sfera* for readers much like himself. But he did treat topics that were typically dealt with by church intellectuals, and he helped spread views that ultimately were considered necessary in a society that was increasingly influenced by developments in technology and science.[8]

The *Sfera* has a long and rich manuscript tradition, attesting to its enormous popularity throughout the Quattrocento.[9] This means that there is ample evidence for considering the work's meaning for scribes and readers. After a brief description of the *Sfera*'s structure and contents, therefore, we will consider the poem in three fifteenth-century manuscripts of the Beinecke Library at Yale University, each of which is significantly different from the other in terms of content and format. The material form in which Dati's didactic poem circulated is as interesting as the themes and images in the text. This sampling of manuscripts represents the understanding of merchants and readers who made, commissioned, or purchased copies for themselves. In short, we will try to answer the following questions: "What do these manuscript copies tell us about the physical world according to its author, the scribes who copied the work, and fifteenth-century readers?" and "What role did the *Sfera* play in popularizing 'science' among merchants, and to what ends?" The ongoing process of secularization that Dati struggled with in his *Libro segreto* is also reflected in the *Sfera* and especially in the manuscript copies that contributed to spreading knowledge about the world. But unlike early modern science that challenged Scholasticism and the Ptolemaic world view, Dati's poem mediated between the old and new paradigms for a secular readership that was ever more curious about the world.

Dati's *Sfera*

Gregorio (Goro) di Anastagio Dati (1362—1435) came from modest origins and made his living primarily in the silk trade. In his *Libro segreto*, he records his successes and failures and the major events of his personal life, such as his several marriages, the births and deaths of his many children, and his involvement in Florentine politics. From his diary, we sense that Dati was a persistent, resilient, and patient man. As a member of the guild of Por Santa Maria, he was eligible

---

[8] Epurescu-Pascovici's analysis of Dati's sense of his own agency helps us hypothesize about authorial meaning in the *Sfera*. Dati would have been aware of the potentially controversial nature of his poem. The author's invocation at the beginning of his poem (bk. 1, *ottave* 1–5) is conventional, but it can also be interpreted as an apologia and confirmation of his good intentions, whatever the subject matter.

[9] Lucia Bertolini, "L'attribuzione della 'sfera' del Dati nella tradizione manoscritta," in *Studi offerti a Gianfranco Contini dagli allievi pisani* (Florence: Casa Editrice Le Lettere, 1984) 33–43. Acccording to Bertolini ("Attribuzione," 35), there are at least 152 extant manuscripts of the *Sfera*. The Beinecke codices are not mentioned in her study.

for political office. Indeed, it was probably because of his equanimous temperament and also because of his modest social status that he was ultimately elected as Standard-Bearer of Justice in 1429, the highest political office in Florence. Dati's older brother, Leonardo, was a prominent Dominican theologian, having served most notably as Prior of S. Maria Novella between 1401 and 1405. Scholars assumed for centuries therefore that the more famous Leonardo (and not Goro) was the author of the *Sfera*. But the didactic poem more appropriately fits with Goro's intellectual profile and commercial interests, and it is written in the vernacular and not Latin. As Bertolini has explained, confusion about authorship was moreover caused by a misattribution in an early, authoritative manuscript.[10] Nevertheless, the overwhelming majority of codices (3:1) attribute the poem to Goro.[11] As we have already mentioned, Dati also wrote a chronicle, the *Istoria di Firenze*, in the early 1400s around the time of Florence's struggle with Milan. Thus his personal and public selves found their expression in his diary and in his didactic poem and chronicle.

Written at the end of the fourteenth century,[12] the *Sfera* is composed of 144 *ottave* that are evenly distributed in four books.[13] Book One deals primarily with cosmology, the zodiac, the planets, celestial phenomena (such as solar and lunar eclipses), and the effects of the heavens on men. Book Two describes the physical and natural elements, the seasons, and Galen's theory of humors that was the basis of medical knowledge from late antiquity through the early modern period. From the heavens to the earth, from the cosmos to the individual soul, Dati engages his reader by moving swiftly between the immanent and the minute. In Book Three, he describes the earth's zones and continents, in particular the Near and Far East and the major seas, and rhapsodizes about Cairo and Egypt, concluding his Asian *iter* with an allusion to *Monte Atlante* that rises in the middle of the African desert. In Book Four he traces a geographical outline from North Africa to Asia Minor, and he concludes his poem rather abruptly with a reference to the *fiume Tanai*, the geographical boundary between Asia and Europe.

By some accounts, the *Sfera* was left unfinished, as the work's continuation by the Dominican friar Giovanni Maria Tolosani de Colle seems to attest. Fra

---

[10] Bertolini, "Attribuzione," 33–35.
[11] Bertolini, "Attribuzione," 39.
[12] Filiberto Segatto, "Un'immagine quattrocentesca del mondo, la *Sfera* del Dati," *Memorie degli Atti dell'Accademia dei Lincei, Classe di Scienze morali, storiche e filologiche* 27 (1983): 147–83. As Segatto notes (148–49), the dating of the *Sfera* is quite problematic. There is no internal evidence, and the manuscript tradition is not helpful in this regard. Scholars have assumed that the *Sfera* is from the late fourteenth century or early fifteenth century when the poet had reached his "maturità anagrafica e intellettuale."
[13] In citing the *Sfera*, I will refer to the book number, the *ottava* or *ottave* (plural) that are numbered in the modern editions, and the line number as well.

Giovanni published his *aggiunta*, later known as *La nuova sfera*, in 1514.[14] The fact that Dati omits a description of Europe and Italy supports this view. It may be the case, however, that the author had ample opportunity to elaborate further, but deemed it unnecessary.[15] The question of the poem's overall structure affects our perception of the work's genre and ultimate purpose. On the one hand, Dati's geographical poem belongs to a long line of medieval didactic poetry describing the cosmos and the world: Dante, Fazio degli Uberti, and Cecco d'Ascoli come immediately to mind as literary precursors, and especially the poet of the *Divina Commedia* figures prominently in the work.[16] The invocation at the beginning of the *Sfera*, for example, reveals his Dantesque sensibility: "Ad ogni cor gentile e mente pura / che desidera intender la ragione / con la qual si governa la Natura" (To each gentle heart and pure mind / that desires to understand reason / with which one rules Nature").[17] But as each of the doctrinal poems are different from one another, so too is the *Sfera* from all of its predecessors. Devoid of Dante's teleological and salvific discourse, Dati keeps his feet firmly planted on the earth even when he is looking at the stars. His aim is more pragmatic: to give readers facts they can use. Unlike Fazio's *Dittamondo*, moreover, the poet of the *Sfera* does not rely on a fictional pretext or framework, avoiding allegorical interpretations associated with similar narratives; nor is he as free-thinking and provocative as Cecco d'Ascoli. Dati's voice in the *Sfera* is willfully self-effacing and not only in the name of 'science.'[18] On the other hand, the *Sfera* foreshadows the travel literature of the Renaissance with its emphasis on navigation, although it is not a *giornale di bordo* or an account of his travels. There is no historical or fictional pilgrim of the *Sfera*, just as there are few extraneous details in this very compact poem. Nevertheless, we sense Dati's excitement and wonder in a few points in the text, for example in the description of Cairo's streets: ". . . la gran città del Cairo che contiene / tanta di gente, ch'è mirabil cosa / vedere in ogni parte le vie piene / per modo, che a cercarla è faticosa" ("The great city of Cairo

---

[14] *La Sfera, libri quattro in ottava rima, scritti nel secolo XIV da F. Leonardo di Stagio Dati aggiuntivi due altri libri e La Nuova Sfera pure in ottava rima di F. Gio. M. Tolosani da Colle, L'America di Raffaello Gualterotti con altre poesie del medesimo* (Milan: G. Daelli e Comp. Editori, 1865).

[15] Segatto ("La *Sfera* del Dati") argues that had Dati wished to include a description of Europe he would have done so in Book III. The omission therefore seems intentional because Dati probably modeled his poem on late medieval pilot books used by merchants. These guides were not typically exhaustive and were often inaccurate. Moreover, whereas the African and Asian coasts were less well known, it would have been less important to describe what was more commonly known to Dati's readers.

[16] Segatto ("La *Sfera* del Dati," 152) provides an excellent overview of the history of Dati criticism and also of the literary precursors of Dati's poem.

[17] Segatto's footnote ("La *Sfera* del Dati," 152, n. 21) lists the most important examples of Dati's references to Dante's *Commedia*.

[18] See notes 6 and 7.

contains / many people, that it is a marvel / to see here streets full everywhere / so that to walk about it is difficult": bk. 3, *ottava* 32, ll. 2–5), where the transitive verb and direct object, *cercarla*, denote "to walk about it", but also connote "to know the city well", as if exploring the city's bustling streets.

Like his medieval counterparts, Dati accepts the Christian-Ptolemaic cosmology, with a heaven above and an inferno below. The *Sfera* reads like a popular compendium of brief interconnected encyclopedia entries written for an audience that has neither the time, nor perhaps the education, to engage in long academic study about cosmology and geography. A good illustration of Dati's clear statement of facts and understated aesthetic appeal is his simple, but not simplistic, description of "air" (bk. 2, *ottava* 9):

> Anchora è bella chagione a pensare
> le qualità dell'aria e sua natura,
> che quanto in alto più potessi andare
> la troveresti più sottile e pura;
> però, alchuno ucello non può volare,
> né sostenersi su per quella altura,
> sostiensi in questa bassa ch'è più grossa,
> perché fa risistenza alla percossa.[19]

Without explaining the science, Dati distinguishes between the levels of atmosphere and introduces "gravity" through the concrete example of a bird's flight. The last verse, "perché fa risistenza alla percossa", the sense of which is "because it resists movement", vividly depicts the interaction between wind and air resistance and the bird's beating wings.

One of the basic truths of medieval life is the influence of the celestial spheres and natural elements on the psychological makeup of individuals. Dati reprises this absolute and relates how the four complexions or bodily humors are interrelated. Echoing Dante again, he puts the burden of responsibility for our actions squarely on our shoulders: "quand'ella al chorpo si lascia ghuidare, / e sèghuita sua bassa chonditioni / perde l'altezza e 'l ben de l'intelletto, / et è per suo, et non d'altrui, difetto." (bk. 2, *ottava* 33, ll. 5–8; MS. 328, fol. 12r). Shortly thereafter (bk. 2, *ottava* 35) he warns against the consumerism and materialism of his age:

---

[19] MS. 328, fol. 8r. "Also, it is beautiful to consider / the quality of air and her nature / that the higher you were able to go / you would find it thin and pure; / so much that no bird can fly / nor live up at that height, / it lives in this lower air that is more dense / because it resists movement."

Citations of the *Sfera* are transcribed from the manuscript sources used in this study. I have not altered the orthography, but have divided words and inserted punctuation to clarify meaning.

> Queste chose chonposte e choruttibili,
> che non possono durare, né chrescer tanto,
> ch'enpian la voglia alli animali sensibili,
> chon gran faticha se n'achuista alquanto,
> chon timore le tieni che sono fluxibili;
> e poi le lasci chon dolore e pianto.
> Chi vede ben ciò ch'elle sanno fare,
> pocho vorrà per esse afattichare.[20]

While the first two books discuss the cosmos and human nature, Books Three and Four clearly delineate the elements of world geography, that is, that part of the world that would have interested his contemporaries most. The author likely used a number of sources including maps, guidebooks to ports (known as *portolani*), and also pilgrims' accounts of the Holy Land. As Raymond Clemens states, "Dati was the only cartographer in the Renaissance to fragment portolan maps and press them into service in an educational primer. His use of the portolan maps indicates his intention of providing the most up-to-date and accurate maps then available for his primary audience: Florentine merchants."[21] The reliance on maps, atlases, portolans, and pilgrims' accounts is also evident from the drawings and colored illustrations in many of the manuscripts. Besides basic figurative and geometric figures, such as spheres to describe the heavens and natural elements, there is the common T=O Map that dates to antiquity:

> Vn T dentro a uno O mostra 'l disegnio
> chome in tre parti fu diviso il mondo,
> e lla superiore è maggior regnio
> che quasi piglia la metà del tondo,
> Asia chiamata; il ghambo ritto è segno
> che parte il terzzo nome dal sechondo,
> Africha, dicho da Europia; el mare
> Mediteran tra esse in mezzo apare.[22]

---

[20] "Worldly things that are made and are corruptible, / that cannot last, nor grow, / that fill sentient beings with desire, / with great difficulty they are acquired in number, / with fear you hold onto them that they are fluid; / and then in pain and in tears you leave them. / He who knows well what they can do, / will want little to struggle for them."

[21] Clemens, "The Newberry *Sfera* and the Study of Renaissance Geography."

[22] Bk. 3, *ottava* 11 (MS. 328, fol. 14v): "A T within an O, the map shows / how the world was divided into three parts, / and the upper is the larger realm / that takes up almost half of the globe, / Asia it is called; the vertical stem is the line / that separates the third name from the second, / Africa, that is, from Europe; the Mediterranean / sea is between them."

Analogous to medieval bestiaries that blended myth and reality, city maps and geographical atlases expressed an "affective experience of the world"[23] and were often influenced by Scripture. In Ptolemaic maps, Jerusalem is at the center of the world and the Holy Lands are prominently featured. This is the case, for example, in Book Three of the *Sfera*. However, as the need for accurate geographic renderings increased during the early modern period, cartography benefited from development of perspective in the visual arts. In many medieval maps, cities and coastlines are outlined in relative proportion, but with Alberti's *Descriptio Urbis Romae*, for example, Renaissance cartography became technically and scientifically more proficient.[24] It is an exaggeration to say that Ptolemaic maps were to the Renaissance and modern cartography what myth is to historiography; but the parallel is intended to underscore the impact of science and technology on "affective experience." It does not in any case explain how readers interpreted medieval maps and other verbal and visual renderings of places and distances. To understand this we need to consider the dynamic between history and myth and between imagined and empirical experience in the production and circulation of texts and images.

Because any map is a metaphor about the world, it bridges time and space and provides extensive quantitative information in a manageable format. Maps frequently tell us as much about their cartographers' intentions and about their audience's understanding as they do about the objective reality they seek to represent. In many illustrated copies of the *Sfera*, for example, the Tower of Babel is depicted as a visible landmark of the Middle East. Reflecting a crucial turning point in the history of humankind, it is the archetype of linguistic confusion and decay and also, by historical association, linked with Islam and the Crusades. The empirical facts of the *Sfera* therefore coexist with deep-seated myths. On an artistic level, Dati and/or his illustrators can be said to use anachronism effectively, similar to Boccaccio's technique in various tales of the *Decameron*, or to Renaissance artists like Masaccio who portrayed biblical figures in fifteenth-century clothing, for aesthetic as well as for ideological reasons. While explicating and reinforcing textual meaning, the maps in the *Sfera* underscore the merchant's obsession with commanding time and space for commercial gain. The telescoping of time and space is evident in the oppositions and in the pithy syntax of the following *ottava*:

---

[23] Naomi Miller, "Mapping the City: Ptolemy's *Geography* in the Renaissance," in *Envisioning the City: Six Studies in Urban Cartography*, ed. David Buisseret (Chicago: University of Chicago Press, 1998), 34–74, here 44.

[24] Miller ("Mapping the City: Ptolemy's *Geography* in the Renaissance," 49) discusses Alberti's integration of perspective into his plan of Rome. In a footnote (71) she discusses the problematic dating of Alberti's map. Originally assumed to have been made in 1435, it was more likely produced in the 1440s, although the date of 1452–1453 has also been proposed.

> Et cho' la charta dove son segniati
> i venti e porti e tutte le marine,
> vanno per mare merchatanti et pirati:
> que' per ghuadagnio e questi per rapina;
> e in un punto richi e sventurati
> sono alle volte da sera a mattina;
> che lla Fortuna in alchun altra chosa
> non si dimostra tanta rovinosa.[25]

In many copies of the *Sfera*, the maps of coastlines encroach the space reserved for the text, blurring the hierarchical relationship between text and image. The complexity of this relationship is even more pronounced in middling-level copies in which the illustrations are hastily executed and are, thereby, less clear and accurate representations of spatial relations. Whether or not the poet conceived of the illustrations by himself or in concert with an artist is unknown, although it is likely that the earliest manuscripts established the convention of representing some features of the text and not others. What is certain is that the imagery contributed to the poem's didacticism and aesthetics and ultimately to its popularity for an audience with one foot in the Middle Ages and the other in the Renaissance.[26]

Beinecke Manuscripts of the *Sfera*

MS. 328

In turning to a discussion of the Beinecke manuscripts, we must remember that each codex is a unique artifact with respect to others, even those that have the same text. The manuscripts in question bear the shelfmarks 328, 943, and 1030.[27] Of the three, MS. 328 is aesthetically speaking the most attractive. A paper manuscript that was likely produced in Florence during the third quarter of the fifteenth century, the codex bears the arms of the Cambio family, although the

---

[25] Bk. 3, *ottava* 4 (MS. 328, fol. 13v): "And with the map on which the winds / and ports and all the waters are marked, / travel the seas both merchants and pirates: / the former by gainful commerce and the latter by violence; / and in one moment they are rich and poor / sometimes from evening to morning / that Fortune in no other matter reveals herself to be so ruinous."

[26] In his analysis of the poem's reader reception history, Segatto ("La *Sfera* del Dati," 176) notes that the average reader of the *Sfera* would have been "anche meno colti e preparati di quelli normalmente raggiunti da altre opere del medesimo genere, quali il *Dittamondo* e l'*Acerba*."

[27] There is also a fourth manuscript of the *Sfera* in the Beinecke collection, MS. 946, that I have examined but have excluded from this analysis because it is similar in type to MS. 943 discussed below.

actual owner has not been identified.[28] As with many other copies of the *Sfera*, the format used was the sesternion or quire of six bifolia (equal to twelve *chartae*) that perfectly suited the structure of the poem. The *Sfera*'s 144 *ottave* were laid out three stanzas per side, allowing for illustrations in the ample external and bottom margins. The layout of the poem also facilitated the transcription of other copies, if not serial production, and explains why it is such a common format for the *Sfera*. Written by one person in a very fine mercantile script, MS. 328 has twenty-nine separate pen illustrations that have been colored in red, pink, blue, yellow, and green washes, a coloring technique that was commonly used in other copies of similar production level. There is a gold capital or *dentelle* on the first *charta* that lends a tinge of luxury to the codex, along with the elegant Humanist *bianco girari* (white vine motif) extending downward in the left margin. [Plate 1] The text has been bound between wooden boards and covered with dark brown sheepskin with remnants of clasps and bosses. The back cover has concentric circles embossed onto it, perhaps intended to mirror the astronomical drawings within the codex.

With respect to the other Beinecke codices, the text of MS. 328 is generally reliable, meaning that the scribe copies carefully from a good model and underscores textual *loci* about which he has doubts or questions (such as in bk. 3, *ottava* 16, ll. 6–7 [fol. 15v] and in bk. 4, *ottava* 14, ll. 4–5 [fol. 21v]). Most of the textual variants are simply morphological or graphological, although there are passages in which all three codices have a different substantive reading. For example, referring to the body type of an individual with a choleric temperament, the text of MS. 328 reads: "di chorpo astuti e di chuor chonditiosi" [bk. 2, *ottava* 29, l. 6 (fol. 11v)], even though the context requires "asciutti" (that is, "thin") and "giudiziosi" ("judicious"). "Astuti" is a simple misreading or a reasonable conjecture on the scribe's part because human physical and psychological features are so closely tied together in the description of the bodily humors. However, the lection "chonditiosi" is incomprehensible and could easily be an anticipation of "chonditione" which appears as the rhyme word of the first verse of the following *ottava*.

The illustrations in MS. 328 have been rapidly executed and are ancillary to the text. The reader would be hard put to interpret the geographical outlines and locations without clearly associating them with the text they are meant to represent.[29] Nevertheless, the watercolor composition of Noah's Ark, the Euphrates

---

[28] For a detailed description of this codex, see Barbara Shailor, *Catalogue of Medieval and Renaissance Manuscripts in the Beinecke Rare Book and Manuscript Library, Yale University*, vol. 2, MRTS 48 (Binghamton, NY: Medieval and Renaissance Texts and Studies, 1987), 146–47.

[29] Mariners and seafaring merchants would have been able to depend on more precise nautical maps than the ones in illustrated copies of the *Sfera*. A. E. Nordenskjöld ("Dei disegni marginali negli antichi manoscritti della Sfera del Dati," *Bibliofilia* 3

Imagination and Pragmatism in Dati's Sfera

Plate 1: MS 328 (Beinecke Rare Book and Manuscript Library, Yale University), c. 1r.

and Tigris rivers, and the Red Sea leap across the folios (15v-16r) and circumscribe part of the *ottava* they are meant to illustrate, as if they were integral to the poem itself. [Plate 2] In another set of drawings depicting the Holy Lands, the cartoon blends a medium-distance view of a church perched on a mountaintop, presumably Mount Sinai, with a bird's-eye image of what is perhaps Galilee (fol. 21v) or the Crusader port of Joppa; whereas the facing folio (22r) contains an image meant to suggest Damascus and possibly Tripoli to its south. [Plate 3] Like the silhouettes on today's road signs, these drawings are purely referential, rather than illustrative or expressive. In most cases, cities are depicted as a circular or straight wall, depending on the perspective, with towers. There is no pretense of accuracy; yet these cartoons reflect shifts in the author's narrative technique and point of view, from the mere mention of place names (corresponding to the bird's-eye view in many of the illustrations) to essential details that lend vibrancy to the geographical inventory (corresponding to drawings that have several figurative elements in them). Text, script, and decoration indicate that the codex was conceived for a consumer of good taste but relatively modest means, and certainly for someone who wanted a reliable version of the poem. The mercantile script is very legible and elegant, and the decoration of the poem's *incipit* reflects the impact of Humanist book production on lower-production-level books. Fifteenth-century readers would have been very familiar with many of the places in the poem, but Dati's popularizing representation places them in a spatial and conceptual relation that is concise, informative, and lively, while also being economically accessible.

MS. 943

A paper manuscript datable to between 1450 and 1480, MS. 943 [Plate 4] contains Petrarca's *Trionfi* and Dati's *Sfera*, a pairing of a literary digest and a cosmological poem.[30] It is clearly not a composite book because the paper stock, quiring, rulings, and even the average number of written lines per folio are the

---

[1901–1902]: 49–55, here 51–52) believed that the illustrations reflected modified versions of maps used in portolani for different compilations and not the regular "portolani normali." Indeed, he hypothesized more specifically (55) that they were copies of maps first used by travelers and Crusaders in the Middle Ages and not the more recent and accurate maps of Dati's time.

[30] MS. 943:

    Francesco Petrarca, *Trionfi*. fols. 1r–47r: Et ei questo mavien per laspre some ... Or che fia dunque arivederla incielo / FINIS

    Gregorio Dati, *Sfera*. fols. 48r-76r: Al padre al figlio allo spirito sancto ... lasciai maggiore il fiume tanaij.

    Paper, *chapeau* or "tasseled cardinal's hat", similar, but not identical, to Briquet 3370 (1465–1467) and 3373 (1474/1483), fols. I (parchment) + 77 (modern numbering in

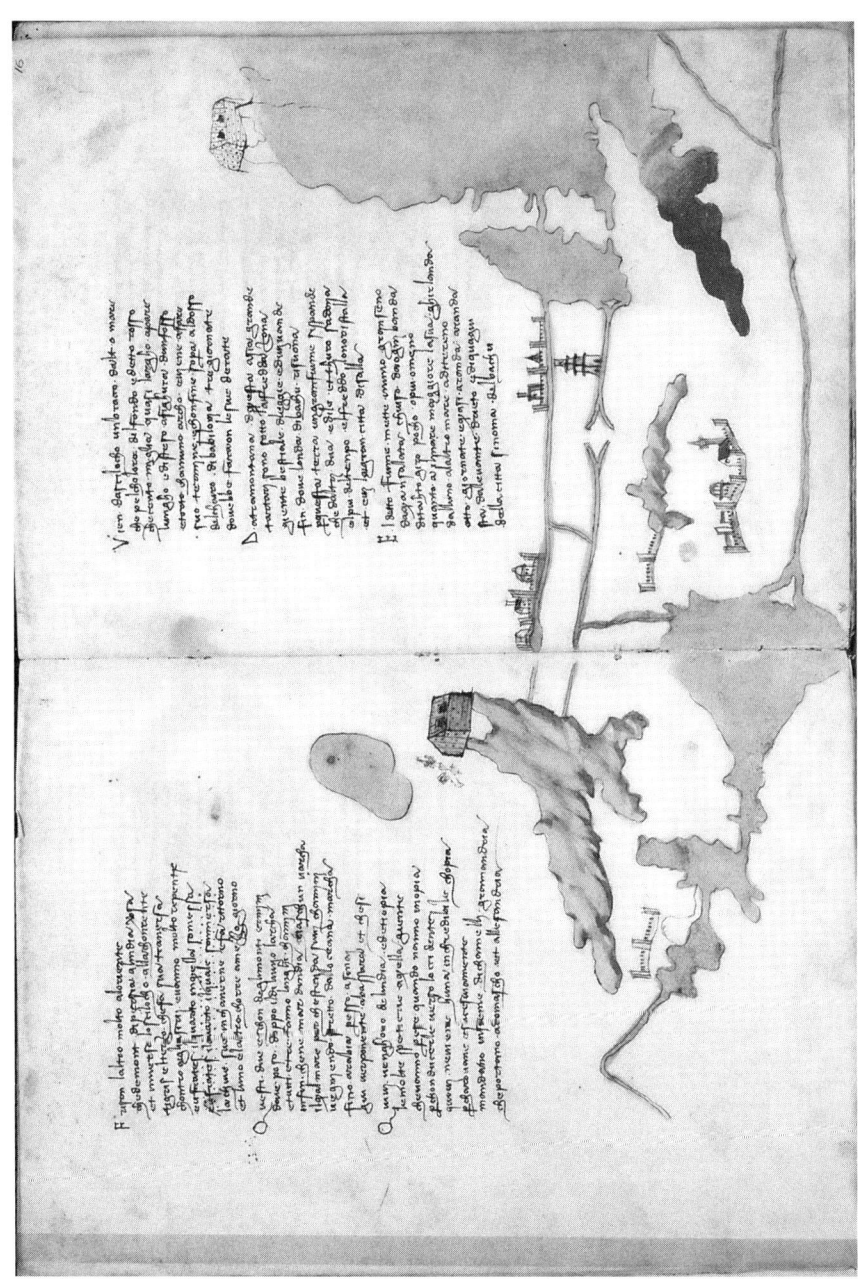

Plate 2: MS 328 (Beinecke Rare Book and Manuscript Library, Yale University), cc. 15v–16r.

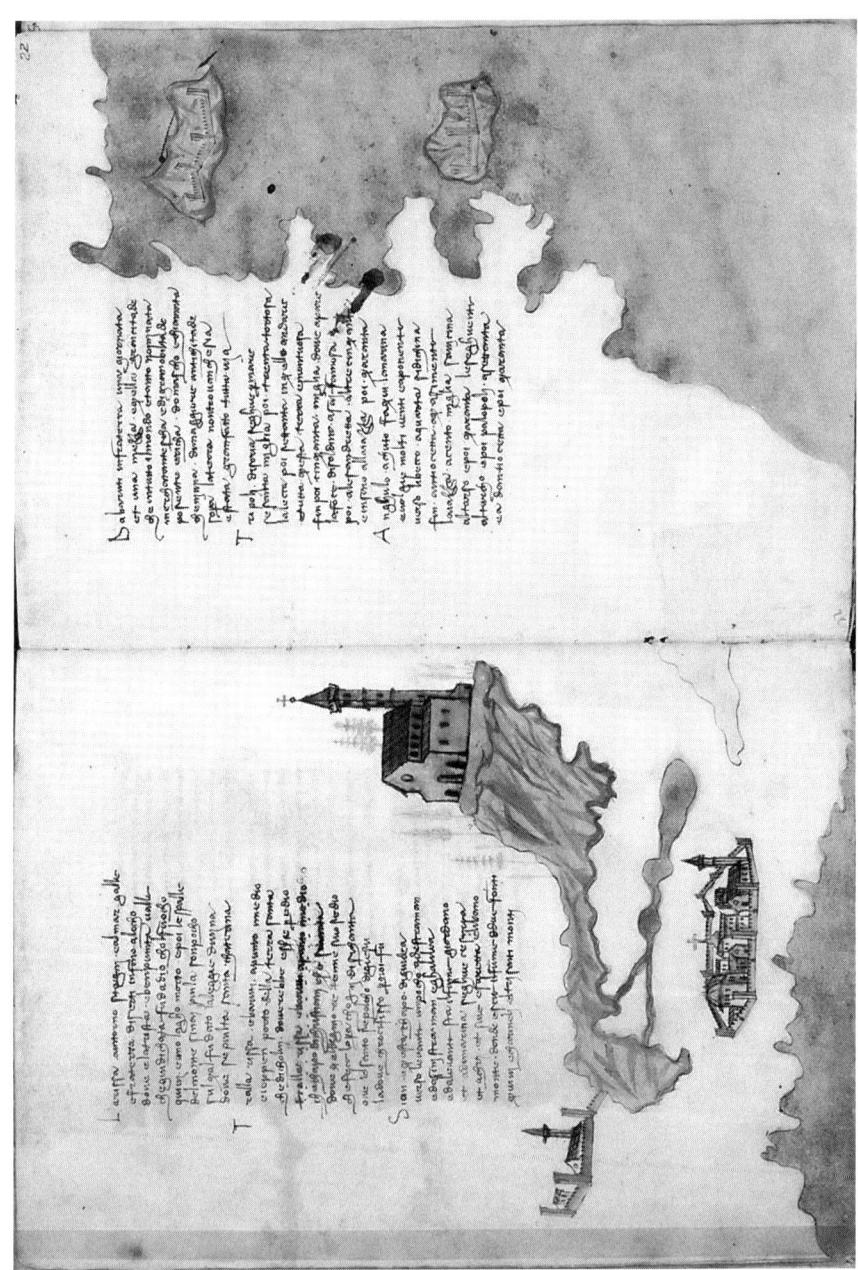

Plate 3: MS 328 (Beinecke Rare Book and Manuscript Library, Yale University), cc. 21v–22r.

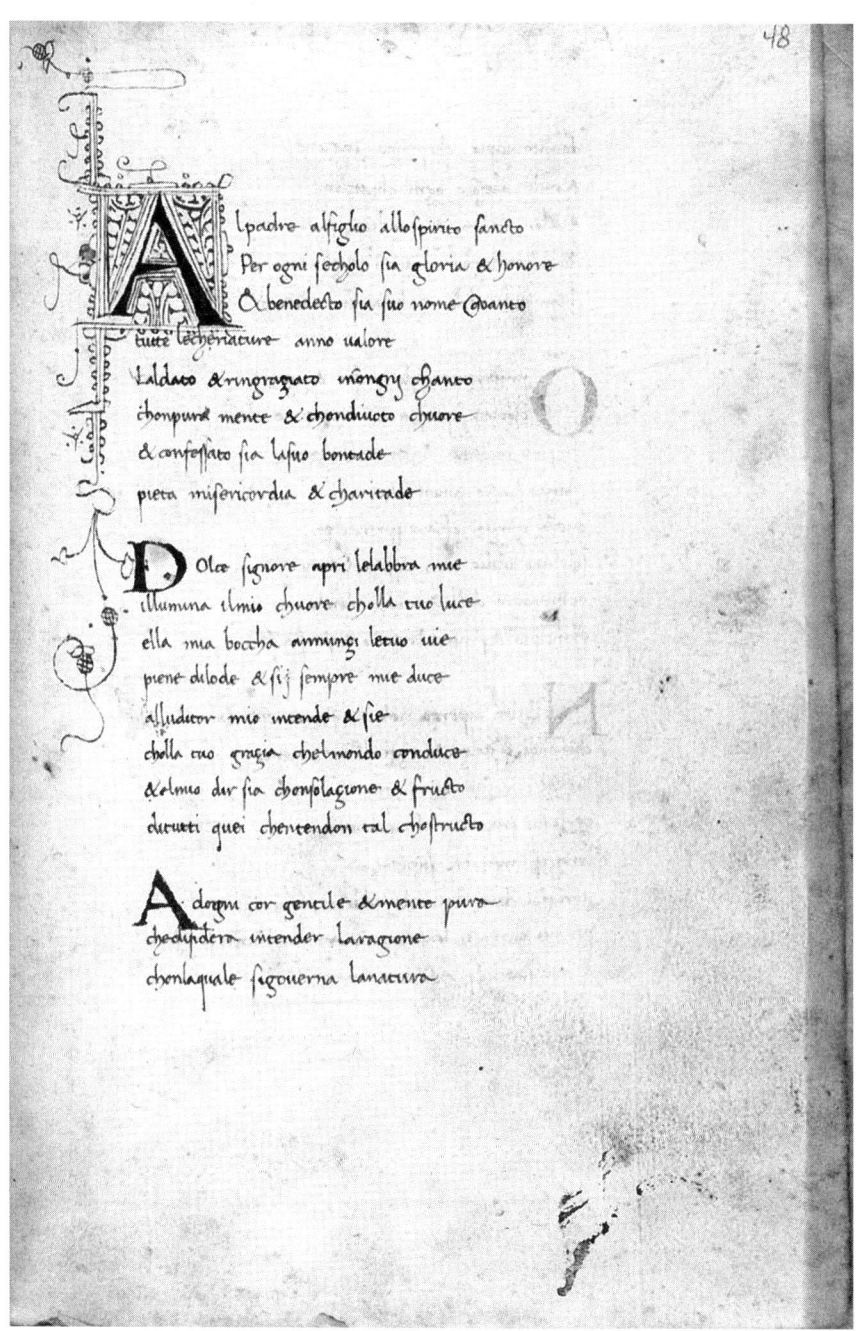

Plate 4: MS 943 (Beinecke Rare Book and Manuscript Library, Yale University), c. 48r.

same for both works, despite their clearly different poetic structures. Each work is in the hand of a different scribe. Written in a very clean and neat *humanistica cursiva*, the codex has simple blue painted majuscules for the beginning of each chapter of the *Trionfi* and for each of the *ottave* of Dati's poem. From the external evidence, we surmise that the scribes or whoever commissioned the manuscript intended for both texts to be paired together as part of the editorial plan and not because they were merely available to be copied. According to Bertolini's census of manuscripts[31] of the *Sfera* in Florentine libraries, there are at least eight other codices that join both works in one volume, although the *Sfera* was often paired with other renowned literary texts, such as Petrarch's *Canzoniere* and Dante's *Comedy*.[32]

The *Trionfi* was a bestseller in the Quattrocento because Petrarch was the paragon for other poets and because his poem in *terza rima* portrays the pageantry and grandeur of ancient Rome. To look at the hundreds of codices that have come down to us, the *Trionfi* was a "must-have" work, and even more interesting are the different kinds and levels of copies that reveal its popularity among readers from different social classes, some of whom could afford deluxe copies and others who were in the market for a plain and unadorned version. This is apparently the case for the *Sfera* as well. The texts of the *Trionfi* and the *Sfera* in MS.

---

pencil, upper right hand corner) + I (parchment). 215mm × 145mm. 23 ruled (dry point) and written lines. Single column text. 140mm × 90mm writing frame.

I 5(-1a), II-IV5, V4, VI-VIII5. Catchwords: vertical, downward, inside of right double line column at the end of each quire.

Written by two scribes (one for each work) in a humanistic cursive. There are blue initials for the beginning of each chapter of the *Trionfi*, except for the first one because of the missing leaf. It probably did have a large decorated initial, perhaps like the one with red flourishes that introduces the *Sfera*. Similar to the *Trionfi*'s chapters, the *Sfera* has small blue initials for each of the stanzas. There is the name "Ruberto" and the initials "GFF" on the recto of the first parchment flyleaf. The back parchment flyleaf has a roughly drawn coat of arms in brown ink of a shield with a large circle around a smaller one in the middle. There are also basic arithmetic and numbers written on the back pastedown.

The binding is fifteenth-century, 225mm × 145mm, of brown leather, with lozenges that have been dry-tooled onto the covers, with remnants of two clasp and catch fastenings on the edges of the boards There is a modern shelfmark, "123", on a piece of paper glued onto the spine.

The codex was likely written in Florence in the third quarter of the fifteenth century.

[31] See Lucia Bertolini, "Censimento dei manoscritti della *Sfera* del Dati," *Annali della Scuola normale superiore di Pisa, Classe di Lettere e Filosofia*, 3a ser., 12.2 (1982): 666–705; 15.3 (1985): 889–940; 18.2 (1988): 417–588.

[32] The manuscripts that have both the *Sfera* and the *Trionfi* in Bertolini's census are the following: II. II. 40, VII. 845, VII. 946, VIII. 54, and Palatino 128 in the Biblioteca Nazionale Centrale di Firenze; Ashburnham 854 and Conventi Soppressi 109 in the Biblioteca Mediceo-Laurenziana; and 1091 of the Riccardiana Library.

943 appear to offer reliable readings, that is, in line with the standard fifteenth-century *vulgata* of both works.[33] They are without illustrations, nor are there spaces set aside for them. It is a fine example of mid-level Humanist book production. Although Dati's science was not cutting-edge, nor was his poetic style a model of literary excellence, the *Sfera* is perceived as a literary, rather than scientific, work, although the boundaries between literature and other genres were more blurred than we usually presume. One reason for the prevalence of didactic poetry might have to do with the fact that meter favored mnemonics, as a learning device; but versification more likely reflects the peculiar history of Italian as a language that developed and spread among the populace thanks to poetry. Dati's audience of readers would have appreciated his simple and clear versification of facts and ideas, and the *ottava* favored a paratactic style of explication.

The practice, moreover, of copying literary *qua* classical and historical texts, such as the *Trionfi*, along with empirical and didactic works, like the *Sfera*, was not uncommon and had long existed. Setting aside considerations about the intellectual differences and divisions between the liberal arts and areas of knowledge in late medieval Italy that would have influenced book production and, therefore, how knowledge circulated, there was a practical and economic reason for copying different works together in anthology form or in miscellanies. A relative lack of available texts and the cost of materials and of copying encouraged individuals to gather them into manageable units. The basic structure of the booklet or quire also lent itself to being bound with other works. But just as the *florilegium*, the quintessential medieval book of knowledge, represents a cultural ideology and pedagogy as well as a convenient practice, the pairing of the *Trionfi* and the *Sfera* entails more than their identity as literature. Taken in the cultural context of mid-fifteenth-century Italy (and, more specifically, Florence where MS. 943 was probably produced), literature and empirical knowledge are symbiotically tied together; it is only subsequently, with the imposition of disciplinary boundaries, that we view didactic literature (with few noteworthy exceptions) with aesthetic skepticism. To refer to Dante's *Commedia* as a didactic

---

[33] The pairing of the *Trionfi* with the *Sfera* is not unique to this codex, as Lucia Bertolini's census of Florentine libraries demonstrates, and it was not likely for editorial reasons only. Petrarch's criticism of astrological determinism in the *Seniles* (I 6) and Dati's view that man is primarily responsible for his actions by controlling his natural impulses (bk. 2, *ottava* 33–36) underscore the emphasis on the role of will in the individual's agency and identity. As Segatto ("La *Sfera* del Dati," 154–55) explains, "Ai tempi in cui veniva composta la *Sfera* non si era ancora sviluppata pienamente quella polemica sull'astrologia che costituì uno dei momenti più significativi del dibattito culturale umanistico e vide intervenire tra gli altri Pico della Mirandola, Pietro Pomponazzi, Girolamo Savonarola. Tuttavia c'era già stato chi, come il Petrarca, aveva difeso strenuamente la libertà dell'uomo e la sua capacità di superare la necessità delle cose e la causalità fisica, negando che gli astri determinassero o anche solo rispecchiassero gli eventi mondani."

poem would possibly diminish its aesthetic achievement for some critics, and yet that is exactly what *il poema* is. The *Trionfi* and the *Sfera* complement one another in MS. 943, the first being an *ekphrasis* of classical culture and history, and the second a capsule representation of the world. In the sense that MS. 934 is a Humanist book, it underscores the centrality of a complex art form, poetry, the epitome of *logos*, as the principal means of imparting knowledge, and it also underscores the civic and practical value of learning beyond the circle of intellectuals and artists. Although he was not a *literatus* (a man of Latin letters) like his brother Leonardo, Dati was a cultural intermediary between Humanists and his fellow merchants.

MS. 1030

The most interesting of the three codices from a literary and cultural perspective is MS. 1030, an anthology containing a variety of works that are thematically interconnected.[34] This paper manuscript of 110 folios copied in Florence and dating from the 1420s contains a section of business accounts, religious sermons, the

---

[34] MS. 1030:
Written in the fifteenth and beginning of the sixteenth century.
1. fols 1r-2r. Inscriptions and entries with dates of 1484 and 1501.
2. fols. 2v-18v. Ricordi, 1423 // Domenicho Antonio di domenicho delmonte asansovino . . . che tu gli presti cio chio o lasciato.
3. fols. 20r-24r. Sermons. Do(meni)ca dopo la penti(coste) // Multi sunt vochati pauci vero electi amen . . . e la madre / di gesu xpo vera dovete sapere charisimi chel nostro signore gesu xpo ordino.
4. fols. 25r-48r. Goro Dati, *La sfera*. Al padre e figlo allo spiritto santo . . . lasia mag(i)ore il fiume tanai.
5. fols. 50r-75r. Brunetto Latini, selections from *Il Tresor* (bks. 3, 4, 5, 8, 9), Et pero le gentti si amagionano sopra . . . po / polo a ttutte umanittade che avere.
6. fols. 76r-81r: Artte di stolomia (Book about prognostications and astrology). Artte di stolomia prencipiatta per giafette figliolo di noe perittrovare il suo figluolo . . . E chosi sara anchora delle femine che / nasceranno in questi sengni.
7. fols. 81v-108r: Detta charttigine e buono portto (Portolan). Detta charttigine e buono porto e a inannsi unisolla pichola dinansi apuntta/lungha circha a 1o miglio . . . qui finisce ilibro del maestro deportti deo graziase (sic).
8. Three unattributed sonnets (*Cara vetoria e de virtù ornata, Com'animal c(h)'è in cac(i)a ad altrui è g(i)oco, Ricordati ora mai c(h)e cener sei*) on a small loose leaf (219mm x 114) inserted inside front cover.
Paper (watermark very similar to Briquet Tour 15864 documented in Lucca, 1419 and Florence, 1422–1427), 110 cc. (109 and 110 are blank), modern foliation in lead in the top right corner of recto and ancient numbering to c. 19 in brown ink, the same used for texts, 295 x 220. Vertical lines ruled in lead, except for *Tesor* and *Artte di Stolomia* written in double columns.
I8(-3a, -6b), II8 (-5a, -7a), III8 (-7b), IV8 (-1a), V-VII8

Sfera, excerpts from Brunetto Latini's *Tresor* in Italian, a curious little tract about astrology (the *Artte di Stolomia*), and a lengthy and fascinating portolan. There are also three sonnets written on a small loose-leaf sheet that was tucked into the codex. All texts are in Italian. The binding, of soft yellowish sheepskin with straps and exposed leather supports, is clearly reminiscent of a merchant's ledger or account book. The volume also has several inscriptions dating to the second-half of the fifteenth-century that indicate its provenance. The codex may have belonged to Pagholo di Lapacio di Jacopo di Firenze, whose accounts for the biennium 1423–1424 are recorded in the first 18 folios, and it was certainly owned by at least three generations of the Florentine Del Sera family: Neri di Miniato, Domenico, and Neri di Domenico. Further research is required, but we can say confidently that Neri di Miniato was active in the wine-sellers guild according to the Florentine *catasto*.[35] Explaining his reasons for handing down this book to his son, Domenico writes:

> Richordo chome morì Neri di Miniato dell Sera in M468 d'aghosto, la vilia di Santo Lorenzo, e laciò questo libro a Domenicho di Neri di Miniato dell Sera, a suo figliuolo, perché si diletava di navichare e voleva sapere più chosse dell mondo, e cierchò asai paesi di tere di mare e vide d'ognie chose per lo mondo. E chosì vole che chi vedrà detto libro voglia vedere le beleze dell mondo per aqua e diventerà praticho e buono merchatante di tuta le merchatantia che vole toscha e di levante o di ponentte; e sarà persona pra-

---

Written in a simple, unadorned *mercantesca* by one hand, with the exception of the *ricordi* at the beginning of the book that is written in another, more cursive, mercantile script.

There are painted initials and illustrations in the section of the *Sfera*, as well as running headers in the *ricordi* section with the dates 1422–1424.

The volume was bound in a fifteenth-century limp vellum binding with three horizontal straps with the metal buckle still extant (albeit detached).

Written quite likely in Florence and mostly during the mid to late 1420s, given the *ricordi* (1422–1424) and the fact that the codex originally belonged to Neri di Miniato Del Sera who died in 1468. The poems seem to have been copied in or around 1501 by Neri's grandson, also named Neri (di Domenico), who owned the volume. The codex was acquired by the Beinecke Library from Bernard Rosenthal in 2003.

[35] From the *Online Catasto of 1427*, it appears that Neri di Miniato became eligible for election to the Vinattieri guild in 1465 and was elected in 1468, but he had died before taking office. His son, Domenico, was in a certain sense even less successful than his father, because he appears to have been chronically in arrears with his taxes and was unable to assume office. The *catasto* also confirms Neri di Domenico's inscription about the date of his birth, 9 May 1483 (*Online Catasto of 1427*. Version 1.3, ed. David Herlihy, Christiane Klapisch-Zuber, R. Burr Litchfield, and Anthony Molho. [Machine-readable data file based on D. Herlihy and C. Klapisch-Zuber, *Census and Property Survey of Florentine Domains in the Province of Tuscany, 1427–1480*] Florentine Renaissance Resources/STG: Brown University, Providence, R.I., 2002).

ticha se seghua detto libro a volere sapere e' buoni paesi da merchatanti; si seghua questi mari che sono da fare uomini industri e navichanti e di buona merchatantia e lascierà buona fine di sé. M480 marzo.[36]

In other inscriptions Domenico records his son's birth in May 1484 and declares having made his will, stating also that "Francesco De sSera" owes him the handsome sum of 40 gold florins. For nearly a century this Florentine family of merchants held the codex dear because of the practical knowledge it contained, but also because the texts reflected the cultural and scientific interests of their social class. If reading informs cultural identity, then the Del Seras wish to be "uomini industri e navichanti e di buona merchatantia," an identity that is grounded in their mercantile experience and culture and one that is also mirrored by the complex of texts.

Like other vernacular anthologies, MS. 1030 is organized according to an editorial plan,[37] as if the principal scribe gathered and copied the works over a relatively short time, perhaps a few months and no more than a few years. Indeed the transcription of the texts (with the exception of the *ricordi* and the sheet of poems) was certainly completed by the end of the 1420s, if not by around 1427. Written in a larger book format (of quires of sixteen folios) than the other Beinecke codices we have examined, MS. 1030 is not the product of a professional scriptorium. Aside from the first section of *ricordi* attributable to Pagholo di Lapaccio di Firenze who uses a rapid and loose cursive, the texts have all been copied in a mercantile script that is far less calligraphic than that of MS. 328. Even more interesting from a philological perspective is the linguistic register and the scribe's use of an everyday, common vernacular that is characterized by popular spellings (such as *grolia* for *gloria*, *sprendore* for *splendore*), the frequent doubling of consonants (especially of "t", as in *spiritto santto*, and *laudatto e ringraziatto*), the "h" after velar consonants (*triangholo*, *chaldi*), and the reinforcement of nasal sounds (*rengno*, *ongni*). The text of the *Sfera* is defective in places or has very different variant spellings of words, although most of the

---

[36] MS. 1030, fol. 2r: "I remember how Neri di Minato del Sera died in August of 1468, on the eve of Saint Lawrence's feast day, and he left this book to his son, Domenico di Neri di Miniato, because he enjoyed traveling by sea and wanted to know many things about the world. And he traveled to many countries by land and by sea, and he saw all types of things in the world; and so he wanted that whoever will read this book will also want to see the beauties of the world by sea and will become an expert and good merchant of all kinds of goods, be they from Tuscany, the East, or the West. And that person will become expert if he follows this book in order to know which are the good countries to do business with. He must travel these seas that make men industrious and seafaring and good merchants, and he will leave a good end of himself. March 1480."

[37] Segatto ("La *Sfera* del Dati," 176, n. 89) states that there is at times an evident compilational criterion, especially with works that immediately precede or follow the *Sfera*.

misreadings can be attributed to the scribe (*lebia* for *labra*, fol. 25r; *argerto* for *argento*, fol. 28v; *chudiziosi* for *giudiziosi*, fol. 35v [the latter, "ch-" for "giu-", being quite possibly a popular form of pronouncing and writing the voiced palatal]). The two missing leaves in the text of the *Sfera* (fols. 43 and 45 according to the modern numbering) are evidence of the manuscript's heavy use.

As for the sequence of texts, Dati's *Sfera* complements and is informed by the *Artte di Stolomia* (the astrology handbook) and the portolan. But it is also connected to the selection of sermons that immediately precede it, as well as to the excerpts of Brunetto's *Tresor* that follow.[38] According to this view, the manuscript as a container of texts is itself a kind of overarching macro-story. Like many other didactic poems, the *Sfera* begins by invoking God's inspiration and guidance. And so the placing of the sermons, these very common and popular narratives celebrating key moments in the Christian calendar, before Dati's poem serves as an apt introduction and possibly an apologia for the poem's potentially dangerous subject matter. The inclusion of passages from the *Tresor*, a work that was produced in the first half of the thirteenth century, is a testament to Ser Brunetto's enduring popularity, despite anachronisms in his encyclopedia. The excerpts from Brunetto's *bestiario* explain natural history and philosophy and complement Dati's treatment of cosmology and geography. MS. 1030 includes selections from Books Eight and Nine that deal respectively with rhetoric and politics. Given Brunetto's standing as one of the most illustrious intellectuals in Florentine history, it is no wonder that a fifteenth-century merchant would wish to possess his own copy of such important texts that also had practical value.

There are twenty-eight hastily drawn illustrations and maps in the text of the *Sfera* in MS. 1030 (one less than in MS. 328), and the scribe/illustrator has clearly written place and object names in bright red ink, a usage that Nordenskjöld believed confirmed his view that the *Sfera*'s illustrations derived from sources older than the "portolano normale." As in other illustrated copies of the poem, the images of coastlines cover the external and bottom margins, surrounding the text (fols. 39v-40r). [Plate 5] Occasionally the illustrator highlights a city, such as Tunis (fol. 45v), by drawing a generic profile of principal monuments and then indicating with a red line where it is located on the North African coast. [Plate 6]

Taken together, the *Sfera* and the other works in this codex are morally and intellectually edifying, as we can readily see from Domenico Del Sera's *ricordo*. And just as the text of the *Sfera* is the expression not only of its author's imagination and cultural identity, but also of his mercantile pragmatism, so too does MS. 1030 reveal a similar sensibility among Dati's readers, the Del Sera family. Literary imagination and mercantile pragmatism are seemingly polar opposites, but they are actually complementary terms in the cultural dynamic of late medieval Italy. Dati's talent for crafting a mental map of the world, using contemporary

---

[38] Segatto ("La *Sfera* del Dati," 153) underscores several textual correspondences between the *Sfera* and Brunetto Latini's *Tresor*, in particular with chapters 121–124.

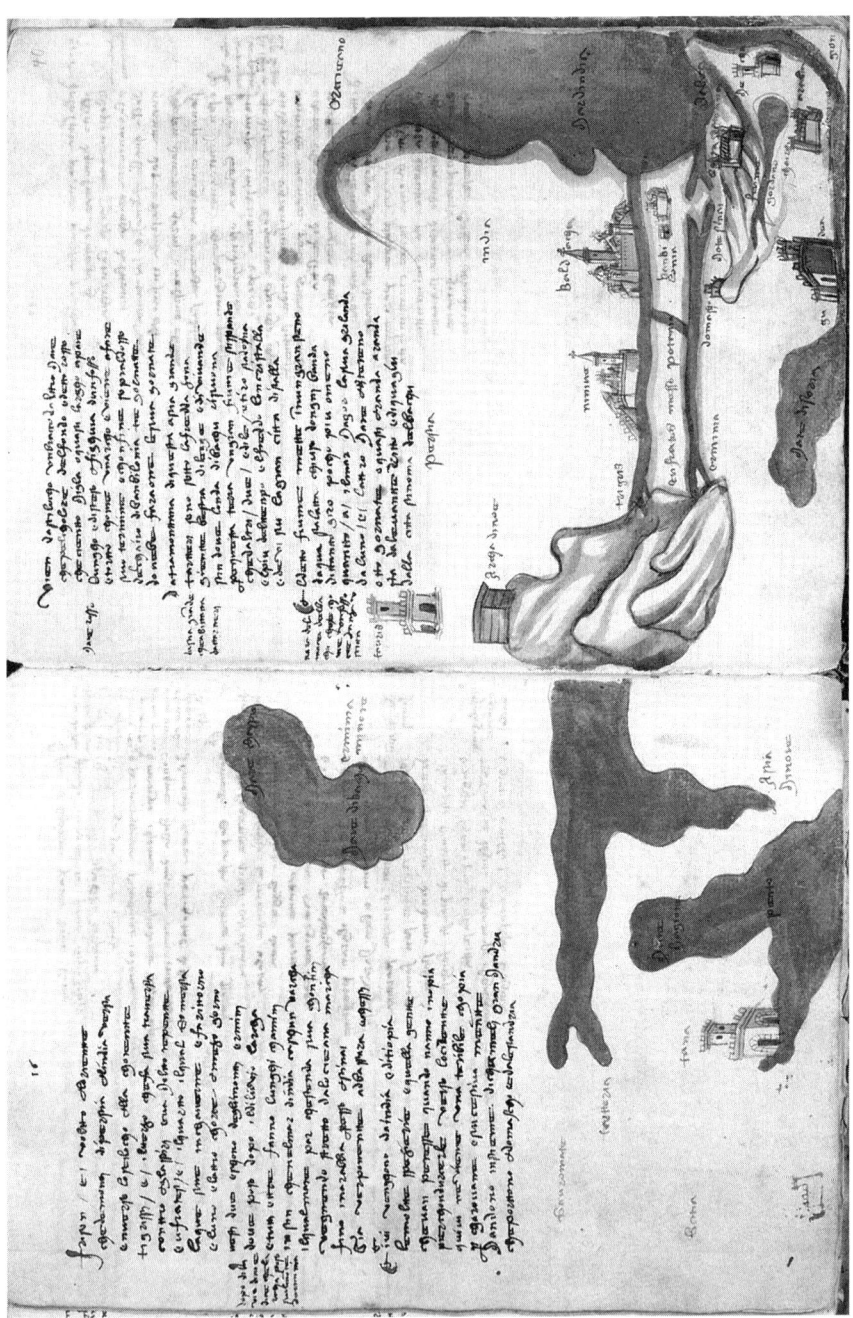

Plate 5: MS 1030 (Beinecke Rare Book and Manuscript Library, Yale University), cc. 39v–40r.

Imagination and Pragmatism in Dati's Sfera

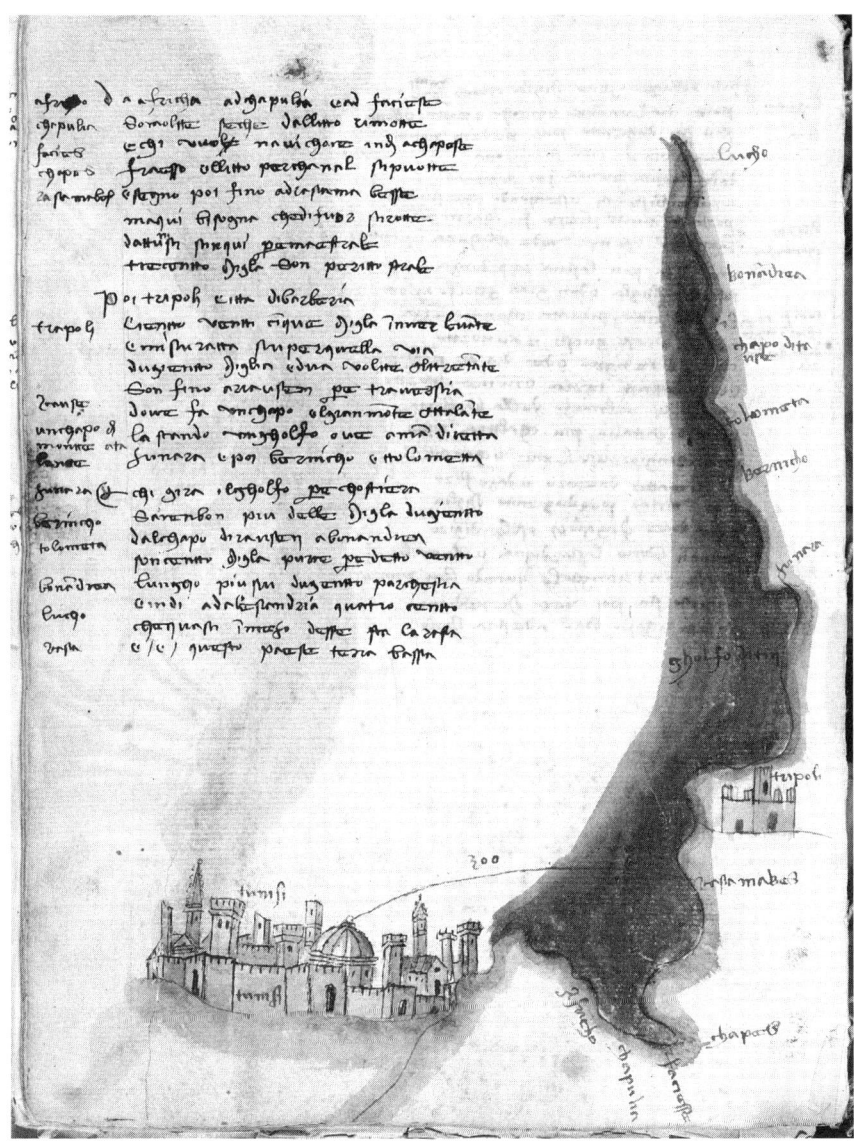

Plate 6: MS 1030 (Beinecke Rare Book and Manuscript Library, Yale University), c. 45v.

science and borrowing extensively from his literary-didactic predecessors, is an example of how literature contributed to developing the merchant's cultural identity. As commerce spread and a burgher class developed in the Italian city-states, the need for an intellectual and professional class arose, and thus Italian literature was born. With good reason the view that literature was a positive cultural effect of economic progress has served as the standard narrative; but it does not explain how literature actually contributed to commerce. Dati's *Sfera* and the manuscripts taken into examination are not merely an instance of literature as the combination of *l'utile* and *il dilettevole*, the useful and the pleasurable (that is, of the importance of literacy and education); rather, the popularity of the *Sfera* among fifteenth-century readers is explained by the fact that literature and art are inherently practical for society, that aesthetics inspires science and commerce, or to say it in the words of Domenico Del Sera, "E chosì vole che chi vedrà detto libro voglia vedere le beleze dell mondo per aqua e diventerà praticho e buono merchatante di tuta le merchatantia,"[39] in which "beauty" and "experience" of the world are inseparable from each other. The fact that readers continued to copy the *Sfera* long after many of its authors' views were superseded by new ideas and discoveries (even with respect to advanced cartography, like Alberti's map,[40] and those from the maritime republics of Genoa and Venice) reveals the work's importance in developing a cultural mindset in the merchant class. This is not to say that Dati's *Sfera* was a direct cause of the spread of mercantilism; but it did promote its ethos effectively. In explaining the book's significance for himself and for his heirs, Domenico Del Sera claims that "si seghua questi mari che sono da fare uomini industri e navichanti e di buona merchatantia e lascierà buona fine di sé."[41] The *Sfera* and the other texts it was often copied with (such as in MS. 1030) were an important resource that had educational value and, as such, they contributed to creating the mercantile *ethos*.

---

[39] "And so he wanted that whoever will read this book will also want to see the beauties of the world by sea and will become an expert and good merchant of all kinds of goods..."

[40] See *Leon Battista Alberti's Delineation of the City of Rome (Descriptio Urbis Romae)*, ed. J.Y. Boriaud, M. Carpo, and F. Furlan, trans. P. Hicks, MRTS 335 (Tempe: ACMRS, 2007).

[41] I re-translate this passage quite loosely, especially the last clause with its rich connotations of "reputation", "wealth" and "self-esteem": "One travels these seas that make men industrious and seaworthy and good merchants, and he will have left much that is good."

Works Cited

Almagià, Roberto. *Monumenta cartographica vaticana*. Vatican City: Biblioteca Apostolica Vaticana, 1944.

Bec, Christian. *Les marchands écrivains: affaires et humanisme à Florence, 1375–1434*. Paris and the Hague: Mouton & Co., 1967.

Bertolini, Lucia. "Censimento dei manoscritti della Sfera del Dati: Manoscritti della biblioteca Laurenziana." *Annali della Scuola normale superiore di Pisa: Classe di Lettere e Filosofia*, 3a serie, 12(2) (1982): 666–705.

———. "L'Attribuzione della "sfera" del Dati nella tradizione manoscritta." In *Studi offerti a Gianfranco Contini dagli allievi pisani*, 33–43. Florence, Casa Editrice Le Lettere, 1984.

———. "Censimento dei manoscritti della Sfera del Dati: Manoscritti della Biblioteca Riccardiana." *Annali della Scuola normale superiore di Pisa: Classe di Lettere e Filosofia*, 3a serie, 15 (3) (1985): 889–940.

———. "Censimento dei manoscritti della Sfera del Dati: I manoscritti della Biblioteca Nazionale Centrale e dell'Archivio di Stato di Firenze." *Annali della Scuola normale superiore di Pisa: Classe di Lettere e Filosofia*, 3a serie, 18(2) (1988): 417–588.

Branca. Vittore. *Mercanti scrittori*. Milan: Rusconi, 1986.

Buonaccorso Pitti and Gregorio Dati. *Two Memoirs of Renaissance Florence: The Diaries of Buonaccorso Pitti and Gregorio Dati*, ed. Gene Brucker, trans. Julia Martines. Prospect Heights, IL: Waveland Press, 1991 (1967).

Clemens, Raymond. "The Newberry *Sfera* and the Study of Renaissance Geography." *Mapline* 94/95 (2002): 1–4 and http://www.newberry.org/smith/Mapline/94-95/94-95feature.html.

Dati, Gregorio. *Istoria di Firenze di Goro Dati dall'anno 1380 all'anno 1405*. ed. Giuseppe Manni. Florence: Stamperia Giuseppe Manni, 1735.

———. *La Sfera, libri quattro in ottava rima, scritti nel secolo XIV da F. Leonardo di Stagio Dati aggiuntivi due altri libri e La Nuova Sfera pure in ottava rima di F. Gio. M. Tolosani da Colle, L'America di Raffaello Gualterotti con altre poesie del medesimo*. Milan: G. Daelli e Comp. Editori, 1865.

———. *Il libro segreto di Gregorio Dati*, ed. Carlo Gargiolli. Bologna: Romagnoli, 1869.

Epurescu-Pascovici, Ionut. "Gregorio Dati (1362–1435) and the Limits of Individual Agency." *Medieval History Journal* 9 (2006): 297–325.

Miller, Naomi. "Mapping the City: Ptolemy's *Geography* in the Renaissance." In *Envisioning the City: Six Studies in Urban Cartography*, ed. David Buisseret, 34–74. Chicago: University of Chicago Press, 1998.

Munsterberg, Margherita. "A Medieval Pilot Book." *Boston Public Library Quarterly* 6 (1954): 114–117.

Nordenskiöld, Adolf Erik. "Dei disegni marginali negli antichi manoscritti della Sfera del Dati." *Bibliofilia* 3 (1901–1902): 49–55.

Segatto, Filiberto. "Un'immagine quattrocentesca del mondo, la *Sfera* del Dati." *Memorie degli Atti dell'Accademia dei Lincei Classe di Scienze morali, storiche e filologiche*, 8th ser., 27 (1983): 147–83.

Shailor, Barbara. *Catalogue of Medieval and Renaissance Manuscripts in the Beinecke Rare Book and Manuscript Library, Yale University*, 2:146–147. Binghamton, NY: Medieval and Renaissance Texts and Studies, 1984.

Viti, Paolo. "Dati, Gregorio (Goro)." In *Dizionario biografico degli italiani*, 33: 35–40. Rome: Istituto dell'Enciclopedia Italiana, 1987.

Section V

Studies on the Italian Renaissance (Fifteenth and Sixteenth Centuries)

The Newberry Library's Italian Prayer Roll: Evidence for Piety and Novelty

Tonia Bernardi Triggiano

Designed and created for a woman who held a special veneration for St. Jerome, Case Manuscript 122 at Chicago's Newberry Library is a product of mid- to late fifteenth-century Tuscany. Delicate illuminations decorate the top and left margins of this elegant roll manuscript and an historiated initial introduces its main text—a laudatory poem to St. Jerome in vernacular Italian.[1] The author of this poem, Battista da Montefeltro-Malatesta (1384–1449), did not own this object nor (to my knowledge) did she ever see it. St. Jerome appealed to early Italian humanists, like Battista, who saw in him the successful coexistence of multiple scholarly and religious traditions. This manuscript piece connects to St. Jerome's world by way of identification, in a nostalgic way, with the era in which the protagonist of its poem worked and lived. It is my belief that MS. 122 was fashioned in a humanistically-inspired frame of mind whereby the resuscitation of the roll form is reminiscent of a bygone era, recalling the *rotuli* of the classical world.[2]

The miniature portrait of St. Jerome housed in the historiated initial "O" is a crucial component of the Newberry roll because while the poem works vigorously to craft a well-rounded verbal portrait of the saint, this representation singularly portrays the penitent saint (he is dressed in a tunic and holds a stone to his breast, see fig. 1). If this rendering upsets the balance intended by the poet, it also serves to connect provenance of the manuscript to fifteenth-century Tuscany. The image of the Penitent St. Jerome is an invention of the Hieronymite groups

---

[1] Raymond Clemens and Timothy Graham, *Introduction to Manuscript Studies* (Ithaca: Cornell University Press, 2007), Chap. 16, "Rolls and Scrolls," 250–58, includes a brief description of Newberry MS. 122. For the source of the Clemens and Graham description, see Tonia Bernardi Triggiano, "Piety Among Women of Central Italy (1300–1600): A Critical Edition and Study of Battista da Montefeltro-Malatesta's Poem in Praise of St. Jerome" (Ph.D. diss., University of Wisconsin-Madison, 1999), 54–56.

[2] The term *roll* most often refers to pieces that are read by holding the piece vertically, while the term *scroll* most often refers to documents that are held horizontally. See Clemens and Graham, "Rolls and Scrolls," 250.

Figure 1. Newberry Library Case MS. 122, upper portion.

that were founded in the early 1400s in and around Florence and were supported financially by Cosimo de' Medici.[3] These male and female associations embraced the notion of penance and looked to St. Jerome as the author of the penitential formula. While the patronage of this manuscript remains unclear, feminine adjectival agreement in the poem testifies to female usage; it is possible that the Newberry roll was present among an association of women who found in St. Jerome a rule of simplicity and an example of ascetic monasticism.

The creator of MS. 122 was easily reminded of the roll form, for it was present in the visual arts in a number of different capacities. Primarily, artists used the scroll form to display the convention of the banderole that related informative text, as in the identification of a figure or to impart a message by inscription. One particularly fitting example is found in the *Penitent St. Jerome* recently attributed, in part, to Fra Angelico.[4] This panel shows a full-length image of the saint in a

---

[3] Eugene F. Rice, Jr., *Saint Jerome in the Renaissance* (Baltimore: Johns Hopkins University Press, 1985), 99–101.

[4] Now at The Art Museum, Princeton University, this panel may have been commissioned by the lay confraternity of Santa Maria della Pietà, also called the Buca di San Girolamo (which, by 1411, moved from Fiesole to Florence's Ospedale di San Mateo, located near San Marco). See Laurence Kanter, "The Penitent St. Jerome in a Landscape," in *Fra Angelico* (New York: The Metropolitan Museum of New York, 2005), 55–57. This catalogue was published in conjunction with the exhibition "Fra Angelico," which was

short grey tunic, cinched at the waist by a rope belt. Set in the usual rocky desert landscape, St. Jerome looks up and holds a stone to his breast in his right hand. In his left hand he holds an unfurled roll with legible writing, upon which is written in Latin in capital letters an abbreviated version of his penitential formula; in essence, the message is a warning to his monks to fast and overcome the luxuries of the body, and to avoid wine and cooked food. In this painting, the roll serves a conventional purpose; although appropriately placed in time, the roll is an object that would have aided the eremitic saint as a tangible reminder of his vow to practices of self-renunciation.[5] This panel is a touchstone to the study of the Newberry roll since the newly-popularized recreation of St. Jerome as a penitent appears here in tandem with the roll as a devotional device.

While the bound volume (characterized by a sewn binding of pages of papyrus, parchment, or vellum) had been in circulation in Europe since the second century, the vehicle of the scroll and roll continued to be used in the Middle Ages in the processing of specific texts, especially those that required a long, easily augmentable writing space.[6] Nevertheless, the reinvention of the scroll as a vehicle of devotional literature in the Renaissance is an especially anachronistic phenomenon considering more fully the time frame in discussion, since mid-fifteenth-century Florence had to wait only two decades before it became a place of modest printed production in 1471.[7] The transition into print further stabilized and industrialized the production of the codex, and yet, on the very eve of the proliferation of the printed document, impulses to create something unique and completely handmade were alive.

---

held at the Metropolitan Museum of Art, New York, 26 October 2005–29 January 2006; Marvin Eisenberg, "'The Penitent St. Jerome' by Giovanni Toscani," *Burlington Magazine* (1976): 275–83. See also Ludovica Sebregondi, *Tre confraternità fiorentine: Santa Maria della Pietà, detta "Buca" di San Girolamo, San Filippo Benizi, San Francesco Poverino* (Florence: Libreria Salimbeni, 1991), 3–23.

[5] A similar rendition of St. Jerome, and one of the earliest representations (circa 1400) of St. Jerome as a penitent, is a fresco at the monastery of Santa Marta in Siena. Against a desert background, he holds a roll in his lifted right hand, the writing upon which is largely illegible due to damage to the fresco. An interesting component of the scene, however, is the figure of a kneeling nun on the left, which may be a portrait of the woman who commissioned the piece. For further discussion of the possible contents of the roll, see Bernhard Ridderbos, *Saint and Symbol: Images of Saint Jerome in Early Italian Art*, (Groningen: Bouma's Boekhuis bv, 1984), 63–72.

[6] Frederick G. Kilgour, *The Evolution of the Book* (New York: Oxford University Press, 1998), 48.

[7] Paolo Trovato, *L'Ordine dei tipografi: lettori, stampatori, correttori tra Quattro e Cinquecento* (Rome: Bulzoni Editore, 1998), 57.

Newberry Library Case Manuscript 122: A Devotional Object

The physical dimensions of a scroll or roll are critical to describing the dynamics of its usage. Newberry MS. 122 measures fully 106 centimeters in length (by 14 centimeters in width).[8] It is made up of two membranes of approximately equal length, which are sewn together. An ivory rod is attached at the top and bottom, the manuscript being inserted through a fissure in the rods, folded over and glued. While the top rod is decorated in relief in a leaf design, the bottom rod is undecorated. A fine metal string is attached to the top rod. The rods themselves taper at the ends where there are attached, at each of the four ends, a screw-on knob.[9]

Both pieces of parchment are in generally good, but fragile, condition. Greater wear at the top visibly obscures the manuscript's illuminations and the first ten lines of its text due to both a large stain on the right and a general darkening of the parchment in the uppermost area. These signs of damage and wear, and the fact that the bottom rod is undecorated, suggest that the manuscript spent a good part of its life with the bottom portion rolled up into the top portion. A significant tear is present at the bottom right side of the manuscript, and there is some damage due to wear and worms that runs vertically along both sides. The text is written on the flesh side, and the number "8000" is written in pencil at the top of the verso.

The illuminations at the top extend horizontally along the top margin 8.3 centimeters and vertically along the left margin 11 centimeters in a traditional Florentine design: acanthus scrolls and figures of a bird at the top and a moth on the left side in blue, yellow, green, and pink with gold accents make up a simple border decoration although the colors are now much faded. A decorated initial "O" painted orange against burnished gold, six lines high (33 millimeters), contains a haloed figure upon a solid dark blue background. The saint is tonsured and bearded and is dressed in a hooded robe that is cinched at the waist and open at the chest. Turned somewhat to his left, he looks upward. He holds a rosary in his lowered left hand, and in the right hand (bent at the elbow to his breast), he holds an unidentifiable object, presumably a stone.[10] Overall, the miniaturist's

---

[8] I would like to thank Franca Petrucci Nardelli, co-director (with Armando Petrucci) of the 1993 Newberry Library Summer Institute in the Italian Archival Sciences, for her supervision in the compilation of this description and in the transcription of its text.

[9] I hesitate to place the rods and string as original to the roll. While it may be that they are a modern addition, it is still my belief that the roll was created with the intention of maintaining some type of horizontal hardware owing to the large empty margins and unfinished edges of parchment at top and bottom.

[10] The rosary is somewhat unusual in that it is not formed as a string of round beads. Rather, it appears to be made of a stiffer material with short spikes marking the prayers.

rendering of the saint is monochromatic and simple: the cloth of the robe is static and the head and elongated neck twist upward unnaturally. The fingers of the right hand are enlarged and do not curl over the object but rather extend fully and flatly.

The text contains fifty-six versal initials alternating in blue and red (marking the tercets of the poem) and one initial "C" in blue with red detail, which marks the beginning of the secondary text, the *Confiteor*. While each of the capitals that marks the beginning of each verse are all stroked in yellow, many capitals are double-stroked with two dots added in the large part of the letter in the same brown ink. A plain flourish in red and blue separates the primary text from the *Confiteor*. Both texts of this manuscript are written in an elegant Italian gothic rotunda script in brown ink in a single column, and it appears that both are of the same hand although the secondary text is somewhat less careful as it omits the use of capitals and permits more abbreviations. Ruling throughout (both horizontally to guide each verse and vertically in double lines on each side of the text to plot the writing space) is done by way of stylus. Writing space measures 98 centimeters by 10 centimeters, framing 173 rhymed verses of vernacular Italian and 11 lines of the *Confiteor*. Patches have worn away in some places due to damage to the parchment and in others due to the use of inferior ink. The incipit of the main text reads "O glorioso padre o almo doctore"; the explicit reads "Ieronimo sancto ora m'aiuta al puncto extremo / Deo gratias Am(en)".

The relatively small size of the roll, the characters of its text measuring less than one half of a centimeter in height, suggests that the manuscript could have been employed by one woman at a time or by a very small group of women, by whom it was unrolled as the verses were said or sung in recitation.[11] The horizontal supports at top and bottom lend strength to the most-handled parts of the roll, and possessing such (even if only later in its life) MS. 122 imitates a herald's document and thus could have served in ambulatory prayer. It was manageable, portable, and easily stored. In comparison to the codex, these are the roll's most attractive qualities especially when considering that these objects were aids in active devotion and not simply vehicles of sacred text. Despite these many useful

---

A type of chaplet, a similar device is found in a painting by the Master of the Sherman Predella, *The Martyrdom of Saint Agnes (?), The Flagellation of Christ, and Saint Jerome in the Wilderness*, Museum of Fine Arts, Boston. Laurence Kanter identifies the object in Jerome's lowered left hand as a rosary and suggests the painting may have belonged to a confraternity specifically devoted to praying the rosary or alternatively to the Compagnia di Sant'Agnese, a Carmelite association in Florence. See Kanter, "Giovanni di Consalvo and the Master of the Sherman Predella," in *Fra Angelico*, 296–97.

[11] Katherine Gill, "Women and the Production of Religious Literature in the Vernacular, 1300–1500," in *Creative Women in Medieval and Early Modern Italy*, ed. E. Ann Matter and John Coakley (Philadelphia: University of Pennsylvania Press, 1994), 64-104, here 67.

attributes, relatively few prayer rolls like the Newberry's remain. Other types of rolls were in circulation, however, and these vary in complexity of elaboration and construction.[12]

Concerning its usage as a devotional object, the Newberry roll fits best among a type of amulet piece that was especially popular among women. These were documents in Latin and/or a vernacular that called upon the intervention of some particular saint. Some were folded and others were rolled, and they were often carried or worn by women for protection and safety in pregnancy and childbirth.[13] Serving a devotional purpose when held in the hand and a protective purpose when worn on the body (either around the abdomen or bound to the leg), these rolls suffered from use and, despite their popularity among lay women, relatively few have survived.[14] While some of these rolls were made simply or carelessly and hence were expendable, others were done by professional hands,

---

[12] Of the professionally made rolls, there are the *Exultet* and *Arma Christi* varieties. See *Exultet: Rotoli liturgici del medioevo meridionale*, ed. Guglielmo Cavallo (Rome: Istituto Poligrafico e Zecca dello Stato, Libreria dello Stato, 1994); T.F. Kelly, *The Exultet in Southern Italy* (New York: Oxford University Press, 1996); R.H. Robbins, "The *Arma Christi* Rolls," *Modern Language Review* 34 (1939): 415–21. Smaller, but sometimes done by a professional hand, are the pilgrimage type of rolls: for a fine example, see Pia Palladino, "Pilgrims and Desert Fathers: Dominican Spirituality and the Holy Land," in *Fra Angelico*, 27–47. Of the unprofessional variety there are account rolls and literary rolls. For an example of an Italian account roll, see *Nuovi testi fiorentini del Dugento con introduzione, trattazione linguistica e glossario*, ed. Arrigo Castellani (Florence: G.C. Sansoni, 1952), 2: 207; for an example of a French literary roll, see *Archéologie du Livre Médiéval* (Paris: Presses du CNRS; Bibliothèque Municipale, 1993), 36. For the genealogy type of roll, see *La Biblioteca Casanatense*, ed. Carlo Pietrangeli (Florence: Nardini editore, 1993), 50–51.

[13] Don C. Skemer, "Textual Amulets for Women," in *Binding Words* (University Park: Pennsylvania State University Press, 2006), 235–84. Some examples include the following: a thirteenth-century French roll: Paris, Bibliothèque Nationale de France, Nouvelles Acquisitions Françaises, no. 4267 (Skemer, "Textual Amulets," 241); a French parchment roll of six membranes, dated 1491: New York, Pierpont Morgan Library, M1092 (245); and an early sixteenth-century English general amulet roll: Oxford, Bodleian Library, roll no. 26 (260). Cf. also G. Peers, "Art and Identity in an Amulet Roll from Fourteenth-Century Trebizond," *Church History and Religious Culture* 89 (2009): 153–78.

[14] Similar in use is an English prayer roll of the fifteenth or early sixteenth century at the Pierpont Morgan Library (M486). Composed of three pieces of vellum, it is quite long, measuring seven feet in length by six inches in width. The text of this piece consists of three prayers in Latin and one in English, plus a poem on the Passion in English. While the prayers are commonly found in other religious books, the poem is unique. With some decorations, M486 shares with the Newberry roll the simultaneous presence of Latin and vernacular religious texts (one common, one uncommon). See Curt F. Bühler, "A Middle English Prayer Roll," *Modern Language Notes* 52 (1937): 555–62.

and the more elegant type, when not in use, was often kept in a sack or case of cloth or leather.[15] Naturally, these were among the more carefully preserved examples and moved with women and families among the contents of their most prized possessions. The prayers maintained on these amulet rolls often invoked the aid of St. Margaret of Antioch, patron saint of pregnant women, while the more general-purpose type invoked a wide variety of saints and martyrs. The quality that these rolls share with MS. 122 is the relationship between object and reader whereby the document becomes an intermediary between disciple and saint.

Battista da Montefeltro-Malatesta: Poet, Diplomat, and Sister of St. Clare

Battista actively composed works of vernacular poetry and Latin prose from the year of her marriage in 1404 to her death in 1449. Writing from outside and inside the cloister, Battista's written production is not extensive, but at the very least she must be credited for paving the way for later Renaissance devotional poets, and in recognition of the diversity of her accomplishments, she indeed warrants a position among the aspiring humanists of her time.

Battista was born in Urbino in 1384 to Antonio da Montefeltro and Agnesina dei Prefetti di Vico, and the political climate at the court of Urbino in the years of Battista's youth was generally one of stability.[16] Antonio was a contemporary of Giovanni Boccaccio and Fazio degli Uberti, and in communication with them, the court of Urbino participated in the early cult of Dante. As a young woman, Battista was educated along with her sister Anna and her brother Guidantonio, and together they studied the works of Dante and were very likely exposed to the works of Petrarch. It is certain that Battista learned the most important pieces of ancient literature, of both the Christian and pre-Christian worlds, and she had a particular interest in the works of St. Jerome. She could read Greek, and wrote in Latin and in the vernacular.

---

[15] The center panel of the Mérode triptych (New York, Metropolitan Museum of Art, Cloisters Collection, Netherlandish, ca 1425–1430, Master of Flémalle, who has been identified as Robert Campin of Tournai) shows an Annunciation scene in which Mary sits near a table with a book in her hands. On the table, under another book, is a partially unrolled scroll, the text of which is written in two columns but is not legible. Both items appear to have been removed from a dark green cloth sack. See Skemer, *Binding Words*, 272–76.

[16] Cesare Cenci, "Il Testamento della b. Cecilia Coppoli da Perugia e di Battista (Girolama) di Montefeltro," *Archivum Franciscanum Historicum* 69 (1976): 219–39; James Dennistoun and Edward Hutton, *Memoirs of the Dukes of Urbino Illustrating the Arms, Arts, and Literature of Italy, 1440–1630* (New York: J. Lane, 1909), 1: 36–41.

Shortly before the death of her father, Battista was married to one of the sons of the Malatesta family of Pesaro. The two families had been rivals for centuries, their strife being appeased only in the years of Battista's young adulthood. Battista found in Pesaro a highly intellectual atmosphere, not wholly unlike her childhood home. Her father-in-law was a strong and capable ruler, and he was known as "il Malatesta dei sonetti" as he avidly wrote and exchanged poetry, and he also retained some of the most learned men of his time. Pietro Turchi was employed by Pandolfo Malatesta, and to him is attributed a significant correspondence with the Florentine chancellor Coluccio Salutati, in the acquisition of books for the library at the Pesaro court. Angelo Galli, one of Petrarch's earliest followers, was also present at Pesaro, as well as the painter Mariotto di Nardo, an associate of Lorenzo Ghiberti.[17]

In 1407, Battista and Galeazzo had a daughter, Elisabetta, and the first years of Battista's life in Pesaro were fruitful and peaceful. By 1410, however, the climate of the Pesaro court began to change as the Malatesta daughters were married off. With Pandolfo's death in 1429 and Galeazzo's decision to live in Tuscany with his natural family, Battista was eventually left in charge of the house. In this phase of Battista's life she is most fluent in prose correspondence in the vernacular; however, she is also credited with an oration in Latin which was addressed to Emperor Sigismund, king of Hungary, when he passed through Urbino in 1433.[18] In returning to Urbino in 1445, Battista began the difficult task of obtaining a dispensation from her marriage, but in 1447 she professed her vows as a sister of St. Clare at the convent of Santa Lucia in Foligno and took the name of Suor Girolama; she was then sixty-three years old. The two years that she lived at Santa Lucia represent the last phase of her literary production, and it is probable that she composed her poem in praise of St. Jerome at that time. Battista died at Santa Lucia on 3 July 1449.[19]

---

[17] Gino Franceschini, "Battista da Montefeltro Malatesta, signora di Pesaro," *Studia Oliveriana* 6 (1958): 7–43.

[18] A. Fattori and B. Feliciangeli, ed., "Lettere inedite di Battista da Montefeltro," *Rendiconti, Reale accademia dei Lincei, classe di scienze morali, storiche e filologiche*, ser. 5, 6 (1917): 196–215. Battista Malatesta, *Oration of Battista da Montefeltro-Malatesta to the Emperor Sigismondo*, translation based on Latin text published by G.B. Mittarelli, *Biblioteca codicum manuscriptorum Monasterii Sancti Michaelis Venetiarum prope Murianum* (Venice: G.B. Mittarelli, 1779), 701–2.

[19] In the convent's diary, the abbess of the Monastery of Santa Lucia recorded this entry describing Battista: "Stecte etiam in questo sacro Monasterio la nobile Madonna Battista, donna del Signiore de Pesaro, chiamata poi sora *Hyeronima*. Questa spectabile madonna, simelmente, era docta in ogni scientia liberale et maxime in strologia, et havea grande cervello in componere et rimare laude, quale gli dictava la mente per el grande fervore et lume de Dio che era in lei, come me hanno referito sore che conversarono con essa": *Ricordanze del monastero di S. Lucia osc. in Foligno (cronache 1424–1786)*, ed. Sr. An-

In the task of identifying Battista Malatesta's place among Italian women writers, one additional document, although not of her hand, warrants attention. In 1420, Leonardo Bruni composed a letter to Battista, most probably upon her request, in which he outlines the most suitable educational program for Battista's daughter.[20] His advice presents a comprehensive approach to education, where both the manner and the style of expression are as important as the acquisition of knowledge itself, the breadth of which should include all of the great names of ancient literature, Christian as well as classical. In this way, Bruni's letter highlights the essential quality of *varietas* in a youth's curriculum. This was a quality already understood by Battista and one that must have figured prominently in her choice of a heavenly patron.

"O glorioso padre, almo doctore": Poem and Prayer

Battista's last will and testament (dated 2 June 1447) lists the contents of her personal collection of books. Among other things, the will describes a volume of St. Jerome's letters, which she passed on to a group of Observant Franciscan men.[21] She specifies in her testament, however, that they may take possession of these letters only *after* her death. Exactly which letters of St. Jerome were included in this volume is not known. Also not known is whether this volume also included a series of three pseudographs written in the fictitious hands of Eusebius of Cremona, St. Augustine, and Cyril of Jerusalem. What is clear, however, is that Battista consulted these letters in the composition of her poem, for certain common episodes, metaphors, images, and vocabulary, as well as literary devices such as the use of direct discourse, are present.[22] Indeed, both Battista and the author of the pseudographs have difficulty in ordering the events of Jerome's life, and

---

gela Emmanuela Scandella and Giovanni Boccali (Assisi: Edizioni Porziuncola, 1987), par. 517.

[20] Leonardo d'Arezzo, *Concerning the Study of Literature, A Letter addressed to the Illustrious Lady, Baptista Malatesta*, in William Harrison Woodward, *Vittorino da Feltre and Other Humanist Educators* (New York: Teachers College Press, Columbia University, 1974), 119–32.

[21] Cenci, "Il Testamento," 222–25.

[22] These three pseudographs appear to be written by the same author. The first is in the fictitious hand of Eusebius of Cremona (who is said to have been Jerome's successor at the Bethlehem monastery) to Damasus (bishop of Portus) and Theodosius (a Roman senator). The second is by a pseudo-Augustine to a pseudo-Cyril of Jerusalem, and the third is pseudo-Cyril's reply to pseudo-Augustine describing the miraculous moment of Jerome's death. These letters began to circulate in Latin at the beginning of the fourteenth century and were soon translated into Italian and incorporated into various types of hagiographical collections and compendia. Since the exact copy of the pseudographs that Battista consulted is not known, I have used the version in Domenico Cavalca

Battista attempts to reestablish the facts but without complete success. In particular, episodes of Jerome's various trips to the Holy Land are confused.

Already in the fourteenth century St. Jerome was the object of a popular cult, and the admiration that grew around his legend was widespread as he appealed to the educated and uneducated alike, to the fervently religious and to the humanist thinker. He was simultaneously scholar and penitent, translator of Hebrew texts and desert father. He was a miracle worker and ascetic, cardinal, cleric, and hermit. "O glorioso padre, almo doctore" reflects this aspect of the saint's popular legend in that it seeks to describe Jerome's many historical and mythical personae, and the resulting portrait reflects the multidimensional quality of his legend. This sort of collective representation of St. Jerome was additionally shaped by the visual arts; while the figure of the Penitent St. Jerome is an invention of the Hieronymite groups of Tuscany born at the beginning of the fifteenth century,[23] already by the middle of the same century the iconographical elements that earlier formed two distinct schools in representation of the Saint—either as scholar or as desert father—begin to appear together. He is less often portrayed indoors, but rather in the wilderness of the desert, near a cave, sometimes before a crucifix. In one hand he holds a stone, usually to his breast, but the objects that once filled his study are not forgotten. Books may be scattered about, or the cardinal's hat might be found on the ground near a scorpion or hanging from a hook in the background.[24]

Close examination of the verbal portrait created by Battista's laudatory prayer discloses a similarly cumulative approach to his representation through an elaborate system of categorization and ordering of his many legendary qualities. Indeed, the careful equilibrium of the poem becomes obvious when Jerome's personae seem to parade, one by one, before the reader (see below, 361-66 for transcription). The result is the creation of a type of patristic *uomo universale*.[25] Jacob Burckhardt coined the terms "many-sided man" and "all-sided man" to describe a phenomenon of the early Italian Renaissance whereby the return to a classically-inspired education combined with new ideals of individual perfection, and St. Jerome was understood by his fourteenth- and fifteenth-century admirers to be endowed with the same objectives. Battista's laudatory poem expresses this notion in two ways: first by means of a figurative "cornucopia" from which flows

---

(ca 1270–1342), *Volgarizzamento delle Vite dei Santi Padri* (Naples: Stamperia del Vaglio, 1871), 3: 3–68.

[23] Millard Meiss, "Scholarship and Penitence in the Early Renaissance: The Image of St. Jerome," *Pantheon* 32 (1974): 134–40.

[24] Many fitting examples of this type of representation of St. Jerome exist: see Ridderbos, *Saint and Symbol*, 79–88.

[25] Jacob Burckhardt, *The Civilization of the Renaissance in Italy* (New York: New American Library, 1960), 125.

a concatenation of titles, and second by an orderly movement of tercets describing Jerome's diverse qualities of saintliness.[26]

Composed in *terza rima*, "O Glorioso padre, almo doctore" presents each tercet as though it were a short stanza; the result is a poem whose syntax is sometimes choppy despite its perfect meter and rhyme. The rhythm changes in the third part of the poem as the balance achieved earlier is purposely abandoned. Throughout the composition, transitions are closely controlled, as movement between tercets often occurs by links based on a simple idea or image. In the first of the poem's three parts, Battista addresses the Saint by way of a *captatio benevolentiae* that spans fifteen verses. Because Battista demonstrates great concern for order in this composition, the first title she gives Jerome characterizes the prominence he held in her devotion in the form of ecclesiastical terms. As Father and Doctor of the Church, Jerome is a teacher, and this is his most common appellation. In the second verse, the first of many images of light appears— a metaphor commonly used to describe the interpretative effect of Jerome's biblical commentaries. The "college" that is recalled here refers to the first hierarchy associated with the institutionalization of the church, as Jerome was ordained a priest in Rome, possibly by Pope Damasus (366–384), and was himself considered for the papacy.[27] The subsequent four tercets each presents a paradigm of Jerome's dual-natured saintliness, and Battista gives equal attention to both his divine and human qualities.

Verse 16 provides the transition to the second part of the poem. By way of the meaning of the verb *contemplare* (v. 15), the reader is prepared to meet the first persona of the saint: Jerome the Scholar. This episode begins in a laudatory tone as Battista comments upon Jerome's accomplishments as a translator who made difficult works more universally understandable. Even though Jerome's revisions were conservative, he was faulted for questioning the authority of, and subsequently for refuting, the popular versions of his time. With verse 28 ("L'anima tua che a Christo avevi oblata")[28] all images of light disappear, and Battista begins to recount St. Jerome's biography. First to be described is Jerome the Ascetic and Desert Father as he repaired to a hermitage outside of Antioch sometime between 374 and 376; he himself reports that in the solitude of his desert cave he spent most of his days in self-mortification.[29] Jerome the Desert Father is then dismissed in verse 42 by way of a summarizing verse ("Vivesti in Bethelem vero

---

[26] For a more detailed discussion of this poem, see Triggiano, "Piety Among Women of Central Italy (1300–1600): A Critical Edition and Study of Battista da Montefeltro-Malatesta's Poem in Praise of St. Jerome," 122–51.

[27] Rice, *Saint Jerome in the Renaissance*, 26.

[28] The verses that are reproduced in this literary analysis will include punctuation and will omit symbols of expansions.

[29] Rice, *Saint Jerome in the Renaissance*, 7.

cenobita"), and the next division of the poem flows into an account of Jerome the Visionary.

By way of war metaphors, Battista characterizes Jerome's visions as victories. Verse 48 ("Del premio eterno qui l'arra obtenesti") describes the earthly guarantee of what he will more fully enjoy after death. Movement to the next division is abrupt (verses 64–70) as she begins to describe Jerome's famous dream trial in which he dreamed that he was accused by the Supreme Judge of being a Ciceronian and not a Christian. He was flogged as punishment for his misplaced attentions and his collection of secular books. When he awoke, his shoulders were bruised and swollen and his face was wet with tears. This was the sign that Jerome needed to take up a more ascetic Christian life, and shortly thereafter he left Rome and went into the Syrian desert. The last verse (verse 70) turns on the adverb *poscia* ("Poscia el tuo tempo tucto a dio donasti"), and the next two tercets demonstrate Battista's sense of balance as she expresses the accessibility of Jerome's scriptural interpretations to all people. The first tercet is devoted to describing all women ("Verginj, coniugate et continente"), while the following two verses are devoted to describing all men ("Clerico, layco, subdito et prelato").

In the passage marked by verses 76 through 86, the pope is hurried upon the scene and Jerome's relationship with the papacy is quickly described: here Battista uses the motif of direct discourse in verses 77 and 78 as Pope Damasus may have related to Jerome concerning Jerome's absence from Rome ("Senza el tuo consiglio / son quasi membro dal corpo tronchato").[30] Battista makes the next transition in verses 85–87 by focusing on the *locus* of Bethlehem as it was the place of the Nativity and of Jerome's first monasteries. Battista looks to the *presepio* and its animals to introduce the story of Jerome and the lion: just as it was fitting for Jesus to be born among the animals in the manger, so was it natural for Jerome to have befriended the lion that came to him there and lay submissively at his feet with a wounded paw.

At this point, and rather abruptly, Battista moves ahead in Jerome's biography to the event of his death. This division (verses 94–120), which extends over nine tercets, represents the longest single episode of the poem and can be subdivided into the moments before, during, and after his death, ending with the appearance of light and angels. The upward movement of his soul is made more glorious by enhancing the notion of death (and thus eternal life) as the saint's final reward. Imbedded in this passage is a verse (v. 104) that includes the reader in the event of Jerome's death and looks toward the last phase of the poem ("Hor mi ricevi però che a te vengno").

The last tercet of this part (verses 121–123) acts as a transition to the final part that centers on the reader ("Multiplicava idio di giorno in giorno / A suplicanti dei suoi benefitij / dei quali io sitibonda a te ritorno"). Gradually, Battista

---

[30] See Cavalca, *Volgarizzamento*, 54 for the passage in which the pseudo-Eusebius imitates this discourse.

changes the subject and perspective of the poem and moves its narration from the past into the present, as the author's clear departure from the telling of Jerome's biography creates a change in focus and tone. Gone are the praises of the saint and the upward movement of laudatory verses. The poem becomes personalized, and a loss of confidence is detected when in this weak moment Battista concentrates upon certain frailties associated with womanhood, calling upon adjectives like *sitibonda* (v. 123) and *asuefacta* (v. 125) and nouns like *serva* and *ancilla* (v. 129). While the poem will conclude on a desperate note, she mirrors her hopes for salvation by reaching out to her patron saint as she humbly requests his intervention to facilitate her entrance into heaven (verses 145–147).

A significant change in style in the last nine tercets of the poem is apparent as Battista narrows the vision of the poem and charges it with passion. The verses begin to tumble upon each other, resulting in a concatenation of desperate cries, and in verses 169–171, she reminds the saint of her pilgrimages to his burial place. The concluding tercet summarizes the message of the poem, restating a plea for protection against Satan, the obstacle that stands in the way of her ascent to Jerome's place of peace. The very last verse ("Ieronimo sancto ora m'aiuta al puncto extremo") reminds the reader of two important facts. First, the author indicates this composition to be her last, as though it were written in her final moments of life. Second, using her last breath to call upon the special help of Jerome indicates the primacy of his devotion in her life. In conclusion, the balance achieved in the most substantial episodes of the poem is upset in the closing section as Battista reveals the doubts and worries that continue to plague her, giving the closing a feeling of catharsis. The poem takes on the dynamics of prayer as the reader departs from the text in the renewed role of protagonist and supplicant.

With this in mind, the presence of the *Confiteor* as an addition to the Newberry copy is an important distinguishing attribute. Because of its confessional nature, the *Confiteor* makes a fitting accompaniment to "O glorioso padre, almo doctore" since in the vocalization of the *Confiteor* audience and officiant become penitents as they first avow sinfulness and then ask forgiveness of God and of each other. Alternatively, the *Confiteor* had a place in the private recital of the Divine Office in which case there would be no requesting of forgiveness outside of God.[31] One need only examine the possessive adjectives incorporated therein to understand for which capacity this version was intended. The Newberry version begins: "Confiteor deo omnipotenti et beate marie semper virgini beato ieronimo et omnibus sanctis. Et *tibi patri* me graviter peccasse per superbiam in lege dei mei cogitatione." This reference to the presence of a male officiant (*et tibi patri*) suggests that this version was most likely intended for oral rather than ocular use and thus in some type of public or semi-private service. It becomes possible, then,

---

[31] J. A. Jungmann, S.J., *Public Worship*, trans. Clifford Howell, S.J. (London: Challoner Publications, 1957), 106.

that these two prayers, appearing together as they do in Newberry Library roll, may have had a place in a service performed by a group of women in some way dedicated to St. Jerome.

"O glorioso padre, almo doctore": Recensio and Examinatio

The notion of shared prayer may be approached by two paths. What may be termed the "proxemic" mode examines the manuscript as a physically accessible object of devotion and further seeks to interpret the tangible relationship between the device and its user. What is most remarkable about MS. 122 is its elegance, for surely it was made to be a *bella copia*, and its good condition further manifests its ownership as a precious item. It comprehensively speaks of refinement, and whether its intended function foresaw active service or a more static aesthetically-driven purpose (as it may have been suspended upon a wall later in its life as a type of *objet d'art*), undoubtedly it was created to be used by a female hand. A supplemental approach to understanding this roll traces the itinerary of the text as it was circulated and copied. What might be termed the "migratory" mode looks to the way the piece made its way into, and took its place in, various collections.[32]

As one of thirteen manuscript witnesses, the Newberry version of the poem "O glorioso padre, almo doctore" occupies a place in a type of family tree or stemma. The tradition of the text and its critical edition reveal that this poem circulated largely in northeastern and central Italy from 1449 to approximately the end of the seventeenth century, and one will find descendants in Chicago, Florence, Pesaro, Rome, Treviso, Vicenza, and Vatican City.[33]

---

[32] This terminology is my own and was first used in a paper titled "Newberry Library's MS 122: Evidence for Women Sharing Prayer" presented at the conference "Devotion Before Print: Art, Literature, Liturgy and Prayer in the Christian Middle Ages," University of Chicago Divinity School, 7–8 April 2006.

[33] Manuscript copies (in codex form) of "O glorioso padre almo doctore" may be found in the following collections: Florence, Biblioteca Nazionale Centrale (3 copies): II, IV, 250: for a description, see Giuseppe Mazzatinti, *Inventari dei manoscritti delle biblioteche d'Italia* (Forlì: Casa Editrice Luigi Bordandini, 1900), 10: 165–86; II, IX, 140 (incomplete); CL. VII, 51: for a description see Mazzatinti, *Inventari dei manoscritti*, 13: 19. Three additional copies in Florence are at the Biblioteca Riccardiana: 1155; 1271; 1406: for descriptions of these, see Salomone Morpurgo, *Indici e cataloghi* (Rome: I Principali Librai, 1893), 15: 185–87. There are two copies in one codex at Pesaro, Biblioteca Oliveriana 454 (Miscellanea), fols. 32–36, 38–42: for a description of this codex see Giuseppe Mazzatinti, *Inventari dei manoscritti delle biblioteche d'Italia* (Florence: Libreria Editrice Leo S. Olschki, 1929), 39: 150. There is one copy at Rome, Biblioteca Nazionale Centrale, Varia 24. There is one copy at Treviso, Biblioteca Comunale, 904. There is one copy at

The re-creation of a text's history by way of its handwritten copies is done by examining variants among all the known versions. While the stemma in itself cannot always specify date and place of origin, the analysis of distinguishing characteristics helps to point to provenance with considerable accuracy. What is most distinct about Newberry 122 is that it is the only one of the thirteen witnesses to appear upon a roll rather than in the more typical codex form, and also that the version contained in the Newberry manuscript is a rather distant relative of any original. There are, to my knowledge, no autograph copies of this poem. The thirteen manuscript copies of "O glorioso padre, almo doctore" demonstrate a generally small range of morphological and lexical variants, the most extreme of which occurs in the Rome witness as the copyist adapted the text to accommodate a male reader.[34] Concerning the Newberry witness, some distinguishing marks include the omission of a complete tercet (probably unintentionally), which reads as follows (as per the base text):[35]

142. Per tuti i divini don di quali imbuto
143. eral tuo mondo chor et p(er) quell opre
144. P(er) la qual di tal gloria fusti i(n)duto

An additional error is found at the end of verse 122 where a letter "d" is added, perhaps as the scribe looked to the first word of the following verse. This extraneous letter is left uncorrected, and it stands outside the period marking the proper end of the verse. Punctuation throughout this version consists solely of a period that marks the end of every verse.

Morphological variants sustained in the Newberry version testify to a language typical of Quattrocento Tuscany primarily in the attribute of being generally free of dialectal influences. A marked attempt at standardization toward a cultivated vernacular, while often maintaining a Latinate orthography, is present (as it is inconsistently present in the base text). A fine example of this trend can be found in rhyming position at verses 5, 7, and 9 whereby the base text demonstrates *sapienza, essentia, scienza* and the Newberry version shows a rectification to the better rhyming *sapientia, essentia, scientia*. A similar phenomenon occurs at verses 41, 43, and 45 where the Latinate orthography is maintained from the base

---

Vicenza, Biblioteca Civica Bertoliana, 205. There is one copy in Vatican City, Ross 424: for a description see P.O. Kristeller, *Iter Italicum, accedunt alia itinera; A Finding List of Uncatalogued or Incompletely Catalogued Humanistic Manuscripts of the Renaissance*, 6 vols. (Leiden: Brill, 1983–1997), 2: 469.

[34] See the following morphological and lexical variants in the Rome witness: at verse 123, "Di quali io *sitibondo* ad te ritorno"; verse 125, "vedi che in essi *assuefatto* sono;" and at verse 129, "a cui per *servo me rendo e si* mi dono".

[35] The copy that serves as the base text is found in Pesaro, Biblioteca Oliveriana, 454, fols. 32–36. A comparison of the orthographical variants in this witness and Battista's personal letters demonstrate this version to be closest to any original.

text in the rhyming *notitia, militia,* and *initia*. A persistent oscillation is present between *cum* and *con* in the Newberry witness while *et* is always favored over *e*. Also consistent is the copyist's use of the more antiquated form of the article *el* in position before a consonant.[36] Often, but inconsistent, is the <ngn> orthography of the palatal nasal as demonstrated in the rhymes at verses 83, 85, 87: *regni, degni, spengni*. A consistent correction occurs in the form of the second- and third-person feminine possessive adjectives in the singular forms of *tua, sua,* and the plural forms of *tue* and *sue* (whereas the base text presents *toa, soa, toe,* and *soe*).[37]

Lexical variants in which the Newberry version represents an independent departure from all other copies (peculiar errors) are found at the following places: verse 105 in which the Newberry witness reads, "El quale morendo le giuste *vie* ai spente" (versus *ire*); at verse 122 in which the Newberry version reads, "A suplicanti dei suoi benefitij" (versus *invocanti*); at verse 141 in which the Newberry version reads, "Che i prophetici *detti in originali* ci spose" (versus *enigmati*); at verse 155 in which the Newberry version reads, "*Dischaccia* si dense tenebre chi veggha" (versus *Fuga*); at verse 166 in which the Newberry version reads, "Solo nella croce abbi gloria ove conficto" (versus *nel vexil me*); at verse 170 in which the Newberry version reads, "Sopra *el sepolcro* ove el tuo corpo giace" (versus *lavello*); and at verse 171 in which the Newberry version reads, "*Humiliati* in terra taggio collanimo offerti" (versus *Prostrati*).

The most significant of these lexical variants is that found at verse 166. The replacement of the vernacular *croce* for the Latin *vexillo* may have served to clarify the copyist's reference to the Crucifixion, but it also modifies the message of the passage. A leitmotif of Battista's writings, the word *vexillo* is used in other poems to recall a more precise significance beyond a simple flag, but rather the red flag that is hoisted above a commander's tent as a signal for battle (a meaning found in Venantius Fortunatus's sixth-century hymn to the Cross, *Vexilla regis prodeunt*, sung in Holy Week). The result of this substitution is twofold: not only does it lessen the graphic depiction of the image of Christ Crucified as the red color of the *vexillo* recalls the blood of Christ's wounds, but the innovation also removes the active gesture of the calling to arms. While the variant *croce* modernizes the Newberry version, it also contributes to the appropriation of the text to the owner of the roll.

The Newberry Library's Italian prayer roll represents a movement from the time and place in which its poem was conceived. What was a product of Battista's lifelong dedication to St. Jerome could have easily been favored by other

---

[36] Arrigo Castellani demonstrates the favoring of *el* to *il* to be present in some parts of Tuscany (mostly in the western parts of the region but also in Lucca and Pisa): *Nuovi testi fiorentini del Dugento* (Florence: G.C. Sansoni, 1952), 1: 44.

[37] These dialectal forms are particular to some of the Northern regions, specifically the Veneto and the Marche. See Pavao Tekavčić, *Grammatica storica dell'italiano* (Bologna: Società editrice il Mulino, 1972), par. 39–40.

Quattrocento women, and to this purpose certainly roll and scroll functioned in their itineraries of devotion and study.[38] While the investigation of ownership lies beyond the scope of the present study, let it be sufficient to maintain that had Battista seen the Newberry Library's MS. 122, she would have been pleased: the miniature rendering of the saint as penitent, the *Confiteor* coda, and, most notably, its roll form are distinctive and appropriate compliments to her poem in praise of her heavenly patron, St. Jerome.

The following symbols will be used in the transcription of the version of "O glorioso padre, almo doctore" sustained on Newberry Library MS. 122.

( ) =   expansion of abbreviation
\ / =   added above or below line
-- -- =   erasure or cancellation, what is contained within reflects correction by copyist
[ ] =   contents illegible, added by way of conjecture

1. O glorioso padre o almo doctore.
2. O sole fulgente electo a quel collegio.
3. Che circundava el supremo pastore.
4. Spirito dotato di tal privilegio.
5. Che i mortali excedevi i(n) sapientia.
6. Vergine sacro et co(n)fessore egregio.
7. Tu contemplavi la divina essentia.
8. Vivendo in carne et lalma in dio rapita.
9. Delle cose future prendevi scientia.
10. Norma di sanctita fu la tua vita.
11. Di pudicitia mirabile exemplo.
12. Tucta di gratia et virtu redemita.
13. Di spirito sancto inmaculato templo.
14. Et per la fe prepugnatore invicto.

---

[38] In another example, the scroll symbolically identifies with the contemporary world as in Pesellino's *Annunciation* (now at the Fine Arts Museum in San Francisco). In an alcove between the figures of Gabriel and Mary stands a cabinet upon which are a codex and a scroll. The book shows its binding on the right which suggests that its text is written in Hebrew; the scroll is opened somewhat and lies horizontally. That Pesellino paired the scroll with the book reinterprets the figure of Mary as a woman of study who sought out both ancient and modern texts, but the binary presence of these literary vehicles may also imply the incarnation as this is the moment in which the prophecy of the coming of Christ is fulfilled. To the Renaissance viewer, the roll takes on the symbolic value of the text appropriate to Mary's time. See Kanter, "Francesco di Stefano, called Pesellino," 269–90.

15. Contra a ongni heresiarcha ti contemplo.
16. Chi ben ruminare vuole cio chai scripto.
17. Collelegante stile ben ti discerne.
18. Riprendere con fervore ciascun delicto.
19. Per questo el ceto clericale te sperne.
20. Con fa\l/sa infamia offuscando el tuo zelo.
21. Ma tua vita exemplare suo dire prosterne.
22. Col sacro studio rimovesti el velo.
23. [Dal] ydioma h[ebrayc]o [dal vo]lume.
24. Che con ambo le mani ci [spe]gne al cielo.
25. Lucerna accesa [di supe]rno lume.
26. In sublime c[andela]bro locata.
27. Che nella chi[esa] splende s[e]nza fume.
28. Lanima tua [cha (Christ)o avevi] oblata.
29. El tuo giogo [suave] et [peso] leve.
30. Lieta porta[va in carita fonda]ta.
31. Con grande austerita sempre] teneve.
32. Alla ragione [e sensi subiu]gati.
33. Ne mai riposo quasi al corpo deve.
34. Cibi squisiti et [mangia]ri dilicati.
35. Tutti aborrendo pane et acqua pura.
36. Dava rist[oro a m]embri attenuati.
37. La sacra pelle avevi arrida et scura.
38. Che sol di[sacch]o i(n) [eremo] vestita.
39. Ora pativa gran freddo ora gram calura.
40. Li visitasti alcuno anacorita.
41. Poi di [loro dando a post]eri notitia.
42. Vivesti [in bethele]m vero cenobita.
43. Assidua [fu la tua] spiritual militia.
44. Ne mai in otio [al]cuno ti disolvesti.
45. Pero che in quello ciascuno male se initia.
46. E perche i(n) ongni prelio sempre rimanesti.
47. [Delli] adversarij tuoi vitorioso.
48. Del premio eterno qui larra obtenesti .
49. Oltre piu volte el tuo sire gratioso.
50. Solevava el tuo spirito a tanta gratia.
51. Che lo vedevi tra li angeli glorioso.
52. Dalla qual visione lanima satia.
53. Molti di stava senza cibo alcuno.
54. O gloria excelsa de tucta la dalmatia.
55. Tu stavi absorto i(n) dio che trino et uno.
56. Dilectandoti i(n) lui con tal dolceza.
57. Che sprimere nol poria calamo alcuno.

58. E ben giusto mi pare che chi dispreza.
59. Tucte le volupta solo idio amando.
60. Tale ora festeggi i(n) mirare sua belleza.
61. Uno i(m)perfecto piacere avesti usando.
62. Di leggere Tulio et Plato tu\o/i divoti.
63. Laudabile exercitio i(n)terpolando.
64. Ma poi per observare ei s(an)c(t)i voti.
65. Facti dinanzi al giudice eternale.
66. Da quello studio e sensi fuoro(n) rimoti.
67. Che lo spirito fu racto al divino tribunale.
68. Dove dio ti fe fragellare sicche giurasti.
69. Mai piu no(n) leggere alcuno libro tale.
70. Poscia el tuo tempo tucto a dio donasti.
71. Verginj coniugate et continente.
72. Con splendida doctrina illuminasti.
73. Di tua mira eloquentia et excellente.
74. Clerico, layco, subdito et prelato.
75. Prendeva cibo a se conveniente.
76. Al successore di Pietro tanteri grato.
77. Che ti scriveva senza el tuo consiglio.
78. Son quasi membro dal corpo tronchato.
79. Et di cio patre no(n) mi maraveglio.
80. Perche dal bon sentier no(n) deviava.
81. Essendo imitator di si car figlio.
82. La cui perfectione si divulgava.
83. Nel secol tuo et yh(es)u col quale regni.
84. La gloriosa fama tua aumentava.
85. O felici que monaci che degni.
86. Fur di star tech[o] al presepio ove nacque.
87. Coluj che con suo morte i(n) noi la spengni.
88. Come tra bruti li nascer li piacque.
89. Cosi un fero animale ti fe subiecto.
90. Che ivi a tuo piedi mansueto giacque.
91. Bensi de vergognare che a(n)tellecto.
92. Non ubbedir [a te] poi chun leone.
93. Indomito adempieva el tuo precepto.
94. Hor quando della terrestre pregione.
95. Dilibero tirarti lalto idio.
96. Et quietarti in sua fluitione.
97. Essendo in mezo del consortio pio.
98. De tuo figliu\o/li et redemtore ti chiama.
99. Dicendo veni ad me dilecto mio.
100. Possiedi el bene che ongni apetito sfama.

101. Poiche combatuto ai si virilmente.
102. Prendil triumpho che tua voglia brama.
103. Et tu a lui o buon yh(es)u clemente.
104. Hor mi ricevi pero che a te vengno.
105. El qual morendo le giuste vie ai spente.
106. Poi duca mio nel qual fiducia tengno.
107. Una mirabile luce ti coperse.
108. Che i(n) te discese dal superno regno.
109. Onde el tuo corpo no(n) potea vederse.
110. Dai discepoli tuoi le cui popille.
111. Dai pianti et lucti loro fuoro asperse.
112. Scorrere ben si vedieno come scintilla.
113. Celeste i(n)telligentie or quindi or quivj.
114. Cherano di tal mistiero liete et tranquille.
115. Alhora quel divino splendore stette ivi.
116. Poi disparendo seco asumpse lalma.
117. Per colloca\r/la ove i(n) perpetuo vivj.
118. Bene ve rimase tua corporea salma.
119. Che odore suave [porgeva dintorno].
120. Teste di tua virtu inclita et alma.
121. Multiplicava idio di giorno i(n) giorno.
122. A suplicanti dei suoi benefitij.d.
123. Dei quali io sitibonda a te ritorno.
124. Dislegami caro padre dai miei vitij.
125. Vedi che i(n)essi tanto asuefacta sono.
126. Che dubio ho di gire aglinfernali hospitij.
127. In te ho posto ogni mia speranza et pono.
128. Che sia mio protectore et sia mio duce.
129. A cui per serva et ancilla sempre mi dono.
130. Lalta tua disciplina che reluce.
131. Nella oscura mia mente pur talora.
132. Adalcuno buono desiderio me conduce.
133. Ma la pena mia e l dolore che macora.
134. E che tal seme no(n) produce fructo.
135. Anzi sie tolto et in me no(n) dimora.
136. O interpetre sacro o divinal co(n)docto.
137. In cui scientia doni lingua i(n)fuse.
138. Colui dal quale se plasmato et prodocto.
139. Per la singulare gratia che i(n) te pose.
140. Quello ingegno perspicace et acuto.
141. Che i prophetici detti i(n) originali ci spose.
142. omission
143. omission

144. omission
145. Te suplico humilemente che tu adopere.
146. Tanto eficacemente con tuoi prieghi.
147. Chio fermi lamor mio nel bene di sopre.
148. Dolce mio difensore el quale non neghi.
149. Mai e tuoi sufragij a chi co(n) fe tinvoca.
150. Ma col suo creatore lunisci et leghi.
151. Quantunche la mia fe sia i(n)ferma et poca.
152. Pure io i(n)te spero et i(n) te mi confido.
153. Che exaudire vogli omai mia voce roca.
154. Abbi pieta di me maestro mio fido.
155. Dischaccia si dense tenebre chi veggha.
156. La semita che mi co(n)duci al somo sido.
157. Lalme tue prece la mia vita reggha.
158. [Guardandomi dal usi]tate colpe.
159. Accioche indarno i tuoi libri no(n) leggha.
160. [Gloperati] dilelecti scrivi et colpe.
161. Nellaflicto mio cuore la cui memoria.
162. Struggiere tucto mi faccia nervi et polpe.
163. Avendo tanto offeso el re di gloria.
164. Almeno i(m)petra per me de humilita lamicto.
165. Che mai no(n) cerchi laude transitoria.
166. Solo nella croce abbi gloria ove conficto.
167. Fu el benigno gesu e nei tuoi meriti.
168. Che mi difenderano nel grande conflicto.
169. Tu fai refugio mio che li membri i(n)erti.
170. Sopra el sepolcro ove el tuo corpo giace.
171. Humiliati i(n) terra taggio collanimo offerti.
172. Guardami adunque mio padre dal saghace.
173. Nostro adversario il quale forte temo.
174. E perche io salire possa alla tua pace.
175. Ieronimo sancto ora maiuita al puncto extremo
176. Deo gratias. Am(en).

1. Confiteor deo omnipotenti et beate marie
2. semper virgini beato ieronimo et omni-
3. bus sanctis. et tibi patri me graviter peccas-
4. se per superbiam i(n) lege dei mei cogitatione.
5. delectatione. obmissione. consensu. visu. ver-
6. bo. et opere. mea culpa. mea grave culpa. mea
7. massima culpa. ideo deprecor beatam & glori-
8. osam virginem mariam. beatum ieronimu(m)
9. omnes sanctos & sanctas dei & te patrem ora-

10. re pro me ad [dominum] yh(esu)m (christu)m patrem omnipo-
11. tentem. peccavi d(omi)ne miserere mei.

Kairos: The Renaissance Reconstruction of the Best of All Possible Times

Giancarlo Maiorino

In W. H. Auden's poem *Kairos and Logos*, time is anchored to the transience of opportunity, whereas the rhetoric of time peaked

> Where conscience worshipped an aesthetic order
> And what was unsuccessful was condemned
> (Kairos and Logos)

While empirical time belongs to Chronos, favorable moments are dispensed by Kairos. He is the Greek god of propitious beginnings, which Auden's "rhetoric of time" links to "the worship of an aesthetic order." The construction of beauty is carried out through the opportunistic vocabulary of possibility and "occasion." The kairotic moment involves a world view pointed toward a perfective, or perfected, sense of plenitude, which Auden links to "punctuality" as the discharge of an action "at an exact moment."[1]

By so doing, Auden highlights essential features of the Renaissance understanding of time, which has been predominantly goal-oriented. In this paper I will center on the concept of the favorable beginning in that earlier phase of the Renaissance known as Humanism. Because of their-newly acquired interest in classical ruins, the humanists understood that the cultural demise of the ancients could become their own, that the propitious could easily turn into the foredoomed. To avoid the fate of simple chronology, the endpoint of which is death, it was a matter of utmost urgency for the humanists that Chronos himself be dismembered, so that Kairos could assert a value-laden concept of time. As a counterweight to the time of loss and nostalgia, Kairos instigated moments which were ground-breaking and future-bound. The very concept of re-naissance/*rinascita* described a rebirth of merit to a propitious beginning.

---

[1] In *W. H. Auden, Collected Poems*, edited by Edward Mendelson (New York: Vintage Books, 1991), 305.

Ancient marble reliefs present Kairos as a slim adolescent with winged feet. The back of his head is bald, so he cannot be seized from behind. His forward motion carries out symbolic commitments to grasp opportune moments, which the poet Pindar identified with the assertion of independent will (*Pythian* 4, 10). Amid the seafaring culture of the Greeks, the term *kairos* sailed westward, where its meaning found literary and visual equivalents, from the Latin *occasio* and *opportunitas* to the humanist *occasione*. Inevitably, transfers and translations accommodated layers of new meanings. After meandering detours out of antiquity and through the deep waters of medieval Christianity, the 'ghosts' of Latin and Greek words for time hovered over the Renaissance.

On Christian grounds, *kairos* has been linked to the tradition of *consecratio*, which pointed to the divinization of the emperor in late antiquity, and to that of *adventus*, which prefigured Christ's own appearance at the center of history. On more secular and collective grounds, the emergence of Imperial Rome as the unifying force of the pagan world, and of Florence at the leadership of the mercantile and artistic Renaissance, foregrounded exemplary instances of kairotic beginnings. Whatever the circumstances, *kairos* celebrates memorable deeds, and *Kaironomia* consists of an encomium of the will-to-invent.

The favorable beginning had to be memorable, and a short list of kairotic texts would have to start with Petrarch's *Triumph of Eternity* (from *I Trionfi*), which outlines a synopsis of verbs and nouns that foreground the Renaissance ideal of human time:

> Quel che l'anima nostra preme e 'ngombra:
> 'dianzi,' 'adesso,' 'ier,' 'diman,' 'mattino' e 'sera,'
> tutti in un punto passeran com'ombra:
>   non avra loco 'fu,' 'sara' ne 'era,'
> ma 'e' solo, in presente, ed 'ora' ed 'oggi'
> e sola eternita raccolta e 'ntera:
>
> All that encumbers us and weighs us down,
> 'Yesterday' and 'tomorrow,' 'morn' and 'eve,'
> 'Before' and 'soon,' will pass like fleeting shadows.
>   'Has been,' 'shall be,' and 'was' exist no more,
> But 'is' and 'now,' 'the present' and 'today,'
> 'Eternity' alone, one and complete.

Thus the Renaissance began in the encomiastic mode of perfected completeness, in which the end exists within the beginning. The favorable beginning linked up to maturity, which, pointing as it did to timeless ideals of perfection immune to decay, was to last forever, at least within the closely-knit boundaries of "an aesthetic order." From poetry to the arts, the architect Filarete was directly familiar with the etymology of *kairos*. In his treatise on architecture, he gave the port of Plusiapolis the name of *"Limen galenokairen,"* which consists of a compound of harbor, calm, and the right, the propitious, place. In the planning of his ideal city, Filarete also sketched a nude figure, the mythic Kairos, "with a wheel under his foot. He had wings on his feet, hands, and shoulders." As the Renaissance gained strength, the semantic meaning of *kairos* served ambitious projects of rebirth. Such a cultural framework inspired the pictorial triumph of Guido da Montefeltro by Piero della Francesca and of Julius Caesar by Mantegna, while Giannozzo Manetti and Pico della Mirandola wrote praises of human dignity that left no room for improvement. Indeed, the re-born or 'new-born' Adam had regained his pre-lapsarian perfection.

As such, perfection identifies a state of being in which beginning and end either disappear or are the same. To borrow from Leon Battista Alberti's conclusive remarks in his treatise *On Painting*, the Renaissance *kairos* had to be "newborn and perfect." Under these conditions, improvement is denied and change can only be for the worse. Such a transformation of the concept of kairotic time dates back to the shift from paganism to Christianity, which linked the birth of Christ to the resurrection of humankind. For Paul Tillich, *kairos* is the "fulfilled moment, the moment of time approaching us as fate and decision." Toward the end of the fifteenth century, Marsilio Ficino, the scholar and leader of the Neoplatonic Academy, made it clear that "the only person never to be affected by misfortune is the one who does not await an end after and beyond the beginning but establishes his own end in the beginning." The humanists did not wait around for luck to strike. As Alberti wrote: "We shall always believe that in political affairs and in human life generally reason is more powerful than fortune, planning more important than any chance event." 'Rule' and 'planning' set up procedures meant to make success endure. Opportunity became systematic and human conduct was steered away from the whim of fortune.

2

At the very beginning of the fifteenth century, the humanist Leonardo Bruni wrote *Laudatio Florentinae Urbis* (*Panegyric to the City of Florence*, 1401–1403). Favoring as he did an idealized view of history, Bruni praised landmarks of Florentine culture by enforcing a poetics of empowerment meant to prevail over the heritage of Antiquity and the Middle Ages. The past had to be dismantled before kairotic choices could reconstruct it outside the womb of chronology. In Florence, mercantile prosperity offered unprecedented opportunities in all fields of human endeavor. Bruni's panegyric illustrates a golden stage in the culture of Florence by making sustained references to the city's architecture, the artistic medium which has always made favorable beginnings resist time. The kairotic moment is one of construction, and the architect is he who begins something. In fact, humankind has constructed hours, days, months, years, centuries, and millennia as methodically as architecture, for time and buildings regulate and shelter our life. While innately temporal, kairotic beginnings occur in physical spaces which tend to be just as propitious.

At the outset of Bruni's panegyric, Florence is recognized as the most splendid city on earth. Set midway between plains and mountains, the city "stands in the center. . .Just as on a round buckler, where one ring is laid around the other, the innermost ring loses itself in the central knob." The geometric components (buckler, circle, knob) of the Brunian landscape amount to a demonstration of achieved perfection. At the center of a sunlit hub, Florence was invested with the mission of extending *studia humanitatis*, vernacular literature, and the arts to the rest of humankind. Such a geometric landscape provides a visual image of time. It is the frozen time of an ideal enclave free from the vicissitudes of natural processes and akin to the clear and dust-settled effects of the pictorial system of linear perspective. In that sense, Bruni described the best of all 'cultural topographies,' one that could accommodate the stability of both utopia and perfection.

The comparisons which Bruni made between Florence and other Italian cities remind us that, whether ancient or Renaissance, the kairotic moment is agonistic and is measured against previous achievements. This attitude ran against the medieval belief that the moderns are dwarfs standing on the shoulders of ancient giants. The humanists were convinced that kairotic beginnings could reverse the terms of that comparison, and Bruni's encomiastic language takes the superlative as the required mode of public expression. To give visual form to the superlative, Alberti's praise of the cupola of Santa Maria del Fiore by Filippo Brunelleschi acknowledged an economic and cultural superiority that cast its long shadow over Tuscan landscapes and European markets. A century later, Michelangelo the Florentine emulated Brunelleschi when he designed the dome of Saint Peter's in Rome. Voicing an anti-classical attitude typical of Modernism at its most radical, Frank Lloyd Wright, who never bought the idea that he was a dwarf perched on anybody else's shoulders, declared that Michelangelo outdid architectural precedents. In fact, he "built the first skyscraper, when he hurled the Pantheon on top of the Parthenon. The Pope named it St. Peter's and the world called it a day."

Although quite invisible, time happens in space. The favorable moment as well as the favorable location led Bruni to call the whole region around Florence "a paradise." While drawing together utopia and heaven, this transcendent imagery generates a sense of fulfilled prophecy. Historical time was fixed into a state of bliss, which reverted back to Bruni's opening image of a heavenly locus by the banks of the Arno. Bruni thus identified "two ways of describing a city: the more polished one worked out by philosophers which exists only on paper and in the mind; and the one corresponding to what we see in practice and reality." In 1401, Bruni wrote that the seeds of the noble arts in Florence were bound to yield great artworks. Favorable beginnings were stretched out to include maturity. Like the seed, the beginning contained the end.

At least in literary treatises and on frescoed ceilings, the humanist Adam was "newborn and perfect," just like Athena from the head of Zeus. Panegyrical images blended the most opportune of times with the best of spaces.

In Florence, *kairos* sketched a perfected history of the future, which, like "paradise," could be neither improved nor diminished. Bruni lived long enough to see that his praise of Florence was fulfilled. Happy endings, however, could not be taken for granted. It often was the case that propitious beginnings failed, and many theoretical plans never saw the light of day. The architect Bernardo Rossellino was charged with planning a new humanist city north of Siena. The favorable moment was offered by the election as pope of Aeneas Sylvius Piccolomini, who took the name of Pius II. He was born in the little town of Corsignano, which he transformed into the city of Pienza. The topography of ancestry made room for that of learning, and the modern Aeneas drew the boundaries of a new place of propitious beginnings. But Pienza never grew beyond the pope's best intentions. The architectural nucleus (church-square-palace) remained an isolated instance. As a symbol, however, Pienza has stood as a gravitational center on any map of Renaissance culture. But its failure to reach fulfillment pointed to a gap which existed between the perfection of the aesthetic order and the instability of socio-political events.

3

Keyed as it was to staging social harmony and civic success, Bruni's panegyric shows a peculiar lack of strife. Yet much was achieved through individual and factional conflicts. In the language of architecture, it suffices to mention the enormous number of towers (*torri*) that affluent families constructed as symbols of their competitive materalism. Even public buildings such as the Palazzo Vecchio in Florence and the Palazzo Ducale in Urbino were fortresses. Alberti opens the fifth book of his architectural treatise by considering "appropriate methods of defense against one's fellow citizens." Before Dante and after Machiavelli, the history of the city was one of unrelenting struggle. Before Bruni, Dino Compagni wrote that "on all sides there are many noblemen, counts and captains, who love the city more in times of discord than in peacetime, and obey it more from fear than love." Inside the city, many citizens were moved by "ill will and competition for office." Language and subject matter foreshadowed the darker *chiaroscuro* of Machiavelli's analysis of human nature at its selfish worst. While Lorenzo Valla criticized Bruni's *Laudatio* because of its exaggeration in light of the factual evidence, Machiavelli believed that Bruni's *History of Florence* brushed aside matters of internal strife too quickly. All this suggests that there was a darker side to kairotic opportunities. Although the rhetoric of praise won the day, concerned voices uttered a parallel, though less overt, rhetoric of blame.

And there lies the human and social problem of fifteenth-century Humanism. What did common people know about the prizes and honors of fame? How could they even begin to think about secular immortality when their socio-economic lot often was deficient even at the level of ordinary existence? Bruni's description of Florence shows no periphery, no poor quarters, and no popular culture. Conspicuously absent from literary and pictorial representations of cities was the world of work. One could ask of Bruni: where are Boccaccio's scoundrels, businessmen, and rogues? Where is the marketplace? This probing into the socio-political effects of the kairotic will-to-invent amid what Lynn White calls "subhistory," Unamuno *"infrahistoria,"* and Michel de Certeau the everyday life of popular culture in *The Practice of Everyday Life* draws a line between positive and negative approaches to favorable opportunities. There is *kairos*, but there is an anti-*kairos* as well. To meditate on these questions is to probe into the implicit shortcomings of the culture of Humanism, and to break open its tightly-knit fringes. To meditate on these questions is also to move beyond kairotic moments and to confront the quotidian life of humankind. We know about humanist correlations between *kairos* and the literary forms of panegyric, epistle, and the treatise. Do praises of folly and quixotic madness fall within the province of Kairos? Is there a favorable beginning for picaresque indigence and Cervantine waywardness?

It has been said that we should be embarrassed by the length of time that the Western tradition managed to get along without the novel. Perhaps we should be just as concerned about the elitist nature of Kairos. In our age, *Kairos* would find himself ill at ease amid low and middle-class enclaves inhabited by men without qualities who are committed to the practice of everyday life. The gendered label of Musil's 'men without qualities' also raises the gendered character of *kairos*. To that extent, a critical assessment of the social no less than the artistic role which *kairos* has played in shaping cultural priorities can gauge the transformation of human consciousness from antiquity to modernity, a transformation which cannot but underline the exclusionary nature of kairotic privileges. Because Kairos is a deity of thresholds rather than of dead ends, one still ought to hope that renaissance may retain its operative linkage to some sense of propitious future.

Because its etymology also points to a passage or opening, *kairos* was related to the Latin *opportunitas*, in the sense of that which offers an opening, an opportunity. Moreover, *opportunitas* was part of the symbolism of Janus Bifrons, the god of beginning whose temple had gates opened toward past and future. Though in a roundabout way, Greek *kairos* and Latin *occasio* somehow re-emerged in the vernacular *occasione*. Semantics underwent an array of adjustments, and philology strained its resourcefulness to find vernacular terms for expressing kairotic concepts. On matters of symbolic figures, Alberti describes a small chapel dedicated to Fame, which is guarded by four priests: Wealth, Power, Action, and Opportunity. Their task is not to let anyone in by chance. While Wealth and Power keep the doors open, Opportunity marks the best moment for entering the shrine. Adaptations of ancient images became typical of 'classical' revivals. At the end of the fifteenth century, Andrea Mantegna painted *Occasio et Penitentia*, two female figures who embody activism and restraint. *Occasio* is portrayed as a figure 'on the run' who is about to jump off the globe. Hair covers only her face, and she has wings behind her left foot. *Occasio* thus takes on a new name and a new form for expressing an older symbol; while borrowing features from Hermes, the painter made *Occasio* female. If the word faltered in the drawn-out process of historical 'conversion,' the semiotic sign did not. In a substantive way, *occasione* was *kairos*' inheritor.

In *The Prince*, Machiavelli described *Occasio* as a figure ever ready to take flight: "My name is *Occasione*, and I to few reveal Myself." Personification pivots on the dynamics of the verb *travagliare* (to struggle), which describes a painful activity, and of *occasione*, which defines the acting out of a decisive moment. Machiavelli understood that assertive choices called for a vocabulary of charismatic word-concepts. By loosening the bonds of Fate and Fortune, *occasione* described the favorable opportunity that made it possible for human virtue (*virtù*) to act successfully. By capturing the struggle between repetition and deviation, *occasione* reveals the kairotic side of human ingenuity as well as the exceptional nature of individual talent.

Machiavelli's kairotic talent is also operative at the very beginning of *Discourses on the First Decade of Titus Livius*, where references to Moses, Cyrus, Romulus, and Theseus take up matters of superior leadership: "Without opportunity, their strength of will would have been wasted, and without such strength the opportunity would have been useless." Machiavelli's concept of *virtù* relinquished half of its power to *fortuna*. Having inherited faith in renewal from Petrarch, Machiavelli quoted his verses in the last chapter of *The Prince*, which predicts the advent of a new culture under the guide of a new leader. From individuals and communities to cultural landscapes, the very concept of re-naissance/rebirth offered an eventful opportunity to redefine human nature on the strength of both pagan and Christian inheritance. Whereas Bruni offered a socio-political vision of blissful permanence, Machiavelli recovered the strife of growth and decay in the world of empirical reality. That was the price which had to be paid whenever attempts were made to steer *kairos* amid the living experiences of humankind.

If we agree that to imagine a language means to imagine a form of life, the humanists imagined a language of charismatic words such as *virtù, grazia, sprezzatura, terribilità, occasione* that in fact projected unique styles of conduct. Gaps, adjustments, and changes in the etymological line between *kairos* and *occasione* reflected the very semantics of rebirth, which itself bridged past and future, burial and disinterment, misreadings of anterior texts and mistranslations of earlier terms. Rebirth turned out to be a frame of mind. The time of the Renaissance *kairos* is the 'better' time of rebirth. *Naissance* is a matter of biology, and biologists teach us that nothing can be born twice. Whenever a rebirth seems to occur, one confronts acts of the mind. In Alberti's words, the humanists tried to make rebirth "newborn and perfect." In that sense, 'renaissance' stood out as the reversal of the medieval 'waning' as well as the reversal of such recurrent concepts as 'autumn,' 'decline,' *decadentismo*, and '*fin de siècle.*'

Once it exhausted its initial potential, however, the humanist rebirth quickly faded away. It did not 'swerve' toward unlimited progress. One might suggest that renaissances are beginnings, they are trajectories of rising excellence. Because they are perfective and utopian, renaissances cannot sustain themselves for extended periods of time in the world of empirical practice; their permanence is mainly cultural. The favorable moment can live forever in the world of art and ideology, where the present can absorb past and future. Even better than the ideal Courtier, who was conceived "without defect of any kind," Michelangelo showed unlimited confidence when he chose to sculpt *David* in the moment before attacking Goliath. Whereas Donatello had portrayed David after he had defeated the giant, Michelangelo staged the moment of an impending engagement, which however leaves no doubt as to the outcome. David's confidence seems to equate history with an ameliorative vision which no foe can threaten. The favorable beginning illuminates the end as well. David's victory is, in fact, a foregone conclusion. Whether it refers to an individual deed or to an epochal landscape, the Renaissance *kairos* could not envision a future different from the present. Petrarch wrote a letter to posterity, and it probably never dawned on him that posterity could develop interests different from his own. He did to humanist heirs what medieval Christianity had done to pagan ancestors: one colonized the past and the other the future.

Indeed, we confront a synoptic vocabulary of time. For the humanists at their kairotic best, the past was reborn for the future's sake. Concerned with such dynamics, Paul Tillich raised a question at once disturbing and provocative: "Is it possible that the message of *kairos* is an error?" At his kairotic best, the humanist would answer that the message is an error only if humankind fails to identify itself with ideal models. By the same token, however, *kairos* is not an error insofar as it spurs people to conceive of such models. That recognition is itself an ameliorative activity. Even in Harold Bloom's study of the anxiety of influence, the Gnome of Error is the one who secures creative or re-creative deviations. In both instances, error is an act at once transgressive and inventive.

Between Early Modern and Postmodern culture, swerves, errors, and disjunctions have been crucial to creation and recreation, reading and rereading. Often, the upshot has unhinged the dialogics of tradition and individual talent by means of 'swerving' compounds that are both spatial and temporal: ex-centric, dis-integrated, dis-located, disjuncted, and, last but not least, deconstructed. The prefix no longer qualifies; it denies. We begin with loss, with *kairos*'s negative 'Other.' The prefix has become the weapon of choice in the arsenal of postmodern erasures, when parodic beginnings are overlaid with the scars of archetypal traces and unmendable fractures. In our culture of parody and referentiality, the concept of beginning has become highly derivative. The single has become plural, and the unique often simulates the counterfeited. The Renaissance *kairos* reconciled beginning with end because it operated on cultural grounds ruled by principles of harmony and proportion, what John Donne called concinnity (*concinnitas*). Today, however, culture is less insulated, and it projects empirical tensions and ideological unrest which make kairotic beginning difficult, if not improbable. In the culture of Pierre Menard's re-writing and of Borges's anecdotal commentaries, it is fair to ask whether we are living in an epoch which is post-kairotic as well.

At a time when the angel of history has been flying into the future backwards while the debris of the dead past has been catching up with him, how could one still believe in propitious beginnings? Instead, we have developed a passion for endings of all kinds, which cannot but inspire cynicism about rebirths. Frank Lloyd Wright ridiculed the idea of the Renaissance rebirth of architecture, which "has been continually re-born for several centuries. . .and now thoroughly dead from repeated 're-birth'." How favorable can any beginning be amid a culture of bits and pieces, and of posthumous echoes after the end of art? But the original artist knows that the past, without being forgotten, must yield to the present; otherwise he becomes a gravedigger instead of a groundbreaker.

Waiting for a different *kairos* to steer us toward a new beginning, after so much anti-kairotic 'waning,' *decadentismo*, and *fin de siècle*, appreciation no less than criticism cannot but lead us to admire the Renaissance reconstruction of the best of all possible times. Although not quite sunlit and somehow removed from the center, the kairotic dream of myth, of history, and of an aesthetic order is still with us. To phrase it in the words of the modern poet Wallace Stevens:

> There was a myth before the myth began,
> Venerable and articulate and complete.

Reading Through the Text: Lives of Saint Catherine of Alexandria by Christine de Pizan and Pietro Aretino

Elizabeth Dolly Weber

In this paper I examine two versions of the life of the same powerful woman, Saint Catherine of Alexandria, arguing that while the stated goals of the authors, Christine de Pizan and Pietro Aretino, are similar, their actual representations of Catherine's life are diametrically opposed. Despite the fact that the same aspects of Catherine's life are highlighted in each version, Catherine's skills as an orator lead Christine de Pizan to present her as the epitome of the authoritative good woman, an unquestionably positive force, whereas in Aretino's version the same power of verbal persuasion allows Saint Catherine to be read as a dangerously insubordinate woman whose unchecked public speech leads to the destruction of her father, her family, and the Roman state.[1]

Saint Catherine of Alexandria was one of the most popular saints of the Middle Ages, and her legend inspired a significant vernacular literary production in both France and Italy.[2] The basic story of Catherine's life is as follows. Catherine was a princess in Alexandria in the fourth century, when Egypt was under Roman rule. Born a pagan, she converted to Christianity. She was extensively educated, and became an unbeatable debater, trained in pagan philosophy

---

[1] This article is part of a book-length project exploring representations of female speech in French and Italian saints' lives.

[2] Catherine's legend was very widespread: medieval versions exist in French, Italian, Greek, Latin, Arabic, German, Hungarian, Czech, Polish, English, Irish, Welsh, and Spanish. For details, see Pamela Gehrke, *Saints and Scribes: Medieval Hagiography in its Manuscript Context* (Berkeley and Los Angeles: University of California Press, 1993), 93; Christine Walsh, *The Cult of St. Katherine of Alexandria in Early Medieval Europe* (Aldershot: Ashgate, 2007); also J. Jenkins and K. J. Lewis, eds., *St. Katherine of Alexandria: Texts and Contexts in Western Medieval Europe* (Turnhout: Brepols, 2003). There are eleven verse versions in French, of which at least one was written by a woman. For edited versions in Italian before 1600, see Anne Wilson Tordi, ed. and trans., *La festa et storia de Sancta Caterina: A Medieval Religious Drama* (New York: Peter Lang, 1997), 17–35.

as well as in Christian theology. At the age of eighteen, she confronted the Roman emperor, Maxentius, and her arguments in favor of Christianity were so articulate that the emperor, unable to silence her himself, summoned the fifty most skilled rhetoricians in the empire to debate her. Although the male debaters were initially scornful of the young girl, Catherine soon reduced them to silence, convincing and converting them. Furious, the emperor had the debaters burnt alive, and tried to force Catherine to abjure her faith with promises, threats, and tortures. Catherine remained firm, and while in prison managed to convert not only Maxentius's wife but also the commander of the army, Maxentius's best friend. Maxentius was forced to execute them both, and these betrayals sealed Catherine's fate. Although she was sentenced to be torn to pieces on huge spiked wheels, God caused the wheels to explode, killing five thousand pagan spectators and converting many others who were impressed by the miracle. After calmly enduring more tortures, Catherine was beheaded, and angels carried her body to Mount Sinai.[3]

The many early medieval French and Italian versions of Saint Catherine's life were based on this passion story or *passio*, which focuses on her debates and situates her as wise, articulate, and independent. By the fourteenth century, however, a new story, the *conversio* or "mystic marriage" version, had appeared and was the most represented in literature and in art.[4] The *conversio* relates the story of Catherine's conversion to Christianity and her symbolic marriage to the Christ child. While the *passio* presents Catherine as a champion for all Christians, the *conversio* presents her as a patron for unmarried young girls. The "mystic marriage" Catherine is slow-witted, sexualized, dependent, indecisive, and virtually mute — a figure antithetical to that of the debater Catherine.

---

[3] For an English translation of the popular *Golden Legend* version (1260; *passio* version only), see Jacobus de Voragine, *The Golden Legend: Readings on the Saints*, trans. William Granger Ryan, 2 vols. (Princeton: Princeton University Press, 1993), 1: 334–41. Maureen Curnow argues that Christine's major source for the Third Book is Vincent de Beauvais' *Speculum Historiale*: "The *Livre de la cité des dames* of Christine de Pisan," ed. Maureen Cheney Curnow (Ph.D. diss., Vanderbilt University, 1975), 189; Quilligan concurs: Maureen Quilligan, *The Allegory of Female Authority: Christine de Pizan's Cité des Dames* (Ithaca and London: Cornell University Press, 1991), 216–17. I have argued that another significant source is Gautier de Coinci's *Vie de Sainte Christine*: Elizabeth Dolly Weber, "The Power of Speech: Models of Female Martyrdom in Medieval and Early Modern French Literature" (Ph.D. diss., University of Wisconsin-Madison, 1994), 164–72.

[4] Giovanni B. Bronzini, "La leggenda di S. Caterina d'Alessandria: Passioni greche et latine," *Atti della Accademia nazionale dei Lincei, Memorie*, 8th ser., 9 (1960): 257–416, here 415, and Louis Réau, *Iconographie de l'art chrétien*, 3 vols. (Paris: Presses Universitaires de France, 1955–1959), 3: 266, date the origins of the mystic marriage version to the late thirteenth or early fourteenth century.

It is thus not surprising that, despite the growing popularity of the mystic marriage version in the fifteenth century, Christine de Pizan chose to showcase the debater Saint Catherine in her 1405 *Livre de la Cité des Dames* (*Book of the City of Ladies*), a project explicitly devoted to rehabilitating and re-authorizing women and to silencing male slanderers of women.

Christine de Pizan's decision to place female saints at the culminating point of her otherwise secular work, the *Book of the City of Ladies*, represents her greatest break with her major source, Boccaccio's *De Mulieribus Claris*, which excludes saints and holy women.[5] This addition reflects her understanding that saints' lives preserve some of the strongest female voices in French medieval texts. The saint's life, and particularly the martyr's life, provides one of the very few medieval fora in which women engaged in an openly political and public discourse. Virtually all of the authoritative women's voices with which Christine de Pizan and her potential readers would have been familiar were those of female saints. Thus it is not coincidence that Christine places a series of female saints' lives at the end of her *Book* and at the summit of her City. Christine's appropriation of the voices of the female martyr saints reveals her own perception of them as authoritative speakers, as well as her expectation that her readers would accept these women as powerful and good.

The Third Book of the *Book of the City of Ladies* is the crown or, more literally, the "roof" of the City of Women. This book opens with the installation of the Virgin Mary as queen of the City, and the rest of the book is devoted to saints and saintly women, who are presented as the most important inhabitants. Introducing Saint Catherine's life, the character Justice remarks that female martyr saints "serve as excellent examples for every woman above all other wisdom. For this reason, these women are the most outstanding of our City."[6] Twenty-nine female saints' lives are recounted in this section, of which two stand out by virtue of their length and position: the life of Saint Catherine of Alexandria, whose prime position as the first non-biblical saint mentioned indicates her importance,

---

[5] Christine probably consulted the 1401 French translation, *Des Cleres et Nobles Femmes* (itself an adaptation), tentatively attributed to Laurent de Premierfait, according to Curnow ("The *Livre de la cité des dames*," 139). See also A. Jeanroy, "Boccace et Christine de Pizan: Le *De Claris Mulieribus*, principale source du *Livre de la Cité des Dames*," *Romania* 48 (1922): 93–105; Patricia A. Phillippy, "Establishing Authority: Boccaccio's *De Claris Mulieribus* and Christine de Pizan's *Le Livre de la Cité des Dames*, *Romanic Review*" 77 (1986): 167–94.

[6] Unless otherwise noted, translations of Pizan are from Christine de Pizan, *The Book of the City of Ladies*, trans. Earl Jeffrey Richards (New York: Persea Books, 1982); here 189. Citations of Pizan in the original are all from "The *Livre de la cité des dames*," ed. Curnow: "Bon exemple a toute femme sus toute autre sagesce . . . [Elles] seront les plus supperlatives de nostre cité" (978).

and the life of Saint Christina, Christine de Pizan's patron saint, significantly placed at the exact midpoint of the third book.

This privileging of the lives of Saints Catherine and Christina is motivated by Christine de Pizan's double desire to give examples of authoritative women speakers and to reduce to silence male slanderers of women. Both Saint Catherine and Saint Christina famously resisted repeated attempts to silence them: Catherine was venerated for her skill as a debater, and Christina miraculously spoke more clearly after her tongue was cut out. While Christine de Pizan's representation of herself as Saint Christine/Christina is crucial to her project of self-authorization, I will here concentrate on Christine's self-identification with Saint Catherine as a learned and authoritative woman.

The framework for the *Book of the City of Ladies* is that the protagonist Christine, discouraged by the overwhelming weight of misogynist "wisdom" condemning the evil nature of women, is chosen as the "champion" of women and commissioned to build a City to defend all women against the slanderous attacks of men. Christine's prime positioning of the life of Saint Catherine ("Et premierement, comme tres excellente, la benoite Katherine")[7] marks her continuing interest in highlighting instances of authoritative female speech and in providing examples of women who literally silence men. Of all the female saints, Saint Catherine was the only one venerated for her intellectual abilities, and in particular for her mastery of oration and debate.[8] She was a symbol of the efficacy and authority of the female voice.

Christine emphasizes the connection between female authority and male reduction to silence in her narration of the initial confrontation between Catherine and the pagan emperor Maxentius. Catherine claims the authority to "correct" the emperor's error with "many wise words."[9] Her power lies in her erudition: thus Christine pointedly identifies Catherine as a female clerk, a "clergesce" who constructs and proves her personal authority as she convinces the pagans of their error by citing their own pagan authorities.[10] Catherine's skillful appropriation of the authority of the classical philosophers she cites, and her clerkly "autto-

---

[7] "The *Livre de la cité des dames*," 978.

[8] The only other female saint venerated in part for her intellect at this time was Saint Catherine of Siena (d. 1380, canonized 1413); Christine does not mention her, but may expect the name Catherine to suggest this double resonance.

[9] "l'empereur prist a corriger de celle erreur par moult sages paroles": "The *Livre de la cité des dames*," 979.

[10] "As a well-lettered woman versed in the various branches of knowledge, she proceeded to prove on the basis of philosophical arguments that there is only one God": *The Book of the City of Ladies*, 220. "Comme grant clegesce et aprise es sciences que elle estoit, prist a prouver par raisons philosophiques que il n'est qu'un seul Dieu": "The *Livre de la cité des dames*," 979.

rité," leave Maxentius and the fifty debaters literally speechless: "[I]l fu tous *esmerveillez* et ne luy sceut que dire."[11]

The implicit parallel between the tasks of Catherine and Christine is clear. Catherine has to first convince the rhetoricians, who are inclined to dismiss her as a mere "pucelle" (young girl, innocent) not worth debating, that she is a worthy opponent. She accomplishes this by showing her mastery of the pagan philosophers, whose ideas she then neatly refutes. In the same way, Christine as narrator of *the Book of the City of Ladies* presents her exhaustive examples and counter-examples as proof that her erudition makes her a worthy commentator; this allows her to claim the authority to re-read, re-interpret, and correct other authoritative (and anti-woman) works.

The goal of the *Book of the City of Ladies* is to create a coherent vision of the true nature of women (as opposed to the false image created by male writers), and by the bulk and force — the authority — of examples to at once *convince* the reader and completely *silence* those writers who have slandered women. The silence of the emperor and the rhetoricians when they are faced with the truth Catherine reveals to them is the silence that Christine de Pizan herself demands from the misogynist writers: either the silence of the defeated or the silence of the converted. In casting herself as Catherine's alter ego, Christine makes it clear that she reads Catherine as a wholly positive woman, and expects others to read her as such.

Pietro Aretino's version of the life of Saint Catherine initially seems to position Catherine in much the same way.[12] He begins the *vita* by emphasizing Catherine's role as an authoritative and persuasive speaker in the dedication to the patron who commissioned the work, mentioning *only* Catherine's oratorical powers, and describing her as "quella vergine che amutì sì grave stuolo di sapienti"

---

[11] "The *Livre de la cité des dames*," 979. "They were all astonished and did not know what to say to her" (my translation). "Esmerveillez" literally means "speechless."

[12] Aretino's literary production, in addition to his letters (published during his lifetime), ranged from pornographic dialogues (1536, 1556) to art criticism, from political satire to pornographic poems. His "Sonnetti Lussuriosi" (1527), for example, were composed to accompany *I modi*, a set of representations of sexual positions so explicit that their engraver was arrested (Bette Talvacchia, *Taking Positions: On the Erotic in Renaissance Culture* [Princeton: Princeton University Press, 1999], 4). Moved perhaps by the spirit, perhaps by the large commissions offered by various patrons, Aretino composed the *Vita di Sa nta Caterina Vergine* and several other religious texts, including *Dell'Umanità del Figliuol di Dio* (1535), *Il Genesi con la visione di Noè nella quale vede i misteri del Testamento Vecchio et del Nuovo* (1539), and lives of the Virgin Mary (1539) and St. Thomas Aquinas (1543). Although all his religious works were put on the *Index Librorum Prohibitorum* in 1558, they were much praised at the time of their composition. For contemporary reviews of the religious works, see Pietro Aretino, *Prose sacre di Pietro Aretino*, ed. Ettore Allodoli (Lanciano: Carabba, 1914), "Introduzione," III-IV.

("that virgin who silenced such a serious group of sages").[13] Significantly, despite the fact that the mystic marriage version of Saint Catherine's life had virtually eclipsed the debater version by the sixteenth century, Aretino chooses to devote the bulk of his retelling not to the story of Catherine's conversion and marriage to Christ, but to the amazing efficacy of Catherine's speech, which he goes so far as to characterize as official authoritative speech: namely, preaching and sermons.[14] However, while Christine de Pizan positioned her 1405 representation of Saint Catherine as one of her final and strongest arguments for the positive power of educated and powerful women, Aretino's 1540 version seems to undermine its own goal of glorifying an authoritative female speaker by allowing or encouraging a negative reading of the same characteristics. Aretino's relentless emphasis on Catherine's verbal conquests—and their violent consequences—points to anxiety about this powerful and insubordinate woman who defied Caesar (as Aretino calls Maxentius), seduced his subjects with her preaching, and essentially led a popular rebellion against the Roman state.

I have argued elsewhere that the possibility of the Christian female martyr saint as a positive symbol of and model for a powerful woman becomes weakened in the sixteenth century owing to a variety of factors, including the humanist revival of the Lucretia story, and the resulting conflation of Lucretia with

---

[13] Pietro Aretino, *Le Vite dei Santi: Santa Caterina Vergine, San Tommasso d'Aquino (1540–1543)*, ed. Flavia Santin (Rome: Bonacci, 1977), 25 (Dedication to the Marchese del Vasto). All translations of Aretino's life of Catherine are my own.

[14] The oldest versions of Saint Catherine's life are the *passio* (debater) plot; the *conversio* (mystic marriage) versions arose later and appear to have been created based in part on a series of iconographical misreadings that transformed her original symbol, the celestial sphere (representing philosophy), into a wheel (the intended torture instrument shattered by a miracle). Finally, in the later Middle Ages, the wheel is read as a wedding ring symbolizing her status as bride of Christ. In the *conversio* versions, Catherine is transformed from an independent intellectual into a dependent bride whose main function is to submit rather than to defy. See Réau, *Iconographie de l'art chrétien*, 3: 266. It seems likely that this "misreading" of iconography stemmed also from an anxiety about the representation of such a powerful and successful woman, as I argue later in this paper.

While there are some references to the mystic marriage in Aretino's version, these passages are greatly minimized with respect to the overall length of the *vita*, and to their relative importance in other versions that include the *conversio*. This despite the fact that Aretino (as an art critic and artist groupie) would probably have been familiar with the many contemporary representations of the mystic marriage of Saint Catherine, among them those of the Italians Filippo Lippi (1501), Boccaccio Boccaccino (1506), Correggio (1526), Parmiggiano (1527–1537), et alii. Aretino's particular friends Tintoretto and Titian painted the mystic marriage in the 1560s and 1570s. See H. T. Blodget, "Titian's 'St. Catherine' in Boston," *Burlington Magazine* 111:798 (Sept. 1969): 544–48; Luba Freedman, *Titian's Portraits through Aretino's Lens* (University Park, PA: Pennsylvania State University Press, 1995).

the female martyrs.¹⁵ At the same time, previously acceptable representations of powerful women outside the realm of martyrdom were re-evaluated and reinterpreted as inappropriate and threatening. Geraldine Johnson details the reduction of positive female images in the public sphere in fourteenth- to sixteenth-century Italy, where she notes the growing discomfort with public statues of powerful women—including the Virgin Mary herself. In 1504, for example, the Florentine city council removed Donatello's *Judith Beheading Holofernes* from its central position in front of the Palazzo dei Priori. That this decision was motivated by anxiety about the public representation of a powerful woman was made explicit by one of the men who argued for removal of the statue: "The Judith is . . . inappropriate in this place because . . . it is not fitting that the woman should slay the man."¹⁶

The statue of Judith, like the typical iconography of female martyr saints and of Saint Catherine in particular, shows a woman wielding a sword and standing on the body of a fallen, defeated man. As the decision to remove Judith makes clear, these symbols of women subjecting men were considered all too easy to "misread," particularly by "unsophisticated" viewers/readers like women, who might feel empowered to emulate this church-sanctioned domination of men. The extent of the official discomfort about representations of powerful women can be inferred from the fact that the statue of Judith decapitating Holofernes was eventually replaced by a statue showing the decapitation of a strong woman by a man, the decapitation of Medusa, in which Perseus, standing on Medusa's fallen body, raises her head like a trophy, and like a warning.¹⁷

Whereas up to this time period, then, images of strong women could be read as saying one thing (Judith as a woman killing a man) and meaning another (Judith as a righteous individual saving her people), the disassociation of the signifier from the signified became increasingly difficult in the sixteenth century, with respect to women and to the body in general.¹⁸ Thus, it may not be a coincidence that in Aretino's version Catherine herself tells the fifty debaters: ". . . [S]pero triofar de voi come . . . la vedova Iudith di Oloferne."¹⁹

---

¹⁵ Weber, "The Power of Speech," 55–114. Cf. Linda C. Hults, "Dürer's *Lucretia*: Speaking the Silence of Women," *Signs* 16 (1991): 205–37.

¹⁶ Geraldine A. Johnson, "Idol or Ideal? The Power and Potency of Female Public Sculpture," in *Picturing Women in Renaissance and Baroque Italy*, ed. eadem and Sara F. Matthews Grieco (Cambridge: Cambridge University Press, 1997), 222–45, here 231.

¹⁷ Johnson, "Idol or Ideal?" 231.

¹⁸ The Council of Trent (1545–1563) would concretize this trend, banning nudity in sacred images in 1563. Cf. Cynthia Stollhans, "Michelangelo's Nude Saint Catherine of Alexandria," *Woman's Art Journal* 19 (1998): 26–30.

¹⁹ Aretino, *Le Vite dei Santi*, 88 : "I hope to triumph over you like the widow Judith over Holofernes."

In this context, it is not suprising that Aretino's choice to represent Catherine as a successful preaching woman turns out to include at least as many negative components as positive ones. Injunctions against women preaching or speaking in public date back to Saint Paul (1 Tim. 2:12), and preaching women in other contexts were routinely condemned.[20] However, Saint Catherine and the other female martyrs, all of whose *vitae* include public speech easily understood as preaching, had hitherto been exempt from this censure. Thus in Aretino's *vita*, the events themselves—Catherine preaching to individuals (the emperor, his wife) and to crowds (the debaters, the general populace gathered to see her tortured—are traditional ones, frequently represented in written and in pictorial versions of her passion. What is new, however, is the introduction of a strongly negative analysis of the effects of Catherine's preaching, hitherto praised for its power to persuade and convert: in this version, it is possible to read Catherine as one of the powerful and anxiety-producing women who "seduce and then slaughter unsuspecting men."[21]

The extended negative analysis of Catherine's preaching is voiced by the Roman emperor Maxentius, who explicitly characterizes Catherine's public speaking as fatal to all those around her: "Le tue prediche, madonna, hanno estinte le turbe dei miseri, e dalle tue persuasioni son derivate le morti dei sapienti . . . il genitor tuo, il tuo proprio padre . . . gli hai procacciato il fine. . ."[22] Although the censure comes from the villain of the story, the very fact that it is articulated here for the first time reveals a narrowing, a closing down of the ways powerful female speech could be read.

Besides featuring Catherine in the now-ambiguous role of preaching woman, Aretino includes significant modifications to the traditional story of her life—which, as he boasts in the dedication, he has amplified from the half-page

---

[20] Katherine Ludwig Jansen, *The Making of the Magdalen: Preaching and Popular Devotion in the Later Middle Ages* (Princeton: Princeton University Press, 2000), 57. Cf. Nicole Bériou, "The Right of Women to Give Religious Instruction in the Thirteenth Century," in *Women Preachers and Prophets through Two Millenia of Christianity*, ed. Beverly Mayne Kienzle and Pamela J. Walker (Berkeley: University of California Press, 1998), 134–45.

[21] Johnson, "Idol or Ideal?" 231.

[22] Aretino, *Le Vite dei Santi*, 109: "Your preaching, my lady, has extinguished the lives of crowds of miserable men, and from your persuasive words have ensued the deaths of wise men. [You procured/caused the death of] your own father." Maxentius continues: "Abbi rispetto alle creature umane, le cui vite si spengono per colpa dei tuoi magici artificii. Noi non ci potiamo imaginare come sia possibile che una donzella equale a te sia crudele come sei tu . . .Tu, tu, figliuola unica del re Costo gli hai procacciato il fine . . ."; "Respect human beings, whose lives were snuffed out by your fault, with your magic. We can't imagine how it's possible that a young woman like you is as cruel as you are . . .You, you, only daughter of King Costos, caused his death . . ." (Aretino, *Le Vite dei Santi*, 109).

of his source to a whole book (140 pages in the modern edition).[23] While he sticks to the general outlines of her life, he is "più libero nel gioco inventivo."[24] The most telling of these re-writings are changes in the role of Catherine's family and in the continual emphasis of the Romanized setting.

In earlier debater versions of her life, Saint Catherine's mother is not mentioned and her father dies while she is still a child. In mystic marriage versions, Catherine's father is dead and Catherine's mother is instrumental in her conversion and marriage to Christ. In neither case is Catherine the cause of the death of her parents. Aretino, however, creates an entirely new parental scenario, one in which Catherine is responsible for her mother's death (in childbirth), her father's death, and the deaths of all her brothers and sisters (siblings never mentioned in any other version). The process of eradicating the entire lineage of King Costos begins in the first moment of Catherine's life, and in the first line of Aretino's version, where her birth effects her father's transformation from strong father to weak mother:

> Da che la madre di Caterina si morì partorendola, Costo, re inclito, di genitore le diventò nutrice, et, dal latte che non potea darle, infuora, intervenivia negli uffici di tutte le cure necessarie al governo di chi nasce."[25]

Costos' feminization leads him not only to wash Catherine's diapers ("scaldare i panni sottili et le fascie candide"), but also to a continuing intimate relationship with her. Noticing that Catherine, even as a young child, disliked "woman's work" ("nel prendere il pettine, le forbici, l'aco e il fuso simigliava un gusto infermo schifo delle vivande"), her doting father allows her to undertake the kind of education reserved for boys, "peroché le scritture erano il vero cibo del suo intelletto."[26]

---

[23] "[My patron wished] che io formi un libro intiero d'una leggenda, che non empie un foglio mezzo . . ." (Aretino, *Le Vite dei Santi*, 25). Aretino does not identify his source, and it is likely that he drew from multiple sources; his version follows the general plot of the *Golden Legend* version, which presents only the debater story, but interpolates scenes from the mystic marriage tradition. Voragine mentions Catherine's father but does not represent him as a full-fledged character (Voragine, *The Golden Legend*, 3:334).

[24] Mario Scotti, "Gli Scritti Religiosi," in *Pietro Aretino nel Cinquecentenario della Nascita: Atti del Convegno di Roma-Viterbo-Arezzo (28 settembre-1 ottobre 1992), Toronto (23–24 ottobre 1992), Los Angeles (27–29 ottobre 1992)* (Rome: Salerno Editrice, 1993), 1:121–42, here 141.

[25] Aretino, *Le Vite dei Santi*, 27: "Since Catherine's mother died giving birth to her, Costos, the illustrious king, was transformed from her progenitor to her nurse, and, though he could not give her his milk, he saw to all the other things necessary for the care of a child."

[26] Aretino, *Le Vite dei Santi*, 27–28: "taking up the comb, the scissors, the needle, and the spindle seemed [in her] a sick distaste for that kind of food;" "since writing [or the

This thorough education is valorized positively by the narrator (it gives Catherine the knowledge of pagan authorities that allows her to defeat her pagan interlocutors) and negatively by most of the commentators in the text itself (it, along with her knowledge of Christian theology, allows her to "seduce" various pagans and leads to their execution). For example, when Catherine attempts to convert her father he is very aware of the fatal effects of her preaching: "Ma chi se potrìa tenere di non attribuirti il nome di crudeltà ché, nascendo, ponesti nella sepoltura chi ti porse nel mondo, vivendo abbatti colui che ti riserba il regno?"[27] He is correct in his assessment of the situation: when he gives in to Catherine's persuasion and converts, a series of events is set off that leads to his death and to the utter annihilation of his immediate and future family.

Catherine herself refuses any negative interpretation of the effects of her preaching; she is confident that the results (conversion, baptism) lead to an ultimately positive result (eternal life) for those she convinces and converts.[28] However, within the context of the narrative, Catherine's persuasive powers, often described as setting on fire the minds and souls of her listeners, seem to lead those who follow her into flames reminiscent of hell rather than of heaven. Catherine tells the crowd of pagans gathered to watch her debate that the power of her oration will set them afire with desire for the right religion: "per opra delle mie parole la timiditade vi si convertirà in ardire, la tepidezza in fiamme."[29] The conversion of the empress (among others) is also framed in terms of incendiary speech: "Il continuo soffiar del vento non accende i carboni, e accesigli non gli aviva, e avivatigli non trae le fiamme che trassero le parole di Caterina dal core della cesarea consorte, poi che l'ebbero avivato e accesso."[30]

These references to figurative fires set by Catherine's inflammatory speech are concretized in the various fires that kill those she converts, from the fire that reduces to ashes the royal palace and her brothers and sisters, to the fire that burns the debaters, to the fire set under the belly of the huge bronze horse in which Catherine's prison guards are burned. This oratorical fire consumes the

---

Scriptures, though Catherine has not yet converted] was the true food of her intellect."

[27] Aretino, *Le Vite dei Santi*, 36 : "But who could hold himself back from giving you the name of cruelty/cruel one, since in being born you buried the one [mother] who gave birth to you, [and] in living you struck down the one [father] who kept a kingdom for you?"

[28] See for example her response to Maxentius' accusations that she has murdered many people: Aretino, *Le Vite dei Santi*, 110.

[29] Aretino, *Le Vite dei Santi*, 44: "By the work of my words, timidity will be converted to ardor, tepidity to flames."

[30] Aretino, *Le Vite dei Santi*, 129: "The continual blowing of wind doesn't light charcoal, and charcoal once lit doesn't burn, and once burning doesn't create such flames as were created by the words of Catherine in the heart of Caesar's consort, once the words had inflamed and lit that heart."

entire royal family and puts an end to the Alexandrian succession; it devastates the intellectual and military assets of Roman Egypt; it puts the succession of Maxentius into question by removing his wife (and thus future heirs). The destruction of the *pater* leads to the destruction of the *patria*.

Not only is Catherine's preaching the match that starts the fires that kill her own family as well as those in power in Alexandria and the Roman empire, it is the germ that starts an epidemic disease: "[Alessandria] potea simigliarsi a une terra stata assai tempo sana, nel cui cerchio la infezion de l'aria comincia a piovere il tosco della peste." This characterization of Catherine's effect on Alexandria is startling: where one might expect a description of Christian conversion as having a healing effect on a sick pagan city, Catherine's conversion campaign is instead described as an "infection" leading to a deadly plague that devastates a once-healthy city.

All versions of Catherine's life describe (in more or less detail) the tortures to which Catherine and her converts are submitted: the intention is to show the fortitude of the saint and the converts as well as the supreme power of God, which allows the Christians to survive without pain a succession of torments, each one of which would obviously be fatal. The analogous failure of the pagans to survive Christian miracles is also described, though not dwelt on. Aretino, however, departs from the typical script in two significant instances: the torture of the bronze horse and the miracle of the torture wheels.

The torture of the bronze horse is not in any other versions of Catherine's story; while Aretino does not invent the kind of torture (roasting in a brazen animal), he adds the torture to Catherine's life, and his choice of a horse, rather than of the typical animal, a bull, is significant. He imagines the ruins of a palace, the only remains of which are a tall staircase surmounted by an enormous statue of Bucephalus, the famous horse of Alexander the Great. In the belly of this immense brazen horse Catherine's prison guards are burnt to death.[31] This extended and seemingly gratuitous reference to Alexander reminds the reader of Alexandria's foundation and pre-Roman history. I would argue that it is in fact an oblique reference to the fall of another empire, the fall of Egypt to the Romans—not under Alexander, but under his descendant, Cleopatra. In fact, while Cleopatra's name is never mentioned in Aretino's text, the specter of that other educated Alexandrian queen who feminized men, did the work of a man, and battled with the Roman Empire subtends the whole work. Cleopatra, like Saint Catherine, was a powerful and seductive speaker. Plutarch says of her, "The

---

[31] Aretino, *Le Vite dei Santi*, 144–47. The use of a brazen bull as an instrument of torture was supposedly invented by the Greeks and used by the Romans; several martyr saints—Saint Eustace, Saint Antipas—were reportedly killed in bronze bulls. Dante mentions the Sicilian bull in *Inferno*, Canto XXVII. However, the bronze horse Bucephalus is Aretino's invention, as is the connection of this type of torture with Saint Catherine.

charm of her presence was irresistible, and there was an attraction in her person and her talk, together with a peculiar force of character which pervaded her every word and action, and laid all who associated with her under her spell."[32]

The connection between the famously sexy queen and the virgin martyr was more obvious in the sixteenth century than it seems today. In fact, Cleopatra was sometimes portrayed as a martyr to love, displaying the asp with which she committed suicide in the same way that martyr saints hold, as symbols of their virtue and sacrifice, the swords that executed them. Without forcing the interpretation, it can be said with confidence that contemporary readers of Aretino's text would have been alive to the historical implications, however subtly alluded to, of an emasculating virago Egyptian princess from Alexandria.

Aretino himself always insisted that his work was political satire, steadfastly defending his pornographic dialogues as political commentaries. It is this deep investment in the political that makes his version of Catherine's life so potentially ambiguous. He chose to emphasize, as previous retellers of Catherine's story did not, the political implications of Catherine's radical refusal to bend to the wishes of the Roman state: in his version she is potentially readable as the uncolonizable Other, the Egyptian wrench in the machine of the Roman Empire.

Another scene unique to Aretino's version that introduces the possibility of a negative interpretation of Catherine's project is the penultimate and most famous miracle of her story, when four spiked wheels designed to rip her body apart are instead destroyed by angels. The explosion of the wheels kills thousands of pagan spectators, but converts many as well; in all other versions of the story the positive effects of the miracle are underlined. Aretino, however, chooses to insist on the very negative effects of the explosion, quoted at length but not in entirety below:

> Onde... dispererso le gravide l'umano seme... morir gli infermi, ismarirsi i giovani, perdettero i sensi i vecchi...
>
> [G]iacevano in terri i corpi infidi con attitudini orride e con gesti brutti. Né si potean guardare senza raccapricciarsi, peroché le ferite che si vedevano in loro erano crudelmente varie e oscuramente diverse, conciosia che i rasoi tagliarono quelle tempie, quei colli, quelle bracchia, quei busti, quelle gambe, quelle coscie, quei piedi, e quelle mani che gli fece tagliare il caso.
>
> I chiodi passarano quei petti, quei dossi, quei costati, quei ventri, quegli stomachi, quei fianchi, quelle faccie e quelle rene... Talché i sangui mescolata con le cervella, e le cervella miste coi sangui, e i sangui e le cervella con le teste aperte, con le carni lacere, erano la minore oscurità che si dimostrasse ivi, peroché la somma di tutta la destruzione dei corpi, appariva nel

---

[32] *Makers of Rome: Nine Lives by Plutarch*, ed. and trans. Ian Scott-Kilvert (London: Penguin Books, 1965), 294.

discopersi là un busto senza il resto delle membra, e qua un membro senza il resto del busto. Qui si vedeva il corpo con una gamba e un braccio, e quivi un petto ritenente in sul collo quasi la metà d'un capo senza altro.[33]

Such a detailed and disproportionately lengthy description of the horrifying and bomb-like effects of this miracle, with its spontaneous abortions, pierced and dismembered bodies, and "rivi de sangue," undermines the ostensible positive outcome. Catherine's miracle, though destined to show the positive power of those under God's protection, paints a vivid picture of the suffering pagan victims, who suddenly seem more sinned against than sinning.[34]

Taken together, these pervasive images of destruction by fire, disease, and extreme violence, underpinned by the subtlest of references to Cleopatra, raise the possibility of a negative interpretation of Catherine's oratorical prowess. It would take only a slight tip in the balance, a small shift in sympathy, to cast Catherine as a negative model rather than a positive one.

The potential for that interpretive shift is latent in Aretino's insistence on the Romanized setting. In every version of her life, Catherine's passion takes place against a vague backdrop of Roman Egypt. Aretino, however, foregrounds that setting, referring to Rome and the Empire in an obsessive manner suggestive of an ulterior motive. The exploration of the meaning of a story about a rebellion

---

[33] Aretino, *Le vite di santi*, 152–53: "There pregnant women lost the human seed ... the ill died, the young became lost, the old lost their minds ...

The pagan corpses lay on the ground in horrible positions, with ugly gestures. Nor was it possible to see them without being horrified, because the wounds visible in them were cruelly varied and grimly diverse, conscious that the razors cut through here temples, here necks, here arms, here chests, here legs, here thighs, here feet, here hands that chance had cut off from them.

The nails pierced through here chests, here backs, here ribs, here bellies, here stomachs, here intestines, here faces, here kidneys ... So that the blood mixed with the brains, and the brains mixed with the blood, and the blood and the brains with the opened heads, with the lacerated flesh, were the least of the horrors shown here, because the greatest of the bodily destruction appeared in the discovery of there a torso without the rest of the limbs, there a limb without the rest of the torso. Here was to be seen a body with a leg and an arm, and there a chest retaining on its neck half of a head, without more."

By contrast, many versions (e.g. the *Golden Legend*; Pizan's version; Mombrizio) note simply that 4000 spectators were killed. Others, such as an Umbro-Senese version from 1394, emphasize the positive effects of the miracle: "cinqemilia di quel popolo moriero, / ed altretanti *se ne convertiero*" (Giovanni B. Bronzini, ed., "Una redazione versificata umbro-senese della leggenda di S. Caterina d'Alessandria," *Accademia nazionale dei Lincei, Rendiconti della classe di scienze morali, storiche e filologiche*, 8th ser., 7 [1952]: 77–106, here 92, my emphasis).

[34] While the tortures of the Christians are also striking in Aretino's version, it is the fact that the torture and the suffering of the pagans is described in such great detail and with sympathy toward the pagans that introduces a new note into the story.

against Rome, or of a Rome divided by two religions, in the particular context of Venice, the Reformation and Counter-Reformation, and in Aretino's work itself, is a subject too broad for the current study. However, I would propose that by consistently referring to Maxentius by his Roman title, "Cesare," or "Imperatore" (rather than by his name), and by emphasizing Roman legal and religious customs in a way unique to this version, Aretino draws attention to the political ramifications of Catherine's project, and leads the reader to think of Catherine as contributing to the fall of the Roman Empire in an unusually vivid and concrete way. The implicit link between the rise of one religion and the fall not only of a religion but of an empire is made explicit in Aretino's version. In this way, Aretino's Catherine is directly comparable to Lucretia, whose "martyrdom" inspired the restoration of the Roman Republic, since Catherine's martyrdom is tied to the ultimate destruction of the Roman state and creation of the Christian empire. Catherine's seductions bring about both personal and political disasters for Maxentius and the empire: first Costos, the local king and ally, is alienated; next the king is publicly and personally shamed when he cannot respond to Catherine's accusations about the Roman idols; then his wife betrays him; and finally he loses the loyalty and support of his best friend and the commander of the Roman army (as well as his two hundred best soldiers). By the end of the tale, the future looks exceedingly bleak for the isolated and impotent Roman emperor and for the empire itself.

In Aretino's life of Saint Catherine, then, we can see the moment in time at which it is no longer possible *not* to read a preaching woman as at best a questionable source of good and at worst a bringer of evil. Aretino's amplification or "fleshing out" of Catherine's legend voluntarily or involuntarily reveals that it is no longer possible to read representations of strong women only as metaphors. Saint Catherine's verbal prowess, which once figured her as a worthy disseminator of God's word, now, in the new atmosphere of the sixteenth century, lets her be understood as an uncontrollable virago whose attempts to topple the pagan idols/Roman state have unsettling resonances in an Italy suddenly full of outspoken Catherines, from the sixteenth-century Italian saints Catherine of Bologna, Catherine of Genoa, and Catherine de' Ricci to Catherine de' Medicis and to Catherine of Aragon, the sister-in-law of Aretino's patron.[35] Indeed, one can read between the lines of Aretino's text the growing anxiety that these monumental Judiths and Catherines might hop off their pedestals and do some damage in the real world.

---

[35] Not to mention Saint Catherine of Siena (1347–1380) and perhaps Aretino's own common-law wife, Caterina Sandella.

Works Cited

Aretino, Pietro. *Lettere*, ed. Francesco Erspamer. 2 vols. Parma: Fondazione Pietro Bembo, 1995.

———. *Ragionamento delle corti*, ed. Fulvio Pevere. Milan: Mursia, 1995.

———. *Sonetti sopra I "XVI modi,"* ed. Giovanni Aquilecchia. Rome: Salerno Editrice, 1992.

———. *Le Vite dei Santi: Santa Caterina Vergine, San Tommasso d'Aquino. 1540–1543*, ed. Flavia Santin. Rome: Bonacci, 1977.

———. *Prose sacre di Pietro Aretino*, ed. Ettore Allodoli. Lanciano: Carabba, 1914.

Bériou, Nicole. "The Right of Women to Give Religious Instruction in the Thirteenth Century." In *Women Preachers and Prophets through Two Millennia of Christianity*, ed. Beverly Mayne Kienzle and Pamela J. Walker, 134–45. Berkeley: University of California Press, 1998.

Blodget, Henry T. "Titian's 'St Catherine' in Boston." *Burlington Magazine* 111:798 (Sept. 1969): 544–48.

Blumenfeld-Kosinski, Renate, and Timea Szell, eds. *Images of Sainthood in Medieval Europe*. Ithaca, NY: Cornell University Press, 1991.

Bronzini, Giovanni B. "La leggenda di S. Caterina d'Alessandria: Passioni greche et latine." *Atti della Academia nazionale dei Lincei, Memorie*, 8th ser. 9 (1960): 257–416.

———. ed. "Una redazione versificata umbro-senese della leggenda di S. Caterina d'Alessandria." *Accademia nazionale dei Lincei, Rendiconti della classe di scienze morali, storiche e filologiche*, 8th ser. 7 (1952): 77–106.

Cairns, Christopher. *Pietro Aretino and the Republic of Venice: Researches on Aretino and his Circle in Venice 1527–1556*. Florence: Leo S. Olschki, 1985.

Christine de Pizan. "The *Livre de la cité des dames* of Christine de Pisan." ed. Maureen Cheney Curnow. Ph.D. diss., Vanderbilt University, 1975.

———. *The Book of the City of Ladies*, trans. Earl Jeffrey Richards. New York: Persea Books, 1982.

———. *Le Livre des Trois Vertus*, ed. Eric Hicks. Paris: Honoré Champion, 1989.

Freedman, Luba. *Titian's Portraits through Aretino's Lens*. University Park, PA: Pennsylvania State University Press, 1995.

Gehrke, Pamela. *Saints and Scribes: Medieval Hagiography in its Manuscript Context*. University of California Publications in Modern Philology, 126. Berkeley and Los Angeles: University of California Press, 1993.

Hults, Linda C. "Dürer's *Lucretia*: Speaking the Silence of Women." *Signs: Journal of Women in Culture and Society* 16 (1991): 205–37.

Hunt, Lynne. "Obscenity and the Origins of Modernity, 1500–1800." In *The Invention of Pornography: Obscenity and the Origins of Modernity, 1500–1800*, ed. eadem, 9–45. New York: Zone Books, 1993.

Jacobus de Voragine. *The Golden Legend: Readings on the Saints*, trans. William Granger Ryan. 2 vols. Princeton: Princeton University Press, 1993.

Jansen, Katherine Ludwig. *The Making of the Magdalen. Preaching and Popular Devotion in the Later Middle Ages*. Princeton: Princeton University Press, 2000.

Jeanroy, A. "Boccace et Christine de Pisan: Le *De Claris Mulieribus*, principale source du *Livre de la Cité des Dames*." *Romania* 48 (1922): 93–105.

Johnson, Geraldine A. "Idol or Ideal? The Power and Potency of Female Public Sculpture." In *Picturing Women in Renaissance and Baroque Italy*, ed. Geraldine A. Johnson and Sara F. Matthews Grieco, 222–45. Cambridge: Cambridge University Press, 1997.

Kienzle, Beverly Mayne, and Pamela J. Walker, eds. *Women Preachers and Prophets through Two Millennia of Christianity*. Berkeley: University of California Press, 1998.

Mulas, Luisa. "L'Aretino e i Medici." In *Pietro Aretino nel Cinquecentenario della Nascita. Atti del Convegno di Roma-Viterbo-Arezzo (28 settembre-1 ottobre 1992), Toronto (23–24 ottobre 1992), Los Angeles (27–29 ottobre 1992)*; 2:535–72. Rome: Salerno Editrice, 1993.

Phillippy, Patricia A. "Establishing Authority: Boccaccio's *De Claris Mulieribus* and Christine de Pizan's *Le Livre de la Cité des Dames*." *Romanic Review* 77 (1986): 167–94.

Plutarch. *Makers of Rome: Nine Lives by Plutarch* ed. and trans. Ian Scott-Kilvert. London: Penguin Books, 1965.

Quilligan, Maureen. *The Allegory of Female Authority: Christine de Pizan's* Cité des Dames. Ithaca and London: Cornell University Press, 1991.

Réau, Louis. *Iconographie de l'art chrétien*. 3 vols. Paris: Presses Universitaires de France, 1955–1959.

Scotti, Mario. "Gli Scritti Religiosi." In *Pietro Aretino nel Cinquecentenario della Nascita*, 1:121–42. Rome: Salerno Editrice, 1993.

Stollhans, Cynthia. "Michelangelo's Nude Saint Catherine of Alexandria." *Woman's Art Journal* 19 (1998): 26–30.

Talvacchia, Bette. *Taking Positions: On the Erotic in Renaissance Culture*. Princeton: Princeton University Press, 1999.

Tordi, Anne Wilson, ed. and trans. *La festa et storia de Sancta Caterina: A Medieval Italian Religious Drama*. Edited and Translated into English, with an Introduction on Saint Catherine of Alexandria's Legend in Medieval Italian Literature by Anne Wilson Tordi. English Translation of the Latin *Passio Sancte Katerine Virginis*, BHL 1663, by Nancy Wilson Van Baak. New York: Peter Lang, 1997.

Weber, Elizabeth Dolly. "The Power of Speech: Models of Female Martyrdom in Medieval and Early Modern French Literature." Ph.D. diss, University of Wisconsin-Madison, 1994.

Walters MS W720:
Chapters to Be Observed by the Singers
of the Cappella Giulia (1574)

Ilona Klein

The manuscript W720 that bears the title *Capitoli che hanno da osseruare gli Cantori della Cappella di San Pietro* is an unstudied and unpublished document held in the archives of the Walters Art Gallery in Baltimore, Maryland.[1] As one of the earliest surviving written texts of its kind, W720 documents in detail the rules that the singers of the Julian Chapel had to obey during the year 1574. The following critical edition of the manuscript and the accompanying English translation are intended to provide materials that will assist Renaissance specialists in a number of areas (art history, philology, history, musicology, Italian studies, and so on).

---

[1] I am particularly and deeply indebted to the kindness and expertise of Prof. Christopher Kleinhenz (University of Wisconsin-Madison) who has reviewed a previous draft of this study: he suggested several corrections to my translation and made copious comments on the manuscript. Prof. Kleinhenz was my professor and mentor when I was a graduate student at UW-Wisconsin, and he taught me paleography and philology, and ignited in me an everlasting passion for old manuscripts. I dedicate this study to him, with much gratitude, affection, admiration, and respect. Also, I am grateful to the College of Humanities at Brigham Young University for providing me with a grant to support some of the research and the writing of this article. I am indebted to the generosity of the Study Abroad Office of BYU for arranging my stay in Rome to consult the necessary archives in the Vatican Library. Dr. Elizabeth Burin and Dr. Roger Wieck, former Associate Curators of Manuscripts and Rare Books of the Walters Art Gallery in Baltimore, extended every courtesy to me during my several consultations of W720. Dr. William Noel, present Curator, has generously provided me with the photo of the coat of arms of W720, and granted permission to include the image in this article. Notwithstanding my gratitude to all who helped in this project, the responsibility for any omissions and errors, of course, remains my own.

The Cappella Giulia

The Cappella Giulia was founded in 1509 and sanctioned on 19 February 1513 by Pope Julius II (hence the Cappella's name), who signed a Bull to this effect just two days before his death. Although perhaps not as well known as the more prestigious Sistine Chapel Choir, the Julian Chapel singers were a very close second.

Unlike the singers of the Pontifical Sistine Chapel, the members of the Cappella Giulia choir also performed outside of St. Peter's in several other Roman churches (e.g. the church of St. John degli Spinelli—destroyed in 1849—mentioned in section [52] of the manuscript). In fact, several buildings in Rome belonged to the Cappella Giulia and were used as a means to increase revenue for the Cappella. The singers themselves received additional payments for services provided beyond those where their attendance was required.

The Papal Bull sanctioning the Cappella Giulia had provided for various administrative jobs, among which was that of "maestro" of music, although no further details were given. Owing to this vague "job description," the responsibilities associated with the post of "maestro" varied greatly, according to the personality of the incumbent.

After 1534, the "administrator" of the Julian Chapel was called the *magister cappellae*, and his duties were primarily supervisory and/or financial. In fact, the *magister cappellae* was a Prefect, a high prelate nominated from among the Canons by the Chapter of Saint Peter who remained in office for one year.[2] In his job as administrator, the *magister cappellae* authorized everyday, routine expenses. For instance, he was in charge of the bookkeeping and of contacting booksellers and bookbinders, among other duties.[3]

The *magister* was assisted by a *puntatore* (a "score keeper," so to speak), a position usually held by one of the oldest among the singers.[4] Following pre-established rules, the score keeper levied fines and penalties on a daily basis, through a well-established system of fines/points, on late and/or absent singers.

Pope Gregory XIII (26 May 1572 – 10 April 1585, the initiator of the Gregorian reform) insisted on hiring only qualified singers for the Cappella Giulia, and reduced the number of singers from twenty-four to twelve, subjecting them to the authority of two *maestri* (one of music, one of grammar). The pope insisted that the singers participate each day in the liturgical activities of Saint Peter's,

---

[2] Giancarlo Rostirolla, "La Cappella Giulia in San Pietro negli anni del magistero di Giovanni Pierluigi da Palestrina," in *Atti del Convegno di Studi Palestriniani 28 settembre–2 ottubre 1975*, ed. Francesco Luisi (Palestrina: Fondazione Giovanni Pierluigi da Palestrina, 1977), 99–283, here 113.

[3] Rostirolla, "La Cappella Giulia," 119.

[4] Rostirolla, "La Cappella Giulia," 112.

from which they could not be excused, except under extraordinary circumstances.[5] All singers were to attend all services.[6]

The Manuscript

W720 was purchased by Henry Walters in 1902 as part of the Don Marcello Massarenti collection (# 477), as confirmed by the large paper ticket glued on the front pastedown, and by the small sticker on the top center of the front cover.

W720 is not a unique document type. Perhaps the most direct and readily available model would be the *Constitution of the Papal Singers*, promulgated in 1545, and reprinted in Haberl.[7] The *Constitution* shows a delegation of authority similar to that seen in W720, and a somewhat similar schedule of fines. In fact, chapter XL of the *Constitution*, entitled "De Punctatore," describes in detail the role of the "score keeper" who was to be elected from among the most senior members of the Cappella, and from among those who had a clear understanding of the rules of the Pontifical Chapel. According to this *Constitution* the "puntatore," once in office, would enforce the Chapel's policies by "keeping score" and fining those singers who were not in compliance.

Although perhaps not unique in content, W720 is a very special document in many other ways. Its probable standing as a *codex unicus* is confirmed by two loose paper receipts housed in the archives of the Biblioteca Apostolica Vaticana.[8] These handwritten slips are signed by Paolo Ghiselli himself; the same handwritten signature is found three times in W720. Both receipts in the Vatican collection explicitly mention the content of W720, referring to it as the "book" (in the singular form) and thus implying that W720 was the only extant original manuscript.[9] The two receipts housed in the Biblioteca Apostolica Vaticana are dated 2 November 1574, and in both of them Paolo Ghiselli points to

---

[5] Ariane Ducrot, "Histoire de la Cappella Giulia au XVIᵉ siècle depuis sa fondation par Jules II (1513) jusqu'à sa restauration par Grégoire XIII (1578)," *Mélanges d'Archéologie et d'Histoire* 75 (1963): 179–240, 467–559, here 468.

[6] Rostirolla, "La Cappella Giulia," 129.

[7] Franz Xaver Haberl, "Die römische 'schola cantorum' und die päpstlichen Kapellsänger bis zur Mitte des 16. Jahrhunderts," *Bausteine für Musikgeschichte* 3 (1888): 96–108. Written in Latin, the titles of some of the chapters of *Constitutiones Cappellae Pontificiae* are "Novus cantor tenetur solvere duos ducatos per cotta," "De silentio observando stante divino officio," "De licentia exeundi extra chorum pro aliquo particulari negotio," "De cantore scandalum faciente," "De cantore infirmo," "De Punctatore."

[8] Both receipts are until now undocumented and unstudied. They are catalogued as Arch. Cap. S. Petri in Vat. (ACSP), Cappella Giulia, nº 429 "XCI — Cantori della Cappella Giulia," p. 134; ARM 20–23.

[9] I have not been able to uncover any other manuscript copies of Ghiselli's text, and I strongly believe that all evidence points to W720 as a *codex unicus*.

his authorship of W720. The content of both receipts is almost identical: Ghiselli authorizes Filippo Coccovagino, the collector ("esattore") of the Cappella Giulia, to reimburse 12 *julii* to Maestro Giovanni da Palestrina for the bookbinding expenses of W720.[10]

The first receipt in Ghiselli's hand reads:

> 1574. 2. Nov. Ordine di pagare a M(aestr)o Giovani da Palestrina Julii Dodici per le carte pecore e per la coperta e ligatura del libro delli Capitoli delli Cantori accomodati da noi. Io, Paulo Ghiselli.

> [2 November 1574. Request to pay 12 *Julii* to Maestro Giovanni da Palestrina for the parchments and for the cover and binding of the book on the Chapters of the Singers arranged by us. I, Paolo Ghiselli].

The second, somewhat longer, receipt reads:

> Io, Paulus Ghisellus, Can(oni)cus et Magister Cappellae. R(e)v(erend)o M(esser)o Philippo, Benefitiale di S(an) Pietro ed Exatore della Cappella Julia, pagarete a M(aest)r(o). Gio(vanni) da Palestrina Julii Dodici: p(er) le carte, Paj(occhi) cinquanta, et per la copperta et legatura del libro delli Capitoli delli Cantori accomodati da noi, che in t(ut)to sono julii 12, et mettetali a conto del mio salario. Dies 2 novembre 1574. Io Paulo Ghiselli.

> [I, Paolo Ghiselli, Canon and Magister Cappellae. Reverend gentleman Filippo [Coccovagino], beneficiary of St. Peter's and collector for the Cappella Giulia, you will pay 12 *julii* to Maestro Giovanni da Palestrina: fifty *baiocchi* for the papers, for the cover and the binding of the book on the Chapters of the Singers arranged by us, for a total of 12 *julii*, and which you should debit to my salary. The day 2 November 1574. I, Paolo Ghiselli.]

Even though Rostirolla documents a different and less detailed entry/receipt for this manuscript, he does not appear to be aware of the existence of W720 ("La Cappella Giulia," 265). The two receipts which I discovered in the archives of St. Peter's in Rome are interesting in that they reveal the particular financing behind the making of W720. Evidently, Palestrina advanced the sum of 12 *julii* for the bookbinder's work, and he was then reimbursed by Ghiselli the following month through what we would define today as an "automatic payroll deduction."

For the edition, I have attempted to reproduce the text as it appears in W720 with the expansion of abbreviations, addition of accent marks, and insertion of punctuation. I have also retained orthographic inconsistencies.

W720 can be divided into several segments, according to topic. For example, sections [2] and [42] discuss in detail the role of the *puntatore* who, as noted

---

[10] Rostirolla, "La Cappella Giulia," 264. Also, Rostirolla identifies Filippo Coccovagino as "esattore" for the year 1574.

above, was charged with assessing and collecting fines from those singers who did not follow the rules of the Cappella Giulia. He accomplished this task by assigning "penalty points" to behavioral infractions: every singer accumulated scores to which a monetary value was given, and then the singer was assessed a corresponding fine. The Italian words used most often in W720 to describe the penalty procedure and fines exacted are "punti" (points) and "puntare" (assign points). For the English version of W720, I have here translated these words interchangeably as "points," "fine," "score" (as nouns), and "to score," "to fine" (as verbs) to allow a better understanding of the original Italian text.

Sections [4] through [45] detail exactly when, why, and how singers could be fined for misconduct. Specifically, a few sections such as [31], [32], and [40] discuss the issue of unjustified vs. permissible absences; [33] treats the issue of surplices not worn, due to laundering; singers' job security and causes for dismissal can be found in [37], [39], and [41], among others. Specific days of duty are detailed in sections [46] through [60]. The addendum to the first part of the manuscript (parts [62] through the end) focuses on disciplinary actions to be taken against singers for behavioral infractions.

From a linguistic point of view, the text of the Walters manuscript is written in a central Italian dialect, with several words showing consistent variants typical of the time and place of composition. For example, we find Latinisms such as *stationi, beneditioni, distributione, lamentatione, vacantie,* as well as etymological *h* (*haveranno, hora, havendo/havuta, habito*). The ecclesiastical, learned form *escusare* (section [19], from Latin *ex-*) appears here, rather than the more common, central-Italian dialectal form *scusare*, and preference is given to the classical Latin form *fraude* for Italian *frode*.

On the other hand, *gir* (for *andare*) appears as a very popular form in central Italian of the time (from the hortative Latin *eìmus* > *giamo* > new verb *gire*). Also, the manuscript attests to the fact that in 1574, in Rome, the general rule that pretonic *a* tends to become *e* before an *r* is in a linguistic transitional phase: *mancarà, cascarà, levarà*; in the simple future, third person singular forms of first-conjugation verbs (*andare* follows the same pattern, *andarà*). These older forms are found alongside newer ones: *mancherà,* in [35] and [41], and *troverà* in [60], [64], and [66].

The example of onomatopoeic *ciarlare* (section [36], from Boccaccio [1375]) is noteworthy. Masculine plural definite articles *li* still retain their Latin derivative origin (from a plausible fusion of *illis* and *illi*). The medieval Latin word *communis* (*commune*, section [6] and others) has not yet begun its (rare) phenomenon of consonantic simplification to *comune* (generally, Italian shows a strong resistance to this tendency). Even though Italian had started to drop *i* after *l* in clerical Latin (*evangelium* > *vangelo*) by the thirteenth and fourteenth century, W720 has the clearly Latinate form *evangelio*.

The manuscript also displays examples of Roman dialect: e.g., gemination of single consonants in the words *doppo* (*dopo* < Latin *de post*) and *sabbato* (*sabato*).

The third person plural present subjunctive of the verb *dire*, *dichino* (for *dicano*, in standard Italian) shows a very strong Roman dialectal formation. Similarly, *l'ultimi* (for *gli ultimi*) is of central-Italian imprint, as is the rhotacism of l ($r < l$): *mercordì* (cl. Italian *mercoledì*) in section [46].

Four types of coins of the Papal States' monetary system are mentioned in W720 in reference to the fines: the *giulio*, the *baiocco*, the *scudo*, and the *carlino*. During the Renaissance, the most important mints in the Papal States were in Rome, Bologna, and Ancona. In 1508 the *giulio* was renamed (from the *grosso carlino*) in honor of Pope Julius II,[11] for he was the first Renaissance pope to have his own likeness used extensively on a coin. This coin, a "grosso largo" (that is, of larger-than-usual dimensions), was struck in silver and had been part of the papal monetary system since the thirteenth century. The *giulio* was worth one-tenth of a *scudo*.

The *baiocco* was worth one-tenth of a *giulio*, or one one-hundredth ($1/100^{th}$) of a *scudo* in 1574, the year in which W720 was written, and it was issued in base silver at that time. The *scudo*, a large silver coin, took its name from the word "shield," for it had armorial insignia on one of its faces. It was introduced as papal currency during the sixteenth century, and after 1545 it was struck in silver. The papal silver "grosso" coin known as the *carlino*, so called after the golden Neapolitan *carlino* of the Middle Ages, was worth one-half of a *giulio*.

In order to give a better idea of the impact which the fines imposed by the Chapel had upon its singers, I offer some terms of comparison from other coeval documents. For instance, according to Rostirolla and Ducrot, Giovanni Animuccia, the *magister cappellae* who immediately preceded Ghiselli, earned 8 *scudi* per month: this was approximately 3 *scudi* more per month than the pay of the adult singers of the Cappella Giulia. In 1575, the year after W720 was written, the *magister* earned 15 *scudi* per month, and the singers' salaries were increased to 7 *scudi* a month in 1578. Children in the choir (typically the soprano and alto voices) earned between 1 ½ and 3 ½ *scudi* per month.

Even more specifically, among the unstudied material contained in Arch. Cap. S. Petri in Vat. (ACSP), Cappella Giulia, n° 429, ARM 20–23 (134), there is a document signed by Paolo Ghiselli ("Paulus Ghisellus, Can[onicus] et M[a]g[ister] Cappell[ae]") that details the payments to each of the singers of the Cappella Giulia for the month of January of 1574. These "Pagam[enti] alli Cantori" ("Payments to the Singers") indicate, among other things, that Petro Aloysio, the *magistro cantorum*, was paid 8.33 *scudi*, that the three *bassi* earned 4, 6, and 7 *scudi* respectively, that three of the four *tenori* earned 4, 5, and 5 *scudi* and that the fourth tenor's salary was pro-rated that month at 1.66 *scudi*. We also learn that the four *alti* earned 5, 5, 6, and 7 *scudi* respectively and that the four *soprani*

---

[11] Giuseppe De Gennaro, *L'esperienza monetaria di Roma in età moderna (secc. XVI–XVIII): tra stabilizzazione ed inflazione* (Napoli: Edizioni Scientifiche Italiane, 1980), 30.

were paid 1, 1, 4, and 4 *scudi* respectively. "Marco [Houtermann] Organista," a.k.a. "Marco Fiamingo," earned 50 *baiocchi* that month, and Dionisio Malatestae, *magister grammatice*, was paid 2 *scudi*.[12]

Physical Description of W720

As noted above, W720, *Capitoli che hanno da osseruare gli Cantori della Cappella di San Pietro*, is a dated, autograph *codex unicus* by Paolo Ghiselli, a Canon of St. Peter's in Rome who oversaw the Cappella Giulia in 1574 in the role of the *magister cappellae*.[13]

The Walters Art Gallery's own files pertaining to this manuscript are helpful in describing the document's physical condition. The binding of W720 is still in its original state: a sixteenth-century dark green morocco (a soft, textured leather made of goatskin) presents a stamped gilt over the foliate design imprinted over the cardboard binding. The coat of arms of Ghiselli is impressed on a small oval leather inset in the center of the front cover. In the center of the back cover, the capital letters DECR. CAP. S.P. (presumably the abbreviated title of the book, rendered as *Decreti dei Capitoli di San Pietro*) are also gilded. The booklet is kept closed by four yellow ribbons of which three still remain.

The manuscript is in parchment, and consists of 22 folios (of which the first and the last are paper), and measures 16.4 x 11.7 cm. Each page is ruled in ochre ink, forming one wide column per page of 19 lines, with 6 mm. separating each line. The ruled column (10.7 x 7.1 cm.) is closed on the right and on the left by single vertical lines. The text, written in central Italian dialect, bears a clear and regular slanting Roman handwriting, in light brown ink. As this critical edition of W720 indicates, the light-brown-ink initial letter of each of the words denoting the twelve months (sections [47] through [58]) has been erased and replaced by a gold Roman capital letter. The collation shows two pastedown paper bifolia flyleaves (folio 1 and folio 22). Upon inspection under ultraviolet light at two different intensities, no watermarks were visible on the paper.

Paolo Ghiselli's signature appears three times: in sections [1], [61], and [79] ({2r}, {16v} and {20r}, respectively). His coat of arms appears not only on the binding, but also on the illustrated frontispiece (see illustration at the end of this

---

[12] Rostirolla, "La Capella Giulia," 246. Rostirolla specifies that Marco Houtermann actually earned a total of 3 *scudi* per month, of which 2.5 were paid by the Chapter and 0.5 by the Cappella Giulia.

[13] Paolo Ghiselli, the author of W720, was both Canon and Maestro di Cappella twice: in 1574, and again in 1578–1579. W720 reflects Ghiselli's double tenure: pages {1v} through {16v} are all written with the same ink and in the same handwriting. Pages {17v} through {20r} display a more mature handwriting (although clearly belonging to the same scribe, Ghiselli himself) and are in black ink.

article). In the upper half of the shield (in the center of the coat of arms), a small but fierce-looking lion, exhaling red flames, holds in its right paw a fleur-de-lis against a light blue background. The lower half of the shield depicts three azure fleurs-de-lis against a gilded background. On either side, the shield is supported by two nude maidens each holding the black tassels of a priest's flat hat hovering above the shield.[14]

Critical edition of W720

{2r} Capitoli che hanno da osservare Gli Cantori della Cappella di San Pietro.

[1] Io, Paolo Ghiselli, Canonico di S(an) Pietro di Roma, Deputato dal R(everen)do Cap(ito)lo alla cura della cappella per l'anno 1574. Dovendo, conforme al mio obligo provedere alli bisogni di essa cappella et principalmente all'officio de' cantori. Ordiniamo che si debbano osservare li Capitoli fatti già li anni passati per li R(everen)di s(igno)ri Maestri di Cappella. Accomodati da me ne l'infrascritto modo, de' quali acciò niuno possa pretender Ignoranza, vogliamo che siano descritti a notizia loro {2v} acciò li osservino, et quelli che trasgrediranno a detti Cappitoli siano puntati secondo l'ordine infrascritto.

[2] In primis, che si debbano fare due Puntatori delli medesimi cantori participa(n)ti, Incominciando dal Decano con il seguente doppo lui. Et debbano puntare tutti dua, per due mesi, et ciasch'uno debba puntare nel suo foglio finita la Messa, o vero il Vespro in presentia delli compag(n)i. Et debbano riscuotere li straordinarij che dà Il Capitolo et la Cappella, et li punti che faranno i cantori. Et questi debbano distribuire tra li participanti mese per mese et, nol facendo, debbano perdere La loro parte che gli toccarebbe tanto de {3r} straordinarij come delli punti. Et finito che haveranno li due mesi, debbano li altri due Cantori più antichi fare nel medesimo modo che haveranno fatto li primi, et così de mano in mano fino a l'ultimi seguendo l'ordine sottoscritto. Et si debba dare la lista delli Punti al pagatore primo che paghi Il mese; et per le loro fatiche debbano havere cioè delli punti cinque per cento.

---

[14] I would like to emend in this respect the notes of the Walters concerning the two leaning human figures on either side of the shield, for their enticing and somewhat seductive position, together with the size and shape of their hips and bosoms, best portrays them as young women, not as *putti* (as the collection's description of W720 indicates). See the illustration at the end of this article.

{2r} Chapters which the Singers of the Cappella of San Pietro Must Observe.

[1] I, Paolo Ghiselli, Canon of San Pietro in Rome, appointed by the reverend Chapter to the administration of the Cappella for the year 1574. In agreement with my obligations, I must provide for the needs of such Cappella, and mainly for the activity of the singers. We enjoin that chapters completed already in the previous years for the Reverend Signori Maestri di Cappella be observed. Arranged by me in the following written fashion, so that no one may claim ignorance of them, we want them to be described for their [the singers'] information, {2v} so that they may observe them. Those who will transgress said chapters will be fined according to these written rules.

[2] In the first place: that among the same participating singers, two are to be designated as score keepers, beginning with the Dean and his immediate subordinate. Both of them are to keep score for two months, and each of them must assign points on his sheet in presence of the co-singers at the end of Mass or of Vespers. They must collect overtime monies paid by both the Chapter and the Cappella, and the points which the singers will accrue. And they must distribute these [monies and fines from points] among the participants month by month. In failing to do so, they will lose their due share—{3r} both overtime and points. At the end of the two months, the next two most senior singers will perform in the same way the first two had, and so on until the last [singers], following the rules described below. The score list is to be given to the payer before he pays for the month. For their labor, [the score keepers] must therefore receive 5% of the points.

[3] Item, che se alcuno de' Cantori haverà ricevuto intieramente li denari del mese, prima che siano consignati li pu(n)ti al pagatore, se, in termine di quattro giorni del seguente mese non darà li suoi punti, cascherà in pena di due giulij, oltre alli punti fatti.[1]

[4] {3v} Item, Nelli giorni communi il punto sarà sei baiochi la Messa, et sei Il Vespro; et si punta in due volte, cioè: Tre baiochi al primo cantar della Messa, et altri tre finito l'Evangelio. Al Vestro[2] tre baiochi al cominciare della prima Antiphona facendosi contrapunto, et tre al cominciare del Hymno. Et quando non si fa contrapunto, Il primo punto si punta al primo cantar della Cappella, et il secondo al cominciare del Magnificat. Et nelle Feste solemni, et nelle stationi,[3] il pu(n)to sarà un giulio alla Messa, et uno al Vespro, partito come di sopra: come sarà segnato nella Tavola delle feste communi.

[5] Item, quando sono Messe Episcopali si punta nel medesimo modo che è detto di sopra. {4r} Nelle feste solenni, et quando antecede a dette Messe Episcopali, o vero, Canonicali Beneditioni, o vero altre cerimonie Eccl(es)iastiche. Il primo punto si punta al p(rim)o cantare apartinente alla Cappella. Il secondo ponto si punta al cominciare del Kyrie, cioè baiochi cinque per punto: che sono in tutto baiochi dieci.[4]

[6] Item, tutte le Feste che corrono fra l'anno, che sono guardate per Roma. Non essendo commune, si punta la Messa baiochi quattro et similmente Il Vespro; et si parte il detto punto come è detto di sopra nelli giorni communi.[5]

---

[1] Also included on this line, in lighter color ink, are two numbers: 6 and 20.

[2] It is evident that *Vestro* represents the scribe's error for the correct *Vespro*.

[3] The word *stationi* appears twice in W720: here and in section [46]. While I take this word to mean "stations" (for Stations of the Cross), there may be a second reading, namely *stagioni* (seasons) which could fit the text as well. My preference for "stations" is based on the wording of section [46] where the word "statione" appears together with "Lent" in the same sentence. Lent is the most appropriate season for the Stations of the Cross (specific locations in the church that correspond to certain precise moments in the Passion), with Good Friday being the most important day to celebrate this prayer service. The alternate reading *stagioni* stems from the fact that the reference in W720 might appear to be a more generic reference to the "Lent season." Linguistically, both readings are justified, because sonorization of $-ti > \breve{g}$ occasionally appears in writings of the time, favored by intervocalic position.

[4] Also included on this line, in lighter color ink, is the number 10.

[5] Also included on this line, in lighter color ink, is the number 4.

[3] *Item*: if any of the singers should receive all of his monies for the month, before his scores have been entrusted to the payer, if he will not give up his score within the four days of the following month, he will incur a penalty of 2 *giuli*, to be added to the points accrued.

[4] {3v} *Item*: during common days, the score will be of six *baiocchi* for Mass, and six for Vespers. Scores are assigned twice, that is to say three *baiocchi* at the song beginning Mass, and another three at the end of the Gospel. At Vespers, three *baiocchi* at the beginning of the first Antiphon with counterpoint, and three at the beginning of the Hymn. When there is no counterpoint, the first point is given at the first song of the Cappella, and the second at the beginning of the Magnificat. And on solemn feast days, and during the Stations,[1] the points given will be one *giulio* for Mass, and one for Vespers, to be distributed as above, as will be marked on the chart of common feast days.

[5] *Item*: for Episcopal Masses, scores are kept in the same way as described above. {4r} During solemn feast days, and when these precede the above-mentioned Episcopal Masses, or, similarly, canonical benedictions, or, similarly, other ecclesiastical ceremonies, the first point is assigned at the first song belonging to the Cappella. The second point is given at the beginning of the Kyrie; namely, five *baiocchi* per point, making a total of ten *baiocchi*.

[6] *Item*: on all feast days which occur during the year and are observed in Rome and which are not common, the score for the Mass is four *baiocchi* and likewise for Vespers. This score is distributed as said above for common days.

---

[1] See n. 3 on facing pages.

[7] Item, Tutti li giorni feriali, non essendo communi,[1] si punta: baiochi tre la Messa, et tre il Vespro, partito il punto come è detto di sopra nelli giorni communi.[2]

[8] {4v} Item, la notte della Natività di N(ostro) S(igno)re q(ue)lli che partecipano al cominciare del primo Hymno perdeno la distributione di due scudi, et al cominciare del Te Deum perdono la distributione delli altri due scudi, cioè di quelli quattro scudi che dà[3] Il capitolo et la Cappella.

[9] Item, chi non participa la sopradetta notte al cominciare del primo Hymno, si punta in dieci baiocchi; et al principio del Tedeum si punta altri dieci non si trovando presente. Et sono in tutto baiochi Vinti.[4]

[10] Item, Li Tre Matutini della Settimana San(ta) al cominciare della prima Antiphona si punta cinque baiochi. Il secondo punto si pu(n)ta al cominciare della prima lamentatione in dieci baiochi: che sono in tutto baiochi quindici.[5]

[11] {5r} Item, quando S(ua) S(anti)tà Viene in s(an) Pietro, et si ca(n)ta il Motetto, si punta al cominciare del Motetto baiochi Vinti; et chi starà senza cotta si punta come se non fosse presente.[6]

[12] Item, Il Venerdì santo si punta il p(rim)o punto al primo cantare che fa la Cappella: baiochi cinq(ue). Il secondo punto si punta al cominciare del passio: cinque altri baiochi. Che sono baiochi dieci.[7]

[13] Item, Il Sabbato S(an)to Il primo punto si punta al primo cantare della cappella: baiochi cinque. Il secondo punto si punta al cominciare del p(rim)o Kyrie: cinque altri baiochi. Che sono in tutto baiochi dieci.[8]

[14] Item, Nel tempo delle Vacantie si punta un giulio la Messa chi non si trova al cominciare dell'Introito. Et similm(en)te un Giulio si punta Il Vespro chi non si trova al cominciare del {5v} Hymno. Et li sopradetti giulij non si partono altrimente in due punti, per esser cosa importante il trovarsi in coro nel cominciare della Messa, et del Vespro.[9]

---

[1] MS *communi* written over *commune*.
[2] Also included on this line, in lighter color ink, is the number 3.
[3] MS *di*.
[4] Also included on this line, in lighter color ink, is the number 20.
[5] Also included on this line, in lighter color ink, is the number 15.
[6] Also included on this line, in lighter color ink, is the number 20.
[7] Also included on this line, in lighter color ink, is the number 10.
[8] Also included on this line, in lighter color ink, is the number 10.
[9] Also included on this line, in lighter color ink, is the number 10.

[7] *Item*: on all weekdays which are not common days, assigned scores are: three *baiocchi* for Mass and three for Vespers. The score is distributed as described above for common days.

[8] {4v} *Item*: the night of our Lord's Nativity, those who participate at the beginning of the first Hymn lose the distribution of two *scudi*, and at the beginning of the Te Deum lose the distribution of another two *scudi*, that is of those four *scudi* which are given by the Chapter and the Cappella.

[9] *Item*: whoever does not participate in the beginning of the first Hymn during the above-mentioned night is fined ten *baiocchi*, and at the beginning of the Te Deum is fined another ten, when still not present, making a total of twenty *baiocchi*.

[10] *Item*: for three Matins during Holy Week, at the beginning of the first Antiphon one scores five *baiocchi*. The next score is set at the beginning of the first lamentation, in the amount of ten *baiocchi*, making a total of fifteen *baiocchi*.

[11] {5r} *Item*: when His Holiness comes to San Pietro, and the Motet is sung, points [corresponding to] twenty *baiocchi* are assigned at the beginning of the Motet, and those not wearing the surplice are fined as though not present.

[12] *Item*: on Good Friday, the first point will be assigned during the first song that the Cappella is to sing: [amounting to] five *baiocchi*. The second score will be given at the beginning of the Passion: another five *baiocchi*, which are [a total of] ten *baiocchi*.

[13] *Item*: on Holy Saturday, the first point is assigned at the first song of the Cappella: five *baiocchi*. The second point is given at the beginning of the first Kyrie—another five *baiocchi*. These add up to ten *baiocchi*.

[14] *Item*: during the holiday period, for Mass, a fine of one *giulio* will be assessed to those who are not there by the beginning of the Introit. And similarly, one *giulio* will be assessed for Vespers to those who are not present by the beginning of the {5v} Hymn. And the aforementioned *giuli* will not be otherwise divided in two different points, for it is important to be ready in the choir at the beginning of Mass, and at Vespers.

[15] Item, che tutte le volte che alcuno de' Cantori lasciarà San Pietro, essendo commune per andare a cantare in altre Chiese, o con q(u)al si voglia compagnia de' Cantori, salvo che con quella di San Pietro, non havendo havuta licenza dal S(igno)re M(aest)ro di Cappella sarà puntato per ciasch'una volta: giulij cinque.[1]

[16] Item, che li Putti siano puntati secondo la provisione che hanno.

[17] Item, Quando si cantano Misse fuori di San Pietro, chi partecipa perde la distributione al cominciare del Kyrie, et finito lo Evangelio perde cinq(ue) baiochi oltre [al]la distributione.[2]

[18] {6r} Item, chi non partecipa si punta dieci baiochi: cioè cinque nel cominciare del p(rimo) Kyrie, et altri cinque finito l'Evangelio. Et sono in tutto baiochi dieci.[3]

[19] Item, Tutti le volte che si comincia la Messa et non sia finito di sonare, non si debba pu(n)tare. Et se alcuno, venendo tardo, si volesse escusare con dire che non sia finito di sonare, et che sia trovato in fraude, si punte un giulio per ciasch'una volta.[4]

[20] Item, Quando se intima la Congregatione che ogn'uno si debba ritrovare sotto pena di un giulio.[5]

[21] Item, Chi non fa la sua settimana secondo la Tavola et ordine delli Cantori in intonare Messe et antiphone, secondo il bisogno appartinente alla Cappella, et chi ma(n)carà {6v} di quest'ordine cascarà in pena di due baiochi per ciasch'una volta: cioè li giorni feriali, et le Feste quattro, et le solenni otto.

[22] Item, che tutti li Cantori nelli giorni co(m)muni et quando si canta Messa Vespro, Processioni, Te Deum, o vero Motetti in san Pietro fuori del nostro Coro, debbano portare la veste sotto la cotta. Et chi mancarà di questo ordine, si punterà un giulio per ciasch'una uolta.[6]

---

[1] Also included on this line, in lighter color ink, is the number 50.
[2] Also included on this line, in lighter color ink, is the number 5.
[3] Also included on this line, in lighter color ink, is the number 10.
[4] Also included on this line, in lighter color ink, is the number 10.
[5] Also included on this line, in lighter color ink, is the number 10.
[6] Also included on this line, in lighter color ink, is the number 10.

[15] *Item*: each time that any singer will leave San Pietro on a common day to go and sing in other churches, or with whichever other company of singers, except that of San Pietro, if he has not received permission from the Signor Maestro di Cappella, he will be fined five *giuli* for each occurrence.

[16] *Item*: that the children be scored according to their own wages.

[17] *Item*: when Masses outside St. Peter's are sung, those who participate will lose the distribution at the beginning of the Kyrie, and once the Gospel is over, they will lose five *baiocchi* besides the distribution.

[18] {6r} *Item*: he who does not participate is fined ten *baiocchi*, that is, five at the beginning of the first Kyrie, and the other five at the end of the Gospel, which add up to ten *baiocchi*.

[19] *Item*: each time Mass begins before the music has ended, one must not be fined. However, if someone should arrive late and use as an excuse the fact that the music was still playing, and should he be found cheating, the penalty is one *giulio* for each occurrence.

[20] *Item*: when the assembly [of singers] is notified that each should be there, under the penalty of one *giulio*.

[21] *Item*: he who does not work during the week according to his schedule and to the orders of the singers by intoning Masses and antiphons, and according to the needs of the Cappella, and he who will not adhere {6v} to this rule will be fined two *baiocchi* for each occurrence: that is, four [baiocchi] during week days and feast days, and eight [baiocchi] during solemn feast days.

[22] *Item*: that all singers must wear garments underneath the surplice during common days, and when they sing the Vespers Mass, during processions, the Te Deum and also for motets in San Pietro outside our chorus. Whoever will disobey this order will be fined one *giulio* for each occurrence.

[23] Item, Tutte le Processioni che si fanno fuori d(e)lla Scala di san Pietro, dove intervengano li S(igno)ri Canonici, a chi non partecipa al cominciare del primo Hymno, o vero Motetto, si punta dieci baiochi. Et cantato il p(rim)o Hymno, o vero Motetto si punta altri dieci baiochi: che sono in tutto vinti baiochi.[1]

[24] Item, chi partecipa cantando Il p(rim)o Himno, o vero {7r} Motetto, perde tutta la destributione; et non vi essendo estraord(ina)rio, perdono i participanti secondo il Capitolo delli non participanti: cioè baiochi vinti, partiti come di sopra.[2]

[25] Item, La Processione delle Palme a chi non si trova presente, si punta in tutto baiochi[3] dieci.

[26] Item, Le processioni che si fanno dentro le scale di S. Pietro si punta due baiochi per ciasch'una volta.[4]

[27] Item, Li due p(un)ti[5] che hanno a S. Biasio il dì dell'ottava del Santiss(im)o Sacramento: l'uno delli due scudi si mette per la Messa, et l'altro per la processione. Pu(n)tati nel medesimo modo che si puntano l'altre Messe et processioni fuor delle Scale di S(an) Pietro.

[28] {7v} Item, che morendo alcuno de' Cantori siano li altri obligati a accompagnare il Morto alla sepoltura. Et chi mancarà sia puntato in un giulio.[6]

[29] Item, che si habbia a cantare una Messa de' morti in termini d'otto giorni a ciasch'uno de' Cantori che morirano; et che alla predetta Messa s'habbiano a ritrovare tutti, alla pena d'un giulio, puntato nel medesimo modo che si puntano gli comuni. Et che si habbia a dimandare licenza al sig(no)r Can(oni)co M(aest)ro di Capp(ella) di poter lasciare l'officio di S(an) Pietro per fare queste due opere pie.

[30] Item, che la spesa che si farà per la sopradetta Messa de' Morti, non la potendo havere in dono dal Sig(no)r Can(oni)co Ma[e]stro di Cappella, l'habbiano a pagare tra Cantori ogn'uno la sua parte.

---

[1] Also included on this line, in lighter color ink, is the number 10.

[2] Also included on this line, in lighter color ink, is the number 20.

[3] MS *baiochi* written over *baiochr*. Also included on this line, in lighter color ink, is the number 18.

[4] Also included on this line, in lighter color ink, is the number 2.

[5] Abbreviations for the word *punti* are created quite consistently in W720 by writing a short vertical stroke on top of the vowel *u*, pu(n)ti. However, in this case the abbreviation seems to be formed by a cursive Greek π, followed by *ti* in superscript.

[6] Also included on this line, in lighter color ink, is the number 10.

[23] *Item*: all the processions which are held outside of the steps of San Pietro, and in which the Signori Canons participate. Whoever does not participate from the beginning of the first Hymn or Motet will be fined ten *baiocchi*. And once the first Hymn or Motet has been sung, one is fined another ten *baiocchi*, which makes a total of twenty *baiocchi*.

[24] *Item*: those who participate by singing the first Hymn or {7r} Motet miss the entire distribution; and since there is no overtime compensation, the participating singers lose according to the rules of those who are not present, that is twenty *baiocchi*, divided as above.

[25] *Item*: those who are not present for the procession on Palm Sunday are assessed a total of ten *baiocchi*.

[26] *Item*: the processions which are held within the steps of San Pietro are worth two *baiocchi* each time.

[27] *Item*: the two points which [the singers] have on Saint Blaise, on the day of the Octave of the Most Holy Sacrament. One of the two *scudi* is given for Mass, and the other for the procession, assessed in the same way in which the other Masses and processions beyond the steps of San Pietro are scored.

[28] {7v} *Item*: when one of the singers dies, the others are obliged to accompany the dead one to the place of burial, and he who is absent will be penalized one *giulio*.

[29] *Item*: a Mass for the Dead must be sung within eight days of the death of each deceased singer, and that all must be present at the above-mentioned Mass, under the penalty of one *giulio*, scored in the same way one scores for common matters. And one must request permission from the Signor Canonico Maestro di Cappella to be able to leave the function of San Pietro in order to attend to these two pious acts.

[30] *Item*: the expenses incurred for the above-mentioned Mass for the Dead, if they are not received as a gift from the Signor Canonico Maestro di Cappella, they must be paid for by the singers, each one his share.

[31] Item, che gli puntatori debbano avertire {8r} chi fusse ammalato, o vero havesse licenza di stare assente per sei giorni, partecipa delli punti di detti sei giorni. Et se passa questo termine non partecipa, né delli sei p(redet)ti giorni, né di quanti starà assente. Et se per Vinti giorni starà assente, non potrà participare per il mese intiero, ancora che serva il restante delli dieci giorni: et questi p(redet)ti dieci giorni si punta ancora che non partecipa.

[32] Item, Chi è fuor di Roma se in termine de Vinti giorni continui non tornerà, non possa participare dell'Introiti che pagano li Cantori, Per quel tempo che sta fuora, ancora che habbia licenza dal sig(nor) Canonico Mastro di Cappella di stare fuori.

[33] Item, Chi non si mette la Cotta et la porta alli tempi debiti si debba puntare come assente; et non sia accettata alcuna scusa eccetto {8v} quando si dà a lavare. Et tutte le volte che alcuno se la levarà alla Messa inanti la beneditione, et al Vespro ina(n)nti al Deo gra(tia)s, sarà puntato come assente.

[34] Item, Chi non ha pagato l'Introito non possa participare di niuno estraord(ina)rio che hanno li cantori, Dentro et fuori di S(an) Pietro, dove intervengano li S(igno)ri Canonici.

[35] Item, Chi andasse fuori di Roma con licenza, o vero fusse ammalato, sia obligato farlo sapere alla Compagnia. Et chi mancherà di questo sarà puntato di continuo come assente, insino a tanto che sia intimata la sua assentia.

[36] Item, Che li Puntatori debbano avertire li cantori di stare in piede alli tempi debiti. Et se ciarlano, l'amoniscano per una volta {9r} et poi li puntino in due baiochi per ciasch'una volta.[1]

[37] Item, S'alcuno delli Cantori si partesse dal servitio della Cappella, o vero per qualche disordine fosse mandato via, se in termine di sei mesi non piglia partito, et poi tornando al servitio di S(an) Pietro possa ritornare nel medesimo loco et ordine che stava prima. Ma passando li sei mesi che non torni al d(et)to servitio, debba tornare come ultimo nella lista de' Cantori. Et se fusse alcuno de' participanti, passando il predetto tempo o termine, non possa participare se di nuovo non paga l'intrata. Et se dentro il sop(raddet)to termine piglia partito in qual si voglia loco, subito pigliato perde ogni sua ragione che pretendesse havere con la Compagnia delli Cantori. Della p(redet)ta Cappella come se fossero passati li sei Mesi.

---

[1] Also included on this line, in lighter color ink, is the number 2.

[31] *Item*: the score keepers must forewarn {8r} that anyone who is ill, or who has permission to be absent for six days, [he] will take part in the score for those six days. If he goes beyond this time, he will not participate in either the six previous days, nor in those when he will be absent. And if he will be absent for twenty days, he will not be able to participate for the entire month even though he may serve for the remaining ten days. And for these above-mentioned ten days, he will be assessed [points] as though he has not participated.

[32] *Item*: he who leaves Rome and does not return within twenty consecutive days may not have his share [of the funds] which pays the singers for the period he is out of town, even though he may have permission from the Signor Canonico Maestro di Cappella to be absent.

[33] *Item*: he who does not wear the surplice at the proper moments will be fined as though absent. No excuse shall be accepted, except {8v} for when one gives it to be washed. For each time that one will take it off during Mass before the benediction, and during Vespers before the *Deo Gratias*, he will be fined as though absent.

[34] *Item*: whoever has not completed the Introit may not share in any of the overtime that the singers do within and outside San Pietro, wherever the Signori Canons are present.

[35] *Item*: he who leaves Rome with permission, or is ill, is obliged to make it known to the Company. And whoever fails to do so shall be continuously fined as though absent until the moment in which his absence is announced.

[36] *Item*: the score keepers must remind the singers to stand at the proper moments, and to warn them once if they chat, {9r} and subsequently fine them two *baiocchi* for each occurrence.

[37] *Item*: should any of the singers leave the services of the Cappella, or else if he should be sent away for disorderly conduct, if within six months he does not find employment and [wishes to] return to the service of San Pietro, then he may return to his same position, and order which he occupied previously. However, should he not return to such service within six months, he must return to the bottom of the list of singers, and should he wish to participate after such time or deadline, he may not do so until he has paid the entry fee again. If, within the above-mentioned time frame, he should gain employment in any other place, as soon as this happens, he will lose any right that he might claim to have with the Company of the Cantori of the above-mentioned Cappella, as though the six months had gone by.

[38] {9v} Item, Tutte le volte che si altera l'hora del sonare Il Vespro, et che non sia intimata alli Cantori, et che per questo disordine non possano venire a tempo, non si possa puntare.

[39] Item, Che niuno de' Cantori possa servire d(e)l suo giorno della settimana a qual si voglia altro Cantore, se non a quelli della parte sua: cioè Basso per basso, Tenore per Tenore, Contralto per Contralto, et soprano per soprano.

[40] Item, Se alcuno de' Cantori, essendo stato male et poi, rihavuta la sanità, andarà per Roma et non andarà al servitio di San Pietro, dal giorno che sarà visto andare per Roma sia puntato come se non fosse stato male. Et volendo andare a spasso, debbia prima andare a consegnarsi alla compagnia, eccetto se havesse havuto licenza dal sig(no)re Canonico Mastro di Cappella.

[41] {10r} Item, che se alcuno de Cantori Venesse tardo, et poiché vedendosi esser puntato si partisse, si debba puntare il doppio.

[42] Item, Che gli Puntatori siano tenuti mostrare li punti alli Compagni che li vorrano vedere, sotto pena di tre baiochi per volta. Et se saranno trovati in fraude siano pontati.[1]

[43] Item, Se lo Vltimo in ordine nella cappella non apparecchia li libri che fanno bisogno per cantare, ciasch'una volta che mancarà sarà puntato in baiochi Vinti per ciasch'una volta. Et quando è il suo giorno Vacante, o vero fusse ammalato, o fusse fuori di Roma con licenza, Il penul(tim)o in ord(in)e si punta nel med(esim)o m(od)o sop(raddet)to.[2]

[44] Item, Niuno de' Cantori possa do{10v}mandare licenza al Sig(nor) Can(oni)co M(aest)ro di Cappella per andare fuori di Roma, o in qual si voglia altro luoco quando alcuno della sua parte fossi fuori con licenza, o vero fusse a(m)malato, et chi mancherà del sop(raddet)to ordine sarà puntato in uno scudo di pena alla Compagnia.[3]

[45] Item, Che li quattro Cantori che offitiano Il Coro, Non possano haver Vancantie eccetto che il suo giorno della settimana. Et, volendo pigliare altri giorni senza licenza del sig(nor) Can(oni)co Mastro di Cappella, siano puntati dal Pontatore di Benefitiati cinque baiochi per ciaschedun giorno. Et le Feste siano puntati en uno carlino. Et quando si offitia in Coro, et che si cantano Antiphone, o Responsorij debbano andare in mezzo del coro dove sta il libro di Canto fermo {11r} et chi mancherà del sopradetto ordine sarà puntato come assente.

---

[1] Also included on this line, in lighter color ink, is the number 3.
[2] Also included on this line, in lighter color ink, is number 20.
[3] Also included on this line, in lighter color ink; is number 100.

[38] {9v} *Item*: every time that there is a change in the beginning hour of Vespers, and should this not be communicated to the singers, and, because of such misunderstanding they will not arrive on time, hence they will not be fined.

[39] *Item*: that none of the singers may exchange his day off with any other singer, except with those of their same voice range, i.e. basses with basses, tenors with tenors, contraltos with contraltos, and sopranos with sopranos.

[40] *Item*: if any of the singers, having first been sick and later feeling well again, shall go around Rome but shall not render his services in San Pietro, as of the day he was seen about Rome he will be fined as though he had not been sick. Should he desire to go for a walk, he must first report to the Company, unless he had received permission from the Signor Canonico Maestro di Cappella.

[41] {10r} *Item*: if any singer should arrive late and—noticing that he is being fined—should leave, he must be fined twice the amount.

[42] *Item*: that the score keepers are obliged to show the scores [accumulated] to their fellow singers upon request, under the penalty [of being fined] three *baiocchi* each time, and if they are found cheating, they will be fined.

[43] *Item*: if the last singer, according to the ranked order of the Cappella neglects to prepare the books which are needed to sing, each time he overlooks this, he will be fined twenty *baiocchi* for each time. And when it is his day off, or else should he be ill, or should he be away from Rome with permission, the second-to-last in the ranked order [of the Cappella will be responsible], and fines will be allocated as above.

[44] *Item*: none of the singers may {10v} ask Signor Canonico Maestro di Cappella for permission to leave Rome or to travel anywhere else when another singer of his same voice range is away with permission or is ill. Whoever disobeys this order will be fined one *scudo* as punishment by the Compagnia.

[45] *Item*: that the four singers who officiate at the choir may not take holidays except on one established day a week; should they wish to obtain more days without permission of the Signor Canonico Maestro di Cappella, they shall be fined by the score keeper of the beneficiaries: five *baiocchi* for each day, while feast days will be scored at one *carlino*. And while officiating at the choir, singing Antiphons or Responsories, they must go into the middle of the choir, where the book of chant is located. {11r} And he who fails to obey the above-described order will be fined as though absent.

[46] Li giorni Communi, et Feste Mobili di Tutto l'Anno: In primis, Tutte le Domeniche, per tutto Il giorno. Item, Tutti li giorni di statione a San Pietro nella quaresima. Item, Il primo giorno di quaresima commune, la mattina. Item, Tutte le esequie comune, la {11v} mattina per tutto l'anno. Il Mercordì, il Giovedì, Il Venerdì et sabbato della settimana santa si pagano scudi due per le lamentationi.

[47] Gennaro.[1] Il primo giorno della Circuncissione, per Tutto. La Vigilia della Epiphania, Il Vespro. Il Giorno della Epiphania, per Tutto. La Cathedra di San Pietro in Roma, per tutto.

[48] {12r} Febraro.[2] Il giorno della purificatione, la mattina. Il giorno di S. Biasio, si paga due scudi la mattina. La Cathedra di san Pietro, La Mattina. L'esequie de PaPa Giulio paga la cappella Due scudi la mattina. Il giorno di San Mattia Apostolo, La mattina.

[49] Marzo.[3] L'esequie di Nicola PaPa terzo[4] {12v} la mattina. Il Giorno di San Gregorio la Matt(in)a. Il Giorno dell'Annuntiatione della Madonna per tutto.

[50] Aprile.[5] Il Giorno di San Marco per la processione paga Il Capitolo Dui scudi, et altri Due la Cappella.

[51] Maggio.[6] Il Giorno di San Philippo et Giacomo, la mattina. {13r} La Messa al Volto Santo si pagano due scudi, Il giorno di santa Petronilla, la mattina.

---

[1] The black-ink capital letter G has been scraped off and replaced with a larger, gilded G.

[2] The black-ink capital letter F has been scraped off and replaced with a larger, gilded F.

[3] The black-ink capital letter M has been scraped off and replaced with a larger, gilded M.

[4] Even though the MS clearly indicates the word *terzo*, this must be regarded as the scribe's error, and *terzo* must be emended with the word *quinto* instead. It was Pope Nicholas V and not Pope Nicholas III who died on 24 March 1455. Hence, memorial funeral services held in March can refer only to those for Pope Nicholas V.

[5] The black-ink capital letter A has been scraped off and replaced with a larger, gilded A.

[6] The black-ink capital letter M has been scraped off and replaced with a larger, gilded M.

[46] Common days and moveable feast days for the entire year. First, all Sundays, the whole day long. *Item*: all of the days during Stations at San Pietro during Lent. *Item*: the morning of the first common day of Lent. *Item*: all common funerals the {11v} morning for the whole year. On Wednesday, Thursday, Friday and Saturday of Holy Week, two *scudi* are paid for Lamentations.

[47] January.[1] The first day of Circumcision, for the whole [day]. The Eve of Epiphany, for Vespers. The day of Epiphany, for the whole [day]. St. Peter's Chair, throughout Rome for the whole [day].

[48] {12r} February.[2] On the day of Purification, in the morning. On the day of St. Blaise, two *scudi* are paid in the morning. St. Peter's Chair, in the morning. The exequies for Pope Julius, the Cappella pays two *scudi*, in the morning. The day of St. Matthias the Apostle, in the morning.

[49] March.[3] The exequies for Pope Nicholas III, {12v} in the morning. The day of St. Gregory, in the morning. The day of the Holy Virgin's Annunciation, for the whole [day].

[50] April.[4] On St. Mark's day, for the procession, the Chapter pays two *scudi*, and another two *scudi* are paid by the Cappella.

[51] May.[5] The day of St. Philip and James, in the morning. {13r} Two *scudi* are paid for the Mass in honor of the Holy Face, and on the day of St. Petronilla, in the morning.

---

[1] These festivities were held on the following days: The Circumcision of Our Lord and Octave of the Nativity (Jan. 1); the Eve of Epiphany and the day of Epiphany (Jan. 5 and 6, respectively); St. Peter's Chair at Rome (Jan. 18).

[2] These festivities were held on the following days: Day of Purification of Mary (forty days after Christmas, Feb. 2); Saint Blaise (Feb. 3); St. Peter's Chair at Antioch (Feb. 22); the funeral for Pope Julius II (the pope who created the Cappella Giulia in 1513, Feb. 21); St. Matthias the Apostle (the current feast is on May 14. This feast used to be celebrated on February 24).

[3] These festivities were held on the following days: the funeral for Pope Nicholas V (see n. 4 on facing page); St. Gregory (March 12); the Annunciation (March 25).

[4] The feast day of St. Mark was held on April 25.

[5] These festivities were held on the following days: St. Philip and James (May 3); I was not able to find a date of celebration corresponding to the festivity of the Holy Face. Perhaps the Mass in front of the Holy Face might refer to a special Mass sung for the Holy Face (i.e., the Veronica which is housed in St. Peter's—now in the area around the high altar) on the day of Saint Petronilla (May 31).

[52] Giugno.[1] Il giorno di santo Antonio di Padoa, la mattina. Il giorno di san Gioan Battista alli Spinelli et si paga uno scudo, per tutto. La Vigilia delli Apostoli Pietro et paolo, per tutto. {13v} Il Giorno di san Pietro et Paolo, per il matutino, si paga scudi due. La Terza Domenica si mostra la Testa di Santo Andrea Apostolo.

[53] Luglio.[2] Il dì dell'ottava delli Apostoli, la mattina. Il dì di San Giacomo, paga la cappella uno scudo. Il giorno di santa Anna la Matt(in)a.

[54] Agosto.[3] {14r} Il Giorno di san Pietro in Vincula, per tutto. La Vigilia dell'assontione, Il Vespro. Il giorno dell'assontione, per tutto. I(l) giorno di S(an) Batholomeo Apostolo, per tutto.

[55] Settembre.[4] La Natività della Madonna, per tutto. Il giorno di San Mattheo Apostolo, per tutto. {14v} Il giorno di San Michele Arcangelo, per tutto, et paga la cappella Vno scudo.

[56] Ottobre.[5] Il giorno di San Francesco, per tutto. Il giorno di San Luca, per tutto. La Vigilia di San Simone et Juda, Il[6] Vespro. Il giorno di San Simone et Juda, per tutto. La Vigilia de Tutti Santi, Il Vespro.

---

[1] The black-ink capital letter G has been scraped off and replaced with a larger, gilded G.
[2] The black-ink capital letter L has been scraped off and replaced with a larger, gilded L.
[3] The black-ink capital letter A has been scraped off and replaced with a larger, gilded A.
[4] The black-ink capital letter S has been scraped off and replaced with a larger, gilded S.
[5] The black-ink capital letter O has been scraped off and replaced with a larger, gilded O.
[6] MS *Il* written over *e*.

[52] June.¹ On the day of St. Anthony of Padua, in the morning. The day of St. John the Baptist at the Spinelli, and one *scudo* is paid, for the whole [day]. The Eve of St. Peter and Paul Apostles, for the whole [day]. {13v} On the day of St. Peter and Paul, two *scudi* are paid for *Matins*. On the third Sunday the head of St. Andrew the Apostle is displayed.

[53] July.² The day of the Octave of the Apostles, in the morning. On St. James' day, the Cappella pays one *scudo*. On St. Ann's day, in the morning.

[54] August.³ {14r} On the day of St. Peter in Chains, for the whole [day]. On the Eve of the Assumption, for Vespers. Assumption day, for the whole [day]. On the day of St. Bartholomew the Apostle, for the whole [day].

[55] September.⁴ The Nativity of the Virgin Mary, for the whole [day]. The day of St. Matthew the Apostle, for the whole [day]. {14v} On the day of St. Michael the Archangel, for the whole [day], and the Cappella pays one *scudo*.

[56] October.⁵ On St. Francis' day, for the whole [day]. On the day of St. Luke, for the whole [day]. On the Eve of St. Simon and Jude, for Vespers. On the day of St. Simon and Jude, for the whole [day]. On the Eve of All Saints, for Vespers.

---

[1] These festivities were celebrated on the following days: Saint Anthony of Padua (June 13); St. John the Baptist (to be celebrated in Rome on June 24, in the Church of the Spinelli which was destroyed in 1849); the eve and the day of Ss. Peter and Paul the Apostles (June 28 and 29, respectively).

[2] These festivities were celebrated on the following days: the Octave of the Apostles (July 6, the eighth and final day of celebration for the feast of Ss. Peter and Paul Apostles on June 29); St. James (July 25); St. Ann (July 26).

[3] These festivities were celebrated on the following days: St. Peter in Chains (San Pietro in Vincoli, Aug. 1; the feast lasted for 8 days); the eve and the day of the Assumption (August 14 and 15, respectively); St. Bartholomew (Aug. 24).

[4] These festivities were celebrated on the following days: Nativity of the Virgin Mary (Sept. 8); St. Matthew (Sept. 21); St. Michael Archangel (Sept. 29).

[5] These festivities were celebrated on the following days: St. Francis of Assisi (Oct. 4); St. Luke (Oct. 18); the eve and day of Ss. Simon and Jude (Oct. 28); the Eve of All Saints' (Oct. 31).

[57] {15r} Novembre.[1] Il giorno de tutti Santi, per tutto. Il giorno delli Morti, la Mattina. Il giorno di S(an)to Maguto, la Mattina, paga la Cap(pel)la i.[2] La Vigilia della Dedicatione della Chiesa, Il Vespro. Il giorno della Dedicatione, per tutto. Il giorno di Santa Chaterina, per la mattina paga il Capitolo Scudo Vno. Il giorno di Santo Andrea Apostolo, per tutto.

[58] {15v} Decembre.[3] Il giorno della concettione, per tutto. Il giorno di San Thomasso paga il capitolo uno scudo, et uno ne paga la Cappella. La Vigilia di Natale, con due dì seguenti, paga Il Capitolo dui scudi, et altri due ne paga la Capp(el)la.

[59] La Vigilia della Circuncisione, Il Vespro. Il dì di Pasqua, Il motetto la Mattina, per tutto. Il secondo dì di Pasqua, Il motet{16r}to, per tutto. Il Terzo dì di Pasqua, per tutto. Il giorno dell'Ascensione si mostra la Coltra, per tutto. La Vigilia della Pentecoste, per tutto. Il giorno della Pentecoste il Motetto, la Mattina, per tutto. Il Secondo giorno della Pentecoste, per tutto. Il terzo dì della Pentecoste, per tutto. La Vigilia del corpo di Christo, Il Vespro. {16v} Il giorno del Corpo di Christo, per tutto. L'ottava del corpo di Christo, la mattina a San Biasio; et il Vespro a San Pietro per causa della processione, et si pagano due scudi: Vno dal Capitolo, et l'altro dalla Cappella.

[60] Item, che ogn'anno si debba cantare una Messa di morti per li cantori defunti dentro l'ottava de ogni Santi, et chi non vi si troverà, si punti un giulio, partito nel med(esim)o modo delli com(m)uni.[4]

[61] Io, Paulo Ghisellj, Canonico et mastro di Capella.[5]

[62] {17r}[6] Capitoli aggiu(n)ti alle antiche constit(uzio)ne di Cantori de La Cappella di sa(n) Pietro.

---

[1] The black-ink capital letter N has been scraped off and replaced with a larger, gilded N.
[2] This sentence has been compressed between the previous and the following sentences. It has been added by the same hand who writes the rest of the manuscript, in a finer pen and in darker ink.
[3] The black-ink capital letter D has been scraped off and replaced with a larger, gilded D.
[4] Also included on this line, in lighter color ink, is the number 10.
[5] Signature of Paolo Ghiselli.
[6] From this point on in the MS, the ink is of a lighter color, apparently the same color of the numbers written in the right-hand margin of the MS, as indicated so far in these footnotes. The writing, clear and regular, seems to be by a different hand.

[57] {15r} November.¹ On All Saints' Day, for the whole [day]. On the Day of the Dead, in the morning. On the day of St. Maguto, in the morning, for which the Cappella pays one. On the Eve of the Church's Dedication, for Vespers. On the day of Dedication, for the whole [day]. On the day of St. Catherine, in the morning, for which the chapter pays one *scudo*. On the day of St. Andrew the Apostle, for the whole [day].

[58] {15v} December.² On the day of the [Immaculate] Conception, for the whole [day]. On the day of St. Thomas, the chapter pays one *scudo*, and another one is paid by the Cappella. On Christmas Eve and on the two following days the Chapter pays two *scudi*, another two are paid by the Cappella.

[59] On the Eve of the Circumcision, for Vespers. On Easter day, the Motet in the morning, for the whole [day]. The second day of Easter, the Motet {16r}, for the whole [day]. On the third day of Easter, for the whole [day]. On Ascension day, the pall is [to be] exposed for the whole [day].³ On the day before Pentecost, for the whole [day]. On the day of Pentecost, the Motet in the morning, for the whole [day]. On the second day of Pentecost, for the whole [day]. On the third day of Pentecost, for the whole [day]. On the Eve of Corpus Christi, for Vespers. {16v} On the day of Corpus Christi, for the whole [day]. The Octave of Corpus Christi, the morning of St. Blaise and Vespers in San Pietro, because of the procession. And two *scudi* are paid, one by the chapter, and the other one by the Cappella.

[60] *Item*: each year, within the Octave of All Saints, a Mass for the Dead must be sung for those singers who have passed away. And those who will not be present will be fined one *giulio*, divided in the same ways as the common days.

[61] I, Paolo Ghiselli, Canon and Maestro di Cappella.⁴

[62] {17r} Chapters Added to the Old Constitutions of the Singers of the Cappella of San Pietro.

---

¹ These festivities were celebrated on the following days: All Saints' Day (Nov. 1); the Day of the Dead (Nov. 2); St. Maguto (St. Malo/Maclovius or Machutus, Nov. 15); the eve and day of the feast of the dedication of the Churches of Peter and Paul (Nov. 17 and 18, respectively); St. Catherine (Nov. 25); St. Andrew Apostle (Nov. 30).
² These festivities were celebrated on the following days: the Immaculate Conception (Dec. 8); St. Thomas (Dec. 21); Christmas Eve (Dec. 24).
³ Ascension Day was celebrated on the Thursday of the sixth week after Easter.
⁴ See n. 5 on facing page.

[63] In prima, si ordina da osservarsi inviolabilm(en)te che ciascuno di essi Ca(n)tori debba esser prese(n)te al primo verso dell'Hinno di Matutino, sotto pena di tre baiocchi. Et parimente se non sarà in Choro al terzo notturno quando si farà l'ufficio doppio: cioè di nove lettioni. Overo se si farà di Feria, o di Santo semplice, al sesto salmo, caderà in pena di dua baiocchi.

[64] Et più, chi di essi Ca(n)tori non si troverà presente almeno alla Gloria del primo Salmo, di Prima, Terza, Sesta et Nona, per ciascuna di esse hore sarà pontato in un baiocco.

[65] Et più, chi no(n) sarà p(rese)nte al primo Kirie della Messa de' Morti caderà in pena di due baiocchi.

[66] Et più, chi no(n) si troverà p(rese)nte alla replica dell'introito della messa gra(n)de perderà due baiocchi.

[67] Et più, chi non si troverà p(rese)nte alla gloria del primo salmo del Vespro caderà in pena di tre baiocchi.

[68] Et più, chi no(n) si troverà prese(n)te alla gloria del primo Salmo della Compieta sarà punito in un baiocco.

[69] Et più, chi non si troverà p(rese)nte al Notturno dell'ufficio dei Morti quando si haverà da dire, perderà un baiocco.

[70] {17v} Et perché dove si tratta del Colto Divino è conveniente non solo stare nel Choro con atte(n)tione et riverenza, ma ancora prestare il debito silentio. Però si ordina che nessuno di essi Cantori presuma né ardisca far tomulto o romore, né ragionare fra essi, né con altri, sotto pena di un baiocco. Et se perseverrà nel ragionare, debba il loro Pontatore radoppiare il ponto per ogni volta che quel Tale sarà ammonito. Et se a[l]l'ultimo vorrà persistere nella sua pertinacia, sarà po(n)tato per tutta la giornata.

[71] Et più, si ordina che il loro Maestro di Cappella debba ogni settimana eleggere dui Cantori: o Soprani, o Contralti per ordine in giro. Che senza replica si essibisca(no)[1] pronti con il libro delle Preci o Litanie ordinate da sua santità. Et l'habbino con Charetà, et Relligione a cantare in Choro, o in Chiesa, et dove sarà bisogno. {18r} Et che gl'altri cantori rispondino unitamente come è debito, altrimente siano pontati in cinq(ue) baiocchi per ciascuno.

---

[1] MS *essibisca(no)* written over *essibisce*.

[63] In the first place, it is ordered and must be duly observed that each of the singers must be present at the first verse of the morning Hymn, under the penalty of three *baiocchi*. And likewise if the singer will not be present in the choir during the third nocturn, when a double office is performed, that is nine lessons; or when the office is held during a feast day, or during a simple holy day, [if not present] at the sixth Psalm, the singer will be penalized two *baiocchi*.

[64] In addition, whoever among the singers will not be present at least for the Gloria of the first Psalm at the first, third, sixth, and ninth [hours], for each of these hours, he will be penalized one *baiocco*.

[65] In addition, whoever will not be present during the first Kyrie of the Mass for the Dead, he will be fined two *baiocchi*.

[66] In addition, whoever will not be present at the reprise of the Introit of the main Mass, he will lose two *baiocchi*.

[67] In addition, whoever will not be present at the Gloria of the first Psalm of Vespers, he will be penalized three *baiocchi*.

[68] In addition, whoever will not be present during the Gloria of the first Psalm of Compline will be punished in [the amount of] one *baiocco*.

[69] In addition, whoever will not be present at the nocturn of the office for the dead, when words are uttered, he will lose one *baiocco*.

[70] {17v} And for that which concerns the Holy Service, it is proper not only to be present in the choir with attention and reverence, but also to remain in due silence. Therefore, it is ordered that none of the singers presume nor dare to cause turmoil, nor to make noise, nor to speak among themselves, nor with others, under the penalty of one *baiocco*. And should he persist in talking, the score keeper must double the points for each time that such individual will be warned. And if, in the end, he will want to persist in his stubbornness, he will be penalized for the whole day.

[71] In addition, it is ordered that every week their Maestro di Cappella will choose two singers, either a Soprano, or a Contralto, alternatively, who, without rehearsing, will be ready to perform [from] the book of the Prayers, or the Litanies ordered by His Holiness. They will sing with charity and piousness, either together with the Choir or in the church, and wherever there might be the need. {18r} And that the other singers must respond in unison as is necessary, or else they be fined five *baiocchi* each.

[72] Et perché si vede che vi sono alcuni di essi cantori che trascuratame(n)te van(n)o fuggendo la schuola di non volere talvolta cantare, né rispondere alle cose che son tenuti, ascondendosi talhor dietro al Lettorino, o dove torna loro comodo, per provvedere a tale inco(n)veniente, si ordina che il loro Maestro di Cappella, o Po(n)tatore ci tenga l'occhio adosso; et gli essorti ad astenersi da tal trascuragine, sotto pena arbitraria. Advertendo che se[1] il detto Pontatore darà occasione da[2] dolersi di lui, cioè che egli no(n) ponti rigorosame(n)te tutte le cose sopradette et quelle che sieguono, caderà in pena di mezzo scudo ogni volta che per sua negligenza sa caderà ne' disordini sopradetti.

[73] {18v} Et più, si ordina che nessun Cantore, ta(n)to Prete qua(n)to Laico, presuma entrare non solo in Choro, ma neanche in Chiesa senza l'habito clericale, cioè: veste lunga, Cotta, beretta et colari lisci, conforme a tutto il clero. Et che finiti gl'ufficij Divini ritornino a spogliarsi nelle loro stanze ove si sono vestiti, sotto pena di perdere tutta la giornata ogni volta che co(n)traverran(n)o.

[74] Et più si statuisce che ciascuno di essi Cantori sieda al luogo suo per ordine, cominciando dal primo Prete, di mano in mano per grado. Et stiano dinanzi al Lettorino, et non dietro, acciò possino vedere quel che hanno a cantare senza impedimento. Et faccino il loro debito sempre con riverenza, charità et religio(n)e.

[75] Et più, che nessuno di essi Cantori presuma partirsi di Choro mentre durano gl'ufficij Divini senza espressa licenza {19r} del Maestro di Cappella, et in sua asse(n)za del Pontatore, i quali no(n) siano però facili a concederglela, eccetto se non fusse qualche urgente necessità. Acciò non si dia campo et addito che il Choro resti solo, overo con poco numero, che sarebbe scandalo di no(n) poca importanza. Et poi che i Cantori ha(n)no a portare sopra le loro spalle questa soma spirituale di tutto il Choro, si sforzino a esser presenti più che possono, 'sendo honore loro, et gloria del signor, sotto pena arbitaria.

[76] Et più, che ogni volta che si verrà al gloria P(at)ri di tutti li Salmi, essi Cantori si levino in piedi con la beretta in mano, 'sendo cosa di molta importanza. Acciò che il Popolo p(rese)nte, sotto questo essempio, stia desto et vigila(n)te[3] ad un atto sì notabile, sotto pena di un baiocco.[4]

---

    [1] The word *se* is inserted as a superscript, and clearly marked as such (^), between *che* and *il*.
    [2] MS *da* written over *di*.
    [3] MS *stia desto et vigila(n)te* written over *stiano desti et vigila(n)ti*.
    [4] *sotto pena di un baiocco* in lighter color ink.

[72] And since one observes that some of these singers carelessly cut school, for they do not want to sing at times, nor be responsible for their duties, hiding at times behind the music stand, or wherever else they may find it convenient, in order to take care of such unbecomingness, it is ordered that their Maestro di Cappella or the score keeper keep an eye on them, and exhort them to abstain from such negligence, under an arbitrary penalty. It is warned that if the above-mentioned scorekeeper should himself become the object of complaints, that is, if he will not penalize rigorously for all the above-mentioned infractions and for those here to follow, he himself will be penalized one-half of a *scudo* each time that for his negligence [the singers] will fall in the aforementioned disorderly conduct.

[73] {18v} In addition, it is ordered that no singer, neither priest nor layman, dare to enter either the choir or the church without the clerical habit, that is the long robe, the surplice, the cap, and the smooth collars, which are the same for all the clergy. At the conclusion of the Holy Services the singers must return to undress in their same quarters where they had dressed, under the penalty of losing the whole day's [wage] every time they transgress.

[74] In addition, it is established that each of such singers will sit at his assigned seat, in the [correct] order, beginning with the first priest and so on by rank. And they [must] remain in front of the music stand, not behind it, so as to be able to view that which they need to sing without obstructions. They also must render their duty always with reverence, charity, and solemnity.

[75] In addition, no singer dare leave the choir while the Divine Services are in progress without explicit permission {19r} of the Maestro di Cappella, or in his absence, of the score keeper, who in turn should not be so easy to grant it, except for some urgent necessity. Such [measures are necessary] so as not to offer the possibility to point out a choir left without direction, or with few singers, which would raise a scandal of no little importance. Thus, since the singers have to bear the spiritual burden of the whole choir, let them strive to be present as often as possible, for this redounds to their honor, and to the Lord's glory, under an arbitrary penalty.

[76] In addition, every time one arrives at the *Gloria Patri*, with all the Psalms, the singers will stand and hold their cap in their hands, [this] being an event of great importance. Therefore the attending populace, through this example, will be impressed and attentive to such a remarkable act, under the penalty of one *baiocco*.

[77] {19v} Et più, che il Maestro di Capella elegga ogni settimana un Cantore eddomedario idoneo et atto, che con ogni studio et diligenza habbia a guidare et ordinare il Choro per evitare gl'errori che molti sono. Et La sera, doppo che sono finiti tutti gl'ufficij Divini, se ne resti in Choro ad acco(m)modare per la seguente giornata l'antifonarij, et libri. Et nell'ufficio doppio, o semidoppio, preintonare l'antifone, ripeterle, segnarle, et prevenire dove sarà opportuno, conforma(n)dosi con la Tavola che affigge il M(aest)ro di Cerimonie. Et che egli sia il primo a levarsi per gir verso gl'antifonarij co(n) prontezza, et decoro. Et che il resto de' Cantori il sieguano co(n) debito modo, acciò si possa con verità dire che la Chiesa di san Pietro è almeno retta, et guidata da persone no(n) meno religiosi, et prudenti di quel che siano sufficienti, et Vertuosi!

[78] {20r} Et più, che il sop(raddet)to Eddomedario debba sempre ammaestrare, et prevenire li soprani Cantori quando vanno a fare e versi, o altra spirituale attione, andandogli appresso per remomorargli le cose che hanno a dire, acciò non dichino o cantino una cosa per un'altra, per la poca isperienza che hanno delle cose di tanta importanza.

[79] Io, Paulo Ghïsellj, Canonico et Mastro di Capella.[1]

---

[1] [79] is in the same handwriting as the first part of the MS, sections [1] through [61]. Signatures appearing in [1], [69], and [79] are identical.

[77] {19v} In addition, every week the Maestro di Cappella will choose a capable and suitable singer of the week. This person will lead and direct the choir with every consideration and diligence to avoid the mistakes which are many. At night, after all the Divine services are over, he will remain at the choir to attend to the antiphonaries and the books for the following day. And when during a double office, or a semi-double office, he will pre-intone the Antiphons, repeat them, mark them, and anticipate them where necessary, conforming to the charts posted by the Master of Ceremonies. Let him be the first to rise and turn toward the antiphonaries, with promptness and dignity, and let the rest of the singers follow him in the right way, so that it may be said in truth that the Church of San Pietro is at least righteous and led by people who are no less religious and prudent than they are efficient and virtuous!

[78] {20r} In addition, the above-mentioned singer of the week must always mentor and supervise the soprano singers when they are about to sing verses or engage in other spiritual action, shadowing them, quietly suggesting to them the things that they must say, so that they do not say or sing one thing for another, due to the little experience which they have with things of such importance.

[79] I, Paulo Ghiselli, Canon and Maestro di Cappella

Works Cited

Adami, Andrea. *Osservazioni per ben regolare il coro de i cantori della cappella pontificia*, ed. Giancarlo Rostirolla. Lucca: Libraria Musicale Italiana, 1988.
Arch. Cap. S. Petri in Vat. (ACSP), Cappella Giulia, n° 429 "XCI—Cantori della Cappella Giulia" ARM 20–23, 134.
Attwater, Donald. *The Avenel Dictionary of Saints*. New York: Avenel Books, 1981.
Brauner, Mitchell P. "Music from the Cappella Sistina at the Cappella Giulia." *Journal of Musicology* 3 (1984): 287–311.
Capelli, Adriano, ed. *Dizionario di abbreviature latine ed italiane*. Milan: Hoepli, 1990.
Cribb, Joe, Barrie Cook, and Ian Carducci. *The Coin Atlas: The World of Coinage from Its Origins to the Present Day*. New York: MacDonald, 1990.
Dean, Jeffrey J. "The Repertory of the Cappella Giulia in the 1560s." *Journal of the American Musicological Society* 41 (1988): 465–90.
De Gennaro, Giuseppe. *L'esperienza monetaria di Roma in età moderna (secc. XVI–XVIII): tra stabilizzazione ed inflazione*. Naples: Edizioni Scientifiche Italiane, 1980.
Ducrot, Ariane. "Histoire de la Cappella Giulia au XVIe siècle depuis sa fondation par Jules II (1513) jusqu'à sa restauration par Grégoire XIII (1578)." *Mélanges d'Archéologie et d'Histoire* 75 (1963): 179–240, 467–559.
Enciclopedia cattolica. 12 vols. Vatican City: Ente per l'Enciclopedia cattolica e per il libro cattolico, 1949.
Frey, Albert. *Dictionary of Numismatic Names*. New York: Barnes & Noble, 1947.
Grandgent, Charles H. *From Latin to Italian: An Historical Outline of the Phonology and Morphology of the Italian Language*. 3rd ed. Cambridge, MA: Harvard University Press, 1927.
Haberl, Franz Xaver. "Die römische 'schola cantorum' und die päpstlichen Kapellsänger bis zur Mitte des 16. Jahrhunderts." *Bausteine für Musikgeschichte* 3 (1888): 96–108.
Hucke, Helmut. "Zu einigen Problemen der Choralforschung." *Die Musikforschung* 11, (1958): 385–414.
Junge, Ewald. *World Coin Encyclopedia*. New York: William Morrow & Co., 1984.
Llorens, José M. "Iconografia e araldica nel fondo musicale della 'cappella Giulia' del Vaticano." *Rivista italiana di musica* 21 (1986): 236–65.
Moroni, Gaetano. *Dizionario di erudizione storico-ecclesiastica*. Venice: Tipografia emiliana, 1841.
———. *Histoire des Chapelles Papales*. Paris: Sagnier et Bray, 1846.
Pei, Mario A. *The Italian Language*. 2nd ed. New York: Vanni, 1954.
Reynolds, Christopher A. *Papal Patronage and the Music of St. Peter's, 1380–1513*. Berkeley: University of California Press, 1995.
Rostirolla, Giancarlo. "La Cappella Giulia in San Pietro negli anni del magistero di Giovanni Pierluigi da Palestrina." In *Atti del Convegno di Studi*

Palestriniani 28 settembre–2 ottobre 1975, ed. Francesco Luisi, 99–283. Palestrina: Fondazione Giovanni Pierluigi da Palestrina, 1977.

Sherr, Richard. "Competence and Incompetence in the Papal Choir in the Age of Palestrina." *Early Music* 22 (1994): 607–29.

———. "From the Diary of a 16th-Century Papal Singer." *Current Musicology* 25 (1978): 83–98.

———. "Notes on Two Roman Manuscripts of the Early Sixteenth Century." *Musical Quarterly* 63 (1977): 48–73.

Weiser, Franz X. *Handbook of Christian Feasts and Customs: The Year of the Lord in Liturgy and Folklore*. New York: Harcourt, Brace & World, 1952.

Figure 1: The illustrated frontispiece of W720, bearing Paolo Ghiselli's coat of arms.

Section VI

Renaissance Petrarchism
and *Petrarchiste*

LETTERE DI UNA DONNA INCERTA: UNPUBLISHED LETTERS AND SONNETS OF CHIARA MATRAINI

Veena Kumar Carlson

In 1953 Luigi Baldacci published his article "Chiara Matraini Poetessa Lucchese del XVI Secolo," in the journal *Paragone*, introducing the poet to modern scholars.[1] His article is part of a process that Pamela Joseph Benson and Victoria Kirkham have described as "the recovery" of women's "largely forgotten history."[2] In *Strong Voices, Weak History* Benson and Kirkham address the treatment of women writers from the medieval and early modern periods: "Women's presence in national literary histories, generally speaking, has been less stable than men's, their niches more shallow or precarious, their memory more quickly occluded by time." This is in fact the case for Matraini, a female lyricist, who wrote her own *canzoniere* and modeled her poetic production on that of Petrarch and his followers. It is only in the last thirty years that the real "recovery" of Matraini's literary production has occurred.

Baldacci, in his article, mentions a man named Cesare Coccapani, describing him as "un oscuro podestà di Modena." However, Baldacci does not elaborate on Matraini's ties to Coccapani. In 1981, picking up the threads of the Matraini story, Giovanna Rabitti published her article "Linee per il ritratto di Chiara Matraini" in *Studi e Problemi di Critica Testuale*. For those interested in Matraini it proved to be a seminal work. Since that time, many scholars have made reference to "Linee per il ritratto" and to subsequent articles published by Rabitti.[3] It is in

---

[1] Luigi Baldacci, "Chiara Matraini Poetessa Lucchese del XVI secolo," *Paragone* 42 (1953): 53–67.

[2] Pamela Joseph Benson and Victoria Kirkham, *Strong Voices, Weak History: Early Women Writers and Canons in England, France, and Italy* (Ann Arbor: University of Michigan Press, 2005), 1.

[3] See Giovanna Rabitti, "Linee per il ritratto di Chiara Matraini," *Studi e Problemi di critica testuale* 22–23 (1981): 141–65; eadem, "La metafora e l'esistenza nella poesia di Chiara Matraini," *Studi e Problemi di critica testuale* 26–27 (1983): 109–45; eadem, "Inediti Vaticani di Chiara Matraini." in *Studi di filologia e critica offerti dagli allievi a Lanfranco*

"Linee per il ritratto" that the general public learns more about a series of letters exchanged between Matraini and Cesare Coccapani. Rabitti presents these letters as a type of "autoritratto." The letters are contained in a manuscript copy from the 1700s, now housed in the Biblioteca Governativa di Lucca.[4] Coccapani was a noble from Carpi (Emilia Romagna) who was in Lucca in 1560 and again between 1592 and 1593. The letters are not dated, but Rabitti tells us that there are sufficient references to date them between 1560 and 1562.

> "Queste lettere, contrariamente ad altre testimonianze in cui la Matraini parla di sè in prima persona, non sono nate per la pubblicazione ma appartengono alla sfera privata e, come sempre in questi casi, presentano una vasta gamma di tonalità e di prospettive: accanto a disquisizioni filosofiche o a riferimenti al mondo della letteratura compare la vita quotidiana con le sue vicissitudini; a fianco della poetessa nella sua veste coturnata entra in scena la donna con i suoi timori e le sue preoccupazioni di tutti i giorni." ("Linee per il ritratto," 150)

Rabitti does an excellent job of providing an overview of the letters. She returns to the subject of these letters in her more recent article "Le lettere di Chiara Matraini tra pubblico e privato."[5] In this work she examines the Coccapani letters and also the letters that Matraini published with her *Rime*. What is interesting to note is that no other scholar, to my knowledge, has studied this manuscript source. All references to these letters by other scholars are done by way of Rabitti's synthesis of them. In my research I have returned to the manuscript letters themselves to explore what they may offer us with regard to Chiara Matraini.

One of the initial observations I made is that many of the letters between Coccapani and Matraini conclude with one or more sonnets. These sonnets have never been published and were not mentioned by Rabitti in her initial findings. In her more recent work she reproduces the first sonnet, but does not address the remaining poems. However, Rabitti does call the sonnets "parte integrante della

---

Caretti (Rome: Salerno, 1985), 225–50; eadem, "Vittoria Colonna as Role Model for Cinquecento Women Poets," in *Women in Italian Renaissance Culture and Society*, ed. Letizia Panizza (Oxford: European Humanities Research Centre, 2000), 478–97; eadem, introduction to *Chiara Matraini, Selected Poetry and Prose*, by Elaine Maclachlan (Chicago: University of Chicago Press, 2007).

[4] Cesare Coccapani, "Lettere e poesie del Sig. Cesare Coccapani auditore di Lucca e di Donna incerta lucchese," in Miscellanea lucchese, MS. 1547, Biblioteca Governativa di Lucca. Quotes from the letters are taken from this collection.

[5] Giovanna Rabitti, "Le lettere di Chiara Matraini tra pubblico e privato," in *Per lettera: la scrittura epistolare femminile tra archivio e tipografia, secoli XV-XVII*, ed. Gabriella Zarri (Rome: Viella, 1999), 209–34.

missiva."[6] In this study I will examine these unpublished sonnets, relating them both to the letters in this collection and also to Matraini's other poetic works.[7]

The manuscript collection begins with an anonymous introduction to Matraini, "Notizie di Chiara Matraini Dama Lucchese." She is described as a "gran Donna" born to a noble family in the middle of the sixteenth century. Scholars have since discovered that Matraini was in fact from a middle-class family, and did not belong to the nobility of Lucca. The anonymous narrator then lists her works: *Considerazioni sopra i sette Salmi*, *Dialoghi spirituali di M.a Chiara Matraini Gentildonna Lucchese*, and the *Orazione d'Isocrate a Domenico*. What strikes us immediately is that there is no mention of her *Rime*, the work for which she is noted today. Next in the introduction, her poetry is mentioned as an aside: "Oltre la Poesia dilettosi ancora la Matraini della musica suonava la Spinetta, e cantava d'ottimo gusto, di modo che La Gioventù Lucchese allettata dalle sue grazie andava a far conversazione a Casa sua, ove alle volte passava buona parte della notte in canti, e suoni, et allegria." At the time, these pastimes were not very common for respectable women and helped to foster negative rumors about Matraini. These rumors are discussed by Rabitti in "Linee per il ritratto," where we learn that Matraini was labeled a "poetessa-strega-cortegiana" in various sixteenth-century sources. Rabitti believes that these comments were made by the wife of Matraini's alleged lover.[8]

The introduction then mentions the portrait commissioned by Matraini that was painted by Alessandro Ardenti. Irma Jaffe has written an interesting analysis of the Ardenti painting.[9] She links it to events in Matraini's personal life and her interest in leaving a legacy in portrait form:

> "It is a portrayal of Chiara as she had come to see herself and wanted others to see her, and visualizes what we have come to know of her and her development: poet; lover; learned intellectual; a woman who has submitted to the power of men but has won the authority to make them kneel by her prophetic gifts; a woman whose life journey has taken her from the perception of earthly love and beauty to the understanding of spiritual love and beauty; a devout believer in her Christian faith; in her life and in her art, the interpreter of Truth: Neo-Platonist to the core." (*Shining Eyes*, 124)

Janet Smarr has recently pointed out that the painting is a visual depiction of the Catholic and also classical traditions from which Matraini draws:

---

[6] Rabitti states: "In coda, quasi marchio autoriale, l'immancabile accompagnamento di uno o più sonetti, come uno 'scolio' in versi, parte integrante della missiva . . ."("Le lettere," 228).

[7] The sonnets are included in an appendix below.

[8] Rabitti, "Linee per il ritratto," 144.

[9] Irma Jaffe, *Shining Eyes, Cruel Fortune: The Lives and Loves of Italian Renaissance Women Poets* (New York: Fordham University Press, 2002).

". . . Matraini had commissioned an altar painting for S. Maria Forisportam, in Lucca, in which she herself was depicted as the Cumaean Sybil pointing to the Virgin Mary foretold in the sybilline prophecies. The painting contributes to our understanding of Matraini's own sense of her curious role in these dialogues. On the one hand her discourse, like the sybil's, is validated by the Catholic truth that it indicates. On the other hand, she cloaks herself at the same time with a classical wisdom that stands outside the church, even while it shows itself to be compatible with and even in the service of that church."[10]

Jaffe, commenting on the relationship between Coccapani and Matraini, points out that other scholars have viewed the two as lovers. Jaffe for her part asserts that there is no indication in the letters to prove that Matraini and Coccapani were lovers. I am inclined to agree with the latter assessment. After studying the letters and sonnets I hesitate to say that the two were lovers. What is readily apparent is a deep friendship and an intellectual exchange on a number of issues.

After the brief biographical statement there follows a letter from Tommaso Bernardi to Eustachio Cabaggi of Carpi dated Lucca, 16 March 1784. This letter confirms certain biographical facts regarding Matraini: that she was married, had a child, and was then widowed at an early age. Following this letter are an additional two letters written from Coccapani to Giorgio Battista Alessandrini. These letters are not relevant to the Matraini collection save for the fact that they confirm that Coccapani was in Lucca in 1592. At this point in the collection one finds the letters between Matraini and Coccapani. The first letter from Matraini to Coccapani starts with a discussion of an "utile libretto di Severino Boetio" that he had sent her. She writes, "m'è stato così caro per come si possa stimare più li tesori dell'animo, che quegli del corpo." She had already seen a copy of the book in Lucca that had been translated by Varchi. She tells him that the book will be useful for her in a certain dialogue that she is writing, that perhaps one day he will see. We then find the first of the sonnets: "Oh quanto d'ogni honore, e reverenza." It is a poem thanking Coccapani for his gift. She writes, "ch'avete oggi a gustar dato al mio ingegno, / Pien di soave humor di sapienza." The word "ingegno" occurs in other Matraini poems, in reference to her own creative capacities and underscoring her confidence in her own poetic ability.[11] She continues, "Gia d'ogni cibo infastidita, e senza; / Gusto avea quasi me medesma a sdegno." The poem is peppered with words associated with food and eating: "frutto," "gustar,"

---

[10] Janet Levarie Smarr, *Joining the Conversation: Dialogues by Renaissance Women* (Ann Arbor: University of Michigan Press, 2005), 93.

[11] See my discussion of "Quel si dolce di gloria ardente sprone": Veena Carlson, "Rime e Lettere: (Self) Representation and Chiara Matraini," in *Medusa's Gaze: Essays on Gender, Literature, and Aesthetics in the Italian Renaissance*, ed. Paul Ferrara, Eugenio Giusti, and Jane Tylus (Boca Raton: Bordighera Press, 2004), 106–23.

"cibo." We learn that, for the poet, reading other works is not simply a pleasurable activity: rather it provides the sustenance for her intellectual growth.

As the letter continues, Matraini makes a comment disparaging her own skill: "gli miei incolti ragionamenti vi porghino tanta delettazione, che v'addolcischino in parte l'amaritudine Loro." Fiora Bassanese writes that self-criticism was a theme common to women writers of the period.[12] However, what we find in Matraini is feigned disparagement. Thus we have a vacillation between pride in her own poetic skills and what I would call false modesty. Matraini thanks Coccapani several times for taking time from his "importanti fatiche" to write to her. She concludes her letter with another sonnet, "Poscia che bel divino idol sacrata."

In his response Coccapani flatters her: "il condimento della vostra m'addolcisca ogni amarezza, essendo tutto zucchero il ragionar vostro," and later "vi replico nuovamente . . . per che ne siate certissima, che il sentirvi m'e di soddifazione infinita." Coccapani tells her that he enjoys her letters and that he will try to write her in the same manner: "quando vi viene comodo di scrivere che io mi sforzerò tuttavia di rubar all'offizio mio tanto di tempo, che non restino vostre senza risposta, e se non vi manderò cose molto alte, standomi nella bellezza che mi trovo, cercherò di dilettarvi con ogni mio potere." His concluding sonnet is in praise of Matraini: "Qual'oggi è piu di me, Donna, beato." He writes that he needs her in order to "cinger gli allori; / Che indarno solo ho senza voi tentato." Perhaps in deference to her skill, Coccapani admits that he needs her aid in order to succeed in writing. He offers her his "alma . . . Per doverci in amor essere unita."

Immediately following is the sonnet "Del naufragio di Malica." I believe this poem was inserted by the copyist and was most likely not part of the original sequence of correspondence, for the following reasons. First, in his preceding letter Coccapani mentions "questo Sonetto, che sarà qui alle spalle di questa." He does not indicate a second sonnet in the letter. Second, it is also the only sonnet in the collection that has its own title. Third, as far as the subject matter, a shipwreck, is concerned, it has no real connection to any of the themes discussed up to that juncture by Coccapani or Matraini. Finally, we see in Matraini's response that she also refers to his "sonetto" in the singular.

In Matraini's response she reiterates her interest in intellectual pursuits: "se Dio non mi priva della mente, non mai sono per abbandonarlo." She tells him of two sonnets that she will include with her letter: one, she states, is "fatto di capriccio." These two sonnets, "Di si bel nodo amor l'anima cinge" and "Se quel soave chiaro alto concento," are examples of Matraini's better poetic production. In the first she writes of love which holds the soul with a "bel nodo." She tells the reader that the heavens have given her "fra tanti amati un dolce solo . . . di cui sempre mi pasco." The second sonnet, "Se quel soave chiaro alto concento," is a Neoplatonic poem in the vein of Vittoria Colonna that borrows vocabulary from

---

[12] Fiora Bassanese, "Gaspara Stampa's Poetics of Negativity," *Italica* 61 (1984): 335–46.

Michelangelo. Much has been noted of the debt that Matraini owed to Colonna. Recently Rabitti has written that Matraini actively modeled herself after Colonna.[13] In the poem the narrator speaks of the harmony of her soul. Her "oggetto divino" is beyond her reach and she cannot attain it with either voice or thought. The last tercet focuses on her ravished body as she tries to "alzarmi da terra":

> Ma per che troppo alla mia debol possa
> L'ardente oggetto mia divino è lunge
> Giugner mai non lo puo voce, o pensiero
> Pur tant'alto è il disio, che m'arde e punge
> Che con la carne travagliata, e legger d'ossa
> Cerco alzarmi da terra al suo bel vero.

Coccapani, in his reply, excuses his tardiness in responding: ". . .vi dono il presente sonetto scusandomi con voi della mia tardità perchè sono occupatissimo et di maniera mi bisogna aver cura delle cose altrui, che mi scordo di me stesso." His sonnet "Quella catena intorno che mi cinge" concludes the letter. This sonnet is clearly a response to Matraini's "Di si bel nodo amor l'anima cinge," echoing her vocabulary and theme. Where she writes "Di si bel nodo amor l'anima cinge, / Di gloria accesa, e di desiri ardenti" he writes "Quella catena intorno che mi cinge, / Di pensieri alti, e di desiri ardenti." We see the repetition of words such as "cinge, desiri ardenti, rallenti, si stringe, finge, spirti, intenti, spinge." While Matraini does speak of her "stato afflitto e lagrimoso," she concludes the sonnet with the positive expression "vivo e nasco." Coccapani takes up the same images, but evokes a cycle of rebirth:

> E nel mio stato amaro, e lagrimoso
> Perchè giammai non abbia fine l'duolo
> Mille volte il di moro e mille nasco.

Matraini begins her next letter by again denigrating her own writing abilities: "non so gia qual frutto da loro si possi cavare, come ella dice, non conoscendo essere buona pianta da produrne." She tells Coccapani that she is also sending him two letters: "gli mando ora due lettere, una al Principe di Salerno, e l'altra non so

---

[13] Benson and Kirkham point out that this is a critical time for all women writers: "For the first time in the western literary tradition, in this period women took inspiration from living or near-contemporary authors of their own sex, either through open citation or implicitly through allusive borrowing" (*Strong Voices, Weak History*, 4). Also Rabitti, "Vittoria Colonna as Role Model." See also Rinaldina Russell, "Chiara Matraini nella tradizione lirica femminile," *Forum Italicum* 34 (2000): 415–27; Luciana Borsetto, "Narciso ed Eco: figure e scrittura nella lirica femminile del Cinquecento," in *Nel cerchio della luna: figure di donna in alcuni testi del XVI secolo*, ed. Marina Zancan (Venice: Marsilio, 1983), 171–233.

ancora a cui dedicarlami, con una novella." These two letters and the short story have, to my knowledge, never been found. In fact, in all of Matraini's known writings there are no *novelle*.

Many scholars have mentioned that Matraini lived away from Lucca for some time. There are several possible reasons for her departure. The first assumes that her departure is tied to the defeat and disgrace of the Matraini family after the uprising of the "Straccioni."[14] The second is that she left after her love affair with a married man ended badly when he was murdered.[15] The third is that her departure was tied to her legal battle to regain her dowry from her son. While there is no way to know for sure, the Coccapani letters seem to support the last reason. In the letter we read: "io mi dogli della mia cattiva sorte, gli dico, che ciò procede per vedermi tolta ogni speranza, della quale se avessi pur una scintilla, l'animo mio non saria cosi oppresso dal duolo. Egli è ben vero che in Dio si deve puonose ogni sua speranza . . . ma io non vedo gia come possi fare a riavere i miei beni." Here, I believe, the poet is referring to the legal battle she faced. At some point during her life Matraini breaks with her only son. She spends much time trying to regain her dowry, and it becomes the focus of many of the letters she sends to Lucca. In fact, records in Lucca indicate that she filed her will four times, perhaps changing it as her relationship with her son changed.[16] As a result, she seems to have a love-hate relationship with the city itself. She writes: "Se a Firenze, o altre terre fusse che accettasse tal cosa con darmi quello, che fosse justo per il mio vivere io lo farei volentieri, perchè a Lucca io non vi torno volentieri, ne mai volentieri vi stei." She concludes with the sonnet "Come da notarist'aspre, e rie catene." The sonnet continues in the Neoplatonic vein noted earlier, with references to "la strada del bene, (il) proprio bene, l'animo, alzarlo . . . dinanzi a Dio." But given the frustration that is exhibited in the letters regarding her legal battle with her son, it is possible that the sonnet makes reference to the more mundane issue of inheritance. In the sonnet she queries "Da qual parte debb'io vedere la spene; / o la strada del bene ch'oggi ho smarrita; / s'indi giustizia, e carità sbandita." Perhaps these lines are a reference to the *giustizia* and *carità* which are lacking in her son.

At this juncture we find a sonnet from Coccapani, "L'aspro giogo che tempo assai vi tiene," with no accompanying letter. It seems to be a response to Matraini's frustration regarding her relationship with her son and the desire to

---

[14] A period of political unrest in Lucca as the working class rebelled against the nobility. See Jaffe, *Shining Eyes, Cruel Fortune*, 105.

[15] See Rabitti, "Linee per il ritratto."

[16] See Rabitti, "Linee per il ritratto," 151–53. Rabitti also states in "Le Lettere" that she believes that the legal battle is one of the primary reasons for the exchange with Coccapani: "Il breve carteggio ruota intorno as un nodo problematico: la difficoltà della Matraini di ritornare in possesso della sua dote e la conseguente causa legale che vede la letterata contrapposta al figlio Federigo Cantarini" (227).

return to Lucca. He writes: "Della prigione vi disegnai l'uscita." He seems to be encouraging her "si cangia il destin malvaggio, e rio."

In the next letter Matraini presents her opinion on the position and perception of the sixteenth-century woman.[17] She states that society limits a woman's participation in "learned activities." Matraini dismisses the idea that women are incapable of science and art. According to her, women suffer from a lack of opportunity, not of ability. She also complains of the paucity of early education for girls, which prevents them from fully experiencing the arts and sciences. She compares the fate of women to that of prisoners: both are restricted in their movements and are kept busy with menial tasks. Matraini refutes contemporary misogynistic ideas, using warlike imagery to underscore that the community of women must unite to resist the misogynists. She writes that women may indeed not be as strong as men, but strength alone is not enough to bring superiority. If that were the case, then bears, lions, and bulls would be superior to man.

She concludes the letter with "Deh quando fia, che da quest'aspri scogli." The sonnet, very similar to religious poems that appear in the latter part of Matraini's *Rime*, again returns to Boethian images and themes common in the poetry of Petrarch and Colonna.

> Deh quando fia, che da quest'aspri scogli
> Ove l'onde nemiche, e i venti fieri
> Sotto nembi del Ciel horridi, e neri
> Mi sospinger, giammai piu mi ritogli!
> Sarà giammai, che di dilor si spogli
> L'Anima, e del suo bene alquanto speri
> Veder pur l'orme, o soliti sentieri
> Segna, et in lieto Porto io mi raccogli!
> Ahime, che longhe, travagliate, e torte
> Son le strade, onde Febo il giorno mena
> Et incauto a passarli è il mio Fetonte;
> Onde gia temo, e veggio lui rea sorte
> Seguir, l'alma del Ciel luce serena
> Non si gli scopre al gran periglio a fronte.

In particular there are two sonnets from Matraini's *Rime* with Petrarchan roots that appear to be quite similar. The poems, which appear next to each other, are religious poems in which Matraini links writing and studying to religion and the endeavor to follow the proper path in the hopes of salvation. The first poem, "Mentre la nave mia colma d'oblio," centers on the poetic metaphor of a boat lost at sea, linking it to the journey towards salvation, a common theme in the Renaissance:

---

[17] I have discussed this in Carlson, "Rime e Lettere: (Self) Representation and Chiara Matraini," 108–12.

> Mentre la nave mia colma d'oblio
> Solcando andava in questo mar di pianto
> E stava a udir delle Sirene il canto,
> Scorta dal vago suo cieco desio.
> Tu solo, immenso, alto, e pietoso Iddio,
> Dal Ciel mandasti il tuo bel lume santo,
> Che scombrò dalle nebbie oscure il manto
> Onde me non vedeva e 'l fallir mio.
> Grazie dunque ti rendo, ed infiniti
> Preghi ti porgo, che 'l mio stanco legno
> Con la sant'aura tua conduchi al porto.
> Fa' che stian sempre i miei pensieri uniti
> A Te solo, e 'l mio cor, l'opra, e l'ingegno,
> Sì che non resti al fin dall'onde assorto.[18]

In the first quatrain she refers to the past in which she was lost at sea and bewitched by the song of the Sirens.[19] Here Matraini, through the use of the gerund ("solcando") and the imperfect ("andava," "stava"), implies that the narrator was lost for some time. The narrator is pulled — as were the sailors — from the proper path, guided by blind desires. It is interesting to note that the gender of the narrator does not diminish the impact of the Siren metaphor. The beauty of the Sirens is not at issue. Matraini focuses instead on the musical seduction of the classical figures. As is common in the Renaissance lyric, Matraini's sonnet turns from the amorous to the religious, so that the beloved is replaced by God. God becomes the desired other and the Sirens merely a distraction from attaining the goal of salvation.

The first line of Matraini's poem is taken from the incipit of a Petrarchan sonnet, "Passa la nave mia colma d'oblio," a poem filled with despair and distress, in which the narrator loses his way while his boat is ravaged by the elements. Reason and skill, "la ragion e l'arte," are lost and he fears that he will not reach a safe port. In Petrarch's poem we note the present tense, "passa," indicating a conflict as yet unresolved. Matraini, however, places her poem in the past, indicating

---

[18] Chiara Matraini, *Rime e Lettere*, ed. Giovanna Rabitti (Bologna: Commissione per i Testi di Lingua, 1989). All subsequent quotations come from this edition.

[19] The Sirens were one of the best-known figures from classical mythology. They were said to be half-woman, half-bird, but possessed incredible musical skills, both vocally and instrumentally. They lived on a rocky island, where they played music and sang to lure and seduce passing sailors. At times sailors were so entranced that they allowed their boats to be destroyed upon the rocks: other times, mesmerized, they would leap overboard, trying to reach the Sirens, only to die on the rocks. It is unclear what the Sirens' motives were, but it has also been written that they devoured the shipwrecked sailors. See Robert E. Bell, *Women of Classical Mythology* (Oxford: Oxford University Press, 1991); H.D. Brumble, *Classical Myths and Legends in the Middle Ages and Renaissance* (Westport, CT: Greenwood Press, 1998) 312–15.

that some resolution has been reached. While Matraini has borrowed the incipit and lexicon of Petrarch's sonnet, her poem finishes on a different note. In the second quatrain the narrator addresses God, who is described as "immenso, alto, e pietoso." He sent a beautiful, holy light that cleared away the cloud that prevented her from seeing her mistakes. For this reason, at the *volta*, she offers him thanks and also prayers. It becomes clear that although she has come to understand her faults she is not completely saved. She asks God for help, in the form of a divine wind that will guide her battered boat to port.

In the last tercet she asks that her thoughts always be united in him; but not only her thoughts, also her heart, her work, and her "ingegno." Matraini's evocation of "l'opra e l'ingegno" recalls Petrarch's "la ragione e l'arte." She asks for divine guidance in order to use her skills and talents in the proper manner. While the pessimism of the Petrarchan sonnet is not reproduced, Matraini borrows heavily from its lexicon and imagery. Petrarch's "Passa la nave mia colma d'oblio" also mentions Scylla and Charybdis, who appear in another Matraini sonnet. "Padre del Ciel, doppo molt'anni e molti" is the poem that follows "Mentre la nave mia colma d'oblio" in her *Rime*:

> Padre del Ciel, doppo molt'anni e molti
> che senza 'l lume tuo da Te son gita
> per quest'ombra mortal chiusa e smarrita,
> prego ch'a buon sentier l'anima volti;
> e fa' si ch'e pensier fallaci e stolti
> che m'han dal dritto tuo sentier partita,
> a più lodate imprese, a meglio vita
> stian sempre, col tuo aiuto, ognor rivolti.
> Trae dalli scogli a più secura parte,
> signor, la vela del mio stanco legno,
> tal ch'io stia lunge da Cariddi e Scilla.
> Raccogli in Te l'alte speranze sparte,
> e volgi questi studî e quest'ingegno
> a più lodata vita e più tranquilla.   (1–14)

Here Matraini borrows from another Petrarchan sonnet, "Padre del Ciel, dopo i perduti giorni." In that poem the narrator addresses his lord and begs for aid in easing the pain of love and help in leading a better life. Matraini's incipit expands the period of time the narrator spent away from God from "giorni" to "molt'anni." In her apostrophe to God she asks for his aid in finding the right path, after having lost her way due to "pensier fallaci."

At the *volta* Matraini returns to the Petrarchan metaphor of the boat, which, however, is not used in his "Padre del Ciel." She asks God to turn her from the rocks to more secure parts; to guide the sail of her tired boat, so that she remains far from Charybdis and Scylla.[20] In the last tercet the narrator asks for divine guidance in her studies and her talent. Her thoughts are scattered, or distracted from God ("raccogli in Te l'alte speranze sparte"), as were Petrarch's ("reduci i pensieri vaghi a miglio luogo"). She wants to turn to a more praiseworthy and tranquil life. The phrase "questi studi e quest'ingegno" also recalls "Mentre la nave mia colma d'oblio," where we see "i pensieri uniti. . .'l mio cor, l'opra, e l'ingegno." In both cases the poet appears to possess the requisite skill and talent but seeks guidance in order to use them properly.

I believe that we must consider one other subtext in the analysis of these sonnets. Matraini is also drawing from Dante Alighieri's *Divina Commedia*. The Dantean subtext is most obvious in word choice and imagery. For instance, in the first half of "Padre del Ciel, doppo molt'anni" words such as "ombra," "mortal," "smarrita," and "sentier" recall the beginning of the *Inferno*, where Dante the pilgrim is lost in the dark wood. But I would also suggest that Matraini is actually referring in these two poems to Ulysses from *Inferno* XXVI.

The figure of Ulysses, hero of the Trojan War, is punished for three things: convincing Achilles to join the Greeks against the Trojans; stealing the Palladium (a wooden image of Pallas Athena which was said to protect the city of Troy); and inventing the trick of the wooden horse that ended the Trojan War. It is Dante's account of Ulysses' death that is interesting in our consideration of Matraini's poetry. Dante presents Ulysses who, in a quest for knowledge, ignores caution and travels beyond the Pillars of Hercules, which "were supposed to mark the western limit beyond which no one could sail and come back alive."[21] Ulysses' misuse of intellect makes him an example for both Dante and Matraini.

---

[20] Along with the Sirens, Charybdis and Scylla were two nautical obstacles that sailors of mythological times had to navigate to avoid. Charybdis was originally a woman who stole cattle from Hercules. For this Zeus struck her with a thunderbolt and she was changed into a monster and cast into the sea. Three times a day she drank in great quantities of water creating dangerous whirlpools, and then vomited whatever she swallowed. Scylla was also a woman who was turned into a monster. The sea god Glaucus loved her, but Circe was in love with Glaucus. Because of her jealousy, Circe put magic herbs in the water where Scylla usually bathed. When she entered the water she was transformed into a monster with six dog heads growing from her groin. She eventually took up a position opposite Charybdis. Here again, as in the case of the Sirens, the mythological figures serve as obstructions in the path to salvation. See Bell, *Women of Classical Mythology*; Brumble, *Classical Myths and Legends*, 305–7.

[21] Dante Alighieri, *The Divine Comedy*, trans. Charles Singleton (Princeton: Princeton University Press, 1980), 1: 465. All subsequent quotations come from this edition.

According to Singleton, Dante's source for the account of Ulysses' death is unknown. This is pertinent because Matraini seems to be drawing from the Dantean text, a text that Singleton states did not appear in any other source:

"The source of Dante's account of the death of Ulysses, which the hero himself relates in this canto, is unknown. It is at variance with the prophecy of Tiresias in the

In the beginning of Canto XXVI, before Dante encounters Ulysses, there is a foreshadowing of what is to follow. Dante, unlike Ulysses, will control his curiosity and intellect, realizing that even intelligence must be guided by divine grace: "e più lo 'ngegno affreno ch'i'non soglio, / perchè non corra che virtù nol guidi" (21–22). Ulysses, then, is an example of how not to behave: he shows the reader that the unbridled quest for knowledge can be destructive. Ulysses begins his story by stating that not even love for his family could dissuade him from knowledge of the world:

> Nè dolcezza di figlio, nè la pieta
> Del vecchio padre, nè 'l debito amore
> Lo qual dovea Penelopè far lieta,
> Vincer potero dentro a me l'ardore
> Ch'i'ebbi a divenir del mondo esparto
> E de li vizi umani e del valore . . .   (94–99)

Not only was Ulysses responsible for his own demise, but he also encouraged others to follow him:

> . . .'O frati,' dissi, 'che per cento milia
> perigli siete giunti a l'occidente,
> a questa tanto picciola vigilia
> d'i nostril sensi ch'è del rimanente
> non vogliate negar l'esperïenza,
> di retro al sol, del mondo senza gente.
> Considerate la vostra semenza:
> Fatti non foste a viver come bruti,
> Ma per seguir virtute e conoscenza.'

Through the misuse of rhetoric, Ulysses convinces his men to join him. Dante here uses Ulysses as a negative exemplum. Matraini in her poems points to the figure of Ulysses, through the metaphor of the ship and the evocation of the Sirens, Charybdis, and Scylla. Ulysses survived encounters with those three obstacles. However, as in Dante, for Matraini the Trojan hero is negative and is ultimately rejected as a model. In Matraini's sonnets the narrator tempers her quest for knowledge and her use of "ingegno," turning to God for guidance. In doing so, Matraini concurs with Dante's presentation of Ulysses.

Odyssey (XI, 134–37)—with which Dante has no direct acquaintance whereby a peaceful death from the sea is predicted for Ulysses . . . Dante's account varies also from the story, current in the Middle Ages, given by the so-called Dictys Cretensis in the *Ephemeris belli Troiani* (VI, 15), of how Ulysses met his death at the hand of Telegonus, his son by Circe. It is possible, as B. Nardi suggests, that Dante's idea was suggested to him by the voyage in 1291 of the Genoese brothers Vivaldi, who sailed out past Gibraltar and into the west, seeking a route to India, and were never heard of again" (456–57).

Matraini returns to her discourse on women in the next letter. She states that strength alone is not enough to put men in a privileged position over women. Although women in general may not be as "robust" as men, they possess no less reason and intellect. Matraini views her current situation as a battle or fight, and adopts the language of war, presenting herself as a leader and warrior protecting those who are weaker. She enters the battleground to fight those who would take away a woman's honor.

In this letter she thanks Coccapani for two sonnets which do not appear to be in the collection. She states that she will not respond to the first poem but will allow "il Serchio" to speak for her in answering the second. What follows are a pair of sonnets between "il Serchio" and "Carpi." Given that Matraini is from Lucca where the river Serchio runs and Coccapani is from Carpi, we can deduce that that they are using senhals[22] for one another. The poems are quite pastoral in theme. What is most interesting are the last two verses in each.

Matraini writes:

La fama, e il grido, che lei chiara noma
L'aura corona avrà del suo Polluce

And Coccapani responds:

La fama, e il grido di lei chiara noma
Chiara risuoni ovunque Febo Luce.

This is a technique that is also found in the initial pages of Matraini's *Rime*. There she uses the sonnets of other men who sing her praises to create the introduction to her collection.[23] Here we see that Coccapani, writing as Carpi, is doing the same. These two poems conclude the correspondence between Matraini and Coccapani.[24]

If these letters were actually written around 1560, as Rabitti asserts, why were the poems not included in later editions of the *Rime*? There were several ways in which they could have been incorporated: the Matraini sonnets could have been included in the *Rime* itself. The sonnet exchange between Coccapani and Matraini could have been included in the introductory section mentioned above. The letters themselves could have been included in the section of letters that we find in the *Rime*. My own conclusion is that, as Rabitti suggests, the letters were too personal and that Matraini chose not to have them included. Another possibility is that, if

---

[22] Invented names for lover and beloved.

[23] See Carlson, "Rime e Lettere: (Self) Representation and Chiara Matraini," 113–14.

[24] There follow three more sonnets with no clear indication of author. There are no letters nor headings with which to place these poems. I have chosen not to include them.

Coccapani and Matraini were lovers, then their story did not belong in the *Rime*, because the collection was based on another love interest.

The "recovery" of these letters and poems allows us to expand our understanding of Matraini's work. We are given a window into her everyday life, both literary and personal. The sonnets become the poetic rendition of her frustrations, joys, and sorrows. Unlike the published *Rime e Lettere*, these poems are closely linked. Each sonnet is clearly connected to the letter that precedes it. It is also apparent that the Matraini letters need to be considered alongside the Coccapani letters: together they form a cohesive unit of statement and response. The investigation begun by Luigi Baldacci in the 1950s continues to bear fruit in the twenty-first century as scholars return to examine the poetic product of Matraini. As Benson and Kirkham state, it is the recovery of "largely forgotten history" that is the critical step in a more complete understanding of the early modern period and the writers who wrote during that time.[25] These letters and poems allow us to consider Matraini as both poet and citizen.

---

[25] Benson and Kirkham, *Strong Voices*, 1.

Appendix

1. Donna incerta a Cesare Coccapani

    Oh quanto d'ogni honore, e reverenza
è il bel frutto gentil mia pianta, degnò
ch'avet'oggi a gustar dato al mio ingegno
pien di soave humor di sapienza.
    Già d'ogni cibo infastidita, e senza
gusto avea quasi me medesma a sdegno,
quando l'alma nel dolce suo disegno
fè desta da tant'alta intelligenza
    Così da un'uom di duol presso che morto
e da Donna più bella assai che il Sole
prendo, e per mezzo vostro ormai conforto
    Ringrazio lor che a coglie eterne, e sole
mi sollevaro, e voi che il mio diporto
s'ete per cui sol par, ch'io mi console.

2. Donna incerta a Cesare Coccapani

    Poscia che bel divino idol sacrato
quasi a Dea con sublimi eterni onori
m'avete in mezzo dei piu santi ardori
dell'alto vostro cor sacrificato;
    Degno è che a voi quel ben sì desiato
cui ricever si deè ne' santi amori
vi doni, ond'ambe insieme i nostri cori
dirsi possino in un amante, e amato.
    Questo dunque vi porgo, e sol ne resta
qui di bearsi nell'amata vista
del caro oggetto pe' darne eterna vita.
    Ma in questa parte qui l'un non s'aquista,
l'altro forse pur fia, se sia con questa
voglia, la gloria mia larga, e infinita.

3. Cesare Coccapani a Donna incerta

    Qual'oggi è piu di me Donna beato
se mi dà il Ciel ch'io possa coglier fiori
in Parnaso, e con voi cinger gli allori
che invano solo ho senza voi tentato
    Felice onesto amore e fortunato
dirò ben io, che tuoi casti favori

ministri all'alme vostre, ove dimori
fra voglie oneste in signorile stato
   Et poi quest'alma a vostre voglie presta
vi porgerò, tutta giojosa in visto
per doverci in amor essere unita.
   Accoglietela intanto, vi sia mista
con la vostra inmaniera, e forma honesta
che di voi non ha stanza piu gradita.

4. Del naufragio di Malica

   Signor che di vendetta il nome hai spento
et sei pietoso a perdonar rivolto,
mirando all'esser tuo via piu che al molto
dimerto altrui, d'amor vero argomento.
   Quall'orribil procela e ch'ora sento
del popol sotto il tuo vessilo accolto
forse è l'amor in odio o in ira volto,
o intepidito, onde a giovar sei Lento.
   Che fia dunque di me senza te o Padre,
in così travaglioso, e gran periglio,
fra rumori, e domestici avversari,
   Se le nimiche opprimon le tue squadre
e profandan le navi, e va in esiglio
il Popol tuo da tè, quai fien ripari.

5. Donna incerta a Cesare Coccapani

   Di si bel nodo amor l'anima cinge
di gloria accesa, e di desiri ardenti,
ch'io prego Lei, che mai non lo rallenti
o il foco ammorzi ov'ella or piu si stringe
   Ma l'cibo ond'ei si dolce alletta e finge
a 'famelici spirti a quello intenti
lieto li porga; e non sian tarde o lenti
l'ore, o il tempo, che al fine oltra ne spinge
   Non fia il mio cor più misero, e pensoso
poiche fra tanti amati un dolce solo
m'ha dato il Ciel di cui sempre mi pasco
   E nel mio stato afflitto e lagrimoso
quel nettar posto ha per temprare il duolo
di cui novellamente or vivo e nasco.

6. Donna incerta a Cesare Coccapani

 Se quel soave chiaro alto concento
ch'ho dentro all'alma, le mie voci, e il suono
conforme avessi onde da quel ch'io sono
tutta mi trasformassi in dolce accento
 Ogni spirto vago, a quello intanto
spererei farlo tal, che ardente sperano
di bel desio di cosi alloro dono
giugner ferialo a quel ch'io provo e sento
 Ma per che troppo alla mia debol possa
l'ardente oggetto mia divino è lunge
giugner mai non lo puo voce, o pensiero
 Pur tant'alto è il disio, che m'arde e punge
che con la carne travagliata, e legger d'ossa
cerco alzarmi da terra al suo bel vero

7. Cesare Coccapani a Donna incerta

 Quella catena intorno che mi cinge
di pensieri alti, e di desiri ardenti,
l'amor non fa che un giorno si rallenti
sento l'alma ch'al cor tutta si stringe.
 Che sebben d'ingannar se stessa finge
mostrando altrove aver li spirti intenti
fin quest'opra d'ognhor in altro senti
son gli [...] ove amor poscia le spinge
 Lieto nel volto, e nel mio cor pensoso
altrui giova a me son contrario solo
e di vano desir sempre mi pasco
 E nel mio stato amaro, e lagrimoso
perchè giammai non abbia fine l'duolo
mille volte il di moro e mille nasco.   [...] [content illegible]

8. Donna incerta a Cesare Coccapani

 Come da notarist'aspre, e rie catene
potrò mai disferrarmi essere ardita
senza quell' aurea chiave onde la vita
libera tenni, e fuor di tante pene
 Da qual parte debb' io vedere la spene
o la strada del bene ch'oggi ho smarrita
s'indi giustizia, e carità sbandita
trovo, onde piu sperai del proprio bene
 Debbo fors'io per tor da servitute
l'animo, ad altro farlo anchor soggetto
senz'alzarlo giammai dinanzi a Dio.

Questo di Liberta, ne di virtute
non saria stato da due dolce eletto
per il breve camin del viver mio

9. Risposta del Coccapani

    L'aspro giogo che tempo assai vi tiene
al collo il primo error ch'hor chiede aita
non vi dess'io ch'a scior forse spedita
per servir ad altrui che mal conviene.
    Ma per levar le luci alme, e serene
dal pianger sempre co'il dolor v'invita
della prigion vi disegnai l'uscita
col nodo scior d'altrui, che vi ritiene.
    Poi che allor vi fia il campo di salute
largo ove drizzate ogn'hor l'oggetto
et havrà il fin, che brama il bel desio
    Converrà insieme in voi allor si mute
la sorte essendo in stato più perfetto
e si cangia il destin malvagio, e rio.

10. Donna incerta a Cesare Coccapani

    Deh quando fia, che da quest'aspri scogli
ove l'onde nemiche, e i venti fieri
sotto nembi del Ciel horridi, e neri
mi sospinger, giammai piu mi ritogli!
    Sarà giammai, che di dilor si spogli
l'Anima, e del suo bene alquanto speri
veder pur l'orme, o soliti sentieri
segna, et in lieto Porto io mi raccogli!
    Ahime, che longhe, travagliate, e torte
son le strade, onde Febo il giorno mena
et incauto a passarli è il mio Fetonte;
    Onde gia temo, e veggio lui rea sorte
seguir, l'alma del Ciel luce serena
non si gli scopre al gran periglio a fronte.

11. Il Serchio al Carpi

    Frenar vedrassi i rapidi torrenti
del ghiaccio sciolti, e l'alma ragione
a mi il bel nome diede Lucomone
irrigar le mie linfe e chiare, e lenti:
    E bei raggi del Sol d'oro Lucenti
produr fiori, erbe, e frondi, alma stagione

recando dal bel frisco montone
a cantar gli auccelletti in dolci accenti
fu dal avenoso alta la testa
levando, alvenir poi della mia Luce
d'edera'ornerò l'antica chioma
    E s'empia voglia altrui piu non l'infesta
la fama, e il grido, che lei chiara noma
l'aura corona avrà del suo Polluce

12. Risposta del Coccapani all'addietro Sonetto

    Serchio, che co tuoi rapidi torrenti
i campi, infesti cui diè Lucomone
il nome, homai la bella regione
lava, e riga con le linfe chiare, e lenti.
    Volve in guisa de sassi aspri e frequenti
erbe, e fiori alla prossima stagione
che sciolta da crudele, e ria prigione
vien la tua ninfa, e a lei ne fa porgenti
    De verdi edere intorte orna la chioma
e dal letto avenoso alza la testa
che piu tempo non è d'odiar la luce;
    E per far piu celebre ancor la festa,
la fama, e il grido di lei chiara nome,
chiara risuoni ovunque Febo Luce

Dissecting the Beloved's Body:
The Blazon and Italian *Petrarchiste*

Fiora A. Bassanese

For lyric poets of the sixteenth century, Francesco Petrarca's *Rerum vulgarium fragmenta*, better known as the *Canzoniere*, was, in Roberto Fedi's words, the "architesto," the archetypal text whose emulation validated its imitator.[1] After Pietro Bembo's canonization of Petrarch as the *primum* in the *Prose della volgar lingua* in 1525, it became an established norm that successful versification could be achieved only through creative imitation. To borrow Fedi's words once again: "This is Bembo's great intuition: imitation means having an identity card, entering into the tracks of illustrious traditions, wearing 'the masters' robes,' in other words: lasting through time."[2] Aspirants from the Alps to the Ionian were expected to embrace this canonized tradition, assimilate it, and echo it. To do otherwise was to court marginalization, criticism, even ignominy. In brief, writers of the Cinquecento adhered to a codified system, wherein the voice of a poet speaks with the intonations, words, imagery, and structures contained in the exemplary models. Acceptable lyric poetry came in one size only: Petrarchism.

But what happens when the imitator is female? With the entry of a substantial number of literate women into the cultural conversation of the day, the potential for female creativity grew as well. Their particular conundrum is quickly summarized: How does one deal with the paradox of being both a *petrarchista* and a woman? What are the strategies for constructing an individual voice when co-opting a male idiom? Moreover, how can a woman successfully and blamelessly adopt the assertive roles of lover and writer in a society that judged womanly *onestà* and *virtù* on the basis of passivity and chastity, in a culture that proposed powerful social taboos against the expression of female desire? Petrarchism clearly designated authorship, or "artistic selfhood," as male. Gary

---

[1] Roberto Fedi, *La memoria della poesia: Canzonieri, lirici e libri di rime nel Rinascimento* (Rome: Salerno Editrice, 1990), 51.

[2] Fedi, *La memoria della poesia*, 37: "Questa è la grande intuizione del Bembo: imitare significa possedere una carta d'identità, entrare nel solco delle tradizioni illustri, vestire 'panni curiali,' in altre parole: durare nel tempo."

Waller has noted that the "structures of power within the language these women use [. . .] create them as subjects, denying them any owned discourse."³ To "own" her discourse and achieve some measure of authenticity, the *petrarchista* must be involved in the process of re-defining gender expectations and challenging conventional definitions of masculinity and femininity. This creates both a societal and a literary dilemma for amatory poets, who inevitably overturn established norms by praising men in a code formulated on the elevation of female subjects, while concurrently gainsaying cultural assumptions of womanly submissiveness and silence. As Ann Rosalind Jones has pointed out, "In the discourse of humanism and bourgeois family theory, the proper woman is an absence [. . .] She is silent and invisible: she does not speak, and she is not spoken about."⁴ One aspect of the reworking of the canonical model undertaken by the *petrarchiste* concerns the construction of the male beloved's material persona and its derivation from the representation of Laura in the *Rerum volgarium fragmenta*.

The process of "gendering" the beloved male was certainly of singular importance in women's love lyric, requiring both creativity and manipulation as these poets walked a tightrope between the literary canon and the canons of propriety. An immediate complication derives from the fact that the male gaze is an essential element in Petrarch's lyric universe, in which the lover's eyes, or the eyes of memory, are repeatedly drawn to the physical body of the beloved. What emerges, however, is a fragmented woman, a compilation of parts. We encounter Laura's hands, feet, hip, breasts, hair, mouth, eyes, even the veils and gloves that concurrently cover and suggest the concealed anatomy, but not a whole person. Given the codification of the love lyric in the Cinquecento, generations of male poets continued to propose a piecemeal representation of the beloved in their imitative verse. In his discussion of French *petrarchisti*, Lawrence Kritzman analyzes the parameters of this imitative choice: "The representation of the woman depicts that of the poet's imaginary projection of the reality of his desire onto an object that is narcissistically subjectivized [. . .] Indeed, bodily representation, realized in the scriptural space onto which the effects of the subject's desire is portrayed, is disclosed as a consequence of the masculine gaze on the represented object."⁵

---

³ Gary Waller, cited in Wendy Wall, *The Imprint of Gender: Authorship and Publication in the English Renaissance* (Ithaca and London: Cornell University Press, 1993), 282. Waller is referring specifically to English imitative writers, but the situation in Italy would be even more pronounced given the hold of Petrarchism in the early Cinquecento.

⁴ Ann Rosalind Jones, "Surprising Fame: Renaissance Gender Ideologies and Women's Lyric," in *Poetics of Gender*, ed. Nancy Miller (New York: Columbia University Press, 1986), 74–95, here 74.

⁵ Lawrence D. Kritzman, "Architecture of the Utopian Body: The *Blasons* of Marot and Ronsard," in idem, *The Rhetoric of Sexuality and the Literature of the French Renaissance* (Cambridge: Cambridge University Press, 1991), 97–112, here 98.

Critics have written extensively on the possible significance of Petrarch's fragmentation of the beloved in the *Rerum vulgarium fragmenta*, often considering it a rhetorical strategy or a sign of the collection itself, whose scattered rhymes, when assembled, produce a satisfactory *literary* whole. As Nancy Vickers demonstrated over twenty-five years ago in a notable essay titled "Diana Described: Scattered Woman and Scattered Rhyme," the Petrarchan exemplum subverts the integrity of the female subject. As Vickers notes, "Laura is always presented as a part or parts of a woman . . . her image is that of a collection of exquisitely beautiful disassociated objects" and her "whole body was at times less than some of its parts." This critic goes on to state that "the isolation of these parts" provided emulators "an attractive basis for imitation, extension, and, ultimately, distortion."[6] For Petrarch, such "dismemberment" of the female form has a literary function: "[he] transforms the visible totality into scattered words, the body into signs"[7] so that the body in the text is transformed into the textual body. Another American critic, Wendy Wall, suggests that the fragmented body becomes "a corporeal sign for the text," therefore an object of dual desire.[8] For Gaspara Stampa (1523–1554) the desire for the beloved is often accompanied by the same desire for words found in Petrarch, whose own lyric lexicon she faithfully reproduces.

In her *Rime*, Stampa utilizes the paradigmatic fragmentation of the beloved's body, as she shifts the gaze of desire from the masculine standard to a feminine variant. Like Laura, Stampa's "conte" is the absent or indifferent beloved, the superior being, and the personification of art, upon which the lover gazes. Like Petrarch's beloved, the male subject is presented as a passive object whose existence is known through his effects on the true subject of the rhymes, the poet-lover. The construction of the masculine figure found in the quatrains of *Rime* 7 can serve as an example of Stampa's imitative strategy:

> Chi vuol conoscer, donne, il mio signore,
> miri un signor di vago e dolce aspetto,
> giovane d'anni e vecchio d'intelletto,
> imagin de la gloria e del valore:
> di pelo biondo, e di vivo colore,
> di persona alta e spazioso petto,

---

[6] Nancy Vickers, "Diana Described: Scattered Woman and Scattered Rhyme," in *Writing and Sexual Difference*, ed. Elizabeth Abel (Chicago: University of Chicago Press, 1982), 95–110, here 96–97.

[7] Vickers, "Diana Described," 103.

[8] Wall, *The Imprint of Gender*, 281. This citation comes from the chapter titled "Dancing in a Net: The Problems of Female Authorship," which contains interesting discussions for the study of women writing within the canon.

e finalmente in ogni opra perfetto,
fuor ch'un poco (oimè lassa!) empio in amore.⁹

(If, ladies, you desire to know my lord,
Look for a gentleman with sweet expression,
Though young in years, old in his intellect;
Image of valor and of warlike glory;
His hair is blond, and his complexion light,
He's tall in stature, with a manly chest,
Seeming perfection in his every act,
But, ah, in love not faithful to his word.)[10]

The fragmentation of the beloved in this sonnet recalls the Renaissance blazon, or *blason*, one means of constructing a paradigm within the conventional boundaries of approved *imitatio*. According to Bernard Weinberg, "the *blasons* (light descriptive poems) [were] started by [Clément] Marot at the court of Ferrara"[11] in the mid-1530s, but it is clear that the cataloguing of body parts is intrinsic to the Petrarchan source. Stampa integrates some attributes that are both conventional and gender-neutral: "vago e dolce aspetto," youth, blondness, fair complexion. These are traditional components of feminine beauty within the canon; essentially, Laura is reconfigured male by Stampa, whose *conte* retains the beauty expected in the figuration of a beloved. The apparent allusiveness of the representation underscores its literariness, thus emphasizing its reiteration of standardized tropes. Yet any feminization of a masculine beloved would be unacceptable to a prevalently male audience; therefore, Stampa goes on to endow her representation with indisputably male gender markings: he is wise and courteous, his bearing is military. Laura's "angelico seno" (angelic bosom)[12] becomes his broad chest, a sure sign of physical strength and virility; her "bionde treccie" or "capei

---

[9] Gaspara Stampa, *Rime*, 2nd ed. (Milan: Rizzoli, 1976), 85. The *Rime* were published posthumously in 1554. The tercets of the sonnet form a self-portrait: "E chi vuol poi conoscer me, rimiri / una donna in effetti ed in sembiante / imagin de la morte e de' martiri, / un albergo di fé salda e costante, / una, che, perchè pianga, arda e sospiri, / non fa pietoso il suo crudel amante." ("If you should care to know me, you might see, / A lady in her manner and appearance / Like Death herself and every kind of sorrow, / An inn of steady faith and constancy, / One who, for all her tears, her ardent sighs, / Can win no pity from her cruel lover." Trans. Laura Anna Stortoni and Mary Prentice Lillie, in eaedem, *Women Poets of the Italian Renaissance: Courtly Ladies and Courtesans* (New York: Italica Press, 1997), 141.

[10] All translations within this essay are my own unless otherwise indicated. This version of *Rime* 7 appears in Stortoni and Lillie, *Women Poets of the Italian Renaissance: Courtly Ladies and Courtesans*, 141. The initial illusion is to Song of Songs 5: 10-16.

[11] Bernard Weinberg, *French Poetry of the Renaissance* (Carbondale: Southern Illinois University Press, 1954), 28.

[12] Francesco Petrarca, *Il Canzoniere*, ed. Nereo Vianello (Milan: Bietti, 1966), 126: 9.

d'oro" (blond tresses)[13] become his "pelo biondo" which can apply to both hair and beard, another sign of masculinity; Laura's face "fra 'l bianco e l'aureo colore" (colored between golden and white)[14] (CXXVII, 49) becomes his "vivo colore" (lively coloring), more an indicator of the horseman and outdoorsman than of the blushing roses of feminine modesty. Both figures are embodiments, however, of the cruel beloved of tradition who is "empio in amore" (pitiless in love). To highlight her subject's masculinity Stampa has proposed the culturally endorsed image of a perfect courtier, a twin of Castiglione's ideal. In a few brief lines of verse, the beloved emerges as the epitome of the knightly gentleman-warrior, a practitioner of what Frédérique Verrier terms "l'Humanisme militaire."[15] Both Laura and not, Stampa's subject has avoided effemination while adhering strictly to the Petrarchan formula.

While a conventional poet, Stampa was not a conventional woman, having been either an "irregolare," as Donadoni asserts, or possibly a courtesan.[16] In the case of "honest" female versifiers from the middle class or aristocracy of the Cinquecento, the construction of a "narcissistically subjectivized" male object of desire posed serious moral and literary obstacles. Like Stampa, two celebrated and highly respected ladies of their day, Vittoria Colonna (1492–1547) and Veronica Gambara (1485–1550)[17] also accepted the hegemony of the Petrarchan model in their amatory poetry, in keeping with the aesthetic lessons found in Pietro Bembo's rhetorical works. The two aristocrats easily adapted to the system of creative imitation Bembo proposed, actively seeking the master's benevolent guidance and stamp of approval. Letters were exchanged between Bembo and these two disciples, who submitted samples of their compositions for his perusal. His responses make it clear that their poems were fine illustrations of the middle style he had declared suitable for the lyric, the characteristics of which were

---

[13] Petrarca, *Canzoniere*, 127: 77 and 84.

[14] Petrarca, *Canzoniere*, 127: 49.

[15] Frédérique Verrier, *Les Armes de Minerve* (Paris: Presses de l'Université de Paris-Sorbonne, 1997).

[16] Eugenio Donadoni, *Gaspara Stampa* (Messina: Principato, 1919). For more information on the inflammatory debate over Gaspara Stampa's identity, whether musical *virtuosa*, mistress, courtesan, or passionate virgin, see the chapter "Fiction and Reality" in Fiora A. Bassanese, *Gaspara Stampa* (Boston: Twayne, 1982), 22–46.

[17] Contemporaries and friends, Colonna and Gambara had much in common. Daughters of the aristocracy, they were well educated, entered political marriages as a matter of course, and held court in their palaces, surrounding themselves with artists, humanists, and assorted intellectuals whom they patronized. Both grew to love their husbands, military men who were often fighting other people's wars. Both were widowed in their thirties, as a consequence of these wars, finding solace in their deep faith. Women of strong moral fiber, Colonna and Gambara found an instrument for self-expression in poetry.

described as "piacevolezza," "leggiadria," "grazia," "vaghezza," and "dolcezza."[18] As Peter Burke notes: "The taste of 'the time' was the creation of particular social groups and expressed their social prejudices."[19] Both Colonna and Gambara were celebrated poets in their own day because they reflected the literary status quo and fulfilled the elite's aesthetic expectations. Imitation provided agency and approbation for these women as poets, as it did for scores of their male counterparts, but, as love poets, moral and aesthetic constraints were also operative for them. Besides having to deconstruct and reconfigure Laura as male, female practitioners also faced the secondary complication of inventing strategies to represent male beauty, for lyric tradition held that beauty was at the heart of love. In the case of Colonna and Gambara, these poets were also not adopting the trope of the cruel, distant beloved, intrinsic to the figure of Laura and utilized by Stampa. In their *rime amorose*,[20] they are celebrating conjugal love, where desire is socially sanctioned and religiously sanctified. Yet, as gentlewomen, they risk criticism, even opprobrium, by representing the bodies of their husbands, their own erotic desire, or marital fulfillment.

In Vittoria Colonna's *rime amorose*, the poet solves these conundrums by capitalizing on her deceased beloved's status as a celebrated *condottiere*, offering a virile counterpart to the womanly Laura. A soldier by temperament, training, and choice, Ferrante d'Avalos as a lyric subject embodies the notions of martial virility found in classical texts and propagated by Humanism. Taking *Rime amorose* 5 as an example, we find that Colonna proposes his archetypal *virtus* in a variant on the blazon. The poet stockpiles martial and manly terminology in the sonnet: "superba insegna" (proud sign), "ardire" (boldness), "il vigor" (vigor), "gli sdegni" (indignation), "l'ire" (rages), "l'invitto valor" (unconquered valor), "virtù, celerità, forza ed ingegno" (virtue, swiftness, strength, and genius), "la chiara fama" (noble fame), "la gloria bella" (great glory), "'l merto" (merit), and, finally, "opre divine" (divine works). The only body fragment allowed to appear is "la forte vittrice mano" (bold, victorious hand), more sword than hand. However, in the controlled language of the *Rime amorose*, Colonna is careful to preserve decorum and *gravitas*, as required by the Bembian code, not permitting her

---

[18] Cited in Peter Burke, *Culture and Society in Renaissance Italy 1420–1540* (New York: Scribner's, 1972), 136.

[19] Burke, *Culture and Society*, 141.

[20] This is the title of the section of Colonna's *Rime* (edited by Alan Bullock) dedicated to her love for her husband, Ferrante d'Avalos. Gambara composed about a dozen pieces dedicated to her husband, Gilberto, which constitute close to a sixth of her known output. See Veronica Gambara. *Le Rime*, ed. Alan Bullock (Florence: Olschki, 1995) and Vittoria Colonna, *Rime*, ed. Alan Bullock (Rome and Bari: Laterza, 1982). All poems cited are taken from these editions and indicated by poem number in the body of the text. Sections of the discussion on Colonna derive from, and are expanded in, Fiora A. Bassanese, "Vittoria Colonna, Christ and Gender," *Il Veltro* 40 (1996): 53–57.

verse to wander from encomium into the suggestion of the erotic, so key to the Renaissance Petrarchan blazon. Colonna's praise is hyperbolic, suggesting the construction of an ideal, rather than a real, subject, more *exemplum* than person. Like an icon, the figure of the dead warrior is static and symbolic, mythic rather than human.

Colonna is composing at a disadvantage. The emphasis on the socially endorsed virility her beloved embodies must be housed in language that does not wander into the erotic. As in Stampa's sonnet, Colonna's verse recalls the figure of the gentleman-knight: the beloved is an exemplary man of arms, worthy of all recognition and honor, "che è il vero premio delle virtuose fatiche" (which is the true prize of virtuous labors) according to Castiglione.[21] While acceptable masculine beauty may be found in strength, muscles, and arms, this formulation is not as congenial to the lyric as it is to the epic tradition. Only a handful of Colonna's poems actually focus on the warrior beloved. In Veronica Gambara's amatory verse, on the other hand, the beloved's forays onto the battlefield are barely referred to, and his absences are easily integrated into the Petrarchan discourse of abandonment and loss. While Colonna eulogizes her husband as hero as a viable literary strategy, in *Rime* 25 Veronica Gambara employs the technique of indirection to express the desire created by the sight of her beloved. Her *condottiere* is described as worthy of Venus's ardor, "perché ne l'arme il bellicoso Marte / vinci d'assai, e di bellezza Adone / cede al tuo paragone" (because in arms you greatly surpass the warlike Mars and, in beauty, Adonis surrenders to your example). By projecting her desire onto the figure of Venus, the poet acknowledges the beloved's allure, masculinity, and sensuality, while preserving personal modesty. It is a shrewd rhetorical tactic to concurrently represent the gaze of female desire ⁻ who is more femininely erotic than Venus?—and avoid the open declaration of the subject's own passion and sexuality. Notwithstanding the repeated references to love, only one body part is privileged and recurring in both Gambara's and Colonna's amatory verse: the eyes.

In Veronica Gambara's *Rime*, the beloved is represented in a cycle of four sonnets dedicated to his bright and clear eyes ("occhi lucenti e chiari").[22] Through synecdoche, the eyes stand for the body of the beloved; their movements and changes capture his character in what can be loosely termed a "blazon" of his eyes. But the sonnets also provide a warehouse of Petrarchan ocular modifiers: rather than being signs of the fragmentation of the beloved's body, however, the eyes function as repositories of his identity. They reflect the multifaceted nature of the beloved in one all-inclusive locus, thus allowing the lover to celebrate the whole of the beloved by focusing on the single anatomical indicator. Among

---

[21] Baldassare Castiglione, *Il libro del Cortegiano*, ed. Ettore Bonora (Milan: Mursia, 1976) 1.18.

[22] These are *Rime* 20–24 in the Bullock edition.

Gambara's best-known lyrics, the four poems dedicated to the beloved's eyes are clearly derivative, as in *Rime* 21:

> Lieti, mesti, superbi, umili, alteri,
> vi mostrate in un punto, onde di speme
> e di timor m'empiete [. . .]
> Or poiché voi mia vita e morte sete,
> occhi felici, occhi beati e cari,
> siate sempre sereni, allegri, e chiari.

> [Joy, sorrow, pride, humility, and arrogance,
> you display all at once, whence with hope
> and with fear you fill me [. . .]
> Since you are my life and death,
> eyes happy, eyes lovely and dear,
> be always serene, lively and clear!][23]

In Gambara's *Rime* 22, the eyes represent the man and his functions as a husbandly beloved. Described as the "vero albergo d'amore" (true residence of love), "fermo sostegno" (steadfast support), "the absence of pain or disdain, the presence of joy," in short, his eyes contain "all that good that Heaven and my good fortune can give me in this mortal life" ("tutto quel ben ch'in questa mortal vita / darmi può 'l Cielo o mia benigna sorte"). This is a declaration of feminine dependency and wifely submission which doubtlessly appealed to Gambara's contemporaries but which certainly presents an individualistic reinterpretation of the canonical source. But the poet's borrowings do not stop at Petrarch.

Gambara was also drawn to the Neoplatonic sources so popular in her day. Marsilio Ficino, for example, considered eyes among the most exalted parts of the body, and sight was deemed the most spiritual of the senses. Even before Ficino and the popularization of Neoplatonic love in Bembo's *Asolani*, the Dolce Stil Nuovo had privileged the beloved's eyes as a powerful instrument of transformation—not of the beloved, but of the observer or lover, as can be seen in a familiar sonnet from the *Vita Nuova*: "Ne li occhi porta la mia donna Amore, / per che si fa gentil ciò ch'ella mira" (my lady carries Love in her eyes, making noble all she gazes on). As Dante explains it, Love is awakened in the beholder: "not only does it awaken where it is sleeping but where it is not in potency; she, acting marvelously, makes it appear . . . this woman turns this potency into act by means of the most noble part of her eyes."[24] In Gambara's verse, the idea of

---

[23] Trans. Richard Poss, "A Renaissance *Gentildonna*: Veronica Gambara," in *Women Writers of the Renaissance and Reformation*, ed. Katharina M. Wilson (Athens, GA: University of Georgia Press, 1987), 47–66, here 58.

[24] Dante Alighieri, *Vita Nuova; Rime*, ed. Fredi Chiappelli (Milan: Mursia, 1971), 46: "non solamente [Amore] si sveglia là ove dorme, ma là ove non è in potenzia, ella,

the transformative power of love, realized through the beloved's eyes, is joined to the narcissistic element typical of Petrarchan discourse. The poems elaborate the lover's response far more than they focus on the actual eyes praised. Like all Petrarchan verse, these compositions are concerned with the speaking I far more than with the object of desire, as in this first quatrain of *Rime* 20:

> Dal veder voi, occhi lucenti e chiari,
> nasce un piacer ne l'alma, un gaudio tale
> ch'ogni sdegno, ogni affanno, ogni gran male
> soavi tengo, e chiamo dolci e cari.
>
> (Seeing you, O eyes serene and clear,
> there rises in the soul such pleasure, such bliss,
> that each hurt, each affliction, each great pain
> I consider mild, and I call them sweet, and dear.)[25]

The contemplation of the beloved's eyes, the poet continues, neoplatonically gives life and pushes away death. Clearly, two sets of eyes are required for Love's transformation to occur; the lover's gaze is as essential to the reception of meaning as the eyes observed.[26]

The importance of seeing, gazing, and looking is also featured in Colonna's *Rime amorose*. References to sight and vision, real, imagined, or dreamt, populate her love poetry. Colonna's language accentuates the importance of both physical and spiritual sight. These are a few random samples, taken from the *Rime amorose*, with the visual references italicized: "l'imagin viva a *l'occhio* riede" (RA1.4); "*Occhi* miei, oscurato é il nostro sole" (RA1. 15); "*veggio* spento il valor" (RA1.19); "vera luce a *quell'occhio* era 'l mio Sole" (RA1.24); "Sperando di *veder* là su il mio Sole" (RA1.37); "l'alma *vede* la sua sì bella" (RA1.60). *Vedere*, "to see," is synonymous with comprehension, knowledge, awareness, perception, foresight, and imagination. As was the case in the *Vita Nuova*, gazing upon Colonna's beloved is transformative of all who come to grasp his significance, his meta-historical role on earth, or his metaphysical import. In poem 62, she imbues the beloved with Neoplatonic absolutes as well, writing: "Ma quanto mai di buon visse fra noi, / quanto di bel per occhio uman si scorse, / anzi la virtù vera e la beltade / in lui rifulser . . ." (Whatever good lived amongst us, whatever beauty human eyes perceive, indeed, true virtue and beauty shone forth in him . . .) in

---

mirabilemente operando, lo fa venire . . . questa donna riduce questa potenzia in atto secondo la nobilissima parte de li suoi occhi."

[25] Translated by Poss, "A Renaissance *Gentildonna*," 61.

[26] A middle-class poet from Lucca, Chiara Matraini (1515–1604?) also penned several compositions dedicated to her beloved's eyes, often utilizing images used by Vittoria Colonna, whom she admired. See the paper by Carlson in this volume.

such a way that those who saw him wondered if glory had already arrived at its noblest age in him.

Vittoria Colonna achieved public encomium for her amatory verse in large part because it was a spiritualized panegyric in honor of a dead spouse. The female author retains *onestà* by virtue of both marriage and death. Except for his sword-wielding hand—quite unlike Laura's "man bianche sottili" (slender white hands)[27]—and intimations of the powerful, battle-hardened body required to achieve military glory, a body never directly described in the sonnets, the beloved of Colonna's *rime amorose* is reduced to a luminous presence, his eyes her stars and beacons. Within the Petrarchan "architesto," Laura's eyes also hold a place of honor among her fragmented body parts: they are "quei begli occhi soavi / che portaron le chiavi / de' miei dolci pensier" (those beautiful gentle eyes that held the keys to my sweet thoughts).[28] Indeed, a cluster of poems dedicated to Laura's eyes appears early on in the *Canzoniere* (specifically 71, 72, 73, 75). Claude Perrus likens these compositions to an "exercise in Stilnovistic form and content" in which the eyes "show the path to heaven, improve the poet as both an individual and a poet" but also blend in with common Petrarchan themes of "curiosity and frustration."[29] Like beacons, they sometimes illuminate the turbulent seas of life, guiding the subject's proverbial fragile boat, a conceit Colonna borrows whole from Petrarch in *Rime amorose* 1.28: "Così il bel lume de' suo' santi ardori / guidi mia nave in queste turbide onde, / tra scogli e tra sirene empie nemiche" (May the beautiful light of his holy ardor thus guide my ship in these angry waves, amidst reefs and wicked, hostile sirens). In many of the love lyrics, Colonna mourns the loss of the living man, the physical being represented by his guiding eyes: "Gli occhi che Morte mi asconde e cela, / Ond'uscio 'l foco ch'ancor l'alma accende" (Death conceals and hides from me the eyes from which emerged the fire that still lights my soul) or "Dove sono ora le mie fide scorte, / e dove tengon volti i chiari rai?" (Where are my faithful guides now, and where have the noble rays turned?).[30]

As is well known, the Petrarchan lover in the *Canzoniere* is affected by the contemplation and observation of the beloved's form. When the object of this

---

[27] Petrarca, *Canzoniere*, 37: 98.

[28] Petrarca, *Canzoniere*, 37: 34–36.

[29] Claude Perrus, "L'image fantastique du corps dans le *Canzoniere* de Pétrarque: de l'anamorphose à la metamorphose," in *La Représentation du Corps dans la Culture Italienne: Actes du Colloque de 1982, Centre d'Études Italiennes d'Aix-en-Provence* (Aix-en-Provence: Université de Provence, 1983), 29–44, here 34: "Les 'chansons des yeux' elles-memes, qui apparaissent de prime abord comme un exercise de forme et de contenu stilnoviste, insèrent dans la thématique sans surprise de la louange (les yeux de Laure montrent le chemin du ciel, rendent le poète meilleur comme individu et comme poète, etc.) des motifs plus complexes ou se melent la curiosité et la frustration. . ."

[30] Colonna, *Rime amorose* 2.39 and 37.

gaze is absent, the contemplation moves inward, originating in memory or fantasy. When the absence is predicated on the death of the subject, a powerful spiritual element is added, one that finds expression in Neoplatonic language and thought. Although Laura's eyes are repeatedly referred to as the source of Amor's arrows and a spur to spiritual awakening, Petrarch does not detail their specific properties; their attributes remain generic. They are known by their beauty, brilliance, and power but not by color, shape, spacing, and so forth. René Stella terms them "ritual signs of a semiotic system" named *lumi, faville*, and *stelle*.[31] For Gaspara Stampa, intent on reinventing the *fabula* of the *Canzoniere* in her own collection, the ocular motif is prominently displayed: her beloved's eyes are referenced repeatedly being the "luci . . . chiare e serene" "ove mirando / perdei me stessa"[32] (clear and serene lights, where gazing I lost myself) or, in a reprise of the typical Petrarchan antithesis of war and peace, "Beate luci, or se mi fate guerra / voi, donde può venir solo la mia pace"[33] (blessed lights, if you make war on me, whence can come my peace). But Stampa does not explore the religious potential of the beloved intrinsic to the Petrarchan model, particularly in the verse composed after Laura's death.

In the section "In morte di Madonna Laura," the illuminating power of Laura's eyes is heightened, as a concentrated spiritual element enters the Petrarchan text, underscored by Neoplatonic language and thought. The beloved's beauty is sublimated by death, augmented by its connection to the divine. As is to be expected, it is this representation of Laura that most inspired the widow Vittoria Colonna's *Rime amorose*, all composed after the death of her spouse.[34] In the *Canzoniere*, Petrarch never ceases referring to the beloved's corporeal self, to a body so prized that the poet continues to describe it here and there throughout the final, commemorative poems of his opus. Colonna opts for the spiritualized version of Laura, a love object transformed into *sole, lume, luce*—sun, illumination, light, and flame. Such terms are also genderless, readily commutable from female to male. Colonna eventually transforms the beloved as hero into the beloved as celestial guide, a Neoplatonic "degna scala del Ciel" (worthy ladder to/of Heaven):[35] his virtue emanates from the true Good; his beauty is the

---

[31] René Stella, "La Représentation du corps dans le *Canzoniere* de Pétrarque," in *La Représentation du Corps*, 45–76, here 62–63: "ne sont que des signes rituels d'un système sémiotique."

[32] Stampa, *Rime*, 33 and 66.

[33] Stampa, *Rime*, 52.

[34] One composition written before the death of d'Avalos survives. Titled "Excelso mio signor, questa ti scrivo," it is an "epistle" written by the faithful wife to her distant husband, represented as the traditional "cruel beloved" who ignores her after having abandoned her to go to war. The poem's style is not particularly Petrarchan. In the Bullock edition, it is placed among the "Rime amorose disperse."

[35] Colonna, *Rime amorose*, 60.

manifestation of a celestial soul. Indeed, Marsilio Ficino had taught that beauty is a manifestation of God and that love—even if originating in material beauty—ultimately reaches towards God. Moreover, even though man employed a body, his rational soul was part of the divine. With death, the beauty of the beloved would ascend heavenward, with the rational soul. Integrating these Neoplatonic lessons into her Petrarchan imitation, Colonna celebrates her continuing love for a deceased beloved, whose role is no longer erotic but abstract. Acquiring transcendent qualities in this altered state, his purpose is to lead the mourning lover upwards, towards the divine light he reflects.

Like Petrarch's dead Laura, the heavenly D'Avalos displays no flaws. Within the development of the *rime amorose*, the love object de-materializes, more angelic projection than man. The lover's eyes continue to view Beauty but the sight is pure light. The desired body is not dismembered but dissolved into evanescence. Such potential was innate in the flesh the poet has metamorphosed into light. In *Rime amorose* 77, Colonna declares that if Nature's "noble thinkers" and believers "avesser del mio Sol mirato i rai, / quei primi avrian da sue grand'opre inteso / che reggeva il bel corpo alma immortale" (would have gazed upon the rays of my Sun, they would have understood from his great deeds that his handsome body bore an immortal soul). As Abigail Brundin notes, "her love is the primary vehicle for arriving at divine fulfillment though the ennobling and purifying effect that the memory of the beloved has upon the poet's heart and soul." [36] The memory of the "amata imagin" (beloved image) results in an immaterial fireworks show: "Mille accese virtuti a quella intorno / scintillar vidi, e mille chiari rai / far di nova beltate il viso adorno" (I saw a thousand burning virtues sparkling around him and a thousand noble rays adorn his face with a new beauty).[37] The two "soli" (suns) that are Laura's eyes have given way to Colonna's "bel Sole" (beautiful Sun), a proper noun, a non-corporeal identity brimming with religious and literary connotations.[38] For "Sole" is also Christ the Redeemer, as well as the pagan Apollo, god of poetry and art.[39] In the end, the true object of desire is spiritual and artistic: a quest for meaning beyond the physical and ephemeral.

It can be argued that Petrarch's fragmentation of the female body led to its reification but also to its use as a trope for literary achievement and rewards. In Nancy Vickers' words: "As Petrarch's readers have consistently recognized,

---

[36] Abigail Brundin, "Volume Editor's Introduction," in Vittoria Colonna's *Sonnets for Michelangelo* (Chicago: University of Chicago Press, 2005), 1–43, here 4. This volume contains an excellent bibliography on Colonna and her times.

[37] Colonna, *Rime amorose*, 85.

[38] A similar progression takes place in Gambara's verse after the death of her spouse: in *Rime* 31, a deceased "bel sole" has replaced Gambara's living "fidato duce."

[39] The significance of Apollo for Petrarch's rhymes is an obvious subtext for Colonna's references to "Sole." See H.D. Brumble, *Classical Myths and Legends in the Middle Ages and Renaissance* (Westport, CT: Greenwood Press, 1998), 28–32, s.v. "Apollo."

Laura and *lauro*, the laurel to crown a poet laureate, are one."[40] Circumscribed by the impositions of imitation, Cinquecento *petrarchiste* nevertheless found ways to accommodate to canonical imagery and language while constructing a subject whose body did not lend itself to the same interpretations and allusions as Laura's but nevertheless functions as such a trope. Whether they sought to translate Laura's beauty and anatomy into a masculine archetype of humanist virility or substitute a single, palatable part—the eyes—for the unwritten whole or metamorphose the beloved's material flesh into immaterial luminescence, Stampa, Gambara, and Colonna formulated socially and artistically acceptable strategies in constructing their male subjects. They escaped the silence of their sex and their sister, the reified and fragmented Laura, by borrowing her lover's words in their own scattered rhymes. Whether masculine or feminine, the poets' gaze becomes contemplative and aesthetic. While Colonna and Gambara's poems are easily situated in the Petrarchan mold, they also resound with other lyric, philosophical, and linguistic echoes that enrich their verse. Their eyes not only gaze into those of the beloved, but also look into the pages of Dante, Ficino, and Bembo, among others, finding inspiration in them all. Eventually, both Gambara and Colonna would be drawn away from the physical to an exclusively spiritual representation of love, having concluded, as Pietro Bembo's Hermit declares in Book 3 of the *Asolani*: "la vera bellezza non è umana e mortale che mancar possa, ma è divina e immortale."[41] (true beauty is not human and mortal, that can die, but it is divine and immortal). All the *petrarchiste* sought another form of divine and immortal beauty as well: art.

---

[40] Vickers, "Diana Described," 107.
[41] Pietro Bembo, *Prose della vulgar lingua; Gli Asolani; Rime*, ed. Carlo Dionisotti (Turin: TEA, 1966, repr. 1989). *Asolani*, Book 3, 17.

Literary Pastimes of a Paduan Jurist: Boccaccio, Petrarch, and Marco Mantova Benavides

Victoria Kirkham

At his death in 1582, aged ninety-three, Marco Mantova Benavides had penned a river of books rising to one hundred titles, the collected wisdom of a legal giant passionate in his bent for humanistic letters.[1] Alongside volume after volume packaged for the law students he taught at Padua stand his poems in the Petrarchan style, written mainly in youth but not published until toward the end of his life, *Rime benavidiane. In gratia di quegli, i quali sono studiosi et vaghi della lingua italiana* (Padua: Lorenzo Pasquati, 1577). To keep them company, this remarkable one-man library preserves a commentary on their source, keyed to Mantova's ruling perspective as a lawyer, *Annotationi brevissime, sovra le rime di M. F. P. le quali contengono molte cose a proposito di ragion civile, sendo stata la di lui prima professione, a beneficio de li studiosi. Hora date in luce, con la tradutione della Canzona Chiare fresche et dolc'acque, Italia mia, Vergine bella, et del sonetto Quando veggio dal Ciel scendere l'aurora, in Latino* (Padua: Appresso Lorenzo Pasquale, 1566). Clearly, the Paduan jurist felt a professional kinship with Petrarch. Even his Italian fiction is veined with vocabulary mined from rhymes that he judged ripe with authority on civil law, the Trecento poet's "first profession."[2] Dante,

---

[1] Counts vary. See the catalogue in Marco Mantova Benavides, *Novelle*, ed. Luigi Pescasio (Mantua: Padus, [1973]), 57–62, taken from A. Valsecchi, *Discorso inaugurale letto nella grand'aula dell'I.R. Università di Padova per l'apertura di tutti gli studi . . .* (Padua: Coi Tipi del Seminario, 1839). Pescasio synthesizes such earlier sources for a useful introductory sketch on Mantova's life and the publishing history of the *novelle*. The jurist's name has variant spellings: Mantoa, Benevides. See now also F. Tomasi and C. Zendri, "Mantova Benavides, Marco," in *Dizionario biografico degli Italiani* (Rome: Istituto dell'Enciclopedia Italiana, 2007), 69:214–20.

[2] Like Petrarch, Mantova assembled his "familiar" letters: *Di lettere famigliari diuerse a diversi regi, cardinali, vescoui, duci, prencipi, senatori, ed altri letterati, et idioti, et non pur maschi, ma etiando femine ualorose, et degne* (Padua: Lorenzo Pasquati, 1578), preserved also in MS at the Marciana (MS. It. X, Cod. 91, vol. 1, *Lettere volgari e latine di*

too, as far as Mantova was concerned, rightly belonged in the circle of illustrious jurists. Their twenty-seven portrait busts adorned a *Wunderkammer* of his *palazzo*, from the field's founding father Accursius (1182–1260), who taught at Bologna and compiled the great medieval concordance of civil law, to the Parisian humanist Guillaume Budé and the recently deceased Andrea Alciati (1492–1550), better known for his emblem book. Just one series in the marvels that made his home a memorable museum, the busts survive as full-page engravings by Enea Vico printed in 1566 at Rome.[3] Rounding out his homage to the Three Crowns of Florence, Mantova performed as a new Boccaccio when he put his hand to creative prose in the vernacular. After a first experiment divided into five "days," *L'Heremita* (Venice: Rusconi, 1521), he produced a trio of *novelle* sent to press in 1530 under the title of the first, *Della ingratitudine novella*. Reprinted only three times, twice in the nineteenth and once in the twentieth century, this tale and its siblings *Della avaritia de' principi moderni* and *Della eloquenza* constitute a small, rarely cited *novelliere* abob in the great sea of stories that flow from Boccaccio's imitators.[4] Mantova exploits the genre for didactic possibilities, inspired philosophically by his firm belief in the powers of law and human reason.

Born in 1489 to a family of Spanish origins, Marco Mantova Benavides studied Latin, Greek, and law at the University of Padua, winning when only

---

Marco Mantova), as noted by Charles Davis, "Ammannati, Michelangelo, and the Tomb of Francesco del Nero," *Burlington Magazine* 118.880 (Jul., 1976): 472–84.

[3] *Illustrium iureconsultorum imagines quae inveniri potuerunt ad vivam effigiem expressae. Ex Musaeo Marci Mantuae Benavidij. Patavini iureconsulti clarissimi* (Rome: Ant. Lafrerij Sequani, 1566).

[4] *L'Heremita*, reprinted in 1525 and 1532, is not a vehicle for short stories in spite of its five-day division. On the first day the author visits a cave-dwelling Pisan hermit in the Euganean Hills, on the second he narrates dreams; the third and fourth days tell of hunting pleasures, and the fifth is a theological dispute on predestination. For the *novelle*, see Marco Mantova Benavides, *Della ingratitudine novella*. [Italy], 1530, 96 pp, which also contains "Della avaritia de prencipi moderni" and "Novella della eloquenza." This edition, of which one copy is listed at Yale by the Library of Congress online catalog, is presumably the same as that referred to by Romagnoli (see below) and Pescasio (above, n. 1) under the title *Novelle tre*. 16th c., 48 fols., "Alla valorosa signora Madonna B.A.C.C.C. (Beatrice) Pia de gli Obici De la ingratidudine Novella." etc. The later reprints are in: *Opere di M. Sperone Speroni degli Alvarotti tratte da' mss. originali*, ed. Natale dalle Laste and Marco Forcellini (Venice: D. Occhi, 1740), which contains "Della eloquenza," erroneously attributed to Sperone Speroni; *Novelliero italiano*, ed. Girolamo Zanetti (Venice: Pasquali, 1754), which contains "Della eloquenza," erroneously attributed to Sperone Speroni; *Novelle scelte rarissime stampate a spese di XL amatori* (London: R. Triphook at the T. Bensley Press, 1814), which contains "Le amorose novelle" by Giustiano Nelli and all three by Mantova; *Novelle di Marco Mantova scrittore del sec. XVI, novellamente stampate a fac-simile del testo originale* (Bologna: Presso Gaetano Romagnoli, 1862; repr. Bologna: Commissione per la Lingua, 1967); and the most recent, Pescasio's edition of 1973.

twenty-six his appointment to the chairs he would famously hold for half a century.[5] Word of his learned lectures drew students from afar to the venerable athenaeum of the Venetian patriciate, men like the Spaniard P. Amato, who translated Petrarch's *canzone* "Italia mia";[6] the Flemish medalist Jacob Zagar, who struck one of his portraits (Titian did another);[7] Antonio Caraffa of Naples, a future cardinal of the church; and Giovanangelo de' Medici of Milan, later Pope Pius IV. His lofty consulting clientele counted Italy's most powerful princes, among them Duke Cosimo I de' Medici and Duke Ercole II of Ferrara, not to mention the Holy Roman Emperors Charles V and Ferdinand II. With his classical humanistic education, Mantova emerged as a defining figure in Padua's intellectual elite. During the 1540s he found an outlet for his vernacular literary hobbies in the city's Accademia degli Infiammati, inspired by Sperone Speroni and brightened for a time by Benedetto Varchi.[8] The polymath Anton Francesco

---

[5] On his appointments to the chaired professorships, see Tomasi and Zendri, "Mantova, Benavides." Between then and his official retirement half a century later, his annual salary rose to eight hundred florins, more than any citizen had ever been paid. Even afterward, he continued active as an adjunct university professor until he was ninety-three. See Irene Favaretto, "Andrea Mantova Benavides: Inventario delle antichità di casa Mantova Benavides—1695," *Bollettino del Museo Civico di Padova* 61 (1972): 35–164. Although his family name and background suggest Jewish origins, he expresses antisemitic sentiments in a *Dialogo brieve et distinto, nel qual si ragiona del duello et si decide ben cento e più quistioni* (Padua: Gratioso Perchacino, 1561). Duelling, he writes, is a heroic and generous act of honor from which Jews are excluded because they are not capable of honor, even if converted and baptized. Cited by Manlio Pastore-Stocchi, "Marco Mantova Benavides e i trecentisti maggiori," in *Marco Mantova Benavides, Il suo museo e la cultura padovana del Cinquecento: Atti della Giornata di Studio 12 novembre 1983 nel IV centenario dalla morte 1582–1982*, ed. Irene Favaretto (Padua: Accademia Patavina di Scienze Lettere ed Arti, 1984), 253–65.

[6] Marziano Guglielminetti, "Petrarca 1566 (Le 'Annotazioni' di Marco Mantova Benavides)," *Revue des études italiennes* 29 (1983): 170–79, here 173 n. 13. Mantova speaks of Amato as "già mio discepolo."

[7] Charles Davis, "Medals of Marco Mantova Benavides by Jacob Zagar and Giovanni dal Cavino," *Studies in the History of Art* 6 (1974): 96–103. Davis dates this medal to ca. 1551–1553. Zagar appears as an interlocutor in one of Mantova's dialogues in his book *Bassanellus, seu Dialogi CC. Juris, additis etiam Dialogo CCI. De elocutione, ac lib. Tribus locorum communium, nec non centuria Stili sacri Palatii apostolici, et Curiae romanae* (Venice: Valgrisi, 1553).

[8] The *Infiammati* were founded 6 June 1540, but flourished only a few years, having ceased to exist by 1545: Richard S. Samuels, "Benedetto Varchi, the *Accademia degli Infiammati*, and the Origins of the Italian Academic Movement," *Renaissance Quarterly* 29 (1976): 599–634. See further Francesco Bruni, "Sperone Speroni e l'Accademia degli Infiammati," *Filologia e Letteratura* 13 (1967): 24–71. For Marco Mantova Benavides's membership in the *Infiammati* as well as his role as a founder of the *Accademia degli Elevati*, see Giuseppe Vedova, *Biografia degli scrittori padovani* (Padua: Coi Tipi della

Doni, writing him in 1550, praises "tante infinite virtù di nobiltà, di dottrina, di splendore, di cortesia e di magnanimità, nate in voi, e sparse, e seminate, sopra li letterati, sopra li scultori, pittori e sopra tutte le sorte di virtuosi."[9] Pietro Aretino sees in him a man "piuttosto re nelle opere, che dottore nelle leggi, come l'umanità benigno, come la cortesia gentile."[10] A list of the many illustrious creative spirits associated with him and his splendid townhouse, "il teatro delle muse e della musica insieme, dove concorrevano quasi tutti i virtuosi della patria," might just begin with Titian, Jacopo Sansovino, Bartolomeo Ammannati, and Pietro Bembo.[11]

By 1541 he had built the home that became both a museum and *cenacolo*, and he turned his attention to creating for it a worthy garden. To frame that open space, he called on Ammannati for a triumphal arch in celebration of the honors he had won as of 1545. Running above symmetrically placed figures of Apollo and Jupiter, a band of relief panels dramatizes Mantova's "conquests": the Emperor Charles V knights him as Count Palatine, the Venetian doge appoints him ambassador to Padua, and Pope Paul III names him to the high Vatican court, the *Sacra Ruota*.[12] This arch led into a landscaped space where Ammannati had already carved and raised for Mantova a giant *Hercules*, the same legendary hero whose image appeared as emblem of the Accademia degli Infiammati.[13] Relief panels at the base of the statue, which is an idealized portrait of the Paduan himself, allude to the legendary hero's labors in a total composition that symbolically asserts the power over animalistic appetites of virtue and reason, *sapientia* and

---

Minerva, 1832–1836), 1:564–79; the introduction to Giulia Bigolina, *Urania*, ed. Valeria Finucci (Rome: Bulzoni, 2002), 37; Valeria Andrea Gallo's article "Giulia Bigolini," on the website "Escridoras y Pensadoras Europeas," at http://www.escritorasypensadoras.com/fichatecnica.php/72 (accessed 23 February 2007).

[9] Doni is quoted by Corrado Lattanzi, "L'attività giovanile di Bartolomeo Ammannati in Veneto," in *Bartolomeo Ammannati scultore e architetto 1511–1592*, ed. Niccolò Rosselli Del Turco and Federica Salvi (Campi Bisenzio [Florence]: Alinea Editrice, 1995), 87–94.

[10] Pescasio, ed., *Novelle*, 18, quoting Valsecchi, *Discorso inaugurale*.

[11] He and Bembo exchange epistolary compliments. The latter thanks him, for example, on 6 April 1539, for his "umanissime lettere" and promises more news soon, when he returns to Padua. See Pietro Bembo, *Lettere*, ed. Ernesto Travi, 4 vols. (Bologna: Commissione per i Testi di Lingua, 1987–1993), 4:200. Lionello Puppi, "Il 'Colosso' del Mantova," in *Essays Presented to Myron P. Gilmore*, ed. Sergio Bertelli and Gloria Ramakus, 2 vols. (Florence: La Nuova Italia, 1978), 2:311–29, mentions a stucco figure Sansovino made for his house, "statua gigantesca . . . coricata."

[12] The Triumphal Arch still stands *in situ*. See for a good photograph Michael Kiene, *Bartolomeo Ammannati* (Milan: Electa, 1995), 38. On Mantova's commissions of Ammannati, see Lattanzi, "L'attività giovanile di Bartolomeo Ammannati."

[13] Puppi, "Il 'Colosso' del Mantova."

eloquentia.[14] So proud was Mantova of his *Hercules* that he publicized the achievement by having its image circulated in an engraving cut by Enea Vico with the inscription, "The 50-foot colossus erected in Padua by the Sculptor Bartolomeo Ammannati." In the picture, Hercules rises not within a residential yard, but over the skyline of Rome, a setting superimposed to declare the monumental classical character of this amazing modern accomplishment. Elsewhere he boasts of it in a literary conversation composed in Padua after a refreshing visit at his country villa, "Il Bassanello." There he had enjoyed reading dialogues by his friend the philosopher Sperone Speroni, ecstatic on the subject of Titian, "whose art isn't art, it's a miracle," and whose colors, like the grass that turned Glaucus into a sea god, make the painter an immortal.[15] If Speroni saw Titian as the greatest artist since Apelles, Mantova muses, imagine what hyperbole would have sprung from his pen had "Ammannati da Settignano" made a *Hercules* for his courtyard like the one he did for mine, "twenty-five feet tall in stone . . . as everyone knows, something that from the time of the ancient masters until our own, no sculptor has ever attempted, much less done, and it certainly is such that it fills whoever sees it with marvel."[16]

Colossi like Mantova's intimated immortality, a theme explicitly carried into the monumental tomb he next had Ammannati make for him.[17] Inspired by the jurist's enlightened philosophy of life and patronage, its complex design presents an ensemble of figures harmoniously arrayed, as if for a stage setting, against the wall of the nave in his neighborhood church, the Eremitani. At the center, beneath the crowning figure of Immortality, sits Mantova, straining forward toward the altar, book in hand, flanked by Honor and Fame, the rewards of his virtues seated just below, Labor and Wisdom. At Labor's foot, the young man

---

[14] Peter Kinney, *The Early Sculpture of Bartolomeo Ammanati* (New York: Garland Publishing, 1976), 128–30, and for illustrations, 331–33.

[15] Marco Mantova Benavides, "Discorsi sopra i Dialoghi di M. Speron Speroni, ne' quali si ragiona della bellezza ed eccellenza dei loro concetti," originally published Venice, 1561; repr. Sperone Speroni, *Opere*, 5 vols. (Venice: D. Occhi, 1740), 5:426–51.

[16] This still standing colossus, the largest created in Italy since ancient times, was to establish the sculptor nationally, anticipating his most familiar and most beleaguered piece in the genre, the *Neptune* fountain in Piazza della Signoria at Florence. On the commission, see Charles Davis, "'Colossum facere ausus est': L'apoteosi d'Ercole e il Colosso padovano dell'Ammannati," *Psicon* 6 (1976): 32–47. According to Puppi, "Il 'Colosso' del Mantova," the *Hercules* may affirm not just reason's power over appetite, but also the superiority of sculpture over painting in the rivalry that gave rise to Renaissance debates on the *paragone*. Ammannati's ancestral village was Settignano, a place of marble quarries near Florence, but he took pride in the citizenship, bestowed by Duke Cosimo I de' Medici, that entitled him to sign himself "Florentine." See below for his signature on Mantova's tomb.

[17] Virginia Bush, *The Colossal Sculpture of the Cinquecento* (New York: Garland Publishing, 1976), 3–4.

who had been responsible for hewing and polishing all these personifications, then setting them into their soaring multi-tiered architectural frame, signed his name: "MADE BY THE FLORENTINE BARTOLOMEO AMMANNATI." At its completion, in 1546, Mantova was nearing sixty, but it would be ten years before serious illness threatened his life. At that time he received a visit from the Augustinian priest Girolamo Negri, who rushed home to compose a worthy funeral eulogy, but the indomitable Mantova recovered, while his embarrassed encomiast preceded him to the grave by twenty-five years. Before reaping the endless renown announced on this tomb, Padua's remarkable professor had the good fortune of living for thirty-six more years on earth.[18]

The decade that saw Mantova busily directing work on his home, garden, and tomb produced an outpouring of publications as well. One can imagine him rapidly penning them at the study desk on which he kept a small bust of Seneca. At Lyons in 1546 appeared his volume *M. Mantuae Bonaviti Iurisconsulti patavini observationum legalium libri X* with a title-page medallion that depicts Mantova in profile bust, as if he were a Roman emperor. Thick with abbreviated references to the authorities who are his sources, this alphabetical reference text in Latin embraces human experience so rigorously that by the end, it has only begun to touch on the c's: "On the Abstract and the Concrete," "On Actions," "On Adultery" ("considered among atrocious crimes"), "On Agriculture," "On Amity" (vs. consanguinity), "On Avarice," "On Alchemy," "On Anatomy," "On Bastards" (a word held "in odium" by the law because it refuses to perpetuate the parents' memory), "On Beards" (priests are not to cultivate them for reasons of cleanliness, but for laymen they are a formal male member and a sign of upright character), and "On Bologna" (famous for its law school).[19] Even as his hairline retreats with passing time, Mantova himself always appears fully bearded on medals that were struck with his image (he gave them as gifts to his friends) and in the life-sized portrait in the round, probably from Ammannati's model, mounted to complete his tomb after he died.[20]

How far Mantova's interests roamed beyond the law, from the bed of humanism on which his learning lay, jumps from the pages of these abc's as it does from an inventory of his other books. Not only did he record his legal opinions

---

[18] Girolamo Tiraboschi reports the anecdote about Negri's premature death notice: *Storia della letteratura italiana dell'abate Girolamo Tiraboschi bibliotecario del serenissimo Duca di Modena*, 10 vols. (Naples: Giovanni Muccis, 1777–1786), 7.2:99. Negri's funeral oration was published in the collection *Jacobi Sadoleti Epistolarum appendix* (Rome: Generosus Salomonius, 1767).

[19] *M. Mantuae Bonaviti Iurisconsulti patavini observationum legalium libri X* (Lyons: Godefridus et Marcellus Beringi, fratres, 1546), esp. 249, 254.

[20] Kinney, *The Early Sculpture*, 140. Favaretto, "Andrea Mantova," reports that Mantova gave the medals with his image to his friends, perhaps in return for things they sent for his museum.

in volumes he himself signed, dealing with both civil and ecclesiastical questions, he also composed commentaries on earlier jurists, such as the treatise by Matteo d'Afflitto and Baldo Ubaldo of Perugia on priestly law, *Tractatus de iure prothomiseos*, published at Venice in 1562.[21] His sense of the law as a living tradition led him into an ideal dialogue with the men who had shaped it, much like the conversations Machiavelli carried on with revered ancients during his painful years of exile in a muddy village to the south of Florence, Sant'Andrea in Percussina. Immersed in the spirit of justice, Mantova researched the lives of his precursors, which he published at Padua in 1555 as *Epitoma virorum illustrium qui vel scripserunt, vel iurisprudentiam docuerunt in Scholis, et quo tempore etiam floruerunt, ordine alphabetico constitutum, quo Studiosi facilius alliciantur ad legendum*. More than that, he brought them into his home, quite literally surrounding himself with them. Their sculpted busts, including Dante's, were a notable part of his extensive private collection. Perhaps the Paduan scholar so honored the great Florentine for his treatise *On Monarchy*, which addresses the separation of powers between church and state, pope and emperor. Surely, too, he had in mind the pilgrim's encounter in *Paradiso* 6 with Justinian, whose canto-long speech is a point of convergence for the *Commedia's* multiple registers of justice — divine, human, moral, political, and poetic. Dante, who had decried the injustice of his times and personal fate as an exile, would doubtless have been pleased to know his standing with a man of such rectitude as Benavides.

The appearance of his *Annotationi brevissime* on Petrarch's *Rime* the same year as the portraits of the jurists, in 1566, suggests a spurt of activity in leisure-time pursuits following his semi-retirement in 1564. Yet even though he is no longer teaching full-time, Mantova connects with Petrarch collegially, a somewhat ironic relationship given the latter's avowed hatred of the subject his father had forced him to study in a misspent youth at the universities of Bologna and Montpellier. As Boccaccio explained it with imaginative flourish in *De vita et moribus Domini Francisci Petracchi de Florentia*, Petrarch could no longer tolerate the "dangerous cavils of the laws and the deafening arguments of the raging forum," once captivated by the Muses, who disdainfully pushed him away from "the laws of the Caesars and the jurisconsults' charts," setting before his eyes Homer with all his fellow poets.[22] A pedagogical intent organizes Mantova's

---

[21] Luigi Moranti, *Le cinquecentine della Biblioteca Universitaria di Urbino* (Florence: Olschki, 1977), 1:487–88, no. 1134: Matteo d'Afflitto, *Tractatus de iure prothomiseos Excellentissimi Iureconsul. Matthaei de Afflict. et Baldi de Perusio nuperrime recognitus* per D. Ioan. Baptis. Zilettum Venetum a plurimis quibus scatebat erroribus vindicatus, candoriq; suo restitutus, ut facile ex aliorum collatione constat. Subsequenti commentariolo Gravissimi Iuris Interpretis, Marci Mantuae Bonaviti Patavini, ad L. Dudum. C. de contrah. empt. Summariisq... (Venice: Al Segno della Fontana, 1562).

[22] *De vita et moribus Domini Francisci Petracchi de Florentia secundum Johannem Bochacii de Certaldo*, ed. Renata Fabbri, in Giovanni Boccaccio, *Tutte le opere*, ed. Vittore

annotations into two books. First comes the commentary, attached to selected lines and poems. The second part is a mini-dictionary of rhetoric, "Petrarch's Artful (*artificiosi*) Ornaments and an Abbreviated Epilogue of What has Been Said Before." Examples drawn from the poet's verse illustrate classical figures of speech, Latin terms alphabetically ordered. Thus for "*Circumlocutio*," Mantova quotes "Il successor di Carlo," "Vicario di Cristo," "dolce ritegno," and "forma miglior," which he glosses as "the king of France," "the pope," "Laura," and "the soul" (*anima*). Under "*Contraria*" he cites a typical Petrarchan oxymoron, "Arder la neve et agghiacciar 'l foco." *Exclamatio* is illustrated by "O inconstanzia de l'umane cose"; *Impossibile* by "Annoverar le stelle," "gridar sanza lingua." "*Invective*" can be seen in the scathing line with a Dantesque ring, "Ite superbi e miseri Christiani." Instances of "*Metaphora*," defined as "*translatio* of things or words," are "Piovommi amare lagrime dal viso," "Ma poi ch'il ciel accende le sue stelle." As Mantova scans the *Rime sparse*, "*Proverbi*" keep leaping to his eye, for he notes a good number of them: "Ama chi t'ama"; "Tutti siam macchiati d'una pece"; "Chi non ha l'oro no 'l perde." Still more fall under the later rubric "*Sententiae*": "Amor rege suo impero senza spada"; "Che poco val contra fortuna scudo"; "correr a morte ogni cosa creata"; "Cosa bella mortal passa e non dura"; "Cose belle non fur mai senz'honestate."[23] Even less than Dante would Petrarch today present himself as a candidate for a legal library, but this volume reveals how readers took possession of the great sonneteer, dissecting his lyric corpus to serve their own purposes.[24] Mantova customizes Petrarch, alighting on passages with legal implications and providing a gloss. To this specialized apparatus he appends a refresher course on rhetoric, mastery of which was essential to any skilled forensic orator. The content of those pithy sayings that the professor abstracts from the poet's story could well stand as a personal credo, illustrating stylistically his endless fondness for apophthegmatic diction.[25]

Branca (Milan: Mondadori, 1992), 5.1:898–911. In a long tradition from ancient times (Virgil, Ovid), Italian poets often had legal training (Pier della Vigna, Cino da Pistoia, Boccaccio himself). Boccaccio exaggerates Petrarch's disdain, playing up a literary topos that makes poets and lawyers eternal enemies. In fact, Petrarch speaks with deep respect for the law in his tirade against an inept practitioner from France, *Invective against a Detractor of Italy*.

[23] For an excellent distillation of Mantova's commentary, see Guglielminetti, "Petrarca 1566," who places him in—or rather, outside—the tradition of Petrarchan studies, especially as represented in the sixteenth century by Bembo and his followers, and profiles Mantova's abundant classical, biblical, and modern sources. On the mainstream tradition and its origins, which Mantova well knew, see Christopher Kleinhenz, *The Early Italian Sonnet: The First Century (1220–1321)* (Lecce: Milella, 1986).

[24] See the examples in William J. Kennedy, *Authorizing Petrarch* (Ithaca: Cornell University Press, 1994).

[25] Much of what Mantova wrote, as Massimiliano Rossi points out, belongs to a popular sixteenth-century genre of collected *loci communes* such as Erasmus of Rotterdam's

Although not published until the 1560s, Mantova's commentary reflects long familiarity with Petrarch and finds its companion in his own verse, *Rime benavidiane*, written, as his subtitle announces, for the sake of those *i quali sono studiosi et vaghi della lingua italiana*. No one should blame him for turning after more serious studies (the volumes of law he has published both large and small) to his maternal tongue, for the Greeks and Romans did it, so too French, Germans, and Spaniards, who nowadays are also eager to learn the Italian vernacular. We are to compare these verses, he suggests, with his own other pieces on "predestination, ingratitude, avarice, and eloquence"; his thoughts on Sperone Speroni's dialogues, and the poetry by Petrarch and his circle, especially Cino. Mantova could have read Cino in the seminal anthology published at Florence by Giunti in 1527, *Sonetti e canzoni di diversi antichi autori toscani*, widely circulated in reprints. Aside from the appeal he had for Mantova as a fellow law professor, Cino features prominently in the Giuntine edition, where Dante has first place and most space, but the poet from Pistoia comes a prominent second, followed by Cavalcanti, Dante da Maiano, and Guittone d'Arezzo.

Distinctly amateur in flavor, the *Rime benavidiane* move like practice pieces through a variety of forms, themes, and occasional topics without any clear story line. A majority are love poems, apparently written in his youth for a lady known by the *senhal* Olimpia. Like her predecessors Beatrice and Laura, she is sometimes far from her lover, who suffers during her absence. In a variation on precedent, this lady travels on a lake by boat, which gives Mantova an excuse to wish he could be her helmsman. Some sonnets pay homage to a powerful family whose emblem is the stork. Others celebrate a girl's decision to withdraw from the world into a "solitary cell," or weep for a young mother's death in childbirth, and several give vent to sorrows visited on the community by plague. Repeatedly it struck in Mantova's century, in 1528–1530, 1555, and 1575–1577, most devastatingly the third time. In these plague sonnets, as in the final penitential *ternario*, the author speaks not as a youthful rhymester, but an elderly man.

> Poverell'io, vecchio, infermo, e stanco,
> a che tempo mi trovo strano et rio,
> nato, pien di paure, o buono Iddio,
> deh, per pietà non mi venir al manco.
> Ecco la peste di ciascun al fianco. (*Rime benavidiane*, 13v)

Reminders of Boccaccio's *Decameron*, which resonate in Mantova's plague poetry, permeate his prose. While still in his twenties he tried his hand at Italian fiction with *L'eremita* (Venice, 1521), which generated sufficient demand for two

---

Adagia. See "Un episodio della fortuna di Giulio Camillo a Padova: l'"anfiteatrino' di Bartolomeo Ammannati per Marco Mantova Benavides," *Bollettino del Museo Civico di Padova* 82 (1993): 339–60.

reprintings, in 1525 and 1532. When in the introduction to his *Rime* he speaks of "predestination," he alludes unmistakably to this little book, which takes up that subject on its fifth "day." The same passage mentions writings on "ingratitude, avarice, and eloquence." These are the themes of his three long *novelle* in the Boccaccian style, each with a moralizing frame that carries instructive words to the famous personage he has chosen as its recipient. As he explains in a preamble to Madonna Pia degli Obici, his first dedicatee, he found time for this project during leisure enforced by a plague epidemic:

> io, havendo tempo . . . perciò che per la mortifera pestilenza, come sapete, celebrate le ferie et delle corti et delle schole, è stato bisogno alle ville fuggire, et a studi più piacevoli, che ordinariamente gli altri non sono, attendere, intendo di ragionarvi et di scrivervi in queste charte, una Novelletta forse non villana, benchè in villa nata et composta (71).[26]

After addressing Ercole Fregoso in the third, as he enters into the matter proper of the story he speaks again of those terrible circumstances, which forced the university of Padua to close in 1528:

> Hor avenne pur che in questi tempi calamitosi et infelici, ne quali non pur la terra nostra, come sapete, ma universalmente tutta la Italia ne è stata vexata, si per la mortifera pestilenza, si etiandio per che era scarso il vivere . . . la maggior parte de scholari a loro paesi se ne tornorono . . . Et l'anno, che di se lassava memoria a molti secoli, che dopo noi verrano, fu della salutifera incarnatione del nostro signore, Mille cinquecento ventiotto. (11–12)

In the first novella, "Della ingratitudine," an ungrateful Venetian disinherits the most deserving of his three sons, Girolamo, who with much sacrifice had accumulated wealth in Alexandria. Shamed, Girolamo goes into exile in Padua, finding refuge in the house of a dyer and hope for an upturn in his affairs thanks to a jurist who will help him break the will. Mantova proudly seizes on the point, "nostra terra, la quale ne è tanto copiosa [of lawyers] quanta altra d'Italia sia, uno armaio di ragioni civili tenuto et reputato era" (75). In a plot that might well serve as a case study for a course on wills and estates, the two bad sons then bribe the dyer to have Girolamo declared insane, but a good priest rallies to his cause and reports the injustice to the authorities. Their representative, an exemplary *podestà*, orders the dyer arrested and Girolamo freed. In the aftermath, the dyer's servants reveal how they have lived for five years in virtual slavery, unpaid, under constant threat. The only debt the dyer has ever honored, it seems, was his niece's dowry. After torture ("molte tratte del fune"), the dyer confesses to his wrongdoings, a fair settlement is reached, and justice prevails. Mantova spells it

---

[26] All citations are from the *Novelle*, ed. Pescasio, here 71. References are hereafter given in the body of the essay.

out precisely, as if he himself had declared the sentence. The dyer is exiled from Padua for ten years, and if caught in the territory, he is to be decapitated because he had usurped powers of the prince and violated the "santo volere della legge naturale: che niuno altrui faccia quello che non vorria che a se fatto ne fusse." At last, Girolamo returns to Venice and succeeds in breaking his father's will, all on his own, without any lawyer, because he is well spoken, "essendo pratico molto et parlatore . . . a cui molto bene la lingua era stata posta in boccha, che molto bene sapea dir il fatto suo" (84–86).

The vice that gives a title to the second tale, "Della avaritia de principi moderni," strikes the young new king of England, in whose court Gianotto, a Venetian harpsichordist, seeks patronage after his wealthy merchant father loses all in a shipwreck and dies. Fortuna, a major player in Boccaccio's peripeties, here too drives events: "se ben la Fortuna gli haveva le ricchezze involate, non però tolto gli haveva la nobilatà de 'l sangue, ne la virtù, ne la grandezza dell'animo" (98). Instead of rewarding Gianotto's art, born of natural talent and disciplined study, the king dismisses him with twenty-five florins and pays two hundred to the musician's companion, a man who had merely made his instrument. Such arbitrary unfairness causes Gianotto to attempt suicide, but his friends prevent the fatal gesture, mistakenly believing that he won't try again, "essendo a ciascuno animale vivente naturale istinto la vita amare più che alcuna altra cosa et la morte a tutto potere fuggire." Nevertheless, once back in Venice, he hangs himself with his sword belt, "et tal fine hebbe il degno et virtuoso uomo, per la ingratitudine et avaritia del Re d'Inghilterra" (99). Gianotto's end marks just the half-way point of the story, a platform for the author's praise of patronage, especially among the ancients. Without that virtue, sadly lacking today—although the story's dedicatee Monsignor Messer Paolo Palavicino is an obvious exception (and so, implicitly, Mantova himself)—men are not human, but more like shadows, statues, and pieces of wood. The Romans, in contrast, were "liberalissimi, magnanimi et splendidi," as we read in examples set by Julius Caesar, Alexander the Great, Octavian, Pompey, and Scipio Africanus. Nevertheless, even if modern-day princes like the king of England have banished magnanimity, a time of restoration will come when our contemporaries imitate such great men as Hadrian, Vespasian, and Trajan.

Mantova's third story, "De la eloquenza," pits against each other two close friends who become rivals for the love of the same married lady. Not surprisingly, she prefers the more comely of the two, Calliplocamo, a Genoese philosopher endowed (as we see from his name) with a beautiful head of thick, curly hair. Phalacro, a short, thin, pale, and bald Paduan lawyer ten years older, rises undaunted to the challenge, applying the power of his persuasive eloquence. Ginaiola, already won over by Calliplocamo, wobbles but comes to the view that she can't have two lovers. Reasoning that there is only one god, one faith, one soul in the body, and one sun in heaven, she settles on the better speaker. In yet another reversal, unexpected after the climate of courtly love in which Mantova steeps this situation, at the end he steps back and judges, sounding not so much like the jurist he actually is but more like Boccaccio's Fiammetta, queen of the "Questioni d'amore" in the *Filocolo*:

> mo è da vedere . . . quale più e da riprendere, o la malignità di Phalacro, in trattare Calliplocamo così come egli nel trattò et per poca occasione la ammistà di molto tempo con esso lui contratta abbandonare, o la leggierezza di Ginaiola, che così tosto si lasciò svilluppare da colui, che ella già mostrò più d'amare, che se stessa. (132)

Mantova rules that Phalacro deserves more disapproval, but he smilingly adds, let's leave them to enjoy their love, as all gentle spirits would wish to do.

The 1530 *editio princeps* establishes a *terminus ante quem* for dating the stories, which internal references date more precisely to the plague of 1528. Implausible as Mantova's plots may be, with twists aplenty to surprise the reader, all three *novelle* hover close in time and place to his historical present. He says he worked on them at his villa, "Il Bassanello," a place bordering on Arquà Petrarca, whose proximity spurred his attempts as a *Petrarchista*.[27] While his protagonists may travel—Girolamo makes a fortune in Alexandria, Gianotto seeks protection in Britain—the spatial center for all three stories is Mantova's own Padua-Venice axis. A feigned journey by Calliplocamo to Genoa, for example, gives the author an excuse for a moment of *campanilismo*. That Ligurian city isn't nearly as old as Padua, which can boast of being even more venerable than Rome, since its founder was Antenore, who aided the Romans. The unnamed new English king, whose youth is an essential ingredient to the tale spun on a sudden and unexpected turn of avarice, usually only a vice of the old, has to be Henry VIII, who ascended the throne in 1509 and ruled until 1547.

Mantova's trio of stories reverberate with his voice as a Paduan humanist who professed the law and patronized the arts. Among his literary sources, Boccaccio predominates, beginning with the plague connection announced in a preamble to the first novella: "per la mortifera pestilenza . . . è stato bisogno alle ville fuggire" (cf. *Dec.* Intro. 8: "pervenne la mortifera pestilenza"). Instead of borrowing Boccaccio's *cornice* with its fictional narrators, as Giambattista Giraldi Cinzio will for his *Ecatommiti* of 1565, Mantova himself narrates in an unmediated first-person voice, not the Author-Character role Boccaccio assumes. Yet he embeds each tale in a "frame," addressed to the high-born person he has chosen as its recipient. These opening and closing remarks, laced with flattery for the dedicatee, provide a moralizing comment. The strategy, which anticipates Matteo Bandello's more secular pattern in his collected *Novelle*, first published in 1554,

---

[27] Rebuilt in later times, the villa's sixteenth-century gate and coat-of-arms still survive. See Maria Lisa Corso and Sandra Faccini, "Cenni sulla casa Mantova Benavides a Valle S. Giorgio di Baone," in *Marco Mantova Benavides*, ed. Favaretto, 271–75.

may be indebted to Masuccio Salernitano, whose *Novellino* Mantova could have known in its 1483 (Milan) or 1484 (Venice) edition.

Speaking in a preamble to the second novella, "Della avaritia de principi moderni" for Paolo Francesco Palavicino, Mantova decries a vice that is surely the greatest misfortune a man deserving of patronage can meet, but, as he asserts in his conclusion, not one of which Messer Paolo could ever be guilty, given his long family tradition of generosity.[28] Gianotto's shabby treatment as an itinerant musician before the king of England illustrates the point, recalling stories from Day 1 of the *Decameron*, when "subita e disusata avarizia" bites Can Grande della Scala, and Bergamino recounts a similar fault in the legendary Abbot of Cluny. In 1.8 Guglielmo Borsiere's tale of the miserly Ermanno Grimaldi leads to a nostalgic outburst about how much more civil and liberal courtiers used to be; so too Mantova laments present mores, contrasting them eloquently with shining examples from "secoli passati"—Julius Caesar's liberality, Alexander the Great, who called his friends his "maggior thesori."[29] The king was sorry for his moment of folly, but too late, after the fact. His regrets elicit language like that of Petrarch's retrospective pentimento (*Rime sparse* 1), "doppo il fatto et le fortune seguite, il pentirsi, e 'l conoscere chiaramente gli errori con poco consiglio commessi" (100).

Pseudonyms like those Boccaccio assigns his narrators return in Mantova's third tale, whose protagonists he claims to protect from displeasure by assigning them invented names, Phalacro ("baldheaded man") and Calliplocamo ("man with beautiful curly hair"). Better at Greek than Boccaccio, the Paduan humanist betrays a heavier hand when it comes to art. His bizarre names, quite lacking in mellifluence, fit implausible characters whose main purpose is to serve as mouthpieces for Mantova's words "On Eloquence," scripted to teach the importance of well-honed verbal skills. Both in love with the same woman, the pair recall Boccaccio's Tito and Gisippo (*Dec.* 10.8) as models of manly friendship.[30] Given the author's text-book thinking paths, they not surprisingly elicit canonical comparisons. Nature has bound them together "non altrimente che si facesse

---

[28] For information on Masuccio, as well as Bandello and Giraldi Cinzio, see "Rinascimento. Cento opere," RAI International Online, http://www.italica.rai.it/rinascimento/cento_opere/masuccio_novellino.htm.

[29] See Victoria Kirkham, "The Tale of Guglielmo Borsiere (I,8)," in *The Decameron First Day in Perspective*, vol. 1 of *Lectura Boccaccii*, ed. Elissa B. Weaver (Toronto: University of Toronto Press, 2004), 179–206.

[30] Tito and Gisippo loved Sofronia, a more honorable woman (as her name suggests) than Ginaiola. See Victoria Kirkham, "The Classic Bond of Friendship in Boccaccio's Tito and Gisippo (*Decameron* X, 8)," in *The Classics in the Middle Ages: Papers of the Twentieth Annual Conference of the Center for Medieval and Early Renaissance Studies*, ed. Aldo S. Bernardo and Saul Levin, MRTS 69 (Binghamton: Medieval and Renaissance Texts and Studies, 1990), 223–35; repr. in eadem, *The Sign of Reason in Boccaccio's Fiction* (Florence: Olschki, 1993), 237–48. In their rivalry for the same woman, perhaps they could also recall Arcita and Palemone in Boccaccio's *Teseida delle nozze d'Emilia*.

già di Castore et Polluce, di Pylade et Oreste, di Damone et Pithia et di molti altri simili" (114). Their speeches are a pastiche of clichés on courtly love sprinkled with clear echoes of Boccaccio. The married Ginaiola, driven by "concupiscibile appetito" reminiscent of Boccaccio's Ghismonda, explains to Phalacro that she will always love his rival, justifying herself in words prompted by the *Decameron* proem: "le quali [donne] niun diporto hanno se non le lor camere, la dove voi ne havete mille da trastullarvi." Phalacro begins secretly hating Calliplocamo, and no wonder, argues Mantova, considering the "potere e forza di questo disordinato appetito, che così noi Amore ne il chiamiamo" (113–16; cf. *Dec.* 2.10.36, where the doddering Pisan judge Riccardo di Chinzica accuses his young wife, happily abducted by the strapping pirate Paganino, of "appetito disordinato").

Mantova likes to set up unexpected situations that defy the odds—a young king struck by the grasping vice stereotypically associated with age, or here a lover who wins the lady even though, by his own account, he is "picciolo di staura et magro et calvo . . . più tosto Spagniuolo, che Italiano" (124). Calliplocamo's eyes may be more handsome, concedes Phalacro in arguing his case before the lady, but you should look to my intellectual eyes. As for his thick hair, that's an ornament more suited to women since "la chioma insania, leggierezza et instabilità ci dimostra." Julius Caesar and Tiberius had no reason to regret their lack of hair because "gravità, maturità, consiglio et pesati effetti" go with baldness. Moreover, "gli calvi sono più feroci." A small catalogue follows, one of Mantova's favorite rhetorical devices, to clinch the point:

> "calvo fu Diogene, Platone calvo, calvo Esculapio et molt'altri. . . . Socrate philosopho sapientissimo, il quale modestissimo ne fu riputato et massimamente in se stesso lodare, non poteo però non gloriarsi, che a Sileno ne fusse simile, il quale ne fu calvo." (125)

Phalacro borrows his apologia from Synesius of Cyrene's classic *A Eulogy of Baldness*. What does it matter, argues Synesius (ca. 370–ca. 413), if a man's head is bald, so long as "his mind is shaggy?" Man, least hairy of the earthly creatures, is the most intelligent.

> You may look at the pictures in the Museum, I mean those of Diogenes and Socrates, and whomsoever you please of those who in their age were wise, and your survey would be an inspection of bald heads. . . There too is the chair of Silenus and his lash. He has been appointed the guardian slave of Dionysus. For I think that, being bald, he must have been also a man of sense, to keep his self-control in the midst of such aberrations. . . Socrates, the son of Sophroniscus, a moderate man in other respects and beyond

anyone of his associates most chary of self-praise, could not but feel pride in his resemblance to Silenus.[31]

Arguing that man's character is defined by his humanity ("humanità"), woman's by her chastity ("honestà"), the bald orator rises to his peroration, ringing with a eulogy of his native city. None other than Mantova's own Padua, its merits begin with its famous men: "Alberto [Magno] theologo scientissimo, ne fu Padoano; . . . Padoano Tito Livio, vero padre della eloquenza et oratore celebratissimo, che le Romane storie maravigliosamente iscrisse. Et simigliatamente Lodovico Odaxio . . ." (129). In the train of Odasio, tutor to Duke Guidobaldo da Montefeltro of Urbino, other notables crowd, including the Romans Cassius and Flaccus; Marsilio of Padua, Pietro d'Abano, Giovanni de' Dondi, the artists Giusto de' Menabuoi, Guariente d'Arpo, Francesco Squarcione, Andrea Mantegna, Bartolommeo Bellano, and Andrea Briosco, known as il Riccio.

Further soundings bring into sharper focus the Paduan professor's literary profile. Punning in a mannerist spirit, he presents his first story to Madonna Pia, "Novelletta forse non villana, benchè in villa nata" (71). Like so many of Boccaccio's, it takes place "non ha guari, nella nostra città." For Florence Mantova substitutes the great center of commerce neighboring Padua and named as the story proper begins in a Boccaccian formula, "Fu adunque nella città di Vinegia. . ." (72; cf. *Dec.* 2.3.6, "Fu già nella nostra città"; *Dec.* 8.3.4, "Nella nostra città"). Insistent semantics define the mercantile milieu within its first page: "mercatantesca," "mercatantie et trafichi," "mercatante," "mercatantie," "traficare et guadagnare," "cavedale accrescere et aumentare," "mercatantare," "mercatanti." Girolamo's other two brothers live "ne gli oci, nelle piume, con tutte gli aggi del mondo delitiosamente" (74; cf. *Dec.* 4.1.33: "quello che gli ozii e le dilicatezze possano"; Petrarch, *Rime sparse* 7.1, "La gola e 'l sonno et l'oziose piume"). To prevent Girolamo from winning his rightful inheritance, the wicked brothers enlist the dyer in a conspiracy to have their sibling declared mad so he won't keep going about "tencionando et chimerizando" (76; "constructing chimeras," "raving") "di questa benedetta heredità di nostro padre." Although a servant woman called Chimera appears in the *Decameron* frame story, Mantova more plausibly remembers a source with the identical verb form, Teofilo Folengo's *Orlandino* (5.64.6), recently

---

[31] Finucci suggests that in its theme of jealousy between two men, Mantova's novella could have influenced the Paduan writer Giulia Bigolina, who knew him and his daughters. See Giulia Bigolina, *Urania*, ed. Valeria Finucci (Chicago: University of Chicago Press, 2005), 24.
  Synesius, *A Eulogy of Baldness*, trans. A. Fitzgerald, sections 5–6, available at http://www.livius.org/su-sz/synesius/synesius_baldness_01.html (accessed 4 February 2007). Also *Elogio della calvizie*, trans. Anna Rotunno (Milan: Biblioteca Ideale Tascabile, 1995).

published in Venice (1526).[32] Bribed by the conspirators, police sergeants come to arrest Girolamo, "con fustibus et la[n]ternis [with sticks and lanterns], come se havessero voluto pigliare Christo un'altra volta" (78). Boccaccio in his *Genealogie deorum gentilium* (15.9.7) quotes the same Latin words from the Gospels, when Judas leads the mob to capture Christ (i.e., Matthew 26:47; Mark 14:43; Luke 22:47; John 18:3). A Judas is just what Mantova makes his dyer, painting him in the blackest terms to personify the "ingratitude" that gives this story its title. Compared to arch-traitors of the Bible and chivalric romance, this unnamed villain is "come un pessimo et scelerato Iuda" (77), "fintamente ridendo da Gano" (79). In one of the Holy Week antiphons Judas is called "pessimus mercator." Gano, descended from Ganelon in the *Song of Roland*, has a long afterlife in the romances, which make him kin to Judas. Thus assimilated, he figures in Folengo's *Orlandino* (1.32.5: "Gano, stirpe di Giuda et omicida") and Pulci's *Morgante*, of 1466–1480 (11.6.5: "Gan come Giuda in fronte usa baciarlo").[33] In Boccaccio's ethical system, which merges Aristotle with the Christian canon of virtue and vice, ingratitude finds no slot among many other human foibles and failings. Mantova's prompt for the topic lies in a classical treasury of behavioral examples, good and bad, Valerius Maximus's *Memorable Doings and Sayings* (5.3).

Mantova, who preaches ethics and civics in traditions from Aristotle and Cicero, practices rhetoric as well in a classical mode. Its key lies ready-made in his *Annotationi* on Petrarch, where he displays masterful control of the tropes and an inexhaustible enthusiasm for proverbial sayings: "l'avaritia d'ogni male radice" (78); "Gli premi sono solazzi delle fatiche et stimoli della virtù" (102). Countless examples float in his flood of Latin writings, illustrating a sixteenth-century intellectual economy of mnemonics.[34] So, too, he laces his vernacular prose, pitched on a high Tuscan register under a Venetian patina, with examples pulled from a phenomenal personal memory. We should learn from the past, he advocates, since "la storia fu ben maestra della vita chiamata" (100). Alas, she has

---

[32] Teofilo Folengo, *Orlandino* 5.64: "Tutto quel giorno e la notte seguente /... vanno di trotto con la mente / chimerizando . . ." For the text see http://www.readme.it/libri/Letteratura%20Italiana/ORLANDINO.shtml (consulted 24 February 2007).

[33] Luigi Pulci, *Morgante maggiore* programmatically links Gano and Judas, cf. also 16.84.7: Gano is "più che Giuda tristo e traditore." The antagonist of Mantova's first novella is a "novo Gano di Maganza" (85). Editions of the *Morgante maggiore* had appeared in Venice in 1494, 1507, and 1517. See the text at http://www.readme.it/libri/0/0102010.shtml (consulted 24 February 2007).

[34] Rossi, "Un episodio," links this aspect of Mantova's academic writing to his acquaintance with Giulio Camillo's theater of memory, plausibly the model for a "little amphitheater" organized around the seven planetary deities that he had Bartolomeo Ammannati build in his house. Passages in his *novelle* illustrate the mental habit of organizing knowledge into numerically parallel taxonomies. See, e.g., his lesson on the seven Christian virtues, the seven vices, and the seven laws—of which he enumerates only six: "Naturale, Mosaica, Profetica, Vangelica, Apostolica et Canonica" (105).

few disciples, and "nessuno [è] prophetta nella patria" (96), alluding to Matthew 13:57, Mark 6:4, Luke 4:24, and John 4:44, as Gianotto bitterly learned when he took the fatal trip to England. Padua's jurist praises Sperone Speroni's *Dialogues* for their wealth of "sentences," more even than Priscian the grammarian and Quintilian ever taught. Speroni has no words "se non belle, scelte, proprie, ed isquisite [e] un artificio maraviglioso nelle sentenze, le quali, come voi sapete, sono come lumi e finestre all'oscurita, come colonne alle cose, che da se non siano troppo forti, ferme e sode." Don't doubt it, affirms Mantova, he will always be read, as we read now Boccaccio and Petrarch, "ne' quali sono ornamenti e modi di parlare." [35] Cicero and Boccaccio silently join hands to define eloquence for Mantova as a power that serves the republic and uplifts the afflicted. Backed by Aristotelianism as was his Boccaccio, he sees it as an essential virtue that "ne fuoco, ne ferro, ne tempo" can prevent from perpetually preserving lives of people whom it has praised (109–10).[36]

The characters who populate Mantova's fiction, it is clear, have much in common with their author—Padua's excellent legal system, under an enlightened *podestà*, vindicates Girolamo, victim of the Judas-dyer; Calliplocamo is a philosopher, as was Mantova's friend Speroni Speroni, a student of Pomponazzi; Phalacro, bald like the balding man who invented him, triumphs through his eloquence, oratorical skill essential to any good forensic lawyer.[37] The jurist's support of the arts and love of music account for his character Gianotto, unusual for his calling as a harpsichordist and pitiful for his strange death, suicide caused by miserly patronage. Gianotto would have done better to perform in Mantova's own home, a museum that held a musical theater. An inventory of its contents, written in 1695 by a great-great-nephew, lists among some seven hundred items portraits of Petrarch, "Madona Lauretta tanto amata e celebrata dal Petrarca," Dante, and Boccaccio. The collection also boasted Titian's portrait of Mantova, works by Tintoretto, a bas-relief attributed to Michelangelo, and prints by Albrecht Dürer. There were many coins, so desirable that the king of Hungary wanted them, but Mantova wouldn't part with these precious objects, tokens of Roman virtue with its currency of gratitude and patronage: "che altro nelle romane monete si ritrova, delle quali ancora la memoria ne è restata: et tante se ne ha, che è una meraviglia, se non liberalità, salute et doni ampissimi; le quali tutte cose alla gratitudine tendono . . . ?" Along with the coins, Mantova had assembled ancient archeological finds, vases, and figurines. Busts of famous men

---

[35] Mantova, "Discorsi sopra i Dialoghi," 5:430–32.

[36] Boccaccio's *brigata* illustrates Aristotle's virtue of speaking well (*eutrapelia*). See Victoria Kirkham, "The Word, the Flesh, and the *Decameron*," *Romance Philology* 41 (1987): 127–49; repr. in eadem, *The Sign of Reason*, 173–97.

[37] See Kinney, *Early Sculpture*, figs. 188–195a, and Davis, "Medals of Marco Mantova Benavides," for reproductions of Mantova's portrait medals, which depict him in profile with a beard and receding hairline.

sat on pedestals in niches around the frescoed walls, a visual counterpart to the exemplary *uomini famosi* whose names he so often reels off in canons in his *novelle*. As models of gratitude, for example, Caesar and Pompey were great; so too Octavian, Hadrian, Trajan, Marcus Aurelius, and Anthony (89). Another room held such natural curiosities as a stuffed crocodile suspended from the ceiling, a hanging lizard, a rock collection, fossils, a unicorn horn, sea shells, and the skeletons of two dead cats.

A third room dedicated entirely to musical instruments became a musical academy, "camerone ornatissimo con organo, clavicembali, viole et altri strumenti musicali fatti da artefici eccellenti, ove si fa accademia delli musici di Padova."[38] Mantova waxes eloquent, and at moments Dantesque, in the philosophical musings that form the second half of his novella about the poorly remunerated keyboard player Gianotto. People today, "poco esperti delle cose del mondo, [vanno] drieto a loro bestiali et men ragionevoli appetiti, le fiere in questo imitando" (cf. *Inf.* 26.97–98: "l'ardor / ch' i' ebbi a divenir del mondo esperto"; *Inf.* 26.119: "fatti non foste a viver come bruti"; *Purg.* 26.84: "seguendo come bestie l'appetito"). No matter where one looks, be it Rome "già capo del mondo, hor coda" (cf. *Dec.* 5.3.4: "In Roma, la quale come è oggi coda così già fu capo del mondo") or any other city, civilization has deteriorated into violence and warfare. Man was made to live in peace, amnesty, and universal concord, unlike the other animals, all with their own natural armor. The ox has horns, the lion claws, the pig teeth, the elephant his trunk, the crocodile his tough skin for a shield (as Mantova's own stuffed reptile could remind him). Everything about man belongs to peace—our eyes that reveal the soul; kisses to conjoin souls; arms for sweet embraces, laughter, and tears. Nature has given man reason and the liberal arts, things that raise him above the level of a beast. Man, in short, is a "simulacro di pace, di amore, di concordia, d'unione, d'amistà, di benevolenza et di charità" (104).

For all the philosophical wisdom and rhetorical arsenal Mantova brings to his fiction, it doesn't rise to poetry. The stories about Girolamo, Gianotto, and Phalacro are a prose fabric woven and knotted to display a didactic design, texts that function as pretexts. They come loaded with lessons, not only on the vice or virtue of the title, but barrages of embedded topics. Yet are they merely "vere e proprie noiosissime declamazioni"?[39] And how can we cut Mantova down, as this

---

[38] Puppi, "Il 'Colosso' del Mantova." See Camillo Semenzato, "Alcune opere della Raccolta Benavides al Liviano," *Bollettino del Museo Civico di Padova* 45 (1956): 89–104, for the coins that Mantova refused to sell to the king of Hungary. Favaretto, "Andrea Mantova," notes that he died without issue, and the contents of his museum were dispersed. Some are today at the University of Padua, at Palazzo Liviano; some at the Biblioteca Marciana in Venice. The musical instruments, originally kept in a walnut cabinet, went to Vienna. Mantova's collection also included music books and portraits of musicians.

[39] M. Pastore Stocchi, "Marco Mantova Benavides e i trecentisti maggiori," in *Marco Mantova Benavides*, ed. Favaretto, 253–65.

same harsh critic has done, labeling him a limited intellectual and failed Boccaccian, because legal studies—and maybe he wasn't very good even at those—had crippled his brain? History documents how his improvised orations, up to two hours at a time, mesmerized audiences; how students flocked to his magnetic lectures, how the Infiammati welcomed him, and contemporaries widely held him in highest esteem.

Mingling the morality tale with the fairy tale, Mantova performs in his composite role as humanistic law professor, avid collector, and liberal patron. The first novella pits litigants like those in the mock practice cases for students. Right struggles against wrong in legalistic situations that border thematically on the fabulistic—the good son disinherited, his wicked brothers, a treacherous landlord, a wise *podestà*—but justice properly administered can set things right. The second advocates restoring and protecting the arts in society by imitating the ancient Romans, excellent in painting, sculpture, music, and architecture (101–2). The third, whose short unhairy protagonist Phalacro towers intellectually with his eloquence, enunciates the credo Mantova holds most sacred, his undying belief in the power of law:

> Che se vogliamo la dignità et grandezza delle sante leggi considerare, troveremo che sono quelle, che 'l mondo tutto governano et reggono, mura et fondamenti delle città . . . salute de buoni, et supplicio de tristi et pessimi huomini, conservatrici de stati della libertà et ultimamente d'ogni bene et che tanto ci fanno essere dalle fiere differenti. (122)

If these fanciful narratives percolate more from the classroom than the slopes of Parnassus, they nevertheless take us back in time for a fascinating guided tour through the author's fertile mind and his culturally rich urban milieu. It is as if he himself were speaking, as indeed he does, while showing us privately his museum, his musical academy, and the flourishing athenaeum of his venerated city, that exalted Padua whose favorite sons throng in a hall of fame at the climax of his final novella.

The Economies of Authority: Bembo, Vellutello, and the Reconstruction of "Authentic Petrarch"

H. Wayne Storey

In 1525, Alessandro Vellutello intensified what would become a long debate about the nature of textual-critical authority in the then newly founded and rapidly changing economy of printed books, a debate that would soon go underground and that lingers to this day under the surface of dogmatic national traditions of textual editing and the general recovery of texts in the context of the history of the book and editorial theory.[1] Then at stake were the ordering and composition of Petrarch's *Rerum vulgarium fragmenta*, or the *Canzoniere*, known to Vellutello as the "Sonetti & Canzoni" that, together with the author's *Triumphi*, became simply, in the second edition (1528), his *Petrarcha*. Today, we seldom consider Vellutello's editions and numerous reprintings as much other than curiosities, in spite of the fact that they formed the textual backbone of sixteenth-century French Petrarchism and were—along with Guglielmo Rovillio's Lyon editions of 1550, 1551, and 1558 and the reprintings of Bembo's first and second editions (1501, 1514)—the *textes de référence* of the Pléiade poets.[2] However, in a more modern sense, Alessandro

---

[1] See Brian Richardson, *Print Culture in Renaissance Italy: The Editor and the Vernacular Text 1470–1600* (Cambridge: Cambridge University Press, 1994); and Paolo Trovato, *Con ogni diligenza corretto: la stampa e le revisioni editoriali dei testi letterari italiani (1470–1570)* (Bologna: Il Mulino, 1991). Richardson's study investigates the nature of editorial processes in Italian book production in the late fifteenth and sixteenth centuries, exploring—on the heels of Trovato's work—the treatment of earlier manuscripts and previous exemplars. The question of the editor's critical authority and assessments of authenticity was, however, more often than not founded on the overall reputation of the scholar-editor or even of the printer.

[2] See H. Wayne Storey, "Canzoniere e Petrarchismo: un paradigma di orientamento formale e materiale," in *Il Petrarchismo: Un modello di poesia per l'Europa*, ed. Loredana Chines, 2 vols. (Rome: Bulzoni, 2007), 1: 291–310, as well as Jean Balsamo, "'Nous l'avons tous admiré: nonsans cause': Pétrarque en France à la Renaissance: un livre, un modèle, un mythe," in *Les poètes français de la renaissance et Pétrarque*, ed. Jean Balsamo

Vellutello was among the first to confront the problematic nature of the authenticity of authorial materials, system, and intentionality and their applications in editing. At the core of Vellutello's method we will find the first letter of the first book of Petrarch's epistolary collection the *Familiares* as the "authorial wedge" in Vellutello's assessment of the authenticity of the codex that will later become Vaticano Latino 3195.[3] Vellutello's editorial disagreements with monumental humanist figures such as Pietro Bembo and the publisher Aldo Manuzio represent a crucial moment not only in the economic history of the book but also in the editorial treatment of material authenticity, intellectual clashes in which he moves the focus of the genre of what we could call the "modern edition" from the text to its critical-biographical and even geographical apparatus. Key to this critical conversion is Vellutello's treatment of that first letter of the *Familiares*, an epistle written—along with the thirteenth letter of the final book (*Fam.* 24.13)—to frame the entire collection of

---

(Geneva: Droz, 2004), 13–32. The influence of Bembo's editions and subsequent editions and commentaries by Alessandro Vellutello, Giovanni Andrea Gesualdo, Guglielmo Rovillio, and other sixteenth-century scholars depended greatly upon the edition used by readers in diverse cultural contexts. For an orientation to the principal commentaries, see Gino Belloni, *Laura tra Petrarca e Bembo: Studi sul commento umanistico-rinascimentale al "Canzoniere"* (Padua: Antenore, 1992). The principal editions considered in this brief study will be Pietro Bembo's *Le cose volgari di Messer Francesco Petrarcha* (Venice: Aldo Romano [Manuzio], 1501); and Bembo's subsequent edition of 1514, particularly important for the shift in the division between the two 'parts' of the *Canzoniere: Il Petrarcha* (Venice: Aldo Romano [Manuzio], 1514 [note, for example, the reediting of Bembo's 1514 edition in *Li sonetti, canzoni et Triomphi di messer Francesco Petrarcha historiati*. Venice: Melchiore Sessa, 1526]); Alessandro Vellutello's two early editions and commentary on the *Fragmenta: Le volgari opere del Petrarcha con l'esposizione di Alessandro Vellutello da Lucca* (Venice: Giovanni Antonio [Nicolini] & Fratelli da Sabbio, 1525), and *Il Petrarcha* (Venice: Bernardino de Vidali, 1528); and Guglielmo Rovillio's expanded Lyon edition and commentary of 1558: *Il Petrarca con dichiarazioni non piu stampate, Insieme alcune belle Annotazioni, tratte dalle dottissime Prose di Monsignor Bembo, cose sommamente utili, à chi di rimare leggiadramente, e senza volere i segni del Petrarca passare, si prende cura* (Lyon: Rovillio, 1558), though it should be noted that Rovillio's editorial project began with his 1550 edition: *Il Petrarca, con nuove et brevi dichiarationi; insieme una tavola di tutti i vocaboli, detti & proverbi difficili diligentemente dichiarati* (Lyon: Gulielmo Rovillio, 1550). See also Nicole Bingen's study "Les éditions lyonnaises de Pétrarque dues à Jean de Tournes et à Guillaume Rouillé," in *Les poètes français de la renaissance*, 139-55.

[3] For the history of Petrarch's ideograph / partial holograph, see Gino Belloni, "Nota sulla storia del Vat. lat. 3195," in *Rerum vulgarium fragmenta, codice Vaticano Latino 3195: Commentario all'edizione in fac-simile*, ed. idem, Furio Brugnolo, H. Wayne Storey, and Stefano Zamponi (Padua: Antenore, 2004), 73–104. The codex Vaticano Latino 3195 is now in color facsimile in Francesco Petrarca, *Rerum vulgarium fragmenta, codice Vaticano Latino 3195* (Padua: Antenore, 2003).

350 letters.⁴ On a theoretical plane, Vellutello's critical explanations in his early editions of Petrarch cause us to call into question the very nature of our own treatment and use of Petrarch's epistolary texts, which had two sometimes separate communicative functions: as independent missives (microtexts) subsequently revised, rearranged, and collected by the poet.⁵ In many cases, these letters come down to us only in their altered, macrotextual forms now part of the *volumen* of the *Familiares*.

For his edition of the *Fragmenta* and the *Triumphi*, Vellutello inherited the editorial lessons of at least four works: Vindelino da Spira's 1470 *editio princeps* of the *Rerum vulgarium fragmenta* (*Rvf*), Valdezoco's 1472 Paduan edition of the same work, Pietro Bembo's Aldine edition of 1501, and the 1507 commentary by Nicolò Peranzone (known also as the Filelfo/da Tempo edition).⁶ In each of these cases, the ordering of Petrarch's poems is founded on the agreement of one or two manuscripts whose authenticity was guaranteed by the poet's own hand (that is, according to the rubric tradition in selected manuscripts such as Laurentian Segniano 1 from the 1420–1430s "Scripto ipsa manu decti Poete"). Bembo's own working copy of the *Fragmenta*, Vaticano Latino 3197, is founded on two—if not three—manuscripts, to which would have been added some of the variants contained in the manuscript bound in white leather and owned in the late fifteenth century by the Santa Sofia family in Padova, the famous partial

---

⁴ All references to the *Familiares* are from Francesco Petrarca, *Le familiari, edizione critica*, ed. Vittorio Rossi, 4 vols. (Florence: Sansoni, 1933–1942), and will be indicated by the book and number of the *familiaris*.

⁵ For a description and analysis of the textual traditions of Petrarch's *Familiares*, see the relevant section of Rossi's introduction in Petrarca, *Le familiari*, 1: xxxv–xxxix; for the role of the revised book as material genre in the construction of the *Familiares*, see H. Wayne Storey, "Il liber nella formazione delle *Familiares*," in *Motivi e forme delle Familiari di Francesco Petrarca*, ed. Claudia Berra (Milan: Cisalpino, 2003), 495–506.

⁶ While each of these editions demonstrates unique traditions of the *Rvf*, Valdezoco's 1472 edition reveals readings that link it closely to Vatican Latino 3195; see "Minimalia" in H. Wayne Storey, "L'edizione diplomatica di Ettore Modigliani," in *Rerum vulgarium fragmenta, codice Vaticano Latino 3195: Commentario all'edizione in fac-simile*, ed. Belloni et al., 388–92; but also Gino Belloni, ed., *Francesco Petrarca, Rerum vulgarium fragmenta, anastatica dell'edizione Valdezoco Padova 1472* (Venice: Regione Veneto and Marsilio, 2001), xxxvi–xlv. The Peranzone edition of 1507 adopts textual and graphological solutions from the fourteenth-century manuscript tradition, such as in MSS. Vaticano Latino 3195, Laurenziano XLI 17, and Morgan M 502. It is important to rectify the confusion created by the recent assignment of the 1472 Valdezoco as the *editio princeps* (suggested in the section dedicated to the *Rerum vulgarium fragmenta*, in Michele Feo, ed., *Petrarca nel tempo: tradizione, lettori e immagini delle opere: Catalogo della mostra Arezzo, Sottochiesa di San Francesco 22 novembre 2003–27 gennaio 2004* [Pontedera: Bandecchi & Vivaldi, 2004], 63), a distinction held, as noted, by the 1470 edition produced by Vindelino da Spira.

holograph of Petrarch's *Fragmenta* that is today Vaticano Latino 3195.[7] A recent article proposes that Bembo never actually saw nor collated the variants of Petrarch's original—which he came to own before his death—into MS Latino 3197 and consequently into the 1501 Aldine edition.[8] Nevertheless, all four of Vellutello's significant predecessors were concerned with the authenticity and "correctness" not only of the texts themselves but with the author's final intentions in the ordering of the poems. None of the first three—Vindelino, Valdezoco, nor Bembo—occupied himself with commentary, but rather produced texts without apparatus. Peranzone's 1507 commentary, fashioned on the model of Filelfo's unfinished glosses, examined the poems as individual units collected within the "textual container" of the edition.[9]

Vellutello's 1525 edition burst onto the scene offering an extraordinary apparatus of information (tables, a life of Petrarch, a treatise on the ordering of the poems, a map of Vaucluse, ancillary poems related to Petrarch's work, and a new kind of commentary) and a new macrotext, or rather two texts: the first reflected and perfected the then standardized view of the bipartition of Petrarch's

---

[7] For the description of Bembo's copy-text for his 1501 Aldine edition, Latino 3197 in the Vatican Library, see the still useful description in Marco Vattasso, *I codici petrarcheschi della Biblioteca Vaticana* (Rome: Tipografia Poliglotta Vaticana, 1908), 15–17. More recently, Carlo Pulsoni and Gino Belloni have reviewed carefully Bembo's contact with and use of Petrarch's "original" in "Bembo e l'autografo di Petrarca: ancora sulla storia dell'originale del *Canzoniere*," *Studi petrarcheschi* 19 (2006): 149–84.

[8] Without the benefit of studies by Belloni ("Nota sulla storia Vat. lat. 3195") and Dario Del Puppo and H. Wayne Storey ("Wilkins nella formazione del canzoniere di Petrarca," *Italica* 80 [2003]: 495–512), Sandra Giarin concludes that Bembo never integrated readings directly from Petrarch's partial holograph (Vaticano Latino 3195): see Sandra Giarin, "Petrarca e Bembo: l'edizione aldina del Canzoniere," *Studi di Filologia Italiana* 62 (2004): 161–93. Citing Frasso's 1984 study of the added and subsequently erased colophon in parchment copies of the 1501 Aldine ("et dallui, dove bisogno è stato, riveduto, et racconosciuto"), Giarin suggests that the added colophon would have served to attenuare Aldo's strident claims of Bembo's use of a manuscript in Petrarch's own hand ("È probabile, infatti, che il Bembo, consapevole di aver licenziato un testo sì fedele alla lezione del suo presunto autografo z, ma forse altrettanto cosciente che esso presentava profonde innovazioni grafiche quali l'interpunzione e l'introduzione del segno diacritico dell'apostrofo, sentisse il bisogno di dichiararlo per attenuare l'affermazione troppo perentoria presente nel colophon ['[. . .] tolto con sommissima diligenza dallo scritto di mano medesima del Poeta [. . .].' Successivamente l'aggiunta venne cancellata perché il Bembo dovette rendersi conto, come ha giustamente ipotizzato il Frasso, che essa, 'anziché sopire ogni perplessità, avrebbe ravvivato i dissensi'" [192]); see Giuseppe Frasso, "Appunti sul 'Petrarca' aldino del 1501," in *Vestigia: Studi in onore di Giuseppe Billanovich*, ed. Rino Avesani, 2 vols. (Rome: Edizioni di Storia e Letteratura, 1984), 1: 315–35.

[9] Peranzone's 1507 edition unsystematically resorts to single- and two-column presentations of Petrarch's poetic texts; see *Petrarcha con doi co(m)menti sopra li soneti [et] canzone / [. . .]* (Milan: Ioanne Angelo Scinzenzeler, 1507).

Fragmenta into two distinct sections: those poems devoted to Laura while she was alive and those poems composed after her death, and the second grouping consisting—at least in theory—of all those poems traditionally contained in the *Fragmenta* but on themes other than Laura and love.[10] This second set of texts (Vellutello's Part III) begins—in fact—with Petrarch's moral-political canzone *Italia mia*. There are, however, three characteristics of his edition which will occupy the literary historian, the editor, and the cultural and editorial theorist. And while no single feature of Vellutello's edition can lay claim to altering the nature and impact of editorial production and consumption of Petrarch's vernacular works, the combined effect of all three made Vellutello's Petrarch not only a widely successful model but also a profoundly influential critical—if not methodological—tool.

The first is his polemical stance toward Aldo Manuzio and, to a lesser degree, Pietro Bembo. This attack, mitigated slightly in the 1528 edition and absent from 1538 on, had the effect of disputing the scholarly claims of Aldo's edition on critical ground that today still defines the more-than-occasional chasm between philology and literary criticism. It also challenged, as we shall see, the economic supremacy of the Aldine version. Vellutello's anti-philological complaint, masked as philological rigor, and the narratively-based reordering of Petrarch's

---

[10] This division into two parts of the *Rvf* relies on historical interpretations present in some but not all fourteenth-century codices of the *Rvf* of the three and a half blank but ruled chartae (49v–52v) ready for use between *Arbor victoriosa triumphale* (*Rvf* 263) on c. 49r and *I' vo pensando* (*Rvf* 264) on c. 53r (H. Wayne Storey, "All'interno della poetica grafico-visiva di Petrarca," in *Rerum vulgarium fragmenta, codice Vaticano Latino 3195: Commentario all'edizione in fac-simile*, ed. Belloni, et al., 131–71, see 147–48), recalled—notably—in the rubric of a fifteenth-century transcription of the probably 1393 Veronese copy of *Rvf*: "Que sequuntur post mortem domine / Lauree scripta sunt . Ita .N. proprio / codice domini francisci annotatum est / (et) carte quatuor pretermisse uacue" (MS. Beinecke M 706, c. 107r [Dario Del Puppo, "Shaping Interpretation: Scribal Practices and Book Formats in Three 'Descripti' Manuscripts of Petrarca's Vernacular Poems," in *Petrarch and the Textual Origins of Interpretation*, ed. Teodolinda Barolini and H. Wayne Storey [Leiden: Brill, 2007], 93–129, see 108–29]). For issues of layout and poetics in Petrarch's own copy of the *Rvf*, Vaticano Latino 3195, especially for cc. 49r and 53r, see Storey, "All'interno della poetica grafico-visiva di Petrarca"; for a discussion of MS. Beinecke M 706, see Del Puppo, "Shaping Interpretation: Scribal Practices and Book Formats in Three 'Descripti' Manuscripts of Petrarca's Vernacular Poems," esp. 108–29. In her essay "Petrarch at the Crossroads of Hermeneutics and Philology: Editorial Lapses, Narrative Impositions, and Wilkins' Doctrine of the Nine Forms of the *Rerum vulgarium fragmenta*," in *Petrarch and the Textual Origins of Interpretation*, ed. Barolini and Storey, 21–44, esp. 26–34, Teodolinda Barolini reviews how Bembo himself vacillated between two versions of this division in the 1501 Aldine, between *Arbor victoriosa* and *I' vo pensando*, and the 1514 Aldine, between *Signor mio caro* (Rvf 266) and *Oimè il bel viso* (*Rvf* 267), editions.

Fragmenta helped to create one of the most economically successful editions of the sixteenth century. The second aspect that distinguishes Vellutello's edition is inextricably bound together with his reordering of the poems: that is his rationale for a biographical and running commentary devoted to Laura and Petrarch's relationship to her memory. Vellutello's revised ordering of the poems and commentary systematically reorganize the sometimes problematic thematic groupings of the *Fragmenta* into a diaristic narrative that spoke to devotees in Italy and France and created the cult of Laura of Vaucluse and of Avignon in works by authors such as Pierre Sala and Vasquin Philieul.[11] It is perhaps not a coincidence that, in a reprise of the 1507 Peranzone edition, Vellutello's dense narrative commentary graphically surrounds and consumes the poems on the page, often destroying the visual integrity of longer poems by separating stanzas with long prose explanations of the biographical nature and even geographical coordinates of the events to which the poems refer. While subsequent editions, such as Guglielmo Rovillio's 1551 and 1558 Lyon Petrarch, will return expressly to Bembo's ordering of the poems, the economic and cultural influence of Vellutello's extensive apparatus and commentary changes profoundly the composition and functionality of Petrarch editions, leading—in fact—Rovillio to include Luca Antonio Ridolfi's complete table of rhyming words so that Petrarchists in the making could imitate more easily their master (the *centoni*).[12] The third and final distinguishing element of Vellutello's edition is his critical method, which we could characterize as a unique combination of textual criticism and interpretation in the service of literary biography. Vellutello is, above all, systematic, developing a methodological approach which imposes order where the materials supply little but fragmented poetic narratives and thematic-linguistic clusterings.

The second, or 1528, edition (not reprinting) of Vellutello's *Petrarca* includes a more moderate criticism of Aldo Manuzio and a muting of the aspersions cast on the cultural icon Pietro Bembo. Three short years after the first edition of 1525, Vellutello is now more succinct in laying out his method for reordering the poems (contained in his "Treatise on the reordering of Petrarch's Sonnets and Canzoni"). From the title page's arrangement of information, we see the edition's priorities: commentary (*espositione*), the commentator (by now synonymous with the edition's principles of reordering), the apparatus (*utilissime cose*), and the ten-year printing and selling privileges guaranteed by the pope and other authorities.

---

[11] For the integration of Vellutello's Petrarchan material poetics in Pierre Sala's *Petit livre d'Amour* (British Library Stowe 955) and Vasquin Philieul's *Laure d'Avignon*, see Storey, "Canzoniere e Petrarchismo," 302–4.

[12] Rovillio's 1558 edition concludes with a "Tavola delle desinenze de sonetti & Canzoni del 'Petrarca' secondo l'ordine delle cinque vocali" on unnumbered pages. Luca Antonio Ridolfi's "Tavola di tutte le rime dei sonetti e canzoni del Petrarca" begins with a new frontispiece and publication information: "In Lyone, appresso Gulielmo Rouillio, 1558, Con Priuilegio del Re per anni diece" and a new sequence of numbered pages.

The treatise on the changed order, which will be abandoned as a separate entry after this edition, acts as a methodological preface to the volume (before all other matters that might pertain to the work—here called "Sonnets and Canzoni" [*Sonetti e Canzoni*]). Vellutello's goals are (a) to undermine the authority of Aldo's word and of the Aldine edition, (b) to demonstrate the principle of chronology in Petrarch's *Fragmenta* (especially evident among the anniversary poems) and thus the validity of his reorganization of the work along narrative lines, and (c) to provide documentary proof that Petrarch's own material practices (outlined in Petrarch's own introductory letter of the *Familiares*) would never have permitted the kind of organized and completed codex that would have corresponded to Aldo Manuzio's claims to having used authoritatively authorial copies of both the *Fragmenta* and the *Triumphi* implicitly guaranteed by Pietro Bembo. Vellutello's rapid summary of the chronological framework of the *Fragmenta* can only support what must be the primary target of his criticism: the authenticity of the codex in the possession of Daniele di Santa Sofia in Padova, the authoritative manuscript Aldo has in mind, and certainly one of the manuscripts both Bembo and he have consulted, but not the only one; and among these codices there is no absolute agreement on the order of the poems. Moreover, in private conversation with Vellutello, the venerable Bembo has apparently confessed his doubts that the codex is Petrarch's "original." Vellutello's final proof rests in Petrarch's own description of the material nature of his working papers in *Familiare* 1.1. In his 1528 introduction, Vellutello reviews the critical considerations of Petrarch's work habits, Bembo's scholarship, and, perhaps most important, Aldo Manuzio's editorial integrity:

> Prima ch' a la vita & a costumi del Poe*ta* o che ad altra cosa p*er*tinente a l'opera si venga, parmi molto necessario il deuerne alcune dire q*uan*to a l'ordine de Son*etti* e de le Canz*oni* mutato da q*uello* ch'esser soleua, per che assai chiaramente mi par uedere qua*n*to ch'esso mutat'ordine habbia da parer nel primo aspetto a tutt'l mondo non solame*n*te strano, ma forse anchor inco*n*ueniente, come de le cose anchora non intese quasi sempre suol auenire, Ma del tutto fuori d'ogni ragione pe*n*so deura parer a coloro, ch'a lor modo interpreta*n*do, credon hauer alcuna co*n*tinuatione nel prim'ordine trouato, Massimame*n*te per esser affermato da Aldo Romano, che vltimamente fece la p*re*sente opera stampare, egli hauerla dal proprio originale e scritto di mano del Poe*ta* cauata, adduce*n*do il testimonio de l'eccellentissimo Messer Pietro Be*m*bo, dal qual dice hauerlo hauuto. [. . .] Ma se io, per euidentissime ragioni prouero, in esso ordine non esser ordine alcuno, ragioneuolmente mi si concedera non esser vero, che Aldo de l'origin[al]e del Poeta habbia quest'opera cauata. Perche quando di sua mano original alcuno se ne trouasse, non è da dubbitare, ch'egli l'haurebbe col suo debito ordine lassato. [. . .]

Ma perche Messer Piero Bembo, col quale sopra di tal cosa ho alcuna volta parlato dice, non da l'originale del Poeta, come Aldo vuole, ma d'alcuni antichi testi, e specialmente i Sonetti e le Canzoni da vno che noi habbiamo veduto, & anchor hoggi è in Padoua appresso Messer Danielle da Santa Sophia, hauer quest'opera cauata, & anchora per hauerne veduto alcuni altri similmente antichi, e nondi meno in molte cose differenti. secondo ch'è piaciuto a gli scrittori, senon de l'ordine, il quale di tutti è vno medesimo, noi habbiamo per cosa certa, che dal Poeta non ne sia stato lassato originale ordinato, ma fu diuersi separati fogli, e che poi l'ordine che parue di darli a colui che fu'l primo a raccoglierla & metterla insieme, tutti gli altri habbiamo seguitato, e di questo ne fa fede quello, che'l Poeta medesmo scriue in vna sua epistola ad Socratem suum ne la quale (essendo gia vecchio) narra, come stando al fuoco, e riuedendo queste sue compositioni, quelle che giudicaua esser degne di lui le lassaua viuere, l'altre le mandaua al fuoco, qua[n]tunque, come pietoso padre, ad alcune ne perdonaua, che non ben degne di viuere le giudicaua essere, il che se fossero state in vno medesimo volume ordinate, non haurebbe potuto fare, e questo basti hauer detto de l'ordine per dimostrar, che l'opera non è stata de l'originale del Poeta cauata, e che da noi a miglior ordine è stata ridotta, E non senza fondamento, perche noi giudichiamo, ch'appresso di coloro, i quali hanno de vestigi di questo Poeta qualche cognitione, l'ordine solamente habbia ad esser in luogo di comento, & a glialtri via da piu ageuolmente ogni sentimento di quella poter hauere.[13]

---

[13] The text is from Vellutello's 1528 *Petrarcha*, 2–3. My translation follows:
"Before presenting the Life and Customs of Francesco Petrarca, or before any other matter which might pertain to the work itself, it seems to me necessary to address the order of the Sonnets and Canzoni, which has been changed from its usual arrangement, because it seems to me clear that this changed order will appear at first glance to the entire world not only strange but also perhaps awkward, as are those things we do not immediately understand. It will, I believe, seem completely unreasonable to all those who—according to their own interpretations—believe they have found some sort of continuity in the first order, which has been confirmed by Aldo the Roman, who recently printed the same work, having taken the text—according to the statement of the very learned Pietro Bembo who declares having consulted it himself—directly from the poet's original and in the poet's own hand. [. . .] But if I can prove with clear reasoning that in [Aldo's proposed] order there is no order at all, it should be reasonably conceded then that Aldo's statement, that he took the text directly from Petrarch's original, is not true. For it is true that if we were to ever find the poet's original in his own hand, there is no doubt that it would contain his intended ordering of the poems. [. . .]
But because Pietro Bembo in fact says—and I have talked with him several times about this very topic, that the text is not taken from the poet's original—as Aldo would have it—but from a few ancient manuscripts, and especially the Sonnets and Canzoni from one [codex] that we saw, and that can still be found in Padua at the home of Daniele of the Santa Sofia family, as well from a few other similarly ancient [manuscripts], which in numerous ways differ according to the interests of their copyists. And if the order

Even to the casual reader of perhaps one of Petrarch's most famous letters, *Familiaris* 1.1, something at least seems amiss here. Near the very beginning of the volume's dedicatory letter to Ludwig van Kempen, the poet's "Socrates," Petrarch describes himself as encircled by disorderly piles of letters and paper ("Confusis itaque circumventus literarum cumulis et informi papiro obsitus" [*Fam.* 1.1:4]). The sixteenth-century man of letters Vellutello could possibly have mistaken the paper—rather than parchment—commonly used, as codex Laurenziano 53.35 demonstrates, for personal correspondence in the mid- to late fourteenth century for the paper of poetic drafts (equally evidenced by Petrarch's draft copies of poems in Vat. Lat. 3196). However, near the end of the letter, it is clear that this preface to the epistolary collection that will be called *Familiarum rerum liber* refers constantly to the book's constituent genre, the epistle: "and so I would repeat in one letter what I had said in another" ("passim in una dictum epystola in altera repeterem meisque" [*Fam.* 1.1:31]), and again later: "as the order of the letters will testify" ("quod epystolarum ordo ipse testabitur" [38]). And, of course, Petrarch's penchant for collecting his works into books runs throughout the letter: "this work [. . .] which I now—advanced in years—gather together and redact into the form of a book" ("huius operis [. . .] provectior recolligo et in libri formam redigo" [45]). We now meet head-on the problem of the clearly macrotextual functionality of Petrarch's opening letter of the *Familiares* and what might well have been Vellutello's knowledge only of its "occasional textual form," or its microtextual character independent of its counterpart, to the same correspondent Socrates, in book 24 with which Petrarch closes the collection (24.13:6 "hic liber satis crevit") and in which our letter 1.1 is literally called a "preface." Numerous sixteenth-century anthologies and miscellanies testify to the vast and independent circulation of individual letters outside the "book form" of the *Familiares*. Few readers and Petrarch admirers and even fewer manuscripts give evidence of the entire epistolary collection from book I to XXIV. Moreover, it is

---

varies (as it does) among these copies, and there is not one order, we can be certain that Petrarch did not leave an original copy with his intended order, but rather various and separate leaves, and that the order in which the first person who collected these leaves and organized them as a collection has been the order that all of us have followed. This state of his texts is verified by the poet himself when he writes in his letter to Socrates ('Socratem suum' [*Fam.* 1.1]), in which he narrates that one day as an old man he was standing in front of the fire and going over the various pages of his own compositions. Those works he judged worthy of him he allowed to survive, the others he threw into the fire. Like a pious father, he pardoned some that were barely worthy of survival. If these compositions had been in an ordered volume, Petrarch would not have been able to [dispose of some and not of others]. And this demonstrates that the order could not have been taken from a Petrarchan original, and we have reorganized the poems in a better order. And with good rationale! for we believe that among those who understand somewhat this poet the order has to serve also as commentary, and that the other [readers] can more easily experience every kind of sentiment the text offers."

hard to imagine that Vellutello could have ignored the methodological evidence that the final letter to van Kempen reveals about the foundation of "chronological order" as the organizing principle of the *Familiares* (24.13:4 ["Hic sane non rerum sed temporum rationem habui"]).

But the subtlety of Vellutello's reading of the first epistle also suprises us. There, embedded in the first pages of the first letter, Vellutello finds the material proof that justifies his own method, as Petrarch notes: "I commited to Vulcan's correction [. . .] a thousand or so of all kinds of occasional *poems* and *private letters*" ("mille, vel eo amplius, seu omnis generis sparsa poemata seu familiares epystolas [. . .] Vulcano corrigendas tradidi" [*Fam.* 1.1:9, my italics]). The image of *fogli volanti*, or single unbound sheets, as the primary material of both Petrarch's letters and his *rime sparse*, or uncollected poems, must have elevated this first — and thus significant — letter to a new status among literary evidence, an evidence whose own material nature was neither questioned nor doubted by Vellutello. The observations of *Familiaris* 1.1 to van Kempen (*Ad Socratem suum*) on the material nature of Petrarch's own production became, not only for Vellutello but for several generations of readers and Petrarchan scholars as well, more powerful than what we know today to be the partial holograph of Petrarch's masterpiece (Vat. Lat. 3195), the codex which Bembo and Vellutello himself apparently consulted in Padua.

The literary-critical apparatus of Vellutello's early editions reflected not only the critic's perhaps unique perspective on the constructedness of Petrarch's work but also the editorial realities of early publishing practices in the competitive environment of Venice's book trade. From studies by Fulin and Brown (respectively in 1882 and 1891) to recent contributions by Zorzi and Plebani (in 1996 and 2004), the complex world of early Venetian publishing and printing has come to light, especially through the study of the legal statutes promulgated to guarantee the protection and rigor of the Venetian press, from editing practices, and the quality of paper stock and type to the various forms of sales and prices of books themselves.[14] This growing corpus of statutes was designed to ensure Venice's relatively unique industry a corner on the market. However, within that market, competition was fierce, particularly after the Venetian Senate decision of 1 August 1517 to revoke all previously granted privileges and to refuse new privileges — or exclusive rights of a sole printer to publish a work — except in the case of newly published works

---

[14] See Rinaldo Fulin, "Documenti per servire alla storia della tipografia veneziana," *Archivio Veneto* 23 (1880): 82–212, 390–405; Horatio F. Brown, *The Venetian Printing Press* (London: John Nimmo, 1891); Marino Zorzi, "Dal manoscritto al libro," in *Storia di Venezia dalle origini alla caduta della Serenissima*, vol. 4: *Il rinascimento: politica e cultura*, ed. Alberto Tenenti and Ugo Tucci (Rome: Istituto dell'Enciclopedia Italiana, 1996), 817–958; Tizina Plebani, ed. *Venezia 1469: la legge e la stampa* (Venice: Marsilio, 2004).

never before printed.¹⁵ The 1517 statute is significant in its language and content, addressing the growing problem of a large number of printers in the city ("impressores librorum in maximo numero") and the practice of requesting privileges to block competing editions and the consequential transfer of printers from Venice to other towns ("aliis viam occludant imprimendi quaedam opera, [. . .] ut plerisque dictorum impressorum alio migrare necesse fuerit").¹⁶ To resolve this growing problem, the Senate elects to concede new privileges only "pro libris et operibus novis, nunquam antea impressis, et non pro aliis."¹⁷ By 3 January of 1534, the Senate must again address the same problem but in terms of the ambiguity of its 1517 determination to grant privileges only for "new works," noting the disastrous state of the "Arte della stampa" in Venice:

> Vedendosi chiaramente come l'Arte della stampa, che soleva esser grandissima in questa nostra città è andata talmente in ruina, che non s'adopera quasi altri libri se non quelli che vengono stampati de terre aliene, et tra le altre cause che hanno prodotto questo, la principal è sta[ta] le tante gratie concesse alli stampatori per questo Consiglio de molti libri non più stampati, i quali dapoi ottenute tal gratie, o per non poter, o per non voler stamparli, tengono oppressa l'Arte, et levano la libertà alli altri stampatori, che quelli stampar non debbino, ita che ne seguita che tali libri sono poi stampati in terre aliene, *privando questa città della utilità publica, et li studenti della commodità universale, et li stampatori del beneficio commune*, [. . .].¹⁸

The statute's assessment of the situation to justify the step in 1534 of eliminating all privileges provides us with a general history of the printing conditions as they developed from 1517 to 1534. The statute also gives us an idea of the industry's importance to the city and of the implications of its decline.¹⁹ It is, of course, in

---

¹⁵ See Plebani, *Venezia 1469*, 30. For a general overview of the Republic's laws governing printing, see Fulin, "Documenti per servire alla storia della tipografia veneziana."

¹⁶ Both quotations are found in Plebani, *Venezia 1469*, 35.

¹⁷ Plebani, *Venezia 1469*, 35.

¹⁸ Plebani, *Venezia 1469*, 36–37 (my italics): "Seeing clearly how the printing industry, which used to be extensive in this city, has gone completely into ruin, that it is almost exclusively the case that only those books printed elsewhere are adopted, and that among the causes that have produced this situation the principal cause has been that so many privileges were granted by this Council for many books no longer printed, privileges which then — either because of the inability or the unwillingness to publish them — are suppressing the printing industry and taking away the right of other printers, who cannot legally print the books, it then follows that such books are printed in other towns, depriving this city of a public good, and students of a universal product, and printers of a common benefit."

¹⁹ The Senate's 1534 resolved the problem by requiring that all editions be submitted to an oversight committee for commerce, the Provveditori di Comun, for case-by-case evaluations (see Plebani, *Venezia 1469*, 37).

this period that Vellutello is preparing and publishing the early editions of his Petrarch. Plus we should keep in mind that in late January of 1527, Venice's Consiglio dei Dieci adds the requirement of a license (*licentian delli Capi del Consiglio de Dieci*) to print works in verse or prose.[20] Consequently we have to consider the legal and economic pressures that weighed not only on Vellutello but on editors in general as they worked within an ever more regulated and competitive industry that was deemed vital to the City of Venice's health and prestige.[21]

On the one hand, it is clear that Vellutello's dramatically altered editing and interpretation of the sequence to the *Rvf* were not driven by the need to produce a Petrarch that was substantially different from the Aldine edition so that he too could win the post-1517 privilege that marks the early editions. On the other, however, it is significant that Vellutello's attacks on Aldo and its exposition of how his own critical judgment of the Petrarch autograph and his edition's apparatus differ from those of Aldo Manuzio are absent from all post-1534 editions and reprintings of the work. In fact, Vellutello's methodological critiques are reserved, after the initial 1525 edition, not for his fellow editor, Pietro Bembo, but for the publisher himself. Vellutello's accusation seems clear as he enlists, as we have seen, Bembo himself in his cause against the "authenticity" of the manuscript at the Santa Sofia household in Padova: it is the publisher—his principal competitor in Venice, Aldo Manuzio—who is misrepresenting the nature of the manuscript evidence. It would seem that this is a publishers' quarrel rather than a scholarly debate between two editors. It is also doubtful that Vellutello's artful argument against Aldo's "erroneous assessment" and his misrepresentation of the Santa Sofia manuscript as Petrarch's authoritative version won the day for many readers. The popularity of Vellutello's version, commentary, and apparatus—maps and all—depended more on the growing cultural taste for literary biography, which enjoyed in some cases virtually a cult status. Vellutello's version of the *Rvf* feeds the passion for the Petrarchan itinerary of Laura of Avignon, satisfying a linear narrative pleasure that Petrarch's actual order of poems frustrates. The extraordinary number of editions and reprintings of Vellutello's Petrarch throughout the sixteenth century underscores the apparent economic success of his version of the *Rvf*.

Vellutello's open defiance of Aldo Manuzio's editorial supremacy and of the traditional treatment of venerated codices in the transfer from manuscript to print in deference to his own interpretative skills as a reader and commentator inexorably linked the textual and economic strata of sixteenth-century literary culture. Nevertheless, there is no modern edition of Vellutello's Petrarch, a widely diffused and read work which helped shape, and to this day still helps explain,

---

[20] The *licentia* was to be determined by two examiners who would then report to the Council; see Plebani, *Venezia 1469*, 41.

[21] Many anecdotal episodes are recounted in Richardson, *Print Culture in Renaissance Italy*.

the literary and editorial history of Italy and France in the sixteenth and early seventeenth centuries.

Works Cited

Barolini, Teodolinda. "Petrarch at the Crossroads of Hermeneutics and Philology: Editorial Lapses, Narrative Impositions, and Wilkins' Doctrine of the Nine Forms of the *Rerum vulgarium fragmenta*." In *Petrarch and the Textual Origins of Interpretation*, ed. eadem and H. Wayne Storey, 21–44. Leiden: Brill, 2007.

Belloni, Gino. *Laura tra Petrarca e Bembo: Studi sul commento umanistico-rinascimentale al "Canzoniere"*. Padua: Antenore, 1992.

———, ed. *Francesco Petrarca, Rerum vulgarium fragmenta, anastatica dell'edizione Valdezoco Padova 1472*. Venice: Regione Veneto and Marsilio, 2001.

———. "Nota sulla storia del Vat. lat. 3195." In *Rerum vulgarium fragmenta, codice Vaticano Latino 3195: Commentario all'edizione in fac-simile*, ed. idem, Furio Brugnolo, H. Wayne Storey, and Stefano Zamponi, 73–104. Padova: Antenore, 2004.

Bembo, Pietro, ed. *Le cose volgari di Messer Francesco Petrarcha*. Venice: Aldo Manuzio, 1501.

———. *Il Petrarcha*. Venice: Aldo Romano [Manuzio], 1514.

———. *Li sonetti, canzoni et Triomphi di messer Francesco Petrarcha historiati*. Venice: Melchiore Sessa, 1526.

Brown, Horatio. F. *The Venetian Printing Press*. London: John Nimmo, 1891.

———. "Shaping Interpretation: Scribal Practices and Book Formats in Three 'Descripti' Manuscripts of Petrarca's Vernacular Poems." In *Petrarch and the Textual Origins of Interpretation*, ed. Barolini and Storey, 93–129.

Del Puppo, Dario, and H. Wayne Storey. "Wilkins nella formazione del canzoniere di Petrarca." *Italica* 80 (2003): 495–512.

Feo, Michele, ed. *Petrarca nel tempo: tradizione, lettori e immagini delle opere. (Catalogo della mostra Arezzo, Sottochiesa di San Francesco 22 novembre 2003–27 gennaio 2004)*. Pontedera: Bandecchi & Vivaldi, 2003.

Francesco Petrarca, *Le familiari, edizione critica*, ed. Vittorio Rossi. 4 vols. Florence: Sansoni, 1939–1942.

Frasso, Giuseppe. "Appunti sul 'Petrarca' aldino del 1501." In *Vestigia: Studi in onore di Giuseppe Billanovich*, 1: 315–35. Rome: Edizioni di Storia e Letteratura, 1984.

Fulin, Rinaldo. "Documenti per servire alla storia della tipografia veneziana." *Archivio Veneto* 23 (1880): 82–212, 390–405.

Giarin, Sandra. "Petrarca e Bembo: l'edizione aldina del *Canzoniere*." *Studi di Filologia Italiana* 62 (2004): 161–93.

Plebani, Tiziana, ed. *Venezia 1469: la legge e la stampa*. Venice: Marsilio, 2004.

Peranzone, Nicolò, ed. *Petrarcha con doi co(m)menti sopra li soneti et canzone: el primo del inge(n)iosissimo miser Francesco Philelpho; l'altro del sapie(n)tissimo miser Antonio da Te(m)po nouame(n)te addito; ac etiam con lo commento del eximio miser Nicolo Peranzone, ouero Riccio Marchesiano sopra li Triumphi, con infinite noue acute & excellente expositiome.* Milan: Ioanne Angelo Scinzenzeler, 1507.

Richardson, Brian. *Print Culture in Renaissance Italy: The Editor and the Vernacular Text 1470–1600.* Cambridge: Cambridge University Press, 1994.

Rovillio, Gu[g]lielmo, ed. *Il Petrarca con dichiarazioni non piu stampate, Insieme alcune belle Annotazioni, tratte dalle dottissime Prose di Monsignor Bembo, cose sommamente utili, à chi di rimare leggiadramente, e senza volere i segni del Petrarca passare, si prende cura.* Lyon: Rovillio, 1558.

Storey, H. Wayne. "Il liber nella formazione delle *Familiares*." In *Motivi e forme delle Familiari di Francesco Petrarca*, ed. Claudia Berra, 495–506. Milan: Cisalpino, 2003.

———. "All'interno della poetica grafico-visiva di Petrarca." In *Rerum vulgarium fragmenta, codice Vaticano Latino 3195: Commentario all'edizione in fac-simile*, ed. Belloni, et al., 131–171.

———. "L'edizione diplomatica di Ettore Modigliani." In *Rerum vulgarium fragmenta, codice Vaticano Latino 3195: Commentario all'edizione in fac-simile*, edited by Gino Belloni, Furio Brugnolo, H. Wayne Storey, and Stefano Zamponi, 385–92. Padova: Antenore, 2004.

———. "Canzoniere e Petrarchismo: un paradigma di orientamento formale e materiale." In *Il Petrarchismo: Un modello di poesia per l'Europa*, ed. Loredana Chines, 1: 291–310. Rome: Bulzoni, 2007.

Trovato, Paolo. *Con ogni diligenza corretto: la stampa e le revisioni editoriali dei testi letterari italiani (1470–1570).* Bologna: Il Mulino, 1991.

Vellutello, Alessandro, ed. *Le volgari opere del Petrarcha con l'esposizione di Alessandro Vellutello da Lucca.* Venice: Giovanni Antonio [Nicolini] & Fratelli da Sabbio, 1525.

———, ed. *Il Petrarcha.* Venice: Bernardino de Vidali, 1528.

Vattasso, Marco. *I codici petrarcheschi della Biblioteca Vaticana.* Rome: Tipografia Poliglotta Vaticana, 1908.

Zorzi, Marino. "Dal manoscritto al libro." In *Storia di Venezia dalle origini alla caduta della Serenissima*, vol. 4: *Il rinascimento: cultura e politica*, ed. Alberto Tenenti and Ugo Tucci, 817–958. Rome: Istituto dell'Enciclopedia Italiana, 1996.